CALHOUN

CALHOUN

American Heretic

ROBERT ELDER

BASIC BOOKS

New York

Basic Books
Hachette Book Group
1290 Avenue of the Americas, New York, NY 10104
www.basicbooks.com

Printed in the United States of America

First Edition: February 2021

Published by Basic Books, an imprint of Perseus Books, LLC, a subsidiary of Hachette Book Group, Inc. The Basic Books name and logo is a trademark of the Hachette Book Group.

The Hachette Speakers Bureau provides a wide range of authors for speaking events. To find out more, go to www.hachettespeakersbureau.com or call (866) 376-6591.

The publisher is not responsible for websites (or their content) that are not owned by the publisher.

Library of Congress Control Number: 2020947717

ISBNs: 978-0-4650-9644-2 (hardcover), 978-0-4650-9645-9 (ebook)

LSC-C

Printing 1, 2020

To Philip, Dalton, Henry, and Caroline,
for all their questions.

There was an infinity of firmest fortitude, a determinate, unsurrenderable wilfulness, in the fixed and fearless, forward dedication of that glance.

—Herman Melville, *Moby Dick*

CONTENTS

I N THE EARLY MORNING HOURS of April 1, 1850, a young New
York journalist named Joseph Scoville sat in a sparsely furnished
room in a Washington, DC, boardinghouse, penning a letter to Thomas
Green Clemson, the American chargé d'affaires in Belgium. "I am
writing this within a few feet of the venerated corpse of Mr. Calhoun,"
he wrote. "I sat up with him the last night. I hardly know where or how
to commence my letter." After relating the details of the famous senator's final hours to Clemson, Calhoun's son-in-law, Scoville closed, "I
have done now with politics. I will never serve under a lesser man, and
his equal will never be found."

In New Haven, Connecticut, the aging Yale tutor and famous
chemist Benjamin Silliman recorded a different reaction to the famous
senator's death. "He was a first-rate young man," Silliman wrote of his
old student, "both for scholarship and talent, and for pure and gentlemanly conduct...but his mind was of a peculiar structure, and his views
also were often peculiar." With sadness, Silliman wrote, "While I
mourn for Mr. Calhoun as a friend, I regard the political course of his
later years as disastrous to his country and not honorable to his memory, although I believe he had persuaded himself that it was right."

As the day progressed a steady stream of visitors came to see the
body, dressed in the same black suit they had seen its owner wear on
the Senate floor. The face, though deeply lined and emaciated by the

ravages of tuberculosis, still projected the fierce will that animated it in life. Preparations for a funeral the following day in the Senate were underway, and the titans of American politics were preparing their tributes. Meanwhile, far to the south in Charleston, South Carolina, a committee was forming to plan the largest civic event in the city's history to welcome home the dead body of the South's fallen champion.[1]

ONE HUNDRED AND SEVENTY years later, on June 17, 2020, amid ongoing protests throughout the country against racial injustice, Charleston mayor John Tecklenburg announced that the city would take down a monument to South Carolina's most famous political figure, which had stood in the city's Marion Square since 1896. "That we as Charlestonians must reckon with Mr. Calhoun's towering and deeply troubling legacy is a given," Tecklenburg said. "That we must allow his memorial to continue to divide our city while we do that reckoning, however, is not a given."[2]

The announcement in Charleston marked the culmination of John C. Calhoun's remarkable reappearance in American national discourse more than a century and a half after his death. In the preceding years, journalists had noted a "Calhoun revival" in American politics, while one historian claimed that a conspiracy concocted by the modern right in the mid-twentieth century to undermine democracy and protect the interests of wealthy elites took its inspiration from him. Following a horrific, racially motivated shooting at a black church in Charleston in 2015, waves of protest against monuments to the Confederacy spread across the country, sparking calls to rename a residential college named for Calhoun at his alma mater, Yale University. A petition to rename Lake Calhoun outside Minneapolis, Minnesota, soon drew more than 1,700 signatures.[3] Meanwhile, in both the United States and Europe during these same years, elections and referendums signaled a simultaneous revival of nationalism and separatism in the world, forces whose history in an American context is impossible to explain without reference to John C. Calhoun.

FAME AND INFAMY ATTACHED themselves to Calhoun early in his life and have persisted since his death in 1850. Born to Scots-Irish immigrants in the backcountry of South Carolina in 1782, Calhoun was educated at Yale and elected to Congress in 1810. He played a central role in the War of 1812, served as secretary of war in the Monroe administration, and then as vice president under two very different presidents, John Quincy Adams and Andrew Jackson. It was during his term as Jackson's vice president that Calhoun drew on arguments first made by Thomas Jefferson and James Madison to craft his doctrine of "state interposition" or nullification, provoking a showdown between South Carolina and the national government. Parting with an earlier generation of southerners who viewed slavery as a necessary evil, as a US senator during the 1830s Calhoun formulated a defense of the peculiar institution as a "positive good" in a white democracy and became the foremost advocate of slaveholders' right to carry their peculiar form of property into the new territories added by American imperialism in Mexico and the West. At the end of his life, in two of the most controversial and consequential political treatises in American history, *A Disquisition on Government* and *A Discourse on the Constitution and Government of the United States*, both published posthumously, Calhoun made the argument that every significant interest in a society should possess ironclad veto power in any legislative process, an idea that he called the "concurrent majority." Calhoun's aim was to save the Union as he thought it ought to be, but his theories helped lay the philosophical groundwork for southern secession a decade later.

Previous accounts of Calhoun's life are of little help in explaining his sudden reappearance in the twenty-first century. The prevailing view of Calhoun among historians for the past half century and more has been that the intellectual father of southern secession and his ideas were as out of place in the modern world as the slave society he defended. In 1948 Richard Hofstadter dubbed Calhoun "The Marx of the Master Class" for his defense of slavery as a positive good, but wrote that Calhoun's political ideas "have little more than antiquarian interest for the twentieth-century mind." "Calhoun," Hofstadter wrote, "was a minority spokesman in a democracy, a particularist in an age of nationalism, a slaveholder in an age of advancing liberties, and an agrarian in a furiously capitalistic country. Quite understandably he developed a certain perversity of mind."[4] In 1984, J. William Harris wrote that Calhoun was "a pre-eighteenth-century republican," and compared Calhoun to a dinosaur who had survived into the age of mammals, "awesome and perfect in its way...but bound for extinction."[5] In a 1993 biography, the historian Irving Bartlett repeated this judgment, writing, "The dominant tendencies of the Western world moved toward human liberty, equality, and nationality, and Calhoun, frozen in time in tiny South Carolina, seemed to defy them all."[6]

It is long past time to reevaluate whether John C. Calhoun was indeed out of step with the flow of history. In order to answer that question we have to consider him anew. It may be an uncomfortable exercise since, if done honestly, it will not confirm our comfortable preconceptions about him or about our history. Just as we can no longer dismiss slavery as a premodern labor system whose influence was restricted to one section of the country, opposed to modernity and antithetical to capitalism, a past that has no connection to our present, so we can no longer dismiss John C. Calhoun as the dark foil of an inevitable American progress and freedom. Instead, in any honest accounting, he belongs at the center of the stories we tell about our past. Unlike a monument, history cannot be torn down and bundled off to some dusty corner of a municipal warehouse without consequences. It must be told, fully, fairly, and honestly, or else we are left with a limited understanding of our past and no way to explain our present.

———

ONE

The People with No Name

B Y HIS OWN INTERPRETATION of its history, John C. Calhoun was born before the Union. Martha Calhoun was three months pregnant with her fourth child when Cornwallis surrendered at York-town, and when the child, a boy, was born in March 1782, there was still no formal peace treaty between England and its former colonies. Rev-olutionary chaos still reigned in the South Carolina backcountry and British troops still occupied Charleston. For the previous two years South Carolina patriots and loyalists had been torturing and killing one another with a ferocity unmatched in any other colony, and in the months after the boy's birth his kinsman Andrew Pickens was still leading military expeditions to subdue Cherokee along the frontier. Martha and her husband, Patrick, named the boy after her brother, who had been killed in front of his own house by loyalists during the war. All around John Caldwell Calhoun the world was bloody and new, still taking on shape and form.[1]

Well before the revolution began, the Calhouns had a long family tradition of pursuing the promise of cheap land to the fringes of the ever-expanding British Empire. Calhoun's father had been born in northern Ireland and emigrated to America as a young boy in 1733 when his parents, Patrick and Catherine Calhoon, as they spelled it then, decided to follow the promising news they had heard about the colony of Pennsylvania. The elder Patrick had been born in County Donegal in the province of Ulster, but the family was only a century removed from Scotland.[2] During the seventeenth century members of the Calhoon family followed the promise of land taken from Catholic landholders by British rulers to northern Ireland, where by 1690 there were 150,000 Scottish Presbyterians.[3]

Even as they took advantage of its expansion, the Calhoons were keenly aware of their status as second-class subjects within the British Empire. As Protestants they enjoyed more rights than Ireland's native Catholic majority, but as Presbyterians and thus dissenters from the established Church of Ireland, they were barred from holding office by the hated Test Act of 1704 yet still forced to pay a tithe to the established church. This double disadvantage, of being Irish in an English empire and Presbyterian in an Anglican country, was a source of deep resentment among the Calhoons' Presbyterian friends and neighbors, who believed they were due the same rights that other freeborn Britons could claim in the decades after the Glorious Revolution. In the years before the Calhoons departed Ulster, some Presbyterian ministers protested their political exclusion and mounted a campaign to repeal the Test Act. Minister John Abernethy inveighed that the act deprived dissenters of "the full possession of their Civil Rights in common with their fellow Subjects." The campaign eventually failed, but it assured that dissenters like the Calhoons who left Ulster in the early 1730s had been shaped by the rhetoric of the effort to repeal the act, which dissenters labeled a "badge of slavery."[4]

Many of the ideas that would shape the history of Britain's North American colonies could be found in Ulster in the years before the Calhoons departed. The ideas of John Locke were just finding their way into Ireland by way of the Scottish universities where most of Ireland's Presbyterian ministers were educated. One of those ministers, Francis Hutcheson, departed Ulster three years before the Calhoons to take a chair in moral philosophy at the university at Glasgow, where he developed the idea of an innate moral sense that would make him a central figure in the Scottish Enlightenment and one of the sources of the Scottish Common Sense philosophy that would dominate American universities like Yale by the beginning of the nineteenth century.[5] In 1747 Hutcheson published *A Short Introduction to Moral Philosophy*, in which he argued that it was the right, and even the duty, of a people to resist and change their system of government when it failed to secure their interests. Intimately familiar with the plight of the Irish within Great Britain, and the plight of Presbyterians within Ireland, Hutcheson applied this logic specifically to the case of a colony separating from its mother country, a radical argument that few other figures in the Scottish Enlightenment were willing to endorse, but which Great Britain's American colonies would eventually embrace. More radical and less widely accepted in America was Hutcheson's extension of the right of resistance to slaves and wives who were treated unjustly by their masters and husbands.[6]

Patrick Calhoon probably knew about Pennsylvania because of the linen trade, which had transformed Ulster society in the first few decades of the eighteenth century. Pennsylvania provided flaxseed for the Irish market and in turn served as one of the primary markets for the linen fabric woven in homes throughout Ulster, including perhaps the Calhoons'. But in the 1720s failing crops combined with rising rents, falling linen prices, and political and religious oppression created a perfect storm of pressures that set off a wave of migration to the American colonies that peaked in 1729 and continued for decades.[7] More than one hundred thousand of Ulster's Presbyterians would make the trip by the eve of the American Revolution, including Andrew Jackson and his wife Elizabeth, who sailed from the northern town of Carrickfergus in 1765 and settled in the Waxhaws region of South Carolina, where their third son, named after his father, was born two years later.[8]

Much of what the elder Patrick hoped Pennsylvania would be as he and his family sailed up the Delaware in 1733 had likely been shaped by reports from acquaintances who had already made the trip. As one Irish observer told an English official, the dissenters heard from friends and relatives that land could be purchased cheap in America, "and that these will remain by firm tenure as a possession to them and their posterity for ever." They also heard that in Pennsylvania they would be "free from all those oppressions and impositions which they are subject to here… that there they have no tythe (or task masters, as they call them) to vex or oppress them…[and] no laws which render them incapable of serving their King and Country." To Patrick and many others, the attractions of Pennsylvania contrasted with the oppressions of Ireland.[9]

After their arrival in Pennsylvania, Patrick and his family made their way inland from the coast to Lancaster County along the eastern side of the Susquehanna River, where by the 1730s large numbers of immigrants from Ireland had already settled. Evidence suggests they settled somewhere in what would become the township of Dromore, near the community of Chestnut Level, and almost certainly with family and acquaintances from Ireland. If the dead are evidence, Calhouns were buried in the cemetery of the Chestnut Level Presbyterian Church until well into the nineteenth century.[10]

Already by the time the Calhoons arrived some in Pennsylvania called the new immigrants the "Scotch-Irish," denoting their mixed origins within the British Empire. Some observers simply called them "Irish." The dissenters themselves rejected both labels. In any case, most colonists agreed the new arrivals were undesirable. In 1729, in his *Pennsylvania Gazette*, Benjamin Franklin noted the "impenitency" of the Ulster migrants, and blamed them for a recent outbreak of smallpox. Another observer called the migrants "the very scum of mankind." As late as the eve of the American Revolution in his famous *Letters from an American Farmer*, Hector St. John de Crèvecœur could still write, "The Irish do not prosper so well; they love to drink and to quarrel; they are litigious and soon take to the gun, which is the ruin of everything." The Calhoons likely arrived with more resources than many of their countrymen, and it appears they put those resources to good use, but Pennsylvanians were not disposed to draw distinctions.[11]

THERE WAS ONLY ONE group of immigrants to North America in the eighteenth century that outnumbered those from Ulster. In Pennsylvania, perhaps on the streets of Philadelphia, young Patrick probably had his first glimpse of enslaved Africans. Like the term "Scotch-Irish," the term "African" was imposed, and would have made little sense to the people from various regions on the west coast of Africa who were given the name by those who enslaved them. During just the decade that the Calhoons arrived in Pennsylvania more than fifty thousand enslaved Africans were sold in ports up and down the Atlantic sea coast, with thirty thousand of them going to Charleston to feed the insatiable demand of South Carolina rice planters exporting to markets in Britain and the British West Indies.[12] One of the Africans who endured the Middle Passage in the 1750s could still recall years later the "pestilential" smell of the hold of the ship that carried him across the Atlantic. "The closeness of the place, and the heat of the climate, added to the number in the ship, which was so crowded that each had scarcely room to turn himself, almost suffocated us," wrote Olaudah Equiano. "The shrieks of the women, and the groans of the dying, rendered the whole a scene of horror almost inconceivable." Two of Equiano's fellow captives threw themselves over the side of the ship and drowned.[13] For Patrick Calhoon and many other dissenters from Ireland, the New World was an opportunity to seek a better life with more political equality and economic opportunity, but as it turned out that dream was sometimes rooted in the nightmares of people like Olaudah Equiano.

Slavery was not central to Pennsylvanian society in the 1730s, but it was not quite marginal, either. By the first decade of the eighteenth century most wealthy households in Philadelphia owned slaves as household servants, and by midcentury enslaved craftsmen were common in the city's trades. In the countryside, enslaved Africans worked alongside European indentured servants growing crops for sale to the Philadelphia market and beyond. The same year the Calhoons arrived, Philadelphia papers carried advertisements for slaves, mostly in very small groups, including one by a Philadelphia merchant named Robert

Ellis with a history of importing slaves from Antigua, who advertised "Several likely Negroe Boys and Girls" for sale.[14] The Ulster Presbyterians showed little aversion to slavery, perhaps because they were accustomed to living with a subjugated Catholic population in Ireland, and by the late 1730s slave ownership was common in Ulster conclaves along the Susquehanna River. Although there is no evidence his family purchased slaves in Pennsylvania, as a boy young Patrick may have heard justifications of African slavery similar to the one Presbyterian minister John Elder gave in a sermon to his congregation in Lancaster County, in which he proclaimed, "The Negroes the Progeny of Ham are the servants of servants and their Country the Market of Slavery."[15]

The biblical story of the curse of Ham in the book of Genesis had served to explain the inferiority and enslavement of black Africans among Muslims, Jews, and Christians for several centuries by the time it appeared in Pennsylvania.[16] But newer explanations were on the horizon as the Enlightenment drive to organize knowledge produced the first efforts to scientifically categorize human beings. In 1735, the Swedish naturalist Carl Linnaeus famously subdivided the human race into Europeans, Asians, American Indians, and Africans, the latter of whom he described as "crafty, indolent, negligent." Most Enlightenment thinkers still held to the common origins of mankind, but the observable fact of African enslavement along with a neoclassical aesthetic of beauty drawn from ancient Greece and Rome led many to agree with David Hume, who in 1748 wrote, "I am apt to suspect the Negroes…to be naturally inferior to the whites." In the eighteenth century these ideas had not crystallized into "scientific" racial theories, but as one historian writes, "the scientific thought of the Enlightenment was a precondition for the growth of a modern racism based on physical typology." Natural rights and the racism that would eventually be used to deny that Africans deserved those rights matured together as cousins in Patrick's world.[17]

Just as the Calhoons arrived in Pennsylvania a radical critique of slavery and the slave trade had begun to emerge within Pennsylvania's Quaker community, a movement that would continue to grow and spread on both sides of the Atlantic as the century progressed. As early as 1688, a petition from four Quaker converts in Germantown condemned Quaker involvement in the slave trade, stating, "We shall doe to all men like as we will be done ourselves…making no difference of what generation, descent or colour they are."[18] Quaker critics condemned not only the cruelty of slavery but also the unrestrained desire for wealth and "luxury" that they believed sustained slaveholding and trading. One of the most influential voices in the middle colonies during the eighteenth century belonged to the Quaker John Woolman, who composed the first part of his *Some Considerations on the Keeping of Negroes* in 1746 after visiting the southern colonies. Woolman observed that "customs generally approved, and opinions received by youth from their superiors, become like the natural produce of a soil," but he begged his Christian readers to reconsider their opinions on slavery. He also cited Genesis, but in this case to argue that "all nations are of one blood." Woolman rejected "the idea of slavery being connected with the black colour, and liberty with the white," lamenting that "where false ideas are twisted into our minds, it is with difficulty we get fairly disentangled."[19] Whether the Calhoons encountered arguments like Woolman's or thought much about them if they did we do not know, but it seems unlikely that they had any moral objections to slavery. Like many other European immigrants to British North America, their concerns were mostly for their own rights as British subjects, not any rights supposedly common to all mankind.

WHEN PATRICK'S FATHER DIED in Pennsylvania in 1741 the elder Patrick did not own any slaves, but he had accumulated a modest estate worth roughly £150, including land, crops, four horses, and a few cows.

Since arriving in Pennsylvania he had also changed the spelling of his name to Calhoun.[20] Within a few years of their father's death, Patrick and his brothers, accompanied by their sister Mary Noble, her husband John, and likely other extended family and friends, took their widowed mother and traversed what would soon be a well-traveled path south from Pennsylvania along the eastern side of the Appalachian mountains into western Virginia, where colonial officials were offering cheap land to new settlers. Repeating a family pattern begun in Ireland a century earlier, the Calhouns settled in Augusta County sometime before 1746 and quickly began accumulating land.[21] In 1749, the surveyor for Augusta County, acting on an order from the governor's council to distribute 100,000 acres of land to settlers, surveyed 159 acres for twenty-two-year-old Patrick along Reed Creek. Patrick's acreage, which the surveyor marked out by imposing arbitrary lines and boundaries based on features of the natural landscape, represented one small part of the larger process in which the vast interior of North America was being transformed into private property and transferable wealth secured by the power of the British Empire and shaped by European notions of property rights.[22] To Patrick, his 159 acres undoubtedly represented independence, the right and duty to participate in politics as a "freeholder," and a space in which to exercise his energy and authority. Patrick and his brothers would eventually amass nearly 1,800 acres in Augusta County.[23]

In 1755, Augusta County held over two thousand white settlers but only forty black people, the second-lowest number of any county in the colony despite having been settled for two decades. Indeed, Patrick may have had more familiarity with slavery from his time in Pennsylvania than in Augusta County. Scots-Irish Presbyterians were the largest single group in Augusta County in the 1740s, and given their tendency to move and settle together, it is likely that Patrick's time in Virginia continued to be defined by the memory of Ireland and by the rituals and governance of the Presbyterian Church.[24]

When Patrick ventured through Rockfish Gap in the Blue Ridge Mountains into the Virginia piedmont to conduct business, he encountered something unique in the British colonies: a two-tiered society in which an attachment to liberty among whites drew its vitality from freedom's opposite, embodied in black slaves. In Virginia the presence of racial slavery served, in the words of one historian, as a "flying buttress to freedom." Between 1700 and 1775 an estimated 140,000 Africans were sold into slavery in the port cities of the Chesapeake.[25] Slavery shaped the way that white Virginians read the warnings of a group of eighteenth-century British writers called the commonwealthmen, who drew from critics of monarchical power such as Algernon Sidney and James Harrington to urge the need to constantly guard liberty against the voracious nature of power. Virginians only had to look around them to see what they would become if they did not resist the first hint of a threat to their liberty, and few questioned the racial distribution of freedom in their society. Indeed, some of the British commonwealthmen such as James Burgh and Andrew Fletcher, both greatly admired by Thomas Jefferson, saw no contradiction between espousing liberty for one class of men while recommending slavery, or near slavery, for the dependent poor, who in their view posed a threat to political stability. By the time Patrick Calhoun arrived in Augusta County, Virginians across the Blue Ridge had followed this prescription. The dissenters had already shown a willingness to embrace slavery for economic gain in Pennsylvania, but in Virginia Patrick may have begun to learn its political lessons, as well.[26]

IN EARLY 1756 PATRICK and his family left Virginia, driven by the growing unrest on the Virginia frontier in the wake of General Edward Braddock's disastrous defeat at the hands of the French and their Indian allies the previous July. This time, a recent treaty between the colonial government of South Carolina and the Cherokee seemed to promise not only cheap land but also a relative reprieve from the conflict upending life on the Virginia frontier. Making their way southward, Patrick and his family passed through the Waxhaw settlement on the border between North and South Carolina where Andrew Jackson would be born in 1767. Pushing on past a trading post called Ninety Six, which represented the boundary of white settlement in South Carolina, the Calhouns finally settled in what would become Abbeville County, on a small tributary of Long Cane Creek that soon came to be known as Calhoun Creek.[27]

As a boy growing up along that creek, John C. Calhoun would read in his father's journal descriptions of the land as it appeared when the Calhouns arrived. It was "in a virgin state, new & beautiful, without underwood & all the fertile portion covered by a dense canebrake, & hence the name of Long Cane." When the Calhouns settled there the area was full of game and only "16 or 17 miles" from the border with the Cherokee.[28] In the first history of the state, published in 1809, the historian David Ramsay wrote that in the 1750s there were so many buffalo in the backcountry, as the piedmont region west of the fall line that separated it from the coastal plain was known, that "three or four men with their dogs could kill from ten to twenty in a day."[29]

Unlike Pennsylvania and Virginia, South Carolina had been a slave society from its beginning. The Barbadian planters who settled the colony sought to replicate their society in South Carolina. Eventually nine of the parishes clustered around Charleston in the coastal area below the fall line, a region known as the lowcountry, would bear the names of parishes back in Barbados. Along with their Anglican parish names, Barbadian planters brought their slaves. In Barbados a 1661 code "for the better ordering and governing of Negroes" strictly defined the relationship between white masters and black slaves and directly influenced a slave code adopted by South Carolina in 1696.[30] In 1669 Lord Ashley, one of the English proprietors of the colony, worked with his secretary, John Locke, who had not yet penned his famous treatises on government, to write the Fundamental Constitutions of Carolina, which promised prospective colonists religious freedom as well as a governmental structure designed to resist the dangers of "numerous democracy" and aristocratic oppression alike. As the Fundamental Constitutions put it, "Noe bodys power…is soe great as to be able to hurt the meanest man in the Country." Ashley and Locke did not feel the need to explain the apparent contradiction between this statement and their guarantee, aimed squarely at enticing Barbadian planters to the colony, that "every freeman of Carolina shall have absolute power and authority over his negro slaves."[31]

The colony imported slaves at a rapid pace. In 1708, the governor of South Carolina reported to the proprietors that enslaved Africans were a majority of the colony's population. By 1720 the ratio of blacks to whites in the colony was two to one, and in some of the parishes around Charleston it was four to one.[32] In the 1730s alone, drawn by a demand for labor to grow rice and indigo, an estimated twenty-eight thousand people passed through the port of Charleston into perpetual servitude, a pace that after a brief interruption in the 1740s would continue until the American Revolution.[33] In 1739 the largest slave rebellion in British North America erupted on the banks of the Stono River near Charleston, mirroring other events in Antigua and Jamaica that year and leaving white South Carolinians with an enduring fear of the dangers posed by living in the midst of a black majority, and yet the Stono Rebellion did little to dampen the colony's demand for slave labor.[34] Three years after the Calhouns arrived in the backcountry the *South Carolina Gazette* reported that over the past ten years more than sixteen thousand slaves had passed through the port of Charleston.[35]

Patrick had picked up the craft of surveying and soon secured an appointment as a deputy for the colony's general surveyor, surveying the land recently acquired from the Cherokee. In the summer of 1758, Patrick surveyed land plats along Long Cane Creek for himself and his brothers, along with other members of their extended family. In the coming years he would survey thousands of acres, literally laying the groundwork for the plantation economy in the backcountry of South

Carolina. Surveying was a pathway to wealth in the South Carolina backcountry, and Patrick was soon one of the wealthiest and most respected men in the district.[36]

It is not clear exactly when Patrick began buying slaves—when his brother Ezekiel died in 1762, Ezekiel's will still listed no slaves as part of his estate—but it is likely that Patrick, as many other backcountry planters did, saw owning slaves as a sign of prosperity.[37] Neighborhood lore in the Calhoun settlement later held that on one of his trips to the coast sometime before the revolution, Patrick returned with a young African boy he had purchased in Charleston riding on the back of his horse. In one of the rituals of enslavement, Patrick renamed the boy Adam, after the father of the human race. Adam would in time become the father of a long line, his family's history intertwined with the Calhoun family's for the next century.[38]

THE MAIN THREAT TO the Calhoun community at Long Canes in the 1750s came not from slave rebellions but from the Cherokee, who took the opportunity of the ongoing conflict between the British and French empires to attack white settlers who had moved beyond the boundary defined by the recent treaty. In the middle of the winter in 1760 two hundred settlers, including the Calhouns, left Long Canes in wagons bound for the relative safety of Augusta, on the border with the neighboring colony of Georgia. A few hours after they set out a group of Cherokee mounted on horseback surprised the wagon train and quickly overwhelmed them, killing Patrick's brother James as well as his Irish-born mother, Catherine Montgomery Calhoun. Twenty-three settlers died in the massacre, and when Patrick returned to the site days later he found bodies "most inhumanely butchered," lying among empty wagons in a burnt clearing. As a young boy John C. Calhoun would have heard the story of his grandmother's death from his father and seen the rough stone marker that Patrick erected to her memory, inscribed "Mrs. Catherine Calhoun Aged 76 Years Who

With 22 Others Was Here Murdered By The Indians First of Feb. 1760." Patrick returned to the frontier after being appointed captain of a troop of rangers, serving until the end of the French and Indian War.[39]

In the years that followed the Long Canes massacre the backcountry descended into a Hobbesian nightmare. Many settlers retreated into forts, where they sometimes died of disease or starved for lack of food. The delicate social fabric of the frontier disintegrated as those left outside the forts helped themselves to the abandoned land and property of the refugees. Even after the war ended in 1763 and settlers began returning to places like Long Canes, the problems persisted. By 1767 armed gangs of bandits openly roamed the backcountry, and reports of theft, torture, and rape prompted little response from the colonial government in Charleston, which was consumed by the controversy with England over the Stamp Act, the 1765 act that imposed a direct tax on the colonies of North America and sparked widespread protest. In a remonstrance to the colonial government in 1767, backcountry settlers complained, "We live not as under a British Government...but as if we were in Hungary or Germany, and in a State of War...having it not in our power to call what we possess our own." The colonial government's failure to defend property rights, which Locke had identified as one of the primary functions of legitimate government, was at the heart of the backcountry's complaint.[40]

One of the forms of property that the settlers worried about most was their slaves. Anglican minister Charles Woodmason reported in late 1767 that land in the backcountry was "unoccupied, and rich men afraid to set slave to work to clear them, lest they should become a prey to the banditti."[41] The situation only further inflamed backcountry resentment at the colonial government's failure to establish a system of courts in the backcountry, or to provide representation for this rapidly growing part of the colony. "We are Free-Men," proclaimed the signers of the remonstrance, "—British Subjects—not Born Slaves—We contribute our Proportion in all Public Taxations, and discharge our Duty to the Public, equally with our Fellow Provincials Yet we do not participate with them in the rights and benefits which they enjoy." The backcountry settlers made essentially the same complaint against the lowcountry that colonial Americans were just then voicing against England, and which the Irish had made against the English earlier in the century.[42]

Some backcountry settlers soon took justice into their own hands. In what became known as the Regulator movement, self-described "men of property" who wanted a return of order formed their own armed bands to counter the "bandits." By late 1768 the Regulators had effectively co-opted the authority of the colonial government in the backcountry, and for nearly three years they controlled most of the territory up to fifty miles inland from the South Carolina coast in defiance of the colonial government. As the minister Charles Woodmason, a friend to the Regulators, observed, "The Country was purged of all Villains, The Whores were whipped & drove off…Tranquility reigned. Industry was restor'd." The powers in Charleston would have disagreed with Woodmason's summary, but there was little they could do.[43]

Patrick sympathized with the Regulators and even signed a pro-Regulator petition in 1769, but like most of the wealthiest backcountry planters he did not openly support or join the movement. Like the Regulators, Patrick undoubtedly found it unfair that the backcountry elected only three of the forty-eight seats in the South Carolina state assembly despite holding a majority of the state's white population. Determined to make the most of what power they had, in 1769 a group of Patrick's neighbors from Long Canes settlement marched nearly a hundred miles to Charleston to cast their votes, where they elected Patrick to one of those seats as the representative of Prince William Parish. In the assembly, Patrick and other newly elected backcountry representatives took part in the passage of an act that established circuit courts, jails, and sheriffs in the backcountry, addressing nearly all of the Regulators' complaints and marking an end of the quasi-rebellion of the backcountry, although the conflict between the backcountry and the lowcountry was far from over.[44]

Resentment over the colonial government's failures and the Regulator controversy meant that backcountry loyalties during the revolution were far from certain. But Patrick's sympathies appear to have been firmly with those resisting British rule. On a trip through the backcountry to whip up support for a boycott of British goods, the Presbyterian minister Gilbert Tennent recorded hostile crowds at several places but a warm reception at Patrick's home at Long Canes, where he spent the night in September 1775.[45] In 1783, when the Peace of Paris ended the war and his son John was a year and a half old, Patrick Calhoun owned sixteen slaves and 2,100 acres of land in the new United States.[46]

JOHN C. CALHOUN WAS five years old in 1787 when South Carolina's delegation to the Constitutional Convention—all from the lowcountry—returned from Philadelphia with the proposal for a new federal constitution. Patrick's previous experience with lowcountry politicians and constitutions may have made him wary of what the wealthy lowcountry delegation brought back from Philadelphia. During his time in the South Carolina legislature, that body passed a new state constitution that allocated the backcountry—which held a majority of the state's white residents—only 64 of the 202 seats in the new state House of Representatives, and attached prohibitive property qualifications to the office of governor and lieutenant governor that seemed designed to exclude parvenu backcountry planters like Patrick.[47] A half century later, when he had become a champion of state rights, John C. Calhoun recalled his father's opposition to the new federal constitution because "it permitted other people than those of South Carolina to tax the people of South Carolina, and thus allowed taxation without representation, which was a violation of the fundamental principle of the Revolutionary struggle."[48] But Patrick's experience as a backcountry planter meant that he undoubtedly had the lowcountry in mind as well as England when he complained of far-off authority.

The influences that shaped the proposed constitution were as abstract and philosophical as the examples of ancient republics, and as immediate and nearby as Daniel Shay's tax rebellion in western Massachusetts and the enslaved people working on plantations in lowcountry South Carolina. The Constitution carefully avoided the word *slavery*, as well as the word *nation*, silences that spoke to the main lines of disagreement during the debates at the convention. The delegates from South Carolina were acutely aware of the hostility to slavery that existed among their northern counterparts and the danger that a stronger federal government could pose to their interests. In the years during and after the revolution, Vermont had outlawed slavery, while Pennsylvania, Connecticut, and New Hampshire had all passed gradual emancipation measures. A wide variety of opinions on slavery existed even in Virginia. For an example of how a federal law might eventually threaten slavery in their states, slaveholders had to cast their memories back no further than 1772, when a Virginia slave named James Somerset ran away from his master during a trip to London and sued for his freedom, making the argument that English law—which did not directly sanction or establish slavery—superseded Virginia law. In a decision that resounded across the Atlantic, chief justice of the Court of the King's Bench, Lord Mansfield, ruled narrowly in Somerset's favor, a decision that had potentially revolutionary implications since it implied that slavery was a local, not universal, institution. From a transatlantic perspective, the issue of slavery's relationship to constitutional law far preceded 1787.[49]

South Carolina's delegation soon made it clear that slavery's existence and protection was a nonnegotiable condition of their participation in the new federal government. As John Rutledge put it, the issue of slavery's safety would determine "whether the southern states shall or shall not be parties to the Union."[50] In response, but without using the word, the Constitution gave slaveholders representation for three-fifths of their slaves, guaranteed that the slave trade would continue for twenty years, lent states assistance in putting down "insurrections," and included a fugitive slave clause that gave South Carolina's slaveholders, as General Charles Pinckney put it, "a right to recover our slaves in whatever part of America they may take refuge, which is a right we had not before."[51] For many antislavery delegates, the three-fifths formula essentially created slaveholders as a new American aristocracy, wielding enormous power with little accountability. "What will be said," asked Pennsylvania's John Dickinson, "of this new principle of founding a Right to govern Freemen on a power derived from slaves...?"[52]

And yet, as opponents of slavery would point out decades later, the Constitution also consistently refused to acknowledge what James Madison called "the idea that there could be property in men," an omission that over the next few decades would fit into an evolving trend in international law, building on the 1772 *Somerset* decision, which saw slavery as an unnatural state that could only be authorized by positive law.[53] Slavery in states where it existed would be recognized, represented, and protected, making the new federal government functionally proslavery, but providing an ambiguity so profound that when the Confederate States of America drew up their own Constitution seventy years later, they made sure it spoke unequivocally on the issue.

During the debate in the South Carolina General Assembly over whether to hold a convention to consider ratification, Patrick's sole contribution was his objection that the new constitution allowed "too great latitude" in matters of religion. There is no evidence he publicly supported James Lincoln, his fellow representative from the Ninety-Six judicial district, who plaintively asked the assembly, "What have you been contending for these ten years past? Liberty! What is liberty? The power of governing yourselves. If you adopt this Constitution have you this power? No: you give it into the hands of a set of men, who live one thousand miles distant from you." Lincoln and three other representatives from Ninety-Six voted against holding the ratification convention. Patrick voted in favor of holding the convention, and the measure passed the General Assembly by a single vote, 76–75. Perhaps because of this vote, Patrick was not chosen as one of Ninety-Six's delegates to the convention in 1788. James Lincoln was, and at the convention voted against ratification along with most other backcountry representatives. Nevertheless, South Carolina ratified the new constitution by a vote of 149–73, mostly on the strength of lowcountry representation.[54]

But how the new constitution would be interpreted, by what rules it could be, and even what sort of a thing it was or if it was finished or unfinished, were still very much uncertain. As James Madison put it to Jefferson, "We are in a wilderness without a single footstep to guide us."[55]

THE FIRST FEDERAL CENSUS, mandated by the Constitution to apportion representation in the new federal government, shows that in 1790 Patrick Calhoun enslaved thirty-one people, nearly doubling the number he listed only seven years earlier and making him the fourth-largest slaveholder in newly formed Abbeville County. The inventory of Patrick's estate after his death six years later lists twenty-six men and women as his property, by far the most valuable of his possessions, with an estimated worth of over one thousand pounds (the transition to the dollar was, at the time, not yet complete in the backcountry). The inventory also included seven feather beds, a measure of Patrick's social status as one of the wealthiest men in the backcountry.[56] Patrick's status, and his role as an elder in the local Presbyterian church he helped to found, made it natural that when a young minister named Moses Waddel came to preach in 1794 he stayed with Patrick and Martha. Waddel would soon marry the Calhouns' daughter Catherine, and he later delighted in telling the story of how that night as he sat before the wide fireplace a door opened and a boy with strong features and a mass of tousled hair, a young John C. Calhoun, peeked out to catch a glimpse of the new minister.[57]

BY THE END OF the summer of 1795 Patrick could feel that he was nearing his earthly end. He wrote to his nephew John Ewing Colhoun, "It cannot be expected my dissolution can be at [a] long period distant…as it is appointed for all men come to die and there is not devise or repentance in [the] grave to which we are all hasting." His combination of common sense and Calvinism showing through, he continued: "Therefore it seems highly reasonable that we should endeavour to redeem our time for our days are not only shorte but full of evil and troubles. May we be diligent through the grace of God enabling us to make our calling election shure, and to live a life of godliness in this sinful and corrupt world." As an example of the world's "degenerasie and corruption," Patrick pointed to "Jay's late treaty with Britain/or ought rather to be called an infamious submission to Britain." Probably Patrick meant Chief Justice John Jay's failure as the Washington administration's representative in the recent treaty negotiations with Britain to end British impressment of American sailors or to secure compensation for slaveholders who had lost their slaves in the late war. His opposition to the treaty was shared by many of Thomas Jefferson's followers, who had begun to call themselves Democratic Republicans. Even in the face of death Patrick carried a fierce Irish hatred of the British and a scorn for "submission." To one degree or another, his son absorbed them both. He would carry his father's postcolonial suspicion of the British Empire for the rest of his life.[58]

John C. Calhoun would later describe with pride Patrick's fierce sense of independence, recalling that the elder Calhoun always "claimed all the rights which nature, and reason seemed to establish, and he acknowledged no obligation which was not supported by the like sanctions." Admiring his father, Calhoun also recalled their differences. "Relying upon virtue, reason, and courage as all that constituted the true moral strength of man, he attached too little importance to mere information and never feared to encounter an adversary who, in that respect, had the advantage over him." In describing Patrick, Calhoun was also casting the shadows of his own self-image back onto his father. Honor, virtue, duty, and reason were ideals that Calhoun adopted and used to explain and justify his actions throughout his life, although he would never underestimate the value of "mere information."

Over the years one conversation with his father in particular stayed with him. Calhoun was nine years old. George Washington was in his first term as president of the new federal government. As Calhoun recalled, Patrick emphasized the need for an equilibrium between individual freedom and government power. He "maintained that government to be best which allowed the largest amount of individual liberty compatible with social order and tranquility." According to Calhoun's memory of the conversation years later, when he was in the midst of his own struggle to shape American government, Patrick held that "improvements in political science" would soon allow "throwing off many of the restraints then imposed by law, and deemed necessary to an organized society." A world of increasing freedom and decreasing government, Patrick believed, was the future. It was a radically optimistic conception of the direction of history, one that for most of his life Patrick's son shared with his father. But the influence and memory of his father was only one of John C. Calhoun's many educations.[59]

TWO

Educations

O NLY WEEKS BEFORE PATRICK'S DEATH, thirteen-year-old John had moved to Georgia to live with his older sister Catherine and her husband, Presbyterian minister Moses Waddel, where he was to attend a school run by Waddel. Disaster struck again almost immediately when Catherine died within weeks of their father. Years later, John recalled that Waddel was soon gone most of the time, "attending to his clerical duties" and no doubt fleeing his grief, leaving the young boy alone on the "secluded plantation" for long stretches of time "without any white companion." Written decades later, the description hints at a feeling of intense solitude and loneliness, even though John was almost certainly not alone. There is no trace in the description of the enslaved people who undoubtedly surrounded him and kept the plantation running in Waddel's absence. Only the word "white" implies other presences unmentioned.[1]

But he remembered the books. Calhoun was surrounded by "a small circulating library," for which Waddel had served as the librarian. The books became the teenaged boy's solace, and years later he could still remember precisely what he had read during those weeks alone in Georgia. He read the French historian Charles Rollin's *Ancient History*, a multivolume work that traced the rise and fall of the Egyptian,

Assyrian, Persian, and Greek empires. The central lesson taught by Rollin, one eagerly absorbed by Americans of the founding generation, was that the course of empires in history was cyclical. They rose to power as virtuous republics and, as empires, just as surely fell due to the rise of vice, luxury, and corruption.[2] Calhoun also read Voltaire's history of Charles XII of Sweden, in which Voltaire portrayed the famous Swedish monarch as a heroic and ultimately tragic figure whose virtues became the seeds of his eventual defeat when they were carried to such extremes that they became vices.[3] He read John Locke's *Essay Concerning Human Understanding* "as far as the chapter on Infinity." Published as part of a campaign biography, the list of texts was no doubt intended to reinforce an image of its subject as intellectually serious, in contrast to others on the national stage in the 1840s, but it also hinted at the way that trauma had seared the memory of those long-ago weeks into a young boy's mind. Exhausted by grief and intellectual exertion, Calhoun recalled that at the end of three months his "eyes became seriously affected, his countenance pallid, and his frame emaciated." When Martha Calhoun heard of John's precarious health, she immediately ordered her son back home.[4]

At home, Calhoun slowly recovered and began engaging in the sorts of pursuits, mainly hunting and fishing, that constituted an education in themselves for backcountry boys. For the next four years, with his two older brothers mostly absent, Calhoun and his younger brother Patrick helped his mother run the plantation. Martha Calhoun had a local reputation as an extraordinarily good manager, and it is likely Calhoun learned a good deal of what he knew about planting from her during those four years, including how to manage the slaves Patrick had left to his wife until his sons grew older or married.[5]

Slavery, as some American observers lamented, was an education in itself. "The whole commerce between masters and slave is a perpetual exercise of the most boisterous passions," Thomas Jefferson wrote in his *Notes on the State of Virginia*, first published in 1785, "the most unremitting despotism on the one part, and degrading submissions on the other." The results, Jefferson thought, were disastrous for the body politic. "With what execration should the statesman be loaded," he asked, "who permitting one half the citizens thus to trample on the rights of the other, transforms those into despots, and these into enemies...?"[6]

But this indictment of slavery's effects transformed itself into a riddle when combined with the other lesson that enlightened observers believed could be learned from the school of mastery. That lesson was the inferiority of black people. Writing about the possible outcomes of emancipation, Jefferson acknowledged, "It will probably be asked, Why not retain and incorporate the blacks into the state...?" In answer, he described what he called the "real distinctions of nature," of "color, figure, and hair." In addition to these, Jefferson wrote, "there are other physical distinctions proving a difference in race." Jefferson noted that blacks possessed a "strong and disagreeable odor," produced, he thought, because "they secrete less by the kidneys, and more by the glands of the skin." Blacks were less susceptible to heat, more to cold, and needed less sleep than whites. Jefferson then leaped effortlessly from supposedly empirical evidence about physical difference to conclusions about intelligence, emotion, and character. Blacks were more sensuous, but also, somehow, less feeling than whites. "Their griefs are transient...In general their existence appears to participate more of sensation than reflection." "Never yet," he wrote, "could I find a black that had uttered a thought above the level of plain narration."[7] This was the problem as Jefferson and others in the founding generation saw it—slavery was a moral and political evil for white and black alike, but the prospect of emancipation only raised more questions since, in their view, black people could never be incorporated as citizens. It was a Gordian knot waiting for an American Alexander.

During the four years on his father's plantation Calhoun grew to adulthood as he absorbed the lessons that slavery taught to young white men of the slaveholding class. The Calhouns no doubt raised livestock and cultivated corn and wheat as well as tobacco, the commercial crop of the backcountry until the turn of the century. John likely worked alongside his mother and the family's slaves in the field, as many backcountry planters did. He had known many of these enslaved people his whole life. There was Adam, the African who had ridden on the back of his father's horse from Charleston, and who now had a family of his own, including a young son named Sawney. There was Tully, Jack, Simon, Rose, Sal, Kate, a little boy named Pompey, and others. Some of them had been taken from the west coast of Africa, probably from Senegambia, Sierra Leone, and Angola, and brought to Charleston, where they had been purchased by a backcountry Presbyterian who had himself been born on the other side of the Atlantic. When Patrick died, their names were recorded in an inventory of his estate next to seventy hogs and forty-five head of cattle.

By this time white South Carolinians had learned to distinguish the different ethnic groups found on the western coast of Africa. From Patrick, or perhaps Martha, John may have learned that Africans like Adam were more desirable if they were Gambian or Mandingo (from Senegambia) and less desirable if they were Congo or Malimbe (from Angola). Also from his father, Calhoun would have learned to talk about slaves like Adam and the others as part of a figurative extended family, as his father frequently had in his letters, referring to "my family, both whites and blacks." No doubt Adam and all the other enslaved people wondered what Patrick's death would mean for them. Sale? Separation of families? And what did they make of this serious young man whom they now had to obey even as they helped him learn how to become a planter? They probably soon saw that they knew more about planting than their young master. Sawney, Adam's son, was a very young boy when Patrick died, but no doubt he listened as his father and the others quietly discussed their future. Sawney could not have known at the time that he would raise a whole family, all enslaved to Calhoun, or that he would outlive this serious young white man to become, eventually, a free man himself. For his part, Calhoun later recalled that these years gave him "a taste for agriculture, which he…always retained." But he undoubtedly learned much more. What he learned, or thought he learned, in those four years would become apparent in the decades ahead.[8]

DURING THE YEARS CALHOUN helped his mother manage his father's plantation an economic transformation was sweeping the Atlantic world, a cotton revolution that would soon reach the South Carolina backcountry. By the 1790s a series of inventions with strange names—the flying shuttle, the spinning jenny, the water frame, Crompton's mule—finally allowed British textile manufacturers centered in Manchester to compete with cheap Indian cottons that had dominated the market for most of the century.[9] This technological leap forward, a key moment in what we call the Industrial Revolution, produced a voracious demand for raw cotton fiber that transformed the peripheral areas of European expansion. Cotton imports from British islands in the Caribbean quadrupled between 1781 and 1791. Outside British areas, the colony of Saint-Domingue became the most important source of raw cotton, as planters there remade the landscape and bolstered their labor force to meet the exploding demand. Nevertheless, by 1791, when the Haitian Revolution birthed the world's first free black republic in Saint-Domingue, disrupting one of the key sources of raw cotton for European markets, demand was already far outstripping supply. After the Haitian Revolution, English manufacturers began desperately looking for new sources of cotton.[10]

They would find it in the American South. Cotton planting was not foreign to Americans, but in colonial South Carolina it placed well behind indigo, rice, and tobacco as commercial crops. In the 1780s planters along the South Carolina coast noticed the rising demand for cotton in England and began raising crops of Sea Island cotton, and South Carolina exports of this variety soon grew from less than 10,000 pounds in 1790 to 6.4 million pounds in 1800. The first significant shipments of cotton from South Carolina and Georgia reached Liverpool in 1795, the year before Patrick died.

But Sea Island cotton could not be grown far from the coast, and the short staple, upland cotton that could be grown further inland was laborious to process due to the small seeds embedded tightly into its fibers. These difficulties nearly caused the cotton revolution to stall out. Then in 1793 a recent Yale graduate named Eli Whitney invented the cotton gin while serving as a tutor on a Georgia plantation. His technological innovation would shape the course of Calhoun's life and career as well as generations of white and black Americans. Whitney's invention increased the productivity of the ginning process by a factor of fifty, allowing short staple to be grown profitably and redirecting the ambitions of a whole generation of white South Carolinians as backcountry planters scrambled for land and slaves to grow the new white gold. Calhoun and his mother may have heard from friends and neighbors about Wade Hampton I, newly arrived to the backcountry from Virginia, who made $75,000 on his first crop of short staple cotton in 1799. The cotton boom was underway.[11]

Calhoun also followed events unfolding beyond the backcountry during those years as Americans continued to argue about the power of the federal government created by the Constitution and its relation to the states. In his farewell address to the nation in 1796, George Washington addressed the fault lines between eastern and western parts of the country revealed by the Whiskey Rebellion, a tax protest that erupted in western Pennsylvania in 1794. Washington warned the nation of the danger of party feelings that coincided with "geographical discriminations, Northern and Southern, Atlantic and Western." The federal government, Washington reminded Americans, was no mere "alliance" of states, subject to negotiation among the different members. True liberty as Americans knew and desired it existed and was only made possible through obedience to the Constitution and the Union it represented, and Washington warned sternly that "all obstructions to the execution of the laws, all combinations and associations, under whatever plausible character, with the real design to direct, control, counteract, or awe the regular deliberation and action of the constituted authorities, are destructive of this fundamental principle, and of fatal tendency."[12]

It was hard to disagree with Washington, but in the summer of 1798 when John Adams's administration passed the Alien and Sedition Acts, restricting foreign immigration and prohibiting criticism of the administration, and then began using them to prosecute Republican (shortened from Democratic Republican) newspaper editors, Thomas Jefferson and James Madison believed that something drastic had to be done to counteract federal overreach. The two founders chose resolutions passed by state legislatures as the instruments of their counterattack. Of the two, Jefferson's resolution for the Kentucky legislature was more radical. In it, Jefferson purposefully described the Union as a "compact," a word that implied the continued existence of sovereign states and granted much less authority to the federal government than Washington had argued for in his farewell address. Jefferson further argued that it was within a state's power to declare an unconstitutional federal law "void & of no force." Jefferson called this action "nullification," a word so pregnant with radical implications that the Kentucky legislature deleted it from the resolution, although the legislature would resurrect the word in a 1799 act repeating its opposition to the acts. Madison's resolution, by contrast, was more of a protest, although he, too, denounced the acts as unconstitutional and declared the states "duty bound, to interpose for arresting the progress of the evil," although he did not say how they should accomplish this. Few other states followed the lead of Kentucky and Virginia, and several northern states passed resolutions condemning them. In 1799, at his most pessimistic, Jefferson raised the possibility of secession to Madison, arguing that Virginia and Kentucky should "sever ourselves from that union we so much value, rather than give up the rights of self government which we have reserved, and in which alone we see liberty."[13] The Virginia and Kentucky resolutions would over time attain sacred status among proponents of state rights for the simple, powerful fact that their authorship conveyed authority on the ideas they contained, which came to be known as the "principles of '98." Yet, aside from their ringing defense of state rights, the fact remained that nobody was quite sure whether what the resolutions recommended was constitutional or what it would look like in practice.[14]

As CALHOUN TOLD IT later, at the end of four years on his father's plantation he had decided to make planting his profession. According to him, it was only a visit by his older brother James in the summer of 1800 that changed his mind. James, who worked in a Charleston counting-house, "strongly urged him to acquire a good education, and pursue one of the learned professions." John objected that the time and expense of such an education would be too much, and that "he would far rather be a planter than a half-informed physician or lawyer." He would only agree to go if James could win their mother's approval and guarantee him funds for seven years of study, the amount of time he reckoned it would take to become properly educated. James agreed.[15]

The very fact that Calhoun had apparently calculated the amount of time it would take to accomplish the sort of education he desired suggests that his horizons were broader than his father's plantation. Where that ambition came from, or how it took shape, is a mystery of human nature that might not be solved even if we had better sources. Perhaps it was a son's desire to emulate his father's example. Or perhaps the histories of empires and great men that he had read when grieving on Moses Waddel's plantation kindled a desire for fame. Or it might be that what he read of politics in newspapers, when he could get them, gave shape to what was clearly an intense desire in a fatherless young man to make something of himself. In 1798 the sixteen-year-old Calhoun got a copy of the *South Carolina Gazette*, published in Charleston, and he pored over this narrow window into the outside world, reading about the debates in Congress over the Quasi-War with France, President Adams's reply to an address from the citizens of York, Pennsylvania, and a public meeting in Charleston. As he carefully filled the edges of the newspaper's pages with his notes, taken with pencil and still visible decades later, Calhoun was already dreaming of a world well beyond South Carolina. And his dreams were not small.[16]

This meant college, but before that it meant a return to Moses Waddel's academy to continue the education cut short by his father's death. And so, in the fall of 1801 Calhoun wrote his cousin Andrew Pickens Jr. that "induced by my own inclination and by the advice of some of my friends, I commenced the study of Lattin the 1st July 1800 at Columbia in Georgia under the Revd. M. Waddel." Calhoun inquired of Pickens—a student at Providence College (later Brown University) in Rhode Island—"which college is in the highest repute northerly," mentioning that he had good reports about Yale.

In the same letter, in the awkward manner of a young man still mastering the epistolary art, Calhoun also relayed the news of his mother's death, "which I expect ere now you have heard." Martha Caldwell Calhoun had died on May 15. "I left her the day before her death," Calhoun wrote. "I never experienced so sever [*sic*] and unexpected a shock…How can I express my feeling when it was announced to me the next day, that she was dead!" For the last four years, Calhoun and his mother had been partners, and during that time Calhoun undoubtedly saw Martha deal with the full array of tasks demanded of a plantation mistress, leaving him with no illusions about women's capabilities. It seems likely that it was also her influence that shaped Calhoun to see women as intellectual peers, if not social or political equals, as he would throughout his life. At the age of nineteen Calhoun had now lost both his parents, and although he still had his brothers and a whole network of Calhouns, Nobles, and Pickens relatives throughout South Carolina, he would have to rely on his own considerable abilities to make his way in the world.[17]

AT MOSES WADDEL'S ACADEMY, the intellectual currents of the Scottish Reformation and the Scottish Enlightenment reached the edges of Anglo-European expansion in the New World, providing the sons of ambitious backcountry planters the cultural and educational capital to compete with the lowcountry elite. Over two decades Waddel presided over a series of backwoods academies that produced some of the most famous South Carolina and Georgia politicians of Calhoun's generation. Waddel's students often completed the first two years of a college curriculum at his academy and then entered college in the junior class, where they were famously well prepared. Calhoun would recall Waddel appreciatively as "pious, zealous, and well versed in Theology generally," a minister whose sermons were addressed "much more to the understanding than to the imagination or passions." It was the kind of religion Calhoun would always appreciate. Calhoun called him "the father of classical education, in the upper country of South Carolina and Georgia." Augustus Baldwin Longstreet, one of Waddel's later students, recalled that Waddel was "of stout, muscular frame, and a little inclined to corpulency...His head uncommonly large, and covered with a thick coat of dark hair." When Waddel grew angry, his enormous, bushy eyebrows met in the middle of his huge forehead.[18] He was also a delightful if long-winded storyteller. "Give me as much & minute news as my old friend Dr. Waddel would in telling one of his long stories," Calhoun would later write his daughter Anna, who understood exactly what he meant.[19]

At his academies Waddel engaged in a kind of social and educational experimentation that was rare for the time. Most of the surviving accounts have to do with Willington Academy, which Waddel established two years after Calhoun left his tutelage, but which still serves as evidence of his educational style. There, spurred on by the necessity imposed by a boarding school with only one building, students built and lived in huts scattered around the central log structure that served as the schoolhouse, from which Waddel would sound a trumpet each morning to call students to class, prompting, as one student recalled, responding trumpet calls from the surrounding huts. The curriculum centered around the mastery of ancient languages, beginning with Greek and Latin grammar, and continuing to the translation of ancient texts, including Cicero, Horace, Tacitus, Caesar, Homer, Sallust, Juvenal, and many others. Students learned the history and geography associated with these authors alongside the texts they translated. Under Waddel's instruction Calhoun first read Polybius, the ancient historian whose description of the Roman constitution had influenced Montesquieu's *Spirit of the Laws*, and who famously argued that the strength of the Roman constitution derived from its incorporation of different types of government—monarchy, aristocracy, and democracy—each of which, if overemphasized or left unchecked, could devolve into their dark counterparts—tyranny, oligarchy, or anarchy.[20]

The standard preparation for class each day was the translation of 150 lines of a text, although some students far exceeded this (the record was George McDuffie, the future governor of South Carolina and US senator, who once translated over a thousand lines of Horace in a single day). Novels were not part of Waddel's curriculum, and neither were plays, with exceptions for Shakespeare, Greek drama, or classically inspired theater (such as George Washington's favorite, *Cato*). A debating society provided future public men with invaluable practice in absorbing a spoken argument, taking notes on the fly, and composing a response without much time to prepare. Classes were held outside under the trees in warm weather, and inside during the winter. "In this way," the historian David Ramsay, whose two sons attended Waddel's school, wrote in 1809, "the classics are taught 190 miles from the Sea Coast...Far removed from the dissipation of cities, and among sober, industrious, and religious people, [pupils] must be studious or lose all character and be pointed at by the finger of scorn." Waddel's school eventually attracted many students from the lowcountry, perhaps because their parents were drawn to the Spartan and republican simplicity of Waddel's school as well as his stellar record of producing prominent statesmen, lawyers, and ministers. Augustus Baldwin Longstreet recalled it as a utopian environment in which the sons of prominent statesmen mixed with the sons of backcountry planters in an austere, orderly, and self-governing scholarly community. It was exactly the kind of school that Thomas Jefferson would have applauded if it had not been run by a Calvinist.[21]

Waddel's Calvinism showed itself in his struggle to overcome the inertia of human nature in his students as he engaged in a grim war against the moral and spiritual effects of the biblical fall on human beings. Hard work and self-discipline, Waddel believed, could be a partial bulwark against the forces unleashed in Eden. Calhoun, with his usual understatement, recalled his brother-in-law as "sociable and amiable, but not without a due mixture of sternness and firmness." Another of Waddel's former students was more vivid, recalling Waddel's "sleepless vigilance over morals and conduct." "He seemed to regard vices as consuming fires," recalled Augustus Baldwin Longstreet, "and he adopted the engine process of extinguishing them." Waddel eventually evolved a democratic style of discipline at his schools that utilized a structure loosely based on Presbyterian church discipline (in which a church session, elected by the congregation, handled infractions) and run entirely by students. The system made insightful use of his students' sensitivity to shame. Physical punishment was not uncommon, but usually imposed only after a trial by a jury of peers, which made the shame of moral lapses the real punishment. Longstreet testified that the "moral reforms" imposed at Waddel's school were still "fresh and vigorous" fifty years afterward in many of his students.[22]

In later years, when asked by a young correspondent for his opinions on the proper education for a statesman, Calhoun advised the young man to become "thoroughly acquainted with the history of the five states of antiquity and the history of England and our country, and to read the best elementary treatises on government, including Aristotle's, which I regard, as among the best." Added to this, "a thorough knowledge of political economy, and of his country in all its relations, external & internal, including its resources, and the character of the people." But even all this, Calhoun wrote, "leaves much, that can only be acquired by actual experience." And all this knowledge and experience would be little use "without the power of speaking & writing well, both of which, in free communities like ours, are indispensible to success." Calhoun owed the beginnings of his education as a statesman to Moses Waddel, a debt he never forgot. The "actual experience" he would acquire for himself.[23]

AFTER TWO YEARS OF preparation with Moses Waddel, Calhoun entered the junior class at Yale in October 1802. In some ways it was an odd choice for the son of a backcountry republican like Patrick Calhoun, but it was a sure sign of Calhoun's ambition. Nothing in the backcountry of South Carolina and Georgia could have prepared him for a bustling commercial port city like New Haven, which at the turn of the century had about five thousand inhabitants. Wide, sandy streets were lined with orderly, white-washed houses, many of them with yards in front and gardens in back. The Yale campus, which had been badly run down in the 1790s, was in the midst of an expansion when Calhoun arrived. Most of the college buildings looked out onto New Haven Green, an unkept common area that one observer recalled was also lined with "barber's shops, several coarse taverns…a poorhouse and house of corrections, and the public jail with its yard." Since the jail doubled as an asylum, "the shrill screams and wild laughter of the insane…mingled with the sacred songs of praise and with the voices of prayer, rising from the academic edifices."[24]

Only a few years before Calhoun's arrival, Yale had been a very different place. Lyman Beecher, the father of the famous abolitionist family who attended Yale in the 1790s, recalled an atmosphere of political and religious (or rather irreligious) radicalism in which students called one another by the names of famous radicals like Rousseau and Voltaire, and Yale president Ezra Stiles sympathized with the French Jacobins.[25] By the time Calhoun arrived, however, Yale's new president, Timothy Dwight, had changed the college's direction decisively, rebuilding and expanding its physical campus and transforming it into a bastion of Federalist politics and revivalist Christianity. Dubbed by one of his enemies the "Pope of New England" for his sway within the Congregationalist establishment and Connecticut politics, Dwight had already been famous as a veteran of the revolution, a poet, and a minister before taking the helm of Yale. Dwight was an "old Federalist" in principles, suspicious of democracy and thoroughly opposed to the politics of Thomas Jefferson and the "Revolution of 1800." According to his critics, Dwight was a secret monarchist who in 1805 forbade students from celebrating the Fourth of July, calling the country's separation from England "unfortunate." This was all exaggerated, but certainly in Dwight and at Yale Calhoun had to contend with a staunch and sincere Federalism that was new to him.[26]

Not everything in New Haven was strange and new. When Calhoun arrived in October 1802, he found a revival going on among his fellow students. In 1801 the Second Great Awakening began in Cane Ridge, Kentucky, in a series of revivals that soon spread throughout the country, eventually reaching even Yale, although Dwight was careful to contrast the orderly and restrained nature of the revival at Yale with the emotional excesses reported at Cane Ridge. Calhoun's future tutor and friend Benjamin Silliman, a professor of chemistry who was converted in the revival, wrote that in the months before Calhoun arrived the campus had become "a little temple: prayer and praise seem to be the delight of the greater part of the students, while those who are unfeeling are awed into respectful silence."[27]

For Dwight the revival was part and parcel of his larger struggle against infidelity at Yale in both its religious and political guises. Dwight fearlessly debated ultimate questions about God and the Bible with his students, famously opening the floor to debate on the question of whether the Bible was really the word of God, confident that reason and moral sense would win the day against atheism and infidelity. Against the skepticism and radicalism of the French philosophers Voltaire, Rousseau, and d'Alembert, whose fruit had showed its rot in the French Revolution so admired by Jefferson and the Republicans,

Dwight arrayed a barrage of Scottish thinkers, composed of Thomas Reid's Common Sense philosophy, Hugh Blair on language and rhetoric, and William Paley and Lord Kames on moral philosophy. These ideas and thinkers were, in their way, conservative, but they were not reactionary. That was their appeal. As one historian writes in describing the Scottish philosophy employed by Dwight at Yale, "It was enlightened, moderate, practical...It could be used to sustain or validate any set of ideas, but was in fact associated with Moderate Enlightenment and moderate Calvinism. It was never anti-scientific or obscurantist, never cynical, and it opened no doors to intellectual or moral chaos." At Yale, in other words, Calhoun was introduced to a creative but conservative strain of Enlightenment thought.[28]

Dwight also fearlessly advocated Federalist ideas against those of the Francophile, and thus suspect, Jefferson and his Republican Party. By the time Calhoun arrived, Dwight had purged the faculty of any French or Republican sympathizers, like Josiah Meigs, who departed in 1801 to become the president of the University of Georgia (where he would eventually be succeeded by Calhoun's old teacher Moses Waddel). Alarmed by the rise of Jefferson and the Republicans, in 1801 Dwight hired Elizur Goodrich, a staunch Connecticut Federalist who had recently been dismissed from his government post in the Jeffersonian purge, to deliver lectures on civil government, Connecticut's constitution, and the US Constitution. Dwight hired other dependable Federalists, like Benjamin Silliman, and then decided what they would teach—in Silliman's case chemistry, even though he had no prior training in that subject. The result was a thoroughly Federalist institution. One of Dwight's critics during these years called Yale "a common sewer for abuse upon republicans."[29]

In fact, it was almost certainly during his time at Yale that Calhoun first heard real arguments for separation from the Union—and they came not from the South but from Federalist New Englanders. In late 1803 and early 1804, in the wake of the Louisiana Purchase and the passage of the Twelfth Amendment, a network of New England and

New York Federalists had seriously contemplated a "Northern Confederacy" that would have counteracted the Jeffersonian and southern hold on the federal government. One of the leaders of the conspiracy, Timothy Pickering of Massachusetts, would later serve in Congress with Calhoun, and Calhoun's future law teacher Tapping Reeve was intimately involved in the plot, as was Aaron Burr. And as one scholar has pointed out, even Federalists who disagreed with the plan in 1803 "did not refute either the idea of, or the justifications for, secession." Although unsuccessful, the conspiracy laid the foundation for another New England revolt during the War of 1812.[30]

CALHOUN'S PROTÉGÉ AND SOMETIME rival James Henry Hammond would later claim that Calhoun "had no youth, to our knowledge. He sprung into the arena like Minerva from the head of Jove, fully grown and clothed in armor."[31] The observation had some truth to it—Calhoun's earliest letters reveal a serious and self-consciously formal young man. But in his first winter at Yale in 1803 Calhoun sounded much like a typical college student missing his South Carolina home in a letter to his cousin Andrew Pickens, who had returned to South Carolina. "Are we not, while in college, insulated from the rest of the world," Calhoun asked, sounding dejected, "and deprived of those enjoyments and amusements, to which the human heart is so strongly enticed?" Calhoun complained that at Yale "day after day presents the same unvariegated scenes; a tiresome sameness; Books, Books, Books engross our whole time and attention." Describing a day in the life of a typical Yale student, no doubt his own experiences related in the third person, he wrote, "The morning bell, ere yet the sun has despeled the darkness, summons him to the chapel. In vain the warm bed entices to indulgence…hastily having thrown on his clothes, half frozen, he repairs to chapel." Calhoun lamented that he spent his days "in pouring over long and abstruse mathimatical demonstrations" and that he studied late into the night, jeopardizing his health.

But the main problem with college from Calhoun's perspective was that the stage was not large enough for his ambitions. Dismissing the "approbation of…teachers and the applause of…competitors," he wrote, "The ambition must be small indeed, which can be gratifyed in college." To Pickens he noted the recent death of their cousin John Ewing Colhoun (yet another American spelling of the old Colhoon), who had been elected a US senator in 1800 as a Republican. Calhoun wrote admiringly of Colhoun's conduct as a politician who had been willing to stand apart from his party when principle required it, writing, "It is probably, dear Andrew, that we shall follow the same presuits [*sic*, pursuits] of life, that he did, let us therefore be ambitious to emulate his virtues and knowledge." Clearly, college was only a waypoint in Calhoun's plan for his future.[32]

Calhoun's political identity was also firmly entrenched, if not fully shaped, when he reached Yale. He was unapologetically Republican, or Jeffersonian, in his sympathies, a rare thing in New Haven. Calhoun later recalled a classmate as "one of the very few, who dared speak out in College in 1803–4 when Federalism was so prevalent at Yale." Others recalled Calhoun in the same way. As one old classmate wrote to him in an 1844 letter, "You have always been the same true and undeviating Republican, in principle and practice, that you were forty years ago." This was not quite a correct assessment of the forty years that came after Yale, but there is no reason to doubt it as a description of Calhoun's college politics. Yet at New Haven and elsewhere, indeed at every point of his education and early career, Calhoun was surrounded by Federalists, many of whom he admired and respected.[33]

Calhoun's willingness to speak out in defense of the principles he had absorbed as the son of an immigrant backcountry planter in South Carolina can be glimpsed in a classmate's notes from November 1803, his senior year at Yale. In one of the twice-weekly "forensic disputations" or debates that formed part of the senior curriculum at Yale, in which students would debate a question for some time before Dwight finally weighed in, Calhoun addressed the question of whether foreign immigration to the United States should be encouraged. Calhoun argued in favor of immigration, pointing out that immigrants would come mostly from Europe's middle classes and that many of the immigrants he knew in South Carolina were "of respectable character & useful members of society." Dwight immediately leaped in, arguing that immigrants had largely supported the uprisings, like the Whiskey Rebellion a decade earlier, in western parts of the country, and were therefore a danger to the republic. But Calhoun, no doubt thinking of his own immigrant family and perhaps of Patrick's sympathy with the Regulators in South Carolina, pressed the point, arguing that immigrants would contribute to American manufacturing, the spread of science, the improvement of agriculture, and would eventually be "assimilated to our own citizens." The same classmate who observed this exchange later wrote a few lines of awful but admiring poetry about Calhoun, whose "soul by the ardour of honour is fir'd/ And by his acquaintance he most is admird/ His science extensive his manners refind/ To strangers polite and intimates kind/ His mind is serene and his judgment is clear/ His love for his friend is unfeign'd and sincere…" Evidently, some of Calhoun's other classmates held similar opinions. At least two of them eventually named children for Calhoun.[34]

During the senior year at Yale, students studied almost exclusively with Dwight, covering the topics of rhetoric, ethics, logic, metaphysics, and the history of civil society. Dwight would cover these topics methodically over the course of the year, mixing lectures on assigned readings with debates on questions drawn from the same readings or on contemporary issues. Students got a heavy dose of theological education, as well, since many of them intended to become ministers. Calhoun's education was shaped by the vestiges of Puritanism and the long tail of the Great Awakening every bit as much as by the Scottish Enlightenment. Every Saturday, students recited from the Puritan author Thomas Vincent's *Exposition of the Shorter Catechism*, after which Dwight would lecture on Christian doctrine and the evidence for Christianity. As the Connecticut winter descended, Dwight would hold classes in the Theological Chamber, a large room on the second floor of the new Lyceum building, where he would often sit with his feet to a fire and his back to the students as he lectured while they took notes.[35]

Calhoun began his senior year reading and listening to Dwight lecturing from Hugh Blair's *Lectures on Rhetoric and Belles Lettres*, in which the Scottish minister covered topics such as the "Rise and Progress of Language," the "Structure of Language," the "Structure of Sentences." In the chapter on style, Calhoun read that perspicuity was the most important element of style, and that a clear and powerful style of writing or speaking was always connected to the clarity of the author's thinking. In other words, a difficult subject was no excuse for a muddled address. "For whatever a man conceives clearly, that, it is in his power…to express clearly to others," Blair wrote. Calhoun would be a model of Blair's instructions throughout his career.[36]

As the New England weather turned colder, Dwight moved Calhoun and his classmates on to logic and metaphysics, where Calhoun encountered William Paley's hugely influential text *Moral and Political Philosophy*, first published in 1785 and a central part of university education in the United States and England for a half century. Paley defined moral philosophy at the beginning of his book as "that science which teaches men their duty, and the reasons of it," and he employed utilitarian reasoning to show that human happiness depended on adherence to three different sets of laws—the law of honor, the law of men, and the law of God, or the scriptures. A contemporary of Jeremy Bentham, Paley was a utilitarian, but of a particular sort. He did not believe that human happiness was furthered by physical pleasure or the absence of pain. Rather, he argued that true happiness depended on social ties of friendship and family, good health, the vigorous pursuit of some worthy end in life, and in the arrangement and encouragement of virtuous habits. "Man," Paley wrote, "is a bundle of habits," and it was much easier to form and follow bad habits than good ones. Acting virtuously was a matter of rightly perceiving and faithfully fulfilling one's duty to one's self, others, and to God, and would lead to both private and public happiness. In charting a course of action, Paley was clear, men should not rely on culture or custom, which could justify almost anything.[37]

Some elements of Paley's philosophy harmonized easily with the Calvinistic view of human nature that Calhoun had absorbed from his family and from Moses Waddel, such as its emphasis on duty as an end in itself and hard-won virtue. But in Paley Calhoun also encountered for the first time a more optimistic Enlightenment conception of human potential and purpose that undergirded the rise of liberal democracy and shaped a whole generation of Americans who would lead the country in the following decades.

Calhoun also undoubtedly took note of Paley's withering criticism of slavery. Paley expressed disgust at Aristotle's "self-evident" assumption that some men were naturally suited to be slaves. Such an assumption was blatantly self-serving, Paley argued, and was far more reflective of Aristotle's own society than any abstract moral law. "I question whether the same maxim be not still self-evident to the company of merchants trading to the coast of Africa," he wrote in a caustic aside. In another part of the *Philosophy*, Paley acknowledged the legitimacy of slavery in cases of war, crime, or debt, but argued that all these instances should be temporary. He singled out the practice of slavery in England's colonies and former colonies as particularly cruel, "a dominion and system of laws, the most merciless and tyrannical that ever were tolerated upon the face of the earth," and he lambasted "the inordinate authority which the plantation-laws confer upon the slave-holder." Paley probably had in mind places like Barbados, but as Calhoun may well have known, South Carolina's slave laws were closely modeled after Barbadian slave society. Thinking of his years spent working among his father's slaves in South Carolina, Calhoun must have felt a twinge of indignation when he read Paley's acknowledgment that his knowledge of slavery was secondhand.[38]

Slavery itself was still present in Connecticut and in New Haven during Calhoun's college years. Calhoun quickly became friends with his tutor Benjamin Silliman, only two years older than Calhoun, who gave his first lecture on chemistry at Yale during Calhoun's senior year. A "fair and portly" young man who wore his long hair "clubbed" behind him in imitation of Washington, Silliman would go on to become one of the fathers of American scientific education and founder of the *American Journal of Science*. Silliman's own education at Yale had been financed by the sale of slaves owned by his grandparents. And just a few years before he met Calhoun, Silliman's mother had been the largest slaveholder in Fairfield, with twelve enslaved people living on the farm where Benjamin lived and worked as overseer for a time after returning from college in 1796. Despite this connection, or perhaps because of it, Silliman was passionately opposed to slavery, at one point penning a poem titled "The Negroe" set at George Washington's Mount Vernon in which an old slave named Yarrow tells the tale of his kidnapping from Africa.[39]

Calhoun also encountered a profoundly conservative strand of antislavery sentiment in the person of Yale president Timothy Dwight, who once compared slavery in the American nation to an "uncur'd gangrene." But Dwight was much more critical of British slavery in the West Indies than he was of the institution in America, which he considered more Christian and domestic. A few years after Calhoun left Yale, Dwight responded to British attacks on American slavery by pointing to the wealth of Liverpool gained in the slave trade and the brutality of slavery in the West Indies. "The Southern Planter, who received slaves from his parents by inheritance, certainly deserves no censure for holding them," he wrote. Calhoun's relationships with Silliman and Dwight apparently did little to sway his beliefs about slavery, beliefs he derived from what the Common Sense philosophy enshrined at Yale taught him was the unimpeachable authority of personal experience. But his time at Yale did familiarize him with a certain kind of antislavery sentiment that appeared to pose little threat to the institution as he knew it.[40]

Calhoun's education at Yale took place at a key moment in a transatlantic scientific debate over the origins and meaning of observable
human differences, a debate in which Silliman and Dwight took sides.
In Benjamin Silliman's poem, part of the tragedy of old Yarrow is that
he has been kidnapped out of his native African environment into an
alien American one unsuited for him, a theme that was part of a larger
environmental theory of race that was widespread in Europe and popular in New England by the turn of the century. In the United States,
the theory drew its authority from a famous 1787 address to the American Philosophical Society by Princeton president Samuel Stanhope
Smith, in which he argued for an environmental theory of race and
criticized Thomas Jefferson's comments about Africans, published two
years earlier in Jefferson's *Notes on the State of Virginia*. The environmental theory of race would support a particular kind of opposition to
slavery, most evident in the colonization movement to send freed slaves
to Africa (despite the fact that many of them had been born in North
America), but it was based less in natural rights rhetoric than in the
belief that Africans were cruelly unsuited to North America. We can
imagine a young Calhoun, perhaps thinking of Adam, Sawney, and
others back in South Carolina, listening intently to Timothy Dwight's
opinion that the differences between white Europeans and Africans
were due entirely to environmental reasons, and that given time black
people in North America would eventually turn white under the influence of a milder climate and a more advanced society, something that
Dwight thought he was already observing among free blacks in New
England.

Dwight's position mirrored the beliefs of many other educated
Americans of the time, including Samuel Stanhope Smith's brother-
in-law and Calhoun's fellow South Carolinian, the historian and physician David Ramsay. But this environmental explanation, which was
compatible with Christian theology of a single creation and could be
used to argue for human equality (although certainly not all its proponents did so), was increasingly challenged at the turn of the century by

other Enlightenment theories such as the idea of polygenesis, championed by figures like Voltaire and the British philosopher Henry Home, Lord Kames, which posited the distinct and separate creation for the different races and lent itself to the relentless drive to classify human beings in the same way that scientific pioneers were doing with other species.[41]

Slavery is not listed as one of the topics of the debates that took place twice weekly during Calhoun's senior year at Yale, although it must have been a topic of conversation between the South Carolinian and his New England tutors and friends. But the debating society at Waddel's academy evidently prepared Calhoun to perform well on other topics, even against so formidable an adversary as Timothy Dwight. After one particularly vigorous exchange with Calhoun over the legitimate origins of political power—Calhoun maintaining the Republican position that it came from the people—Dwight proclaimed that Calhoun "had talent enough to be President of the United States," an observation and prediction that the twenty-one-year-old Calhoun took deeply to heart.[42] Certainly Calhoun was talented and admired enough that the young South Carolinian was given the honor of delivering one of the orations at Yale's graduation, which he planned to give on the topic of "the qualifications necessary to constitute a perfect statesman." Calhoun had his own future in mind and did not shy away from the inevitable comparison of his own qualifications to those of the "perfect statesman," a mark of the unshakable self-confidence that appeared early and never left him. But he never delivered the address, falling seriously ill with "a very severe dysintery" in August 1804 before commencement in September.[43]

In late September, graduated from Yale and contemplating his future plans, Calhoun traveled to Newport, Rhode Island, where Floride Bonneau Colhoun, the wealthy widow of his cousin, the late senator John Ewing Colhoun, had invited him to come visit her and her family at their summer home before they sailed back to South Carolina in November.

THREE

The Science of Law

NEWPORT IN THE FALL WAS an exhilarating experience for a young man used to South Carolina's lingering summers. Soon after his arrival from Connecticut, Calhoun wrote to his cousin Alexander Noble that Newport had "one of the most delightful climates on earth, it seems to possess all that can contribute to the pleasure of man." Still, not everything was to Calhoun's liking, and in the next breath he pronounced Rhode Island "much inferior" to the rest of New England in its "civil situation…manners, customs and moral and religious character." Shaped by his backcountry Presbyterian upbringing and his college years in the "Land of Steady Habits," as Connecticut was called, from early in his life Calhoun showed a clear preference for the more ascetic ways of life found in areas of the country dominated by Puritans and Presbyterians.[1]

In Newport Calhoun met his wealthy cousin by marriage, Floride Bonneau Colhoun, the widow of the late US senator John Ewing Colhoun, his first cousin.[2] The son of Patrick Calhoun's older brother Ezekiel, John Ewing Colhoun had served in the revolution and eventually served in the South Carolina legislature before being elected to the Senate, where he served only one year before his death. Floride was the daughter of a wealthy planter, Samuel Bonneau, who owned extensive rice plantations in the lowcountry. The Bonneaus were Huguenots, the descendants of French Protestants who fled France after Louis XIV revoked the Edict of Nantes in 1685; many of them settled in coastal South Carolina. The marriage, which united descendants of the Scottish and French wings of the Calvinist Reformation, made Colhoun a rich man and linked the backcountry Colhoun/Calhoun family to the lowcountry elite, part of an ongoing process of unification between the planter classes in both regions.

After her husband's death Floride and her three children, John Ewing, James Edward, and her namesake Floride Bonneau, continued to be generously supported by her husband's estate, which she might justifiably have considered hers from her father. The estate's accounts, kept by Charleston lawyer Henry W. DeSaussure, recorded numerous charges between 1803 and 1811 "for wine, sugar, brandy, coffee, tea, cloathings…furnished to Mrs. Colhoun for the use of herself and her family." DeSaussure, a lowcountry Federalist, also invested heavily on Floride's behalf in the new Bank of the United States, buying nearly $20,000 of stock between 1803 and 1807.[3]

As was the custom among wealthy lowcountry families, Floride hired tutors for her children, including young Floride, who had been born on her father's Rice Hope Plantation in Berkeley County, South Carolina, in 1792. Floride was twelve years old in 1804 when Calhoun came to Newport, and was being tutored in reading, writing, and music, including the fashionable "piano forte." In Newport, the Colhouns attended Trinity Episcopal Church, where the young Floride sometimes filled in for the church organist. She also knew how to ride a horse. In 1810 the estate accounts record $27 spent "for saddle and bridle for Miss Floride."[4] It seems that Floride raised her children as the members of the wealthy lowcountry elite that they were, a very different experience than John C. Calhoun's backcountry upbringing; his four years hunting, fishing, and running his father's plantation with his mother; and his education at Moses Waddel's backwoods academy.

Nevertheless, Calhoun soon endeared himself to his young cousins and to his cousin's widow, who quickly came to depend on him for advice. He would later confess to her, "I know not why, from my first acquaintance with you at New Port, I have loved you as a mother."[5] Certainly his attachment to Floride and her family filled a void for a studious young man who had no father and mother of his own, but it strains credulity to believe that the ambitious young Calhoun did not immediately see the advantages of cultivating a relationship with his wealthy kinswoman. His years with his mother likely served him well in his relationship with Floride, another widow with young children, and the two would correspond extensively for the next few years, he always addressing her in letters as "Dear Madam" and she adopting "Dear John." His letters to her are so lengthy and numerous, far outnumbering his correspondence with anyone else during this period of his life, that one wonders whether Calhoun secretly had the thought that at thirty-nine his cousin's rich widow was not at all an old woman.

Floride's letters reveal a woman with a fatalistic sense of life as well as a deep and fervent faith. Relating an illness in one of her first letters to Calhoun, she wrote of the "unspeakable blessing, that I the most helpless of mortals have been brought to put my whole trust and confidence in Him who has enabled me to say *His will be done*, should I be obliged to return Home." On one occasion a few years later, Floride took in a sick young stranger at her plantation in St. John Parish and nursed him for two weeks until he finally died, writing to a friend that she had "the satisfaction to see him become a Christian" before his death. In an emotional letter to her son James, written in 1819 when he was a midshipman on the frigate USS *Congress*, Floride wrote, "I can entertain but little hope of seeing you again, a heart rending thought indeed," and informed him that she "continually intercede[s] at the throne of [God's] grace" asking for James and her other children to experience the "transforming influence of his Holy Spirit."[6]

Just as at Waddel's school and at Yale, Calhoun continued to be surrounded by vibrant expressions of religious faith that were transforming the religious landscape of the new nation. He never experienced the dramatic conversions that many of his classmates at Yale underwent or that Floride prayed her children would, but in his letters to Floride he frequently acknowledged God, though in an impersonal sense that contrasted with but was sensitive to Floride's evangelical fervor. On one occasion, after relating news of the good health of their South Carolina friends, he wrote, "How thankful we ought to be to the author of all good for this high favor." Floride clearly worried about his religious condition, and in one letter he assured her that he was not offended by her concern for the state of his soul. "I receive with gratitude your friendly advice and anxious solicitude for my welfare on the all important subject of religion," he wrote. But he also quickly changed the subject.[7] His daughter Anna, his closest confidant, later recalled that her father never talked about his personal beliefs in her presence, although she insisted that he read the Bible "constantly & earnestly" and was always interested in religion.[8] Calhoun would always be drawn to the more rational forms of Christianity that he associated with the progress of human knowledge, but he was never hostile to the evangelical Christianity that surrounded him his entire life. He was simply, and completely, without the particular spectrum of emotions in which evangelicals like Floride expressed themselves.

CALHOUN SAILED BACK TO Charleston with Floride and her children in November, and in December he began studying law at the firm of Henry W. DeSaussure and his partner Timothy Ford, a connection no doubt facilitated by Floride. Returning to the seat of lowcountry power and elegance with a Yale education, the support and friendship of his cousin's wealthy widow, and as the student of one of Charleston's most prominent lawyers, Calhoun was poised to enter the South Carolina elite.[9]

Calhoun's time in DeSaussure's office exposed him to a stream of political thought that differed from both the backcountry republicanism of his childhood and the antislavery Federalism he had encountered in New England. The main currents of DeSaussure's lowcountry

Federalism can be seen in the political battle over representation in the South Carolina legislature that took place a decade before Calhoun arrived in Charleston, a continuation of the conflict between the low-country and backcountry that had been left unresolved by previous constitutional settlements. The episode involved in microcosm many of the arguments that would eventually make DeSaussure's young apprentice famous. It began in 1794 when a young, ambitious lawyer and politician named Robert Goodloe Harper, who at the time was living in Ninety-Six district, published an explosive indictment of the lowcountry-dominated state legislature, calling for a change to the South Carolina Constitution to account for the backcountry's larger white population. Arguing that representation should be based solely on population, not property, Harper boldly asserted the very Jeffersonian principle "that equality was the natural condition of man" and that any system of representation that did not represent each citizen equally was a form of tyranny.[10] Harper compared the decadent lowcountry with the industrious backcountry, and in a phrase that raised eyebrows and blood pressures in Charleston, he wrote that while the lowcountry "wishes for slaves; the [backcountry] would be better without them."[11]

Harper's *Address to the People of South Carolina* provoked numerous published responses from both DeSaussure and his law partner Timothy Ford. In his response, DeSaussure warned of the consequences of blindly applying abstract principles like equality, especially in a slave society. Did Harper really mean that equality was the natural condition of man? DeSaussure thought not. "Such is the state of society in South Carolina, that if this principle…was adopted and reduced to practice, it would instantly free the unfortunate slaves…and this fine country would be deluged with blood, and desolated by fire and sword," he wrote. "Nor would the ruin be confined to the low country." DeSaussure pointed southward to Haiti, in the throes of a revolution, to prove his point. In fact, he argued, inequality for some—in the form of slavery—could deepen an attachment to liberty in others. "It has been remarked of the ancient free states of Greece," wrote DeSaussure, "that their knowledge of the horrors of domestic slavery, which prevailed among them, rendered them more fiercely jealous of their liberties than any other people in the world."[12]

Timothy Ford made the point even more forcefully in his own attack on Harper. "Liberty is a principle which naturally and spontaneously contrasts itself with slavery," he wrote. "In no country on earth can the line of distinction ever be marked so boldly as in the low country…the instant a citizen is oppressed *below par*…in point of freedom, he approaches to the condition of his own slave, his spirit is at once aroused, and he necessarily recoils into his former standing." Just as antislavery advocates used reason and evidence from the natural world to argue for the principle of human equality and freedom, DeSaussure and Ford utilized reason and history to reach an opposite conclusion— that the love of liberty thrived in the presence of slavery.[13]

DeSaussure also attacked Harper's claim that representation should be based solely on population. A government in which representation was based on the principles of equality and free white population, DeSaussure argued, in which the backcountry would greatly outnumber the lowcountry, would threaten the rights of property and leave the lowcountry vulnerable to democratic tyranny. "It would, in its unprotected state," DeSaussure wrote of the lowcountry, "perhaps offer strong temptations to power to abuse it, and load it disproportionally." If Harper's proposals were put into practice, DeSaussure warned, the lowcountry could not be expected to submit willingly. "Countries become united by their reciprocal utility to each other…," he wrote. "Remove or weaken these bonds of union, or render them odious, and so diverse are the circumstances of the two countries, that it is probable an immediate separation would follow." As a boy in the backcountry, Calhoun had undoubtedly heard his father complain of the lowcountry's control of the state government. He may well have heard his father and uncles discussing Harper's *Address*. Reading law in the Charleston offices of DeSaussure and Ford he encountered, quite literally, the other side of the argument. He remained a son of the backcountry and the same convinced Jeffersonian that he had been at Yale, but in time he would come to see DeSaussure's and Ford's side of things more clearly.[14]

It may also have been from DeSaussure that Calhoun picked up a saying that he would repeat and adhere to throughout his life. On the title page of a volume of case law that DeSaussure published in 1817 there is a quote in Latin from Francis Bacon's collected works that reads, "Justitia best belle omnibus quod aequm est," which translates "The duties of life are more than life." The phrase came from a famous letter Bacon wrote to the Earl of Buckingham in which Bacon expressed his satisfaction at having heard all the court cases before him even though he was working himself to death. The phrase would become Calhoun's mantra, reflecting a stoic outlook that fit his temper better than evangelical fervor, although he never attributed the saying to Bacon or to DeSaussure.[15]

DESPITE HIS INCREASING TIES to the lowcountry, Calhoun's stay in Charleston did not impress him. In fact, the beautiful houses and lavish lifestyles of the Charleston elite grated on his backcountry sensibilities, and their apparent laxity in matters of religion struck him as of a piece with their indulgence and excess in other areas. Relaying the news that a religious revival had broken out in the city, he wrote to Floride, "What a happy change to that place; which in every thing was so extremely corrupt; and so particularly inattentive to every call of religion. I hope, and think it probable, that this happy change will extend itself from the city to the country. Surely no people ever so much needed a reform as those in the parishes near Charleston." Unfortunately, the reports of a revival were unfounded. "Every friend to religion and that place must regret it," he wrote, knowing Floride would agree.[16]

Five months after he arrived in Charleston he was on his way back north again, once again accompanying Floride and her family. He had determined to study the law in Litchfield, Connecticut, where he had heard of a law school that provided a type of practical, scientific training that was the first semblance of formal legal education in the country. Calhoun carried with him a letter from Henry DeSaussure introducing him to none other than DeSaussure's onetime enemy Robert Goodloe Harper, who was now a famous lawyer and Federalist fresh off a successful defense of Supreme Court Justice Samuel Chase against an impeachment attempt by Jeffersonians in Congress. DeSaussure congratulated Harper on his victory over the "wild measures of democracy" and introduced Calhoun as "the son of old Patrick Calhoun and a near relation of our late respected friend Mr. J.E. Colhoun." "This young southerner," DeSaussure wrote, "has been educated at New Haven, and has acquired more knowledge than is usual at his age...there are indications of a superior mind."[17]

It was on the same trip that Calhoun met the very source of DeSaussure's fears about the "wild measures of democracy." The reference, in a letter to his cousin Andrew Pickens Jr., is so brief that some biographers have doubted Calhoun's meeting with Thomas Jefferson happened at all. Noting public speculation about the destination of a French fleet, Calhoun casually mentioned to his cousin that "I heard the President (I got acquainted with him at Washingt[o]n) predict the fleet's destination."[18] It is tempting to imagine the scene—the young Calhoun meeting the sixty-two-year-old author of the Declaration and of the Kentucky resolution that first introduced the idea of nullification into American political discourse. One observer in 1790 described Jefferson as a tall, slender man, in clothes too small for him, who sat "on one hip commonly, and with one of his shoulders elevated much above the other...He spoke almost without ceasing; but even his discourse partook of his personal demeanor. It was loose and rambling; and yet he scattered information wherever he went, and some even brilliant sentiments sparkled from him." In 1804 a puzzled British observer again noted Jefferson's mismatched clothes, writing that the leader of the Republican Party's appearance was "very much like that of a tall, large-boned farmer."[19]

One wonders very much what the two men talked about besides the French fleet. Perhaps about their mutual love of what they would have called "farming." Calhoun never again mentioned the meeting, but Floride's son James Edward Colhoun, then a child, also recalled that it happened. If so, it was a meeting between two men—one young, one old by the standards of the day—who had much in common politically in 1805, between one man who had helped to birth the American nation and one who would set the stage for its unmaking, partly by relying on the sage of Monticello's own ideas.[20]

On reaching Connecticut Calhoun took a series of stages to Litchfield, where he had arrived by late July. On the last leg of his journey, from Hartford to Litchfield, he found himself on the stage with a portly, red-faced man who turned out to be Tapping Reeve, the famous proprietor of the law school in Litchfield that Calhoun was traveling to attend. Calhoun wrote to Floride that on the ride to Litchfield he found Reeve "open and agreeable," but in many ways the young South Carolinian and his new teacher could not have been more different. Reeve famously argued his legal cases with such passion that he frequently forgot to finish sentences, leaving the jury and judge—even speech itself—far behind in his flights of rhetoric. He was so absentminded that one resident of Litchfield recalled seeing him wander down the street, deep in thought, holding the empty bridle of a long-escaped horse. After the death of his beloved wife in 1797, Reeve had married his housekeeper, solidifying a local reputation for eccentricity.[21]

Despite all this, Reeve was also widely acknowledged as perhaps the most brilliant legal mind of his generation and a long parade of students—beginning with his brother-in-law, the future vice president Aaron Burr—had made their way to Litchfield to seek out Reeve's instruction since the 1780s. For the first half century of the nation's existence Reeve's law school was the most prominent and respected seat of legal education in the country. By the time it closed in 1834 the school had educated over one hundred members of Congress, three Supreme

Court judges, and scores of state judges throughout the nation. What Reeve could not have known in 1805 was that the tall young southerner sitting across from him in the stage that day would be the closest he would ever come to placing one of his students in the White House.[22]

If he knew much about Reeve, Calhoun probably did not tell him about his detour to meet Jefferson. Firmly entrenched in Connecticut's political elite, which sided wholly with the Federalists as party sentiment emerged in national politics during the 1790s, Reeve was also a pious Congregationalist who feared the irreligion and disorder of the Jeffersonian Revolution of 1800 and saw the law as a tool to blunt its force. Indeed, many Connecticut Federalists saw the law school at Litchfield as the heart of a counteroffensive against the rising tide of Jeffersonian democracy and an anchor of stability in a period of economic uncertainty. One historian of Reeve's school has called it "a propaganda mill for the Federalist vision of social order" and Litchfield itself a "Federalist utopia" where as late as the 1820s old men were still wearing silk stockings and knee breeches.[23] Calhoun came to Litchfield just as the school was beginning to attract more students from beyond Connecticut, but he was one of the few southerners and even fewer admirers of Thomas Jefferson. Whether Calhoun wore the pantaloons and loose, long hair that visibly marked many young Jeffersonians we cannot know, but on the inside he was a Jeffersonian through and through.[24]

At first, Calhoun missed Floride and her family, although he described even the course of his emotions with rational detachment. "For two or three days, after I left New-Port," he wrote to her, "I felt much of that lonesome sensation, which I believe everyone experiences after departing from those with whom he has been long intimate. However by mingling and conversing with others, I have felt it much diminished; and by a few days application to studies, which to me are highly interesting, I have no doubt it will be entirely removed."[25]

His studies soon consumed all Calhoun's time, and, just as he suspected, his loneliness left him. "I return…with much pleasure to the cultivation of Blackston's [*sic*] acquaintance," he wrote to Floride, refer-ring to William Blackstone, the eighteenth-century English jurist who in 1765 had published the first comprehensive interpretation of British common law. Calhoun's mention of Blackstone points to the main rea-son that many students attended Reeve's school: in the early nineteenth century there was no comprehensive commentary on an "American" system of law available in print, and the customary practice of reading law with a practicing lawyer was notoriously haphazard and exploit-ative. Reeve's innovation—what separated his school from the older apprenticeship model of learning the law—was his organization of the study of law into a series of topics that he covered in daily lectures over the course of fourteen to eighteen months. Just as Blackstone's *Com-mentaries*, originally delivered as lectures, had offered the first system-atic overview of English common law, so Reeve's lectures offered what could be considered the first comprehensive summary of the law in America, although one still substantially based on Blackstone. Unlike Blackstone, Reeve never published his lectures. They survive only in the notebooks kept by his students.[26]

Students' days were ordered by the clock, an emerging characteristic of the market economy in which they would work. They attended ninety-minute lectures in the morning in the small, one-room building next to Reeve's house on South Street in Litchfield. The house had no heat, even in winter, and students sat at wooden desks while Reeve perched at the front of the room on a high wooden chair to give his lectures. Students spent the rest of the day exploring the day's topic in the school's large library, perhaps reading relevant sections of Black-stone, and copying the lectures and their research notes into bound folio volumes that would provide them with an invaluable advantage over competitors once they began to practice law. It was a process that assumed independently motivated students, and Calhoun reported to Floride that "in order to take the course of law lectures, not as they usually are; but as they ought to be, I find, I must devote almost the whole of my time to that purpose."[27]

Students left Tapping Reeve's school with what was, in effect, a comprehensive legal textbook. Another important innovation that Reeve imported from English practice was the holding of a moot court every week, where students would read a hastily prepared statement on some legal question and be judged by Reeve or James Gould, who had joined the school as Reeve's partner in 1798.[28] Calhoun's longtime friend and political ally Virgil Maxcy, who evidently heard the stories when he visited Litchfield the year after Calhoun left, wrote that Calhoun "usually prepared himself by reflection on the subjects proposed for discussion, but rarely, if ever, committed to writing the arrangement of his topics, or took notes of the arguments of those who preceded him. He relied on his tenacious memory for preserving the order established in his own mind."[29] For an aspiring politician, it was excellent practice.

In their lectures Reeve and his partner Gould presented the law as "an orderly science revolving around a set of crucial principles." Reeve, in particular, portrayed himself as a scientist uncovering the deeper principles on which the law rested through a process of "historical deduction."[30] This modern approach to the unwieldy body of custom, precedent, and statutes that constituted the common law tradition trained Calhoun to view legal and, later, constitutional matters as involving deep, sometimes unspoken principles that undergirded and gave meaning to the text of a law or piece of legislation, but which might not be apparent on a literal reading. This scientific approach to the law also meant that the education at Litchfield was practical, not political. Students at Litchfield in 1805 may have heard plenty about Reeve's Federalist sympathies outside the classroom, but inside it they heard nothing about contemporary politics.[31]

To begin the year, Reeve gave a series of lectures on "Domestic Relations," the first of which was on "Master and Servant."[32] In the lecture, Reeve defined a master as "one who, by law, has a right to a personal authority over another," and he defined a servant as "such person over whom such authority may be rightfully exercised." The kind and extent of a master's authority and a servant's duties depended on the role and position of the "servant," and in his lecture Reeve outlined six different categories: slavery, apprenticeship, menial servitude, day labor, agents, and debtors assigned to service. Calhoun may have been surprised to hear that Reeve counted attorneys as a category of servant (as agents), although with a very specific set of duties.[33] Reeve's lecture on masters and servants was part of a view of society in which a person's social position, age, sex, race, and gender assigned to them different rights and duties. In this way, the law simply reflected the variety of organic social relationships that made up society, and slavery was only one of many hierarchical, reciprocal relationships that characterized a functioning society. In the same way that Thomas Jefferson claimed in the Declaration to be describing the world as it was, a world in which all men were created equal, and in the same way that Thomas Paine ridiculed monarchy as a human invention not justified by reason or nature, so Reeve and other conservatives claimed the law was a science that only reflected the world as it was. And that world, they said, was a hierarchical world in which propertied white men had the most liberty but also the most responsibility. Nearly everyone in Calhoun's world claimed to have reason, nature, and science on their side.

On slavery, Reeve struck a delicate balance. The practice could not be justified by either natural or English common law, he argued, following Blackstone, and yet since slavery was part of the law of the land it had to be accorded space in Litchfield's practical curriculum.[34] Following Reeve's lecture Calhoun may well have pulled the first volume of Blackstone's *Commentaries* off the shelf—it was one of the few books students were allowed to take back to their rooms, and given Calhoun's approach to his studies it seems likely that he took advantage of this privilege. On "negro slavery," in particular as practiced in the eighteenth-century British Empire, Blackstone was clear: it could not exist under English law. "This spirit of liberty is so deeply implanted in our constitution, and rooted even in our very soil, that a slave or a negro, the moment he lands in England, falls under the protection

of the laws, and with regard to all natural rights becomes...a freeman."
Only a few years after Blackstone published his *Commentaries*, the decision in the 1772 Somerset case concerning a runaway slave in London
would be widely interpreted as confirming this judgment.[35]

If Calhoun kept reading, he found that Blackstone did not limit his
condemnation of slavery to the sacred soil of England, but embraced a
vision of natural rights that precluded a state of servitude in which "an
absolute and unlimited power is given to the master over the life and
future of the slave...indeed it is repugnant to reason, and the principles
of natural law, that such a state should subsist any where." Blackstone
also bluntly dismissed the three ancient legal justifications for slavery—
capture in battle, self-sale, and hereditary slavery—as "built upon false
foundations."[36]

Crucially, Blackstone's criticism of slavery was limited by his narrowly defined version of slavery as absolute power over another human
being. He believed that masters could be entitled to the "perpetual service" of a servant if that service had been acquired "by contract or the
like." Observing that capture in battle could give the captor "a sort of
qualified property" in a captive until his ransom was paid, Blackstone
wrote, "this doctrine seems to have been extended to negro-servants,
who are purchased, when captives, of the nations with whom they are
at war...though, accurately speaking, that property consists rather in
the perpetual service, than in the body or person, of the captive." But
Blackstone's use of the term "property" in referring to the service a slave
might owe a master immediately exposed the ambiguities and contradictions of African slavery as it had emerged in the Atlantic world over
the past century. Were slaves persons with rights, or were they (or their
labor) property? Or both?[37]

Blackstone did not answer these questions. But at the beginning of
the second volume, on property, Blackstone observed—not writing
about slavery—"There is nothing which so generally strikes the imagination, and engages the affections of mankind, as the right of property;
or that sole and despotic dominion which one man claims and

exercises over the external things of the world, in total exclusion of the right of any other individual in the universe." American slaveholders would apply a similar definition of property to their slaves, which would make any challenge to the system of slavery all the more inflammatory.[38]

CALHOUN'S NATURAL PROCLIVITIES FOR study were encouraged by the vaguely hostile Federalist environment of Litchfield. "I take little amusement; and live a very studious life," he wrote to Floride. "This place is so much agitated by party feelings that both Mr. Felder and myself find it prudent to form few connections in town. This, though somewhat disagreeable is not unfavorable to our studies." John M. Felder, a fellow South Carolinian, was one of Calhoun's closest associates in Litchfield and a political ally. When a local newspaper editor, Selleck Osborn, was imprisoned for his biting criticism of the local Federalist establishment, Calhoun and Felder were the only law school students who dared to march in a procession to salute Osborn in his jail cell.[39]

But whatever he told Floride, who after all was his patroness, Calhoun obviously found time to enjoy Litchfield, which was known for its lively social life. Law students—however studious—were still young men, and one student recalled that "often the midnight air resounded with the songs of midnight rioters."[40]

Other aspects of social life in Litchfield were highly refined thanks to the presence of Sarah Pierce's Litchfield Female Academy. Pierce, the formidable Puritan proprietor of the academy, felt strongly that women were the intellectual equals of men, telling one graduating class that their education had been designed "to practically vindicate the equality of the female intellect."[41] This intellectual equality was intended to serve the ends of the emerging ideal of republican motherhood, in which women were responsible for instilling in their sons the virtue on which the country's future depended, but it was nevertheless a remarkably egalitarian vision for the time. Pierce's views fit well with Tapping Reeve's controversial position in his famous lecture on "the law of baron and femme" that women, even when married, had the right to hold property for themselves.[42] Calhoun, already comfortable in his relationships with necessarily independent women like his mother and Floride, socialized with the students of Pierce's academy at the balls, on sleigh rides, and at other social events designed to facilitate interaction between eligible law students and potential partners and train young men and women for the elite social settings that lay in their future. In January he wrote Floride, "We have excellent sleighing here. I was out last evening for the first time this season; and found it very agreeable. It is a mode of conveyance that the people of this state are very fond of." In typical fashion, he recommended the practice to Floride, noting it was also "very conducive to your health." Calhoun did not mention what company he had on the sleigh ride, but we may assume he was not alone.[43]

By April, Calhoun was considerably less enamored of the Connecticut winter. "What a cold, disagreeable spring we have had," he wrote. He was recovering from a severe cold and was tired of Litchfield. He wanted to visit Newport, he wrote, but "everything must yield to improvement at present." He asked Floride to give his love to her children. "Tell James I wish to hear him read the bible very much; and that I hope he will learn from it to be a good boy."[44] Three months later the weather was better and Calhoun was nearing the end of his studies at Litchfield, but also running short of money. He wrote Floride that his brother James had abandoned his mercantile business in Charleston for the life of a planter, a change that Calhoun approved of but that left his brother temporarily without funds to support him. "If you can make it perfectly convenient to supply me till the fall you will oblige both my brother and myself," he wrote, asking Floride for two hundred dollars. He received his diploma from the law school at the end of July.[45]

By December he was back in Charleston, having made the trip back to South Carolina on horseback alone. "In a tour so long, and without a companion, and a stranger to the road I necessarily experienced many solitary hours," he told Floride. "My reward was the perpetual gratification of curiosity in passing through a country entirely new to me, romantic in a high degree, and abounding with many objects of considerable novelty."[46] As he passed through Pennsylvania and Virginia, Calhoun no doubt thought about his parents and uncles, who had made the same trip fifty years earlier. But he undoubtedly also thought about the future that lay ahead in South Carolina now that his ambitious and careful preparation was complete.

FOUR

"I Am Your True Lover, John C. Calhoun"

ALHOUN ARRIVED IN CHARLESTON IN December 1806, where he continued reading law in Henry DeSaussure's law office for the next six months. Combined with the time he spent in DeSaussure's office before leaving for Litchfield, this meant that Calhoun would eventually spend nearly as much time reading law with Henry DeSaussure as he had spent at Tapping Reeve's school. While in Charleston, he boarded with a French Protestant minister, Martin Detargney, on Church Street, and kept to himself. "Since my arrival here I have been very much a recluse," he told Floride. Charleston never exercised its famous charms on Calhoun.[1]

But fate soon offered Calhoun the opportunity he had been waiting for to enter public life. In June he returned to Abbeville, the town nearest to his father's plantation and all his Calhoun relatives, where he continued reading law with George Bowie, a local attorney who was married to one of his cousins, in order to fulfill a requirement for joining the South Carolina Bar. He had only been back in Abbeville a few weeks when news arrived that on June 22 a British ship, HMS *Leopard*, had attacked and boarded the USS *Chesapeake* off the coast of Virginia, looking for deserters from the British Navy. The attack spelled the beginning of the end of Thomas Jefferson's efforts to keep the United

States neutral in the wars between Great Britain and France, which had begun when Napoleon Bonaparte came to power in the wake of the French Revolution and would continue until his defeat at Waterloo in 1815. A succession of American presidents during these years would try to follow George Washington's advice to steer clear of involvement in European conflicts, but the fact that the United States traded with both nations, as well as Great Britain's desperate need for sailors and their failure to carefully distinguish between British deserters and American citizens in filling this need, made American ships prime targets. Both Britain and France had been guilty of not respecting the neutrality of American shipping, but British dominance on the water meant that Great Britain had been the worse offender, and the attack on the *Chesapeake* was seen as a brazen insult to American sovereignty.

The attack provoked public meetings across the country, including in South Carolina. In early August a gathering of citizens at the Abbeville Courthouse elected Calhoun's cousin Joseph as the chairman of a committee charged with drafting public resolutions to express their outrage. The committee then chose the newly returned, northern-educated son of old Patrick Calhoun to draft the resolutions, which were subsequently published in newspapers across the state.

The resolution itself reads like the work of a young man conscious of the occasion, still leaning for help on the elevated and formal style of the college debating society and the moot court, but nevertheless absolutely clear about the argument he wanted to make. As he would so many times in the future, Calhoun argued that the issue at stake was a principle, one that could not be compromised without ruin. Britain's insult to the nation's honor threatened the very existence of the United States as a sovereign country since a nation depended for its existence on the acknowledgment of its peers. Just as a man who failed to respond to an insult proved that he was no true man of honor, a nation that failed to respond to an insult proved that it was no true nation. In the United States, of course, the national honor resided in and must be defended by the people, "in whom the Sovereignty of the country ultimately resides." To fail to respond to the British attack on the *Chesapeake* "would disgrace our character abroad, and exhibit us a degenerate and pusillanimous people." Americans were a peace-loving people, and their long suffering in the face of British insults proved it. But Great Britain, Calhoun wrote, "seems determined to demonstrate, if possible, that our Love of Peace, instead of a noble principle and a generous sentiment, is only mean sufferance, and stupid insensibility." The United States had to respond, either commercially or militarily, and the resolutions offered the Jefferson administration the support of the citizens of Abbeville in whichever course it chose.[2]

Even more than the resolutions, Calhoun's performance at the gathering in Abbeville launched his political career. His friend Virgil Maxcy later recalled that the crowd requested Calhoun to address them when his resolutions were proposed. "The assemblage was very large," Maxcy wrote. "It was the first time he was brought before the public." The last time many of those gathered at the courthouse had seen Calhoun he had been a teenager. But he was undeniably one of them. Now he was also the product of the best education the country could provide, certainly one of the best-educated men in that part of South Carolina, and he addressed his fellow citizens with an argument that confirmed their deepest feelings and sentiments about the crisis. Calhoun's reputation as an orator would later rest mainly on his powerfully logical arguments, not his style, but his address that day hit the mark. George Bowie's younger brother Alexander, who was present at the meeting as an eighteen-year-old, remembered that Calhoun's performance "astonished every body."[3]

As HE WAITED TO draw on the political capital he had earned at the Abbeville Courthouse, Calhoun finished his legal apprenticeship—South Carolina law required a year as a clerk in a law office before applying to join the bar. He continued with George Bowie for the rest of the year, applied, and was admitted to the bar in December 1807 just as Thomas Jefferson passed the disastrous Embargo Act, which shuttered American ports in an effort to coerce the British into respecting American rights. Calhoun immediately opened an office in Abbeville, and for the next three years he practiced law as his political career and his personal fortunes took shape.[4]

Shortly after returning to Abbeville, Calhoun told Floride, "I... cannot but think this part of South Carolina very much improved of late; and that it still is in a state of progressive improvement." One mark of that improvement was the fact that the region was increasingly known within the state as the upcountry, a term that connoted progress and political equality with the older, wealthier lowcountry. Calhoun noted that there were "simernaries of learning"—schools like Waddel's—dotting the upcountry. The progress he expected was in the "society, morals, and information" of the region, which he hoped would soon equal "any other part of the United States."[5]

Part of the changing face of the upcountry was due to the religious revival emanating from Cane Ridge, Kentucky, which reached the region in 1802. Eventually known as the Great Revival, the religious awakening swept increasing numbers in the upcountry into Presbyterian, Baptist, and especially Methodist churches. In 1799, roughly 8 percent of the adult white population in the upcountry were members of a church. By 1810 the number was 23 percent, or about fourteen thousand people, with many more attending services.[6] Calhoun likely approved of this change, although like other observers, especially Presbyterians, he may have been troubled by the emotional and sometimes physical expressiveness of the converts. After growing dramatically between 1790 and 1800, the upcountry's population was churning during this period as large numbers of people moved in and out of the region. In this environment, the revivals performed a social as well as spiritual function, knitting together a highly mobile population into churches that became important institutional expressions of community in a rapidly changing society.[7]

In addition to religion, the advances Calhoun grouped together as "progress" were also the result of a cotton boom—the first in the South—that would continue in the upcountry until around 1820, firmly entrenching cotton and slavery in the upcountry and finally aligning the political and economic interests of the upcountry and the lowcountry. Elites in both areas had been cooperating since the 1790s on a series of initiatives, including public schools and transportation measures such as canals, that were designed to render the rowdy citizens of the upcountry less of a political threat through education and commercial links to the lowcountry. Most of these initiatives had failed, but cotton succeeded.[8] Eli Whitney's cotton gin allowed upcountry planters to plant short staple cotton that thrived in the soil of the upcountry, and by 1800 planters like the transplanted Virginian Wade Hampton I were starting to reap huge profits in the upcountry from the combination of cheap land, enslaved labor, and cotton. Hampton earned $75,000 on his first cotton crop in 1799, and by 1810 he was making profits of $150,000 annually. By the time he died in 1835 Hampton was one of the richest men in the South. Since they already possessed the land and slaves that cotton growing required, the Calhoun family profited from the boom, as well. Calhoun's older brother William became known around Abbeville as "Cotton Billy," and owned thirty-one slaves by 1820. In 1793, the year Eli Whitney invented the cotton gin, the entire state of South Carolina had exported only ninety-four thousand pounds of cotton, almost all of it the Sea Island cotton grown near the coast. By 1811 the upcountry alone exported over thirty million pounds of short staple cotton.[9]

Others besides Calhoun noted the progress that came with the cotton boom. In 1809, South Carolina historian David Ramsay marveled at the progress of the upcountry and attributed it largely to short staple cotton. In particular, Ramsay noted that cotton had benefited the "poor white men" who had previously been of "little account other than as overseers." "In estimating the value of cotton," Ramsay wrote, "its capacity to excite industry among the lower classes of people, and to fill the country with an independent industrious yeomanry, is of high importance." The main advantage of cotton, Ramsay observed, was that it could be grown by those with little capital and no slaves. But of course, most of those who grew cotton hoped eventually to join the slaveholding class, and in the first two decades of the nineteenth century many in the upcountry did. In 1800 about 25 percent of upcountry white families owned slaves. By 1820 that number was nearly 40 percent. One scholar estimated that the number of slaves grew by 194 percent between 1790 and 1810. If lowcountry elites like Henry DeSaussure had once worried about the upcountry's commitment to slavery, by the early nineteenth century they worried no longer. For Calhoun and others, the lesson of the cotton boom was an enduring vision of slavery working hand in hand with what he and others saw as moral and economic progress.[10]

Not everyone agreed. In fact, during the first decade of the century, some of the Presbyterian clergy in the upstate viewed the contagion of cotton and slavery with dismay. Presbyterian ministers William Williamson and Robert Wilson, the latter of whom served the church founded by Patrick Calhoun at Long Canes, were so disgusted with the spread of slaveholding that they left the state in 1804 and moved to Ohio, where Williamson emancipated his slaves and encouraged his relatives to do the same. Wilson's successor at Long Canes, the minister Daniel Gray, compared the upcountry's growing attachment to slavery to the "fleshpots of Egypt." This variety of religious antislavery would be nearly extinct in the upcountry by 1820, but for a time at least, the egalitarian theology spread by the turn-of-the-century revivals supported a short-lived strain of antislavery sentiment.[11]

Some even closer to Calhoun may have had doubts about the institution, as well. The same summer that Calhoun made his political debut in Abbeville, Henry DeSaussure wrote to Floride Colhoun advising her that he wished to use the surplus funds from the estate that year to buy slaves instead of stock in the National Bank (as he had done previously) in light of the impending ban on the transatlantic slave trade, set to take effect on January 1, 1808. "As soon as this prohibition takes effect," he wrote, "negroes will rise in price, and this will continue to be the case for a considerable time." The need to buy slaves was particularly pressing since the estate of Floride's late husband held plenty of land to be passed down to each of her children upon their marriage or coming of age: "But when the negroes come to be divided among them, the number will be small for each." DeSaussure then noted, "Yet as you have scruples on the subject, I should be reluctant to make purchases without your concurrence."[12] If Floride had doubts about slavery, or at least about the slave trade, she would not have been unusual among the southern elite in 1807, although doubts were rarer in South Carolina than in Virginia. Nevertheless, slave ships poured into Charleston harbor in the year before the slave trade officially ended, disembarking more than eighteen thousand enslaved people to be sold in the city's slave markets in 1807 alone.[13]

CALHOUN'S LAW PRACTICE PLUNGED him deep into the inner workings of cotton production and slavery in the upcountry during these years, and at the bottom of many of the cases he tried were legal questions created by treating people as property. In early 1809 Calhoun argued a case in the Chancery Court at Abbeville in front of his mentor and Floride's lawyer, Henry DeSaussure, who served as judge for the court. Calhoun served as attorney for a man named Robert Elgin who was being sued by his wife's children from her first marriage over the ownership of two enslaved women, Phoebe and Nell, and their children, who the first husband had left to his heirs at his death twenty-five years earlier. The lawsuit centered on a subsequent agreement that had given his wife the use of the two women while she lived, an arrangement that transferred their temporary use to her second husband, Robert Elgin, when she remarried. Now, twenty-five years later, her children claimed that Elgin and their mother had moved from Maryland to South Carolina in order to avoid the terms of the will, especially the loss of Phoebe's and Nell's six children, who were now adults and, in DeSaussure's words, "prime negroes," making them extremely valuable. They wanted the court to force Elgin to provide security—a guarantee to return the two women and their children when their mother died.

Calhoun's task was to prove Elgin's ownership of Phoebe and Nell's children. In legal terms, Elgin was a "tenant" who had been leased the use of the two women, and in his argument Calhoun relied on the well-established principle that "in leases for years, of stock, the young ones proceeding from them, during the lease, belong absolutely to the lessee as profits arising and severed from the principle." This precedent, he argued, "would be more forcible as applied to negro slaves, than to cattle or other stock; on the principle of humanity in keeping the parents and children together," and because it gave "an interest in the children to the intermediate tenant, who has the care of the females when pregnant and their support after delivery, and the nurture of the young ones, long useless and always chargeable." Calhoun's argument relied on a version of what would eventually become a standard defense for slavery: that treating slaves as property gave masters a financial interest in the wellbeing of their slaves. In his notes on the case, DeSaussure observed, "There is great force in this argument."

Since the will had been drawn up in Maryland, Calhoun also pored over available case law until he found confirmation that Maryland law agreed with him. DeSaussure eventually ruled that Elgin had to provide security to his wife's children for Phoebe and Nell, but not for their children since they belonged to him. In a cruel irony, this meant that even though Phoebe and Nell were kept with their adult children for the moment, they would eventually be separated from them on the death of Elgin's wife, who was already "aged and infirm" at the time of the trial. In the end it was clearly property rights, and not considerations of humanity, that were most important in South Carolina law. In the long argument over where slaves should fit in a Lockean scheme of government—whether they possessed the inalienable rights to life and liberty that belonged to all men or whether they were the chattel of owners whose property rights must be protected by any legitimate government—Calhoun worked within and shared the assumptions of a legal system that came down firmly on the side of slaveholders. All of his northern education had not changed that.[14]

The law was always a means to an end for Calhoun. After practicing law in Abbeville for more than year, Calhoun lamented to Floride that he was not able to visit her in Charleston because he had to be in court. "I feel myself now and while I continue in the practice of the law almost as a slave chained down to a particular place and course of life," he wrote, using a simile that every white South Carolinian understood. "I still feel a strong aversion to the law; and am determined to forsake it as soon as I can make a decent independence; for I am not ambitious of great wealth."[15]

Calhoun's disregard for money would eventually haunt him, but wealth was never his goal in life. He was always after something more immaterial but, most of his contemporaries agreed, more worthwhile and lasting: fame. To be remembered, to leave one's name in the book of history, all the ancient writers Calhoun had read at Moses Waddel's academy taught, was one of the highest and best accomplishments in human life. Ever since leaving his father's plantation Calhoun had single-mindedly pursued a college and legal education as a means of becoming a public man. The ancients also warned that ambition without virtue was dangerous, and along with his intense desire for distinction, from very early on Calhoun clearly had firm beliefs, including a strong sense of duty and a set of political commitments that he had retained even in the Federalist dominated environs of Yale and Litchfield. And yet his ambition was a powerful, primordial force in his life, shaping the application of his principles in ways that he rarely acknowledged to himself or to others.

His speech in Abbeville in the summer of 1807 put Calhoun on the political map in the upcountry, and the following summer and fall he began his political career in earnest, running for the state legislature. Given Calhoun's later reputation as a theoretician, his success in this early political campaign is a reminder that he was also a formidable campaigner. In the upcountry, he had to be. South Carolina's state government was famously undemocratic in its upper reaches—the state legislature appointed the governor and virtually all other important offices, for which there were usually also high property qualifications. But at the local level citizens of the upcountry during these years practiced an "informal, but direct and intimate, style of democracy" in which candidates for the legislature and Congress campaigned vigorously for their neighbors' votes.[16] During the year that Calhoun was in Litchfield studying law, his Yale classmate Edward Hooker—who hailed from the Federalist stronghold of Connecticut—visited upcountry South Carolina and described the plain style of democracy he found there. Hooker admired the solemnity and simplicity of a church service he attended, but was shocked by the bare feet and shirtsleeves of the men and by women wearing men's hats. At another service Hooker witnessed a candidate for political office, Colonel Lemuel Alston, working the crowd, and noted sarcastically that "from the Colonel's demeanor, a superficial observer would suppose he really came thither to worship God but an adept in the science of human nature, would…be apt to guess that he came to worship the people." Alston reportedly placed a large Bible in the front room of his home as soon as he started campaigning. At the town of Pickensville on Election Day, the "astonished" Hooker described a scene of "noise, blab and confusion" as three candidates for Congress and numerous candidates for the state legislature plied potential voters with speeches, whiskey, and professions of faith in the political creed of Thomas Jefferson. "The minds of uninformed people were much agitated," wrote Hooker in disgust, "and many well-meaning people were made to believe the national welfare was at stake and would be determined by the issue of this back-woods election." One candidate at least had the decency to offer voters whiskey indoors at the local tavern, while another "had his grog bench in the middle of the street and presided over the whiskey jugs himself." In addition to the smell of whiskey, the air was full of "swearing, cursing and threatening," and handbills accusing various candidates of Federalist sympathies or financial fraud circulated through the crowds. Hooker wrote that the whole scene was "highly alarming, when viewed by one who considers…what inroads are made upon the sacred right of suffrage." The frenzy of democracy in the upstate produced exceptionally high levels of voter participation as well as high levels of turnover in political office until at least the 1830s.[17]

In October 1808, Calhoun was elected to the South Carolina House of Representatives from the Abbeville district. We can assume he engaged in some of the same sort of politicking as the candidates Hooker observed two years before. But voters could also be sure that the son of Patrick Calhoun was a reliable Republican, and the number of Calhouns who were elders in Presbyterian churches throughout the upcountry proved his religious bona fides better than a prominently placed Bible ever could.

CALHOUN ARRIVED IN COLUMBIA, the state capital, in late 1808, just after a special session of the General Assembly had passed an amendment to the South Carolina constitution that finally settled the long-running argument about the balance of representation between the upcountry and lowcountry. The Compromise of 1808, as it would be called, was a victory for the upcountry, but it also provided long-term security for the lowcountry against the sorts of populist attacks that lowcountry Federalists like Henry DeSaussure had feared in the 1790s. It provided that representation in the South Carolina House of Representatives would be determined by a formula that weighted population and property equally, while giving each election district as well as the old parishes of the lowcountry one representative in the state senate. This meant that, by 1810, the upcountry would control the House, while the lowcountry would control the Senate, providing each region an effective legislative bulwark against the other. Just as importantly to the upcountry, the amended constitution provided that reapportionment based on the new terms would occur regularly every ten years, ensuring that the rapidly growing white population in districts like Abbeville would continue to gain political power in the years ahead.[18]

Thirty years later, Calhoun described the significance of the compromise as he saw it in private correspondence, writing, "We are almost entirely free from party politicks, as far as our State Legislature is concerned...This results from our peculiar political institutions, which from the admirable adjustment of the conflicting political elements of the State, prevents any one from gaining the ascendancy and oppressing the other, and thus preserves harmony, and produces that tendency to union, which so strongly characterizes our State, and gives it that disperportional weight in the Union, compared to its population & wealth."[19] In his posthumously published *Discourse on the Constitution and Government of the United States*, Calhoun would hold up the Compromise of 1808 as an example of a constitutional arrangement that had protected liberty and allowed for coexistence in the face of deep differences of interest. It did this, he would explain, by giving each section of the state the power to defeat any potentially oppressive legislation, with the result that each section had to consent to pass any significant measures.[20] The result, Calhoun and many others in South Carolina believed, was political harmony and union. The compromise and the long history of conflict between the upcountry and lowcountry over the principles and distribution of representation that preceded it were the seeds of Calhoun's most famous contribution to political theory, the concurrent majority, the idea that significant interests in a society should have the power to protect themselves through a legislative veto, and that important legislation should be passed by consensus, rather than a majority.

In 1808 the compromise was real—both the lowcountry and upcountry got and gave in the arrangement, but Calhoun's later analysis obscured the way in which the state had become unified by a common economic interest in slavery during the decade preceding the compromise. The rapid spread of slaveholding in the middle and upper parts of the state during the cotton boom had erased the hard distinctions that had characterized the two parts of the state in the 1790s. If viewed from the perspective of slaveholding, instead of regions, in 1810 under the new compromise black-majority districts held only two seats fewer in the lower house than white-majority districts, while black-majority districts easily controlled the upper house, and by the time Calhoun lauded the compromise in 1838 black-majority districts controlled both the upper and lower houses by clear majorities. In other words, slavery was responsible for the harmony and union that Calhoun so valued just as much as the state's political arrangements, though both played a role.[21]

Calhoun's view of the compromise also papered over the way that a growing Republican political ascendancy in the state—even in the lowcountry—created a situation in which beleaguered lowcountry Federalists saw the compromise as their last chance to maintain their influence in the state legislature. (A bill proposing to assign representation entirely on the basis of white population, obliterating lowcountry influence, had been narrowly defeated in 1807.) The compromise was made in the same spirit as the founding of South Carolina College, established by the legislature in 1801 and opened in Columbia in 1805. As Henry DeSaussure wrote of the motives behind the institution's founding, "We of the lower country well knew that the power of the State was thence forward to be in the upper country, and we desired our future rulers to be educated men."[22]

The ink was barely dry on the compromise when upcountry representatives began pushing the state government to eliminate property and tax qualification for voting, a measure that would further benefit the white-majority districts in the upcountry. Since 1790, South Carolina had required voters to own fifty acres of land or to have paid tax that would indicate property worth roughly this amount. Calhoun was soon appointed to chair a committee that proposed an amendment to the state constitution eliminating these requirements, a sure sign that he was already acknowledged as one of the ablest upcountry representatives despite his age and recent election. The resulting amendment, eventually ratified by the General Assembly in 1810, declared that "every white man of the age of twenty-one years...being a citizen of this State...shall have a right to vote." The amendment made a six-month residency in the state the only qualification for voting, essentially implementing universal white male suffrage.[23]

South Carolina was only the second of the original thirteen states, after Vermont, to depart from longstanding British and colonial precedent and embrace universal white male suffrage, making it one of the most radical democracies in the world in 1810.[24] Paradoxically, at least to us today, it was also the state with the highest proportion of black slaves as part of its population, with about two hundred thousand slaves constituting roughly half the state's population in 1810.[25] Yet as debates over universal white male suffrage in other states, such as Virginia, would show in the coming years, the presence of a large and potentially rebellious enslaved population was a powerful incentive to enfranchise white voters, giving them a stake in preserving the social and political order of the state and also enlarging the militia, frequently composed of eligible voters, in the event of a slave rebellion.[26] White South Carolinians, especially in the black-majority lowcountry, certainly knew about the abortive uprising of a slave named Gabriel Prosser in 1800 in Virginia, and by 1804 the most successful slave revolt in the Western Hemisphere resulted in the Republic of Haiti just off their shores. All this helps to explain how Calhoun's proposed amendment achieved the two-thirds majority it needed for ratification despite lowcountry domination of the state senate.[27]

Calhoun held a lifelong belief in the wisdom of the people, properly consulted, so there is no reason to believe he was not sincerely committed to broadening the reach of democracy as he understood it. But as the future would show, Calhoun also understood that a common economic and political interest in slavery made a broad commitment to white democracy possible in South Carolina. The amendment made South Carolina into a new type of democracy that sprang up on the staple-producing fringes of European conquest, a democracy whose breadth and depth among whites depended on the existence of a demarcated, disenfranchised, and enslaved black population. As slaveholders themselves soon realized, the best historical parallels to their peculiar society were not found in the mixed government of England or the revolutionary ideals of France, but in ancient Greece and Rome. And even those societies were not perfect parallels since the new racial democracies eventually came to depend on the emerging categories of race produced by the Enlightenment. The popularity of the amendment among South Carolina voters would help propel Calhoun's career to new heights.[28]

Calhoun soon found himself immersed in the day-to-day work of governing, especially in that peculiar democratic form, the committee. On November 29, 1808, the day after he took his seat in the house, he was appointed chairman of the Committee on Claims. In this role, Calhoun was responsible for reviewing petitions made to the assembly by citizens for damages or reimbursement. During the time Calhoun served on the committee a number of the petitions were made by slaveholders seeking reimbursement for slaves executed by the state for crimes. In one case in November 1809, a man named John Earle petitioned the legislature to be reimbursed for a slave, Lew, who had been executed "for having committed a rape upon a white woman." In an ironic contradiction of slaves' legal status as property, these slaves were tried, often before a hastily convened "freeholder" court composed of a few citizens and a justice of the peace, and then executed, sometimes hung by a local sheriff. But in such cases owners' property rights had to be respected, and so the state found itself in the position of having to reimburse owners for the privilege of executing enslaved people who were also valuable property. Slaveholders petitioning for reimbursement to Calhoun's committee were usually successful, and the reimbursement for an executed slave was always the same: $122.44. In a single session in December 1809, Calhoun in his role as chair of the committee recommended that two slaveholders be reimbursed for their executed slaves and that a man named James Bird and his brother, both veterans of the revolution, be compensated for "services rendered during the last war" based on the committee's conclusion that "the petitioner and his brother were faithful soldiers in the cause of our country during nearly the whole of the revolution." That Calhoun could recommend two revolutionary veterans be repaid for their patriotic service and two slaveholders be reimbursed for their executed slaves in the same report offers a vivid illustration of how, in South Carolina, the revolutionary ideals that Calhoun and many other supporters of Thomas Jefferson believed in existed alongside a deep-seated view of slaves as property. Indeed, for many white South Carolinians, one of the defining ideals of the revolution was the protection of their property rights, including the right to petition the state for reimbursement when their slaves were executed.[29]

Some of the petitions that came before Calhoun's committee offered clear evidence of an undercurrent of resistance among the enslaved. One slave, Jack, was executed for "wounding a white man," perhaps in a fight. William Smith petitioned the court to be reimbursed for his slave George, who was executed for setting fire to a "cotton machine" (probably a cotton gin or press). James and Elizabeth Kennedy petitioned for reimbursement for one of their slaves who had been executed after somehow obtaining a pistol and shooting Elizabeth, wounding her.[30] These petitions undoubtedly reminded Calhoun and his fellow legislators of the ever-present threat of a slave rebellion. They may also have reminded Calhoun of an event that occurred in 1798 while he was helping his mother run the plantation in Abbeville. That year, a slave named Will who belonged to Calhoun's cousin John Ewing Colhoun—Floride's husband—was accused of poisoning his master at Colhoun's upcountry plantation near Twelve Mile River. Colhoun became very sick and suspicion soon settled on Will, who confessed, or was coerced into confessing, that he had tried to poison

Colhoun with the help of some enslaved women. A freeholder jury that included Revolutionary War hero Andrew Pickens, Colhoun's kinsman, convicted Will of the poisoning, as well as of "attempting to seduce other negroes out of the state." Will was hung, and three other slaves suspected of helping him had their ears cropped and were sentenced to be whipped. One of them, a woman named Sue, was sentenced to be whipped a hundred times. Calhoun likely heard about the poisoning since he was living in the upcountry in 1798 and it involved two of his close relatives. As he read the petitions that came before his committee from across the state with this event in the back of his mind, Calhoun could not have had the illusion that all slaves were happy with their lot.[31]

SOMETIME IN THE SPRING of 1808, Calhoun visited Floride and her family at her Bonneau's Ferry plantation on the Cooper River near Charleston and made the discovery that her daughter, Floride, his first cousin once removed who he had not seen for two years, was now a young woman. No more would he write to her mother "Give my love to the children," as he had in a letter two years earlier. Perhaps on the spot, but certainly over the next year, while Floride was back in Newport, Rhode Island, with her family, Calhoun developed a settled desire to marry the young, dark-haired daughter of his wealthy kinswoman. Apparently, the elder Floride at first withheld her permission for the courtship to move forward. Calhoun had all the signs of a successful career in politics ahead of him, but he was not wealthy by lowcountry standards, and Floride was only sixteen. But when she visited Bonneau's Ferry again in the summer of 1809, without her daughter, Calhoun raised the subject of the relationship again and asked for Floride's permission to move forward in what amounted to a marriage proposal. Floride evidently asked for time to think and consult her daughter, who had remained in Newport. A few days later Calhoun visited a friend who was about to be married and soon found himself overcome by his desire to marry. "It…called up strongly in my mind another subject of interest more important to myself. You know the one I alude [*sic*] to," he wrote to the elder Floride. "It will be useless for me to conceal from you my increased anxiety on that subject. The more I reflect on it, the more indisoluably does my happiness seem to be connected with that event. If, I should finally be disappointed by any adverse circumstances, which heaven forbid, it will be by far the most unlucky accident in my life…Do make no delay in writing to me."[32]

By the time Calhoun wrote good news was already on its way from Newport. When he received the elder Floride's reply indicating her daughter's willingness to marry him, Calhoun dissolved into relief, and immediately wrote thanking her "for the promtitude [*sic*] of your communication; which has released my mind from no small degree of anxiety. I can scarcely describe my emotions, when I saw your well known hand writing with the New Port post mark." Seeming surprised by his own emotion, he wrote, "This language does not correspond with my former opinion on this subject. I formerly thought it would be impossible for me to be strongly agitated in an affair of this kind." That opinion, he admitted, had been "wholly unfounded." Writing that he had told no one in South Carolina, even his brothers, about his feelings for her daughter, he asked Floride's permission to write "to the object of my affection." Floride gave her permission, but fearing the rumor mill that would begin if letters to both Florides were seen in the mail, Calhoun evidently enclosed his first few letters to her with his letters to her mother, whom he gave permission to read them before resealing and delivering them.[33]

Even as Calhoun and her mother exchanged letters, rumors circulated in Charleston that Floride was already engaged, which worried Henry DeSaussure, who in addition to managing her mother's estate also served as a kind of surrogate father to Floride. In a letter to Ezekiel Pickens—the executor of John Ewing Colhoun's estate—in July 1809 DeSaussure referred to "the report about F. which gave us so much uneasiness," and Mrs. Colhoun felt the need to quash a "foolish report" in Charleston that Floride was engaged to be married, or already had been married, in Newport. Calhoun told the elder Floride that he had encountered these same rumors in Charleston, although he professed "it is quite unaccountable how such an impression should become so universal."[34] Perhaps the rumors were false, or perhaps they actually concerned Calhoun himself, and not some anonymous northern suitor, but they also hint at the possibility that the younger Floride may have had different ideas about whom she should marry than her mother and Calhoun did. Whatever the case, in the coming months Calhoun and the elder Floride discussed the proposed marriage with DeSaussure, who immediately approved the match.[35]

Calhoun spent the rest of 1809 and all of 1810 in the grip of what he described to the elder Floride as the "sweet pain" of anticipation and absence, even as he continued to practice law and carry out his legislative duties.[36] He corresponded extensively, if one-sidedly, with the elder Floride—"I could write you by every mail were I not apprehensive of fatiguing you," he wrote, noting elsewhere that he wrote eight or nine letters to her one—although his letters were now mostly about her daughter. "I know much happiness, or much misery is the consequence of marriage," he wrote, obviously expecting the former.[37] In the summer of 1810, Calhoun described a long ride back to Abbeville from Charleston during which he was absorbed with thoughts of Floride. "I am not much given to enthusiasm," he wrote to her mother, "nor to anticipate future happiness. But I cannot, now, refrain my hopes of joy."[38] He constantly fretted about travel arrangements and any hint of illness in Floride's letters, and he eagerly anticipated his attempts to be a good husband. "No task will be half so sweet to me," he wrote, "as to make her, as happy, as the conditions of this life will permit."[39] Calhoun's letters to and about his family would always be the exception in his correspondence, periodic effusions of emotion amid the steady flow of ruthless reason.

It was difficult to wait. "Time hangs heavily on my hands," he wrote to the elder Floride in the summer of 1810, "tho' I endeavor to make it pass as pleasantly as possible by close application. I have not read so intensely since I commenced the practice of law; as I have this summer." Forty-four years later, Alexander Bowie, the son of the lawyer with whom Calhoun studied law in Abbeville, recalled that during the summer of 1810 he had often accompanied Calhoun on the three-mile walk that Calhoun made every morning, a habit that Calhoun would keep up in one form or another for most of his life. During the walk, Bowie recalled, Calhoun would choose a subject for reflection and concentrate his entire attention on it, telling Bowie "that to this end he had early subjected his mind to such a course of rigid discipline, and had persisted without faltering, until he had acquired a perfect control over it" and could focus his full attention on a subject "until he was satisfied with its examination." Calhoun's powers of concentration and his ability to comprehend an issue in all its facets and unintended consequences would become legendary, and his physical and mental habits undoubtedly helped. Yet, as he confessed to the elder Floride, that summer he often found it "impossible to divert my thoughts from her on whom they naturally concentrate." He also spent time that summer scouting for land that might serve as a suitable place to build a home for Floride, his eye settling on a place near his brother Patrick's plantation, although he wanted to wait to commence building so that "I shall be able to consult yours and Floride's tastes." Sometime that year he bought over eight hundred acres on the Savannah River and began to build a house.[40]

Unfortunately, none of Floride's letters to Calhoun from this period, if she wrote any, have survived, a pattern that would continue throughout their marriage. In the first surviving letter from Calhoun to Floride in September 1810, his tone is awkwardly formal, tinged with uncertainty about how to address her, but full of excitement. "I rejoice, my dearest Floride," he wrote, "that the period is fast approaching when it will be no longer necessary to address you through the cold medium of a letter." Launching into an uncharacteristically florid discourse on the nature of married bliss, Calhoun somewhat lectured his future bride, "To be united in mutual virtuous love is the first and best bliss that God has permitted our natures. My dearest one, may our love strengthen with each returning day, may it ripen and mellow with our years, and may it end in immortal joys." Elaborating on Floride's "beauty of mind," her "amiable and lovable character," and her "personal beauty," Calhoun reached for language to describe his devotion to her, settling on a martial theme. "Such, my dear Floride, are the arms by which you have conquered, and it is by these the durability of your sovereignty is established over your subject whom you hold in willing servitude." He closed the letter by writing "I am your true lover, John C. Calhoun."[41]

Calhoun was just as idealistic when Henry DeSaussure raised the possibility of a marriage contract, a legal agreement that would secure part of Floride's inheritance from her father's estate exclusively for her and her future children, placing it beyond his control. Calhoun wrote to her mother that "duty" required him to express his opinion, despite it being "indelicate" to raise the issue. "From prejudice, or reason," he wrote, "I have always been opposed to marriage settlements…In that state there should be but one interest, one happiness & one destiney [*sic*]. That entire confidence, which is reposed by a female in the object of her choice, in placing both her honor and property in his custody give rise to the most sacred and tender regard. A marriage settlement implies distrust." Obviously, Calhoun had not absorbed his old teacher Tapping Reeve's ideas on the legal status of married women. There would be no protection of minority rights in the Calhoun household.[42]

At the end of his first letter to Floride in September 1810, almost as an aside, Calhoun mentioned his political future. "In a week the election for Congress will take place," he wrote her, referring to the contest for a congressional seat made up of Abbeville district and adjacent Newberry and Laurens districts. "My opponent is Gen. [John] Elmore of Laurens," he wrote, "but it is thought that I will succeed by a large majority."[43] Calhoun's confidence was well placed. His cousin Joseph, who had occupied the seat in the US House of Representatives for two previous terms, had chosen not to run for a third term, perhaps because he saw the swelling support for Calhoun in the upcountry. The election was held on October 8 and 9, and on October 20 the *Charleston City Gazette* reported that Calhoun had received 610 votes to Elmore's 235 in Newberry and a majority of the votes even in Elmore's home district of Laurens. Abbeville, Calhoun's home turf, was a foregone conclusion, and two days later the same paper noted, "There is no doubt of the election of this gentleman."[44] Persuaded by his family name, his militant regard for national honor in the continuing conflict with England, and his devotion to Jeffersonian republicanism in the form of an expanded democracy for white men, voters had elected Calhoun to Congress.

Governor John Drayton published the official results of the election in Charleston newspapers on Christmas Day 1810, and two days later Calhoun obtained a marriage license from the Charleston District Court of Ordinary for his marriage to Floride. The license listed the Reverend Theodore Dehon, who had been Floride's minister in Newport and was now, perhaps through her mother's influence, the presiding minister of St. Michael's Episcopal Church in Charleston. The ceremony took place on January 8, probably at Bonneau's Ferry.[45] Calhoun was twenty-eight, and Floride was a month short of nineteen. "I, in every event of my life, seem to myself more fortunate than I deserve," Calhoun observed to Floride in a letter just before their wedding.[46] Yet his success in marriage and politics were both the result of no little amount of calculation and preparation. Calhoun's marriage to his wealthy cousin cemented his own rise in social status and served as an example of the recent unification, facilitated by cotton and slavery, between the upcountry and lowcountry elite in South Carolina. His election to Congress similarly secured his political fortunes, assuring him a national audience in the midst of an impending international conflict with Great Britain that would birth a new generation of American political leaders. He had no intention of wasting the opportunity.

FIVE

"The Road That All Great Nations Have Trod"

WHILE HIS TERM OFFICIALLY BEGAN on March 4, 1811, Calhoun had to wait several months before the first session of the Twelfth Congress actually met in Washington in November. Calhoun and Floride spent part of the time at her mother's plantation at Bonneau's Ferry near Charleston, and part of the time in Abbeville, perhaps living with Calhoun's brother since there was as yet no house built on the land Calhoun had purchased nearby. Calhoun and Floride were not long in starting a family to occupy the yet-to-be-built house. Floride became pregnant almost immediately after the wedding, and in May Calhoun reported to her mother, who had returned to Newport, that Floride was "in good health and sperits...and feels less sickness than what I believe is usual in her condition."[1]

During the year of waiting Calhoun continued to practice law and oversaw, with Henry DeSaussure, the dividing up of Floride's mother's estate so that he and Floride could have her inheritance. "The division of property in the lower country has been made," he reported to Floride's mother in May. "It will also be made in the upper as soon as Mr. [Ezekiel] Pickens goes up."[2] Surely part of this process involved dividing the slaves that belonged to the estate of the late John Ewing Colhoun, Floride's father, but the parting of friends and family in the slave community that happened whenever white people got married lay hidden behind the language of a "division of property."

In the Charleston newspapers, Calhoun followed the unfolding standoff between the United States, England, and France. Ever since the Napoleonic wars between England and France renewed in 1803, both nations had sought to cut off American trade to the other. In 1807 England passed "Orders in Council," which declared that any neutral ships wishing to trade with France must first visit England and pay duties. In response, Napoleon issued the Milan Decree, declaring that the French would seize any ship that followed the English mandate. This left American merchants in a quandary, a situation that worsened, if that was possible, when in response to the British attack on the *Chesapeake* Thomas Jefferson issued his disastrous embargo at the end of 1807, plunging the nation's port cities into an imposed desuetude. The embargo was replaced a year later by the narrower Non-Intercourse Act, and in his law practice Calhoun observed the dampening effects of both measures on the cotton boom that had been in full swing throughout the upcountry. After the failure of trade restrictions, in 1810 Congress reinstated trade with both nations but offered to reward a recognition of America's neutral shipping rights by either nation with a trading ban on the other.[3] During the summer and fall of 1811, Charleston newspapers reprinted news from abroad about the progress of the Napoleonic wars and issued flaming denunciations of English violations of American rights. Both England and France were guilty of transgressions, everyone agreed, but in the view of a June 15 article reprinted in the *Carolina Gazette*, England should be held the "first aggressor."[4] Most Republicans, and certainly Calhoun, agreed.

Reading the Charleston papers during these months would also have revealed to Calhoun the hemispheric implications of the conflict in Europe. In 1807 Napoleon had kidnapped the Spanish monarch Ferdinand VII and the next year established his brother Joseph on the

Spanish throne, setting off a guerrilla war in Spain and destabilizing the Spanish empire in America. In February 1811 the *Carolina Gazette* published a letter from an American observer in Caracas who reported that Venezuela was on the verge of establishing a constitutional republic founded "on the great basis of the people's rights." That Fourth of July, toasts throughout the United States also toasted South American independence as Americans linked their resistance to the despotic tyranny of England and France to South America's rebellion against Spanish rule. It seemed that the New World was in the final throes of freeing itself from the Old.[5]

Calhoun stayed in South Carolina just long enough to witness the birth of his son, Andrew Pickens Calhoun, on October 15, and named for the Revolutionary War hero who had married Calhoun's first cousin Rebecca. But within days he was on his way north to attend the opening of the Twelfth Congress, which would convene a month early at the request of President James Madison. In order to avoid the tedious overland journey, he likely boarded a ship in Charleston bound for Philadelphia, or perhaps Baltimore or Norfolk, and from there took a stage or horse to Washington.[6]

By the time Calhoun arrived in Washington on November 6, Congress had already been in session for two days. The day before he arrived President Madison had delivered his annual message to Congress. Having accepted Napoleon's dubious promise to respect American shipping, Madison singled out Great Britain for its "hostile inflexibility, in trampling on rights which no independent nation can relinquish," and calling on Congress to speed up military preparations and subsidize domestic manufacturing crucial to the war effort. Madison also reminded Congress of the ongoing independence movements in South America, linking events in "the great communities which occupy the Southern portion of our hemispheres" to the United States' ongoing struggle for independence and calling on Congress to "take a deep interest in their destinies, to cherish reciprocal sentiments of good will…and not to be unprepared for whatever order of things may be ultimately established." It was, as Madison said, a "momentous epoch" in world history.[7]

Calhoun took a room at a boardinghouse with two other South Carolina representatives, the burly fellow Abbeville native Langdon Cheves, already a political veteran although only six years Calhoun's senior, and the young and newly elected William Lowndes, who was exactly Calhoun's age. The day after Calhoun arrived Lowndes wrote home glowingly, "I had heard a very favorable character of him, but this did not at all lessen…the pleasure of an acquaintance with a man, well informed, easy in his manners, and I think amiable in his disposition. I like him already better than any member of our mess, and I give his politics the same preference." Lowndes and Calhoun, both in Washington without their families, would grow to be close friends, and Calhoun would eventually name his youngest son after Lowndes. "Our society is delightful," Calhoun wrote home a few weeks later. "This place is quite gay, during the session; but I do not participate in it much myself. You know I never had much inclination to such enjoyment." The boardinghouse seemed to attract the more bellicose members of the new Congress who favored war with England as the only way to preserve national honor. Felix Grundy of Tennessee roomed there, as well, and it quickly became a kind of headquarters for the emerging war party among the Republicans. The "war mess," it was soon called, although the noise created by the Cheveses' two children sometimes made it difficult to talk politics.[8]

In the same letter, Lowndes mentioned, "We have, too, the honor of having the Speaker among us." Soon after Calhoun arrived he met "the Speaker," a talented young politician named Henry Clay from Kentucky. Only five years Calhoun's senior, Clay had previously served in the Senate and was already known as "the Western Star" for his precocious political talent. He was tall, towheaded, and rail thin, and his face never seemed to stop changing expressions, as if he were constantly trying out different moods during conversation. His mouth, which was so wide he had trouble whistling, frequently slipped into a smirk when he made a point at an opponent's expense. A spellbinding orator with a deep, rich voice—"his voice filled the room as the organ fills a great cathedral," one observer recalled—Clay was also a gifted raconteur who loved gambling, drinking, and especially talking. His political gifts were perfectly suited to his era, and by the time Calhoun arrived in Washington he had already been appointed speaker of the house, a role that he would transform into one of the most powerful positions in the national government. Clay was an avowed war enthusiast and expansionist who the year before had declared in a speech in the Senate his hope for "a *new* United States" that included the entire continent east of the Mississippi, including British Canada and the Spanish colony of East Florida (encompassing most of what is now the state of Florida east of the Apalachicola River). Matched in ambition although nearly opposites in temperament, in 1811 Calhoun and Clay shared a commitment to the democratic ideals of Thomas Jefferson's Republican Party and an equally strong conviction that the demands of national honor made a departure from those Republican principles unavoidable. Their futures were intertwined with the country's, and with each other's.[9]

Like Calhoun's boardinghouse, the new Congress was full of new faces, 63 of them in the House of Representatives alone out of its 142 total seats.[10] In both the House and the Senate the Republicans were firmly in control, although hardly united. The historian Henry Adams, grandson of John Quincy Adams, would later observe that the distinguishing characteristic of the Twelfth Congress was that "the active leaders were young men," men like Clay, Cheves, Lowndes, Grundy, and John C. Calhoun. None of them was over forty, and Calhoun was not yet thirty. They had no memory of British rule, although some, like Calhoun, carried a fierce family resentment of English tyranny. Most of them were born before the Constitutional Convention in 1787. As Adams noted, Calhoun and his young colleagues had also come of age politically after the Revolution of 1800. They were not old enough to remember when the Republicans had been an opposition party during the 1790s, and as a consequence felt a little freer to dissent from the "principles of '98" that had been forged in opposition to the Federalist administration of John Adams. As Adams wrote, somewhat acidly, they were "bent on war with England" and "willing to face debt and probably bankruptcy on the chance of creating a nation, conquering Canada, and carrying the American flag to Mobile and Key West."[11]

Adams was halfway right, but what he failed to grasp in retrospect was how widespread had been the conviction on both sides of the Atlantic in the years before 1812 that the continent of North America could not remain permanently and peacefully divided between a young republic and a monarchy. The border with Canada, especially, was seen as an unstable line that could easily collapse northward or southward. Since the revolution, the British—including loyalists who had fled to Canada—had predicted that the American experiment would fail and the colonies would beg to be reincorporated into the mother country. Some Americans feared this possibility, as well, while others gazed north (and south) in the confidence that the future and the continent belonged to the United States. Part of what inspired British confidence was the impotence of the American central government, which they thought too weak to hold together long on its own, let alone to fight a war. One British spy described the country as "that crazy coalition of heterogenous interests, opinions and prejudices" and wrote of the central government, "Seventeen staves and no hoop will not make a barrel that can last long."[12] The task in front of Calhoun, Clay, and the war party was to rehabilitate (or rather, to create) a military and navy, both of which had been decimated by Jefferson's parsimonious administration, into forces that could resist British encroachments. They also had to bring Congress to the realization that war was necessary if the American republic was to endure among the community of nations. To do that they would have to overcome Republican fears about standing armies (and navies), taxes, and the authority of the central government.

Standing squarely in their way was the cadaverous figure of John Randolph, a congressman from Virginia and the leader of a group known as the Old Republicans or the Tertium Quids (Latin for "a third something") to distinguish them from the new breed of nationalists in the party. Randolph was a proud devotee of the Republican state rights doctrines of 1798 as embodied in the Virginia and Kentucky resolutions, and he once memorably summed up the principles of the Republican Party as "love of peace, hatred of offensive war, jealousy of the State Governments towards the General Government...a dread of standing armies; a loathing of public debt, taxes, and excises; tenderness for the liberty of the citizen, [and]...Argus-eyed jealousy of the patronage of the President."[13] He was a self-professed aristocrat and Anglophile who did not relish the prospect of war with England. A slaveowner who at his death in 1833 owned 383 human beings, Randolph professed a lifelong hatred of both slavery, which he once called "an evil daily magnifying," and abolitionists, whom he dismissed as radical utopians, "quacks," and tools of northern mercantile interests. Unlike most other white southerners of his generation who decried slavery as a necessary evil, Randolph freed every one of his slaves when he died.[14]

He was also, by one description, "a flowing gargoyle of vituperation" who would sweep into the House chamber wearing spurs and carrying a riding whip with his hat pulled down almost over his eyes and his hunting dogs trailing close behind. He had a high, shrill voice that spectators found captivating, and during his harangues, which he made often, Randolph slashed the air with his long index finger as if it were a weapon. His face was deceptively boyish, beardless and smooth, until closer examination showed the deep lines wrought by nearly continuous illnesses and pain that he treated with drugs, laudanum, morphine, and opium. On the floor of the House Randolph was a brilliant, sometimes entertaining, and unpredictable nuisance, but a dangerous one to interrupt. Benjamin Ruggles of Ohio once described a twelve-hour speech by Randolph in which the Virginian poured contempt on every national figure except "George Washington and himself," and covered every topic "from the creation of the world to the present time." Henry Clay had been elected speaker by the Republicans partly because they believed he alone might be able to control Randolph, or to meet him on the dueling field if it came to that, which was a distinct possibility.[15]

For his part, Randolph quickly took Clay and Calhoun's measure. "They have entered this House with their eye on the Presidency," he wrote to a friend of the two, "and, mark my words, Sir, we shall have war before the end of the session." He was not wrong on either count.[16]

CLAY RECOGNIZED CALHOUN AS an ally from the start, and less than a week after Calhoun arrived Clay appointed him to the influential Foreign Affairs Committee, chaired by Peter B. Porter of New York and tasked with determining the foreign policy response to the crisis with Great Britain. The committee also included John Randolph.[17] On November 29 the committee returned an initial report, likely written by Calhoun, that amounted to an open call to prepare for war.[18] It began by rehearsing the offenses of Great Britain and France against the neutrality of American shipping, but ultimately made clear that the impact on American commerce was only one consideration, and not the most important. Another was, according to the report, "the unhappy case of our impressed seamen." Playing on the explosive juxtaposition of white freedom and black slavery, and on widespread reports that impressed American sailors were being whipped by the British, the report charged that Great Britain "enslaves our seamen." This treatment of free white men like slaves was intolerable. "By as much as life & liberty are more estimable than goods," the committee wrote, "so much more impressive is the duty to shield the persons of our seamen." In the end, the report made clear, the nation's honor was at stake. In words that Calhoun would echo in a different context decades later, the committee wrote, "To wrongs, so daring in character, and so disgraceful in their execution, it is impossible that the people of the United States should remain indifferent. We must now tamely & quietly submit, or, we must resist." The committee proposed six resolutions, including raising ten thousand additional regular troops, calling for up to fifty thousand volunteers, outfitting and repairing the woefully deficient navy, and arming private merchant vessels for self-defense.[19]

In the days following the report Calhoun rose to comment on a bill that apportioned representatives based on the most recent census of 1810. The House had proposed a ratio of thirty-seven thousand people per representative and sent the bill to the Senate, which amended the number to thirty-five thousand and returned it to the House. This small change occasioned Calhoun's first speech before Congress. A few days earlier William Lowndes had written home that as a new congressman he had not yet dared to comment publicly other than voting, but Calhoun had no such inhibitions.[20] Some of his older colleagues must have raised their eyebrows at this preposterously self-confident newcomer as Calhoun defended the constitutional right of the House to determine its membership without interference from the Senate. It was true, he admitted, that the reapportionment bill had to pass through the Senate, but "I consider this a case of omission in our excellent Constitution—of that kind which must take place, perhaps in all free constitutions…but particularly in one like ours, formed by the foresight of wisdom, not by slow and successive experience." In this case, Calhoun declared, "the veto of the Senate is no longer the means of protection to itself, but becomes a fatal means of assailing this House." Calhoun trusted that the Senate had the country's best interests at heart, he said, but that was not the point. "Faith," he declared, "is an article of religion, but not of politics."[21] The speech shows that from the very beginning of his political career, Calhoun conceived of the Constitution as a speculative work in progress that contained "omissions" and must be shaped by subsequent experience. His position was contested by James Fisk, who decried Calhoun's speech as a declaration of war on the Senate and declared that the framers of the Constitution had given the Senate veto power "for good reason, no doubt."[22] Back in Charleston, the *Carolina Gazette* praised the "warm, animated and truly eloquent remarks of Mr. Calhoun…which does much credit to himself and his constituents."[23]

A week later Calhoun was back on the floor of the House, but this time his target was John Randolph, not the Senate. Two days earlier Randolph had launched a characteristically vitriolic attack on the report and resolutions of the Committee on Foreign Affairs, on which he had served along with Calhoun. Playing his appointed role as a guardian of true Republican principles, Randolph denounced the committee's call for regular troops—what he felt would amount to a standing army—as a danger to the republic since no war had been declared. Was this report a declaration of war, he asked, or an empty threat? Finally, Randolph darkly reminded the House of "the danger arising from the black population" in the event of a war. He warned that the doctrines of the French Revolution had spread to the slave population in the last twenty years, carried by "peddlers from New England" and even by masters (here perhaps Randolph meant his fellow Virginian Thomas Jefferson) who "unthinkingly…cherish these seeds of self-destruction to them and their families." "You have tempted [the slave] to eat of the fruit of the tree of knowledge…you have opened his eyes to his nakedness," Randolph warned, speaking as much to his fellow southerners as to the whole House. "Now…you are called upon to trust to the mere physical strength of the fetter which holds him in bondage." Randolph vividly described the fear of slave revolts that had spread through white Virginia society in the last decade.[24]

Several Republicans tried lamely to respond the next day, but Randolph had so colorfully pointed out the contradictions between the course the war party was pursuing and Republican principles—"What Republicanism is this?" he had scoffed in closing—that their attempts to reconcile the two were awkward and unconvincing.[25]

Calhoun took the floor on December 12, after being too sick to speak the previous day.[26] One New York newspaper noted that "Mr. Calhoun is to speak tomorrow; he is a new member—rather eloquent in his words, but rapid in his delivery." In contrast to Randolph's extravagant display of sarcasm, wit, and oratory, Calhoun's speech was a carefully crafted barrage of logic that demolished each of Randolph's points with surgical precision, the effect of the whole growing with each successive point, which came on relentlessly, one after another. Was the report a declaration of war? Of course it was. "Indeed the report could mean nothing but war or empty menace," Calhoun declared. "I hope no member of this House is in favor of the latter." Was the country unprepared for war? If so, whose fault was that? Instead of using it as a limpid excuse to avoid the inevitable, "let us remedy the evil as soon as possible," he proposed. Randolph had demanded to know why exactly the country should go to war. But, Calhoun countered, if Randolph acknowledged the ongoing offenses of England, which he must, the burden of proof was on *him*. "Were I to affirm the House is now in session, would it be reasonable to ask for proof?" Calhoun asked. Randolph had pointed to "the evils always incident to war, no matter how just and necessary" as a reason for keeping peace, but as Calhoun declared, this logic was only "calculated to produce unqualified submission to every species of insult and injury." To Randolph's fear of the dangers of a standing army, Calhoun responded succinctly, "I think a regular army raised for a period of actual hostilities cannot be called a standing army." With a blizzard of numbers—"1,000,000 tons of shipping, a trade of nearly 100,000,000 dollars; manufactures of 150,000,000, and agriculture of thrice that amount"—Calhoun demolished Randolph's argument that the country could not afford the war and denounced as a libel on American patriotism his claim that the country would not pay the taxes it would require. Would the war be expensive? Yes. But Calhoun rejected this "'calculating avarice'…only fit for shops and counting houses." "Whenever it touches sovereign power the nation is ruined," he declared. Honor was the only principle that should guide the nation's response.

As for Randolph's fears of a slave insurrection, Calhoun scoffed, "of the Southern section, I too have some personal knowledge, and can say, that in South Carolina no such fears in any part are felt." Claiming inaccurately that "even in our Revolution no attempts were made by that portion of our population," Calhoun dismissed Randolph's claims with a shrug, claiming that most of "our ignorant blacks" had never even heard of the French Revolution. Even if Calhoun was sincere, Randolph's fears were certainly shared by many white southerners, especially in places like Virginia and Louisiana, where only the year before the largest slave rebellion in the young nation's history had emerged on the German Coast near New Orleans. When the war eventually broke out, many in Louisiana and the Mississippi territory were as afraid of their slaves as they were of the British.[27]

The speech showed the influence of Calhoun's Federalist education and his preternatural sense of certainty. In a sweeping pronouncement, he offered what amounted to his own theory of nationalism: "I only know of one principle to make a nation great, to produce in this country not the form but real spirit of union, and that is, to protect every citizen in the lawful pursuit of his business. He will then feel that he is backed by the government, that its arm is his arms, and will rejoice in its increased strength and prosperity. Protection and patriotism are reciprocal. This is the road that all great nations have trod."[28]

As Henry Adams later observed, there was no Republican principle more dearly held by those of an older generation than that the United States should *not* follow the examples of other "great nations"—but this was the genius of Calhoun's address. "Little could be added to what Calhoun said," Adams later wrote, "and no objection could be justly made against it, except that as an expression of principles it had no place in the past history of the Republican party." Calhoun had boldly, brilliantly made his own way.[29]

The speech put Calhoun's name in newspapers all over the country and on lips all over Washington. Finally, someone had taken Randolph's measure and put him in his place. More than that, Calhoun had made the case for war seem clear, even irrefutable, and in response the war Republicans lavished him with praise. Some newspaper accounts noted Calhoun's unique style. "He is a logical and argumentative speaker, which makes him a great acquisition to the house," wrote one admiring correspondent for a New York newspaper who was weary of the gilded oratory that was "fashionable" in the House.[30] The *Richmond Enquirer* published Randolph's and Calhoun's speeches at full length together, ignoring all the other intervening speeches. Thomas Ritchie, the *Enquirer*'s editor, described Calhoun glowingly as "clear and precise in his reasoning...felling down the errors of his opponent with the club of Hercules." Calhoun was not eloquent in a traditional sense, Ritchie wrote, "but like Fox in the moral elevation of his sentiment." And in words that would prove true, if not quite in the sense he wrote them, Ritchie proclaimed, "We hail this young South Carolinian as one of those master spirits, who stamp their name upon the age in which they live!" Considering what the future held, it was ironic indeed that Ritchie compared Calhoun to the radical English statesman Charles James Fox, who had defended the excesses of the French Revolution against the attacks of his colleague Edmund Burke, but it shows how Calhoun's contemporaries viewed this young Hercules from South Carolina.[31]

Randolph responded, predictably, with sarcasm and bile. He made reference to "unfledged political pedagogues" on the floor of the House, and groused privately to a friend about the "Yale-College Orator" who "has not been educated in Connecticut for nothing." He observed that Calhoun had the "savage ferocity of the frontier man," and combined the "cold unfeeling Yankee manner with the bitter and acrimonious irritability of the South." Despite the fact that Calhoun would later come to appreciate Randolph, they were never friends or allies.[32]

As CHRISTMAS APPROACHED, THE weather in Washington was cold and windy, and the Potomac was frozen. At Calhoun's boardinghouse, the boat bringing coal across the Potomac had sunk, leaving them to burn only wood—"a bad substitute," wrote William Lowndes—in the fireplaces. Surrounded by beautiful natural scenery, the city itself was hardly worthy of the name in the opinion of some foreign observers—"scattered houses...intersected with woods, heaths, and gravel pits," wrote an English dignitary in 1808. Lowndes determined next winter to take up residence in nearby Georgetown in order to enjoy "the comforts of a city." There was a social life to be had in Washington, including Dolley Madison's famous dinners, but Calhoun and Lowndes mostly stayed in (their housemate Henry Clay, on the other hand, mostly stayed out). Calhoun was invited to a ball and Christmas dinner by the French ambassador, who was no doubt delighted that the United States seemed poised to declare war on England, but he declined. As he wrote to his mother-in-law, he didn't think it proper, especially "as our oponents [*sic*] accuse us with partiality towards France."[33]

The early months of 1812 found Calhoun strongly supporting preparations for war in the House and frequently sparring with John Randolph.[34] When the House became embroiled with the Senate in a debate over the number of troops to raise and how and when to appoint officers, Calhoun announced that he would vote against any further amendments to the measure in the House because he wanted as much "unanimity and decision" as possible. The time was past for quibbling, he argued, and public opinion had begun to doubt whether Congress was serious in its intent.[35]

Accepting the imperative of war, Calhoun also accepted the logical consequences of that conclusion, even as many of his fellow Republicans gagged on their principles. When Secretary of the Treasury Albert Gallatin presented a thorough and frank report on the possible costs of the war and proposed an equally frank combination of loans and taxation to raise the funds, including taxes on sugar, spirits, stamps, and carriages, many Republicans shrank back. An army was one thing, taxes another. As Henry Adams later noted, "nothing but a Sedition Law was wanting" to make Gallatin's proposal identical to the Federalist programs of the 1790s.[36] Calhoun by contrast accepted Gallatin's proposal with equanimity, writing to his brother Patrick a few days later,

"To lay a tax is a painful thing; but we must either submit [to England] or have money." He also regretted that the House had so far refused to raise an adequate naval force, which some Republicans feared even more than a standing army. "I am sorry for it," Calhoun wrote, "I think we could by a small Navy have peace and commerce."[37]

One night in February, Calhoun and others in Washington were awakened by a mild earthquake. "We had several shocks last night. In what will they terminate[?]," Calhoun wondered to a friend, James Macbride, in Charleston. In March, a much more powerful earthquake far to the south devastated the city of Caracas in the newly declared republic of Venezuela, where the young revolutionary Simón Bolívar helped to dig through the rubble in search of survivors. When news of the devastation reached Washington, Nathaniel Macon of North Carolina proposed an exception to a recently passed embargo in order to send shipments of flour directly to Caracas, which many considered a sister republic in need. When John Randolph used the occasion to inveigh against the embargo, Calhoun rose to object that Randolph had inserted "party feelings" into a measure that aimed to aid "the sacred cause of distant and oppressed humanity." Calhoun then proposed a motion budgeting $50,000 in aid to Venezuela, which was quickly passed.[38]

Consumed with politics and the war, Calhoun rarely wrote home that winter and spring, and received few letters from home in return. The scarce letters from Floride, no doubt busy with a new infant, nevertheless pained Calhoun, who missed his family. "I dreamed all night last night of being home with you; and nursing our dear son; and regreted when I awoke to find it a dream," he wrote Floride in March, noting that it had been a month since he received a letter from her. Perhaps because of the loss of his father when he was a boy, but also in keeping with a growing emphasis in American culture on the family as a sanctuary from the travails of life, Calhoun would always, and only, reveal his emotions in his correspondence with his family and, especially, his children.[39]

AFTER MONTHS OF DELAY and argument, by late spring it was clear that war was at hand. In late May, John Randolph got wind that President Madison was about to ask for a declaration of war and launched into a volcanic denunciation of the administration on the floor of the House. When he could bear it no longer, Calhoun rose and interrupted, objecting that as the question of war was not yet before the House, Randolph was out of order. William M. Bibb, serving as speaker while Henry Clay was temporarily absent, ruled that Randolph could continue, upon which Randolph sarcastically thanked Calhoun for giving him a rest and resumed his speech. When Henry Clay entered in the midst of the speech and resumed his chair as speaker, Calhoun immediately rose and objected again, declaring that surely Randolph wouldn't mind a second break since he had so appreciated the first. This time Clay sustained Calhoun's demand, sparking a heated debate that poured over into the pages of the newspapers all over the country. But the message was clear: there was to be no more debate. With Calhoun's help, Clay would keep the opposition off the floor.[40]

On June 1 President Madison recommended that Congress declare war on Great Britain, citing especially the issue of impressment, which Calhoun and other war Republicans had emphasized as a grave affront to the nation's honor. Two days later, the Committee on Foreign Affairs, which Calhoun now chaired, declared emphatically that the United States must defend itself on the world stage "or submit to the most shameful degradation." After submitting the report, Calhoun immediately submitted a declaration of war with Great Britain, and in a secret session the next day the House passed the measure 79–49, with southern and western representatives overwhelmingly voting for the war and the Federalist bastions of New England, New Jersey, and New York voting strongly against it. The Senate passed the measure 19–13 on June 17, and that day Calhoun penned a brief note to his cousin Patrick Noble back in Abbeville. "I have but a moment to inform you that war is declared against Great Britain," he wrote tersely. The next day Madison signed the bill, and Calhoun and his messmates had their war.[41]

SIX

"The Great Gun of the Party"

N O ONE IN THE UNITED STATES could have known that across the Atlantic two days after the American declaration of war Britain rescinded the Orders in Council that forced American ships to pay duties to England before trading with France. If the war had only been about trade this news, once it crossed the ocean, should have stopped it. But the war Republicans, Calhoun and Clay in particular, had made war primarily on the demands of national honor and the issue of impressment, not commerce. The issue of impressment in particular involved a principle that lay at the heart of the American experiment—the idea that a citizen could choose to be part of the United States and become a naturalized citizen. Britain's refusal to recognize the naturalization of British subjects who had chosen to become American citizens made every impressment a repetition of the American Revolution in microcosm. And to be an American citizen was, by definition, to not be a slave. Calhoun and the war Republicans frequently portrayed impressment as a kind of enslavement that subjected free, white American citizens to the kind of shame endured by black slaves. As Calhoun declared in January 1813 against complaints that the war should end, the central issue of the war was not the Orders in Council and their effect on trade, but "the liberty of our sailors and their redemption from slavery."[1]

In addition to a defense of national honor, many Americans initially saw the war as an opportunity to expand the country—north to Canada, south to Florida—and to suppress what many believed was a Native American conspiracy with the British in the Northwest. Calhoun himself overconfidently predicted that within four weeks of the war's beginning, "the whole of Upper and Lower Canada will be in our possession."[2]

In fact, back in South Carolina that fall after Congress adjourned, Calhoun followed in the newspapers the disastrous defeats that accompanied American military efforts on the Canadian border throughout 1812. In early September the *Charleston City Gazette* reported that General William Hull and his men had surrendered to a British force at Detroit "without striking a blow."[3] In October, the British overwhelmed a temporarily successful American force under the command of New Yorker Stephen van Rensselaer at Queenstown Heights on the British side of the Niagara River, partly because the New York militia refused as unconstitutional the command to cross the river into a foreign country to reinforce their fellow Americans. In early 1813, by which time Calhoun was back in Washington, word came of the defeat and massacre of American soldiers by Indians allied with the British on the Raisin River in the Michigan Territory. The only bright spots in the first year of the war came, surprisingly, at sea, including in August 1812 the defeat of the HMS *Guerriere* by the USS *Constitution*, and in October, Stephen Decatur's celebrated victory over the HMS *Macedonia* off the Canary Islands.[4]

Calhoun arrived back in Washington for the Twelfth Congress's second session in November, having been reelected while at home to the Thirteenth Congress, which would convene at the end of 1813 if the United States still existed as an independent nation. One Charleston paper, noting his reelection, described Calhoun as an "undeviating republican," which would have made John Randolph snort.[5]

Calhoun had cemented his departure from Republican orthodoxy before leaving Washington that summer. He and fellow South

Carolinian Langdon Cheves introduced a bill to suspend the non-importation acts that were part of the so-called restrictive system that Republicans hoped would put pressure on the British. Part of a Republican political tradition rooted in the patriotic boycotts of the revolutionary era and running up through Jefferson's disastrous embargo in 1807–1808, at various times the restrictive system included both embargoes that forbade any trade whatsoever and non-importation laws that kept foreign ships from American shores. It was particularly burdensome to the merchant class of New England, and by opposing it Calhoun leveraged an honest conviction into political capital with the Federalist opposition. When William Richardson of Massachusetts moved instead for a direct repeal of the acts, which would be in effect an admission that the entire restrictive philosophy was a failure, Calhoun supported the repeal and condemned the assumptions on which the restrictive system rested. "It does not suit the genius of our people, or that of our government, or the geographical character of our country," he announced. "We are a people essentially active...distance and difficulties are less to us than any people on earth." Because of the "arbitrary laws" required to enforce a restrictive system, Calhoun argued, "it renders government odious" to the "farmer enquiring why he cannot get more for his produce; and he is told it is owing to the embargo." Human nature was such that the farmer would blame the government, no matter how good the reasons for the embargo. Governing in a democracy, Calhoun declared, could not be based on coercion, and should never pit the interests of citizens against that of the government, but should instead seek to always align them as much as possible. Union was a matter of interests and affection, and the latter depended greatly on the former. "Interest," Calhoun declared, "has a wonderful control over sentiment. Even the more refined and elevated, the moral and religious sentiment may be considered as ultimately resting on it." It was a statement that would have shocked republicans of the eighteenth century on multiple fronts, but it showed how well Calhoun grasped the driving force behind the politics of nineteenth-century America.[6]

Later that year in another speech on trade Calhoun made clear that he believed "cold calculation of interest alone" was not enough to sustain the fabric of Union. Such a calculation, he warned, "is too weak to withstand political convulsions." But still he did not advocate virtue, the byword of republicanism, instead describing how "the love of greatness—the consciousness of strength" stimulated attachment to the Union. "So long as an American is a proud name, we are safe; but that day we are ashamed of it, the Union is more than half destroyed." Self-interest, strength, and pride were Calhoun's recipe for a durable Union.[7]

With support from Calhoun, Cheves, and William Lowndes, the repeal of the non-importation acts almost passed. Even though it failed, it signaled a departure so profound that Henry Adams later called it "a blow at Madison, which belittled Jefferson, and threw something like contempt on the Republican party from its beginning… down to the actual moment." Yet Calhoun did all this with such care that Adams considered the speech against the restrictive system a masterpiece of statesmanship. "With a single gesture, this young statement of the new school swept away the statesmanship of Jefferson and Madison, and waved aside the strongest convictions of his party." Once again, Calhoun proved both his independence and his political savvy. He would need support in New England, New York, and Pennsylvania if he ever launched a presidential bid.[8] His position also aligned with many lowcountry planters in South Carolina, whose longstanding opposition to trade restrictions arose from selling rice and indigo on the international market. Calhoun would continue to oppose his fellow Republicans on the restrictive system for the rest of the war, laying the foundations of a lifelong commitment to free trade.[9]

Fighting a war required both men and money in amounts that the United States had never raised before, and in the session that began in November 1812 Calhoun first faced the realities of fighting a war in a divided country. Over the next two years Calhoun and the war Republicans in Congress struggled to fulfill the Madison administration's requests against the efforts of an increasingly determined minority opposition. Again and again, sometimes in the face of facts, Calhoun insisted that the war was working, or in any case that a vigorous military response was the nation's only and best option for bringing Britain to the bargaining table.

It did not help that, like many Republicans, he had little confidence in James Madison, whose eagerness to negotiate a peace, Calhoun believed, undermined the resolve and effectiveness of the war party in Congress. "Our executive officers are most incompetent men…," he wrote to an acquaintance in Charleston at the end of the year. "We are literally boren [*sic*] down under the effects of errors and mismanagement. I am sorry to say that many of them lie deep; and are coeval with…Mr. Jefferson's administration." Privately, he warned, "I do believe the Executive will have to make a disgraceful peace." Although Madison's replacement of his secretaries of war and the navy in January 1813 signaled a welcome resolve to fight, Calhoun and his colleagues in the House still felt that the weight of keeping up the war effort fell mostly on them.[10]

In the House, Calhoun and his fellow war Republicans faced a determined combination of New England Federalists and Tertium Quids who continued to claim that the war was illegitimate and therefore that any measures passed to support it were unconstitutional. Over the course of 1813 and early 1814 Calhoun developed an argument about the proper role of a minority party in a democratic government that he hoped would prevent what was in his view a disloyal minority from derailing the war. Minority parties were a relatively new phenomenon at the time, unique to the few modern nation-states that sought to incorporate any element of democracy into their constitutional governments. The founding generation, most notably James Madison himself in *Federalist* no. 10, had been concerned in a somewhat different sense with the problem of "factions," and the 1790s had seen the emergence for the first time of an opposition in the form of the very party to which Calhoun himself now belonged. But while the existence of parties had become universally acknowledged, their role and form, especially when in the minority, was not fully worked out. How far could a minority go and for how long could they continue in opposing the majority or an administration before crossing a line? In England the idea of a "loyal opposition"—essentially a shadow government opposed to the governing coalition but still fundamentally devoted to the nation in the person of the monarch—had emerged during the eighteenth century, bloomed during the colonial crisis of the 1770s, and would reach maturity by 1830. But in the United States, in which there was no monarch to embody the nation, and in which the democratically determined will of the people carried more constitutional weight than it did in England, the role that this sort of an opposition should play remained unclear.[11]

It was clear to Calhoun that the opposition coalition had gone too far. In late 1812, James Monroe, serving as acting secretary of war, had asked Congress for an additional twenty thousand men to fight the war. In a fierce attack, John Randolph charged that Calhoun and the war Republicans had departed from the "minority principles of '98," most importantly the principle of rigid opposition to the power of the central government. Randolph used words like "fear," "dread," and "loathing" to describe traditional Republican antipathy to the central government, and accused Calhoun and the other war Republicans of abandoning the faith of their political fathers. On January 14, 1813, Calhoun responded by pointing out that Randolph and his fellow Quids had sought election to the very level of government they claimed to fear. He ridiculed their inconsistency in asking voters to "trust the government to those who are hostile to it! Who prefer their own interests and rights, to its interest and rights!" If the "principles of '98" as Randolph had stated them were indeed the principles of the Quids, Calhoun declared, they could maintain their principles and show their patriotism by determining "ever to remain in a minority" where they "perhaps may be of some use."

Instead of constantly looking back to 1798, Calhoun urged Randolph to look at his *"present* political creed," which was destructive of the war effort and thus of the nation itself. Present circumstances, not stale principles, should determine their actions. Randolph's opposition "cannot be dictated by a love of country," Calhoun said, "and is inconsistent with the duty which every citizen is under to promote the prosperity of the republic." Calhoun believed that the only solution was the "virtue and intelligence of the people," whom he hoped would vote Randolph and others out of office.[12]

INSTEAD THE VOTERS ELECTED reinforcements. When the first session of the Thirteenth Congress convened in special session in May 1813, Calhoun got his first look at the new congressman from New Hampshire, a young lawyer named Daniel Webster. Webster had a striking physical appearance, tall and solidly built with jet-black hair and intense, deeply set eyes. His dark complexion—which he got from his mother, a descendant of Welsh immigrants—gave rise to a pejorative nickname, Black Dan. But it was Webster's voice that would keep him at the forefront of American politics for the next four decades. Where Calhoun eschewed the oratorical style of the age, Webster embodied it. His striking physical appearance and his deep, richly textured voice lent a gravity to the lofty sentiments he expressed that could sweep away an audience. After one of Webster's famous speeches a seasoned political observer recorded that he had never been "so excited by public speaking before in my life. Three or four times I thought my temples would burst with the gush of blood." Ralph Waldo Emerson would later claim that for many Webster was "the representation of the American continent." His sweeping prose in praise of the Union, meticulously crafted and obsessively revised before publication, would be memorized by generations of American schoolchildren.[13]

But Webster's arrival in Congress that May was not a good sign for the Union. In a widely published address known as the Rockingham

Memorial the preceding fall he had written that the war threatened one of the central aims of the Constitution, indeed of any legitimate government—the protection of commerce. Addressing President Madison, he openly threatened a "separation of the states." "We are, Sir, from principle and habit attached to the Union of the States. But our attachment is to the *substance*, and not to the *form*…If the time should ever arrive, when this Union shall be holden together by nothing but the authority of Law…We, Sir, shall look on that hour, as the closing scene of our country's prosperity." Webster vividly described how the Union could fall apart, foreshadowing with such precision complaints that Calhoun himself would make in the coming decades—albeit from a different point on the compass—that it is impossible not to wonder if Calhoun was influenced by them. Disunion would happen, Webster warned, "when one portion of the Country undertakes to controul, to regulate, and to *sacrifice* the interest of another—when a small and heated Majority in the Government, taking counsel of their passions, and not of their reason, contemptuously disregarding the interests, and perhaps stopping the mouths, of a large and respectable minority, shall by hasty, rash, and ruinous measures, threaten to destroy essential rights; and lay waste the most important interests." Webster was not an advocate of what would later be called secession. He saw it as a disastrous outcome that should be avoided at all costs. But, like other New England Federalists ten years earlier, he did not question its legitimacy as a last resort.[14]

Webster's first act in Congress was to propose a series of six resolutions demanding explanations of Madison's conduct and the extent of his knowledge in the lead-up to war, essentially a recapitulation of the Federalist charge that the war had been made under false pretenses. To Webster's surprise, Calhoun announced that he would vote for the resolutions without amendment in the interest of transparency, skillfully defusing the resolutions as a possible rallying point for the opposition or an occasion for oratory, which was what Webster wanted. Nevertheless, Webster soon took John Randolph's place as the most vocal opponent of the war party.[15]

The unrest in New England surfaced in Congress in other ways that summer, as well. On June 29, Federalist Timothy Pickering of Massachusetts, who had played a central role in the plot for a "Northern Confederacy" while Calhoun was at Yale, read a statement of protest from the state of Massachusetts against the war from his seat in the House. While being careful not to affirm too strongly the Republican "principles of '98," the memorial complained that Massachusetts's rights were being violated by the war. "The States, as well as the individuals composing them, are parties to the national compact," it read, in a blended interpretation of the origins of the Constitution. Massachusetts had only consented to join the Union for the protection of its commerce, the memorial stated, and it had paid a heavy constitutional price for that protection—"the representation of slaves" in the national government. It was this "very unequal portion of political power…conceded to the Southern States" that was to blame for the war and for the violation of Massachusetts's right to have its commerce protected. Nowhere did the document threaten secession, but in the context of Webster's Rockingham Memorial the preceding fall the issue loomed large, and Jonathan Fisk of New York, a Republican who must have momentarily forgotten Jefferson's Kentucky resolution, immediately objected to what he called the "unprecedented" notion that "the Legislature of a State could be authorized to form themselves into a board of censors on the conduct of the General Government." Another member complained that he had not been able to hear Pickering read the memorial, which sparked a debate on whether it should be printed. Some found it too objectionable to be distributed, but Calhoun assented to the printing on the condition that his vote should not "be conceived as in any way countenancing the doctrines it contained."[16] About this time he wrote to his friend James Macbride back in South Carolina, "Party sperit is more violent than I ever knew. In what it will terminate is impossible to conjecture." But he was grimly resolute that "no threat of disunion shall shake me," writing that he still trusted "the intelligence, the virtue and the tone of public sentiment."[17] Other Republicans would soon threaten the seditious

Federalists with force, but Calhoun never went this far. Possibly this was because he did not need to—the war Republicans after all held a majority—but also no doubt because it would have contradicted his entire stated understanding of the nature of the Union, making him an easy target for the barbs of John Randolph.[18]

The war itself intruded on Congress in mid-July. As James Madison lay seriously ill with malaria in the stifling summer heat, Philip Stuart of Maryland rushed into the House chamber and announced that British ships were on their way up the Potomac, less than sixty miles from Washington. In the ensuing uproar over whether members of Congress should aid directly in the defense of the city, Henry Clay complained, "Gentlemen, if we do arm and take the field, I am sure we shall be beat, if there is not more order kept in the ranks than in this House." After bombarding Alexandria, the British fleet retreated, but it was a sobering reminder of the nearness of the British threat.[19]

By late summer Calhoun was back in South Carolina, where he would remain until December when Congress reconvened. He spent most of his time at the plantation he had purchased a couple of years earlier in the upcountry on the Savannah River about three miles south of Willington, and an easy day's journey from all the Calhouns, Pickens, and Nobles families around Abbeville. Twenty years later, one visitor recorded traversing a "hilly and unfrequented road" through low hills that suddenly gave way to a view of the "once handsome house" and, below that, the river. A plat of the property made for Calhoun in 1817 shows 840 acres and a house where he, Floride, and little Andrew lived. The plat does not show the dwelling places of the enslaved people—some probably inherited by Floride from her father's estate—who made living there possible and, Calhoun no doubt hoped, profitable. Later in his career Calhoun would hold up the plantation household with a beneficent master at its head as the paradigmatic model of southern society, and the plantation at what came to be called Bath was his first experience playing the role of an independent planter.[20]

He was also about to become a father again. Floride had become pregnant with their second child when Calhoun was home from Washington in the spring, and she would give birth to a daughter at the Bath plantation in January while Calhoun was away in Washington. Over the next sixteen years Floride would give birth to ten children, three of whom would die in early childhood. What Floride, the daughter of lowcountry wealth, thought of being secluded on an upcountry plantation waiting to give birth we unfortunately do not know. But given the dangers to mother and child that childbearing involved at that time, her own ordeal was certainly not less harrowing, and involved a good bit more actual danger, than what her husband was contending with in Washington.[21]

IN DECEMBER, CALHOUN RETURNED to Washington to find the opposition at fever pitch. Despite isolated military successes, such as Oliver Hazard Perry's naval victory over a British squadron on Lake Erie in September and William Henry Harrison's victory at the Battle of the Thames in October, the war was not going well. In fact, the news was grim on nearly all three fronts. American forces had failed to conquer or even achieve a symbolic foothold in Canada. The British had finally brought their naval superiority to bear, establishing a naval blockade from Long Island to the mouth of the Mississippi, but leaving the New England coast open in a blatant effort to encourage separatist sentiment. And in October, while Calhoun was still in upstate South Carolina, the newspaper in nearby Pendleton published a report that hundreds of white settlers had been slaughtered by Creek Indians at Fort Mims in the Mississippi Territory, about forty miles north of Mobile. If Calhoun read it, he must have thought about his grandmother, Catherine, who had been killed by Indians in a massacre in 1760. After relating how the Creeks burned many of the settlers alive inside their houses, and how the attackers had been supplied with weapons and powder by British ships from the Bahamas, the writer of the Pendleton newspaper report concluded of the southwest territory, "I see no hope for the salvation of this country."[22]

President Madison put a match to the powder keg by requesting a renewed embargo almost as soon as Congress reconvened, a measure that many understood to be aimed squarely at New England, the only part of the country not already blockaded by the British. The measure quickly became a test of party loyalty rather than a debate over a policy measure, and the House went into a secret session for two days to debate the bill. Calhoun remained uncharacteristically silent during the debate, evidently refusing to introduce the bill although he eventually voted for it, as he later claimed, to maintain party unity at a moment of crisis.[23]

In the charged atmosphere of the secret session Philip Grosvenor of New York—by most accounts a hothead—charged that Calhoun did not want the proceedings published because it would expose his inconsistency on the restrictive system to the public. He then launched into a long attack on Calhoun, and at least one Federalist member present in the House that day thought Calhoun showed remarkable forbearance in not responding to Grosvenor's "philippic."[24] But when Calhoun felt his honor had been questioned, he responded, as one newspaper from Grosvenor's home state reported, "rather passionately and improperly." Grosvenor leapt up to respond, only to be gaveled down by Clay, leaving the *New York Evening Post*'s breathless correspondent to write, "I can hardly believe it will rest here."[25]

Grosvenor soon issued a formal challenge to a duel, which was to take place on the Virginia side of the Potomac at noon on December 27, which would allow time for surgeons from Baltimore to be on hand. Henry Clay served as Calhoun's second, leaving the House to adjourn for the day when he failed to appear in the chamber on the morning of the duel. Senator Rufus King of New York served as a second for Grosvenor. As fate would have it, Grosvenor arrived on the site an hour before daybreak to practice and was promptly apprehended by an alert Virginia magistrate, while back on the other side of the Potomac the seconds worked out an agreement that both Calhoun and Grosvenor found acceptable. Washington breathed a sigh of relief as the New Year approached. It would not be the last time Henry Clay forged a compromise involving Calhoun.[26]

It seems remarkable to us today that Calhoun would accept Grosvenor's challenge, putting his career, his ambitions, and possibly his life at stake with Floride back in South Carolina about to give birth to their second child. But Calhoun likely believed he had little choice. The opponents of dueling often portrayed it as irrational violence, but Calhoun, as usual, was acting according to a coldly rational understanding of what was at stake. Honor had its own logic. A man, like a nation, could not let a challenge go unanswered and expect to keep his reputation or retain the respect of his peers. In Calhoun's world, this fact was as inarguable as the rising of the sun, and the demands of honor and duty as Calhoun understood them often dictated his political and personal actions like an invisible and, to some, inscrutable road map.

AT THE END OF December, days after the near-duel, the British ship *Bramble* brought the shocking news of Napoleon's defeat at Leipzig, a decisive turning point in the war between Great Britain and France that would soon leave Great Britain freer to focus her immense resources on North America. By coincidence or not, the same ship carrying the news of Napoleon's defeat also carried a British offer of direct negotiations to end the war. Madison quickly accepted the offer in light of the Leipzig news, and commissioned a negotiating committee whose makeup—including Henry Clay and John Quincy Adams—signaled seriousness of purpose. As Henry Adams later wrote, "From that moment the New England Federalists no longer doubted their own power," and were even more determined to frustrate the measures of the war party, who for their part were even more determined to keep up the war effort in order to secure the best possible outcome from the negotiations.[27]

On January 15, 1814, days after it became public that Madison had accepted the British offer of negotiations, and as Federalist attacks in Congress swirled toward a crescendo, Calhoun set aside the issue at hand—a bill to lengthen enlistments—and instead addressed Congress on the larger question of the limits of political opposition in a democracy. He pointedly used the word "faction," which conjured fears of self-interested groups that might co-opt the government for their own purposes, a possibility Madison had famously warned against in his argument for the Constitution as creating a country too large for any one faction to gain control. Calhoun warned instead of minority factions so determined to undermine the public will that they committed, in a phrase he adopted from Felix Grundy, "moral treason." He argued forcefully that it was not legitimate for the opposition to frustrate Republican war measures when the country had decided through its regularly elected representatives to go to war. He cited the examples of Athens, Carthage, and Rome, the speeches of Cicero, the "orations of Demosthenes," and the ancient historian Polybius to argue that the "fell spirit of factious opposition" had been fatal to ancient republics. He denied that the constitutional right to "liberty of speech" included the right to deliberate and destructive obstruction in a time of war. (Weeks later Calhoun praised the Romans as a "wise and virtuous people" because they "considered it a crime in a citizen to doubt the justice of the public cause.") Most strikingly, Calhoun invoked the minority's duty to submit to "the will of [the] majority" even when they disagreed with it. Still, Calhoun refused any but democratic remedies to the problem, appealing to the "good sense and the virtue of the people" as the only solution.[28]

Later, Calhoun would point to the exigencies of war to explain some of his positions during this period, and it was certainly true that he and others, with justification, believed the very existence of the country was at stake. It was also true that the Constitution contemplated war as a special circumstance. But Calhoun's defense of the will of the majority and his fierce attack on a minority opposition that often accused the central government of violating state rights nevertheless stands in striking opposition to what he would later argue. At least one of his colleagues, the Federalist Richard Stockton, found the speech overly didactic, and complained of having to sit through "lectures learnedly prepared."[29]

In early February Calhoun received word—though not from his wife—that back in South Carolina Floride had safely delivered a baby girl. "My inclination would be to call her by the name which you and your mother bear," Calhoun wrote to Floride, but professed he would be pleased with "any one that you and your mother think proper." The little girl was named Floride. Calhoun also begged for more letters and asked for news of his little son, whom he worried was suffering from a lack of attention with the arrival of the baby. "Andrew appears to be forgot," he wrote. "None of the letters from home for some time mention him. I hope he is doing well. Kiss him for me."[30]

Meanwhile, Calhoun was all business back on the floor of the House, which was in the midst of an extensive and acrimonious debate—eventually consuming over 250 pages in the *Annals of Congress*—over the revelation that a new loan for $25 million would be required to support the war.[31] Inevitably, the debate over the loan became a debate over the causes of the war, especially the issue of impressment. The American Constitution formalized a new conception of national belonging that was, in the words of one scholar, "contractual and volitional, not natural and perpetual."[32] (Of course, not all Americans had chosen to come voluntarily, and with a certain grim logic those of African descent were not considered subjects for naturalization, which in the words of the Naturalization Act of 1790 was only available to "free white persons.")[33] Impressment reduced the issue to one all-important question: whether a British subject could renounce his country of birth and be naturalized as an American citizen, making him immune to British claims on his service in a time of war. The British claimed he could not, and that such individuals were subject to impressment even when sailing under the flag of their "new" nation. Great Britain acted on this argument with a vengeance. From the renewal of the Napoleonic wars in 1803 to 1811, Britain impressed some ten thousand men into its navy who claimed to be American citizens, and the majority of these claimed naturalized citizenship.[34]

Some in Congress agreed with Britain, especially since it conveniently countered the war Republicans' main argument for the war. On February 14, 1814, during the debate over the loan, the Federalist Alexander Hanson of Maryland denounced the "new-fangled doctrines" of naturalization and cited the authority of Blackstone, who had written that "natural allegiance is perpetual."[35] Only days before, Calhoun had declared that the United States was not protecting "British traitors," but only "such as had incorporated themselves into our political society according to our laws." Philip Grosvenor could not contain himself, interrupting Calhoun to say that he doubted "whether, according to the principles of public law, we can deliver a citizen from his allegiance to his native country." Calhoun responded incredulously that he hoped Grosvenor was not arguing that "persons who…have forsworn foreign allegiance, and become citizens, should not be protected whilst fighting under our banners?" Perhaps thinking of his own immigrant family, Calhoun consistently and tenaciously defended the principle of volitional citizenship for free white men that set the United States apart from most European countries. It would not be the last time he argued for "new-fangled doctrines."[36]

As the debate on the loan bill continued, and increasingly became a debate on the war itself, many waited for a definitive response from Calhoun. On February 18 the correspondent for the *Boston Daily Advertiser* wrote from Washington that "Mr. Calhoun, the great gun of the party, may…be expected to be let off before the present war of words is finished."[37] And indeed, on February 25, the same day that Henry Clay sailed from New York at the start of a stormy journey across the North Atlantic to make peace, Calhoun gave his most extensive and forceful defense of the war on the floor of the House.[38] In order to respond to Grosvenor and other supporters of the natural allegiance argument, Calhoun had been poring over the accepted authorities on international law: Hugo Grotius, Samuel von Pufendorf, and especially Emer de Vattel's *Law of Nations*, first published in 1758 and in the United States in 1796. Nowhere, according to Calhoun, did these theorists grant the right to impressment the British claimed. "They minutely state the cases in which a belligerent may enter a neutral vessel for the purpose of search. Why not this also?" Calhoun asked. Anticipating the response that custom, not law, authorized the British practice, Calhoun contended that the protection of citizens was an even older and more weighty custom of nations than impressment.

But the heart of Calhoun's speech was his accusation that the British had been trying for decades to establish what he called a "universal monopoly" over the nations of the Western Hemisphere. "Neutral commerce...will be annihilated," Calhoun warned. "Nor will the evil stop there," he predicted. Economic subjugation was only a presage to political domination, and so it must be seen and resisted for what it would become as much as for what it was. "It will be asked how can you counteract it? I answer, by the measure now pursued; by force; by war; not by remonstrance, not by negotiation; and still less by leaving it to itself. The nature of its growth indicates its remedy. It originated in power, has grown just in proportion as opposing power has been removed, and can only be restrained by power. Nations are, for the most part not restrained by moral principles, but by fear."

Calhoun denounced the "despondent and slavish belief" that "we must submit...and hug our chains," or that forbearance in the face of naked aggression was a virtue. "It is more easy to maintain than to wrest back usurped rights," he declared, and there was no excuse or remedy for the moral failure of submission. "Wrongs submitted to produce contrary effects in the oppressor and oppressed. Oppression strengthens and prepares for new oppression; submission debases to farther submission. The first wrong, by the universal law of our nature, is most easily resisted...Let that be submitted to; let the consequent debasement and loss of national honor be felt, and nothing but the grinding hand of oppression can force to resistance. I know not which to pronounce most guilty; the nation that inflicts the wrong, or that which quietly submits to it."

The speech was a sweeping denunciation of the policy of the previous three administrations, an iconoclastic combination of republican ideas about the nature of power and the logic of honor applied to foreign policy. Where traditional republicanism focused on the issue of restraining the grasping nature of power within a state by way of a virtuous citizenry and a well-constructed constitution, Calhoun declared that in the wider world of nations power could only be countered with power, force with force. America would do well to avoid "entangling alliances," and Calhoun was clear that he did not advocate an American version of British imperialism, but the United States could not afford to avoid acting on the international stage. Furthermore, while eighteenth-century republicanism contemplated all sorts of ways that a people could be morally debased to the point that they no longer had the virtue to sustain independent government—such as luxury, vice, or patronage—Calhoun argued that shame and submission carried the same corrosive potential.[39]

In the wake of the speech, Federalist newspaper editors oscillated between portrayals of Calhoun as a formidable enemy and denunciations of the "puerile declamation" of a "presumptuous stripling." In the end, the loan bill passed the House on March 3 by a vote of 97 to 55.[40]

Before leaving Washington in April, Calhoun presided with pleasure over the final and total repeal of the restrictive system, which the Madison administration had finally decided to jettison. In a speech to Congress, Calhoun insisted that the repeal include both the embargo and the non-importation acts. This provoked some protest from Rhode Island and Pennsylvania, where nascent manufacturing industries had benefited greatly from the shield provided by non-importation against British goods. Calhoun reassured them that even after the repeal of the restrictive system his position was that "certain manufactures in cottons and woolens, which have kindly taken root in our soil, should have a moderate but permanent protection ensured them." In other words, a tariff. It was one indication that Calhoun's thoughts were beginning that spring to move beyond the war.[41]

On the day that Congress adjourned its spring session, April 18, the Washington newspapers carried a letter from General Andrew Jackson announcing his stunning and bloody defeat of the Creek Indians at Horseshoe Bend at the end of March.[42] Jackson would negotiate an unusually harsh treaty later that summer that punished Creek allies along with Creek enemies and transferred nearly twenty-three million acres of land—most of what is today southwest Georgia and central Alabama—to the United States. Floating down the Alabama River to Mobile through the new territory, Jackson imagined the "elegant mansions, and extensive rich & productive farms" that would soon line the banks. Jackson's was not a vision of a Jeffersonian yeoman's republic, but of a coming cotton kingdom.[43] Jackson's punitive treaty with the Creeks and his daydream on the Alabama River were integrally connected to the war being fought in Canada, the Great Lakes, and on the waves of the Atlantic. All were part of a struggle for continental supremacy in which the young United States sought to replace Great Britain's central role in a process one historian has called "war capitalism"—the appropriation of native land by state force for individual and national economic gain. As Calhoun well understood and articulated that spring in his description of Britain's attempt to establish a "universal monopoly" on trade in the Western Hemisphere, economic power and profit were intertwined with political and military power. The war was fundamentally about whether the United States would continue to be the periphery and subject of this process, or whether it would take the reins on the continent of North America.[44]

CALHOUN RETURNED TO SOUTH CAROLINA in April, where he found little Floride and the now nearly four-year-old Andrew. The summer began with good news—an American triumph at the Battle of Chippewa on the Niagara River in July that most Americans welcomed as a restoration of national honor. But the late spring and early summer also brought news of the complete collapse of Napoleon in Europe, which left Britain to focus on the upstart Americans and placed the American negotiating delegation in Ghent at a distinct disadvantage. Having been charged to negotiate for an end to impressment and the surrender of Canada to the United States, the American delegation were flabbergasted by British demands that they give up American fishing rights in Canadian waters, part of Maine, and accept a buffer zone between the Ohio River and the Great Lakes in order to protect Britain's Indian allies.

Then at the end of August the British struck a humiliating blow. Overwhelming local militia, British forces entered Washington on the heels of a fleeing James Madison and proceeded to burn the city, including the White House and the Capitol building, to the ground. The war might have ended there if the British had not been turned back at Baltimore by the stubborn defenders of Fort McHenry, a spectacle that led a young lawyer named Francis Scott Key to pen a poem in their honor.[45]

When Congress reconvened in September Washington still smoldered from the British attack. Calhoun was nearly a month late, having fallen ill, but he took his seat on October 19 in time for the debate over the proposed British terms of peace, which the Madison administration was determined to reject. Partly to spite Madison and the war Republicans, the Federalists argued that the United States should accept the terms as the best that could be expected and as the just deserts of an unjust war. Calhoun rejected this argument, reminding the House that "England dreaded a continuance of the contest" as much as the United States did since the situation with Napoleon was still volatile and England's now-uncontested commercial dominance "is calculated to raise up powerful enemies on the continent." "Our very preparation for a vigorous war will make her dread the contest," he declared. England, Calhoun believed, was bluffing.[46]

Calhoun must have seemed overly optimistic, even deranged, to many of his colleagues as they crowded together to listen to him in the main room of Blodgett's Hotel, one of the only structures to have survived the British attack. To many of them it seemed that the American experiment was unraveling before their eyes. The capital was in ruins, the country was nearly bankrupt, and the Royal Navy controlled the coastline and was actively engaged in discussions with communities in New England about making a separate peace. The small island of Nantucket, with little choice, had done just that in August; and in November the Federalist governor of Massachusetts Caleb Strong sent a secret emissary to Nova Scotia to ask for British protection.[47]

Calhoun was fully aware of where all this might lead. In early November he wrote his cousin Andrew Pickens, "They threaten a devision in N. England and many here dread it." When the Federalists actually met in Hartford, Connecticut, at the end of the year, they compiled a list of constitutional demands that aimed to break the sway of the Virginia dynasty in American politics. They also demanded that naturalized citizens not be allowed to hold political office. For the moment, they did not propose secession. Had the war dragged on long enough for a second planned meeting to occur in June, however, it is likely that the more radical voices would have had the upper hand.[48]

But as it turned out, Calhoun was right about circumstances in Europe tipping the scales in the United States' favor. Late in 1814, with negotiations at the Congress of Vienna in doubt and the resumption of war in Europe a real possibility, British officials instructed their peace delegation in Ghent to put an end to the troublesome American war. The resulting treaty that the Americans at Ghent hastily signed on December 24 restored boundaries, including Indian territories, to their 1811 locations, and pushed negotiations over fishing waters off to a later date. Most infuriating to the likes of John Randolph and Daniel Webster, the treaty said nothing about impressment. The administration and the war Republicans, including Calhoun, would argue that this was logical and acceptable since peace in Europe ended the circumstances Britain had used to justify the practice, but this was a half-hearted and deceptive response. Other Federalists pointed out that after all the clamoring for Canada, the United States had not gained a square foot of it. Still, as Henry Clay wrote of the treaty, "We lose no territory, I think no honor." And honor, after all, had been the whole point.[49]

News of the treaty reached New York City on February 11, and took two more days to reach Washington. Calhoun was still unaware of it when he scrawled a hurried letter to Patrick Noble on the eleventh just as the mail was closing in Washington to inform him of "the glorious news that the British have evacuated the Island of Orleans." Calhoun breathlessly reported four thousand British casualties, "with Packenham and Gibbs killed and Kean dangerously wounded." The real number was closer to half that, but it was a remarkably lopsided American victory nonetheless. Like most Americans, Calhoun heard the news of Andrew Jackson's stunning victory at New Orleans shortly before hearing of the peace treaty, a sequence that cemented the impression that America had won the war. Two weeks later an exultant Calhoun wrote to his brother-in-law John Ewing Colhoun, a captain in the United States Army, describing his "extreme delight that the just and necessary war which we had been compeled to wage with England has been brought to a termination so advantageous and glorious to our country." Calhoun, like the entire nation, was flushed with the adrenaline of victory.[50]

Calhoun had good reason to be exultant. The traditional view of the War of 1812 as a somewhat farcical draw in which the United States was extremely lucky has some merit but obscures the war's real effects, which only began to be realized in the following decades. After the unfortunate timing of the Federalist Hartford Convention, which now appeared unpatriotic if not outright treasonous, upcoming elections would leave Republicans in complete control of the government. And despite being fought after the war was technically over, Andrew

Jackson's victory at New Orleans reinforced a strain of traditional British wisdom that American wars were a losing proposition and made a generation of British military and political leaders unwilling to attempt another invasion. Finally, the combination of Jackson's subjugation and dispossession of the southern Creeks, and the British abandonment of their Indian allies in the Treaty of Ghent meant that native peoples would no longer be able to mount any real resistance to the rabid energies of American expansion. As one of the British delegates to Ghent wrote privately, "I had, till I came here, no idea of the fixed determination which prevailed in the breast of every American to extirpate the Indians and appropriate their territory." This appropriation, already in progress, would be carried out with grim determination in the coming decades, part of it under Calhoun's direction.[51]

FOR CALHOUN, IT WAS a moment of personal vindication such as few statesmen ever experience, but his public triumph was soon tempered by personal tragedy. Having played an important role in defeating the greatest empire in the world, within days of arriving home Calhoun found himself kneeling helplessly with his wife beside the bed of their one-year-old daughter Floride as she gazed around with "wildness in her eyes," vomiting and flushed with fever. The little girl became sick around midday on April 6 and died early the next morning, before a doctor the frantic parents had sent for could even arrive. In a letter to his mother-in-law, the little girl's namesake, two days later, Calhoun seemed unable to make sense of what had happened. Relating the "heaviest calamity that has ever occurred to us…the death of our interesting and dearest daughter," the young father was clearly in shock. With the blunt incredulity of grief, he wrote, "She was in the bloom of health on Wednesday morning…and was a corps the next day," and he struggled to make sense of the fact that "she had just begun to talk and walk; and progressed so fast in both as to surprise every one," and yet she was now suddenly "gone alas!"

Feeling the need to console his equally distraught wife, Calhoun fell back on the familiar doctrines of his Calvinist upbringing to make sense of the loss. He tried to tell Floride that death "is the lott of humanity," that "Providence may have intended it in kindness," and that their daughter "is far more happy [in heaven] than she could be here with us." But it was no use. Southern women like Floride Calhoun were often acculturated to blame themselves for the loss of a child, a cruelty compounded by the fact that depression after such a loss was often seen as a lack of proper resignation to divine will. Unable to console himself, Calhoun should not have been surprised that his rationalizations of a loss beyond reason failed to comfort his wife, and his despair at his failure—"every topic of consolation, which I attemp [*sic*] to offer but seems to grieve her more"—is some measure of an emotional distance between them that would not lessen with time. Calhoun would become famous for revealing the elemental logic of an argument or a piece of legislation, but he at times failed to comprehend the vast areas of human nature that had a hidden logic all their own.[52]

SEVEN

"Let Us Conquer Space"

CALHOUN TRAVELED THE LAST FIFTY miles to Washington for the opening session of Congress in December 1815 on the deck of a modern marvel. "You are moved on rapidly without being sensible of it," he wrote excitedly to Floride of his trip up the Potomac by steamboat. "I hope by another session there will be one from Charleston to this place."[1] Early steamboats inspired a similar sense of awe in many who rode or even watched them, and it is easy to see why. For most of history human beings had to ally with the forces of nature, harnessing wind and water to make their way across oceans and down rivers. But these new technological wonders—machines made of wood and metal, powered by steam—could overthrow time, space, and nature itself, traveling upriver against the current. To many Americans they seemed like symbols of the nation itself, something new in history. But the symbolism was ambiguous—despite Calhoun's assurance to Floride of their "safety, ease, and expedition of traveling," steamboats had a troubling tendency to explode, strewing mechanical and human wreckage along the nation's riverbanks. Nevertheless, steamboats would soon transform the Mississippi's massive watershed into a commercial highway for cotton and slaves. In 1815 less than twenty steamboats reached New Orleans via the Mississippi. Five years later the number was two hundred.[2]

Calhoun's ride up the Potomac happened at a key juncture in global economic history. The Treaty of Ghent left the United States poised to exert control over most of the North American continent, including the Mississippi's watershed. Meanwhile, in England, the demand for raw fiber to feed the ever-expanding capacity of the cotton textile industry far outstripped the supply available from traditional source regions such as India, where an embedded system of tenantry frustrated British attempts to reshape production to meet the demand. A plantation economy utilizing enslaved labor and capable of producing cotton on an industrial scale had begun to emerge in the West Indies and in Brazil at the end of the eighteenth century, especially on the island of Haiti, but the Haitian Revolution disrupted this promising stream of white gold, while in Brazil sugar eclipsed cotton as the dominant crop. This cleared the way for the American South to dominate, and a cotton boom had already begun in Calhoun's native upcountry during the first decade of the nineteenth century. But Adam Smith's invisible hand alone could not supply this kind of demand. It would take the power of the state. The United States in the early nineteenth century represented the only place in the world where a planter class wielded the political power necessary to appropriate land and allocate labor swiftly enough to produce cotton on a scale that matched the insatiable appetite of the cotton mills of Manchester.[3]

For nearly a decade after the war Calhoun played an integral role in this national and international process, shaping domestic and foreign policy to both nurture the American economy and protect it from British competition. In early 1816, as Congress deliberated what to do in the wake of the war, Calhoun compared the United States to the mythical Hercules contemplating a choice between a life of ease and a life of "labor and virtue." To Calhoun, as to Hercules, the choice was clear: "May this nation, the youthful Hercules, possessing his form and muscles, be enspired with similar sentiments and follow his example."[4] If Congress and the president would only act, Calhoun understood, the momentum and national pride created by victory over Britain could be harnessed and channeled into policies that would unify, strengthen, and enrich the country. His efforts would lead him even further from the old republican orthodoxies, but the fact that his own future and the country's were so perfectly aligned made it hard to resist the feeling that he was on the side of history.

THE MOST IMMEDIATE CONCERN for Calhoun and his colleagues was that peace might not last. Only two weeks after learning of the treaty, Calhoun wondered "whether the soreness of [Britain's] recent defeat would produce a disposition to remain at peace or to retaliate." A year later in Congress he still confidently predicted "future wars, long and bloody" with England.[5] Best then to stay prepared. Or rather to actually prepare, since the main lesson that Calhoun took from the recent war was that a naïve republican ideology about centralized authority and standing armies had nearly cost the country its very existence. As a result, the Fourteenth Congress that opened in December 1815 was one of the most consequential in American history, setting the stage for the next half century by taking on a slate of issues, including proposals for a new national bank, a tariff, internal improvements, and military reforms—all designed to strengthen the country internally and defend it from external threats both military and economic. In all these efforts Calhoun played a central role.

The First Bank of the United States, chartered in 1791, had been a central part of Alexander Hamilton's financial plan to unify the new nation and strengthen the central government. This made the bank a target for Republicans, who finally achieved their goal when its charter came up for renewal in 1811. During the war the disastrous effects of letting the bank, and with it the federal government's credit, expire became evident in the government's constant near-bankruptcy and scramble for loans. As early as 1813, states like New York and Pennsylvania energetically petitioned Congress to reestablish a national bank. Calhoun supported these efforts from their beginning, at least in theory, lamenting before Congress, for example, that the difficulty in financing the war had been primarily a consequence of "the single fact, that we have no proper medium commensurate in its circulation with the Union, that it is all local."[6]

But at the end of 1814 when the Committee on Ways and Means put forward a bill to establish a bank along lines proposed by Madison's new secretary of the treasury, Pennsylvanian Alexander J. Dallas, Calhoun balked. The bill proposed, as he put it, "a machine for lending money" to the government for the war, not a bank, and paid little attention to the other benefits that a bank could provide or the damage it might do. To the delight of the Federalists and the consternation of the administration, Calhoun decided he could not support it. Instead, he essentially replaced the Dallas plan with his own bill in a resolution the *National Intelligencer* called "ingenious and elaborate," proposing to eliminate ties between the bank and the government, greatly restricting the president's power over the bank, and eliminating its more partisan features.[7] Federalist Samuel Taggart of Massachusetts wrote to John Taylor of Virginia that Calhoun's resolution was "a change in the whole complexion of the bill," and that the Federalists preferred Calhoun's bill to Dallas's.[8] It was a brash move for a young politician who would later admit that "the whole subject of banking, theoretically and practically, was...new" to him, but Congress overwhelmingly approved Calhoun's bill, a measure of his ability to craft a proposal that appealed to multiple and frequently opposed constituencies.[9]

Whatever its political virtues, experienced observers doubted the proposal's financial efficacy. New York financier and fur baron John Jacob Astor wrote to Calhoun congratulating him on a bill "certainly calculated to place the whole community on a more equal footing as to the advantages arising from the institution than the original Bill." But Astor gently expressed his doubt as to "whether this plan will produce the same good effect on public credit." Without a close connection to the government, Astor pointed out, there would be no reason for investors to prefer this bank over other ones. Dallas and Madison also resisted Calhoun's plan, pleading that a machine for lending money was exactly what the government needed to fight the war.[10]

Peace opened the door to compromise. In his annual message to Congress in December 1815, Madison renewed the call for a national bank, but this time more along the lines Calhoun had proposed. With the war over, the bank's purpose would be to impose discipline on the currency by restoring specie payments (the requirement that banks redeem their notes with gold and silver) and reining in the runaway credit practices of state banks, a purpose in line with Calhoun's resolution during the war. As Calhoun declared during the debate over the subsequent bill, the state banks could not be expected to rein themselves in. Their only aim, he declared, was "gain, gain; nothing but gain…Those who believed the present state of things would ever cure itself…must believe what is impossible; banks must change their nature, lay aside their instinct, before they will aid in doing what it is not in their interest to do."[11]

After Madison's message, Speaker of the House Henry Clay immediately appointed Calhoun chairman of the Committee on a Uniform National Currency, and a few days before Christmas, Calhoun sent a brief note to Alexander Dallas with the news that his committee had determined to introduce a new bank bill. The two men met that evening to talk over the details. While previous efforts to justify the bank had appealed to the "necessary and proper" clause to justify a bank, provoking objections from strict constructionists, in their final effort Calhoun and Dallas shifted the justification to a different constitutional anchor, arguing instead that the Constitution's "Coinage Clause" gave Congress the duty and power to regulate currency. If they had hoped to satisfy constitutional critics, they were disappointed. An article titled "Constitutional or Unconstitutional?," published in Philadelphia and reprinted in Charleston, argued that Calhoun's bank bill was "the most daring attempt ever made in congress on states rights" since it allowed the federal government to regulate banks chartered by states.[12] John Randolph sneered that the bank was equivalent to "getting rid of the rats by setting fire to the house."[13] Nevertheless, Madison signed the bank into existence in April 1816.[14]

During the same session, when Congress considered the establishment of additional military academies to train officers for a future conflict with England, Calhoun argued specifically for multiple and geographically diffuse military academies. A single, central academy "would principally be filled with the sons of wealthy men" who would not, Calhoun bluntly asserted, be either the most talented or the most motivated. "Where, in this country, shall we look for genius and talent?" he asked. "Most indubitably in the middle ranks, in the lower ranks in preference to the higher; not that these classes actually contain a greater portion of talent, but that they have stronger stimulants to its exertion. Rich men, being already at the top of the ladder, have no further motive to climb." Calhoun undoubtedly had his own backcountry upbringing and ambition in mind.[15]

At the end of January, Calhoun's fellow South Carolinian congressman William Lowndes proposed a continuation of the direct taxes levied during the war in order to fund a permanent, professional military establishment. The proposal provoked fierce attacks from John Randolph and his allies, throwing the whole array of national projects Calhoun was working toward into doubt. In a major speech on January 31, Calhoun argued that all the great historical republics had required sacrifices, including military service, of their citizens. "I know that I utter truths unpleasant to those who wish to enjoy liberty without making the efforts necessary to secure it," he announced. "It has been said by some physician that life is a forced state; the same may be said of freedom. It requires efforts; it presupposes mental and moral qualities of a high order to be generally diffused in the society where it exists."

What mattered, Calhoun argued, was that the "moral power" of the government over its citizens not be destroyed by levying "heavy and unnecessary" taxes that would damage the delicate fabric of trust on which government sovereignty in a republic depended. Distinguishing between what he called the physical and moral power of government,

Calhoun argued that the latter was much more important and consisted in "the zeal of the country, and the confidence in the administration of its government." Without this, "We had better give up all our physical power" since in a republic the exercise of physical power could only be legitimate when exercised in the context of moral power. If taxes were laid "wisely, necessarily and moderately," then an "intelligent and virtuous" citizenry would support them. Sovereignty in a republic, as Calhoun described it, was a delicate balance between the Lockean assent of a high-minded citizenry and the moderate and reasonable demands made by a just government in order to provide them the benefits they sought. The bill passed, but not before John Randolph darkly reminded Calhoun that the most beautiful features of the Constitution as the basis of a "federative" government could become instruments of oppression in a "consolidated" government. "The gentleman," Randolph said in a sort of grudging compliment, "[is] too deeply read in Aristotle, too well versed in political lore, to deny the fact."[16]

Calhoun also made clear that he was in favor of a new tariff to protect manufacturing interests vital to any future war effort, something he had hinted at as a balm to the manufacturing interests when the restrictive system had been repealed during the war. Singling out "our woolen and cotton manufactures," Calhoun also made clear that the importance of the tariff was not the financial benefit it would provide them, but the advantage it would confer upon the country at large in the event of a possible war. In a speech supporting Lowndes's revenue bill, Calhoun also extended a call for a greatly strengthened navy. To him, the revenue bill, the tariff, the navy, the military academies, the bank, and soon internal improvements, were all of a piece.[17] John Randolph, though from the opposite side of the room, saw it the same way, writing to friends back in Virginia of "the new system which out Hamiltons Alexander Hamilton."[18] Randolph was right. Where Hamilton's system had been designed based on an Atlantic-focused economy and had in many ways taken for granted English commercial supremacy, the measures Republicans proposed during the Fourteenth Congress attested to the assumption of a whole continent and the hope of a whole hemisphere under American control.[19]

During the war Calhoun had remarked approvingly of the growth of manufacturing in the country, the unintended fruit of the war and the restrictive system. Cut off from British competition and driven by necessity, the growth of cotton manufacturing in particular had been astounding. Between 1807 and 1815, the number of mechanical spindles in the United States grew from 8,000 to 130,000. By 1809 there were sixty-two textile mills housing these spindles, concentrated in the North, with twenty-five more under construction, and by 1815 manufacturers had achieved enough political clout to lobby successfully for their interests in Congress. During the war there were even scattered manufacturing efforts in states like South Carolina and Georgia, giving some southerners hope that a regional industry would emerge.[20]

The tariff bill that William Lowndes eventually introduced was designed to protect this domestic industry, which many viewed as essential to any future war effort, against the flood of cheap British goods that were already appearing since the war ended. Lowndes's bill included a 20 percent duty on cheap cotton cloth, which Calhoun supported as "ample protection," but during debate advocates of a more heavily protective tariff, including Henry Clay and Daniel Webster, inserted a temporary 30 percent duty on cheap cotton cloth partly in response to the lobbying efforts of Francis Cabot Lowell, head of the Boston Manufacturing Company.[21]

John Randolph railed that the proposed tariff was nothing less than a tax on consumers that would fall heaviest on "poor men, and on slaveholders."[22] On April 4, as Randolph angled from the floor to postpone the tariff bill indefinitely, Samuel D. Ingham of Pennsylvania left the chamber and found Calhoun in a nearby room working on the details of his bank bill. Ingham begged him to come and answer Randolph in order to show the administration's support for the bill and to keep members from leaving the chamber to escape Randolph's interminable eloquence. Calhoun protested that he had not planned to give a speech, but eventually gave in to Ingham, put away his pen, and hurried to take the floor against Randolph. He would later claim that the speech was off the cuff and did not represent his true thinking, but as late as 1823 he was still pointing correspondents to it as a reliable guide to his views. Apologizing for his lack of preparation, Calhoun launched into a defense of the tariff that soon extended well beyond the military necessities of supporting manufacturing to the nature of wealth and political economy. "Neither agriculture, manufactures, or commerce, taken separately, is the cause of wealth," he maintained, "it flows from the three combined." The only part of the formula lacking to any substantial degree in the United States was manufacturing, which the government could play a role in fostering until it was "grown to a certain perfection." He noted that an unintended consequence of the recent war had been to "divert a large amount of capital to this new branch of industry"—therefore, all the government had to do was provide these infant industries just enough protection to "put them beyond the reach of contingency."

Calhoun knew that some of the objections to the encouragement of manufacturing stemmed from a Jeffersonian belief in the enervating political effects of industrial labor, and he acknowledged that previously manufacturing had required a "minute sub-division of labor" that was "undoubtedly unfavorable to the intellect." But recent improvements in technology—"the great perfection of machinery"—had solved this problem, Calhoun believed, as men had now only to tend the machines that performed the most mind-numbing elements of this labor. He asserted that these industries "furnished new stimulus and means of subsistence to the laboring classes of the community." Manufacturing represented human progress, and Calhoun was in favor of progress. In closing, Calhoun allowed himself an uncharacteristic bit of oratory that he much later downplayed as "hasty and unguarded expressions." Noting that the tariff would help "bind together more closely our widely-spread Republic" by increasing internal trade, he proclaimed that "the liberty and the union of this country were inseparably united!"[23]

The tariff of 1816 passed with the support of a third of southern representatives, both Republican and Federalist, a surprisingly high number considering what the future held. The evidence suggests that many southerners and Republicans especially saw the tariff as a patriotic and temporary measure that was necessary for military reasons and preferable to direct taxation as a means of raising revenue and paying down the national debt. Meanwhile, many New England representatives abstained from the final vote, a measure of the divisions that existed between the interests of the shipping industry and the nascent manufacturing industries in states like Massachusetts.[24]

Calhoun would later portray his support for the tariff as rooted mainly in military necessity and the need to stay vigilant in an unstable world. "Bonaparte had but recently been overthrown," he recalled in 1833, "the whole southern part of this continent was in a state of revolution, and threatened with the interference of the Holy Alliance [Britain, Austria, Russia, and Prussia]." But it is clear Calhoun clearly saw the tariff as more than a matter of military necessity and that he was conscious and supportive of the tariff's protectionist nature, which he supported at least until American manufacturing had matured. He never mentioned the tariff as a revenue measure to pay down the national debt.[25]

The United States was far from alone in the years after 1815 in seeking to protect infant cotton textile industries from a flood of cheap British cloth. Between 1818 and 1824, Prussia, Austria, Russia, France, and Italy all passed high tariffs for similar purposes. Over the course of the eighteenth century, European countries—especially Britain—had transformed the world into what one historian calls an "inside" of law, custom, order, and industrial production in the home country, and an imperial "outside," where military and state power expropriated land, removed native peoples, and utilized enslaved people to produce staple crops and luxuries for consumption on the "inside." The United States' origins were as part of Britain's "outside," but with the tariff of 1816 and the internal improvements bill later that year, they made a bid to build their own "inside" while maintaining an "outside" on their own continent. Henry Clay would eventually call this effort to create a "home market" the American System, and Calhoun was an early supporter.[26]

BACK IN SOUTH CAROLINA that summer, Calhoun claimed with satisfaction in a letter to Alexander Dallas, "I hear not one objection to the bank, Tariff, or taxes." At the same time, Calhoun wrote to Dallas that he expected "great changes" in the election that fall owing to a growing popular backlash over a different bill that had provoked comparatively little debate in Congress that spring. "The compensation bill is much objected to," he wrote. "I find in my own district very considerable dissatisfaction at it." The compensation bill, proposed by Richard M. Johnson of Kentucky, proposed to change the payment of members of Congress from a per diem rate of $6 to a per-session rate of $1,500 because Johnson thought the per diem rate encouraged "constant and never-ending debate." Calhoun had supported the bill, observing that Congress had lost many "young men of genius, without property" who had to leave because of the paltry salary that came with representing the American people. Calhoun even argued that the per-session rate should be increased to $2,500 in order to allow members' families to come with them to Washington, an idea that, if he had pressed it and succeeded, might have been the end of his political career. In the end, Johnson's version of the bill passed the House in an 81 to 67 vote by representatives blithely unaware they had just committed political suicide.[27]

The compensation bill set off a nationwide uproar at the prospect of politicians voting themselves a raise. The anger against the bill was so great in Calhoun's own district that his cousin Colonel Joseph Calhoun, who had stepped aside to let Calhoun run in 1810, decided to run against him in the election that fall. Three other candidates also joined the race. Calhoun's cousin John Noble wrote from Charleston, "Your friends here, feel much anxiety, as to your reelection." Calhoun later recalled that he was advised to apologize and throw himself on the voters' mercy, as many of his colleagues were doing, but he refused. Instead, he held two public meetings at the Edgefield and Abbeville courthouses where he explained his reasons for supporting the bill. The direct approach paid off, and Calhoun was reelected that fall despite the general slaughter of his colleagues over the compensation bill. In the end, half of the Senate and two-thirds of the House were not re-elected that fall. Only two of the seven South Carolina representatives who voted for the bill were returned to the House.[28]

In December, Congress reconvened for its "lame duck" session, in which the current Congress met once more after their successors had been elected (a tradition that continued until the Twentieth Amendment finally ended it in 1933). At the beginning of this session, Richard Johnson proposed repealing the now-infamous compensation bill, arguing that even though the bill had been completely justified, he was still bound by the extremely clear and loudly expressed will of his constituents to repeal it. Many others who had endured uncomfortable summers in their home districts agreed. Calhoun was in the unique position of having refused to apologize, as even the mighty Henry Clay had been forced to do, and having been vindicated by reelection. This gave him the ground to make a bold argument against representatives mechanically following the instructions of their constituents, although he did not see his stance as a rejection of the people's will.

Calhoun first made a mock apology for "committing an unpardonable error, in presenting arguments to this body" when the ears of the House had been "sealed against truth and reason" by "Instructions!" Would his fellow congressmen, he asked, blindly follow the instructions of the people even into the abyss? "Suppose," he asked, "a party were to spring up in this country, whose real views were the destruction of liberty; suppose that by management, by the patronage of offices, by the corruption of the press, they should delude the people and obtain a majority...what then will be the effect of this doctrine?" Calhoun warned that "surely such a state of things is not impossible." Calhoun challenged his colleagues to find the idea that representatives were bound by the will of their constituents in any of the "free governments of antiquity." The idea, he said, had only sprung up in England as an excuse for members of Parliament to use when they wanted to vote against the king. In support of his position Calhoun cited Edmund Burke, who famously argued that a representative owed his constituents the use of his reason and judgment on their behalf, not complete submission to their will. Calhoun made clear that he was not in favor of representatives ignoring the will of the people—they were duty bound to listen—but he located the ultimate source of the people's will in the Constitution, not the changing whims of the electorate. "The Constitution is my letter of instruction," Calhoun declared. "Written by the hand of the people, stampt with their authority, it admits of no doubt as to its obligation." Calhoun warned that if congressmen were merely unthinking extensions of their electorates, and poorly paid to boot, then the patronage of the executive branch and the lure of presidential appointments would quickly make the House subservient to the executive branch. Calhoun did not know it, but he would soon have to face this temptation himself.

The next day, none other than Calhoun's old would-be dueling opponent Philip Grosvenor declared his admiration for Calhoun's speech on the floor, comparing him to an eagle among "groveling buzzard[s]" and predicting that Calhoun would someday fulfill "the high destiny for which it is manifest he was born." Back home in South Carolina, the editor of the *Camden Gazette* enthused, "Never have we seen a more full display of manly independence, virtuous patriotism, and sound political doctrine," and called Calhoun "this American Aristides," invoking the Athenian statesman revered for his sense of justice and honor.[29]

LIKE MANY AMERICANS, DURING 1816 Calhoun cast a sympathetic eye southward on the ongoing revolutions in South America. Despite the popularity of anticolonial rebels like Simón Bolívar of Venezuela, the Madison administration was eager to maintain official neutrality in the revolutionary struggle between Spain and her New World offspring. In January Calhoun opposed an administration-backed bill that would have imposed harsh penalties on American citizens who sold ships to known belligerents against Spain. He acknowledged the need for neutrality, but argued that the bill went too far. He compared the southern revolutions to "our situation in '76" and professed his sympathies with the rebels and his belief that the United States, while remaining neutral, "should do nothing to weaken their efforts or injure their cause." Calhoun's words were especially significant since American newspapers for months had been full of the news of Bolívar's alliance with the black republic of Haiti and his subsequent antislavery proclamations in June and July 1816, which were reprinted in papers throughout the country, including in Charleston and in the *Camden Gazette* in August while Calhoun was at home. In one of these proclamations, Bolívar wrote that "nature, justice, and policy, demand the emancipation of the slave; henceforward there shall be known in Venezuela only one class of men—all shall be citizens." Despite this, most white Americans and even most white southerners continued to support the revolutionaries in 1816, seeing Bolívar's antislavery edicts as a recruitment tactic and a necessary condition of throwing off Spanish rule.[30]

Nor did South Carolinians apparently connect what was going on in South America to two separate slave insurrection scares that occurred in the state in 1816. The first occurred outside Charleston, where a community of runaway slaves began raiding lowcountry plantations, sparking fears of a Haiti-like rebellion until the governor called out the state militia. Then, in July, a supposed plot in Camden sent ripples of fear throughout the entire state and led to the execution of five alleged insurrectionaries. Instead of connecting this resistance to South America, many observers, including the editor of the *Camden Gazette*, blamed the spread of evangelical Christianity among the slaves for the uprisings, all the while publishing glowing reports of Bolívar's antislavery proclamations. In early 1817 Calhoun shared with his fellow white southerners a tendency to see the South American revolutions as a hemispheric triumph of republicanism rather than a threat to slavery, but the ground underneath him was shifting.[31]

Many white Americans in the early nineteenth century drew moral distinctions between the institution of slavery itself, the interstate slave trade within the United States, and the transatlantic slave trade. Almost everyone could join in enlightened condemnation of the transatlantic trade, which had officially ceased in the United States in 1808 but continued unabated between western Africa and other New World slave societies like Brazil and Cuba. A number of white southerners, as we will see, also had misgivings about the interstate slave trade that fell along a spectrum between humanitarian concern and self-preservation. Many others, including Thomas Jefferson, were willing to condemn slavery itself but believed that western expansion would provide a space for the "diffusion" of the enslaved population that would ameliorate conditions for slaves, prevent slave revolts, and perhaps even lead to the end of slavery itself at some future time. Then there were those who saw slavery as a moral and political evil that must be reckoned with.[32]

Calhoun's personal views on slavery during these years can be pieced together from passing mentions in speeches, fragments of evidence, and from silences. In 1816 Calhoun openly condemned the transatlantic slave trade from the floor of the House. In the midst of making the point that a treaty with a foreign power could not override the Constitution on any point, however much it might be desired, he used the constitutional sanction of the slave trade until 1808 as an example. As Calhoun knew, it had been the demands of South Carolina's representatives at the Constitutional Convention that resulted in the continuation of the trade, and he openly lamented his state's role in furthering what he called an "odious traffic." As recorded by a newspaper reporter and published in the third person, as many political speeches of the day were, Calhoun declared "he [Calhoun] would speak plainly on this point; it was the intention of the Constitution that the slave trade should be tolerated till the time mentioned. It covered him in confusion to name it here[.] [He] felt ashamed of such a tolerance, and took a large part of the disgrace, as he represented a part of the Union, by whose influence it might be supposed to have been introduced."[33]

Calhoun's central point was that no treaty could have changed the fact that the Constitution protected the transatlantic slave trade until 1808, but he went out of his way to denounce it, placing himself with the mainstream of American public opinion at the time.

Some white southerners even condemned the swiftly growing interstate slave trade that was driving a steady stream of slaves from the older seaboard states into the new cotton country of the Southwest. This sentiment could be found even in South Carolina. By 1820, the majority of the state's population was enslaved, which—combined with the unrest of the recent war and the panic caused by the 1816 insurrections—led some white South Carolinians to look for ways to prevent the enslaved population from growing even larger. Proposed measures included a ban on the interstate slave trade and even mentions of colonization. Borrowing from moral condemnations of the transatlantic trade, proponents of these measures often cast them as a humanitarian matter as well as a security concern. South Carolina governor David R. Williams urged the legislature to stop the "remorseless, merciless traffic which brings among us slaves of all descriptions from other states," and called the trade "a reproach to our morals and an outrage to our feelings." With temporary support from the upcountry in the wake of the Camden insurrection scare, in 1816 the legislature passed a ban on importing slaves into the state, then repealed it two years later. Other southern states, including even Mississippi, which joined the Union in 1817, contemplated similar bans. In 1818 the Mississippi legislature denounced slavery as "condemned by reason and the laws of nature," but as Mississippi politician George Poindexter apologetically pointed out to Congress, white southerners had no choice. "It would be a blessing could we get rid of them," he acknowledged, "but the wisest and best men among us have not been able to devise a plan for doing it." In the end, apologies and legislation like the South Carolina ban proved no match for the skyrocketing demand for enslaved labor, enabling some white southerners like Poindexter to give the impression of taking the moral high ground by apologizing for slavery but all the while ensuring that no real threat menaced the institution.[34]

There were also, of course, many Americans who opposed the institution of slavery itself, and at least one person who read Calhoun's comments on the slave trade assumed that he was one of them. During the summer of 1816 when Calhoun was at home in South Carolina, he had written to contacts in the North connected to the burgeoning cotton textile industry, which he had just helped to protect, to recommend the services of a friend, John McCalla, a cotton agent who worked for a Charleston firm buying cotton in and around Augusta, Georgia. One reply came from Isaac Briggs, a northern engineer involved in the cotton industry. Briggs was a Quaker, and he assured Calhoun that he would give McCalla's name to his friends in the cotton textile business. "To be of service to thee or to any friend of thine will be to me a gratification," he wrote, applauding Calhoun's efforts to protect manufacturing. Then, at the end of his letter, Briggs addressed "another subject, which I deem of immense importance to our country generally...It is slavery." Making clear that he was not interested in casting blame for the origins or continuation of the institution, Briggs lamented "the existence, in our otherwise happy land, of the slavery of one degraded Class of human beings." He called slavery "a stain on our national character...a moral and political poison...it suffers not liberty to rest on the broad basis of the rights of *man*." Briggs pointed out that the growth of slavery was a problem especially for the South. "In its progress, it is more and more impairing your political strength...I hope, you, my friends of the southern states, will explore the rich resources of your own minds for a remidy." "On this point," Briggs wrote, "I have not the smallest doubt, we think alike."[35]

If Calhoun replied to Briggs, it would certainly have been an illuminating window into his thinking on slavery in this early part of his career, but no reply exists. His silence probably carries its own meaning. Calhoun's condemnation of the "odious traffic" of the transatlantic slave trade did not extend to the interstate slave trade, let alone to slavery itself. In fact, during 1816 Calhoun was buying slaves in exactly the sort of interstate transactions that the South Carolina legislature banned later that year. In June 1816 while he was at home in South Carolina, and as rumors swirled of a slave insurrection in Camden on the Fourth of July, Calhoun purchased two slaves named Tomkins and Anthony from Virginia slave traders named Jacob Fowler and William Hix who were passing through South Carolina. He paid Fowler and Hix $1,400 for the two men. Slave traders like Fowler and Hix were an essential part of the burgeoning interstate slave trade, middlemen who profited by creating a marketplace that provided slave owners liquidity for their human property on one end, usually in the older seaboard states like Virginia, and the ability to purchase enslaved labor on the other, usually in the cotton-growing regions that had emerged in upcountry South Carolina and were quickly spreading west to Alabama and Mississippi. In between transactions, traders erased the personal histories and distinguishing characteristics of individual slaves, sorting them into categories by gender, age, and ability, and assigning them the labels—prime field hand, carpenter, cook, housekeeper—that would determine their price on the market. Slave owners like Calhoun were then able to purchase exactly the kind of labor they needed and to know something of what that labor would cost.[36]

One difficulty with this system, as many slaveholders understood all too well, was that the market was often rigged. Slave traders found ways to buy low and sell high, often concealing illness or injuries and inventing personal histories and fictitious reasons that slaves had been sold by previous masters. When he bought Tomkins and Anthony, Calhoun did not know the truth about them, which was that Fowler and Hix had bought the two men from the Virginia state penitentiary, where they had probably been sentenced to death. Slave traders could buy condemned slaves from the state of Virginia by providing a bond that they would sell the slaves outside the country, but the temptation to erase an enslaved person's history and sell them to some unsuspecting planter the next state over was often too great.[37]

In this case, Fowler and Hix made the mistake of selling the two convicts to a distinguished and well-connected young member of the House of Representatives. In August, having somehow discovered the fraud, Calhoun wrote to US Attorney for the District of Virginia William Wirt to see if there was anything that could be done. Wirt replied that he had forwarded Calhoun's request to William Poindexter, speaker of the Virginia Senate and a lawyer who practiced in the county where the slave-trading firm did business, assuring Calhoun that Poindexter was an expert "in matters of this sort" who would be able to get his money back for him without a costly lawsuit. In January 1817, Calhoun wrote Poindexter an extensive letter detailing the fraud and giving him names of witnesses in Virginia who could testify to the identity of the two slaves and to the fact that Fowler and Hix had bought them from the penitentiary.[38]

If Calhoun got his money back from Fowler and Hix, it was not through the courts. A Virginia court awarded him a mere fifteen dollars in damages in the case three years later.[39] Whether Tomkins and Anthony remained in South Carolina, returned to Virginia to meet their fate, or were sold farther south or outside the country, we do not know. Despite his denunciation of the transatlantic trade and perhaps due to his experience of the cotton boom and its benefits in the upcountry, Calhoun never expressed moral misgivings about the interstate trade, and in fact participated in it. In this sense, Calhoun mirrored the sentiments of his native upcountry and the expanding cotton frontier and not the elite misgivings that were still fashionable in Virginia and lowcountry South Carolina.

THE LAST GREAT PROJECT of the congressional session that began in December 1816 was the most important one to Calhoun. Writing to Alexander Dallas that summer after the passage of the bank and the tariff, he had confessed his anxiety about whether "the other great measures contemplated" in the upcoming session would succeed.[40] The bank and the tariff were pieces of Calhoun's larger economic and political vision, a vision that still required a national transportation network in order to unlock the economic potential of the vast American continent. Such a network was particularly important to the South, where large swaths of the country lacked easy access to the coast or to a river such as the Mississippi. As a child in the upcountry, Calhoun had often heard his father and uncles and their neighbors complain about the difficulty of transporting crops to market in Charleston and the political intransigence of the lowcountry, which had a rich network of rivers and little desire to spend money to build roads or canals that would not benefit them. During his brief time in the South Carolina legislature, Calhoun had supported a petition to build a turnpike from the upcountry into Tennessee, and while in Congress he had seen forlorn petitions from New York and Pennsylvania for the national government to assist them in constructing canals to connect the manufacturing and shipping industries on the coast to the interior of the continent. Now he had the opportunity to accomplish something that would simultaneously benefit the nation and fulfill his own ambitions.

Building roads and canals was expensive, of course, but the bank bill passed in the first session provided a possible source of funding in the so-called "bonus" of funds that would accrue to the national government as a shareholder. In mid-December 1816 Calhoun introduced a motion to form a committee that would examine using this revenue "as a permanent fund for internal improvement," and two days before Christmas he reported a bill to establish "a fund for constructing roads and canals."[41]

In a speech that would mark the culmination of his career in the House, Calhoun argued for the bill as nothing less than a new economic charter for the nation, which had emerged victorious from the recent war with Great Britain and now seemed poised to spread across the whole continent. In a country so vast as the United States already was, he said, it was unreasonable to leave the construction of roads and canals to individuals and to states. "Many of the improvements contemplated," Calhoun asserted, "are on too great a scale for the resource of the states or individuals." Calhoun also argued that the roads and canals were necessary to equalize the effects of unequal government spending, which must at times—here, he used the example of the recent war—be focused on certain parts of the country despite the fact that taxes were drawn, or were supposed to be drawn, equally from every section. At the heart of Calhoun's case for the bill was his ambition that a modern transportation network such as the one he had proposed could enable the creation of a democratic republic larger than any ever before seen in human history—and save the United States from the only real threat to its future. "No country, enjoying freedom, ever occupied any thing like as great an extent of country as this Republic," he acknowledged. In a nod to Montesquieu, he stated, "One hundred years ago, the most profound philosophers did not believe it to be even possible." Thus far, the "happy mould of our government" that blended "the state and the general powers" had allowed the country to achieve something Montesquieu and others thought impossible. But this novel mixture of state and federal governments, the very source of America's history-defying feat, was also its greatest weakness since it "exposes us to the greatest of all calamities, next to the loss of liberty, and even to that in its consequence—*disunion*." Added to this, the country was still "rapidly…[I] was about to say fearfully growing," and therefore increasing the opportunity for the kind of division that might ultimately lead to fracture. During the debate over the tariff in the previous session, Calhoun had sounded similar notes, warning that

he [Calhoun] had often and long revolved it in his mind; and he had critically examined into the causes that destroyed the liberty of other states. There are none that apply to us, or apply with a force to alarm. The basis of our Republic is too broad and its structure too strong to be shaken by them…but let it be deeply impressed on the heart of this House and country, that while [the founders] guarded against the old they exposed us to a new and terrible danger, disunion. This single word comprehended almost the sum of our political dangers; and against it we ought to be perpetually guarded.[42]

Now Calhoun reasoned that connecting the country with a network of roads and canals carrying goods and information would erode stubborn local interests and sectional jealousies and spread "a perfect unity…in feelings and sentiments." Calhoun described how this would work, evoking an imagined community connected by roads and canals carrying mail and newspapers across the continent, in the process fostering a body politic harmonized by a common American identity:

> Those who understand the human heart best, know how powerfully distance tends to break the sympathies of our nature. Nothing, not even dissimilarity of language, tends more to estrange man from man. Let us then…bind the Republic together with a perfect system of roads and canals. Let us conquer space. It is thus the most distant parts of the republic will be brought within a few days travel of the centre; it is thus that a citizen of the West will read the news of Boston still moist from the press. The mail and press…are the nerves of the body politic. By them, the slightest impression made on the most remote parts, is communicated to the whole system; and the more perfect the means of transportation, the more rapid and true the vibration.

Modern nations were made in time by human action, out of the materials at hand, not born fully formed with their destinies predetermined.

Calhoun's bill did not propose specifics, but he hinted he was in favor of following a plan devised by Albert Gallatin ten years earlier when he described in general terms a "principal artery" that would connect Maine to Louisiana, with other projects connecting the Great Lakes to the Hudson River (a reference to the Erie Canal, which began construction that year) and the Atlantic port cities—"Philadelphia, Baltimore, Washington, Richmond, Charleston and Savannah"—to the western states. Naturally, there would be objections that these projects would benefit some parts of the Union more than others, but Calhoun declared, "In a country so extensive, and so various in its interests, what is necessary for the common good, may apparently be opposed to the interest of particular sections. It must be submitted to as a condition of our greatness."

Perhaps the most significant obstacle to the bill was a disagreement about congressional authority, which President Madison, in urging a system of internal improvements in his annual message the previous December, had hinted might have to be overcome with a constitutional amendment. Article 1, section 8 of the Constitution directed that "Congress shall have Power to lay and collect Taxes, Duties, Imposts and Excises, to pay the Debts and provide for the common Defence and general Welfare of the United States." Calhoun thought the "general welfare" clause more than sufficient for the purpose he had in mind, dismissing the argument of strict constructionists that the taxing power contained in the first clause of the sentence did not refer to the phrase "to pay the debts and provide for the common defense and general welfare" that followed it. Surely the framers of the Constitution were not such clumsy writers. The passage meant what it meant. "[I am] no advocate for refined arguments on the Constitution," he asserted. "The instrument was not intended as a thesis for the logician to exercise his ingenuity on. It ought to be construed with plain, good sense." This did not mean that the national government could ride roughshod over states that objected to such projects, but Calhoun was confident that reason and nationalistic sentiment would lead all the states to cooperate even with federal projects that might at first appear to benefit one state or section more than others.[43]

Calhoun's passionate defense of the bill helped carry it over the finish line, but only barely. It passed the House four days later by an 86 to 84 vote. With New England united against the bill and the South divided, the states of Pennsylvania and New York provided Calhoun's main support. Just before the final vote, representative Thomas R. Gold of New York, no doubt thinking of the canal that would begin construction later that year in his own state, declared that Calhoun deserved "the thanks of his country" for his statesmanship.[44] The bill passed the Senate later that month and went to President Madison for his signature. For the moment, it appeared that Calhoun had secured the final piece of a sweeping legislative agenda that would transform the country economically, unite it politically, and might conceivably propel him into higher office.

Or at least it might have if James Madison had been able to overcome his conscience. On March 2, Calhoun called on Madison at the rooms the president and his wife rented in a town house at the corner of Pennsylvania Avenue and Nineteenth Street to pay his respects as Madison prepared to leave office and Calhoun prepared to leave for South Carolina. Calhoun congratulated Madison on the president's successes and expressed his "happiness" at their cooperation. Then he turned to go. When he was nearly at the door, Madison called him back, deciding at the last minute that he must tell Calhoun in person his decision to veto the internal improvements bill. Madison had—belatedly—decided that the Constitution simply did not grant Congress the powers the bill assumed.

Calhoun was stunned. He protested with good reason that he had believed his bill was fully in line with Madison's expressed wishes and that he would never have forced Madison's hand or exposed himself to the embarrassment of a presidential veto if he had known Madison's heart on the subject. He begged Madison to reconsider, but it was no use.[45]

In his public statement on the veto, issued the next day and published in newspapers throughout the country, Madison expressed his hope that the Constitution could be amended, but stated his belief that at present the power Congress claimed "cannot be deduced from any part of it, without an inadmissible latitude of construction." It was a direct and humiliating contradiction of Calhoun's cavalier denunciation of "refined arguments." Privately, Madison was also wary because the fund established by the bill was not tied to specific projects. It seemed too open an invitation to patronage and graft. In his autobiography, Martin Van Buren, no disinterested observer, later called Calhoun's bill "a striking and alarming illustration" of his early constitutional views, which Van Buren described, relishing the irony of hindsight, as "latitudinarian in the extreme."[46]

Calhoun would later disavow the constitutional arguments he made that winter, essentially agreeing with Madison in both the president's public and private doubts, but at the time, the extremely public failure stung. Understanding this, and sharing Calhoun's frustration with Madison's newly discovered scruples, Henry Clay sought to soften the blow by publicly exercising the speaker's prerogative to vote and putting his name down first in the vote to overturn Madison's veto. But not enough of Calhoun's colleagues were willing to go on record against the author of the Constitution, and the effort failed.[47] Madison's veto proved to be a moment of historical contingency that shaped the course of the next fifty years. Without federal assistance, some states, like New York, would successfully bring to completion massive internal improvement projects such as the Erie Canal, finally completed in 1825, that would transform the economy and society of their surrounding regions. But most, especially southern states, would not. Calhoun's vision of a nation bound together by a network of canals and roads came partly true anyway—transportation and communication revolutions transformed American life over the next few decades. But the Erie Canal, the steamboat, and the US Post Office that helped propel these changes were only a shadow of what Calhoun imagined that spring because they reached and influenced different parts of the country unequally.[48]

Ironically, it was one of Calhoun's minor efforts that winter that left perhaps the most lasting impact on American national identity and remains the most visible in the nation's capital today. Pickaxes and shovels funded by the federal government were one way to bind the nation together; the artist's brush was another. At the same time that he was forcefully advocating for the internal improvements bill,

Calhoun also quietly chaired a committee that commissioned four huge paintings by the artist John Trumbull, a student of the great Benjamin West, commemorating key moments in the revolution. Overcoming objections by some in Congress to the federal government becoming a patron of the arts, Calhoun and others argued that the cost of the paintings was a small price to pay for the premium they would yield in patriotic feelings and as an example of virtue for future generations. And since the revolutionary generation was aging, time was short. One of the most striking aspects of the life-size paintings Trumbull eventually produced, which today adorn the rotunda of the United States Capitol, was his inclusion of individual studies of many of the main characters on both sides of the conflict, painstakingly collected in America and Europe over several years. Trumbull's evocations of the signing of the Declaration of Independence, the surrender of Burgoyne, the surrender of Cornwallis, and the resignation of Washington, continue to be central to American identity, the most famous artistic renderings of the American founding era.[49]

THE DAY AFTER MADISON vetoed the internal improvement bill, James Monroe took the oath of office on a hastily erected outdoor platform in front of the temporary Capitol building. The event had to be held outdoors because Henry Clay, upset at having been passed over for the secretary of state post in favor of John Quincy Adams and hoping to embarrass the new president, had refused to rearrange the furniture in the House chamber for the occasion. The outdoor inauguration soon became a tradition. Monroe's presidency continued the Virginia dynasty that the Federalists considered the most egregious proof of the advantage that the three-fifths clause gave to the slaveholding states, and Adams's appointment was Monroe's attempt to placate New England. As Calhoun hurried home to South Carolina, the words of Monroe's expansive inaugural address may have stayed with him. He may have felt a twinge of anger as he recalled Monroe's qualified endorsement of internal improvements "always with a constitutional sanction." Outlining all the natural, commercial, and political advantages of the growing country, Monroe boasted of Americans' unprecedented levels of individual freedom, asking, "On whom has oppression fallen in any quarter of our Union? Who has been deprived of any right of person or property?" These questions sound strangely oblivious to us today, but Calhoun no doubt agreed with Monroe that these were purely rhetorical questions. American citizens were the freest people in the world. Monroe's presidency offered the hope that perhaps the American political system would finally escape partisanship and achieve the harmony that many ancient and modern political theorists believed would result from properly balanced institutions. The so-called era of good feelings had begun.[50]

Calhoun also carried with him the knowledge that Monroe had tried to placate Clay by offering him the post of secretary of war, which Clay rejected in a rage. Over the summer, with Calhoun back in South Carolina, a succession of candidates turned down the post until finally on October 10 Monroe sent Calhoun a letter inviting him to join the administration. Characteristically, Calhoun had little doubt about his suitability for the job. After all, he had been deeply involved in military matters in the late war and since the peace had frequently offered strong opinions on the shape of the postwar military establishment. But some of his friends, including William Lowndes, who had also been offered the post and turned it down, counseled him to decline, advising him that he would be giving up his place in the House just as his talents as an orator and a legislator were reaching their height. As Calhoun later recalled, Lowndes and others also believed that his "talent lay more in the power of thought than action" and that the bent of his mind was "more metaphysical than practical." Calhoun thought they were wrong. Or, if they were right, he believed the cabinet post represented a chance to "strengthen [his practical and administrative abilities] where they were naturally the weakest" and prove himself capable of more than a good speech.

It also occurred to him that the House would be too small a stage for his ambitions now that "most of the great questions growing out of a return to a state of peace had been discussed and settled." With an uncanny ability to foresee the course of events, Calhoun believed the greatest opportunity for distinction in the coming years would be in the executive branch. Added to this, both his predecessors in the office—Monroe himself and William Crawford—had become presidential candidates during their tenure in the War Department. It was not the State Department, to be sure, but it was perhaps the next best thing. Thus, despite his own warnings about the lure of presidential appointments, he dashed off a brief note of acceptance to Monroe in early November and quickly made preparations to move his family to Washington.[51]

Two weeks later Calhoun and his family set off for Washington in a coach driven by a slave named Hector. With them in the coach were little Andrew and a nine-month-old baby girl named Anna Maria. In between the death of their daughter Floride in 1815 and the birth of Anna Maria in 1817, the Calhouns had lost another child, a daughter named Jane who was born in January 1816 and died sometime before Anna Maria's birth in February 1817. With their two devastating losses in mind, the Calhouns could not help but be anxious as they set out for Washington with both their children suffering from a fever and chills. After the first day, a relieved Calhoun wrote to Floride's mother that little Anna Maria had improved and Andrew's appetite was returning. "The children stand traveling much better, and are far less troublesome than we expected," he reported. Hector also drove with unexpected care and skill, neither of which were qualities he had been known for before. Calhoun reported to his mother-in-law that "Floride's confidence in his driving is completely restored." Little Anna Maria would survive to become her father's favorite child, a daughter he doted on and who returned his affection, and the only one of his children with whom he really shared his love of ideas and politics. Perhaps sitting in her father's lap, she jolted along the thirty miles a day toward Washington.[52]

EIGHT

Secretary of Improvement and Empire

A S THE CALHOUNS' CARRIAGE BUMPED along north to Washington in late 1817 guided by the careful hands of Hector, thousands of other Americans were streaming west. General Andrew Jackson's punitive treaties with the Creek Indians after the Battle of Horseshoe Bend and his subsequent treaties with the Cherokee and Chickasaw had opened up vast tracts of land in the Southwest for white settlement, and the defeat of Tecumseh's Pan-Indian alliance in the recent war placed the United States firmly in control in the Northwest, which over the next few years grew nearly as fast. Mississippi's petition for statehood would be accepted a week after the Calhouns arrived in Washington, and for four years in a row beginning in 1816 the December session of Congress welcomed new states into the Union, alternating between slave and free states—Indiana joined in 1816, Mississippi in 1817, Illinois in 1818, and Alabama in 1819. In 1818 Congress passed a law redesigning the American flag, which still had only thirteen stars, instructing that a new star be added every time a state joined the Union. It would fall to Calhoun as secretary of war to oversee the design of the new flag during his first months in office.[1]

The allure of cheap land taken from Indians and skyrocketing cotton prices sparked a frenzied wave of migration from the older

seaboard slave states—Alabama fever, some called it—as white southerners moved west to seek their fortunes. The fever dream was financed
by the rapid proliferation of banks like the Planters' and Merchants'
Bank in Huntsville, Alabama, which opened a few weeks before the
Calhouns started for Washington. Thanks to Secretary of the Treasury
William Crawford, the Huntsville bank became a depository for the
new Bank of the United States, and the bank's directors used those
large deposits to make loans to settlers eager to buy the land and slaves
that it took to grow cotton. By 1819, the government land office in
Huntsville had sold $8.5 million of public land, more than any other
land office in the country. Between 1810 and 1820 Alabama's population
increased by a factor of twelve, to 128,000, while Mississippi's doubled
to 75,000 despite the fact that most of the state was still in the hands of
the Choctaw and Chickasaw. Not all the new residents came willingly.
In the decade leading up to 1820 slave traders carried over 120,000
people from the seaboard to the southern interior, marking the beginning of one of the largest forced migrations in human history. The revolution that had begun in the South Carolina upcountry in Calhoun's
youth gathered speed in the new cotton country, deepening the association for most white southerners between slavery and progress and
closing the window of possibility that slavery would ever die of natural
causes. As Calhoun's friend, the territorial governor William Bibb,
wrote to him in early 1818, referring to Alabama, "It is the Eden of the
nation."[2]

AMONG THE POLITICAL CLASS of Washington there was great curiosity to see how Calhoun's widely acknowledged brilliance would
translate into the business of administration. A profile of the new cabinet members published in November in the *City Gazette* (a publication that would prove to be one of the administration's and Calhoun's
bitterest enemies) observed delicately that while Monroe's new secretary of war had "astonished all who heard him by the rapidity and fire

of his eloquence, and the quickness and accuracy of his mind" during his time in the House, he might also "perhaps from his youth and the character of his intellect, be too fond of novelties that are only calculated to surprise and dazzle." No doubt this was a reference to Calhoun's recent legislative agenda and his sweeping ambitions for the nation, and the writer expressed the hope—forlorn as it turned out—that "age will mellow his mind."[3]

Reaching Washington on December 2, the Calhouns took up temporary residence with Calhoun's friend and fellow South Carolinian William Lowndes. They just missed seeing Floride's brother James Edward Colhoun, who set sail from Norfolk on December 4 as a midshipman aboard the vessel *Congress*, which carried a group of American commissioners to Buenos Aires to assess the wisdom of recognizing the newly declared South American republic of Argentina.[4] As Floride began taking and making calls on women like Margaret Bayard Smith, wife of the *National Intelligencer* editor Samuel Harris Smith, establishing the social connections that facilitated politics in the nation's capital, Calhoun took the measure of the other members of Monroe's cabinet.[5] Three of them he already knew. William Crawford of Georgia, Calhoun's old classmate at Moses Waddel's backwoods academy and his immediate predecessor in the War Department, now served Monroe as secretary of the treasury. Crawford was a big, broad-faced man whose sociability belied a shrewd political infighter. Everyone knew that Crawford held presidential ambitions, and he had been in the running for the nomination against Monroe. Calhoun also knew Attorney General William Wirt well enough to have asked him for help when he had been defrauded by Virginia slave traders a year earlier. Benjamin Crowninshield of Massachusetts had served James Madison as secretary of the navy when Calhoun had championed the navy's cause in Congress, and he now continued in that role under Monroe.

Only three days after he arrived in Washington Calhoun was at the president's house when Secretary of State John Quincy Adams called, a situation that would repeat itself endlessly over the next several years. The scion of one of America's first political families, Adams was fifteen years older than Calhoun, short, stocky, brilliant, and constantly brooding in the pages of his diary, which he filled with his expansive hopes for the American nation and caustic observations about the inferior and small-minded people who ran its government. He had been serving the country overseas with great distinction for the entire time Calhoun had been on the national stage, and had even helped negotiate the Treaty of Ghent. Though the two men would eventually occupy opposite ends of the American political spectrum, especially on the issue of slavery, Adams and Calhoun shared a lofty ideal of statesmanship in a republic, an ambition to expand the country across the continent, and a preference for reason over empty rhetoric. They immediately gravitated toward one another. From the start of their frequent and intimate interaction in cabinet meetings, Adams was impressed with Calhoun's independence and intellect, noting in one early meeting, "Calhoun thinks for himself, independently of all the rest, with sound judgment, quick discrimination, and keen observation. He supports his opinions too with powerful eloquence."[6] Adams appreciated directness, a quality that in his view was in lamentably short supply in Washington, and Calhoun's frank style suited him.

When Adams arrived that day in early December, Monroe and Calhoun may well have been discussing how to deal with a developing crisis of authority involving Andrew Jackson. Earlier that year the War Department had transferred an engineer from Jackson's Southern Division to the Northern Division without consulting him, and after learning of the transfer Jackson issued his own order that nobody under his command was to comply with any further War Department orders unless first authorized by him. Monroe tried to defuse the situation and delicately convince Jackson he was wrong, but Jackson refused to back down. There matters stood when Calhoun arrived. According to one sympathetic biographer, the incident showed Jackson at his "egotistical worst."[7]

Calhoun instantly realized that the authority of his office was at stake but also that his appearance in the midst of the spat was an opportunity. His role was similar to that of a second in a duel—since he was not the offending or offended party, he was free to make an honorable settlement between the administration and Jackson. In his first weeks in office he drafted an order, which Monroe showed to John Quincy Adams on Christmas Eve, directing that "as a general rule, all orders will issue in the first instance, to the commanders of division," but retaining for the War Department the right to issue orders directly when "the public interest may require it," in which case a copy of the order would be sent to the division commander "for his information." Calhoun issued the order on December 29, and had it published in Washington newspapers, publicly committing himself to the position. On the same day, he wrote Jackson a lengthy explanation that portrayed the order as according "substantially with your view in relation to this subject." Jackson believed he had won, but Calhoun had cannily preserved the War Department's authority and its right to issue independent orders as long as he simply copied Jackson.[8]

There were larger crises brewing, as well. When he arrived at his office in Washington, Calhoun found a letter waiting from Major General Edmund Pendleton Gaines of the Southern Division informing him that on November 12 Gaines had attacked and burned a Creek village on the border with Spanish Florida. After the recent war Spanish Florida had become a refuge for Creek Indians dispossessed by the Treaty of Fort Jackson, known as Seminoles, and for escaped slaves. Georgia slaveholders were particularly worried that Florida would serve as a nursery for a Haitian-style revolution. A year earlier, Gaines had been the commander in charge of an attack on the so-called Negro Fort on the Apalachicola River in Florida in which 270 residents of the fort, mostly fugitive slaves who had escaped from surrounding states, had been killed. Even after the destruction of the fort, bands of Seminoles continued to make attacks across the border into Georgia and then slip back into Florida. Gaines's attack was meant to put a stop to these raids, and he wanted permission to pursue the Seminoles into Florida.

Soon after being sworn in, on December 16, Calhoun issued an order directly to Gaines authorizing him to cross the Florida border and attack the Seminoles "unless they should shelter themselves in a Spanish post," in which case Gaines was to notify the War Department. Calhoun copied Jackson on the order, following the procedure he would outline in the coming weeks. The same day in Nashville an impatient Jackson wrote a letter to the War Department warning that "the protection of our citizens will require the wolf be struck in his den." Jackson was clearly itching for a fight. Ten days later Monroe called a cabinet meeting to discuss events in Florida, which as everyone could see presented a clear threat—especially to slaveholders in Georgia and the Alabama territory—but also an opportunity to demonstrate that Spain could not exercise meaningful sovereignty over Florida and should therefore sell the colony to the United States. Later that day, Calhoun issued Jackson orders to travel south and assume command of the widening conflict.[9]

Whether by mistake or on purpose, in his orders to Jackson, Calhoun did not repeat his injunction to Gaines to avoid direct conflict with the Spanish. Calhoun would later claim, and apparently really believed, that Jackson should have understood himself as bound by the previous instructions to Gaines, which Jackson had certainly seen. But it remains the case that Calhoun did not explicitly repeat those instructions in the December 26 letter ordering Jackson south to take command, instead using the vague phrase that Jackson was authorized to take "necessary measures" to end the danger of Indian attacks. This was a curious omission for so important a caveat. Sending Andrew Jackson into a tense situation with ambiguous orders, Calhoun and Monroe had to know, was like turning a wild bull loose at a White House dinner party.

Added to this was the fact that Monroe and Jackson were communicating independently. Two days after the cabinet meeting and

Calhoun's orders to Jackson, Monroe wrote directly to Jackson suggesting pointedly that "possibly you may have other services to perform" in addition to suppressing the Seminoles. Immediately understanding the potential of the moment, Jackson wrote back proposing a back-channel authorization of the invasion and occupation of Spanish Florida. Just give the word, Jackson wrote, "and in sixty days it will be accomplished." Monroe never replied and later claimed that he was ill and never read the letter. This meant that Jackson marched south armed with pregnant silence from Washington and his own clear ideas about what needed to be done.[10]

FROM HIS TIME IN the House, Calhoun had a hard-won education in the workings of the American military establishment and its deficiencies in wartime. He believed that the vast and continuing expansion of the United States required a different, more aggressive stance. In addition to personal political advancement, the cabinet appointment offered him the opportunity to redesign the American military for a new era, and Calhoun's frustrations with the old model were part of the reason he took Monroe's offer. He hated inefficiencies and anachronisms. A recent account identifies two of the defining characteristics of the nation-states that emerged across the world during the nineteenth century as the formation of "militarized industrialized states with new capacities for empire building" and the invention of state bureaucracies run according to principles of "rational efficiency."[11] Of course, these developments did not simply happen of their own accord like the weather. Individuals in positions of power made them happen at particular moments in time, and over the next few years Calhoun was one of the central figures responsible for changes that transformed the United States into a modern nation-state capable of projecting its power across a continent or an ocean.

The task confronting Calhoun in the War Department was herculean. In 1817 the department was a sprawling entity responsible not only for national defense, but also for nearly every facet of the rapidly expanding American empire, including what would later be included under the Department of the Interior and the Bureau of Indian Affairs. This meant the cramped offices of the War Department, located temporarily in the so-called "Seven Buildings" on the north side of Pennsylvania Avenue, were the central dynamo for a bureaucratic engine that drove an endless cycle of exploration, expropriation, and settlement. From Calhoun's perspective it must have often seemed that his department was simply struggling to keep up with the amazing expansion of the country and the relentless westward pressure of its citizens.

In early 1818 Calhoun oversaw thirty-four clerks[12] and another eighteen Indian agents and factors (who ran government trading posts) outside Washington,[13] a pitiful number considering the scope of their duties. And then, of course, there was the army, which by the time Calhoun took the oath of office had been reduced to about eight thousand soldiers, engineers, and staff—far below its recent wartime strength. In Calhoun's view the army's size was completely inadequate when considering the growth of the country and the demands made of the army even in peacetime.[14] In 1818 alone Congress appropriated over $7 million to the War Department in fifty-seven separate allotments for purposes that included repairing roads, funding the United States Military Academy at West Point, paying the soldiers serving in the Seminole War under Andrew Jackson, and surveying land recently ceded by Indians in the Illinois and Missouri territories.[15] At the end of 1818, Calhoun estimated that the department's expenses in the following year would exceed $8 million at a time when the government's total annual spending rarely surpassed $20 million.[16] Though his position may have carried slightly less prestige than others, the new secretary of war controlled a sizable chunk of the national government's finances.

Calhoun later claimed somewhat self-interestedly that when he took over, the department "was almost literally without organization." This was not completely accurate, and surely would have been disputed by Calhoun's predecessor William Crawford. But there was some truth to Calhoun's claim—at least one other official who served under Calhoun recalled that the department was "a literal chaos" when Calhoun took office.[17] And only a week after taking office Calhoun wrote to Charles Ingersoll, "The farther I look into its concerns, the more am I impressed with the magnitude of [my] duties. I believe, I may say, little heretofore has been done to give exactness, economy, and dispatch to its monied transaction[s]."[18] He was right about that. Besides incoming and ongoing business, there was a massive backlog of financial claims on the War Department, some of which dated "almost from the origin of the government" and which altogether totaled some $40 million.[19] Even William Crawford had begged for a general reorganization of the army and its staff, which had ballooned rapidly during the war and then shrank just as quickly, leaving convoluted chains of command and outdated, unspoken, or simply missing regulations, a situation that obliged the secretary to weigh in directly on all sorts of decisions, large and small. The combination of backlog, chaos, and regular business meant that, as Calhoun later recalled, it often required "fourteen or fifteen hours of severe daily labour" just to keep up.[20]

In response, Calhoun set out to transform the War Department into a modern bureaucracy, with all the impersonality and efficiency associated with the term. In his 1843 campaign biography Calhoun would craft an image of himself as an administrative autodidact who quickly mastered and unraveled the byzantine workings of the War Department, but it is clear that he sought out advice from others. These included Crawford, Monroe, and especially Jacob Brown, commander of the Northern Division and the US Army's highest-ranking officer, to whom Calhoun confessed his "want of experience" and his need for advice and Brown's cooperation soon after taking office.[21] A few months after taking office, Calhoun wrote to his friend Senator Charles Tait of Georgia, describing his situation. "I do trust, I will be able to reduce the War Dept. to more method," he wrote, "but, I find, it must be the work of time. It is dangerous to reform, before we know the precise state of the disease."[22]

Despite this sense of caution, when the Senate's Committee on Military Affairs asked Calhoun to propose a bill reorganizing the army's staff in February 1818, he jumped at the chance. The resulting bill, which Calhoun wrote in a week and later called "very much my own conception," passed in April, enacting a sweeping reorganization of the War Department and the army. The bill effectively centralized control of the army in Washington, eliminating staffing redundancies in the Southern and Northern Divisions and creating the offices of surgeon general, quartermaster general, and commissary general, all of which reported directly to Calhoun. The bill also confirmed the president's, and thus Calhoun's, authority to determine rations for the army. Over the next year Calhoun corresponded with the new surgeon general Joseph Lovell on the details of a standardized diet "with a due mixture of animal and vegetable food" for the nation's soldiers, including Lovell's hopes for substituting a mixture of vinegar and water—"the principle drink of the French soldier"—for the whiskey American soldiers customarily received. An easier change would be an allowance for regional differences in diet: the army would provide its soldiers bacon and cornmeal in the South and pork and wheat flour in the North, a change that Calhoun explained to Congress was "much more congenial to the habits of the people in that section of our country."[23]

Calhoun's main tool was that cogwheel of all modern bureaucracies, the regulation. By 1818 Calhoun was already issuing regulations by the dozen, defining War Department policy on everything from housing and firewood allowances for staff officers to the rules governing the granting of government pensions for military service, a major part of the department's work. One forlorn applicant for a pension in late 1818 lamented that his multiple claims "now lie entombed in some abyss about that office which seems to be fast devouring its contents." Calhoun was determined to fix this situation by putting in place regulations that allowed his subordinates to make decisions, approve claims, and answer requests without his direct input. He later recalled with pride that by the time he left office "the secretary had little to do beyond signing his name" and deciding the few cases that fell outside the regulations. "It literally almost moved of itself."[24] During the same time, Calhoun commissioned Winfield Scott to rewrite the field regulations for the army, and in 1821 Scott published his 355-page *General Regulations for the Army*, which governed every aspect of US Army operations and its soldiers' lives for decades. Calhoun's reorganization of the War Department would be adopted in other areas of government, most notably the Post Office, and would remain substantially unchanged until the twentieth century, with the irony that when Abraham Lincoln went to war with the Confederacy he did so with a War Department largely of Calhoun's making. The South would have Calhoun's arguments, but the North would have his war machine.[25]

Then there was the United States Military Academy at West Point. Under its new superintendent Sylvanus Thayer and with Calhoun's strong support, West Point diverged from other institutions of higher education in the United States by employing a "practical" scientific and mathematical curriculum modeled on France's École Polytechnique. In essence, what Thayer and Calhoun created at West Point was the military equivalent of Tapping Reeve's law school, an educational institution focused on modern scientific practice, not classical theory. It was also markedly democratic. You did not have to know Latin or Greek to study at West Point, as most colleges required. At a time when England still assumed an aristocratic model of military leadership in which traditionally educated elites with a supposedly natural gift of leadership commanded social subordinates, the American military would now be led by practically educated citizen soldiers from all walks of life. When he was forced to defend his department's expenditures, including West Point, in the lean times of 1820, Calhoun argued that it was folly to depend on supposed natural leaders or the appearance of the rare natural military genius in times of war. What was required instead in the modern world was a scientific approach to the art of war. "No government," he reported to Congress in December 1820, "can in the present improved state of the military science, neglect with impunity to instruct a sufficient number of its citizens in a science indispensable to its independence and safety."[26]

Calhoun also shaped the future of the military and the country by making appointments of cadets to the academy. In Congress only a few years earlier Calhoun had warned that a single, central military academy would simply reinforce social hierarchies instead of providing an education to the talented and ambitious sons of the middling ranks. Now he held the authority to determine exactly who would benefit from a West Point education. Of the thousands of letters that arrived at the War Department offices addressed to Calhoun every year, hundreds were requests for a slot at the military academy, often written by prominent men on behalf of relatives or protégés. It was hard to refuse President Monroe, who wrote requesting an appointment for Nicholas Trist, a young protégé who had studied law with Thomas Jefferson and would eventually negotiate the Treaty of Guadalupe Hidalgo that ended the Mexican-American War in 1848. But Calhoun did initially refuse him, writing that there was no space at the academy that year. (When Monroe wrote back that he knew of a local cadet who would not be able to attend, and asked that Trist be able to take his spot, Calhoun conceded.) Andrew Jackson wrote on behalf of his nephews. And one day in 1824 a tall, dark-haired seventeen-year-old from Virginia personally delivered his letter of introduction from William Henry Fitzhugh, who described the young man's prominent family, his "amiable disposition, & his correct and gentlemanly habits." Calhoun admitted Robert Edward Lee as a cadet the next year. All in all, Calhoun seems to have struck a middle course, making appointments that he could not refuse, and others that accrued him political capital, while still keeping the academy open to talent from all ranks of society. As Calhoun had predicted, those with friends in high places certainly had a better chance at a slot, but not always, as evidenced by an 1824 letter from eleven incensed citizens of Indiana who wrote to protest that Calhoun had appointed two "clodhoppers" to West Point over the grandson of a prominent Revolutionary War veteran.[27]

WHITE AMERICANS' INSATIABLE DEMAND for land required Calhoun to devote a large amount of his time during these years to convincing Indian tribes to sign treaties in which they gave up claims to eastern lands in return for lands in the West, often along the Arkansas River. Calhoun or his Indian agents negotiated ten such treaties with Indian tribes during August, September, and October of 1818 alone, and Calhoun would preside over dozens more during his tenure.[28] After negotiating one of these treaties with the Miami in late 1818, Indian agent Jonathan Jennings reported to Calhoun that he had obtained for the United States more than seven million acres of land in Indiana "not equaled by any in the state."[29] As Calhoun saw it, he was engaged in the project of establishing his political idol Thomas Jefferson's vision of an agricultural republic, a vision that had always been predicated on the removal or assimilation of the Indians. But in dealing with Indians, Calhoun's commitment to the ideals of democracy, progress, enlightenment, and reason in government took on a more disturbing character, although one by no means unique to him.

In his negotiations with Indian tribes Calhoun and his head Indian agent, Thomas L. McKenney, considered themselves to be advocating not only for the best interests of the nation but also for the best interests of the Indians. Despite their insistence that they were motivated by good intentions and respect for Indian autonomy, these assurances always came with a silent, and sometimes not so silent, threat. "The President, however, by no means wishes that force or threats should be used to cause their emigration," Calhoun wrote to an Indian agent negotiating with the Six Nations in New York in May 1818. But just two months later, to Governor Joseph McMinn of Tennessee, who was negotiating with the Eastern Cherokee, he could write, "Let them reflect how nation after nation have sunk before the United States, and they will see the necessity of coming into our views."[30] Calhoun dictated policy from Washington while on the ground agents used a combination of threats, bullying, and bribery to force tribes into ceding millions of acres to the United States. After tribes signed the treaties, the yearly annuities often paid to them as part of the terms became another means that Calhoun could use to assure peaceful cooperation with the treaty's stipulations, which usually dictated removal west or private "reservations"—small plots of privately owned land—for those who stayed behind.[31]

After a year as secretary of war, in late 1818, Calhoun expressed his views to Congress in a lengthy report that remains one of the best windows into his thinking on Indian policy. In it, he rejected the existing policy of treating Indian tribes as independent nations (a policy he would nevertheless abide by during his time in office) and instead frankly advocated for a paternalistic government program aimed at integrating Indians into the American experiment whether they wanted to or not. "Our views of their interest, and not their own, ought to govern them," he wrote. "By a proper combination of force and persuasion, of punishments and rewards, they ought to be brought within the pales of law and civilization...Such small bodies, with savage customs and character, cannot, and ought not, to be permitted to exist in an independent condition in the midst of civilized society." In Calhoun's view, the Indians would either be civilized and incorporated into American society, move west, or else inevitably become extinct. They could not continue to exist as they were. Calhoun expressed his argument in terms of a moral imperative on the part of the government to protect the Indians from extinction, against their own wishes if necessary. "The Indians are not so situated as to leave it to time and experience to effect their civilization," he warned.[32]

Calhoun believed his goal was already being accomplished by the so-called factory system, a network of government-run trading posts that dispensed food and supplies to Indians. Calhoun and Thomas McKenney saw the trading posts, which preceded Calhoun's tenure in office, as a possible means of teaching "the more helpless parts of our Family" the arts of agriculture and civilization.[33] Calhoun was well aware of critics, especially the businessman John Jacob Astor and his American Fur Company, who charged that the factory system was a government monopoly, and that a more agile and responsive free trade system would better serve the interests of the Indians. In his report to Congress, Calhoun objected that the Indians were too easily taken advantage of to be left to the "competition of private adventurers." He proposed a two-tiered system in which the government would license a few large companies like Astor's to do business with nearby tribes on the edge of white settlement. These companies would be under close government supervision and the licenses would be so expensive as to prohibit much competition and make the cost of noncompliance with government regulations too expensive to ignore. Farther west, he proposed the formation of an entity along the lines of the British East India Company—a government-controlled trading company open to investors at the price of one hundred dollars a share that would have the exclusive right to trade and have the protection of the American military in fending off foreign rivals. Strikingly, Calhoun viewed this as a democratic measure that would allow a broader swath of Americans to share in the profits of the fur trade. "The profit of the trade with the Indians has, at all times, been confined to a few individuals," he asserted, "and it is highly probable that a greater portion of the community would participate in it, by carrying it on in the manner proposed."

Calhoun knew that his proposals ran counter to Adam Smith's free trade doctrines, which were increasingly popular, especially in the South. "All of these provisions, however necessary in the Indian trade, would be absurd in any other branch of our commerce," he acknowledged. But, he argued, "a nation discovers its wisdom no less in departing from general maxims, where it is no longer wise to adhere to them, than in its adherence to them in ordinary circumstances." Calhoun argued that the principles of free trade assumed a certain level of civilization and a certain kind of society—they were not universal truths to be applied at all times in all situations. Just as Indians could not yet be expected to participate in American democracy, neither should they be forced unprepared and unprotected into the market. In

1824 Congress finally abolished the factory system against Calhoun's recommendations, leaving the trade completely to private traders licensed by the War Department, although Congress adopted Calhoun's recommendation that traders post high bonds in order to ensure compliance and less competition. To oversee this compliance, Calhoun established within the War Department the Bureau of Indian Affairs, which manages the relationship between the United States and Indian nations to this day.[34]

Calhoun's confidence in his approach to dealing with the Indians was bolstered by his belief that he had science on his side. Since the late eighteenth century, scholars of the new "science" of population in Europe—most famously Thomas Malthus, but also Adam Smith—had looked to North America and its Indians as a kind of natural testing ground for their theories. The most notable of these theories proposed that societies advance through stages of civilization, and that even supposedly primitive, low-density populations like the Indians of North America might eventually be able to progress to a higher state of civilization by practicing settled agriculture. The danger, these writers felt, was that the Indians might be overwhelmed by their proximity to more advanced, denser populations of white Americans before they could become civilized, leading to their extinction.[35]

Directly or indirectly, Calhoun was clearly influenced by this thinking. Writing to Cherokee agent Return Meigs, Calhoun predicted that the Cherokees' future was bleak "unless they will condense their population, take reservations, become farmers and mechanics, and be admitted to privileges of citizens."[36] To another Indian agent in New York he wrote, "Experience proves, that when surrounded by the whites, they always dwindle and become miserable."[37] To Joseph McMinn, governor of Tennessee and agent to the Eastern Cherokee, he wrote, "I do not see what an intelligent Cherokee has to hope, situated as his nation is, except in emigrating to the West, or taking reservations, and settling down under the fostering protection of our laws. As our population grows dense around them it will be out of the power of the government itself to protect them in their present condition." The logic of population theories lent American expansion an air of inevitability that was both politically and morally convenient for Calhoun. Most of the advocates of removal portrayed it, contradictorily, as both an opportunity for tribes like the Cherokee to maintain their independence—what Agent Meigs in a letter to Calhoun called "their darling, extreme liberty"—and also as a bid to buy time so that when the tide of white settlement inevitably reached them once more the Indians might be ready to become citizens. "By removing West," Calhoun wrote McMinn, "the Cherokee nation will obtain time, before they can be crowded by the whites, to become civilized, and capable of enjoying the advantage of equal laws."[38]

As harsh and condescending as Calhoun's approach to the Indians was, his openness even on a theoretical level to the idea that Indians could eventually become American citizens is striking given what the very near future held. A decade later the advance of scientific theories of race would harden white Americans' attitudes against the very possibility of integrating Indians into American society. But in the early 1820s Calhoun had only to look over the extensive and optimistic reports of Thomas McKenney, his head of Indian Affairs, on the network of Indian schools funded by the War Department to find evidence for his belief that Indians were capable of "civilization."[39] The schools, most of which were founded by missionary boards or religious denominations, were funded out of an ominously named "Civilization Fund" that Congress had established in 1819 at Calhoun's urging in order to hurry along assimilation. Strikingly, from our perspective today, there were no objections to the government funding religious organizations to accomplish this education, and Calhoun corresponded with a wide array of ministers and missionary organizations, and even one Catholic bishop, engaged in establishing schools for the Indians.[40] Calhoun commissioned one of these correspondents, the Reverend Jedediah Morse, father of Samuel Morse, the telegraphy pioneer, to write a report on the conditions of the Indians of North America in order "to devise the most suitable plan for their civilization and happiness." Morse submitted an amazingly detailed report after two years of travel.[41] In 1822 Calhoun reported to James Monroe that the War Department was overseeing fourteen schools with a total of 508 students at a cost of nearly $16,000. Only two years later, the project had expanded to thirty-two schools and over 900 students.[42] In 1828 the *Cherokee Phoenix* reported that some of the young scholars at one of these academies in Kentucky were named after Calhoun, although exactly who did the naming is unclear.[43]

Writing to Monroe in 1822, Calhoun portrayed the schools as a grand experiment. "It was thought advisable, at the commencement of the system, to proceed with caution," he wrote, in order that "the system adopted for the civilization of the Indians have the fairest trial." But now Calhoun was emboldened by the experiment's apparent success. "Experience has thus far justified those policies which have been adopted," he wrote. Calhoun explained that he now felt it was possible for Indians to achieve a level of education "equal to that of the laboring portion of our community"—by which he probably meant poor whites, not slaves. However, he thought the question of higher attainments was still an open one, expressing a hint of doubt about Indians' capacities. "The interesting inquiry remains to be solved," he added, "whether such an education would lead them to that state of morality, civilization, and happiness, to which it is the desire of the government to bring them; or whether there is not something in their situation which presents insuperable obstacles to such a state?" In other words, only time would tell.[44]

Calhoun knew firsthand of one example that suggested Indians were capable of the highest levels of achievement as white Americans conceived of such things. His name was James Lawrence McDonald, a young Choctaw who was the protégé of Thomas McKenney. McDonald lived with McKenney's family in Washington and became acquainted with Calhoun during Calhoun's first two years at the War Department. The young man soon proved so academically gifted that

McKenney asked Calhoun's advice on what to do with the talented youth. "Make a lawyer of him," Calhoun replied briskly. Calhoun authorized McKenney to pay for McDonald's legal education out of his office's funds, and when McDonald left to study law, he sent a letter of thanks to Calhoun that the secretary admired so much he kept it to show to friends as an example of Indian excellence. McDonald continued to keep Calhoun apprised of his progress, and McKenny later recalled, "Mr. Calhoun thought, on reading these letters, that few men, no matter how highly gifted, or thoroughly educated, could excel them." McDonald became America's first Indian lawyer, and after completing his legal training he returned to his people in Mississippi.[45] Calhoun and McDonald would meet again a few years later when the young lawyer served as part of a Choctaw delegation to Washington in 1824 to negotiate a treaty. McDonald's skill made the negotiations "more of an up-hill business than I had ever before experienced in negotiating with Indians," McKenney remembered. "I believe Mr. Calhoun, who negotiated the treaty, thought so too." Indeed, the negotiations with the Choctaw that year represented a new development in the relationship between the American government and the Indians in which Indians increasingly decided to fight expansion with the legal and rhetorical tools of their opponents. The Choctaw left Washington with a better deal than they could have possibly negotiated without McDonald's help.[46]

But as evidence that Indians could, if they wanted to, assimilate and achieve equality with whites, McDonald would prove an ambiguous example. Incredibly talented and oriented toward the models of achievement offered to him by white society, but also deeply conscious that white society would never fully accept him, McDonald was a tortured soul. He committed suicide in 1831 by jumping from a bluff outside Jackson, Mississippi, reportedly after his proposal of marriage had been rejected by a white woman. By then, the racial categories that white Americans used to order their world had shifted to a degree that left little room for James McDonald.[47] His death would make a deep impression on Thomas McKenney, who became a strong advocate of removal after McDonald's death in the belief that whites would never fully accept Indians.[48]

IN EARLY JULY 1818 Calhoun returned to Washington after a tour of the Chesapeake with President Monroe to survey sites for planned fortifications and a brief visit to his plantation in South Carolina. Upon arriving in Washington, he found that one of his slaves was missing and the town was consumed with talk of what Andrew Jackson had done in Florida, where Jackson had been sent earlier that year by Monroe and Calhoun with ambiguous orders to subdue the Seminoles. The missing slave was Hector, the careful carriage driver who had piloted the Calhouns to Washington months earlier. Calhoun suspected that Hector had escaped to Philadelphia, so he wrote to his friend Congressman Charles Ingersoll of Pennsylvania, asking for help. "During my late absence, one of my domsticks without any just provocation left me," he wrote, adding that he suspected Hector had been "under the seduction...of some free blacks near me." Calhoun asked Ingersoll to employ a "constable, or agent"—in other words, a slave catcher—in Philadelphia to look for Hector, whom he described as "about 25 years of age, very black, under the middle size, compactly formed; he speaks slow with a feeble voice, and his upper eye lids hanging very much over his eyes give him a dull and sleepy appearance." Evidently, Hector was not as dull or sleepy as he looked, for two months later he was still missing. For Calhoun, it was a firsthand lesson in the allure of freedom for the enslaved and the difficulties of recovering runaways from a free state.[49]

Before leaving Washington with Monroe, Calhoun learned that Jackson had attacked the Spanish fort at St. Marks, where the Indians he was pursuing had taken refuge and that, as John Quincy Adams noted in his diary, "a Scotchman by the name of Arbuthnot was found among them, and Jackson appears half inclined to take his life." Jackson was more than half-inclined, as it turned out. Jackson executed

Alexander Arbuthnot, a Scottish trader, and Robert Ambrister, a one-time Royal Marine, both of whom he found with the Seminoles and suspected of inciting and arming the Indians. Jackson mailed his report on the courts-martial to Calhoun on May 5, but the report was lost or stolen in the mail and did not reach Washington, so Calhoun and Monroe left on their fortification tour without knowing the full extent of what Jackson had done. In June while Calhoun was in South Carolina, newspapers in Charleston and Camden trumpeted Jackson's occupation of Pensacola, taking for granted that it would mean war with Spain. So Calhoun knew as he hurried back to Washington that an international crisis was brewing, although he may not have known that it would involve Britain as well as Spain. Most disturbing to Calhoun and the rest of Monroe's cabinet was the fact that they had heard none of the news from Jackson himself due to the lost report, leaving John Quincy Adams to face the apoplectic British and Spanish ministers without any explanation for Jackson's behavior.[50]

Jackson's actions put Monroe and his administration in an impossible position. If they publicly announced that Jackson had not been authorized to take Pensacola, they risked the ire of Jackson's rabid followers and, no small consideration, of the general himself. But if they did not disavow Jackson's actions, which would amount to confirmation that he had acted according to his orders, then Speaker Henry Clay and his allies in Congress would pounce on an opportunity to accuse the president of usurping Congress's constitutional authority to make war. Failure to break with Jackson might also mean open war with Spain at the very moment that John Quincy Adams was in the midst of delicate treaty negotiations with the Spanish minister, Luis de Onís, over the possible acquisition of Florida.

With the summer heat in Washington so oppressive that John Quincy Adams began each morning with a bath in the Potomac, Monroe's cabinet met several days in a row beginning on July 15 to discuss what to do. Everyone except Adams agreed that Jackson had disobeyed his orders and that the administration should say so publicly and return

Pensacola and the other Spanish garrisons Jackson had taken. Adams argued that Jackson's actions should be used to force Spain to the bargaining table over Florida, and he lamented to his diary that evening "that there is not vigor to bear out the bold energy of Jackson." Calhoun, who was, Adams thought, "generally of sound, judicious and comprehensive mind, seems in this case to be personally offended" by what he considered Jackson's open defiance of the War Department's instructions. Adams seemed surprised to see Calhoun's usual rationality overridden by emotion, but he failed to grasp that Calhoun took Jackson's actions as an insult, a violation of his honor. Over the next few days, Calhoun continued to be the most vehement voice in the room against Jackson. "Calhoun principally bore the argument against me," Adams noted on July 20, "insisting that the capture of Pensacola was not necessary upon principles of self-defense, and therefore was both an act of war against Spain and a violation of the Constitution." Privately, Calhoun wrote to Charles Tait of Georgia that same day, "As you know, the act was unauthorized; and done by Jackson on his own responsibility. The place of course will be yielded up to Spain."[51]

Monroe indeed determined to eventually return Pensacola and St. Marks to Spain, although delaying long enough to help give Adams the bargaining leverage he sought in negotiating what became the Transcontinental Treaty of Washington, or the Adams-Onís Treaty, signed the following year, which added Florida and opened the way for the United States to lay claim to the continent all the way to the Pacific. But Monroe also tried mightily to soften the blow to Jackson. The administration's public stance, which Monroe delicately explained to Jackson on July 19, was that Jackson had made an honest mistake, misunderstanding his orders but acting honorably in a difficult situation, and so was not to blame even though his prizes had to be returned to Spain. Monroe reported to Calhoun a few weeks later that Jackson "strenuously" disagreed with this interpretation.[52]

For the rest of 1818 and into the next year, Jackson sparred privately with Monroe and publicly with Congress over his conduct. Monroe privately urged Jackson to write to Calhoun explaining his position, assuring Jackson, inaccurately, that Calhoun had "very just and liberal sentiments on the matter" and would respond "in a friendly manner." Jackson refused. Calhoun refused a similar request from Monroe, insisting that the orders had been clear and also wishing to avoid open conflict with Jackson. So when Jackson appeared in Washington in January 1819 to defend his conduct to Congress he directed his considerable rage instead at Henry Clay and at William Crawford, whom he believed had been his main opponents in the administration. Calhoun and Jackson meanwhile enjoyed a friendly relationship, with Jackson blissfully ignorant of Calhoun's true feelings and Calhoun doing nothing to enlighten him. One morning in early February on his way to work John Quincy Adams met Jackson on the street and Jackson informed him that he had dined the night before at Calhoun's home with "a few military friends." Floride, who had to prepare for the event, called it a full-blown "ball" to a friend back home. But Floride apparently knew as little as Jackson about her husband's real views on the general's Florida escapade. A few days before Jackson dined with the Calhouns, Floride described listening from the gallery to some of the speeches railing against Jackson in the House. "I am sorry congress has abused him so much, respecting the Seminole War," she wrote to a friend, "as I am confident he acted to the best of his knowledge, and further, in censuring him, they must my husband, as he directed him in one of his letters to act to the best of his knowledge." Both Floride and Jackson would eventually find out the truth, but it would take years.[53]

NINE

"To the Western Confines of the Continent"

T HROUGHOUT JANUARY AND INTO FEBRUARY, as Congress debated censuring Jackson for exceeding his orders, the country was descending into a deep economic depression that would become known as the Panic of 1819. Toward the end of the previous year, Calhoun had written his cousin Patrick Noble that he was worried about "the state of our paper currency which in many parts of the country is much disordered." Calhoun had good reason to be worried. Earlier that year the Bank of the United States, concerned about the flood of credit that had washed over the country during the last two years (in part to finance the expansion of cotton into the Southwest), moved to constrict the money supply by making fewer loans, calling in debts, and refusing to accept any bank notes not redeemable in specie. In addition, abundant grain crops in Europe and the so-called Corn Laws in Great Britain, which set prohibitive import duties on foreign grains in order to protect the British landed gentry against competition, led to a steep drop in grain prices. Then at the end of 1818 word arrived that the price of cotton in Liverpool had dropped by half overnight as British manufacturers tried to source raw cotton from India to drive down high prices and escape their growing dependence on the American South. The depression that followed would last until the mid-1820s and was one of the worst economic disasters in American history, the first time that many Americans experienced the endless boom-bust cycle that is a defining characteristic of modern capitalism. The depression and resulting calls for austerity throughout the government would place serious obstacles in the path of Calhoun's visionary efforts to transform the nation's military. More than that, the depression would color how Calhoun and many others viewed almost everything in the coming years.[1]

The economic chaos spreading across the nation was soon matched by political chaos. On February 8, 1819, the House vindicated Andrew Jackson on all counts as its members bent to public opinion, rocketing his popularity to new heights. Five days later the House took up the Missouri territory's application for statehood.[2] Everything was routine until Representative James Tallmadge of New York proposed an amendment barring any further importation of slaves into Missouri and proposing a scheme of gradual emancipation similar to what many northern states had implemented. As the southerners in the House erupted, Thomas Cobb of Georgia warned Tallmadge, "You have kindled a fire which all the waters of the ocean cannot put out, which seas of blood only can extinguish."[3] Tallmadge's amendment passed narrowly in the House along sectional lines, but failed in the Senate on the strength of the southern vote, leaving the issue unresolved until the Sixteenth Congress reconvened in December.

Well before Tallmadge put forth his amendment on the floor of the House there had been a fight brewing over the extension of slavery into new states joining the Union. Since the Constitutional Convention northern states had decried the outsize influence that the three-fifths clause gave to the South in the national government, while for their part southern states watched with apprehension as the free states' representation in the House grew with every federal census. Twice in the months before the Missouri debacle began, northern congressmen had unsuccessfully proposed blanket bans on slavery in *any* state added to

the Union in the future. In the intervening months between the defeat
of Tallmadge's amendment and the new Congress, there were calls
throughout the North for Tallmadge's prohibition to be applied to the
rest of the Louisiana Purchase, to Spanish Florida, to Texas, and any
future territory "from the Mississippi River to the South Sea." The
prospect of such a ban terrified seaboard states like Virginia where
slaveholders like James Monroe believed that the diffusion of the enslaved population was essential to their safety and, in Thomas Jefferson's tortured logic, to the end of slavery itself. Clearly, there was more
at stake than Missouri.[4]

By the time of the Missouri crisis, John Quincy Adams and
Calhoun had become as friendly as two fiercely ambitious and
independent-minded men could be. In December 1819, as the House
once more took up the Missouri question, Adams offered Calhoun the
chance to fill the vacant ambassadorship to France, urging him that "as
I expected more from him than from any other man living, to the benefit of the public service of this Nation, I wished from purely public
motives that he could go and spend some time in Europe, because I was
convinced it would much enlarge his sphere of usefulness." Calhoun
declined, saying he could not afford the expense since an ambassador's
salary was so low, something Adams had to grudgingly concede.[5]

A few weeks later Adams dropped by Calhoun's office and they
quickly fell into conversation about "the Slave question." Calhoun told
Adams he doubted the issue would lead to disunion, but that if it did
the South would be forced into an alliance "offensive and defensive"
with Great Britain, a prospect Calhoun did not relish at all since, as
Adams immediately pointed out, this would be returning to colonial
status. "Yes—pretty much," Calhoun replied to the astonished Adams,
adding that the North "would find it necessary to make their communities all military." The two talked for hours, so long that Calhoun
missed his dinner. "This conversation with Calhoun led me into a momentous train of thought," an agitated Adams wrote that evening as he
considered where it all might lead.[6]

In the end, southerners in Congress successfully fended off the most dire threats to the expansion of slavery. On March 3, 1820, the president called his cabinet together to ask their opinions on the bill that would become known to history as the Missouri Compromise. Missouri would come into the Union without restrictions on slavery, Maine would come in as a free state, and a line at 36°30' on Missouri's southern border would divide the Louisiana Purchase between future slave states such as Arkansas (and, southerners soon hoped, Texas) and future free states to its north. Monroe took the unusual step of asking his cabinet to submit their written opinions on two questions: Did Congress have the constitutional right to prohibit slavery in a territory? And, if so, did the prohibition in the bill, which banned slavery from the territory "forever," continue after statehood? On the first question, Adams recorded in his diary, Calhoun and the whole cabinet agreed that Congress had the power to prohibit slavery in a territory, even though, as Adams carefully noted, the southern members of the cabinet admitted there was no "express power to that effect given in the Constitution." But a divide quickly opened on the second question—whether congressional authority extended into statehood. Wirt, Crawford, and Calhoun believed that it did not. Adams believed it did, arguing that no state could establish slavery where it did not exist. As his authority he appealed not to the Constitution, but to the Declaration of Independence.[7]

This divide was in keeping with a theme that had emerged during the congressional debates over Missouri. Antislavery advocates had frequently cast the extension of slavery as a moral issue, appealing to the Declaration, while southerners cast the issue as a constitutional one that threatened the equality guaranteed to all states. Indeed, Adams's use of the Declaration was part of much broader shift in which a surge of historical interest in the revolution "sacralized" the Declaration and made its sentiments available for political uses.[8] "The Declaration of Independence, not only asserts the natural equality of all men, and their unalienable right to Liberty," Adams argued to his southern colleagues in the cabinet, "but that the only *just* powers of government are derived from the consent of the governed." And how, he asked, could slaves ever be construed as consenting to their enslavement? It was a bold argument, and not one Adams was willing to make in public. Undoubtedly thinking of his political future, Adams asked Monroe to be excused from expressing this opinion in writing. Crawford objected, no doubt relishing the political damage the opinion would do to Adams in the South. Calhoun, who had been silent for most of the lengthy debate, now jumped in, saying he "thought it exceedingly desirable that no such argument should be drawn up and deposited."

Instead, Calhoun proposed a lawyerly solution. What if, he asked, the second question were changed to ask "whether the 8th Section of the Bill [which prohibited slavery "forever"] was consistent with the Constitution?" Then, Calhoun explained, he and the others could answer affirmatively, since they believed the "forever" could not apply to statehood, and Adams could reply in the affirmative, too, since technically he based his argument on the Declaration, not the Constitution. Adams quickly agreed to Calhoun's proposal. Many years later the existence of the responses that Monroe requested that day would become the subject of considerable controversy for Calhoun.

After the meeting Calhoun and Adams walked home together, as they often did, and Calhoun tried to explain the southern point of view to his very northern friend. Calhoun complimented Adams, acknowledging that the principles he had expressed were "just and noble." But, Calhoun explained, "in the Southern Country, whenever they were mentioned, they were always understood as applying only to white men." Echoing Henry DeSaussure and Timothy Ford, who had defended lowcountry slave society against the attacks of Robert Goodloe Harper in the 1790s, and influenced by his firsthand view of the effects of the cotton boom on the upcountry, Calhoun explained to Adams that slavery "was the best guarantee to equality among whites. It produced an unvarying level among them. It not only did not excite, but did not even admit of inequalities, by which one white man could domineer over another." Here, in its essence, years before he made it publicly, was the argument that would eventually be Calhoun's claim on history: that racial slavery in a democracy made up of white men was no contradiction at all. "I told Calhoun I could not see things in the same light," a dejected Adams wrote that night.[9]

Calhoun's formulation to Adams that afternoon was different in one crucial respect from the arguments made by DeSaussure and Ford twenty-five years earlier. DeSaussure and Ford had openly acknowledged the "horrors" of slavery, arguing that it was revulsion at this spectacle that produced a fierce attachment to liberty among whites. Their argument rose from a strain of Federalist and republican thought that emphasized liberty, not equality, as the highest political good—and which, for that reason, viewed a hierarchical society as acceptable and even desirable. Calhoun focused instead on equality, which he considered the "genius of the age," arguing that slavery produced a more democratic society for white people. This was not primarily a theoretical or abstract argument. In good rational and scientific fashion, Calhoun's conclusion came from observation and experience, from what he had witnessed in the upcountry during his lifetime. Although Adams did not fully grasp its significance that evening, on their walk he heard a preview of how Calhoun would radically refashion the argument over slavery for a more democratic era in the years ahead.

The conversation exposed a deep divide between Americans like Adams, who reasoned that slavery was wrong based on an abstract belief in natural rights common to all mankind, and Americans like Calhoun who proceeded from a more historical and circumstantial definition of rights as the result of belonging to a particular political community. By virtue of their history first as English subjects and then as American citizens, Calhoun believed, he and his family belonged to the political community of the United States and were entitled to its benefits. Conversely, by virtue of history and circumstance, blacks did not and therefore were not. The difference between Adams and Calhoun could also be glossed as a disagreement over how Locke's famous

Second Treatise should be applied to slaves. Where Adams believed that slaves were part of Locke's community of the governed whose assent was a precondition of legitimate government, Calhoun viewed slaves as property, which, according to Locke, it was one of the fundamental purposes of government to protect. Calhoun's view made the protection of slave "property" one of the most essential rights of white citizens, and Adams understood the magnitude of the difference. Earlier in the crisis, he had written, "I take it for granted that the present question is a mere preamble; a title page to a great tragic volume." That evening he wrote in a dark mood, "If the Union must be dissolved, Slavery is precisely the question upon which it ought to break."[10]

ONLY WEEKS AFTER THE Missouri crisis seemed over, another crisis erupted. Henry Baldwin of Pennsylvania, chair of a newly created Committee on Manufactures, introduced a new tariff bill in the House designed to aid manufacturers hurt by the ongoing economic crisis and to head off the specter of riot and revolution among unemployed northern textile mill workers. Baldwin's tariff was dramatically more protectionist than the 1816 tariff that Calhoun had helped to pass, proposing to raise the average duty on goods like cotton, woolens, iron, and hemp to about 33 percent from the current 25. Voices from the South and North alike decried the tariff as an ominous sign of the growing political power of manufacturers in the country. One New York editor wrote that the bill's effect would be "to create and support a new interest, that of manufacturing at the expense of agriculture and commerce—and finally create a monopoly in the hands of a certain portion of the community, while the other parts of it are virtually taxed for its support." Calhoun's friend William Lowndes, one of the architects of the 1816 tariff, concluded that under the new bill southerners would be taxed more heavily than any other Americans without seeing a single benefit, and he worked tirelessly to unite southern planters and New England merchants against the bill. Like Lowndes and for similar reasons, Calhoun opposed the tariff, but his position in the cabinet kept him out of the fray.

Just as opponents of the Missouri Compromise had wielded the Declaration of Independence, opponents of the tariff now appealed to a different sacred text. During the debate on the tariff in the House, Congressman Mark Alexander of Virginia read a passage from Adam Smith's *Wealth of Nations* from the floor, employing Smith's defense of free trade and his opposition to government restriction to batter Baldwin's protectionist bill. Massachusetts's Harrison Gray Otis likewise used Smith to portray the tariff vote in the Senate as a monumental decision. "On one side have been ranged the [protectionist] economists and cyclopedists," he announced, "and on the other side the disciples of the celebrated Adam Smith." Smith's doctrines of free trade had long been popular among South Carolina's coastal rice-planting elite, but in the face of higher tariffs their appeal was growing, and not only among southern cotton planters.

In the end the tariff bill passed the House on the burgeoning strength of the middle states, especially New York and Pennsylvania, revealing that the most populous northern states could now push legislation through the House with only a little help. But just like Tallmadge's amendment, it failed in the Senate, where the South and maritime New England combined to defeat it. The issue was far from dead.[11]

The debates over Missouri and the tariff put Calhoun in a delicate position as he looked toward the future. Opposition to Tallmadge's amendment and the Baldwin tariff had united the various political factions in South Carolina, while support for them was centered in the very states, Pennsylvania and New York, where Calhoun's positions on internal improvements and support for domestic manufacturing had won him a following that would be essential in any future presidential election. Indeed, James Tallmadge was an ally of Calhoun's on the issue of internal improvements, and the two had worked closely together after Calhoun's departure from the House. So when Henry

DeSaussure wrote to Calhoun telling him that some prominent citizens in South Carolina believed that the Missouri crisis was only a presage to emancipation, and that there was open talk of disunion back home, Calhoun expressed "surprise and deep mortification." Of course the South would choose disunion over emancipation: "Against such an attempt the South would be as one man." But, he wrote his old mentor, "The fact is, that the Missouri question had no connection with emancipation. Its object was political power and preeminence." Calhoun believed there was no desire for emancipation in the North, despite some of the inflammatory rhetoric during the Missouri debates, and even if there was the South was completely safe in the Union. "With wisdom and moderation the slave holding States will ever have influence not only sufficient for their protection, but to secure their just weight in the Union," he wrote. "They have always had it; and they, in my opinion, possess great and permanent political advantages, to maintain their respectability and just influence." He begged DeSaussure not to let such a "dangrous [*sic*] mode of thinking" take root.[12] To a similarly apprehensive Andrew Jackson, Calhoun wrote with more than a whiff of wishful thinking that "the agitators of that question [Missouri] have, in my opinion, not only completely failed, but have destroyed to a great extent their capacity for future mischief."[13] Calhoun believed, or at least hoped, that the issue was settled for good.

THERE WERE OTHER REASONS for Calhoun to be somewhat distracted from politics during the debates over Missouri and the tariff. In the spring of 1820 the Calhouns suffered a deeply personal but very public tragedy, the loss of another child. "We had the misfortune to loose our youngest child Elizabeth, a few weeks since," Calhoun wrote to Floride's brother James Edward in early May.[14] In contrast to the agony evident in Calhoun's description of their first daughter's death, the brief mention of Elizabeth's death seems terse, but it was no doubt a wrenching loss. In between the births of little Anna and the infant

Elizabeth, Floride had miscarried in November 1818, but soon became pregnant with Elizabeth, who was born in South Carolina in the fall of 1819. Calhoun had been present in South Carolina for Elizabeth's birth, and on the way back to Washington with his family soon afterward he had become dangerously ill, stopping at the North Carolina border to recover. Unexpected death was a given in the Calhouns' world, and it could come for anyone. When the baby fell sick in March, she provoked a torrent of sympathy from elite Washingtonians. Monroe himself visited every day, and his daughter Eliza Hay came to sit up at night with the child. Louisa Adams, wife of John Quincy Adams and a southerner though raised abroad, visited often and did the same. The writer Margaret Bayard Smith, wife of *National Intelligencer* editor Samuel Harris Smith, described the house the Calhouns had moved into in 1818 so full of well-wishers that she had to leave for fear of doing more harm than good. "I never in my life witnessed such attention," she wrote, adding, "all this was not a mere tribute to rank," but instead resulted from "that good will which both Mr. and Mrs. C. have universally excited, they are really beloved." Elizabeth died on March 22, the same day that Henry Baldwin introduced his tariff bill in the House. Her funeral train was attended by "an unusually long train of carriages." She was the third little girl the Calhouns had lost in five years.[15]

Floride was pregnant almost constantly during the Calhouns' Washington years, and in Washington birth could be as public as death. At a cabinet meeting in April 1824 Calhoun was missing, and Secretary of the Navy Samuel Southard was sent to ask his opinion on a decision, arriving at the Calhouns' house just in time to be present for the birth of little Martha Cornelia. Southard returned and announced both the safe delivery and Calhoun's opinion to the cabinet.[16]

Despite her frequent pregnancies Floride became an influential figure on the Washington social scene, which in many ways was just another arena of conquest and combat for the city's political class, one in which women like Floride played prominent roles. The Calhouns frequently held large parties attended by a who's who of the capital city.

At one of them in 1819 Margaret Bayard Smith recorded "five rooms crowded," and reported with exhaustion, "I have seen everyone I know for the first and last time this winter." No wonder that Calhoun thanked his New York City friend Joseph Swift for procuring him a shipment of Madeira wine in 1821, since his wine cellar was almost empty. "Nothing could come more apropos," Calhoun wrote. "My stock is so far reduced as to require to be replenished, and I had just been thinking how I could effect it to best advantage."[17]

At the Calhouns' parties Margaret Bayard Smith especially enjoyed her conversations with the secretary of war—"You know how frank and communicative he is," she wrote to a friend. After one dinner she and Calhoun discussed Henry Clay's attack on Andrew Jackson's Florida escapade until late in the evening while across the room Floride played the piano.[18] Over the years many observers would comment on Calhoun's combination of intellectual intensity and what his daughter Anna later called his "almost childlike simplicity of manner," an openness and honesty that could be disarming.[19] Less cerebral personalities sometimes found him tedious—"too intellectual, too industrious, too intent on the struggle of politics to suit me except as an occasional companion," Alabama congressman and Calhoun ally Dixon Lewis once complained.[20] But, like Margaret Bayard Smith, women frequently appreciated Calhoun's willingness to engage them about ideas. Varina Davis, wife of future Confederate president Jefferson Davis, who met Calhoun and carried on a correspondence with him in the 1840s, later recalled that his letters to her were "written as though to an intellectual equal...he assumed nothing except a universal, honest, co-intelligence between him and the world, and his conversation with a girl was on the same subjects as with a statesman."[21]

Playing host in Washington was expensive, and Calhoun's lament to Floride's brother John Ewing that he was "in great need of money" was soon a constant refrain. In fact, the Calhouns probably could not have afforded their constant hospitality if Floride's mother had not lived with them for significant stretches of their years in Washington.

Calhoun meanwhile continued to help his mother-in-law manage her plantations back in South Carolina as well as coordinate affairs of her estate with Henry DeSaussure. Even a cabinet post did not pay well enough to support a Washington lifestyle, and it seems certain that Calhoun and Floride continued to depend on the largesse of Floride's mother.[22]

For her own part, the elder Floride seems to have viewed Washington as a new, broader field for evangelizing. In the fall of 1822 a yellow fever epidemic and a religious revival struck the city at the same time, and by mid-October there were revival meetings in churches and private homes nearly every night as droves of people converted and dozens more died in the epidemic. The Presbyterians even began singing Methodist hymns after their services, a sure sign that something unusual was happening. In the heat of the revival old Mrs. Colhoun went out repeatedly—once in the midst of a rainstorm—"to beat up recruits" for the nightly church meetings. But she never convinced her daughter or son-in-law to attend the meetings, Margaret Bayard Smith observed, writing that the younger Floride, "with many others, disapprove of them." Perhaps Floride shared Smith's feeling that the public conversions and outbursts of emotion on display in the revival were "repugnant."[23]

What Calhoun thought of his mother-in-law's religious fervor he never said, but clearly during these years his adherence to the Calvinist doctrines of his upbringing had loosened. In 1820, along with John Quincy Adams, Calhoun contributed money for the construction of a building for Washington's First Unitarian Church. The church, designed by the architect Charles Bulfinch, who also designed the US Capitol, opened its doors in 1822.[24] Whether Calhoun regularly attended is doubtful; a donation to help build a church was not the same thing as being a member, but there is reason to believe Calhoun took a real interest in Unitarianism. William Seaton, publisher of the *National Intelligencer* and another of the church's founders, recalled that when Calhoun delivered his donation for the church's construction he told Seaton that "Unitarianism was the true faith, and must ultimately prevail over the whole world." This was no small matter, since Unitarianism was profoundly at odds with the religious orthodoxy of Calhoun's family and community in South Carolina. Unitarians not only rejected what William Ellery Channing, one of the most famous Unitarians of the day, called the "irrational and unscriptural doctrine of the Trinity," but also jettisoned other traditional and supposedly irrational Christian doctrines such as original sin and the Calvinist idea of divine election to salvation and damnation.[25] It eventually became common knowledge back in South Carolina that Calhoun's religious beliefs were not in line with the tenets of evangelical Christianity that now predominated in the upcountry.

Calhoun's gravitation toward Unitarianism seems to have been the natural result of his temperament, his devotion to reason, and his embrace of progress. Unitarians, it was said, embraced the unity of God, the brotherhood of man, and the neighborhood of Boston, and indeed they were mostly New Englanders like John Quincy Adams. It was a rational and optimistic faith that appealed to Americans, including Calhoun, who believed they were living in a unique epoch of human history marked by freedom, toleration, and progress in all areas of human understanding. Some of the first advocates of women's rights in England, including Mary Wollstonecraft, were Unitarians, and in the years ahead the denomination would include several of America's foremost abolitionists, such as Theodore Parker and Julia Ward Howe. In 1820 Calhoun seems to have agreed with the Unitarian belief that the dawn of an era in which reason should govern everything, including religion, was upon them. When First Unitarian Church held its first service in the new building in 1822, the Reverend Robert Little proclaimed, "Shall it be said that we have left no useful memorial behind us?...Forbid it, Gracious Father! These walls will, I trust, bear witness that our lives have not been altogether useless to mankind. Some I hope may be better and wiser for our exertions in the cause of truth."

Little's sermon harmonized easily with Calhoun's personal motto: "The duties of life are greater than life itself."[26]

If Calhoun ever attended services at First Unitarian, he was likely alone. Floride continued to attend the Episcopal Church, and in later years Calhoun usually accompanied her. Even if his religious sympathies were with the Unitarians, his political instincts kept him from proclaiming them too loudly. That would not do in South Carolina. With a fervent evangelical, a proper Episcopalian, and a Unitarian-leaning lapsed Presbyterian all living under one roof, dinner conversations at the Calhoun house in Washington during these years may have been almost as lively as the debates over Missouri and the tariff in Congress.

IN THE FALL OF 1820 Calhoun made a whirlwind trip through the North, his first extended visit to the region since leaving Tapping Reeve's law school. The trip's stated purpose was to inspect military fortifications and posts, but Calhoun was also surely testing the waters for a presidential run, and the reception he received was encouraging. At Ballston Spa in New York admirers threw a ball in Calhoun's honor at the famous Sans Souci Hotel, where his entrance was greeted by a band playing "Hail Columbia."[27] In Boston the naval hero Commodore Isaac Hull, commander of the USS *Constitution* during its famous fight with the *Guerriere* during the War of 1812, rolled out a similar greeting for Calhoun at a "very splendid ball" at Charlestown's Navy Yard.[28]

Calhoun had the opportunity to see firsthand the growth of industry in the North when he visited the brand-new Barrett, Tileston, and Company dyeing facility on Staten Island, just opened the year before by a group of investors from Boston. According to one newspaper, Calhoun was especially struck by the "great mechanical ingenuity" of the machinery, some of which had been patented by the owners. At a dinner held in one of the buildings at the site that afternoon Calhoun left his audience no doubt that he was a friend of the nation's burgeoning manufacturing interests. After others offered toasts to "domestic industry" and to "the Government of the United States—may its protecting hand never be withheld from Domestic Enterprise," Calhoun rose and toasted "Mechanic ingenuity—may it give as much prosperity to our Manufactures, as enterprize has given to our Commerce."[29] At a dinner that included many of the state's political elite, including the governor, mayor of New York City, and Vice President Daniel Tomkins, Calhoun gave his audience no reason to doubt his commitment to an economic vision that included protection for domestic industries. But careful observers may have noticed that his praise of mechanical ingenuity did not explicitly endorse the tariff. Nevertheless, Calhoun's stock was high in New York. Upon his departure, the editor of the *National Advocate* remarked that Calhoun's "rapid advancement is the result of talent, industry and correct moral and political conduct, and we trust our young fellow-citizens, will pursue the same persevering and enterprising path, that our Country may be always supplied with men of equal worth and genius."[30]

Calhoun also clearly took the opportunity during his trip to gauge northern opinions on Missouri and slavery. New York, after all, was James Tallmadge's state, and just as Calhoun set out on his trip the Missouri crisis flared back to life when the new state's proposed constitution was found to include a ban on free blacks entering the state. Opponents immediately decried the ban as unconstitutional, throwing the entire compromise into doubt. On the eve of his trip, Calhoun wrote to his Maryland friend Virgil Maxcy of his disappointment that the Missouri issue had resurfaced. Perhaps thinking of Henry DeSaussure, he wrote that he could "scarcely conceive" of anything that could divide the Union except for "a belief in the slave holding States, that it is the intention of the other States gradually to undermine their property in their slaves and that disunion is the *only means* to avert the evil."[31]

Yet Calhoun found nothing on his northern journey to support such a belief on the part of the southern states, confirming what he had told Henry DeSaussure. Over the next year Calhoun repeatedly warned friends and correspondents about the dangers of indulging their unfounded fears about northern motives, or allowing their fears to be manipulated by those in pursuit of political power. One frequent correspondent was Charles Tait, a Virginian who had served as a senator from Georgia before succumbing to Alabama fever and moving west, where he became Alabama's first federal district judge in 1820. The Missouri crisis convinced Tait that the North was bent on emancipation and political domination of the South, and he wrote Calhoun repeatedly in 1820 and 1821.

After a series of exchanges, Tait finally provoked a gentle rebuke from Calhoun. "I can not but think, that the opinion, which you have formed is erroneous," Calhoun wrote. Northerners had not been motivated by "a hatred to the South," but rather saw the question of Missouri as a simple moral question about the "extension, or limitation of slavery…They viewed it in some degree in the same light, that they would the opening of the ports to the introduction of Africans." Calhoun tried to convince Tait that northerners' desire to limit slavery's expansion did not constitute a mortal hatred of the South. If the South misunderstood this fact, or was deceived into believing it by its own unscrupulous politicians, there could be serious consequences. "Were we to act on the supposition, that we cannot trust…we would be no longer one nation," Calhoun warned. "Thus virtually separated we ought to prepare to an actual separation. Distrust must engender distrust. We will not trust them, they will not trust us. Conflict must follow, thence violence and thence disunion. I would neither give, nor exercise power under such circumstances. It must be exercised over a prostrated enemy, and not over freemen delegating it for the advantage of the whole." Calhoun ended by writing, "When I see one of your age, experience, wisdom and virtue thinking as you do on this point, I confess, I am alarmed."

In 1820 and 1821 Calhoun had a clear personal interest in maintaining southern confidence in the Union, which he hoped to lead, and in putting the best face on northern intentions, but his description of the way politics should work and his faith that the American people could get it right despite a few designing politicians are strikingly idealistic. "Our true system," he encouraged Tait, "is to look to the country; and to support such measures and such men, without regard to sections, as are best calculated to advance the general interest. If there are adequate virtue and intelligence in the people, as I firmly believe there are, those individuals and sections of [the] country, who have the most enlightened and devoted zeal to the common interest must have also the greatest influence." Calhoun honestly believed that if he or any politician aimed for the "common interest" rather than personal aggrandizement, the people would support him. Of course, left completely out of Calhoun's calculations of the "common interest" were enslaved people whose fate rested, in part, on the outcome of a disagreement between white people.[32]

When Calhoun warned Tait about the politics of fear, he had South Carolina in mind. As DeSaussure had warned him, the fights over Missouri and the tariff had given oxygen to the so-called "ultra" state rights party in South Carolina led by the irascible Senator William Smith, whom one historian called "a curious cross between a brawling frontiersman and a Bible-belt divine." By the early 1820s Smith had become an avowed enemy of Calhoun's on account of Calhoun's support for an expansive conception of the federal government's constitutional powers and his conspicuous lack of support for Smith's political career. With a base of support in Calhoun's own upcountry backyard, Smith and his followers brutally attacked the more popular Calhoun and William Lowndes on account of their economic nationalism, especially their support for unconstitutional measures such as internal improvements. Of Smith and the ultras, Calhoun wrote to Charles Tait, "I cannot but deprecate any attempt to diminish [the powers of the general government] below, what a fair construction of the constitution would give. There is a vast space between a fair and practical construction of that instrument, and one which in every instance construes rigidly against it." Under such a reading, Calhoun warned, "the powers of the Union would be reduced almost to nothing."[33]

That same fall Calhoun recommended to his friends a series of anonymous essays published in an Augusta, Georgia, newspaper that, in his words, "discuss with much abilities the subject of State rights; and indicate a sound mode of thinking among the most intelligent in that quarter." The essays were by Calhoun's young protégé George McDuffie, another product of Moses Waddel's backwoods academy whose education had been paid for by Calhoun's older brother, and a new member of the House of Representatives who would soon offer his body, and nearly his life, on the dueling field in defense of Calhoun's honor.

In answer to the attacks of Smith and his allies, McDuffie mocked their "visionary" fears of the powers of the federal government, and warned that the doctrine of "state rights" was a tyrannical idea that ran counter to the "great conservative principle" that all governments, general and state, were rooted in the authority of the people, not the "rulers" of a state. In South Carolina, where the state legislature wielded enormous power, this was a boldly nationalist and democratic argument. "The general government," wrote McDuffie, "is as truly the government of the whole people, as a state government is of part of the people." He then viciously accused the ultras of seeking power out of jealousy. "Ambitious men of inferior talents," he wrote, "finding they have no hope of being distinguished in the councils of the national government, naturally wish to increase the power and consequence of the state governments." Smith would be defeated in a Senate race by another Calhoun protégé, Robert Young Hayne, in 1822, much to Calhoun's satisfaction, but Smith and the ultras did not disappear.[34]

FAR BEYOND THE POLITICAL fault lines developing in South Carolina, Calhoun paid close attention to revolutionary developments in

Europe and South America. In addition to newspapers, which Calhoun consumed as voraciously as any of his contemporaries, he also read the most recent accounts of European politics written by American travelers.[35] Furthermore, Monroe's practice of consulting on important matters with his entire cabinet meant that Calhoun was frequently called on to give opinions on foreign policy, including discussions of one of the most famous foreign policy statements in American history, the Monroe Doctrine.

Beginning in 1820 a series of uprisings in Spain, Portugal, Italy, and Greece seemed poised to upend the old order in Europe. Like many Americans, Calhoun assumed that the germ of liberty was spreading. In April 1821, Calhoun wrote Charles Tait, "The genius of the age...has become wholly hostile to the existing order of society. The essence of feudalism was lords and vassals; that of the genius of the age is equality." Even if the Holy Alliance—the monarchies of Russia, Austria, Prussia, and France—successfully quashed the uprisings, Calhoun predicted, "The sperit will break out at some other point, not so easy to control."[36] Clearly, Calhoun considered himself on the side of the "genius of the age" despite being a slaveholder. He saw no connection between the feudalism of Europe with its lords and vassals and the slaveholding society of the South. Indeed, he saw them as fundamentally different, part of two opposite sides in an ongoing struggle between despotism and liberty.

Not even the discovery of a vast rebellion plot in Charleston in the summer of 1822 led by a free black carpenter named Denmark Vesey convinced Calhoun that the contagion of liberty burning through Europe and South America had spread to the people in his society most conspicuously deprived of liberty. In July 1822, South Carolina governor Thomas Bennett, three of whose slaves were involved in the plot, asked Calhoun to send soldiers to guard Charleston. By then Vesey and more than thirty of his fellow revolutionaries had been hung, but the fear of a slave revolt still gripped the city. Calhoun granted the request, ordering a company of soldiers from St. Augustine, Florida, to move up the coast to Charleston, using the power of the American state to secure the property rights of South Carolina slaveholders. Like most white southerners, Calhoun did not immediately see any connection between the Vesey rebellion and the Latin American revolutions, whose strong antislavery character was particularly evident in the nascent Colombian republic's "free womb" law, passed in 1821, which ensured gradual emancipation. Had he connected these struggles, Calhoun might have been expected to disapprove of the Latin American revolutions— after all, the Charleston revolutionaries had planned to escape to Haiti, by now allied with the revolutionary leader Simón Bolívar. But Bolívar and Haiti were allied against the Spanish effort to reimpose colonial rule, and in the early 1820s that covered a host of sins. On the other hand, everyone knew that Vesey and his co-revolutionaries had been captured in possession of some of the antislavery speeches from the debates in Congress over Missouri, a vivid lesson in the dangers of openly discussing the morality of slavery at home.[37]

Over the next two years the European powers of the Holy Alliance successfully turned back the tide of change in Europe, and by late 1823 the Monroe administration feared they had cast their gaze abroad and were plotting to quash the young republics of South America. Based no doubt on his experience of living through an invasion by a foreign power, Calhoun took the threat of the Holy Alliance very seriously— John Quincy Adams thought him "perfectly moonstruck" by the idea. Earlier that year Calhoun had written to Andrew Jackson that he saw the beginning of "a mighty contest...to crush every vestige of liberty on the Continent of Europe," and he feared greatly that it would extend across the Atlantic. He was particularly concerned that a possible war between Great Britain and the Holy Alliance would give Great Britain an opening to take Cuba. "That England looks to that island, and will be ready to seize on it, if a favorable opportunity offers, can hardly be doubted," he wrote Jackson, warning that British possession would threaten coastal trade and communications between New Orleans and Atlantic ports. "Without Cuba our confederacy is not complete; and with it in the hands of the English, the best line of communication between the extreme parts, would be intercepted." At a cabinet meeting a few months earlier, John Quincy Adams noted, "Mr. Calhoun has a most ardent desire that the Island of Cuba should become a part of the United States," both to keep it from the British and to prevent it from being "revolutionized by the Negroes."[38]

Then in November came a proposal from the British foreign secretary, George Canning, to issue a joint declaration with Great Britain warning the Holy Alliance against interfering in the New World. The catch was that the United States would have to forswear engaging in such interference itself, including in Cuba or Texas. In a series of lengthy cabinet meetings that month, Calhoun argued strongly in favor of accepting Great Britain's invitation. Calhoun believed that by doing so, the United States would bring Great Britain onto the side of liberty against the forces of reaction in a hemispheric battle for freedom, a view shared by Thomas Jefferson, who wrote to Monroe urging him to take the opportunity to "bring [Great Britain's] mighty weight into the scale of free government." Calhoun also saw in a joint declaration the opportunity to secure from Great Britain a promise not to colonize Cuba for itself, while leaving open the possibility that Cuba might someday choose to join the United States of its own free will. He believed that if the Holy Alliance invaded Latin America, it would soon set its sights on the United States. As Adams later summarized, Calhoun warned in one meeting that "violent parties would arise in this country and we should have to fight upon our own shores for our own institutions." Adams thought Calhoun was deluded, calling it "one of Calhoun's extravaganzas," but Monroe largely shared Calhoun's views.[39] And on the threat posed by the Holy Alliance and England, so did Andrew Jackson.[40] For his part Adams argued that the United States gained nothing by cooperating with Great Britain and should issue a unilateral declaration of its principles and a warning to all European powers, Great Britain included, that the United States would not permit meddling in the Americas.[41]

Adams won the argument over what would eventually be known to history as the Monroe Doctrine, but Calhoun's different approach has sometimes obscured the fact that he and Adams largely shared the same goal, even if they disagreed on the nature of the threat. Both men believed, in the words of one historian, "that the security of the United States required more than just the safety of its borders—it required an entire hemispheric system conducive to its political system and economic practices." In three paragraphs in his annual address crafted mostly by Adams but with Calhoun's endorsement, Monroe offered a strong dose of anticolonial and nonintervention sentiment that left the door wide open for the possible expansion and influence of the United States in the Western Hemisphere. The statement was both anticolonial and imperial at the same time, contradictory in exactly the same ways that the nation and Calhoun himself were in their domestic policies toward the Indians, where he embraced the methods of empire for the ends of expanding the reach of American democracy. Ironically, Monroe's warning did little to stave off the Holy Alliance, which Adams was correct in thinking had little interest in American excursions. But the statement set off nearly a century of fierce competition between the United States and Great Britain for commercial and political influence in South America and the Caribbean that shaped Calhoun's outlook on the world for the rest of his life.[42]

LOOKING BACK AT HIS accomplishments as secretary of war in an 1843 campaign biography, Calhoun drew special attention to his directive to army surgeons at every post throughout the country to keep a record of the diseases they encountered and the treatments used, as well as a detailed record of the weather using "thermometers, barometers, and hygrometers" that he distributed to them. By 1843 this had resulted in nearly a quarter century of record keeping and two separate volumes on the medical statistics and weather of the United States, and the biography stated confidently that the practice, which was now being used in

England, "will in time lead to most interesting discoveries in the sciences of medicine and meteorology generally."[43] Calhoun viewed himself during his secretary of war years as an agent of progress in an enlightened era, and this view extended well beyond his role in advancing scientific knowledge. By the early 1820s, with the presidential contest of 1824 taking shape, he could point to accomplishments such as his reorganization and modernization of the War Department and the army, his implementation of a democratic, mathematical curriculum at West Point that took advantage of the latest in military science from France, his ongoing construction of modern fortifications at vital strategic points around the country, and the launch of major exploratory and scientific expeditions into the vast western expanse of North America. He could point to millions of acres of Indian lands opened to white settlers through, in his view, peaceable and fair treaty negotiations, and he could point to the hundreds of Indian students who were learning the arts of civilization at missionary schools funded by his department.

That vague and weighty word, *civilization*, summed up for Calhoun the ultimate end of his efforts, combining his belief in democratic government, rational religion, and enlightened science. In North America the United States was the embodiment of civilization writ large as well as a specific type, American civilization, that was unique and unprecedented in human history. American civilization had a destiny and a direction—it went forward, into the future, and westward, across the continent. Calhoun took it for granted that American civilization included slavery, just as it included Indian removal. Today, of course, we can see that the nation taking shape after 1815 was not only a new civilization but a new sort of empire as well, one that wielded its power always with an eye to its own interests, which were the interests of white Americans. Every empire in history has believed in its own righteousness and benevolence, and dissenters, like the Indians, who have resisted the supposed inevitability of progress have always been labeled as backward and recalcitrant. That Calhoun did not see this is unsurprising, although it does not absolve him of blame. It was as inconvenient for him to see himself that way in his day as it is for us to consider ourselves in a similar light today.

During his very first year in the War Department, Calhoun commissioned an expedition to establish a fort at the mouth of the Missouri River, in what is today Montana. In his orders to Thomas Smith in St. Louis, Calhoun was frank that one purpose of the fort was to "extend and protect our trade with the Indians," but he also saw a higher, more symbolic purpose in the expedition. Acknowledging that "the remoteness of the post will, in some respects, render it unpleasant to those who may be detailed for the service," Calhoun wrote, "the glory of planting the American flag at a point so distant on so noble a river, will not be unfelt. The world will behold in it, the mighty growth of our republic, which but a few years since, was limited by the Allegany; but now is ready to push its civilization and laws to the western confines of the continent."[44] As 1824 approached, there were few figures on the national stage who could legitimately claim to have had a larger hand in the progress and prospects of American civilization than Secretary of War Calhoun.

TEN

"I Am with the People, and Shall Remain So"

ONE SWELTERING JUNE DAY IN 1823, John Quincy Adams arrived at the Washington studio of the portrait artist Charles Bird King and found Calhoun already there, sitting for one of the multiple sessions that it took to complete a portrait from life. King's portrait of Calhoun shows a face with the strong, angular features that marked other Irish Presbyterians, like Andrew Jackson, below curly, jet-black hair. Calhoun's large, deep-set, dark eyes project an energy, intelligence, and intensity that observers commented on throughout his life. "*I believe they give out light in the dark,*" the English writer Sarah Mytton Maury once marveled. He looks surprisingly youthful for his forty-one years.[1]

By the time he sat for King that summer Calhoun was one of several candidates pursuing the presidency, although some thought he was still too young and too ambitious. One evening as Calhoun and William Seaton, publisher of the *National Intelligencer*, walked along the banks of the Potomac, Seaton asked Calhoun what he would do if he won the presidency since after one or two terms he would find himself still in the prime of life with nothing left to accomplish. Seaton recalled that Calhoun replied without pausing, "I would retire and write my memoirs."[2] A song reprinted in a Connecticut newspaper listed objections to each of the potential presidential candidates in the 1824 election and noted only that Calhoun was "too young." The song's author preferred Secretary of the Treasury William Crawford.[3] Calhoun characteristically interpreted even this objection as an advantage, as he wrote his brother-in-law, "as there is no other objection to me but age...my chance will finally be the best."[4]

In the end, three members of Monroe's cabinet—Calhoun, Adams, and Crawford—ran for president, while Henry Clay and, by 1823, Andrew Jackson both pursued their ambitions from Congress. All the candidates called themselves Republicans, but they each represented a somewhat different combination of coalitions that existed under that fragile appellative umbrella in the early 1820s. One dimension of the race centered on the difference between nationalist Republicans like Calhoun and Adams, who supported the Monroe administration; nationalist Republicans like Clay, who did not; and Old Republicans like Crawford, who advocated for state rights, strict construction of the Constitution, and a stranglehold on federal spending. In the wake of the Missouri crisis, another dimension of the race concerned slavery. John Quincy Adams was the only candidate with clear antislavery sentiments. The other four candidates were slaveholders, although as a supporter of the American Colonization Society and the author of the Missouri Compromise, Henry Clay held some appeal for antislavery moderates.[5]

Crawford was the presumptive favorite. He had stepped aside for Monroe in 1816, and in addition to his seniority in the political establishment the big Georgian had emerged as the leader of the Old Republicans, often called the Radicals. The Panic of 1819, which many Americans blamed on the Bank of the United States, and the Missouri crisis, which left many slaveholders wary of federal power and sympathetic to state rights, put further wind in Crawford's sails. Crawford could not only claim the mantle of Jefferson and the Revolution of 1800, as most of the candidates did, he could also claim the quiet support of the aged Jefferson himself. Meanwhile, Calhoun's record as an advocate of internal improvements, a strong military establishment, and his support for the tariff of 1816 made him popular in many northern states, especially New York and Pennsylvania. He also appealed to southerners who favored the Monroe administration but could not overcome their suspicion of Adams's antislavery opinions.[6]

Calhoun's campaign for the presidency started out on a shaky note when the South Carolina legislature jumped the gun and nominated William Lowndes for president instead of Calhoun in December 1821, nearly three full years before the election. As one later observer put it, "It is hard now to believe that there was a time when South Carolina preferred *any one* to Calhoun," but Lowndes had won widespread support for his successful opposition to Baldwin's tariff the year before. Calhoun may also have detected the old lowcountry condescension toward the upcountry in the choice since, as future South Carolina governor James Hamilton Jr. reported to Lowndes, support for his nomination came mainly from Charleston. The "very rash and foolish movement in relation to Mr. Lowndes," as Calhoun called it to Virgil Maxcy on New Year's Eve 1821, had the potential to embarrass Calhoun by showing that he was more popular in states like Pennsylvania than in South Carolina. For the time being, the two friends decided to let matters run their course, but Lowndes's untimely death a few months later left the way clear for South Carolina to eventually unite behind Calhoun.[7]

From the beginning Calhoun and Crawford were mortal enemies. In March 1821, just as Monroe began his second term, Congress voted to impose draconian and damaging cuts to the military establishment Calhoun had worked so hard to build up for the past several years. The ostensible reason for the cuts was the ongoing financial damage done by the Panic of 1819, but to Calhoun, the cuts looked like an effort on Crawford's part to undermine his accomplishments. As Calhoun wrote in a letter to Andrew Jackson, "What part he may have taken, I cannot say, but it is certain that his personal friends have many of them been very active to embarrass." The cuts forced Calhoun to stop construction on several fortification projects around the country and to make painful and politically dangerous cuts to the army's personnel. Many of these decisions would reverberate for years to come, especially the dismissal of Andrew Jackson himself, who subsequently became for a short time the governor of Florida before being appointed to the Senate to represent Tennessee.[8] Luckily for Calhoun, Jackson also blamed Crawford for his predicament. The cuts in turn provoked a congressional investigation that in April 1822 vindicated Calhoun but left him fuming because it was leaked that the committee's vote to absolve him of any wrongdoing had been close. He raged to John Quincy Adams about Crawford's treachery, exclaiming that "there had never been a man in our History, who had risen so high, of so corrupt a character, or upon so slender a basis of service."[9] Crawford's allies in Congress also revived an accusation that Calhoun had profited from his office by inappropriately awarding a War Department contract to a man named Elijah Mix early in his tenure as secretary. Calhoun hurriedly composed a lengthy response to the accusation accompanied by documentary evidence, and his protégé George McDuffie demanded that Calhoun's defense be read aloud to the House, after which the House voted 131 to 20 to pay the contract, vindicating Calhoun and embarrassing the Radicals. "My friends have had a signal triumph," he crowed to Virgil Maxcy on May 6.[10]

The hatred between Crawford and Calhoun nearly cost Calhoun's young ally George McDuffie his life later that year in South Carolina when he fought two widely publicized duels with Colonel William Cumming, a veteran of the War of 1812 and prominent Crawford supporter. The feuds concerned a series of newspaper articles McDuffie had written attacking the state rights party in South Carolina and Georgia, which was supporting Crawford for president. "It originated in the rivalry between Crawford and Calhoun," a disgusted John Quincy Adams wrote of the controversy, which filled the newspapers that summer and fall. Calhoun, he noted, "does not talk of it with pleasure."[11] McDuffie and Cumming met on the Savannah River near Augusta in mid-June, and the first reports that reached Washington indicated that McDuffie had been killed, leading a dejected Calhoun to write to Micah Sterling of New York, "our friend is no more." In a sorrowful mood, Calhoun wrote, "He has not left behind him one of his age of equal promise. It has overwhelmed us all with grief." But the next morning brought news that McDuffie was not dead, although he had been seriously wounded by a bullet that was lodged near his spine, an injury that would plague him for the rest of his life. Elated, Calhoun dashed off a short note to Sterling: "Never did my feelings undergo so great a change in so short a time." McDuffie and Cumming would meet again in December, when McDuffie would again be wounded, this time in the arm.[12]

THROUGHOUT THE CAMPAIGN CALHOUN believed that his principled, rational, and republican record would appeal to Americans of all stripes and sections. He had neither the sectional associations of Adams, nor the radical proclivities of Crawford. "I stand on the great Republican cause, free alike from the charge of Federalism or Radicalism," he wrote Virgil Maxcy.[13] "I can conciliate all. I belong to no section or particular interest," he wrote to General Jacob Brown in August 1823 as the contest heated up. "It has been my pride to be above all sectional or party feelings and to be devoted to all of the great interests of the Country."[14] A biographical sketch of Calhoun published in New York in 1823 bore the title "Measures, Not Men," summing up his appeal as a pragmatic politician and able administrator.[15]

Calhoun was evidently popular even with those who couldn't vote for him. A New York newspaper editor in early 1824 remarking on Andrew Jackson's popularity among women noted with surprise that "he has more ladies electioneering for him than the young Hercules of the War Department."[16] If those women could have voted, perhaps Calhoun's youth might not have been such a liability. It certainly did not deter the faculty of Yale College, who seemed to tip their hand by awarding Calhoun an honorary doctorate in law in 1822.[17]

Calhoun hoped virtue and pragmatism would win the day, but people still needed to be reminded. He threw himself into the race in the most energetic way a candidate could at a time before active and open campaigning became the norm, essentially acting as his own campaign manager. He corresponded extensively with allies in Illinois (Senator Ninian Edwards), Ohio (Judge John McLean), Michigan Territory (Lewis Cass), Maryland (Virgil Maxcy), Pennsylvania (Samuel D. Ingham), and New York (Samuel L. Gouverneur and Henry Wheaton). "The way ought to be prepared by conversation and correspondence, where it can safely be done, previously to any publick demonstration," Calhoun wrote to Cass in late 1821.[18] He constantly assessed his chances, always favorably in order to encourage his supporters. In March 1822, before it became clear that Andrew Jackson's candidacy would transform the race, he wrote to his brother-in-law, "My own opinion is that the contest will be between Adams, Crawford, and myself."[19] After years during which his personal correspondence had dwindled under the weight of his responsibilities in the War Department, Calhoun's numerous letters to political allies giving advice and passing on encouraging news from other states offer striking evidence of a fierce ambition he strained not to acknowledge. "In a single mess, I was informed yesterday…that there was nine of the Penn. members in my favor," he crowed to Maxcy at the end of 1821.[20] He always portrayed his own potential election as incidental to "the cause," by which he meant the Monroe administration's policy goals as well as the principles of Jeffersonian Republicanism.

Newspapers were the main way to shape public opinion, at least the opinion of those who mattered, and in 1822 Calhoun started his own paper, the *Washington Republican*, with his old War Department employee Thomas McKenney at the helm.[21] He also paid close attention to Crawford publications like Thomas Ritchie's *Richmond Enquirer*, frequently advising his allies how to respond to attacks on him in print. In 1823 Ritchie's paper published a lengthy five-part denunciation of Calhoun alleging that he had no talents worthy of the presidency, that he had entered into a secret agreement with John Quincy Adams to foil Crawford, and that he played fast and loose with the Constitution. "Above all, give me one not like Calhoun, with whom the sacred constitution of his country will mean anything or nothing…but give me one who knows and feels that instrument was intended to limit power," the *Enquirer* shrilled, referring to Calhoun's support for the tariff of 1816, the Bank of the United States, and internal improvements. The Virginia volley was answered by a five-part reply in the New York *Statesman*, a Calhoun paper, in which the author detailed Calhoun's "faithful and unslumbering" protection of the Constitution during the War of 1812 and rebutted the argument that federal sponsorship of internal improvements was unconstitutional. "He is truly of the Jefferson school," the *Statesman* thundered. If he was elected, the author declared, "we should see Mr. Calhoun adopt a bold, comprehensive, vigorous, and enlightened system of his own, equal to the expectations of the Union."[22] This, of course, was exactly what Crawford supporters and state rights advocates feared. Later that year, Ritchie's paper again warned of Calhoun's grasping ambition for the presidency. "The sanguine man grows more aspiring with success," Ritchie himself wrote, arguing that Calhoun was too inexperienced for the highest office. "He is for clutching the fruit, while it is yet in the blossom."[23]

It was likely to counter those attacks from state rights supporters and the ascendant Old Republicans that in April 1823 Calhoun traveled to John Taylor's Caroline County, Virginia, home to seek Taylor's support in his presidential run against William Crawford.[24] To some of Calhoun's friends, it must have seemed a strange choice. Thirty years older than Calhoun, Taylor was a staunch Old Republican, a defender of state rights who believed that the only true source of wealth came from the soil. Taylor had been sounding the warning bell about the consolidation of federal power his entire career, but his tone had grown more urgent since 1819, when the Supreme Court ruled in *McCulloch v. Maryland* that Maryland did not have the right to tax the United States Bank branch within its borders, a precedent that Taylor and many others viewed as a highly dangerous contradiction of state sovereignty. In

1822 Taylor published a lengthy pamphlet titled *Tyranny Unmasked*, in which he attacked manufacturers' demands for a higher tariff as an unconstitutional attempt to steal wealth from the agrarian South through a subtle, supposedly neutral mechanism. Taylor's pamphlet was partly a response to Daniel Raymond, a Connecticut graduate of Tapping Reeve's law school, who published his influential *Thoughts on Political Economy* in 1820, arguing that the interests of the nation as a whole outweighed any sectional or individual interests and that a protective tariff was the surest route to shared prosperity. "A nation is a UNITY," Raymond wrote, "and possesses all the properties of unity…a unity of rights, a unity of interests, and a unity of possessions."[25]

Taylor, in contrast, believed that the United States, which he called a "confederation of republicks," had only survived so far because of its unique separation of powers, a principle that Taylor argued applied not only to the legislative, executive, and judicial branches of the federal government but also between the federal government and the states. As Taylor pointed out, the constitution granted every branch a veto in order to preserve its powers. Why, he asked, would the framers have given this protection to every branch and level of the government *except* the states? He asked readers to imagine an article in the Constitution reading, "Congress shall have power, with the assent of the Supreme Court, to exercise, or to usurp, and to prohibit the states from exercising, any or all of the powers reserved to the states…" But this was exactly what was happening, Taylor believed, and in addition to the *McCulloch* decision he pointed to another 1821 Supreme Court decision in which the court had upheld the operation of a national lottery against a Virginia law. And, of course, he pointed to the tariff. The solution, Taylor wrote, was for states to exercise their "negative" or "veto" against federal power, although he did not clearly explain how this would work in practice.[26]

Tyranny Unmasked was advertised extensively in Washington newspapers throughout 1822 and 1823.[27] Even if he had not read it, Calhoun must have been aware of it before his visit to Taylor. In any case, during

Calhoun's visit the presidential aspirant and the old senator discussed Taylor's arguments extensively, establishing where they agreed and disagreed. "I went over the ground very fully with Col. Taylor," Calhoun wrote to Virgil Maxcy in November.[28] Calhoun was clear they still disagreed on much, but it is easy to imagine that he may have been attracted to Taylor's elegantly articulated views because Taylor fully acknowledged that the federal government also had important powers that it must exercise and protect against the states, which were just as likely to abuse power. "Until men are cleansed of ambition," Taylor wrote, "[abuse of power] is to be expected in both the federal and State departments."[29] Taylor's acknowledgment of the federal government's legitimacy and important role offered a version of state rights doctrine that was less extreme than, for instance, John Randolph's, and would not represent a complete disavowal of Calhoun's record, making Taylor an ideal ally if Calhoun was going to try and break Crawford's support among state rights advocates.

Calhoun succeeded. A few days after the visit he wrote Virgil Maxcy, "I have no more decided friend than Col. Taylor…His differing with me on constitutional points will only add to the weight of his opinion."[30] Indeed, Taylor finally supported Calhoun over Crawford for the presidency, a sure sign that Calhoun at least convinced Taylor he was not an advocate of a consolidation of power in the federal government. Years later, in 1828, with a specificity that seemed to indicate a particular event or moment, Calhoun wrote that he had distrusted the "American System"—the combination of protective tariffs and internal improvements advocated by Henry Clay—for "the last five years," or since 1823. In 1838, describing how his appreciation of "the old Virginia school of politics" had grown, Calhoun cited Jefferson and John Taylor as two of its primary representatives whom he most admired. It would seem that, at least in hindsight, his visit to Taylor was a definitive moment.[31] But whatever change had begun to take place that year in his thinking, Calhoun for the moment kept to himself.

After his visit with Taylor one can detect a subtle change as Calhoun began to proclaim that while he was not opposed to the judicious use of federal power, neither was he an enemy of state rights. In August Calhoun vented his frustration privately to his New York ally Joseph Swift, writing that "great injustice is done me in Virginia...by an unaccountable misconception of my political principles." He claimed, somewhat brazenly, "that there is not on record a single expression of mine in relation to the construction of the Constitution, which would offend the most rigid defender of State rights."[32] Even if it was true that Calhoun had never directly attacked state rights, his protégé George McDuffie had, and Calhoun certainly knew that his own public reputation was that of an energetic and enlightened apostle of national power. Yet in response to Virginia congressman Robert Garnett's inquiries that summer about his views on state rights, he wrote in greater detail:

> If there is one portion of the Constitution, which I most admire, it is the distribution of power between the State and General government[s]. It is the only portion, that is novel and peculiar. The rest has been more, or less copied; this is our invention and is altogether our own; and I consider it to be the greatest improvement which has been made in the science of government, after the division of power into Legislative, Executive, and judicial. Without it, free States in the present condition of the world could not exist, or must have existed without safety, or respectability. If limited to a small territory, they must be crushed by the great monarchical powers...but if extended over a great surface, the concentration of power and patronage necessary for government would speedily end in tereny. It is only by this admirable distribution, that a great extent of territory, with a proportional population and power, can be reconciled with freedom.

In other words, by its novel division of powers between state and general governments the United States Constitution had proven wrong

Montesquieu's famous dictum that in order to preserve liberty republics must be small in size. Calhoun's phrasing even paralleled Montesquieu's famous passage on the topic, which Calhoun may have encountered quoted in *Federalist* no. 9. Calhoun was clear that he valued the "actual distribution of the two powers, which is made by our Constitution. Were it in my power, I would make no change."[33]

AS THE CONTEST MOVED into 1824, Calhoun's greatest fear was that the will of the people would be thwarted by "a dexterous use of what is called party machinery." Martin Van Buren's Albany Regency in New York was one example of this dangerous trend.[34] But Calhoun also decried the use of the congressional caucus nomination, in which congressional Republicans gathered and unofficially selected their preferred candidate for president, all but assuring his election, as fundamentally undemocratic. Calhoun's opposition to the caucus was no doubt partly motivated by the fact that in early 1824 it was William Crawford's last hope. In a twist of fate that may well have changed the course of history, the Georgian had suffered what was probably a stroke in September 1823 and could barely keep up the appearance of a campaign, leaving his supporters to try and manufacture a caucus nomination in his absence. Instead of the caucus, Calhoun favored leaving the decision to popular election of presidential electors by district within states, a method that was already typical in western states. In private, he even went so far as to propose that "the virtue and intelligence of the people are sufficient to a wise choice without the intervention of electors, caucuses, or the aid in any shape of political managers."[35] Calhoun had his finger on the public pulse. The growing popular consensus against the caucus as antidemocratic doomed Crawford by making many congressmen unwilling to participate. "It will at best be a caucus of Mr. Crawford's friends," Calhoun wrote confidently at the end of January 1824, "and will do him no good." He was right. When the caucus was held the next month only sixty-six members of Congress showed up to nominate Crawford.[36]

Throughout the election Calhoun was keenly aware that he had to win Pennsylvania in order to win the presidency, especially since the support of the other largest state, New York, was uncertain. Just as had been the case with the tariff votes, these two states together wielded enormous influence. "It is certain that the election is with Pennsylvania & New York," he wrote Virgil Maxcy in 1823. Hoping to sway New York's nomination, he wrote to friends in Pennsylvania urging them to nominate him as early as March 1823, but the effort stalled as support for Andrew Jackson's candidacy surged.[37]

In February 1824 the Jacksonian wave that had been building throughout the country since 1822 finally caught up to Calhoun. On the twenty-seventh, Calhoun wrote in shock to Virgil Maxcy that he had suffered an insurmountable defeat in Pennsylvania, which had unexpectedly nominated Jackson for the presidency. Sensing that Calhoun's cause was waning and Jackson's waxing, his main Pennsylvania supporter, George Dallas, had switched his allegiance to Jackson at the last minute, dooming Calhoun's chances. Calling the nomination of Jackson "as unexpected to me as it could have been to any of my friends," Calhoun took some small comfort that at least the nomination contributed to "the great point of defeating the Radicals." But, he sighed, "taking the U.S. together I never had a fairer prospect than on the day we lost the State."[38]

It was one sign that Calhoun's judgment of his chances was not far off the mark that he soon became the favorite choice of Jackson supporters everywhere for the vice presidency, which was elected separately from the presidency. In Pennsylvania he had been nominated alongside Jackson for the second slot, and resolutions passed in North Carolina and Tammany Hall in New York soon made the same recommendation.[39] But for someone as ambitious as Calhoun this did not ease the sting of defeat. In April he reflected philosophically to Lewis

Cass that defeating Crawford was what really mattered. "Personally, I have but little ambition," he avowed.[40] The immense energy that Calhoun had put into the contest belied this ritualistic republican declaration, and acquaintances noted how deeply Calhoun felt the loss. Washington socialite Margaret Bayard Smith noted that "Mr. Calhoun has removed to his house on the hills behind George Town and will live I suspect quite retired the rest of the session. He does not look well and feels very deeply the disappointment of his ambition."[41]

THE "HOUSE ON THE hills behind George Town" was a princely place to nurse disappointed dreams. In 1822 Calhoun's mother-in-law had purchased the magnificent Oakly estate in Georgetown for $10,000, a sum that Calhoun worried to John Ewing Colhoun was too much "as she has no need of it."[42] But old Floride Colhoun had her own plans, and by the next summer the Calhouns were living at Oakly, later known as Dumbarton Oaks and made famous by the 1944 conference there that gave birth to the United Nations. In addition to an imposing Federal-style brick facade, which matched Calhoun's rising national stature, and spacious parlors for entertaining, the thirty-acre estate gave the Calhoun children some much-needed legroom. "We are on the heights of Georgetown, and find the residence delightful," Calhoun wrote James Edward Colhoun in August 1823, reporting with pleasure the effects of the "fine air and abundant exercise" on the children.[43] By 1823 Andrew, the oldest, was eleven and "a stout, hearty boy," while Anna Maria—"slender and sprightly"—was six. Patrick, born in 1821 following the death of little Elizabeth, was only two, with "fair complexion" and blue eyes.[44] And new Calhouns continued to appear almost every year in Washington. John Caldwell was born in May 1823, Martha Cornelia in April 1824, and James Edward in 1826. The last of the Calhouns' children, William Lowndes, would be born in 1829.

Calhoun reported each birth to relatives back in South Carolina with pride, but we have no letters from Floride, who was pregnant and caring for small children, although no doubt with help from her mother and slaves, nearly the whole time the Calhouns lived in Washington. Indeed, it is easy to imagine that her mother purchased Oakly to make life somewhat easier on Floride, who in addition to nearly constant pregnancies had lost a child in a traumatic and public way two years before. Despite all this, Floride fulfilled her duties as a member of Washington society and the wife of an ambitious man, throwing the balls that were expected of Monroe's cabinet members and their wives, who set the social calendar in place of the socially reticent Monroes. The elegant and learned Bostonian George Ticknor, professor of languages and literature at Harvard, proclaimed the Calhouns' Washington balls "the pleasantest of the ministerial dinners, because he invited ladies," and recalled Calhoun on those occasions as "the most agreeable person in conversation at Washington," while recalling Floride condescendingly as "a very good little woman, who sometimes gives a pleasant ball."[45] It is one of the minor injustices of history, and a source of frustration for a historian trying to get at Floride's experience, that perhaps the best record of her life in Washington during this period was left by the acrid pen of Charles Wilkes. Wilkes would later win infamy as the tyrannical captain of the United States Exploring Expedition from 1838 to 1842 and, later than that, for nearly bringing England into the Civil War on the Confederacy's side in the *Trent* affair. He met Floride at a Washington ball in 1825 and wrote that she was "queer," with a "small face and head, overhung large ears," and "black eyes and freckles." He described her habit of tilting back in her chair and feeling her chin "as if she was feeling her beard," and Wilkes was annoyed that the mother of several young children talked about Anna Maria losing her baby teeth.[46] Floride deserved better.

Calhoun was a more attentive father than husband, at least if one judges from his surviving correspondence, and having his children around him in Washington—Anna Maria and Patrick were "at my elbows" as he wrote their uncle James Edward on one occasion—was one of his greatest pleasures.[47] Anna later recalled how during the years the family lived in Washington she and the other Calhoun children would listen for their father to arrive home from the War Department and then "rush to meet him & be taken in his arms for our usual *game of romps*."[48] Calhoun never mentioned the romps in his letters, but he did reflect on fatherhood. "To be placed in the relation of father," he wrote to his brother-in-law John Ewing Colhoun on the birth of Colhoun's first child, "is among the greatest changes which we experience through life." In a reflective mood, he wrote, "I find my children the great solace of life, and midst all of the anxiety which must occasionally be felt, there is still that which makes you feel how much more happy you are with them and how disconsolate you would be without them."[49] As his children grew older, and especially with the prospect of four more years in Washington looming before him, Calhoun felt a constant tension between the childhood he wanted for them, back home in the South Carolina upcountry among a loving web of Calhouns, Nobles, and Pickens, and the childhood they were living in Washington. "I feel it quite a misfortune that we cannot bring them up in Carolina among their relations," he wrote to John Ewing. "I, for my part, love the tie of relationship, and believe that those who are under its influence are usually more disposed to a virtuous life."[50]

EVEN IF CALHOUN WANTED to retire to his house in Georgetown and lick his wounds after the Pennsylvania debacle, his role in the administration and his sense of duty to Monroe kept him firmly in the public eye. He continued to host a steady stream of Indian delegations from every part of the country, from the mostly "civilized" Georgia Cherokee, who departed in June after making it clear they would not willingly give up any more of their lands, to a delegation of six western tribes later that summer whose members John Quincy Adams described as covered in red paint during their audience with Monroe and whom Adams thought "most savage." Calhoun's mother-in-law and two of Calhoun's children, probably Andrew and Anna Maria, were present for at least one of these formal audiences.[51] (It was at one such meeting a few years earlier that Calhoun managed to make a lifelong enemy of a Tennessee Indian agent named Sam Houston, one of Andrew Jackson's favorite protégés, who appeared with a Cherokee delegation dressed in native attire himself. Calhoun waited until the delegation departed before severely upbraiding Houston, mortally offending the touchy future Texan in the process.)[52]

In mid-August Calhoun left his family to take a three-week trip into the Allegheny Mountains on horseback and foot with army engineers to survey possible routes for a Chesapeake and Ohio canal that would connect the Chesapeake Bay to the Ohio River. In April Congress had passed a bill that promised to bring Calhoun's dreams of internal improvement to fruition, authorizing the president to survey routes and procure estimates for roads and canals of "national importance."[53] The *Daily National Intelligencer* in Washington published regular reports from the trip, including the moment when Calhoun and his engineers tested the water flow of Deep Creek in the mountains of Allegany County, Maryland, and determined that it could fill a sixty-foot lock in thirteen minutes. The editor reported that Calhoun considered the question of the canal's practicality "settled," and, ever-mindful of how to channel public enthusiasm toward the public interest, Calhoun suggested the most difficult section of the canal through the mountains should be built first in order to convince public opinion that it could be done.[54] A few months later, he wrote Virgil Maxcy that he believed the project was so great "that it can only be effected by the nation. It is too great to be executed by a Company, or by the States, through which it will pass." Even if the project were less "stupendous," Calhoun wrote, the "necessity of the concurrence of three states, each of which has a powerful opposing interest, would, I fear, long postpone the period of execution."[55] Part of the canal, the less difficult section along the Potomac River to Cumberland, Maryland, would be completed in the coming years, but the most difficult part, from Cumberland through the Alleghenies to Pittsburgh, would never be built.

That fall as Americans eagerly anticipated the results of the election, Calhoun played host to a living embodiment of the American Revolution, an aged but still hale Marquis de Lafayette, who was touring the United States at Monroe's invitation in anticipation of the nation's fiftieth anniversary. The French "hero of the two worlds" arrived in New York to a rapturous welcome and made his way down the coast, reaching Washington in October. Since Monroe's involvement might be seen as a political stunt, it fell to Calhoun to represent the administration as Lafayette wound his way through Virginia to Yorktown for the anniversary of Cornwallis's surrender on October 19. "Yesterday passed off remarkably well," Calhoun wrote Monroe the next day, remarking with admiration on Lafayette's graceful and appropriate conduct of himself and on the vivid displays of national feeling that accompanied his appearances. Calhoun accompanied the old revolutionary hero to Norfolk, Williamsburg, and finally to Richmond, where he was particularly stirred by an emotional reunion between Lafayette and a group of veterans of the revolution. The meeting, he later wrote Monroe, was "really affecting." Lafayette continued to Monticello, where he would see Jefferson, while Calhoun, not wanting to be seen as taking advantage of the moment for political gain, returned by stage to Washington and his family.[56]

BY THE END OF the year, as voting results came in, it was clear that although Andrew Jackson had a plurality of both popular and electoral votes, no candidate would be able to reach the required majority in the Electoral College. Under the Twelfth Amendment this situation threw the election into the House of Representatives, where every state delegation would cast a single vote. It was equally clear by the end of the year that Calhoun had been elected vice president in a landslide, with support from both Jackson and Adams voters. In the final count Calhoun received 182 electoral votes, while the next nearest candidate, former senator Nathan Sanford of New York, received 30.[57] Just as surely as it showed Andrew Jackson's widespread popularity, the voting showed that Calhoun had not been wrong about his ability to appeal to a national electorate without the intervening mechanism of a caucus nomination. And Calhoun was already thinking ahead. "By the true theory of our Constitution, it ought naturally to stand in succession," he wrote Lewis Cass of the vice presidency, especially when chosen by the people and not "made by a caucus."[58]

By November Calhoun was exultant at the defeat of the Radicals. "Our Country has a right to rejoice," he wrote Joseph Swift. "The over-throw of the most dangerous faction, which has ever appeared in our country, is complete."[59] To another correspondent he wrote that now the race was between Adams and Jackson. "Let either succeed," he wrote, "the victory will be equally decisive."[60]

Yet on the whole Calhoun clearly preferred Jackson. Throughout the election, before and after Jackson's strength as a candidate became clear, the military hero and the secretary of war had exchanged a series of letters brimming with mutual declarations of political and personal admiration. "I find few with whom, I accord so fully in relation to po-litical subjects, as yourself," Calhoun wrote on one occasion. In the Hero of New Orleans Calhoun saw not only similar political principles—a shared commitment to Republicanism and a strong mil-itary establishment—but also an approach to life and politics that he believed mirrored his own. "I have a thorough conviction, that the no-ble maxim of yours, to do right and fear not is the very basis, not only of Republicanism," Calhoun wrote, "but of all political virtue; and, that he who acts on it, must in the end prevail."[61]

Principles might win in the end, but in the shorter term Henry Clay's political skills proved more decisive. Having come in fourth in the Electoral College and thus ineligible for the House vote, by early January 1825 Clay had decided to throw his support behind Adams, partly because he feared Jackson's populist style of politics and doubted the old general's adherence to the central tenets of the national Repub-licans, and partly because it would be much easier for him as a westerner to succeed Adams as president. After a meeting with Adams on the night of January 9, Clay left believing that in return for his support he could choose his cabinet post in an Adams presidency, and he went to work. In a momentous vote on February 9, the House elected Adams the next president of the United States on the first ballot, throwing Jackson's supporters into a fury at the blatant, though perfectly constitutional, disregard for the wishes of the people.[62] Calhoun, who had certainly preferred Jackson but had seen Adams as an acceptable choice if duly elected, was horrified at what appeared to him to be a new threat to democracy from a wholly unexpected direction. In a terse letter to Virgil Maxcy days after the crucial vote, he wrote, "Things have taken a strange turn…Form no opinion from what you see on the surface."[63] When Adams announced his intention to appoint Clay secretary of state, Jackson's supporters screamed their belief that a "corrupt bargain" had given Adams the presidency. There was, strictly speaking, nothing illegal or unconstitutional about such a bargain, and political horse-trading would become increasingly common in the years ahead. In addition, Clay was the most logical choice for a cabinet post among the presidential candidates, the only one who combined nationalist policies with even a hint of doubt about slavery. Nevertheless, in 1825 the alleged agreement between Adams and Clay smacked of exactly the kind of corruption that Americans tutored in republican principles had been taught to fear.[64]

Adams, for his part, had known that Calhoun supported Jackson but characteristically saw malice where there was only preference. He now saw Calhoun and the "Calhounites" as the main threat to his administration. Two days after the fateful House vote, Calhoun warned Adams through an intermediary that Clay's appointment would provoke a disastrous reaction and recommended his ally Joel Poinsett instead. Adams took the suggestion as a threat. In the days after the election, as old alliances dissolved and new ones coalesced in response to the news, Secretary of the Navy Samuel Southard and Adams commiserated at "Mr. Calhoun's present conduct and movements," and

Daniel Webster, who now represented Massachusetts in the House of Representatives, told Adams that his opinions of Calhoun had "undergone a change," which was convenient for a man seeking the favor of the new president. Within days of the fateful vote, Adams believed he already saw a "system of opposition as formed by Mr. Calhoun…to bring in General Jackson as the next President."[65]

Although he did not give enough credit to Calhoun's motives, Adams was not completely wrong. In addition to his own frustrated ambitions, Calhoun's genuine horror at the way that the will of the people had been thwarted, constitutional or not, played a large role in his opposition to what he and others began to call "the coalition" between Adams and Clay. To him, the agreement between the two men violated the unstated moral dimensions of the Constitution. The episode marked the beginning of his disillusionment with the idea that implied or assumed limits on power were sufficient to safeguard republican liberty. Years later, in 1838, he would date the descent of the republic into a "deeply diseased state" to that fateful year.[66]

On March 4, 1825, Calhoun rose and made his way to the Senate chamber, where according to custom the Senate's oldest member administered the oath of office to the new vice president. As it happened, that was the fifty-eight-year-old Andrew Jackson, and as the old hero administered the oath looking into Calhoun's eyes, both of the men must have felt a silent bond solidified between them.[67] Writing Joseph Swift six days later, Calhoun called the apparent deal between Adams and Clay "the most dangerous stab which the liberty of this country has ever received," and vowed, "I will not be on that side. I am with the people, and shall remain so."[68] And the people, he had little doubt, were with Jackson.

ELEVEN

"The Impression, That I Acted Under the Force of Destiny"

THE CALHOUNS LEFT WASHINGTON FOR South Carolina in early April, reaching Pendleton in the upcountry after a journey of nearly two weeks over bad roads and with a lame horse.[1] They would remain in South Carolina for the entire summer and fall of 1825, staying with family in Pendleton and Abbeville and at their Bath plantation. In the weeks after arriving back in South Carolina, Calhoun accepted invitations to speak at several nearby events held in his honor. At one such dinner held in Abbeville, near where he had been born, Calhoun spoke to a crowd that included relatives and old friends, laying out the elements of his political creed. "From the commencement of my public course to this day," he told the crowd, "I have under all circumstances been directed by one great leading principle, an entire confidence in the virtue and intelligence of the American people." He gave a carefully worded defense of his entire record, including his support for a bank—"the restoration of specie currency," he delicately called it—as well as for "due protection" for manufactures. He did not speak the word *tariff*. Even in front of a friendly crowd, he knew these topics would be controversial, but Calhoun believed in standing on his record—it had always worked for him—and he thanked the audience for how they had "nobly sustained all these measures," which even if it wasn't completely true was an artful display of deference to the popular will. It also showed that he did not realize how much had changed in South Carolina.[2]

The Calhouns' stay in South Carolina was the longest period of time Calhoun had spent in the state since at least 1819. He soon realized that the upcountry was no longer the upwardly mobile, progressive, enlightened, and profitable place he remembered from his last visit at the end of the recent war. The change was both economic and political. The Panic of 1819 and declining cotton prices had wreaked havoc on the entire state—whereas the pervasive cotton culture had once unified the state politically, now it meant that no part of the state was spared from the economic devastation. Further, many South Carolinians blamed the situation not on overproduction in the Southwest, in states like Mississippi and Alabama, or on their exhausted soil, or on English speculation in the cotton market, but rather on the new tariff passed by Congress in May 1824.

Calhoun had mostly been able to avoid commenting on the tariff during the election, but some of his lieutenants had not been silent. George McDuffie had fiercely attacked the measure in debate, denying that there was anything truly national about the bill and accusing John Tod of Pennsylvania, the bill's sponsor, of "distinctly arraying against each other the interests of two different sections of the Confederacy." Observers took note of McDuffie's new state rights tone, and objected to his inflammatory use of the term "Confederacy" to describe the Union. Calhoun's newspaper, the *Washington Republican*, also published attacks on the tariff, leading House speaker Henry Clay to fear that Calhoun's position on the tariff was changing. The bill that finally passed increased the minimum duties on imported cloth from twenty-five cents a yard to thirty-five cents, while also raising the duty on coarse cottons to a prohibitive 100 percent. It also raised duties on other goods to an average of about 35 percent. Every single southern senator voted against the bill with the exception of Andrew Jackson and John Eaton of Tennessee. No less an authority than Thomas Jefferson, not long for the world, told one visitor that the tariff took "a shilling off of every dollar the southern people paid."[3]

To many South Carolinians the economic and political danger posed by the tariff was part of a metastasizing threat to slavery that came at a particularly sensitive time. The census of 1820 had revealed that for the first time since the revolution white South Carolinians were outnumbered by their slaves, and no sooner had white South Carolinians absorbed this fact than Denmark Vesey's rebellion plot in Charleston vividly illustrated the danger of such a situation.[4] In the aftermath of the plot's discovery and in direct violation of international treaties ratified by Congress, the South Carolina legislature passed a law requiring that any black sailors arriving in Charleston on foreign ships be jailed and held until their ship's departure to prevent interaction with enslaved Charlestonians. They were especially afraid of sailors from the black republic of Haiti. When Supreme Court Justice William Johnson condemned the law and Secretary of State Adams politely requested that the "inconvenience" of the law be removed, the South Carolina Senate passed a defiant resolution declaring that "the duty of the state to guard against insubordination or insurrection…is paramount to all *laws*, all *treaties*, all *constitutions*."[5]

A number of other developments around the country gave South Carolinian slaveholders reason to worry. In early 1824 the Ohio legislature had passed resolutions recommending that the national government formulate a plan of gradual emancipation modeled on those that had been enacted after the revolution in many northern states. To the horror of many slaveholders, eight northern states endorsed Ohio's recommendation. Then Senator Rufus King of New York introduced a resolution recommending that the sale of public lands be used to fund the emancipation of the slaves. Thomas Ritchie of the *Richmond Enquirer* wrote in amazement of this "spirit of innovation" running rampant across the land. "We thank all these gentlemen for their kind intentions," wrote Ritchie, "but we should desire to know by what authority they pretend to interfere? Where is the clause of the Constitution, which gives the United States one atom of jurisdiction?"[6] In South Carolina, Calhoun arrived home just in time to read in the *Charleston Mercury* the resolution of the South Carolina Association, a group of lowcountry planters formed in the wake of the Vesey plot, who declared the doctrine of state sovereignty "the ark to which we must ultimately look to our safety." Calhoun soon began to realize the depth of these changes in the state.[7]

CALHOUN SPENT THE SUMMER in Pendleton and Abbeville seeing friends and family, and he spent the early fall at his Bath plantation near Willington, trying to put it back into order.[8] His financial situation was, as would be usual in the years ahead, precarious. He had lost most of the previous year's cotton crop to a fire, and the crop he found at the Bath plantation was "indifferent." With cotton prices plummeting it was not a hopeful situation, but Calhoun eagerly wrote to his old secretary Christopher Vandeventer in Washington requesting him to order four "two-horse" plows and a new kind of corn-sheller, which Calhoun had recently seen in operation. As he prepared to leave for Washington in October, Calhoun requested his mother-in-law, who would be staying behind in Pendleton, to let the house slaves help with getting in the cotton crop and to leave instructions for the overseer when she left for the lowcountry.[9]

By the time his family returned to Washington in October, Calhoun could see that his place on the political landscape back in South Carolina was as uncertain as the situation that awaited him in Washington. During the presidential election the year before, the intellectually formidable president of South Carolina College, Thomas Cooper, had published a pamphlet titled *Consolidation* in which he criticized Calhoun by name. Cooper described how Madison had vetoed Calhoun's attempt to fund internal improvements, which Cooper sarcastically called "these splendid projects of Mr. Calhoun."[10] Even more worrisome for Calhoun, the South Carolina legislature had that same year narrowly rejected a set of resolutions denouncing his nationalist policies—due only to the strenuous objections of his ally Eldred Simkins. Now in late 1825 there were rumors that the coming legislative session would see them resurrected. Weeks after Calhoun departed, his old enemy William Smith did just that, and this time the resolutions were approved by overwhelming majorities in both the House and Senate. Their success represented a dramatic public repudiation of all the policies and positions that Calhoun had defended in his upcountry speeches that summer. The ground back home had shifted, and Calhoun would have to decide how to respond.[11]

As THE CALHOUNS MOVED back into Oakly, Calhoun prepared to fulfill his only real duty as vice president—serving as president of the Senate. Calhoun had been in the Senate chamber before, of course, but as he approached the nearly complete new Capitol building, rebuilt after the War of 1812, he must have felt a new chapter about to begin. With its high, flat center dome (the modern dome was still under construction more than three decades later at Abraham Lincoln's first inauguration) and neoclassical style, the Capitol building proudly announced the American claim to be descended from the ancient republics of Greece and Rome. Some foreign visitors declared it "superior to any legislative hall in Europe." Inside, the House chamber took up the second floor on the south side, with the Senate chamber on the north. The Senate chamber was smaller, shaped in a semicircle like a Greek theater, with Ionic columns supporting a gallery on the east side. The acoustics of the room, nearly everyone agreed, were abominable.[12] Calhoun could not have known when he first sat down in his chair that December that this chamber would be his field of battle for the remainder of his life.

A young Josiah Quincy, son of the Harvard president and a future mayor of Boston, recalled Calhoun from these years as a "striking looking man…with thick hair, brushed back defiantly."[13] He soon made it clear that he intended to take his office much more seriously than his predecessors, who had been absent so often that the Senate had fallen into a tradition of relying on a president pro tempore (or pro tem) elected by the senators. Calhoun, by contrast, would be in his seat every day the Senate was in session, and he soon raised eyebrows by exercising the right of the "presiding officer" to appoint committees, an authority that previous vice presidents had not used. Adams and his supporters complained that Calhoun had stacked the Senate committees with the administration's enemies, and regardless of political party, and Calhoun's energetic exercise of his authority soon led the Senate to change its rules.[14]

When he took his seat, Calhoun did not anticipate being part of a "systematick opposition" to the Adams presidency, much less being part of a party in our modern sense of the word. As he wrote in June 1825 to Joseph Swift, he did not believe that "the kind of opposition which exists habitually in England and long existed in this country, belongs naturally to our system."[15] By his own account nearly two decades later, his opposition to the administration crystalized in response to Adams's first annual message to Congress that December, which was filled with "bold Federal and consolidation doctrines" and "wild measures of policy."[16] In truth, while Adams certainly laid out a bold and sweeping vision of the country's future in his annual message, announcing "the spirit of improvement is abroad upon the earth," he proposed little that Calhoun had not publicly supported himself as recently as that summer, and was careful to stress the continuity between Monroe's administration and his own.[17] But as Calhoun wrote to Joseph Swift, "The friends of State rights object to it as utterly ultra," and even those, like Calhoun, "who in the main, advocate a liberal system of measures," thought Adams had gone too far.[18] Further, Adams had included a harangue to Congress on their duty to vigorously exercise the powers delegated to them by the Constitution. "To refrain from exercising [these powers] for the benefit of the people themselves," Adams wrote, "...would be treachery to the most sacred of trusts." Certainly as he listened, Calhoun must have realized that South Carolina was in no mood to welcome any hovering "spirit of improvement."[19]

One truly new measure that Adams included in his address was a proposal for the United States to send commissioners to the planned Pan-American conference in Panama City, convened by Simón Bolívar, where many southerners accurately feared that the subject of slavery in the Americas would be discussed. Especially ominous was the news that representatives from the black republic of Haiti would attend. That summer in South Carolina Calhoun had read the rumors in newspapers that the Adams administration might recognize Haiti, and based on his personal knowledge of Adams's beliefs about slavery, he gave the rumors some weight. "I see the recognition of the independence Hayti begin to be spoken of in the Northern papers," he wrote to Samuel Southard, who had served as Monroe's secretary of the navy, from Pendleton in August. "It is a delicate subject, and would in the present tone of feelings to the South lead to great mischief." Tellingly, Calhoun focused not on the act of recognition itself but on the question of "what would be our social relations with a Black minister at Washington? Must he be received or excluded from dinners, our dances and our parties, and must his daughters and sons participate in the society of our daughters and sons?...Small as these considerations appear to be they involve the peace and perhaps the union of this nation." Clearly, Calhoun's sympathy for possible revolutions in Europe and actual revolutions in South America did not extend to Haiti.[20]

Adams's proposal sparked a firestorm in Congress that raged throughout the first half of 1826. The depth of the reaction was partly an effect of the increasingly bitter political environment, as Jackson supporters like New York senator Martin Van Buren and Calhoun saw an opportunity to embarrass Adams and Clay on foreign policy, but it was also a reaction to a perceived threat to slavery that seemed suspiciously of a piece with recent events. As Calhoun listened silently from his chair, his old enemy John Randolph, now a senator representing Virginia, raged for hours on end about a "Holy Alliance of Liberty" among the republics of the Americas that would lead to a race war in the South. Aiming for the incendiary heart of the matter, Randolph warned of "negroes for our task-masters, and for the husbands of our wives." Randolph described the way the antislavery cause in England had evolved from a war against the slave trade to a war against slavery itself, and he stressed that the slavery question was "not a dry rot that you can cover with a carpet…it is a cancer in your face." "It must not be tampered with by quacks," Randolph warned, "who never saw the disease or the patient, and prescribe across the Atlantic." Everyone knew that Randolph was a brilliant crank, but even close allies of Calhoun like the refined young South Carolina senator Robert Young Hayne voiced similar sentiments, if in more temperate language, assuring the Senate that if slavery was ever questioned "the whole South will be as one man."[21]

Randolph filled the Senate chamber that spring with personal and political insults to Adams and his administration, and despite his energetic use of his office in other areas Calhoun did nothing to restrain him. Understandably, Adams and his supporters found this infuriating. Finally, on March 30, 1826, Calhoun twice stopped Senator Mahlon Dickerson of New Jersey from interrupting Randolph as the Virginian spoke at length on his motion to table a resolution. Calhoun acted according to his understanding of the Senate's rules—motions to table a resolution did not allow for debate. Randolph could speak only because he was the one making the motion. All the same, Calhoun's intervention was too much for some of Adams's supporters, and two of the administration's newspapers attacked Calhoun in print for the episode, also merrily spreading the rumor—which ran counter to the narrative of cooperation between Randolph and Calhoun—that Randolph had addressed Calhoun as "Mr. President of the Senate and Would be

President of the United States, which God of his infinite mercy avert."
On April 15, Calhoun felt he had to justify his actions, announcing that
after careful study of the Senate's rules he believed that only other
senators—not the vice president—had the right to call a fellow senator
to order for words spoken in debate. But the newspaper attacks on
Calhoun continued, prompting an anonymous "Western Senator" to
defend Calhoun in the *Daily National Intelligencer* on April 24. The
next day, none other than Mahlon Dickerson himself defended Calhoun in the same paper, writing that the vice president had managed
the situation exactly according to Senate rules.[22]

Then, on May 1, the DC *National Journal* published a letter from an
anonymous correspondent calling himself "Patrick Henry," who attacked
Calhoun on grounds he could not ignore. The author accused Calhoun
of abdicating the single most important and self-evident function of a
presiding officer of a deliberative body, the preservation of order. By this,
of course, the author meant stopping Randolph's soliloquies—"the irrel-
ative rhapsodies of a once powerful mind." In language that suspiciously
echoed Adams's annual message to Congress a few months earlier, the
author wrote, "It is a distinctive beauty of the republican system, that as
the People delegate to their agents no superfluous power, every power
which they delegate, implies a duty to be discharged." Calhoun, the
anonymous author charged, had abrogated his constitutional duty. The
accusation struck directly at Calhoun's sense of himself. And the author
did not stop there, calling Calhoun "the residuary legatee of General
Jackson's pretensions to the Presidency" and mocking his April 15 speech
to the Senate as belonging in a "museum of logical curiosities." Most
inflammatory was the author's savage accusation that in his "inconstant,
experimenting, and reckless ambition," Calhoun resembled another vice
president, the notorious traitor Aaron Burr.

Calhoun and many others instantly assumed that "Patrick Henry"
was, in fact, John Quincy Adams.[23] Calhoun responded three weeks
later on May 20, a delay probably explained by the fact that his son
James Edward Calhoun, named after Floride's brother, had just been

born when Patrick Henry's first letter appeared.[24] Answering under the name "Onslow" after a long-serving speaker of the British House of Commons, Calhoun vigorously defended his actions by referring to the Senate's constitutional right to set its own rules. His was merely the power of what Vice President Thomas Jefferson had once called "umpirage," an appellate and passive, not active, authority.

The differences between Calhoun and "Patrick Henry" unfolded over the course of the next five months in a total of eleven letters—five from Patrick Henry and six from Calhoun. Amid the blizzard of logic and citation of historical precedents from both sides of the Atlantic, a deep divide emerged between the two writers over the sources and exercise of power in a constitutional republic. The exchange revealed a new emphasis in Calhoun's thinking on the old republican theme of the adversarial relationship between liberty and power. Patrick Henry held that the vice president's authority as presiding officer came from a "deeper, holier foundation" than the Senate. The appointment of the vice president as the president of the Senate in the Constitution implied the powers to carry out that role. Those powers were, in Henry's words, "inherent" in the office and carried the obligation to exercise them on behalf of "the people."

Calhoun scoffed at this interpretation as a step toward tyranny. "You perceive perfection only in the political arrangement, which… gives power to a single will," he wrote. "Napoleon Bonaparte, Oliver Cromwell, Julius Caesar, and every other successful usurper of the People's rights, have all traced their power to the gift of the People." The Constitution's delegation of power to the Senate was equally the gift of the people, Calhoun argued, and more crucially, it was part of the Constitution's separation of powers. Much better, Calhoun wrote, "that a public officer should construe his own powers strictly, so as to have them enlarged if necessary, than to assume doubtful powers, particularly when those powers are invidious in their nature, and likely to be abused." Newly returned from a dramatically changed political environment back home and facing an administration that he and many others considered illegitimate, the Patrick Henry–Onslow debate reveals Calhoun in the midst of rediscovering parts of the Jeffersonian Republican creed that he had been accused of abandoning.[25]

BY THE TIME CALHOUN wrote the last Onslow letter, he and his whole family had unexpectedly moved back to South Carolina, the result of a crisis that unfolded over the spring and early summer. After a bout of worms and thrush in the household full of small children in April, in May the whole house came down with severe cold and fever. Calhoun and Floride's attention was at first consumed with Anna Maria, who suffered a temporary but frightening deafness after a dangerously high fever. In the midst of this, five-year-old Patrick fell from a rocking chair and injured, perhaps broke, his elbow, and after "much pain" and lying on his back for four days still had to wear a sling. Pulling on a grandmother's heart strings, Calhoun wrote to his mother-in-law that when little Patrick injured his arm, "he wished for wings that he might fly to you to nurse him." "But these cases were all light compared to John's," Calhoun reported with anguish to old Floride at the end of May 1826. His three-year-old namesake "has been at the point of death." Indeed, Floride's brother James Edward, who had been staying with the Calhouns, had set off to Norfolk to board a ship for Rio de Janeiro with the impression that he had said his last goodbye to his little nephew. By the time Calhoun wrote to his grandmother, John was still ill but seemed likely to recover, from a combination of skillful care from two doctors and "kind Providence."[26]

But young John's illness lingered, and the combination of illnesses and accidents evidently convinced Calhoun and Floride that it was time for the family to move back to South Carolina. There were financial factors at work, as well. In mid-June Calhoun wrote to Floride's brother John Ewing that "the great fall in the price of our staple commodity and impossibility of reducing our expenses…have induced us to change our arrangement of fixing our residence here, instead of the

South." He thought they would be back in South Carolina by October, and asked John Ewing to send some enslaved carpenters, for whom he would pay his brother-in-law "the ordinary rate of compensation," to begin repairing Clergy Hall, a property owned by Floride's mother near Pendleton. The Calhouns planned to use Clergy Hall as a temporary residence until they could build a new house nearby. Driven by exigencies of the moment, but also guided by a long-held desire for their children to grow up in South Carolina among family, Calhoun and Floride had evidently decided that this would be a permanent move.[27]

When John's illness worsened, the family left Washington early in desperation—"one remedy only remained, and that was to travel"—on July 19, traveling slowly in a rocking carriage and stopping often. By the time they reached Salisbury, North Carolina, John had become so sick they had to stop, fearing the worst. But instead of dying, John rallied, and by the time they reached Pendleton days later he had almost fully recovered. "On the very day of our arrival, his cough ceased, and has not returned," a relieved Calhoun wrote James Edward several months later. "It looks almost like a resurrection." John's miraculous recovery confirmed Calhoun and Floride's belief that the environment in Pendleton was infinitely healthier for the children than Washington, both morally and physically.[28]

The Calhouns moved into Clergy Hall during the summer and by that fall had settled into a regular rhythm of life. The youngest three children were tutored at home by "Miss Mary Ann Bell." Andrew, the oldest, attended a school in nearby Pendleton, while nine-year-old Anna Maria lodged with Calhoun's friend Eldred Simkins's family in Edgefield, where she attended the Edgefield Female Academy. Female academies were a new development in the South and a relatively progressive phenomenon—institutions where girls often learned not only the domestic arts but also many of the same subjects studied by boys. The Edgefield Female Academy advertised spelling, grammar, and reading for young students like Anna, as well as grammar, geography, natural and moral philosophy, history, chemistry, and logic for older students.[29] Elite southern parents like the Calhouns saw these subjects as appropriate for daughters who would, they assumed, become wives and mothers, and according to one historian the girls who attended these academies received a "surprisingly thorough education." Perhaps Calhoun remembered his experiences with the young women of Sarah Pierce's Litchfield Female Academy and aspired to the same level of refinement and education for Anna. The schools also inculcated the social graces expected of young southern women, who "learned to measure their success based on their ability to please others and earn their love."[30]

Clergy Hall itself evidently exceeded the Calhouns' expectations, for by December they had decided to live there permanently, and Calhoun wrote James Edward, "I have commenced improving by adding largely to the old establishment." Built in 1803, Clergy Hall had originally been a parsonage for the nearby Hopewell-Keowee Presbyterian Church, which meant that Calhoun and his new residence had roughly the same relationship to Presbyterianism. The house was exactly the sort of structure that a sober-minded but prosperous upcountry Presbyterian congregation would build for its minister, and its dignified simplicity fit Calhoun's changing political identity better than the majestic Oakly, which Calhoun rented to his friend Christopher Vandeventer on their departure from Washington and later sold for his mother-in-law at a loss of two thousand dollars.[31] Still the Calhouns needed more space than the original structure could provide. The house would soon become Floride's personal project, and a family story soon emerged that every time Calhoun went away to Washington, Floride added a room to the house, eventually building a total of ten new rooms.[32] From then on, when he went to Washington, Calhoun would usually live at a boardinghouse as he had done when he first arrived there as a young congressman.

Calhoun also may have begun building the slave quarters that a reporter observed on the property in 1849. Built within sight of the main house on a slightly lower hill, the quarters consisted of stone dwellings, "joined together like barracks," with gardens in front of the structures. At some point after the Calhouns took up residence in Clergy Hall, the slaves from the Bath plantation must have made the trip there for the first time. It is likely that Sawney, Adam's son, who by 1826 was about thirty-one years old, made the trip along with his family. At Clergy Hall, Sawney would become "Old Sawney" and he and his wife, Tilla, would produce a rebellious brood that included his son Sawney Jr. and a daughter, Issey, who would stubbornly refuse to conform to their enslavement.[33]

Calhoun spent most of the following year in South Carolina, only traveling to Washington, alone, for the winter session of Congress. It was a marked change from his years in the War Department when he had lived almost exclusively in the capital. In Washington that winter he found that old accusations of misconduct related to the Elijah Mix contract scandal in the War Department had once again reared their head, the work of friends of the Adams-Clay Coalition, he was sure. "The whole weight of the administration has been brought to bear on me," he wrote to Micah Sterling in December with a whiff of martyrdom.[34] Calhoun took the unprecedented step of demanding a full investigation of the accusation by the House of Representatives, in effect publicly challenging his accusers to produce their evidence. After several weeks the committee vindicated Calhoun from even "the slightest suspicion," despite the fact that it was composed by his enemies. "A life of spotless political purity bore me through every difficulty," he wrote to his brother-in-law James Edward.[35]

Before leaving Washington again Calhoun cast a fateful vote, breaking a tie in the Senate in order to table a new tariff on woolens that had narrowly passed the House in early February. Although it was the first time he publicly voted against a tariff, it was probably not a hard decision. The woolens bill seemed almost intended to vindicate the accusations that many opponents of the 1824 tariff had leveled against it. While that tariff had protected more than ninety different items from foreign competition, the woolens bill protected only raw wool and coarse woolen cloths of the kind worn by most poor and middling Americans. The new bill did this by subjecting foreign woolens to a duty of nearly 200 percent, effectively eliminating any competition from abroad. Wool producers and manufacturers argued that they needed increased protection to survive, while the bill's opponents saw the bill as the clearest example yet of a small privileged class using the mechanism of the government to protect themselves at the expense of their fellow Americans. As Calhoun's friend and ally Samuel Ingham announced on the floor of the House, the bill seemed to him nothing more than "an effort among a powerful class of men...to persuade Congress to make up to them the loss of a bad season's business." The fact that the bill had so many enemies even in traditionally tariff-supporting states like Pennsylvania meant that Calhoun had little trouble deciding on his vote, and did not feel the need to explain himself.[36]

But the defeat of the woolens bill enraged its supporters and galvanized supporters of protection more generally. Calhoun was barely back in South Carolina when the defeated manufacturers and their allies in other industries began to organize a convention to be held in July in Harrisburg, Pennsylvania, to demand more protection from the government. It was a bold move, bound to be controversial. Conventions were understood as political instruments, and to many it seemed that the manufacturers were coming out into the open and declaring a war for control of the government. In a way they were, for as one of the convention's supporters explained, they were trying to sway "public opinion, which, in a government like ours, directs all things and conquers all things."[37]

It was an admission that played to southern fears, and not just about tariffs. In the summer of 1827 a lowcountry planter named Robert Turnbull began publishing articles in the *Charleston Mercury* that portrayed the current craze for tariffs and internal improvements as a threat to slavery. If Congress could use the "general welfare" clause to pass tariffs, build roads and canals, and fund the migration of free blacks back to Africa, Turnbull warned, there was no reason they could not use it to abolish slavery. In fact, during the same session as the woolens bill, the American Colonization Society had applied for a federal appropriation. Devoted to the removal of free blacks back to Africa, the ACS was the mildest of American antislavery organizations. Even some slaveholders like Henry Clay were members. But primed by events of the last five years, South Carolina's slaveholders saw in the ACS application the first move in a cunning plot to deprive them of their property outright or to reduce its value to nothing, which to them amounted to the same thing. The simple act of debating slavery at all, Turnbull warned, could undermine the value of slave property and destroy the wealth of the entire planter class. Turnbull pointed his readers to the British West Indies, where the ongoing movement for emancipation in England had done just that as the planters helplessly watched the value of their human property evaporate. "There must be no discussion," Turnbull insisted. "Discussion will cause DEATH and DESTRUCTION to our negro property." "Let us say distinctly to Congress, 'HANDS OFF,'" he wrote. "If this fails, let us separate. It is not a case for reasoning or negotiation." When they were published in pamphlet form as *The Crisis*, Turnbull's articles became the *Common Sense* of the state rights revolution, and Calhoun could not have helped but notice that Turnbull blamed him and his nationalist policies for the "secession" of South Carolina from the state rights fold. "The best men are often mistaken," Turnbull wrote of Calhoun in *The Crisis*. "Let us hope never to see the doctrines…in which he bore so conspicuous a part, again in fashion below the Potomac."[38]

At another meeting that summer in Columbia to protest the woolens bill and the Harrisburg convention, the irascible English immigrant Thomas Cooper, president of the South Carolina College and a full-throated proponent of state rights, openly announced that "we shall before long be compelled to calculate the value of our union" and warned that the situation was "fast approaching to the alternative of submission or separation."[39] Significantly, while Turnbull was more concerned with the threat to slavery and Cooper more concerned with the tariff, neither saw much constitutional middle ground. Disunion was the only alternative to submission.

CALHOUN REJECTED THE THREAT of disunion as both dangerous and unlikely, and in a letter to his northern friend Samuel Ingham he dismissed "the imprudent decleration of such men as Dr. Cooper."[40] If he saw in the tariff a threat to slavery, real or potential, he did not mention it in his correspondence, although considering the amount of ink he spilled warning southerners not to view the Missouri Compromise as a threat to slavery, his silence on the tariff in this regard is significant. But by July 1827, as he watched from amid the ongoing construction at Clergy Hall, Calhoun was increasingly convinced that something more serious than the conflict between Andrew Jackson and the Coalition was brewing. "I see a great crisis before us," he wrote to Virgil Maxcy on the day before Thomas Cooper's Columbia address, "which even the Presidential election, important as it is, does not carry us over."[41] Furthermore, Calhoun became convinced, looking around at his own precarious finances, that the 1824 tariff really did impoverish southerners. For the first time, he openly embraced the economic diagnosis, if not the remedy, of tariff opponents like Cooper. "I hold it certain, that at present, we are the only real contributors to the national Treasury," he wrote to Littleton Waller Tazewell, who had replaced John Taylor as a senator from Virginia when Taylor died in 1824. "*We alone pay without indemnity.*" And at a public dinner in Pendleton two days later a new note of pessimism appeared in the toast Calhoun offered to "the Constitution of the United States, intended for the protection and happiness of the whole, may it never be perverted into an instrument of monopoly and oppression." In private, he admitted to Tazewell, "the more I reflect, the more I despond."[42]

Calhoun's diagnosis of the problem in 1827 quickly moved from economics to politics. As he wrote to Tazewell in August, "To the reflecting mind, [the tariff issue] clearly indicates the weak part of our system…The freedom of debate, the freedom of the press, the division of power into three branches…afford, in the main, efficient security to the *constituents against the rulers*, but in an extensive country with diversified and open interests, another and not less important remedy is required, *the protection of one portion of the people against another."* The danger manifesting itself in Harrisburg that summer was that a majority or a powerful minority would use this weakness to annex to itself the profits of the country and transform those profits into political patronage, securing its political dominance and creating an unholy feedback loop of ever-increasing tyranny. "Now that the disease is manifest," Calhoun wrote, "every virtuous friend of the country ought seriously to direct his attention to discover what is the effectual remedy."[43]

It was a conclusion that would have monumental effects on American history, in part because of the ironclad certainty with which Calhoun held his conclusions once he reached them. His diagnosis drew on traditional fears of factionalism that had preoccupied framers of the Constitution like James Madison, who famously argued in *Federalist* no. 10 that the very size of the new republic would decrease the chance that any one faction would be able to co-opt its government. Madison had thought of factions as occurring mostly at the state level, like Van Buren's so-called Bucktails in New York, and assumed that vast distances and the difficulties of travel and communication would mitigate the passions and strength of factions, making them too feeble to operate on a distant national government where they would in any case be only one among many. But the world had changed. By the 1820s the steamboat, the canal, the turnpike, the post office, and the ever-expanding world of print had made the nation more interconnected in exactly the way that Calhoun had once hoped it would be, although not to the extent that he had envisioned. By overthrowing the tyranny of distance and the difficulties of communication that Madison had assumed, Americans had also paved the way for the formation of huge national factions, such as the so-called manufacturing interest and, soon, organized political parties, that Madison and the other founders could never have imagined. Some American politicians like Martin Van Buren and, eventually, Andrew Jackson reacted to this new reality by turning a vice into a virtue, arguing that national political parties with clear principles and a responsibility to voters were the antidote to secretive and self-interested factions. Other observers would conclude that party machinery played an important role in mitigating the unfiltered passions of popular democracy. Calhoun instead saw a fundamental threat to the balance of the system, and to democracy itself. Political parties, as they were emerging in the new environment, were not only a symptom of the disease, they were part of the problem.[44]

Almost as soon as he diagnosed the disease, Calhoun was drawn to the idea of a state veto on federal power as the most obvious solution, although he had not worked out the details of how such a veto would function. "After much reflection," he wrote Tazewell at the end of August, "it seems to me that the despotism founded on combined geographical interest, admits of but one effectual remedy, a veto on the part of the local interest, or under our system, on the part of the States." He acknowledged there were important questions related to its constitutionality. "How far such a negative would be found consistent with general power, is an important consideration, which I waive for the present," he admitted. In particular he asked the older lawyer's opinion on the constitutionality of the Judiciary Act of 1789, which had long been a subject of irritation for state rights proponents, including John Taylor. The act had established the federal court system, and the 25th section of the act gave federal courts the authority to review decisions from the highest state courts that raised constitutional issues or conflicted with federal law. Without the 25th section of the Judiciary Act, Calhoun believed, the state veto would already exist in practice, and it would be much easier to repeal an unconstitutional law than to change or reinterpret the Constitution. Calhoun hardly ever asked for opinions, so it seems likely that he was sounding Tazewell out. As he wrote,

"It ought not to be considered too late to enquire, by what authority Congress adopted it, and how far it can be reconciled with the sovereignty of the States, as to their reserved rights?" It was the first time Calhoun had stated a belief in state sovereignty so unequivocally.[45]

EVEN AS HE BEGAN considering other alternatives, Calhoun remained hopeful that the presidential election of 1828 would remedy matters, at least in the short term, by placing Andrew Jackson in the White House. As the election neared, Calhoun attempted to keep protégés like the increasingly radical George McDuffie in check in order to maintain unity among Jackson's allies. Now that he had parted ways so decisively with Adams, a Jackson victory was also the only way to keep his own path to the presidency open.

It helped that Martin Van Buren, now working actively for Jackson against Adams after being a Crawford man in the 1824 election, was committed to keeping Calhoun vice president as a way to stave off the vice presidential candidacy of Van Buren's New York rival DeWitt Clinton. Imperturbable, balding, and unfailingly polite, Van Buren's impeccable outer facade hid both his burning ambition and his unrivaled skill as a political power broker. During the election of 1828 he emerged as the primary architect of the party structure that would define American politics, and against which Calhoun would define himself even as he worked within it. But for the time being they were allies. At the end of 1826, in a private meeting, Calhoun and Van Buren had agreed to try to unify the Calhounites and the Crawford Radicals of 1824 behind a Jackson candidacy in an effort to infuse republican political principles into a campaign that had so far centered mostly on the Hero of New Orleans's personal popularity. Van Buren even made a trip south to woo erstwhile Crawford followers to the Jackson banner and help forge a national political party that included "the planters of the South and the plain Republicans of the North." On that trip, Van Buren made it clear that Calhoun's position alongside Jackson on the ticket was nonnegotiable, a bitter pill for many Crawford supporters to swallow. But swallow it they did, including even Calhoun's old enemy Thomas Ritchie of the *Richmond Enquirer*.[46]

Van Buren, however, was playing his own long game. It seems likely that Crawford himself told Van Buren the secret of Calhoun's opposition to Jackson's actions in Florida during the Seminole War, a secret that the wily Van Buren urged him to keep until the time was ripe. What part Crawford or Van Buren may have played is unclear, but sometime during 1826 or early 1827 a letter from Monroe to Calhoun written during the Florida crisis of 1818 disappeared, or was stolen, from Calhoun's correspondence, and found its way to Jackson. The letter revealed the consensus in Monroe's cabinet that Jackson acted against his orders, although it did not reveal Calhoun's view specifically. After discovering Jackson was aware of the letter, Calhoun corresponded extensively with Monroe over several months in order to get their story straight—the cabinet had agreed that Jackson had disobeyed his orders, though perhaps through an honest mistake. Calhoun then carefully opened up a correspondence with Jackson, who responded immediately that the letter "truly astonished me" and reiterated that his orders, which had come directly from Calhoun, had clearly authorized his actions. Jackson offered no middle ground of interpretation. In response, Calhoun warned Jackson that the letter was an attempt to drive a wedge between them, assured him ambiguously that whatever the technicalities nobody had doubted his "honest and patriotick motives," and urged that the events were "matters of history, and must be left to the historian, as they stand." Perhaps because the election was imminent, Jackson let the matter rest there. But it was clear that the alliance between Calhoun and Jackson had begun to show signs of cracking almost before the cement set.[47]

John Quincy Adams, meanwhile, viewed his vice president's movements in early 1828 with a frustration bordering on rage. "Calhoun is a man of considerable talent, and burning ambition, stimulated to frenzy by success, flattery, and premature advancement," Adams fumed in his diary. "Governed by no steady principle; but sagacious to seize upon every prevailing popular breeze to swell his own sails…[he is] the dupe and tool of every knave cunning enough to drop the oil of fools in his ear."[48] Adams always indulged in the worst possible interpretation of his political enemies' actions, but if he really thought that Jackson and Van Buren were duping Calhoun, he underestimated his old friend.

IN THE SPRING OF 1828 Calhoun revealed publicly his political change of course by casting a tie-breaking vote in the Senate in favor of an amendment to dramatically restrict appropriations for internal improvements. In response to a barely veiled denunciation of his reversal by Senator James Noble of Indiana, Calhoun explained that he had always believed and still did that internal improvements on a truly national scale were constitutional since they benefited all Americans equally. But he had always feared that without a comprehensive plan, appropriations would be "diverted from national to local objects; and… be made subservient to political combinations." As an example, Calhoun pointed to a recent bill for a canal in Illinois that proposed to pass through federal lands but would only be free for Illinois residents. He could have pointed to similar bills over the preceding two years for canals and roads in Indiana, Illinois, Michigan, and Alabama, none of which he had in mind twelve years earlier when he urged his fellow congressmen to conquer the continent with a national system of roads and canals. Better, Calhoun now argued, to cut off national funding for such projects at the source than to have it turned into a contest for political spoils in the service of such narrow interests.[49]

The real fight brewing in Washington that spring, however, was over the proposal for a new tariff in response to the demands of the Harrisburg Convention. The new bill, written by Martin Van Buren's ally Silas Wright of New York, dramatically raised duties on a whole raft of manufactured and raw materials in an effort to win support from both northern and western representatives. Van Buren and

Wright then convinced Calhoun and his followers to cooperate with a political plot that would backfire spectacularly and shape the course of the next five years of American history. Under the guise of defeating the bill, Van Buren evidently urged Calhoun to direct southern representatives to vote against amendments removing some of the bill's most objectionable features—including reducing duties that southerners thought were too high and raising duties on woolen manufactures that New Englanders thought were not high enough—in the hopes that this would drive some Adams men from New England to vote against it alongside southerners, thus dooming the bill to failure. In a political game of smoke and mirrors, this result would allow northern Jackson supporters like Van Buren to support the bill as their constituents wanted, and would cast Adams and his followers as opposed to their constituents' will. But it would also—Van Buren promised—result in the bill's final defeat, as Calhoun and the South wanted. And so, as George McDuffie would later recall of the plan with chagrin, "We determined to put such ingredients into the chalice as would poison the monster."[50]

The problem was that a few New Englanders in the House proved willing to pass the imperfect bill anyway, and at the end of April they did just that. Still, Calhoun believed the measure could be defeated in the Senate, perhaps by his own vote, just as the woolens bill had been the year before. In early May as the bill was making its way through the Senate, he wrote James Edward that the bill's passage was "doubtful."[51] Then, in a surprise maneuver that Calhoun and other southerners would long hold against him, Van Buren reversed course and supported amendments in the Senate that soothed New England's objections and assured the bill's final passage with the provisions most hated by the South still intact. When Van Buren announced his vote on the amendments in the Senate, one observer recalled that Virginia senator Littleton Waller Tazewell looked as if "he had been struck by a bullet" and murmured, "Sir, you have deceived me."[52] From his chair presiding over the Senate, Calhoun may have murmured the same thing. He would later claim that the tariff "was passed by a breach of faith. We were deceived."[53] Calhoun and the South would now have to drink the poisoned chalice themselves. At a stormy meeting of the South Carolina delegation to Congress, held at Robert Young Hayne's Washington residence immediately after the tariff passed the Senate, the prospect of disunion reared its head. But in the end, the meeting decided to try and restrain what they knew would be the violent reaction of their constituents until Jackson and Calhoun were safely elected.[54]

Calhoun reacted to the tariff's passage with a sense of resignation. As he prepared to leave Washington on May 15, two days after the tariff passed the Senate, he wrote to his old college friend Micah Sterling in a reflective mood. "I certainly have had great difficulties to contend with," he wrote, ostensibly about the election, "but truth will in the long run prevail. I have ever relied on it as my only guide under every difficulty." Then, perhaps partly to prepare Sterling for what the future held, he continued, "I know not, that it is even a merit in me. I cannot do other wise. Whether it be too great confidence in my own opinion I cannot say but what I think I see, I see with so much appearant clearness, as not to leave me a choice to pursue any other course, which has always given me the impression, that I acted under the force of destiny. With such an impression, I meet with clearness all events let what will come." Conscious of having disclosed more than usual, he added, "I ought not perhaps to speak so freely of myself, but to a friend, who has been such under all circumstances, for more than a quarter of a century, I may disclose without the imputation of egotism the secret movements of my mind."[55] Ambition always drove Calhoun's actions more than he acknowledged, but at critical moments in his life that ambition diverted in its course, altered by the crystalline certainty of his conclusions and his sense that duty and destiny made their own demands on him. One gets the sense that in May 1828 even Calhoun briefly marveled at the turn his destiny was taking.

The reaction to the tariff in South Carolina was every bit as violent as the delegation in Robert Hayne's Washington parlor had anticipated. When news of its passage reached South Carolina, the ships in Charleston's harbor flew their flags at half-mast.[56] In June a public meeting in the lowcountry district of Colleton adopted a fiery appeal to the governor written by a young member of the South Carolina legislature named Robert Barnwell Smith, who would later change his last name to Rhett, urging "resistance...openly, fairly, fearlessly, and unitedly."[57] George McDuffie, unable to restrain himself any longer, returned to South Carolina and gave a widely read speech declaring that "the people of one portion of the union were corrupted, bought and sold by the money of another part"—he meant the West—and that "none but a coward could longer consent to bear such a state of things."[58] McDuffie proposed a counter-tariff on northern goods as a response, something that made little economic sense but played well to the mood of the state. The mood Calhoun found in his own part of the state when he returned home can be judged from a toast he gave at a public dinner in Pendleton on the Fourth of July, where he raised his glass to "the Congress of '76. They taught the world how oppression could be successfully resisted; may the lesson teach rulers that their only safety is in justice and moderation."[59] Unlike McDuffie, Calhoun still believed the crisis could be averted by statesmanship—his own as well as, he hoped, that of northern friends.

His friends and allies from outside the state wrote to Calhoun warning him to stay clear of the mushrooming madness. From Maryland, editor of the *National Intelligencer* Samuel Smith wrote that the Colleton statement and McDuffie's speech had "distressed me beyond any words" and told Calhoun that his friends "are apprehensive that it will be attributed to you."[60] Duff Green, the excitable editor of the *United States Telegraph*, wrote in the same vein, warning Calhoun that his popularity might be irreparably damaged in the country if he allowed himself to be associated with McDuffie's inflammatory rhetoric.[61] South Carolina's extreme reaction, especially McDuffie's proposal of a tax on northern goods, had alienated many potential northern allies in shipping centers like New York. Some people, Green warned, even believed that Calhoun wanted disunion so that he could become president of a separate southern republic.[62] Even James Monroe wrote Calhoun that he viewed the uproar in the South as extremely unfortunate, not only because he thought the tariff was constitutional, but because the southern states would suffer the most from disunion since in the wars that might follow, Monroe stated baldly, "their slaves would be excited to insurrection."[63]

In response, Calhoun assured his friends that South Carolina's attachment to the Union was still strong, although not indestructible, and he openly proclaimed that he believed the tariff was unconstitutional and that South Carolinians were right to connect their economic plight to its operations. "I can speak from experience," he wrote Samuel Ingham. "My property has ceased to give profits, which I believe is true of 9/10 of our planters." It was not at all surprising that southerners "reduced to poverty by the acts of the government, as they believe, should be deeply excited."[64]

The "hasty and warm expression of opinion" was not what worried Calhoun most about the situation. "These are nothing," he wrote to Samuel Smith at the end of July. Instead, he looked ahead to the long-term consequences of the rift. "I look to the steady alienation of affection, and distrust of our government which must follow," he wrote. "It is this only which can make two of one people."[65] "In my opinion to save us from corruption and disunion a radical change is necessary," Calhoun wrote to his worried friend and ally Postmaster General John McLean that summer. "We must return to the primitive principles of our government. The States must have the power really intended by the Constitution, in order, not to destroy, but to save the Constitution and the Union." Calhoun hoped that after Jackson's election there would be an "equalization of the burdens and benefits of the Union, as the certain means of preserving our excellent institutions."[66]

Calhoun never renounced his Jeffersonian faith in the people, but the tariff prompted him to rethink his views of human nature and democratic government. He believed in the republican idea of a virtuous citizenry who were able to put the country's interests above their own, but he also held the somewhat contradictory view that what bound citizens to the nation was mostly self-interest. Calhoun's view rested on the optimistic assumption, taken from Scottish Common Sense philosophy, that a reliance on simple reason would show a virtuous citizenry how to balance the two. But the tariff made Calhoun confront the possibility that self-interest was, on occasion, likely to win out—that tyranny might come from "the *community itself*," as he wrote to John McLean that summer.[67] The question for him was: Why?

As he searched about for answers, Calhoun felt the pull of the old familiar Calvinist doctrines about human nature. People, his old teacher Moses Waddel had insisted, were naturally selfish and prone to self-deception as a result of the fall. The tariff crisis started Calhoun thinking about the ways that physical distance combined with these traits of human nature might distort how people understood the country's interests, making them less sensitive to the rights and priorities of those far away. The nation was undergoing remarkable advances in transportation and communication, but these advances had so far only produced national economic and political factions—they were not enough to bind the nation together so completely as to eliminate significant regional differences of interest or erase the distorting effects of distance.

This unexpected situation, Calhoun believed, revealed a flaw in the founders' plan that required modification in the light of experience. To John McLean he dismissed "the usual answer that it is the will of a majority, and the minority ought to acquiesce," an answer he had found compelling only a few years before when it was not South Carolina doing the acquiescing. Instead, he wrote, the conflict could only be resolved by "respecting the interest of all of the parts, the weak, as well as the strong." Knowing McLean would not like his answer, Calhoun wrote, "It would indeed be a calamity to me…to travel in a political road without having you as a companion."[68] Calhoun clearly knew he was setting out on a different path through unmapped territory.

WORKING, READING, AND WRITING that summer and fall in his newly constructed office—a separate, small building just behind Clergy Hall—Calhoun worked out in letters to correspondents the arguments he would soon hurl at the tariff.[69] In early November William C. Preston, the new speaker of the South Carolina House of Representatives and one of the more radical opponents of the tariff, wrote to Calhoun requesting him to draft a statement laying out the constitutional case against the tariff and for the state veto. Seeing an opportunity to shape the developing crisis, Calhoun instantly agreed, asking Preston to procure data from recent years on imports and exports.[70]

A little more than two weeks later Calhoun had completed a draft of what would be known as the *South Carolina Exposition*, a document of roughly forty-five pages in its published form containing a formidable combination of economic, historical, and constitutional reasoning. It marked an intellectual as well as political departure for Calhoun, and the first clear example of the theoretical brilliance Calhoun was capable of when he sensed a visceral, systemic threat. His most innovative—and potentially destructive—arguments in the years ahead would be produced from a defensive posture.

Calhoun began the *Exposition* by noting that the Constitution allowed Congress to levy taxes and tariffs only as a means of bringing in revenue; a desire to encourage manufacturing could be only a secondary or incidental consideration. This, he claimed, had been the case with previous tariffs, like the tariff of 1816, which of course he had supported. The new tariff, however, raised rates to prohibitive levels far beyond the needs of the government—they were clearly designed, Calhoun argued, for the express purpose of protecting manufacturers, a purpose that had been discussed and rejected at the Constitutional Convention. The national government, he pointed out, was now drawing nearly its entire revenue (94 percent in 1828)[71] from a tariff paid by roughly one-third of the population for the exclusive benefit, as he claimed, of the other two-thirds. To the argument that the tariff's burden was divided equally since all the nation's consumers, not just southern ones, paid higher prices for their goods under its effects, Calhoun responded that while this might be true, the South was the only part of the nation that saw no benefit from this sacrifice. While the national government's coffers filled with tariff revenues, and while the bank accounts of northern manufacturers and the tax revenues of northern state governments swelled from the profits of inflated prices, the South alone sacrificed. "We are the serffs [*sic*] of the system," he wrote bitterly, "out of whose labour is raised, not only the money paid in to the Treasury, but the funds, out of which are drawn the rich reward of the manufacturer and his associates in interest." It was an intentionally provocative image of exploitation put in terms no slaveholder could misunderstand.

In a striking use of Adam Smith's idea of the invisible hand, Calhoun argued that the tariff was unjust because it would force southerners to involuntarily reallocate their capital to manufacturing at a competitive disadvantage and in ways not suited to their traditional pursuits, which had been adapted to their climate and geography. They would be forced to become the "rivals, instead of the customers of the manufacturing states." Probably southerners would fail, Calhoun wrote, and remain economically degraded by the northern tariff interest. But what if they succeeded? Then the danger was even greater. Nowhere in the *Exposition* did Calhoun cast the tariff as an immediate threat to slavery, but if southern planters became successful manufacturers, he warned, one reason would be the advantage provided by slave labor—an imbalance that northern workers would surely find unacceptable. Northerners, he wrote, "would not tolerate that those who now cultivate our plantations, and furnish them with the material, and the market for the products of their arts, should, by becoming their rivals, take bread out of the mouths of their wives and children." It was a prescient recognition that slaves *were* a laboring class comparable to northern white mill workers, but one that could be more completely and cheaply exploited for competitive advantage.[72]

Calhoun realized that the heart of the problem was that the North and the South had a different orientation to the global marketplace. "We cultivate certain great staples for the supply of the general market of the world," he wrote. "They manufacture almost exclusively for the home market." These orientations were inherently at odds, and Calhoun urged manufacturers to look toward the foreign market instead of concentrating narrowly on the national one.

Some modern economists who have studied the tariff have concluded that Calhoun and southerners who opposed the tariff were not wrong about its operation, but neither were northern manufacturers, whose businesses likely could not have survived more direct competition with the British juggernaut in the decades before the Civil War.[73] But even if parts of Calhoun's economic analysis were correct, it is also clear that he overlooked or ignored just how much slaveholders benefited economically from state power in other ways, especially the way that the United States government had, under his own watch as secretary of war, used its military power and treasure to obtain massive swaths of land from the Indians to keep the cotton revolution rolling. As James Monroe had reminded him that summer, the South benefited from the Union as much as any other section, and was in some ways more dependent on its protection.[74]

Having laid out the economic problem, Calhoun's *Exposition* spelled out a political solution. "Universal experience in all ages and countries…teaches that power can only be restrained by power, and not by reason or justice," he wrote. "This great principle guided in the formation of every part of our political system. There is not an opposing interest, through out the whole, that is not counterpoised." States and the national government were both sovereign within their own spheres of reserved or delegated powers, but without the means to protect that sovereignty, it became meaningless. The national government, he pointed out, had protected itself against the encroachment of state power with the Judiciary Act of 1789, giving the Supreme Court the right to review the decisions of state supreme courts. Now he proposed a corollary for the states.[75]

Calhoun insisted to friends and allies that the state veto, also called state interposition or, most popularly, nullification, was not a new or radical idea. "It is not a new doctrine," he wrote to John McLean, pointing to the *Federalist Papers* and the Virginia and Kentucky resolutions.[76] Nevertheless, Calhoun's proposal in the *Exposition* was different and more theoretically refined than anything Jefferson, Madison, John Taylor, Robert Turnbull, or Thomas Cooper had described. Most significantly, Calhoun proposed that the state veto should be implemented by a special convention, not the state legislature. The special convention had at least three advantages in Calhoun's mind. First, it would function as a conservative safeguard, slowing the process down and making it less susceptible to passions of the moment. Second, the convention had the advantage of being undeniably the purest and most direct expression of the people's will since it was the same mechanism through which they had ratified the Constitution. Finally, Calhoun believed this method would be much less susceptible to a legal challenge that might find its way to the Supreme Court, where the Judiciary Act gave the courts and the national government the upper hand over state legislatures.

Having laid out how the process might work, Calhoun next considered one of the gravest objections to the veto: that it would lead to chaos and an unresolvable stalemate between state and national governments. If there were no higher power to resolve the stalemate, this would be true, Calhoun acknowledged, but there was a higher power, the "creating and preserving power" that when exercised by three-fourths of the states could amend the Constitution. Calhoun envisioned a process in which a state veto would prompt an appeal by the federal government to amend the Constitution in order to grant itself the power in question. If the attempt failed, the state would be vindicated. If it succeeded, he wrote, "a disputed power will be converted into an expressly granted power." Calhoun implied that a state like

South Carolina would have to accept the result—"to deny or resist it, would be, on the part of the State, a violation of the constitutional compact, and a dissolution of the political association." In other words, a constitutional amendment that granted the federal government the power in question and met with the approval of three-quarters of the states would be binding even on states that disagreed. Calhoun took for granted that "dissolution" of the Union would occur if a state continued to resist, but he cast that resistance in a negative light, as the result of a "violation" of the Constitution on the part of the state. Some of the more radical state rights advocates found this aspect of Calhoun's argument horrifying.[77]

More than a purely defensive strategy, Calhoun viewed the state veto as a way to continue perfecting the Constitution by periodic appeal to the purest source of authority, the people. This aspect of Calhoun's theory was perhaps the most novel, distinguishing his formulation from what earlier advocates of the veto had in mind. Where John Taylor had once scoffed at the idea of "perpetual appeals to the people upon every collision of opinions,"[78] Calhoun wrote that very thing into the *Exposition* as a response to the objection that the state veto would produce only stalemate. With the precedent of state interposition and the process of appeal to a national convention established, he wrote, "all controversies between the States and General Government would be adjusted, and the Constitution gradually acquire all the perfection of which it is susceptible. It is thus that the creating becomes the preserving power; and we may rest assured it is no less true in politics than in theology, that the power which creates can alone preserve—and that preservation is perpetual creation. Such will be the operation and effect of State interposition."[79] Often seen exclusively as a defensive statement of state rights doctrine, which it certainly was, what is often missed is that in the *Exposition* Calhoun also offered a remarkably dynamic and creative vision of the Constitution and a Union that was constantly being adjusted and perfected by the creative tension between state and national power. It may have been, as many charged, completely unworkable and dangerous in its tendencies, but it was certainly not unimaginative. By giving theoretical justification and a concrete process to the vague doctrines that had characterized the idea of state interposition before the *Exposition*, Calhoun revolutionized the debate over state and federal power. The consequences would be vast.

IN THE SHORT TERM, a division over strategy within the South Carolina legislature meant that they did not call a convention or exercise a state veto of the tariff, at least not yet. They did order several thousand copies of the *Exposition* printed in the hopes of winning allies against the tariff throughout the country, although a committee chaired by Speaker William C. Preston eliminated from the published version Calhoun's proposal that the state veto should be done by convention, and not the legislature, a central part of his argument. Calhoun would have to clarify the published version's confusions in other writing. In the end, the legislature adopted a short list of resolutions drafted by Preston's committee and known as the *Protest* that repeated some of Calhoun's main points and made South Carolina's case to the nation.[80]

The *Exposition* is usually seen as a reversal in Calhoun's thinking, a pivot away from his earlier, optimistic nationalism, to a more reactionary ideology focused on state rights. Certainly the *Exposition* marks an important change, but Calhoun was tacking into the wind, not reversing course. His goal was to keep South Carolina in the Union by preempting many of the more radical elements of the discourse in the state, preserving his own place on both state and national stages, while also setting forth his sincere conviction that the tariff was unconstitutional. Calhoun was trying to find a way to preserve the structure of the Union consistent with the principle that power ultimately resided in the people, although the people of the states. While other state rights advocates saw only a choice between domination by the federal government or disunion, Calhoun worked creatively, almost desperately, to find the resources for a solution within the system itself.

Not everyone saw it that way, of course, and Calhoun's theory had critics across the spectrum of American politics. In James Madison's posthumously published *Advice to My Country*, written once the fruit of Calhoun's *Exposition* had ripened, the ex-president warned against "disguised" enemies of the nation who professed to love the Union while secretly seeking its destruction, and whom he compared to "the Serpent creeping with his deadly wiles into Paradise."[81] Along with Madison, many nationalists pointed out that Calhoun's theory would allow a state to defy the federal government as long as it could convince a mere one-quarter of the other states that it was right, leaving the Union a hollow shell without any real power. On the other hand many state rights advocates viewed the high-flown arguments of the *Exposition* with distrust since Calhoun's creative defense of state rights violated their strict constructionism, which had no room for a constantly changing Constitution. Calhoun's ideas were thus viewed as dangerously restrictive on the one hand and dangerously expansive on the other.

FOR THE MOMENT, AT least, Calhoun appeared to have short-circuited some of the more radical rhetoric about disunion while setting forth his own theory of the state veto. When he agreed to write the *Exposition*, he warned Speaker Preston against acting precipitously. "There has been heretofore a want of caution on this important point, which has exposed us to great danger," he wrote. "Our measure [the state veto], however sound, however justified by the noble example of Virginia in [17]98, will appear at first to all our friends, *novel, bold and even dangerous, and to those exact tribute from us, treasonable.*" Best to make the argument and then wait to see if time, reason, and cooperation with other states would make a difference, Calhoun urged the younger man. "As our cause rests in truth and the Constitution, it will gain daily, till it will finally prevail, if we act with wisdom and moderation."[82]

At the end of the *Exposition*, Calhoun expressed the hope that the "great political revolution" of the presidential election that fall would bring in an "eminent citizen" who would restore the "pure principles of our government."[83] By the time the *Exposition* was published, with its author's identity anonymous but widely suspected, it was clear that Andrew Jackson had indeed been elected the next president of the United States, with Calhoun as his vice president, in an election that announced the arrival of a new kind of popular democracy in the United States. Calhoun and many other opponents of the tariff were hopeful that Jackson would take their side; despite his vote for the tariff of 1824 in the Senate, he was a loud proponent of state rights. But nobody really knew for sure where Old Hickory stood on the matter. They would soon find out.

TWELVE

"There Shall Be at Least One Free State"

W HEN FLORIDE CALHOUN STEPPED INTO her Washington parlor one afternoon in early January 1829 and found Tennessee senator John Eaton and his new bride Margaret standing there, she must have felt a little trapped. The slave who had announced the visitors had not given their names, and now Floride had one of the most notorious women in Washington standing in her parlor. She treated them with "civility," as her husband later recalled, and they gingerly discussed the "relation, which Mrs. Eaton bore to the society of Washington" before the Eatons took their departure, leaving as they went one of the calling cards that in the rituals of social Washington obligated Floride to return the visit.

Calhoun was not at home when the Eatons came, but on his return that evening Floride told him what had happened and they went to bed knowing they faced a dilemma. Margaret Timberlake's marriage to John Eaton that New Year's Day had caused a scandal in Washington society in the weeks before Andrew Jackson's inauguration. Margaret was the daughter of a well-known tavern keeper, and her previous husband had committed suicide at sea, it was rumored because of the ongoing relationship between Margaret and Eaton. She had not grieved as thoroughly or deeply as many thought she should before marrying

Eaton—which to many observers only confirmed the rumors. In fact, nearly everything about Margaret was scandalous by the standards of Floride Calhoun's contemporaries. Margaret was vivacious, loud, uncommonly direct in her speech, and familiar with men in ways that made their wives uncomfortable. Margaret Bayard Smith, Floride's friend and one of the social arbiters of Washington society, had already declared Eaton's new wife anathema based on rumored youthful indiscretions while working in her father's tavern. One of the ruder jokes circulating Washington in the days before the Eatons appeared in the Calhouns' parlor was the popular jibe that Eaton had "just married his mistress—and the mistress of 11-doz others!" To Floride and others who took seriously their roles as social guardians of Washington society, Margaret Eaton was a threat to the purity and order of the social fabric, which undergirded and was linked directly to the order and purity of the republic.

The Eatons had simply been fulfilling their social duty: it was customary for senators and their wives to call on the vice president and his family first before receiving a return visit. But it was also a test to see if they would be accepted into Washington society. As the vice president's wife, and thus one of the bellwethers of the social scene, Floride's decision would carry great weight.

The morning after the Eatons' visit Floride informed Calhoun that she had decided not to return their call. Calhoun would later recall that he agreed, even though "I foresaw the difficulties in which it would probably involve me." He approved of the moral grounds on which Floride made her decision and, he wrote, "I viewed the question involved, as paramount to all political considerations, & was prepared to meet the consequences, as to myself, be they what they might." Calhoun would often be accused in the coming months of having created the Eaton controversy for his own political gain, but given the political price he eventually paid, it seems much more likely that he indeed approved of or was at least unwilling to override Floride's judgment. As Floride's decision rippled through Washington, other prominent

socialites took her lead and also snubbed Margaret. At the Inauguration Day events in March, including the swearing-in, the raucous
White House reception, and the grand ball where Calhoun and Floride
presided as the guests of honor, the women of Washington took care
not to notice or speak to John Eaton's new wife.[1]

Margaret Eaton's main defender, as it turned out to Calhoun's misfortune, was Andrew Jackson, who saw in the rumors and social snubs
aimed at his old friend's new wife echoes of the insults that he believed
had hurried his own wife, Rachel, to an early grave only months earlier.
Jackson had been planning to appoint Eaton as his secretary of war,
and when he learned of the widespread opposition he would face on
account of the scandal surrounding Margaret, he raged, "Do you suppose that I have been sent here by the people to consult the ladies of
Washington as to the proper persons to impose my cabinet?"[2]

The Calhouns left Washington for South Carolina soon after the
inauguration (the Senate, over which Calhoun presided as vice president, would not reconvene until December), but over the next months
Jackson would wage an unprecedented campaign to vindicate Margaret Eaton's character, gathering evidence and witnesses, and devoting
an entire cabinet meeting in September to her defense. But even his
own household was divided, as his wife's niece Emily Donelson, who
filled in as White House hostess for her uncle, took the side of Eaton's
enemies.[3] In April, a dejected Virgil Maxcy wrote to Calhoun, "It is
come to this that all our glowing anticipations for our country…must
submit to the melancholy conviction, that the U.S. are governed by the
President—the President by the Sec. of War—& the latter by his
wife."[4]

All the time, Martin Van Buren, who had been rewarded for his
loyalty with an appointment as Jackson's secretary of state and remained behind Calhoun in Washington, began to see that the Eaton
affair could be used to his advantage. Nearly everyone acknowledged
that Van Buren and Calhoun were the two most likely successors to the
aging and infirm Jackson, who had initially said he would serve only

one term. With Calhoun safely back in South Carolina and Jackson ever more enraged at Eaton's plight, the dapper widower from New York who had no wife to negotiate with decided, as he later recalled, "to treat every cabinet member and family equally." Van Buren's kindnesses to Margaret Eaton, including making pointedly public social calls on the family, went a long way toward ensuring Jackson's favor as the two men talked about the Eaton affair on their long horseback rides together. At first inclined to blame Henry Clay, by fall Jackson began to associate the opposition to Margaret Eaton with Calhoun's desire to eliminate Eaton as a possible competitor for the presidency. Many in Washington put the shift down to Van Buren. John Quincy Adams remarked with glee, "Calhoun heads the moral party, Van Buren that of the frail sisterhood."[5] As one of Henry Clay's correspondents put it at the time, "[Van Buren] has availed himself of the Case of the Lady to commit himself with Eaton…to obtain the confidence of the President. This is the nucleus of the Van Buren party & Calhoun is forever extinguished."[6] This was overstated. Calhoun was far from finished, and there had been deep differences developing between Jackson and Calhoun well before the Eatons appeared in Floride's parlor. Nevertheless, it was true that Floride's decision gave Van Buren an opening to drive the wedge deeper.

OVER THE SUMMER AND fall Calhoun watched from Pendleton and corresponded extensively with Duff Green, Virgil Maxcy, and other allies as the new administration took shape and the Eaton affair continued to mushroom. Even before leaving Washington, Calhoun had expressed disappointment over some of Jackson's cabinet choices, writing his old friend Christopher Vandeventer that the cabinet "does not fully meet public expectation" and that Jackson had not consulted "prominent friends" in his decisions.[7] As the year progressed, signs only increased that Van Buren, not Calhoun, had the president's ear. Calhoun was especially stung by Jackson's failure to appoint his close friend

Virgil Maxcy treasurer of the United States, and although he petitioned John Eaton to give Christopher Vandeventer a job as chief clerk of the War Department, a post Vandeventer had held under Calhoun, Eaton did not oblige.[8] True, Calhoun's ally Samuel Ingham received the influential secretary of the treasury position, which the vice president hoped would be a help in the fight against the tariff, but as he wrote Ingham that summer, "The highest offices, at least, are going too uniformly in a certain direction," by which he meant old Crawford men who were now shifting their allegiances to Van Buren.[9]

Calhoun had hoped to fight the tariff on international turf, as well as at home, perhaps by encouraging Jackson to use his treaty powers to liberalize trade and decrease duties on both sides of the Atlantic. He was disappointed when his ally, Virginia senator Littleton Waller Tazewell, turned down the post as ambassador to Great Britain. As he wrote Tazewell, "the more I reflect on it, the more deeply am I impressed with the belief, that at London & Paris the death blow may be given to that odious system of monopoly, which is now praying on the vitals of the community."[10] "It is difficult to imagine," Calhoun wrote to William Cabell Rives, a former representative from Virginia whom Jackson sent to Paris, "how much the civilization and happiness of our race depends on a free and unrestricted commercial intercourse."[11] Calhoun realized that the debate over free trade, national interest, and protectionism was larger than the tariff, and he began to pay close attention to British debates concerning the so-called Corn Laws, which protected British crop producers, mainly the landed gentry, against foreign competition.[12]

Before Calhoun returned to Washington for the December session of Congress, in August he and Floride welcomed another son, William Lowndes, named after Calhoun's first messmate and old ally. It was probably because of the birth that Floride did not accompany Calhoun back to Washington, although some interpreted her absence as a desire to avoid the all-consuming drama of the Eatons. Calhoun's oldest son, Andrew, did accompany him to Washington, and then continued on to

Yale, where he planned to join the junior class despite the fact that, as Calhoun wrote his old professor Benjamin Silliman in October, Andrew was a little behind in his study of "Conick sections and Trigonometry." Calhoun begged Silliman and Yale president Rev. Jeremiah Day to select a good roommate for his oldest son. "I would deem an idle and immoral room mate a great misfortune," wrote Calhoun with the understandable concern of a parent sending a child off to college but also a hint of doubt about Andrew's capacities to withstand temptation.[13]

ANDREW JACKSON'S FIRST ANNUAL message to Congress, submitted on December 8, 1829, dashed any hopes that he would move quickly against the tariff. Jackson announced that while he wished all nations would drop their "complicated restrictions" against one another's commerce, nevertheless "we must ever expect selfish legislation in other nations, and are therefore compelled to adapt our own to their regulation." This would be difficult, and he wrote of trying to balance "the conflicting interests of our agriculture, our commerce, and our manufactures." He proposed lowering duties on only two items, tea and coffee, which were not produced in the United States, a small consolation to tariff opponents. Most disturbing to Calhoun, Jackson acknowledged that the tariff revenue would soon pay off the national debt, but instead of proposing to lower or eliminate the tariff at that point, as Calhoun had hoped, Jackson instead proposed distributing the resulting excess revenue from the tariff to the states according to their representation in Congress. Elsewhere, Jackson also announced his administration's position that eastern Indian tribes must either move west or be subject to state law where they were, the culmination of his longstanding belief that the more gradual approach pursued by Calhoun as secretary of war had been misguided. And in a brief paragraph at the end of the address he announced his opposition to rechartering the Second Bank of the United States, the bank Calhoun had helped establish in 1816, claiming the bank had failed in "the great end of establishing a uniform and sound currency." The address was a road map of the next seven years, and it would not be a smooth journey.[14]

A FEW DAYS AFTER Christmas, Calhoun sat in his chair under a gilt eagle presiding over the Senate as Senator Samuel Foot of Connecticut submitted a resolution that inadvertently touched off one of the most famous debates in, and about, American history. Foot's resolution to limit the sale of public lands in the West provoked an indignant response from Thomas Hart Benton of Missouri, a tall, broad-faced, blustering force of nature, who charged Foot and other northern senators of trying to keep the workers in northern manufacturing plants from emigrating west. Agreeing with Benton, the eloquent and sophisticated Robert Hayne of South Carolina compared the proposal's effects to that of the tariff on the South, accusing Foot of trying to create a "manufacture of paupers" to supply industrialists with perpetually cheap labor. Hayne then shifted his attention to focus entirely on denouncing the tariff. "We stand towards the United States in the relation of Ireland to England," he declared. "The fruits of our labor are drawn from us to enrich other and more favored sections of the Union."[15]

As fate would have it, one of Hayne's colleagues in the Senate that day was Daniel Webster, in his first term as a senator from Massachusetts after a meteoric rise in national politics. Having begun his career defending state rights and threatening disunion against Calhoun and his allies during the War of 1812, Webster had by 1830 evolved in exactly the opposite direction of Calhoun, toward a more robust nationalism. Sensing a dangerous alliance emerging between the West and the South, as well as an opportunity to address the South Carolina doctrine of nullification head-on, Webster replied the next day, bypassing most of Benton's arguments and going straight for Hayne's comments on the tariff and the dangers of national consolidation. He pointed out that New England was not at fault for the origins of the tariff of 1816, which they had opposed, or even the tariff of 1824. They had been forced to adapt. Why shouldn't the South have to do the same? Then, refuting Benton's charge of eastern hostility to the West, he claimed that one of the greatest benefits to the western lands, the Northwest Ordinance, had been drawn up by a Massachusetts man, Nathan Dane. The benefit, Webster made deadly clear, was the ordinance's interdiction on slavery in the territories. "It impressed on the soil itself, while it was yet a wilderness, an incapacity to bear up any other than free men." The rest of the country, Webster implied, would have been better off had they instituted such a ban.[16]

Five days later Hayne replied. He pointed out that the South knew Nathan Dane not as the author of the Northwest Ordinance, an honor that belonged to Jefferson, but as a member of the traitorous Hartford Convention, which had flirted with secession at the end of the War of 1812. He reminded Webster of the senator's opposition to a failed tariff proposal in 1820 on exactly the same ground that South Carolina now took. He defended slavery, reminding Webster that New England had profited in the past from the slave trade and profited still from slavery, and asserted that abstractions about freedom or slavery were beside the point. "Finding our lot cast among a people, whom God had manifestly committed to our care, we did not sit down to speculate on abstract questions of theoretical liberty. We met it as a practical question of obligation and duty. We resolved to make the best of the situation in which Providence had placed us, and to fulfil the high trust which had developed upon us as the owners of slaves."[17]

As Calhoun listened, perhaps his mind began to work, realizing that the defensive posture Hayne took on slavery—southerners had to "make the best" out of an unfortunate situation—admitted a presupposition that weakened his argument. Hayne finished by defending nullification, rehearsing the Virginia and Kentucky resolutions and reading letters from Jefferson himself. There is no evidence for the oft-repeated story that Calhoun passed notes down to Hayne during his speech, but at the same time, everyone present knew that Hayne was expressing arguments that originated from the vice president.

The next day, dressed in his trademark blue suit coat with brass buttons and a starched white shirt, Webster returned to the floor and took the starch out of Hayne. The climax of Webster's address was a warning against the dangers of nullification and a panegyric on his enduring love for the Union packaged in a stirring evocation of his own death.

> When my eyes shall be turned to behold, for the last time, the sun in Heaven, may I not see him shining on the broken and dishonored fragments of a once glorious Union…Let their last feeble and lingering glance, rather behold the gorgeous Ensign of the Republic…not a stripe erased or polluted, nor a single star obscured—bearing for its motto, no such miserable interrogatory as, What is all this worth? Nor those other words of delusion and folly, Liberty first, and Union afterwards—but…that other sentiment, dear to every true American heart—Liberty and Union, now and forever, one and inseparable![18]

Webster's second reply to Hayne, memorized by generations of American schoolchildren, was a turning point in the debate over nullification and an important moment in Americans' evolving understanding of what the Union meant. By the force of his oratory Webster cemented into the public conversation exactly what Calhoun had sought over and over to deny: that nullification and disunion were of a piece. This idea would be instrumental in the next three years of the country's history.[19]

MANY OBSERVERS EXPECTED JACKSON to take Robert Hayne's side against Webster. After all, everyone knew that Jackson admired Hayne, hated government consolidation, and was a known supporter of state rights. Instead, the debate deeply disturbed Jackson, especially the mentions of nullification and disunion, neither of which fit into his conception of state rights. Webster's masterful framing of nullification as unpatriotic and treasonous, and his linkage of liberty and Union as indivisible, appealed tremendously to Jackson's sense of nationalism. When Duff Green's *United States Telegraph* published a program for the upcoming celebration of Thomas Jefferson's birthday on April 13, someone, likely Van Buren, convinced him it was an open endorsement of nullification—which claimed the precedent of Jefferson's Kentucky resolution—and he decided to say something that would make his position clear. The president prepared three different potential toasts, and then settled on the one that would best convey his sentiment with fierce economy.[20]

There were well over a hundred guests at the Indian Queen Hotel on the night of the dinner, including congressmen, officers of the army and navy, and distinguished citizens. The celebration had been underway for hours when the prepared toasts began. The tension in the room ratcheted up when the Pennsylvania delegation, anticipating abuse to the tariff, walked out in a planned protest. In fact, at first most of the toasts were unremarkable, but as they proceeded Jackson would later recall that he became uncomfortable, believing some of the toasts—such as Robert Hayne's to "the *Union* of the States, and the *Sovereignty* of the States"— were too pointed to ignore. When the prepared toasts ended, Jackson rose to give the first of what would be dozens of volunteer toasts. In the crowded room, some onlookers stood on their chairs to hear what he would say. Legend has it that he looked straight at Calhoun and offered, "Our Union, it must be preserved." As Martin Van Buren, no disinterested observer, would later remember it, "The veil was rent."[21]

Now by custom it was Calhoun's turn. Memories of the moment vary, mostly depending on whether the person doing the remembering favored Calhoun or Jackson, but some later accounts recalled Calhoun visibly pale while others described him shaking with controlled emotion as he rose and replied, "The Union, next to our liberty most dear;

may we all remember that it can only be preserved by respecting the rights of the States and distributing equally the benefit and burdens of the Union."[22]

Like many historical moments whose meaning takes shape mostly in hindsight, observers initially disagreed about the significance of the exchange, a sign that Calhoun's shifting position on the national stage was not yet broadly apparent. In the days after the dinner the anti-administration *Daily National Intelligencer* leaped at the opening to wreak havoc, portraying the dinner as practically a nullification rally and gleefully holding up Jackson's toast as evidence of a rift in the president's party. Significantly, though, the *Intelligencer* editors, who had not been present at the dinner and thus perhaps did not have the advantage of seeing the exchange, saw Calhoun's toast as equally celebratory of the Union, an interpretation echoed back in South Carolina by Benjamin F. Perry's *Greenville Mountaineer*, one of the most vehement voices against nullification in the state. Soon, the dueling toasts would come to be seen as the first open exchange in a deepening struggle, but for the time being this was not clear beyond a small circle of observers.[23]

Perhaps it was the exchange that famous evening that convinced Martin Van Buren and others around Jackson that it was time to excise Calhoun from the Jackson coalition before an opposition movement began to coalesce around him. Or perhaps, as one of Jackson's biographers concluded, it was Jackson himself who decided to sever ties with the South Carolinian.[24] In any case, three days after the Jefferson dinner, Senator John Forsyth of Georgia wrote to William Crawford, informing him that Jackson had learned "by some means" of a conversation Forsyth had with Crawford during which the latter mentioned that Calhoun had advocated "arresting and trying General Jackson" for disobeying his orders during the Seminole War. Forsyth now asked Crawford's permission to confirm the conversation to Jackson. Crawford responded two weeks later, confirming that Calhoun had indeed argued that Jackson "should be punished in some form," although Crawford denied that Calhoun had ever wanted Jackson arrested.[25]

The distinction mattered little to Jackson's sense of honor. On May 13, 1830, the president's nephew Andrew Jackson Donelson delivered a letter to Calhoun from Jackson with the Crawford letter enclosed demanding an explanation. Jackson quoted some of Calhoun's letters that he claimed proved that Calhoun had approved his course of action in Florida.[26] Immediately realizing the importance of the moment, Calhoun dashed off a terse reply the same day, perhaps with Donelson waiting to carry his note, remarking that he would respond in full soon but that in the meantime "I cannot repress the expression of my indignation at the affair" and at the "secret and mysterious attempts…to injure my character."[27] Like Jackson, Calhoun was always willing to play the martyr and see a conspiracy, but in this case he may have been right.

Calhoun sprang into action gathering information. On the weekend after receiving Jackson's letter, he made a hurried visit to James Monroe, and continued to correspond with the ex-president over the next two weeks. He also wrote William Wirt, Monroe's attorney general, who had been part of the cabinet meetings in question. Both men agreed that it had been the general consensus of the cabinet, including Crawford, that Jackson had gone beyond his orders, and that only John Quincy Adams had defended Jackson. They both remembered that Calhoun had pushed for an inquiry, but also that he had given his "hearty concurrence" with Monroe's decision to portray Jackson's actions as an honest misunderstanding. Crawford had also claimed in his letter to Forsyth that the cabinet had discussed Jackson's secret January 6, 1818, letter to Monroe offering to take all of Florida if Monroe approved. But both Monroe and Wirt denied the letter had ever been discussed. Calhoun even wrote to Postmaster General William Barry to ask about the amount of time a letter would have taken to reach Nashville from Washington in 1818 in order to prove that Jackson could not have received a reply to the letter before he departed Nashville for Florida in late January.[28]

On May 29 Calhoun responded to Jackson at length and in a formal tone that clearly indicated he was writing with an eye to the whole business being made public. From the very first lines it was clear that Calhoun understood Jackson's letter as a charge of dishonesty, an accusation freighted with moral significance in the honor culture that both men inhabited. "I wish to be distinctly understood," Calhoun wrote with cold fury, "that, however high my respect is, for your personal character, and the exalted station, which you occupy, I cannot recognize the right on your part to call in question my conduct on the interesting occasion, to which your letter refers. I acted on that occasion in the discharge of a high official duty, and under responsibility to my conscience and my country only." Calhoun was effectively pulling retroactive rank on Jackson, reminding him that at the time of the Seminole War, Calhoun had been his superior. In the rest of the letter Calhoun meticulously demolished Jackson's argument, reconstructing the course of events evidently from his own records and from those he had gathered from Monroe and Wirt to show that Jackson had never received the authorization he claimed and that only a generous interpretation of his actions by Monroe had saved him. Calhoun practically dared Jackson to make the whole thing public.[29]

Even Jackson's most sympathetic biographer places the responsibility for the break in relations on Jackson. But while the facts were on Calhoun's side when it came to Jackson's orders, it was also true that there had been a distinct difference between Calhoun's role in the cabinet meetings and the impression that he gave to Jackson ever afterward. It was this difference, as much as a disagreement over orders, that hurt Jackson's pride and made him feel he had been lied to. For Jackson loyalty and consistency were everything, while Calhoun was always able to rationalize apparent inconsistencies in ways that made logical, if not emotional, sense.[30]

Jackson's advisor William Lewis later recalled that he had never seen Jackson more upset than he was when he received Calhoun's letter, a bold claim considering Jackson's temper. To Jackson, Calhoun's letter was an admission of a betrayal that connected the hostility to Margaret Eaton, the anti-tariff movement, and the broader resistance he faced during his presidency to his vice president's ambition to succeed him. In effect, the scandal drew all the swirling problems of Jackson's administration to a point in the person of John C. Calhoun. In his reply to Calhoun, Jackson wrote bitterly, "I…never expected to have occasion to say of you, in the langauge [*sic*] of Cesar, *et tu Brute*."[31] By August, Jackson was writing to Lewis describing Calhoun as an "ambitious demagogue," who was leading young politicians like Robert Hayne and South Carolina governor James Hamilton Jr. astray with his nullification doctrines and would "sacrafice friends & country, & move heaven & earth, if he had the power, to gratify his unholy ambition."[32] Meanwhile, Calhoun wrote to Virgil Maxcy that in his continuing exchange with Jackson, "I am determined to keep my temper, but not to yield the hundredth part of an inch."[33] Upon his return to South Carolina, Calhoun offered a toast at a Fourth of July dinner in Pendleton warning against "consolidation and disunion—the two extremes of our system." In August, for the first time, he began signing his letters from Pendleton as coming from "Fort Hill" instead of Clergy Hall, a reference to a fort that had stood nearby during the American Revolution and perhaps a sign of the battle Calhoun saw ahead.[34]

Jackson was not the only one who assumed that Calhoun was driving events in South Carolina. Some of Calhoun's friends, especially Duff Green and Virgil Maxcy, begged him to use his influence to put an end to a movement that they feared would irreparably damage his national standing. Green assured him, "*You* are to be the sufferer."[35] Calhoun replied with frustration to Virgil Maxcy, "My friends, out of the state, seem to think…that [my duty is] to step forward in order to arrest the current of events. They appear to take it for granted, that it is in my power." Only Jackson could stop the course of events in South Carolina, Calhoun wrote, by relieving the state's burden. Nevertheless, Calhoun assured Maxcy that if he really thought disunion would result from nullification, "I would not hesitate, devoted to our system of government as I am, to throw myself in the current with the view to arrest it at any hazard." Calhoun simply did not accept the accusation, hurled by Webster and Jackson with great effect, that nullification would inevitably result in disunion.[36]

CALHOUN HAD SO FAR engaged in little of the fearmongering about slavery that increasingly characterized the debate over nullification, even in the upcountry. But by the fall of 1830 he had begun to think more seriously about what lay behind the divide in interests between northern manufacturers and southern planters. Many southerners had been alarmed that spring when Congressman Charles Mercer of Virginia introduced a bill allocating federal funds to aid the work of the American Colonization Society in transporting freed slaves to Africa. Calhoun seemed to have this on his mind months later when he wrote to Virgil Maxcy, "I consider the Tariff act as the occasion, rather than the real cause of the present unhappy state of things. The truth can no longer be disguised, that the peculiar domestic institution of the Southern States, and the consequent direction, which that and her soil and climate have given to her industry, has placed them in regard to taxation and appropriations in opposite relation to the majority of the Union." This realization, Calhoun told Maxcy, made it all the more important that South Carolina hold true to her reserved rights now, for if she yielded in the case of the tariff she could never reclaim them, and they would see eventually "their domestic institutions subordinated by Colonization and other schemes, and themselves & children reduced to wretchedness."[37]

WHEN CALHOUN REACHED WASHINGTON again at the end of 1830, he found the rumors about his feud with Jackson still swirling. The Jackson camp had started another newspaper, the *Washington Globe*, under the editorship of Kentuckian Francis Preston Blair, that would not be subject to Duff Green's sympathy for Calhoun in the *United States Telegraph*. In one of the *Globe*'s first issues Blair announced that Jackson would not decline to serve a second term.

Determined not to let rumor, the *Globe*'s attacks, or Van Buren's machinations completely undermine his influence or stain his honor, Calhoun made the decision to publish all the correspondence on the Seminole War between himself and Jackson. In preparation, he sent the collections of documents he intended to publish to John Quincy Adams for review, and he had Duff Green submit the collection to John Eaton so that he could show them to Jackson before Green published them in the *Telegraph*. But Eaton never showed Jackson the letters, and when they appeared in the *Telegraph* on February 17, 1831, Jackson's rage knew no bounds.[38] The correspondence, along with Calhoun's prefatory statement addressed "To The People of the United States," was reprinted in pamphlet form, and Calhoun eagerly circulated it in the weeks after its publication. The Jackson press attacked the pamphlet and Calhoun viciously, but others not usually inclined to side with Calhoun judged it effective. Henry Clay observed that Calhoun "must be allowed to have attained the advantage."[39] It had to be more than coincidence that not long after the pamphlet was published Virgil Maxcy facilitated the beginning of a rapprochement between Calhoun and John Quincy Adams.[40]

The presidency was certainly still on Calhoun's mind, and he continued to be viewed as a contender for the nation's highest office. As Calhoun made his way back to South Carolina in March 1831 he attended an enthusiastic dinner arranged by Virginia governor John Floyd, who made it clear that he would support Calhoun for president over Jackson. A few days later, over breakfast in Columbia with Henry DeSaussure and James Henry Hammond, a fiercely ambitious young lawyer and the editor of the pro-nullification newspaper *Southern Times*, Calhoun charted a path that he believed might lead him to the presidency. That path involved passing a constitutional amendment to give the West the internal improvements it sought, reducing the tariff to levels sufficient to provide revenue for the federal government but keeping high duties on the most important manufactured goods, and, of course, giving the South free trade. As Hammond walked out with Calhoun after breakfast, Calhoun assured him that he would not abandon the fight against the tariff, and would "throw himself entirely on the South and if possible to be more Southern." Obviously, the tension between Calhoun's presidential aspirations and the need to maintain his influence back home were on his mind. Hammond noted Calhoun was "much less disposed to harangue than usual" and observed a "listlessness" about him that showed that "his mind was deeply engaged."[41]

THAT MAY, JAMES HAMILTON Jr., South Carolina's foremost nullification organizer, launched an unprecedented campaign to rally democratic popular support for nullification, building on the success of the nullifiers in the 1830 elections in the state. As part of the effort, at a dinner on May 19 at St. Andrew's Hall in Charleston, George McDuffie gave the sort of speech worthy of a revolutionary. A terrifically ugly man, with deep-set eyes, a huge protruding nose, and perpetually disheveled black hair, McDuffie looked like a Presbyterian minister prepared to preach the horrors of hell. Instead, that night he preached the horrors of "the Union, such as the majority have made it," proclaiming, "I say it in the spirit of the decalogue, 'I will not bow down and worship this false idol.'" Their ancestors had rebelled against England over a "miserable tax of 3d. a pound on tea," McDuffie reminded them, spitting out the question, "Great God! Are we the descendants of those ancestors?" These were not the mild and moderate colors Calhoun had painted nullification with in the *Exposition*.[42]

Upon reading McDuffie's speech, Duff Green wrote to Calhoun that it had caused him "a fealing [*sic*] of distress you cannot imagine," and that unless Calhoun acted quickly to separate himself from McDuffie, "it seales your fate."[43] Perhaps more consequential than Green's appeal in driving Calhoun to action were calls like the one addressed to him in the anti-nullification *Camden Journal*, which put the matter in terms of the openness and honesty that honor required. "You are charged with having sanctioned the doctrine of Nullification," wrote the *Journal*'s editor, Constans Freeman Daniels, demanding that Calhoun openly declare his position and adding, "You are not the man to mystify or equivocate."[44]

Calhoun knew the moment had come. His mind had been made up about the issue for four years, and his authorship of the *Exposition* was widely assumed, but he had kept silent in public for fear of damaging his presidential prospects. Even now, he could change course and come out against nullification, joining the substantial group of moderates and unionists that still existed in South Carolina, men like James Louis Petigru, Hugh Swinton Legaré, and Daniel Huger. On July 4 this group held a public meeting at First Presbyterian Church in Charleston and read a fiery and threatening letter from Andrew Jackson in which Jackson promised to uphold the "high and sacred duties" entrusted to him by the Constitution.[45] Joining them would have endeared Calhoun to many nationally, perhaps even increasing his slim chance to challenge Jackson. But it is unlikely Calhoun ever considered this possibility. When his mind reached a conclusion, it latched and held firm. Moreover, going over to the unionists would leave him no ability to rein in the ascendant radicals, including his own lieutenant McDuffie, who were in his view as much a threat to the balance and stability of the Union as the majoritarian tyranny of the tariff. With resignation Calhoun wrote Virgil Maxcy, "[McDuffie's speech] brings matters to a point; and I must meet it, without delay & manfully."[46]

DURING THE NEXT FEW weeks Calhoun worked constantly in the little office behind the main house at Fort Hill. It was there that he composed what came to be known as the Fort Hill Address—perhaps on the very desk he had used in the House of Representatives during the War of 1812, which had been given to him as a gift.

The tone of the address, first published in the *Pendleton Messenger* on August 3, 1831, was deliberately moderate, no doubt to set it off from McDuffie and other firebrands whose incendiary style was alienating even state rights proponents outside the state. Calhoun put the difference of opinions on nullification down to the "great diversity of the human intellect," and admitted that though he was sure of his argument, "the error may possibly be with me," though he added, "but if so…I have not been able to detect it."

The address focused primarily on the historical relationship between the state and general governments, rehearsing all the historical precedents, especially Jefferson's Virginia resolution (a more radical 1799 version of which had recently been discovered and spread by the nullifiers). Rebutting arguments that Webster had put forward during his debate with Robert Hayne, Calhoun asserted that the Constitution was a "compact" between what were in essence independent nations. This was the core of Calhoun's constitutional theory, a presupposition from which, if accepted, all else flowed with an irresistible logic: the states were sovereign entities that preceded the Union, had delegated specific powers to the federal government to be exercised for their common good and protection while retaining all other powers for themselves, and had the final authority to interpret the terms of that agreement. Quoting Jefferson's Virginia resolution at length, Calhoun asserted that from the compact theory flowed the "right of interposition…be it called what it may, State right, veto, nullification, or any other name." (In fact, Calhoun almost always avoided the word nullification, seeing it as too negative in connotation for the positive sense in which he wished the measure portrayed.)

At some point in the future, Calhoun believed, or said he believed, the "advance of knowledge" might bring about a situation in which "all the guards of liberty may be dispensed with," when every part of the community would consider not only its own interests but those of others. But, he wrote, "I fear experience has already proved that we are far removed from such a state; and that we must, consequently, rely on the old and clumsy, but approved mode of checking power, in order to prevent or correct abuses." In closing, Calhoun wrote that he had stated his opinions in order that South Carolina might be fairly understood, but professed to have little hope of changing anyone's mind. Such a hope, he wrote, would be evidence of "a profound ignorance of the human heart." It was a remarkable statement about the realities of human nature for someone who had always been so devoted to the natural power of reason and argument.[47]

The address was reprinted in newspapers and pamphlets throughout the country under the title "Opinions of the Vice-President on the Relations of the States and General Government."[48] It would become a part of Calhoun's legend that he turned his back on his own presidential ambitions for the sake of his native region and state. This overstates what Calhoun knew at the time, but certainly he realized it would not help his chances. "I know not how it will be received to the North," he wrote Virgil Maxcy, "tho I suppose not with much approbation."[49] A year later, as the presidential election approached, he told Samuel Ingham that he was willing to be nominated for the presidency, as some were urging, but acknowledged that his name "would way down any ticket…in the Tariff states."[50]

Alongside the publication of the Fort Hill Address, the popular organizing campaign for nullification remained in full swing in South Carolina. If Calhoun's *Exposition* and Fort Hill Address became the systematic theology of the movement, convincing many uncertain about the constitutionality or wisdom of nullification that it was a legitimate and moderate measure, the new States Rights and Free Trade Association, formed in Charleston that July, provided, quite literally, the catechism of the movement. Intended for "the common man with no other qualification than common sense," and incorporating answers to questions such as "What is a tariff?" and "Is it not in our interest to encourage home industry rather than foreign?" (the answer, of course, was no), the *Catechism on the Tariff* published in 1831 was one of the tools in an unprecedented and brilliantly organized campaign to turn public opinion in South Carolina toward nullification over the coming year.[51] Calhoun, meanwhile, believed in watching and waiting—and he told his younger and more impetuous kinsman and ally Francis W. Pickens that he was "decidedly against active operations" that summer, hoping that national opinion would change.[52]

IN THE MIDST OF the political furor over nullification that summer, an enslaved man named Aleck who worked in the Calhouns' house ran away. "Aleck…gave us the slip yesterday and is now in the woods," Calhoun wrote his brother-in-law James Edward on August 26, three weeks after publishing the Fort Hill Address. Aleck, he believed, might be headed for the Bath plantation near Abbeville, and he asked Edward "to give Mr. Gibson my overseer immediate notice in order that he may be also on the look out." Aleck had "offended" Floride in some way, and she had threatened the house slave with a "severe whipping." If Aleck were caught, Calhoun instructed, "have him severely whipped and sent back immediately."[53]

Aleck ran away just as news of a slave rebellion in Virginia was electrifying the South and the nation. Nat Turner's rebellion began early in the morning of August 22 and by the time Aleck escaped three days later the rebellion was over, fifty-odd white people and scores, perhaps hundreds, of enslaved people were dead, and Nat Turner himself was still on the loose. He would not be caught for six weeks. The rebellion was a turning point in the national debate that convinced many white southerners that attacking slavery was tantamount to inciting mass murder.[54]

It is not clear if Calhoun had heard of the rebellion or whether he connected Aleck's escape to it, but his mood at the end of August was already dark. He had been forced into the open politically, with uncertain results. Three weeks before Aleck's escape Floride had miscarried in what was at least her twelfth pregnancy, and by late August her health was still dangerously precarious. By this time Calhoun also knew that he would have little or no cotton crop to sell that year. Heavy rain had caused the Seneca River to overflow its bounds, flooding many of his fields, including fifty acres of cotton and nearly all his corn. Although he did not know it yet, Calhoun had also lost his entire crop at the Bath plantation, leaving only about fifty acres of salable cotton from his entire crop on both plantations. It was "a calamitous year to me," he wrote to James Edward a few days later once he understood the whole extent of the damage.[55]

Aleck, meanwhile, was captured by a man named Hiram Keller the day after he ran away. He had been found near Abbeville, just as Calhoun had suspected, and as was usual in such cases, Keller billed Calhoun $3.97 for "catching and jailing" Aleck.[56]

Perhaps venting his frustration by exercising control over something—the one thing completely in his power—Calhoun determined to teach Aleck a lesson. Abbeville planter Armistead Burt, a political ally and protégé who was married to Calhoun's niece, had taken charge of Aleck, and Calhoun wrote to him with instructions. "As I am desirous to prevent a repetition," he wrote, "I wish you to have him lodged in jail for one week, to be fed on bread & water and to employ someone for me to give him 30 lashes well laid on, at the end of the time." During the same period, punishments imposed on slaves by the freeholder courts, composed of local landowners that tried slaves in the region, ranged from a low of five to a high of thirty-nine lashes for serious offenses, and juries sometimes specified whether the lashes were to be "light" or "well laid on." Calhoun closed his letter by congratulating Burt on the state of anti-tariff sentiment in Abbeville. "Our cause is founded in truth and must prevail; or the liberty of the country be lost."[57]

That Calhoun could order the brutal punishment of one of his slaves for running away at the same moment that he was pouring all his intellectual energy into preserving his own and his neighbors' liberty offers a stark reminder that when Calhoun and many other Americans used words we still use today, words like *liberty* and *democracy*, they attached to them different, unspoken meanings that must be kept in mind as we read and struggle with their arguments. As Calhoun had once told John Quincy Adams, white southerners simply did not consider the sentiments that Thomas Jefferson had expressed in the Declaration to apply to slaves (the statement could have easily applied to many white northerners, as well). So concerned with power being checked and bounded to preserve liberty for himself and his fellow white Americans, Calhoun saw no contradiction in exercising the most extreme and total form of power over Aleck, a form of power that John Locke had aptly called a state of war. So conscious in one sphere of "how little regard we have for the interests of others while in pursuit of our own,"[58] he saw no contradiction in bending the lives and interests of all those enslaved at Fort Hill to his own will. It is tempting to focus on the contradiction, and to chalk this up to an innate human capacity for self-deception and hypocrisy. Calhoun's own Calvinist family would have understood this interpretation. But it is not the whole story. The apparent contradiction between black slavery and white freedom had a hidden inner logic, a logic Calhoun had once explained to John Quincy Adams on a walk home during the Missouri crisis. In 1831 few had yet expressed it openly, and fewer still had theorized on it, but in the years ahead Calhoun would do just that.

At the beginning of 1832, Calhoun was back in Washington, where he relished casting the tie-breaking vote to kill Jackson's nomination of Martin Van Buren as ambassador to England, a nomination that signaled Van Buren's favored status as Jackson's successor. The opposition to Van Buren's nomination in the Senate also represented a gesture of goodwill toward Calhoun by an anti-Jackson coalition hoping to win him over more completely to their side. Thomas Hart

Benton later recalled Calhoun saying that Van Buren's failure to win approval would "kill him, sir, kill him dead. He will never kick, sir, never kick." The failure did not kill Van Buren, but Calhoun must have relished the small taste of revenge, although he would never have admitted the pleasure.[59]

At the end of the session, John Quincy Adams, now back in the House of Representatives after his defeat by Jackson in 1828, shepherded through a skillfully crafted compromise tariff that under other circumstances might have satisfied Calhoun, and which did satisfy many other southerners. In an attempt to appease the nullifiers and build a larger coalition against Jackson, Adams's tariff reduced rates more or less back to the 1824 levels, and the bill passed the House with substantial support from the South and a final tally in favor 132 to 65. In the Senate some of Adams's most liberal concessions to the South, including the removal of a minimum tax on cotton textiles, were put back into the bill, but it still passed the Senate 32 to 16, although with only two votes from the South. Many northerners and southerners viewed the new tariff as an acceptable compromise that preserved the protective system while softening it, and hoped that it would end the crisis. But as Calhoun wrote to nullifier and ally Waddy Thompson on July 8 as he prepared to leave Washington, "The question is no longer one of free trade, but liberty and despotism." Calhoun and most of the nullifiers in South Carolina refused to accept any bill that included protectionist elements.[60]

In August, Calhoun responded to a public request from South Carolina governor James Hamilton Jr. to elaborate on his views about nullification, although after the *Exposition* and the Fort Hill Address it seemed impossible that Calhoun would have much more to say. He did. In a lengthy and widely republished reply to Hamilton, Calhoun repeated his argument that the Union was a compact of the several states, that nullification was not the same thing as secession or disunion. Most significantly, he laid out a distinction between the usual operation of the government formed by the Constitution, under which a simple majority might make laws that were binding so long as they were in line with the delegated and reserved powers of the national and state governments respectively, and what he called the "concurrent majority," the authority that had brought the Constitution itself into existence and which was therefore required to modify it or to resolve any fundamental disagreement. The balance and equilibrium of the system could only be preserved, Calhoun wrote, by "maintaining the ascendency of the CONSTITUTION MAKING AUTHORITY OVER THE LAW MAKING—THE CONCURRENT MAJORITY OVER THE ABSOLUTE MAJORITY." Legislative majorities could make laws, and so long as those laws adhered to the Constitution, those laws must be respected and could be enforced. But legislative majorities could not change the Constitution. Only the people of the states could do that through the process outlined in the Constitution itself. Nevertheless, Calhoun realized that the Constitution was not always clear, and must be interpreted. Thus the power to interpret the Constitution was the wellspring of all power in the system, and could not be left to the system itself, either to majorities in Congress or to the Supreme Court. In the final instance, the power to interpret or change must always refer back to the people of the respective states met in convention, the creative power that had created the Constitution. And only a consensus of three-fourths or more of those state conventions could be considered a legitimate authority, the voice of "the people" of the United States. This is what Calhoun meant by the concurrent (i.e., consensus) majority, which would eventually be his main contribution to constitutional thought.[61]

AS THE FALL ELECTIONS approached in 1832, the growing divide in South Carolina over nullification gave way to violence. In Greenville in August unionist newspaper editor Benjamin F. Perry killed nullifying editor Turner Bynum in a duel. In Charleston, nullifiers and unionists marched and countermarched, exchanging blows and bricks and only narrowly avoiding large-scale bloodshed.[62] The debate took on such existential and apocalyptic stakes that a religious revival broke out, part of a wave of revivals that had begun the previous year, bringing about a large number of conversions, especially in the lowcountry, which had previously resisted the sort of evangelical religion prevalent in the upcountry. In fact, what became known as the nullification revivals completed the unification of the state that had begun with the spread of slavery and cotton to the upcountry in Calhoun's youth, with waves of religious fervor sweeping back down into the lowcountry like a returning tide, tying the state together "like a great family" in the words of one observer. Some cynical observers saw the adoption of evangelical religion by prominent nullifiers like Robert Barnwell Smith and Colonel Charles Cotesworth Pinckney as a convenient way to appeal to parts of the state population that had previously been ignored. "It is like Mahomet's faith," the despondent unionist James Louis Petigru wrote in October. "They combine war and devotion…fanaticism of every kind is on the increase."[63]

One view of Calhoun's role in the crisis can be seen in an anonymous, satirical pamphlet published in 1832, titled *Memoirs of a Nullifier*. Sympathetic to the nullification cause, the pamphlet relates the story of a hapless southerner who is duped by the Devil into selling his soul. Just as the Devil is about to take his due, a messenger appears to call him to a Unionist meeting in Charleston, which the Devil rushes off to attend, giving his victim time to find some escape. The young victim quickly seeks out "three famous conjurers" from South Carolina sitting around a pot like the witches of *Macbeth*, one of whom was a "tall and slender man, with an eye of extraordinary brilliancy…In his presence, almost every one felt that undescribable power, by which the superior spirit sways the minds of other men." The figure sat, "waving his wand" and "reading from a paper dated, 'Pendleton, July 26, 1831,' and called an 'Exposition.'" The conjurers agree to concoct a solution to free him from his agreement with the Devil, and into the pot they dump writings by Jefferson, Turnbull's pamphlet *The Crisis*, speeches by McDuffie and Hayne, and bones of their revolutionary ancestors. The result is a goddess-like figure who appears from the pot and, upon the Devil's return, puts him to rout. When the astonished King of Hell asks for her name, she replies that her name is "NULLIFICATION." There could hardly be a better illustration of the kind of dark magic that some believed Calhoun had concocted, but many South Carolinians embraced it with open arms.[64]

On election day, October 8, 1832, the nullifiers' superior organizational skills and Calhoun's continued advocacy on behalf of the doctrine resulted in statewide victory for the nullification party. "Our election takes place today," Calhoun wrote Virgil Maxcy, expressing confidence that his allies would win. "A convention of the State will certainly be called and the [tariff] act nullified." Such a convention, Calhoun predicted, would not bring disunion, anarchy, or civil war, but rather would provide an important opportunity for the states to "adjust all constitutional differences, and thusly restore general harmony. We have run nearly fifty years on the first tack. It is a wonderful run; but it is time to bring up the reckoning, in order to take a fresh departure."[65]

On November 24 a convention called by the state legislature nullified the tariffs of 1828 as well as the more moderate one passed earlier that year, proclaiming that the acts would no longer be enforced in the state beginning on February 1, 1833. The ordinance required an oath from state officials to support it, and warned that any interference by the Jackson administration, especially an attempt to close the port of Charleston, would be seen as cause for leaving the Union. Days later, the legislature appointed Robert Hayne as governor and, on December 12, elected Calhoun to fill the remainder of Hayne's term as senator. Calhoun sent his resignation as vice president on December 28 from Columbia, and departed immediately for Washington.[66]

BY THE TIME SOUTH CAROLINA nullified the tariff it was clear that Andrew Jackson had resoundingly defeated Henry Clay to win a second term, with Martin Van Buren as vice president. At first, nobody was sure exactly how Jackson would respond to nullification. After all, he had recently looked the other way as the state of Georgia ignored a Supreme Court ruling that interfered with their designs on the Cherokee lands within their borders, and earlier that year in his veto of the recharter of the Second Bank of the United States Jackson had portrayed the bank as an abuse of federal power. On December 10, in a proclamation on the acts of South Carolina, Jackson made his position absolutely clear. He declared nullification "incompatible with the existence of the Union, contradicted expressly by the letter of the Constitution, unauthorized by its spirit, inconsistent with every principle on which it was founded, and destructive of the great object for which it was formed." He utterly denied the compact theory, maintaining that the United States was a "government, not a league," that the Union had preceded the states, and that it acted directly for and on the people of the whole country. Finally, he forcefully addressed the impossibility of secession, arguing that states surrendered "essential parts of sovereignty" when they joined the Union.[67] In fact, while Jackson's proclamation was heralded by many, it was such a sweeping assertion of the power of the national government and the durability of the Union that it essentially reified many of the nullifiers' accusations and horrified many state rights advocates—even those who opposed nullification. In South Carolina, as the import of Jackson's message sank in, the nullifiers tried unsuccessfully to purchase 120,000 pounds of gunpowder from a Delaware company that firmly refused the order. But Jackson was not as intransigent as he seemed. Even as he held out the threat of force, he immediately began fashioning an olive branch in the form of a revised tariff.[68]

CALHOUN'S ARRIVAL IN WASHINGTON to take his seat in the Senate was greeted with great curiosity on account of his changed and central role in the unfolding national drama. "Will his high soarings end in disappointment and humiliation or be drowned in blood?"

wondered Margaret Bayard Smith as Calhoun made his way toward Washington. "However he may now err, he is one of the noblest and most generous spirits I have ever met with. I am certain *he* is deceived himself, and believes he is now fulfilling the duty of a *true patriot*."[69] Few were so evenhanded about Calhoun, who had always inspired strong reactions but now became one of the most divisive figures in American politics, a role he would play on and off for the rest of his life. Earlier that year his old nemesis John Randolph, a fervent state rights proponent who thought Calhoun's nullification a fanciful abstraction, had written to Andrew Jackson about Calhoun's turn. "Calhoun by this time must be in hell," Randolph wrote. "He is self-mutilated like the Fanatic that emasculated himself."[70]

Calhoun took his seat on January 4. He would remain in the Senate, with only short interruptions, for the rest of his life. It was in many ways the best and perhaps only space in the rapidly changing American political environment suited to his temperament and talents, and as its president for the previous eight years he had mastered its rules and customs. After this long apprenticeship, he took up his role at a moment of extreme crisis.

Calhoun entered the Senate chamber a little late on the morning of January 16 just as Felix Grundy, his old messmate and now a devoted Jackson man, was in the midst of reading a message from Jackson requesting Congress to authorize him to enforce the collection of tariff revenue. The message was milder than his proclamation a few weeks earlier, and arguably asked for powers the president already had, but the resulting bill, called the Force Bill by its opponents, would be one of the most controversial acts of legislation in American history.

As he listened Calhoun realized instantly, as he wrote to Armistead Burt later that day, "that it ought not to pass without a blow."[71] Twenty-one-year-old Charles Cotesworth Pinckney was in the gallery that day, and years later as an old man he recalled that as Calhoun rose "there was hushed silence in the Senate chamber, and the deep emotion of the speaker was reflected in the faces of his auditors. He apologized for his excitement, on the ground that he had not spoken in a deliberative assembly for sixteen years." Pinckney recalled Calhoun pacing like a cornered lion: "His back was against the railing which separated the Senate from the lobby. There was a long desk before him. He had pushed the chairs out of his way, to the ends of the desk, and delivered his speech walking rapidly from side to side of his cage."[72] Admitting that he was out of order, Calhoun denounced the request as rank tyranny by the executive, declaring with barely restrained fury, "We are threatened to have our throats cut, and those of our wives and children" for resisting the tariff by constitutional measures. He quickly apologized for his "warmth," but the president's request for the Force Bill perfectly illustrated what Calhoun saw as the threat of a consolidated government and a tyrannical demagogue.[73]

Calhoun was sure Jackson had gone too far, and he immediately wrote to James Hamilton back in South Carolina, urging him to act "prudently" and to "give no pretext for force." He was convinced that both the public and Congress were coming around to South Carolina's perspective. At a January 21 meeting in Charleston, members of the nullification convention agreed to postpone putting their measure into effect, and declared that they were willing to pay lower duties if Congress passed them. It was an opening for a compromise.[74]

At the same time he was declaring his willingness to use force, Jackson was also working behind the scenes to negotiate such a compromise in the form of lower tariff rates. But the administration's efforts ended up going nowhere, mostly because advocates of the tariff found the cuts too severe. Then Henry Clay stepped into breach. Seeing an opportunity to avert crisis and claim the credit for himself rather than leaving it to Jackson, Clay began secretly visiting manufacturers and talking to friends. He also talked to Calhoun, and found that they agreed on one thing: Jackson should not get the credit for a compromise. Around the time of this meeting young Charles Cotesworth Pinckney encountered Calhoun and found him "smiling, even buoyant," which Pinckney thought odd given the circumstances. When Pinckney expressed his fear that there might be a war, Calhoun told him not to worry. "General Jackson, reckless as he is, can scarcely involve the country in that calamity," Calhoun assured him. "Depend upon it, sir, there will be no war. Nullification is a peaceful remedy."[75]

On February 11 Clay announced to surprise that he would bring his own compromise bill forward in order to preserve both the Union and some semblance of protection. Clay proposed the tariff rates be lowered over ten years, with the most dramatic cuts being reserved for 1841 and 1842, effectively ending protection for many industries but giving them plenty of time to plan for it. One northern paper accused Clay of "parricide" for killing his own creation, but most acknowledged that Clay was patriotically playing a role that few others on the stage could have filled. The next day Calhoun rose and dramatically announced that he would support Clay's bill in order to preserve the Union and because it gave a fair deal to manufacturers. The gallery of the Senate erupted into cheers, whistling, and stamping that only ended with the threat to clear the galleries.[76]

Later that week, on February 15, Calhoun began a two-day assault on the Force Bill and two very different antagonists, Andrew Jackson and Daniel Webster, who had unexpectedly found themselves on the same side in response to South Carolina's intransigence. Webster and Calhoun had been circling one another for weeks, both waiting, preparing, letting others debate, trying to get the advantage of rebuttal that Webster had used so magnificently in his debate with Robert Hayne. But Calhoun finally plunged ahead, while those in the galleries, which had been crowded for weeks in anticipation, tried to stay warm on one of the coldest days of the year, with snow falling heavily outside.[77]

The heart of Calhoun's argument was that the Union was a compact of sovereign states that could never be held together by force without irreparably altering the nature of the Union and the Constitution itself, as he claimed the Force Bill did. "I go on the ground that this

Constitution was made by the States; that it is a federal union of the States, in which the several States still retain their sovereignty," he argued. "In spite of all that has been said, I maintain that sovereignty is in its nature indivisible...we might as well speak of half a square, or half of a triangle, as of half a sovereignty. It is a gross error to confound the *exercise* of sovereign powers with *sovereignty* itself, or the *delegation* of them with a *surrender* of them." On that stormy day, Calhoun finally made the analogy that he had delicately skirted until then, asking, "Does any man in his senses believe that this beautiful structure—this harmonious aggregate of States, produced by the joint consent of all— can be preserved by force?...No, no. You cannot keep the States united in the constitutional and federal bonds by force. Force may, indeed, hold the parts together, but such union would be the bond between master and slave; a union of exaction on one side, and of unqualified obedience on the other."

It was both a clear statement of Calhoun's long-held idea of the nation as held together by bonds of affection and interest, and an astonishingly frank admission that slavery was, in fact, what John Locke had called it: a state of war between master and slave. That, Calhoun warned, was what the Union would be reduced to if Jackson's request were honored. Whether Calhoun thought of old Adam, of Sawney, or, perhaps, of Aleck, we cannot know.[78]

Webster rose to reply as soon as Calhoun sat down. Skillfully choosing his targets, Webster focused on the two legs of Calhoun's argument: the compact theory and the idea that a state had the right to interpret the Constitution for itself. Webster declared that the people of the United States were "one in making war, and one in making peace; they are one in regulating commerce, and one in laying duties of imposts." He appealed to the preamble of the Constitution, and asserted that the Constitution had created the Union as "perpetual and immortal." "The majority *must* govern," Webster insisted. "In matters of common concern, the judgment of a majority *must* stand as a judgement of the whole." Webster concluded by averring that he had no fears for the Union, because the people, including the people of South Carolina, would sustain it. Webster's claims about the power and durability of the Union were more sweeping and more forceful than any that had previously been made, and proved central to the countervailing doctrine of perpetual Union that would shape a generation of Americans, including a young Abraham Lincoln.[79]

Several days later, Calhoun took the opening provided by Webster when he admitted that if Calhoun was right about the compact theory, he was right about everything. Calhoun had the secretary of the Senate read sections of Webster's second reply to Hayne from three years earlier in which Webster had called the Constitution a "compact" and a "bargain." As the secretary began reading, Webster reportedly asked, "What is that?" And when told it was his own speech, he demanded to see the text, looked at it for a moment, looked over at Henry Clay, and shrugged—as if to say, Charles Pinckney thought, "he has me." Many of the senators in the chamber, understanding what Calhoun was about to do, began to smile.[80] Did not these terms, used by Webster in his most famous speech, grant Calhoun's premise, Calhoun asked? He continued, quoting extensively from Massachusetts's ratification of the Constitution, which called the Constitution "an explicit and solemn compact…to form a more perfect union." And he quoted from Jean-Jacques Burlamaqui's *Principles of Natural and Political Right*, in which the Swiss political theorist wrote of governmental covenants, "It is evident that…each of the contracting parties acquires a right not only of exercising the power granted to it, but also of preserving that original right."[81] During the speech John Randolph, who hated Webster even more than he hated Calhoun, and who had to be carried into the chamber to listen to the debate, was heard yelling at someone whose headwear obscured his view, "Take away that hat. I want to see Webster die, muscle by muscle."[82] An English visitor in the galleries turned to the young Charles Pinckney and declared, "Sir, your nullifier has eaten Webster up!" Three years after the Civil War, in 1868, Alexander Stephens, lately vice president of the failed Confederacy, used the speech to defend secession, exulting that the argument was "a crusher, an extinguisher, an annihilator!...This speech of his was not answered then, it has not been answered since, and in my judgment never will be, or can be answered while truth has its legitimate influence, and reason controls the judgment of men!"[83] In any case, Webster never made a substantial reply to Calhoun, although perhaps because he considered the issue exhausted.

OPINIONS HAVE ALWAYS BEEN divided about whether Calhoun or Webster won the debate. Webster was the superior orator, as even Calhoun would have admitted. But John Quincy Adams, no friend of Calhoun's theories and a fair judge of logic, admitted that Calhoun's compact theory was a hard one to rebut. "He hung his cause on a broken hinge," Adams wrote of Webster's soaring appeal to nationalism.[84]

More interesting than who won the debate is that Webster and Calhoun represented two different conservative outlooks on historical change. Calhoun argued that the nation had changed and required regeneration, an adaptation to new circumstances by applying first principles to craft new safeguards for liberty. What the nation needed, as he wrote to Virgil Maxcy the previous summer, was a "fresh departure," by which he meant a refashioning of the old principles for the unforeseen changes that had occurred.[85] Webster meanwhile asserted the timeless nature of the Union, but in fact, as one of Webster's biographers pointed out, "read back to 1787 what had occurred since that date." Webster was willing to defend the present as the product of history. Calhoun, on the other hand, used the past to prosecute the present.

Also striking is that both men appealed to the people as the ultimate arbiters of the Constitution and the Union, but they conceived of those people in crucially different ways. Webster's argument in essence was that Locke's moment of consent had happened once and for all with the formation of the Constitution, which had been ratified by the people at large, and that sovereignty now resided in that Constitution and the Union it created on behalf of the people. Meanwhile Calhoun's argument posited that Locke's consent of the governed could be continually reinvoked through the mechanism of the state veto as a wellspring for the perfection of the Constitution and the preservation of liberty. In many ways, Webster's argument was the more traditionally conservative.

CONGRESS PASSED BOTH CLAY'S compromise tariff and the Force Bill on March 1, leading Henry Clay to call it the most important day in congressional history. Andrew Jackson and Van Buren were inaugurated on March 4, and on the same day Duff Green published the text of the Force Bill in the *Telegraph* in columns bordered in black—a show of mourning for the death of the Constitution. By then Calhoun was already speeding his way back to South Carolina over frozen roads, often riding in an open mail cart exposed to the weather because it promised to get him back before the meeting of the nullification convention on March 11. Calhoun took no open part in the convention, but his influence clearly prevailed as the convention accepted the compromise that he had helped to craft and repealed the nullification ordinance. For good measure the convention also nullified the Force Bill, a sign that the compromise was in reality only a cease-fire.[86] Calhoun wrote to Christopher Vandeventer two weeks later about what he hoped would be a concerted resistance to the dangers of "consolidated government." "I have no doubt the system has got its death wound. Nullification has dealt the fatal blow. We have applied the same remedy to the blood act [Force Bill]…Other States may live under its reign, but Carolina is resolved to live only under that of the Constitution. There shall be at least one free state."[87] Yet while Andrew Jackson's actions and the Force Bill divided his state rights supporters in states like Georgia, Virginia, and New York, none joined South Carolina, and nullification soon became known as the Carolina doctrine.[88]

IN ONE SENSE THE nullification crisis was part of an argument continuing down to our own day about the relationship between the
nation-state and the market. Calhoun's defense of South Carolina
slaveholders' right to choose what they grew, whom they sold it to, at
what price, and in which market, was rooted in the fact that southern
slaveholders had chosen to participate in an international market while
northern manufacturers had chosen pursuits that required insulation
from that market. Calhoun and South Carolina, often portrayed as isolated during the nullification crisis, were in fact driven by their deep
integration into what one historian has called the empire of cotton, a
global marketplace that helped lay the foundations of modern capitalism and whose beating heart lay in Manchester, England—not in
Lowell, Massachusetts, or in Washington, DC. In 1829 Calhoun wrote
to Samuel Ingham about the East India Company's efforts to nurture
alternate sources of trade besides the United States, especially cotton,
observing that the tariff kept the South from competing in the "general
market of the world." Southern planters, Calhoun observed, did not
suffer because of the low prices offered by the market for their cotton,
but from "the high proportional price of their supplies, occasioned by
the restrictive system." In the coming decades, and over the next century, the world would become more amenable to South Carolina's argument as the market acquired an aura of natural law that many
believed could not be denied, even by national interest. In the meantime, Calhoun's fears were misplaced. As much as British manufacturers might have liked to, it proved difficult for them to find cheaper
sources of cotton than the American South. Slavery was infinitely more
responsive and malleable to the demands of the market than the
peasant-based production of places like India.[89]

In another area, many historians have adopted the criticisms of Andrew Jackson, and indeed of many state rights advocates at the time, in
calling Calhoun's theory and South Carolina's practice fundamentally
undemocratic.[90] Indeed, even if it worked exactly as he envisioned it
working, Calhoun's machinery of state interposition would have

allowed a state to interpret the Constitution for itself as long as it could convince a mere one-fourth of the other states of its case, thwarting the three-fourths majority required to expressly grant the power in question. But this view is predicated not only on sidestepping or dismissing Calhoun's presuppositions and his own descriptions of his theory, but on our modern conception of American democracy, which takes the frame of the nation-state for granted.

Calhoun's own conception of his creation was that it was a democratic solution for a democratic excess, a return to the pure, direct form of democracy of his youth in upcountry South Carolina. Alexis de Tocqueville, who toured America in the midst of the nullification crisis, believed that a commitment to democracy and equality was, in fact, making Americans more like each other and more similar in interests. By 1827 Calhoun had drawn the opposite conclusion. The tariff and burgeoning threats to slavery convinced him that the nation was now too large and diverse in its interests to be ruled by the will of a majority who, because of distance and human nature, could not fairly balance their own interests against those of their countrymen. In response, Calhoun created a mechanism to counter that will and to reestablish the direct link between the government and the governed on the principle that "those who make and execute the laws should be accountable to those on whom the laws in reality operate," as he had written in the Fort Hill Address in a maxim that he believed constituted the purest essence of democracy. Chastened, but still a Jeffersonian at heart, Calhoun's insistence that nullification had to be the work of a state convention, not a legislature, grew out of his belief that governments were simply "agents" of the true sovereign power, the people of the states. "The sovereignty resides elsewhere," he wrote in his public letter to James Hamilton in the summer of 1832, "in the people, not in the Government; and with us, *the people* mean *the people of the several States*."[91]

Perhaps the main objection to seeing Calhoun's arguments as democratic is that he made them in defense of the property rights and economic interests of a slaveholding minority that did not represent even all the white population in the South, and which lived by exploiting enslaved people for profit. But as deep as this contradiction seems to us, and as deep as it seemed to many of Calhoun's contemporaries, it was not a contradiction to him, as the coming years would show.

THIRTEEN

"I Think, I See My Way Clearly on the Slave Question"

M Y DEAR MARIA," CALHOUN WROTE at the end of 1831 to his daughter Anna Maria, now fourteen, who had recently left home to attend a school in Columbia, "I have been waiting some time to hear from you...I do not know, that I ought to censure you for your aversion to writing, as I believe it is in some degree hereditary" (a reference no doubt to Floride). He urged her to overcome this trait because he wanted so badly to hear from her. "You must write to me without delay and give me a full account of everything; the course of studies, the teachers; what you are learning...who are your room mates; and who your particular companions," he pleaded, writing that he looked forward to reading letters filled with her "vivacity, and good sense."[1]

Calhoun needn't have worried. Anna, or Maria, as he sometimes called her, was never at a loss for words. "You provoking creature you," Anna scolded her closest friend Maria Simkins affectionately in 1833 in her first surviving letter, "what made you damp all my hopes by even hinting such a thing as your not coming [to visit Fort Hill]." She proceeded to convey all the gossip from Pendleton and demand the same from Simkins. About the same time she mercilessly needled her bachelor uncle James Edward with the prospect of "some intelligence" about "your old flame Miss Sara DeSaussure (slanderously called 'Old Sal')." Anna had her father's incisive intelligence and evidenced an early interest in politics, something Calhoun relished and encouraged. "I am not one of those, who think your sex ought to have nothing to do with politicks," he wrote in 1832. "They have as much interest in the good condition of their country, as the other sex," although he quickly qualified that "it would be unbecoming them to take an active part in political struggles." Perhaps unsurprisingly, Calhoun was not a suffragist. Nevertheless, he began sending Anna copies of his speeches and updates on political goings-on from Washington, "as you are so much of a politician." From 1831 to the end of his life, Calhoun would enjoy a nearly constant stream of correspondence with Anna when they were apart, fulfilling a need for intellectual and emotional companionship that he never found with her mother. Their relationship was the deepest and most important relationship of his life, and perhaps of hers.[2]

Calhoun's utter delight in Anna probably had something to do with his disappointment in his oldest son, Andrew. Calhoun learned in August 1830 that Andrew had been expelled from Yale along with some fifty of his classmates as a result of a disagreement with the administration, and had left debts unpaid behind him in New Haven that Calhoun was still dealing with in early 1831. Andrew enrolled at South Carolina College but soon dropped out, determining to make his way without an education, which in the South meant planting. On January 3, 1833, as Calhoun was traveling to Washington during the final stage of the nullification crisis, Andrew married Eugenia Chappell, the daughter of one of Calhoun's old congressional colleagues, only to see her die in childbirth thirteen months later at Calhoun's Bath plantation, leaving a little daughter "with the loveliest smile that you ever looked upon," as the grief-stricken Andrew wrote to his uncle James Edward days after his wife's death. The child lived only a few months longer. Indeed, Andrew seemed to attract misfortune and tragedy, and for the rest of his life Calhoun would battle the consequences of his son's decisions.[3]

The rest of the children were still too young to frustrate their father's ambitions. Calhoun's next oldest son, Patrick, would enter West Point in 1837, while the three youngest boys—John Caldwell, James Edward, and William Lowndes—ran wild at Fort Hill, enjoying the benefits of the educational philosophy that Calhoun outlined in an interview with Oliver Dyer in 1849, when he described how South Carolina boys were encouraged to ride horses, shoot squirrels, and jump fences before pursuing intellectual advancement. (During the interview he pointed at Dyer's associate, a cerebral young northerner with a large head, as irrefutable evidence of the northern method.) Considering the results this philosophy had produced by 1849 in his own sons, it is remarkable that Calhoun still thought it worth recommending. Anna's younger sister Martha Cornelia was only eight years old in 1832 and suffered from some sort of degenerative condition—family tradition held it was caused by a fall from a swing—that left her partially disabled, as well as partially deaf. During the 1830s Calhoun and Floride sought medical advice on Cornelia's condition from specialists across the country with no luck, but Cornelia developed the same cheerful disposition that Calhoun prized so much in Anna, and when traveling he frequently bought her presents.[4]

IT WAS THROUGH ANDREW during the summer of 1833 that Calhoun contracted a touch of the mania set off by a mini gold rush in neighboring Georgia on lands recently taken from the Cherokee. Sometime that summer Calhoun discovered that Andrew had purchased an interest in a Georgia gold mine, following the lead of his uncle John Ewing, Floride's brother, who a year earlier had unexpectedly spent $12,000 on a nearby mine that he described breathlessly to family as "rich, or richer, than any mine yet discovered." It was already clear to most of the family by 1832 that John Ewing was not good with money, and it cannot have been a welcome sign of Andrew's judgment that he had copied his uncle.[5]

Perhaps to save his son from the consequences of his impetuous decision, Calhoun took over Andrew's interest in the mine and traveled to the hopefully named mining town of Auraria, Georgia, in June to survey his new investment. Calhoun decided that the mine, called the O'Bar mine after its previous owner, had potential despite his son's impetuous decision, leading a relieved Andrew to write his uncle James Edward, "I am glad of it, for independent of other considerations, I will again regain my reputation." Calhoun immediately began corresponding with Nicholas Biddle, head of the beleaguered Bank of the United States, asking advice on how to exchange gold from the mine to the mint for hard currency. Once he was back in Washington, Calhoun submitted a bar of gold from the O'Bar mine to the mint and received more than $600. Over the next few years Calhoun would buy an interest in several other mining properties in Georgia, putting enslaved men from Fort Hill to work there as miners.[6] He also succeeded in getting a branch of the US Mint established in Dahlonega, where it would be easier to process the gold he hoped the mine would produce.

CALHOUN TRAVELED BACK TO Washington in November 1833, stopping in Charleston to deliver a triumphant address and lay the cornerstone for a monument to the recently deceased radical Robert Turnbull. He occupied very different positions in the state he left behind and the national government he journeyed toward.[7] In South Carolina, Calhoun's central role in bringing the nullification crisis to what many considered a successful conclusion had cemented his alliance with the most radical elements of the nullification party and secured his popularity. Having learned from experience the power that unwavering support from his home state gave him in a crisis, Calhoun would cultivate and maintain a firm grip on South Carolina politics for the next seventeen years. From Washington he corresponded with lieutenants like his young relative, the radical nullifier Francis W. Pickens, to guide affairs back home. Meanwhile opponents like the brilliant young anti-nullifier and future unionist Hugh Swinton Legaré could date their status as political exiles to the nullification crisis.[8] A year after the end of the crisis Calhoun wrote Anna from Washington that another anti-nullifier, South Carolina congressman James Blair, had "under the joint effect of Brandy & opium, and a false political position blew out his brains with a pistol." "He had long indulged in bad habits," Calhoun wrote, making no distinction between Blair's personal and political faults.[9]

Calhoun's view of the country and its prospects had darkened considerably over the past five years. To his brother-in-law James Edward he expressed his skepticism that the republic could last another fifteen years considering the "decay of honor, honesty, and patriotism, and the growth of the opposite vices." "It must be arrested," he wrote, "or revolution will be the alternative."[10] But mixed with these dark predictions was always a seam of Calhoun's unrelenting optimism that time was on his side. "Our cause is gaining daily," he wrote to James Edward in a constantly repeated phrase two years later.[11]

In Washington, Calhoun found himself the leader of a small but powerful minority of nullifiers and state rights advocates who were aligned with neither the Jackson administration nor the powerful opposition associated with Henry Clay. "No measure can be taken but with our assent, where the administration & the opposition parties come into conflict," he wrote Pickens after assessing the lay of the land in December.[12] Although naturally inclined to cooperate with Clay against Jackson, Calhoun was prepared to make the most of his situation.

His first opportunity was the escalating battle between Jackson and Congress over the Second Bank of the United States. In 1832, the bank's president, Nicholas Biddle, had applied to Congress to recharter the bank four years early, daring Jackson to follow through on his threats against the bank, which had influential supporters in Congress, during an election year. Jackson took the dare. When Congress approved the bank's new charter, Jackson vetoed it on July 10, 1832, denouncing the bank for its dangerous and undemocratic concentration of wealth and power and declaring that "the rich and powerful too often bend the acts of government to their selfish purposes." Unsatisfied even to let the bank live out its original charter, Jackson soon determined to withdraw all the government's deposits from the bank, effectively killing it, but two successive secretaries of the Treasury (appointed by Jackson!) refused to remove the deposits, objecting that it was unconstitutional to do so since the bank's original charter, approved by Congress, was still in force. So Jackson removed both secretaries one after the other and temporarily installed future Supreme Court Justice Roger B. Taney, who began diverting government deposits to so-called pet banks all over the country at the end of 1833 under a dubious interpretation of his constitutional authority. Biddle soon retaliated by severely contracting credit, causing an economic crisis that he hoped would hurt Old Hickory.[13] Some observers believed that Calhoun would be the beneficiary of Jackson's impetuous acts. "Mr. Calhoun sits there perfectly happy," Daniel Webster observed in January 1834. "And well may he so sit. He sees hundreds flocking to his standard in consequence of these abominable measures."[14]

Calhoun entered the fray with a speech on January 13, 1834, supporting two measures by Henry Clay to censure the president for his impulsive removal of the deposits from the Bank of the United States. Supporting Clay and the bank against Jackson was an easy decision for Calhoun, particularly since South Carolinians in general favored the bank. In his speech Calhoun dissected and dismissed the constitutional arguments of Roger Taney. For Calhoun, the bank war was in reality a struggle between the executive and legislative branches for control. He defended the Bank of the United States as the only legitimate and most efficient vehicle to accomplish Congress's responsibility to regulate the currency. As Calhoun saw it, the only true alternative was "to divorce the government entirely from the banking system."[15]

But this was not Calhoun's goal, at least not yet. After the Senate censured Jackson, in March 1834 Calhoun supported Daniel Webster's unsuccessful proposal to continue the charter of the Bank of the United States for another six years in a lengthy speech that even the *Washington Globe* acknowledged for its "great art and adroitness." In the weeks leading up to Calhoun's speech, the Senate had been deluged with "memorials" or petitions from various parts of the country, especially the North, begging the government to do something about the financial chaos unleashed by Nicholas Biddle's contraction of the bank's credit.[16] The battle in the Senate surged back and forth between friends and enemies of the bank, with some of the speeches going on for days at a time. French observer Michel Chevalier noted with amusement Calhoun's jibe during the debate that Thomas Hart Benton had taken more of the Senate's time (four sessions) attacking the bank than the French people had needed to complete their revolution.[17]

In his own speech, Calhoun took full advantage of his independence to appeal to both Jacksonian hard money advocates and the banking interests represented by Webster. Calhoun tied regulation of the currency to the government's fundamental duty to protect property rights. "If we suppose the entire currency to be in the hands of one portion of the community, and the property in the hands of the other portion," he warned, the portion with the currency would be able to manipulate the value of the other portion's property and eventually "possess themselves of it at their pleasure." Then, breaking with most bank advocates—and to the wonder of the *Washington Globe*—Calhoun admitted that the country's currency was diseased. While gold and silver coins minted by the government were the legal currency of the country (here he agreed with Jackson), the actual currency was a vast flood of paper notes unbacked by anything but greed. Calhoun pointed to the proliferation of banks in the past several years, claiming that at least 450 unregulated banks existed with a capital of $145 million, "and the whole of this immense fabric standing upon a metallic currency of less than fifteen millions of dollars." It was a recipe for financial disaster.

Despite this, Calhoun rejected an immediate return to gold and silver as too radical, and he refused to side with Thomas Hart Benton of Missouri, who soon earned the nickname "Old Bullion" for his advocacy of a return to hard money. Instead, Calhoun suggested, the solution to the currency crisis could be found in the very bank that Jackson blamed. "We must, in a word, use a bank to unbank the banks," Calhoun announced in a genius turn of phrase, arguing that the Bank of the United States could play a regulatory role in restraining other banks, essentially the same one he had envisioned for it when he helped to create it in 1816. But, he warned, it must be done gradually instead of trying to immediately substitute specie simply "on the ground that the Constitution intended" it. Principles must yield, at least temporarily, to reality, he acknowledged, or disaster would ensue. As the incredulous editors of the Jacksonian *Globe* put it, Calhoun's "remedy for the evil of *banking* brought about by the present system of *banking*, is to continue it." How could the supposed champion of state rights advocate such a solution, the *Globe* asked? By justifying the bank "not as a bank, but as a *means of regulating the currency.*"[18]

It was a conservative and statesmanlike solution to reform, but also a remarkable statement from the man who had only recently administered a radical shock to the system on exactly the same principled constitutional grounds that he now declared impractical. Calhoun always professed to take the world as he found it, not as he wished it to be, and he *was* often willing to limit his ambition to moderate solutions that avoided drastic or sudden change. That was, of course, his view of nullification—that it avoided the extremes of majority tyranny and disunion by providing a safety valve for state dissent. But like most conservatives, indeed like most people throughout history, Calhoun picked which realities to accommodate, which to resist, and which to fight for.

IN APRIL 1834 CALHOUN mounted a quixotic effort to repeal the Force Bill. Even though it was scheduled to expire in a few weeks, Calhoun believed it was important to repeal for fear that it would "live forever" and be used as a precedent "to confer on the Chief Magistrate, similar, or even more dangerous powers."[19] A few weeks later, he convinced his Senate colleagues to formally refuse a message from Jackson protesting the Senate's decision to censure him over the removal of deposits. As usual, Calhoun saw a deep and elemental principle at stake, in this case "whether *the President has a right to question our decision.*" It was an issue of the separation of powers, and Calhoun saw in the protest an attempt to set the stage for further encroachments. "The President is an old tactician," Calhoun warned, "and understands well the advantage of carrying on a defensive war with offensive operations."

Calhoun was especially offended by the claim Jackson made in his protest to be the direct representative of the American people and the embodiment of their will. "What effrontery! What boldness of assertion! The *immediate* representative!" Calhoun declared in disgust, pointing out that Jackson was technically elected by the Electoral College. No one part of the government represented the people exclusively, and besides, Calhoun snorted, Jackson claimed to be a state rights man! Jackson's real game was the accumulation of power, and in this quest he tried to "excite the sympathy of the people, whom he seeks to make his allies in the contest," Calhoun warned, scorning the emotional and nationalistic appeals that were at the heart of the emerging arena of presidential politics. "He tells them of his wounds—wounds received in the Revolution—and of his patriotism; of his disinterestedness; of his freedom from avarice or ambition; of his advanced age. And finally, of his religion…Can we mistake the object?" In Jackson's claim to be the only authentic representation of the people's will Calhoun saw the makings of a demagogue, and he laid out a vigorous constitutional defense of the Senate's independence. "I shall take my stand at the door of the Senate, if I should stand there alone," Calhoun announced. In the end he didn't have to stand alone. The Senate voted 25 to 17 to approve Calhoun's motion that the president had no right to question the censure.

Calhoun also noted in passing the revival of an old term from the American Revolution among Jackson's enemies—a coalition that included onetime Adams supporters as well as National Republicans like Henry Clay and Daniel Webster. They had begun calling themselves the Whigs, a pointed reference to the party that had opposed monarchical power in England. Calhoun noted the revival with pleasure, and warned Jackson's supporters that they had brought the revolutionary references upon themselves by supporting the president's king-like pretensions to power. But he abjured the term for himself. "I am content with that which designates those with whom I act," he announced, referring to the so-called nullifiers. "It is, I admit, not very popular, but is at least an honest and patriotic name. It is synonymous with resistance to usurpation—usurpation, come from what quarter and under what shape it may." The Whigs, Calhoun as much as said, were too focused on one possible abuse of power while ignoring others, such as the tariff, while the Democrats focused on the bank at the same time they overlooked executive overreach. Despite the fact that some of his old nullification allies were drifting into the Whig orbit in the fight against Jackson, Calhoun viewed himself standing at the head of a political movement that stood for balance, equilibrium, and the proper separation of powers against the forces of consolidation and demagoguery.[20]

AFTER SPENDING SO MUCH time in South Carolina over the previous few years, and with his family settled in the upcountry among a dense web of relatives, Calhoun was increasingly conscious of his personal as well as political isolation in Washington. He longed for letters from home, and eagerly read Anna's. Near the end of the Senate's session in May, as Washington emptied, Calhoun wrote to her that if it were not for her letters, he would "not have heard a word about the Humming birds, their familiarity, the vines, their blooms, the freshness of the spring, the green yard, the children's gardens," or about "Patrick's mechanical genius…every item of which excited agreeable associations, but accompanied with the painful recollection of my long absence, from those so dear to me."[21] He also congratulated Anna for her tutoring of her younger siblings—"your little scholars," he called them—promising to bring "the prettiest books" he could find home from Washington. He was especially pleased that Anna had gotten her younger sister Cornelia to be "fond of her books." "The mode you have adopted proves, that you are not a little skilled in the knowledge of the operation of the human mind," he wrote.[22] As he was preparing to leave Washington, he wrote, "I cannot describe my desire to see you all, after so long an absence."[23]

Calhoun's longing for his family probably had something to do with the fact that Floride, Anna, and little William Lowndes, the youngest, accompanied him back to Washington at the end of 1834. Floride may have been reluctant, recalling the Eaton debacle. But for seventeen-year-old Anna it was the first time she had been to Washington as a young woman and the first time she was able to satisfy her political interests firsthand. For the first winter, at least, she also had her close friend Maria Simkins at her side. Anna frequently accompanied her father to the Senate chambers, watching from the gallery as her father did the people's business. It was a very different life from floating on a mill pond all day in a feed trough, as she had done that spring. Yet Anna took to Washington naturally, and it must have delighted Calhoun to watch his lively young daughter become a fixture of the capital's social scene.[24]

She would become his regular traveling companion to Washington over the last sessions of the Jackson administration, sharing his life in ways from which Floride understandably demurred. They shared a harrowing journey with the South Carolina delegation in December 1835, when a winter storm battered their steamship the *South Carolina* so badly that they had to put in for the night on the North Carolina coast at the mouth of the Cape Fear River and trudge through sand up to their ankles to the public house, which Anna described as a "miserable hovel" to Maria Simkins. "Pa was so [sea] sick the whole time, he could not get out of his birth, and Col. [William] Preston nearly as bad," she wrote.[25]

In Washington during the 1835 and 1836 sessions, when Floride stayed home, Calhoun and Anna stayed with the rest of the South Carolina delegation at a boardinghouse run by a woman named Lindenberger where, as Anna informed Maria, "I am the *only young person.*" In addition to Calhoun and Anna, the mess during the winter of 1835–1836 consisted of "Col. & Mrs. [William] Preston, Col & Mrs. [James] Hammond, Col. & Mrs. [Francis W.] Pickens…Gen. Waddy Thompson, and Col. James Preston." "You see we do not want for military honors," Anna informed Maria.[26] Calhoun's political isolation meant that when alone in Washington he rarely went out, a pattern familiar to him from his days as a Jeffersonian in Litchfield, but with Anna to accompany him he rediscovered some of the social pleasures of Washington life. They attended a party at Secretary of War Lewis Cass's house (Anna reported to Maria that there had been "little or no change in the fashion, since last winter"), and Anna, perhaps with Calhoun, attended General Alexander Macomb's patriotic drama *Pontiac*, which depicted the siege of Detroit in three acts. Anna declared it "the most ridiculous bombastic and utterly nonsensical assemblages of farrago that the imagination ever conceived."[27]

On the other hand, two years later Calhoun and Anna laughed all the way through actor James Hackett's performance in *The Lion of the West: Or, a Kentuckian in New York*, in which Hackett played Colonel Nimrod Wildfire, a barely disguised version of Tennessee congressman David Crockett, who by then had died at the Alamo. In the play, Wildfire travels to New York City to enlighten a refined foreign traveler, Ms. Amelia Wollope, who is gathering information about Americans for readers back in England. In one scene, Wildfire yells, "Let all the fellers in New York know I'm half-horse, half-alligator, a touch of the airth-quake, with a sprinkling of the steamboat!" In another scene the intrepid frontiersman sends a king of clubs up to Wollope as his calling card. As Calhoun and Anna knew, the Wollope character was based on Frances Trollope, whose *Domestic Manners of the Americans*, published in 1832, had outraged many American readers with its derogatory conclusions about the undeveloped nature of American civilization. *The Lion of the West* was Hackett's revenge on behalf of his fellow citizens, and Anna wrote her brother Patrick, "I never saw father laugh so much or seem to enjoy himself more."[28]

Not everyone saw this side of Calhoun. When the British writer and pioneering sociologist Harriet Martineau met Calhoun in Washington in early 1835, his utter certainty unnerved her. "He is wrought, like a piece of machinery, set a-going vehemently by a weight," she later wrote in wonder, adding, "I never saw anyone who so completely gave me the idea of possession." Listening to Calhoun at Washington gatherings that winter, Martineau went through a series of reactions in succession, first "intellectual reverence," then "regret," and finally "absolute melancholy" in the belief that his ideas, so forcefully expressed and fervently believed, were likely to cause great harm. "There is no hope that an intellect so cast in narrow theories will accommodate itself to varying circumstances," she despaired, "and there is every danger that it will break up all that it can, in order to remould the materials in its own way." "The cast-iron man," she famously called him, "who looks as if he had never been born and never could be extinguished." And yet even Martineau also noted Calhoun's "moments of softness, in his family... a relief equally to himself and others...as touching to the observer as tears on the face of a soldier."[29]

Many days Anna could be found in the Senate gallery, but she also migrated across to the House when a member of the South Carolina delegation, such as cousin Francis Pickens, was expected to give a speech. When the mail came to Calhoun's Senate desk, he would have the doorkeeper of the Senate deliver letters from home to Anna in the gallery immediately so that she did not have to wait until later that evening to read them. After the Senate ended its work for the day, she and her father discussed the day's debates back at the boardinghouse with the rest of the delegation. She often gave Maria detailed reports on particularly exciting speeches, such as the one by Senator Benjamin Watkins Leigh of Virginia in January 1836 on the "abolition question," which Anna described as "one of the strongest law arguments made on any question." At some point during this time, Anna also began to serve as her father's secretary, writing letters and copying important documents for him. It was a role she relished, and the most direct participation in politics that a woman of her day could achieve. As one historian has recently observed of James Polk's wife Sarah, who was far more influential in Polk's career than Anna was in Calhoun's, conservative women stood behind some of the most important conservative statesmen of the antebellum era.[30]

Anna fully absorbed and shared her father's political views. When she accompanied William C. Preston, whose prominent role in the nullification crisis had earned him South Carolina's other seat in the Senate, and his wife on a trip through the North in the summer of 1836, she marveled at the "comparatively miserable appearance of our southern country" to the North. However, she put the difference down to "our money and labour unjustly taken from us" and not to the existence of slavery itself, as many white northerners were beginning to do. Despite the disparities, the trip made her even more conscious of and attached to her southern home. "I shall return home as much of a glorifier as the Gen. [Waddy Thompson]," she wrote Maria in reference to her father's ally, one of the more bombastic nullifiers.[31]

It is clear that Anna not only absorbed her father's arguments but could deploy them with a skill all her own. Of meeting Anna in Washington during these years, Bostonian Josiah Quincy later recalled, "I have rarely met a lady so skillful in political discussion as was Miss Calhoun." Nearly fifty years later the Harvard-educated Brahmin still remembered "the clearness with which she presented the Southern view of the situation, and the ingenuity with which she parried such objections as I was able to make." From such a small sample he concluded that elite young southern women before the Civil War received an education and inculcation into politics "unknown among their sisters of the North." Perhaps, but Anna, as her father knew, was special.[32]

As anna watched from the galleries in 1835 and 1836, Calhoun continued his delicate alliance with the Whigs in his assault on Andrew Jackson. In January 1835, as the Jackson administration was celebrating paying the final installment of the national debt, he introduced a motion to form a committee to study the extent and influence of executive patronage—the president's authority to make appointments and reward his followers—which Calhoun claimed had increased precipitously. Calhoun's motion was timed to take advantage of a devastating bipartisan report that had just been published, revealing that the Post Office, the largest and most extensive government agency, was rife with fraud and corruption. In the interests of impartiality Calhoun recommended that the committee on executive patronage be formed from the three parties that really existed in the Senate—Clay's Whigs, Jackson's men, and his own, composed mostly of state rights advocates disgruntled with Jackson. When the motion passed, he and Senator George Bibb of Kentucky were appointed for the state rights party, Samuel Southard of New Jersey and Daniel Webster for the opposition, and Thomas Hart Benton and David King of Georgia for the administration. Benton, as Calhoun well knew, had authored a similar report in 1826 against the Adams administration, so it would be hard for him to object to a similarly searching report now.[33] Once the committee had formed, Calhoun dashed off letters to various officials requesting numbers of employees and pensioners, using his knowledge of the departments of the government to assure that the committee would have the most complete account.[34]

In the midst of the committee's work, Calhoun's friend and neighbor, South Carolina representative Warren R. Davis, became sick, and on the morning of January 29 he died with Calhoun and other members of the South Carolina delegation at his side. According to the story that circulated in Washington in the days that followed, Davis had told Calhoun, "I hear they are giving you rough treatment in the Senate," and his dying plea to Calhoun had been "to guard your looks and words so as that no undue warmth may make you appear unworthy of your principles." Calhoun told Harriet Martineau that he was deeply moved by the dying man's appeal, remarking, "This was friendship—strong friendship."[35] After a sleepless night at the dying man's side, Calhoun reported Davis's death to the Senate and offered a resolution that the Senate adjourn for Davis's funeral the next day, which would also be attended by the president.[36]

The next day, as mourners left the Capitol building after the funeral through a heavy mist, a deranged painter named Richard Lawrence stepped forward and attempted to shoot Jackson twice, his pistols both misfiring but prompting utter mayhem as Jackson, cane raised, lunged toward his assailant as others around him tackled the would-be assassin and subdued him.[37]

Many of Jackson's supporters assumed that the attempt was directly or indirectly the work of Jackson's enemies in the Senate, a notion that was only reinforced when Lawrence loudly proclaimed his preference for Webster, Clay, or Calhoun as president. The next day the *Washington Globe* laid the attempt on Jackson's life at Calhoun's feet, charging that his incendiary rhetoric about Jackson as the next Julius Caesar had motivated the attack. Calhoun asked the secretary of the Senate to read the column before the Senate, portraying it as an attack on free speech and further evidence that Jackson was trying to muffle dissent. "It asserts that he who denounces abuses and corruption, be they ever so great, instigates assassination!" Calhoun declared, reserving the right to heap abuse on Jackson's overreaches whenever he felt it was warranted.

It would not be the last time that Americans debated the relationship between political rhetoric and violence, and in this instance Calhoun upheld the absolute right to criticize those in power.[38]

True to his word, Calhoun's committee on executive patronage reported its findings a week later, describing in a seventy-six-page report a vast increase in spending and patronage by the government between 1825 and 1833 along with the eye-popping statistic that one hundred thousand people now depended on the federal government for employment or pensions. In Thomas Jefferson's republic this was a terrifying prospect, and the Senate made sure the people knew, ordering ten thousand copies of the report printed and including easy-to-read tables and statistics showing the growth on a year-by-year basis. For good measure they voted to include Thomas Hart Benton's 1826 report with the new report just to illustrate how much Jackson's supporters had been required to bend their former principles.[39]

After reporting the committee's findings, Calhoun introduced three measures designed to limit executive patronage: a bill to repeal the so-called Four Years Law, which limited public officials' tenure in office, a bill to regulate the "Pet Banks" that had received the deposits of the defunct Bank of the United States, and a resolution proposing a constitutional amendment for the distribution of surplus government revenue to the states according to their representation in Congress. Calhoun had vehemently opposed the distribution of surplus revenue as a perverse incentive for continuing the tariff when Jackson first proposed it, but now that the protective principle had been set on a path to extinction and executive patronage was the main threat, he changed course. If there were to be a surplus, better the states should have it than the president. The first two bills passed the Senate by significant majorities, with many Democrats voting alongside Calhoun and the Whigs, but failed in the House, where Jackson men still had the upper hand. Calhoun himself tabled the resolution for a constitutional amendment after it became clear that it was not going to achieve the necessary two-thirds majority. Nevertheless, all three issues would re-surface in the future.[40]

During the debate over the report Thomas Hart Benton, smarting after Calhoun illustrated his hypocrisy by reading long passages from his 1826 report on the Senate floor, took issue with a phrase from the report that had described how patronage turned officeholders into "corrupt sycophants and supple instruments of power." Claiming that Calhoun had him in mind, which might well have been true, Benton pointed directly at Calhoun and bellowed that it was "a bold and direct attack upon truth."

The Senate dissolved into an uproar. Everyone knew that this could easily lead to a duel. Indeed, Benton had famously once brawled with Andrew Jackson himself before becoming Old Hickory's loyal follower, and he seemed to be baiting Calhoun. After a lengthy and heated de-bate, and once Martin Van Buren could make himself heard, the vice president declared that Benton's comment had not been out of order. Daniel Webster appealed the decision on Calhoun's behalf and the Sen-ate overruled Van Buren, who then confessed that he did not know ex-actly how to proceed. At that moment, Calhoun rose and said that he hoped Benton might be permitted to finish his speech. Many observers were deeply impressed by Calhoun's restraint and sense of decorum. As Harriet Martineau recalled, "He sat in stern patience, scarcely moving a muscle the whole time; and when it was all settled in his favor, merely observed that his friends need not fear his being disturbed by an attack of this nature from such a quarter." Many observers recalled Warren Davis's dying plea, and attributed Calhoun's restraint to his promise made to a dying friend. "It was great, and would have satisfied the 'strong friendship' of his departed comrade," observed Martineau. But Calhoun was also deftly insulting Benton by declaring his challenge unworthy of notice, a claim of superiority. And after Benton finished what Marti-neau derided as an "absurdly worded" speech, Calhoun resumed and drowned "Old Bullion" with a flood of figures and statistics.[41]

FOR THE FIRST HALF of 1835 Calhoun was completely engrossed by his attack on the Jackson administration, but events in the summer of 1835 decisively changed the course of his career and the course of the country. During the nullification crisis Calhoun had largely avoided the fearmongering tactics of Robert Turnbull about slavery, although he acknowledged that slavery was the root of the South's different economic and political interests within the Union. He shared the opinion of many of his allies and southern colleagues that any threat to slavery should be met head-on, but his wide national correspondence gave him a better vantage point than most to conclude, accurately, that the threat was not substantial or imminent. That changed in the summer of 1835.

Even before that summer it was clear that the world was changing in ways that threatened the interests of the South's slaveholding class. While the Denmark Vesey plot in 1822 had begun a transformation in South Carolina politics, the more successful Nat Turner revolt in Southampton, Virginia, in 1831, in which fifty-odd white people lost their lives, sent shock waves throughout the South, raising fears of a Haitian-style revolution. Different parts of the South responded differently to the threat. In upper-South states like Virginia, one historian has recently shown, many legislatures concluded that "a whiter state was a safer state," openly debating plans of gradual emancipation and forced colonization to the horror of those in lower-South states like South Carolina. In the lower South, state governments reacted by passing bans on teaching enslaved people to read and write, restricting the movement of enslaved people, revoking freedoms for free blacks, and, since both Vesey and Turner had been connected to religious communities, closely regulating black worship.[42]

The debates in Virginia in particular produced the first stirrings of a different sort of argument about slavery that departed from the defensive posture taken by most southerners since the revolution. In 1832 Thomas Roderick Dew, a young professor at the College of William and Mary in Williamsburg, Virginia, published a widely read review of the debates in which he dismissed emancipation and colonization as "utterly impracticable." Instead, Dew encouraged white Virginians to allow the workings of the market and the internal slave trade to whiten the state by gradually sweeping the enslaved population out of Virginia into the new slave country of the Southwest, leading to the "ultimate extinction" of slavery. But Dew also blamed the tariff, not slavery, for Virginia's economic woes, and he denied there was anything unrepublican about slavery, arguing that slavery produced a "spirit of equality" among whites. Meanwhile, Calhoun's Senate colleague Benjamin Watkins Leigh rebuked the Virginia legislature for even discussing the possibility of emancipation. "All our institutions are founded on the principle, that every man's private property is absolutely his own, and that he holds it independently of the power of the legislature and the will of the majority," Leigh warned, giving the Lockean gloss on slaves as property, "and when that principle shall be abandoned, republican government must be destroyed with it." These were the seeds of a proslavery argument that abandoned the older ground that slavery was a necessary or inherited evil, but the emphasis of both Dew and Leigh was much more on the obstacles to any form of emancipation than on the virtues of racial slavery.[43]

The Vesey and Turner rebellions lent momentum of a different kind to the work of black abolitionists and their white allies who formed a second wave of antislavery activism that had begun in the 1820s. In contrast to the first wave of the antislavery movement in the revolutionary era, which had focused on ending the slave trade, achieving gradual emancipation, and winning limited rights for black people in many northern states, the second-wave abolitionists increasingly proclaimed what one historian has dubbed "interracial immediatism." The free black abolitionist David Walker's pamphlet *An Appeal to the Coloured Citizens of the World* appeared in 1829, and the white abolitionist William Lloyd Garrison began publishing his *Liberator* newspaper in 1831, employing his tactic of "moral suasion" to convince white Americans that slavery was an evil that must be abolished immediately. Despite Garrison's intended audience, 450 of the *Liberator*'s subscribers in its first year were African Americans, a reflection of the sources of support for the second wave of abolitionism and a measure of how deeply unpopular the abolitionists were with white Americans, even in the North. Dozens of local antislavery societies sprang up throughout the North, including one in New Haven started by the son of Calhoun's old Yale teacher Timothy Dwight. Scorning the old gradualist or colonization schemes, they denounced slavery in moral terms and demanded immediate and uncompensated emancipation. In 1833 Garrison and the evangelical silk magnate Arthur Tappan (whose brother Lewis was also a famous abolitionist) founded the American Anti-Slavery Society at a meeting in Philadelphia's Adelphi Hall, which was owned by a black benevolent society. Black abolitionists like the dentist James McCrummell played key roles as managers.[44] Significantly, from the very beginning the AAS was transatlantic as well as interracial, with links to abolitionist societies in England.

Calhoun was certainly aware of the abolitionist groundswell. In January 1834, a few months after the founding of the AAS, he wrote to Francis Pickens about a rumored bill proposing to abolish slavery in the District of Columbia and colonize free blacks using government aid. "Such a move, should it be made," Calhoun wrote, "can only be considered as the commencement of the work of immediate emancipation over the whole of the South, to which event it will certainly lead if not promptly met by the entire slaveholding states, with the fixed determination to resist at any hazard."[45] A few days later, during his speech on censuring Jackson for removing the bank deposits, Calhoun made an offhand reference to the frightening prospect that Congress might use the general welfare clause to place public funds "in the hands of the fanatics and madmen of the North, who are waging war against the domestic institutions of the South, under the plea of promoting the general welfare."[46] But aside from these passing comments he showed markedly little interest in these "fanatics and madmen" before 1835.

From an international perspective, the most earthshaking change in Calhoun's world in the early 1830s was Great Britain's compensated emancipation of nearly eight hundred thousand slaves throughout its empire. This, too, was related to the resistance of enslaved people in the form of rebellion. While white southerners were still on edge in the months after the Turner uprising, the so-called Baptist War slave rebellion broke out in Jamaica on December 27, 1831. The Jamaican uprising was only the latest in a series of Caribbean slave revolts that went back to a rebellion in the British colony of Demerera (part of modern-day Guyana) in 1823, to another rebellion in Barbados in 1816, and to the Haitian Revolution itself. But the Baptist War involved nearly sixty thousand slaves and played a significant role in the popular support that sustained the passage of the British Slavery Abolition Act of 1833, which ended slavery throughout the British Empire except in territories belonging to the East India Company.[47] Suddenly, nearly everywhere they looked—to the American North, where gradual emancipation measures had eliminated the institution by the late 1820s, to British Canada, to the new South American republics, and now in the Caribbean— American slaveholders were surrounded by free societies.

It is not much of an exaggeration to say that British emancipation transformed the Western Hemisphere nearly overnight from a place in which the existence of chattel slavery was taken for granted into a place where it was possible to imagine freedom as the default position and slavery as artificial. In 1772, Lord Mansfield's *Somerset* decision had declared that slavery had no place in British law or on British soil, but the ruling had no effect outside the British isles. International law still held to a principle of comity, or respect for the contradictory laws of other nations in the interest of international trade and harmony, under which the rights of slaveholding nations and slaveholders were respected even where slavery did not exist by law. In this era freedom was, to use Calhoun's own phrase from 1816, a forced state. In 1833, suddenly, the most powerful empire in the world changed sides and adopted the so-called freedom principle, the idea that freedom was the default position and slavery the forced state, depending for its existence on establishment in positive law. Over the next decade this idea would transform US constitutional law as antislavery jurists and politicians gradually accepted it.[48]

THE TRANSFORMATIONS WROUGHT DURING the early 1830s came home to South Carolina on July 29, 1835, when the steamboat *Columbia* sailed into Charleston harbor from New York carrying the mail. Only three weeks earlier, rumors of a massive slave insurrection in Mississippi had provoked a frenzy that led to the hanging of several slaves and two white men suspected of helping them, putting the South on edge for fear of another Nat Turner–style revolt. It was at that moment that the AAS used the mechanism of a newly expanded US Post Office to launch a direct mail campaign, the first in American history, inundating the country with pamphlets meant to convince white Americans of the evils of slavery. Instead, they nearly provoked a slaveholders' revolution. In Charleston an angry crowd two thousand strong burned William Lloyd Garrison and the Tappan brothers in effigy and incinerated the offending pamphlets, which many slaveholders saw as a deliberate attempt to incite a slave rebellion. The city council soon appointed a committee that included Robert Hayne and Henry DeSaussure to guard against possible mob violence of both white and black varieties. Across the South more than 150 of what one historian calls "grassroots antiabolition meetings" were held to meet the threat.[49]

One of those meetings was held at Farmer's Hall in Pendleton, a few miles from Fort Hill. On September 9 the building was "filled to overflowing" and the meeting elected a twenty-member committee that included Calhoun and former Bank of the United States president Langdon Cheves to write a report and resolutions on the crisis. The report denounced abolitionists as "moral incendiaries" and "Fanatics of the North" who were constructing "infernal machines...for the destruction of the people of neighboring sovereignties." It called on northern states to suppress the efforts of their citizens "according to the rules of international law," taking the ground that the states were separate nations and insisting on the principle of comity. They also demanded that the federal government restrict the transmission of incendiary material through the mail, made clear that they expected Congress to address the matter, and threatened secession if their demands were not met, although they professed not to believe it would come to that.[50]

The mail crisis and the Pendleton meeting were both a mandate and an opportunity for Calhoun, a moment when duty, destiny, and his political goals seemed to realign. Frustrated in his hopes that the friends of state rights would flock to the nullification banner, Calhoun saw that the outpouring of anger directed at abolitionists and their pamphlets could serve as a rallying point to unify the slaveholding states for a larger political purpose. Ever since the 1824 election Calhoun had seen a unified South as a possible bulwark, first against the corruption and tyranny of the Adams-Clay coalition, then against the tariff majority, and now against Jackson, if only the states would act together. Now, it seemed they might, if only on this one issue.

Before the mail crisis that summer Calhoun had described Jackson's selection of Van Buren to be his successor as nothing less than a transition to a kind of monarchy with a "hereditary chief magistrate," and lamented "our present divided condition" to Francis Pickens. If a successful opposition to Jackson and Van Buren were to be mounted, he wrote, "the first thing is to harmonize the slave holding states." "With union among ourselves all would be safe; without it all must be lost. But how is this union to be effected?" In a letter that does not survive Pickens evidently suggested a means of uniting the states, perhaps by emphasizing the growing threat to slavery, but Calhoun dismissed the "great and ruinous consequences to which you allude" as too distant to arouse unity. "It must be something more near and visible, growing directly out of the present current of events," Calhoun wrote.[51]

As the mail crisis erupted, Calhoun wrote Duff Green that all signs showed "that the South will be unanimous in their resistance…even to the extent of disunion, if that should be necessary to arrest the evil. I trust, however, that it may be arrested far short of that extremity." Two weeks after the Pendleton meeting, Calhoun told his brother-in-law James Edward, "I think, I see my way clearly on the slave question," writing that he expected "an entire triumph on our own conditions; to be followed by unbounded prosperity in the South & an universal rise in property of every kind."[52]

Clearly, Calhoun sensed a political opportunity in the mail crisis, but the intensity of his reaction is evidence of the deeper threat he now sensed in the abolitionist onslaught. The political scientist Corey Robin brilliantly describes the conservative intellectual tradition in the United States as a "meditation" on the "felt experience of having power, seeing it threatened, and trying to win it back." Many in Calhoun's day agreed that slavery was the clearest example of tyrannical power. But in Calhoun's view he defended not tyranny or power in the abstract but self-determination, liberty, sovereignty, and the rights that his society awarded white men in relation to their property, including property in enslaved human beings. From the beginning of his career in the war against England to the end of his life, Calhoun lived by the maxim that the power sufficient to threaten these things could only be resisted by power sufficient to defend them. Nothing else, not reason, not virtue, not human sympathy, would suffice. In the coming years, Calhoun was determined to demolish any possible avenues that might allow the power of the national government to threaten slavery, but he could also sense that in the end this would not be enough. Changing notions of what is honorable and shameful in society, especially a democratic society, often precede moments of political change. He was deeply conscious that just such a cultural change had ended the transatlantic slave trade and then slavery in the British Empire as the result of a successful propaganda campaign, one of the first in modern history. He was determined not to cede that kind of moral high ground to the abolitionists in the United States. Honor and shame were directly connected to political power, and in the face of the attacks contained in the abolitionist pamphlets that now blanketed the country, the old "necessary evil" apology for slavery smacked too much of submission and shame.[53]

Yet reducing Calhoun's response to a simple defense of, or against, power can fail to capture the historically and culturally specific aspects of what people in the nineteenth century called "the springs of human action." It cannot capture Calhoun's sense of righteous indignation at being insulted by people who, in his view, had the audacity to call on the power of the national government to interfere in the households of their fellow countrymen a thousand miles away and call it morality. It cannot capture an instinctual resentment that had been passed down the generations in Calhoun's family, carried with them from Ireland and nurtured in the conflict between upcountry and lowcountry in South Carolina, the fear of being second-class citizens, deprived of their full rights on account of their religious identity or the place they made their home. That his rights existed alongside and depended on slavery, a complete annihilation of another's rights, was no contradiction at all to Calhoun, as it had not been to his father, or to his father's father, whose identity as a British subject in Ireland had been partly defined by the subjugation of the native Irish. The rights that Calhoun cherished and defended had little to do with the universal human rights that Thomas Jefferson appealed to in the Declaration. Instead, he believed his rights were the product of history, of the particular way in which his society was configured. This made them no less valid or worth defending. In fact, it made defending them all the more important. He also felt deep in his bones and as certainly as he had ever felt anything that the way of life he had inherited from his father, the way of life that he reveled in as master of Fort Hill and longed for when in he was in Washington—the experience of mastery, of power, but also of community, of family, and of home—was not wrong. Slavery was part of who he was, a generational atrocity woven so seamlessly into the fabric of his identity that he could not imagine himself, his family, or the South without it. And so he would defend it.

FOURTEEN

"It Is Our Thermopylae"

D ESPITE THREATENING INTERNATIONAL AND DOMESTIC developments, slavery and cotton in the South had never been more profitable than they were in the first half of the 1830s. British cotton textile manufacturers did not stop buying slave-grown cotton from the American South just because their government had abolished slavery. British manufacturers had begun to look to India as a possible alternate source of raw cotton, but the East India Company had thus far been unsuccessful in transforming the Indian countryside to meet their needs. The British government's Slavery Abolition Act cut off what until the 1820s had been a significant flow of raw cotton from the British West Indies, and by the 1830s the American South was providing the majority of cotton to meet the insatiable and growing appetite for white gold both in Manchester and in other emerging industrial centers in Europe and the American North. Despite misgivings about their dependence on a single region and a slave economy, cotton manufacturers across the world had little choice if they wanted to stay in business.[1]

Through the early 1830s, money had poured into the South to expand cotton production and meet the growing demand, especially in the new cotton country of the Southwest, but by 1835 this wave of investment was reaching a peak. In the first half of the 1830s prices for cotton in New Orleans increased by 80 percent, and in 1835 alone the federal government sold three million acres of land in Mississippi, more than had been sold throughout the whole country a few years earlier. In 1836 the *Natchez Courier* estimated that white Mississippians had bought ten thousand slaves on credit at an average price of $1,000 over the preceding year. Ironically, the new abolitionists had attacked American slavery at a moment when, despite abolitionist successes in Great Britain, it was strong and growing.[2]

Andrew Calhoun was one of many young men in the 1830s who hoped to profit from the boom and redeem his failures. Repeating a long family tradition of traveling to the outskirts of empire in the pursuit of opportunity, at the end of 1834 he traveled to New Orleans and from there north into Alabama looking to become a cotton capitalist. No doubt worried about his son's judgment, Calhoun wrote warning him to "take a full and accurate view of all the advantages and disadvantages of the country" before investing money that Calhoun had arranged to be lent to Andrew by Ker Boyce, one of the wealthiest men in South Carolina. Calhoun recommended "publick lands on Red River [Louisiana]," and in anticipation of Andrew's investment Calhoun made one of his own. "I have effected the purchase of Uncle John's negroes for you," he wrote. "I think it in the main a good purchase. I cannot but think negro property will [increase?] high as it is now." While he waited to see what his son would do, Calhoun put John Ewing's slaves to work at his O'Bar mine in Georgia, where Calhoun told his manager that he had to clear at least $120 per hand a year to make the investment as profitable as growing cotton.[3] While Andrew was away seeking his fortune in the Southwest, his eleven-month-old daughter died of illness in the care of his late wife's parents in Columbia.[4] He also failed on this trip to find a plantation to buy, and so for the time being his father probably left John Ewing's slaves at the mine.

CALHOUN'S VIEWS ON SLAVERY were rooted in his personal experience, especially life at Fort Hill, and in the particular context and history of upcountry South Carolina in the first decades of the nineteenth century. Calhoun knew from experience that the intimacy of slavery often resulted in a connection, however unequal, between slaves and masters, and he apparently never questioned whether slaves returned the affection that masters sometimes developed for particular enslaved people. "We...can easily enter into your feelings, at the loss of a faithful domestick raised in the family," he wrote Virgil Maxcy in 1822, a few days before rumors of the Denmark Vesey plot swept through Charleston. "In such an one the character of a slave is in great measure lost in, that of a friend, humble indeed, but still a friend."[5]

Calhoun may well have been thinking of Adam's son Sawney, who became known as Old Sawney at Fort Hill. He had known Sawney since the enslaved man's birth on his father's plantation when Calhoun was about twelve years old. In his old age, after Calhoun's death, Sawney would recall for white visitors his memories of plowing next to Calhoun under the hot South Carolina sun when they were young men. (The family acquaintance who recorded Sawney's story remarked that while slavery may have tainted manual labor among many whites, he had often seen members of the Calhoun clan behind the plow.)[6] Sawney's long association with Calhoun occasionally stood him in good stead against Floride's wrath, providing the only kind of protection afforded to enslaved people. Like Sawney, many of the enslaved people who lived at Fort Hill had long histories with the different branches of the Calhoun family.

When he walked out of the back of Fort Hill to his office, Calhoun could look down from the elevation of the main house about an eighth of a mile past the horse stables and carriage house to the long, low, barracks-style slave quarters, where in 1830 most of the thirty-seven enslaved people at Fort Hill lived. By 1840, from a combination of purchases and inheritance from Floride's mother, there would be seventy-seven enslaved people living at Fort Hill. Some of them, like Sawney, had belonged to Calhoun's father, while others, like husband and wife Polydore and Monemi, had belonged to Floride's father. Monemi told a visitor to Fort Hill in 1849 that she was 112 years old and had sixty-three descendants living among the Calhoun slaves. When Floride sold Fort Hill to Andrew in 1854 after Calhoun's death, there were fifty slaves living there, and the inventory listed them in several family groups.[7]

Historians have argued over the existence and meaning of a paternalistic ideology among slaveholders, and especially whether that ideology was opposed to the market forces of capitalism. Without entering too deeply into that debate, it seems clear that Calhoun viewed his relationship to the people he owned through the lens of duty and obligation, as he did nearly everything else in his life. In 1844 when a Boston admirer sent Calhoun an article clipped from an abolitionist newspaper that accused Calhoun of selling the wife of one of his slaves "for a harlot" to an Alabama planter, Calhoun replied indignantly. "My character as a master is, I trust, as unimpeachable, as I hope it is in all the other relations of life," he wrote. "I regard my relation to those who belong to me in the double aspect of master & guardian, and am as careful to discharge the duties appertaining to each, as I am those, which appertain to the numerous other relations in which I am placed."[8] What Calhoun meant by this in his own mind can be seen in an 1845 letter to his son-in-law Thomas Green Clemson in which he gave his "strong objections" to the practice of "hiring out," an arrangement in which masters leased enslaved people to other slaveholders for a period of time. "The object of him who hires, is generally to make the most he can out of them, without regard to their comfort or health, and usually to the entire neglect of the children and the sick," Calhoun wrote. He did not rule out the practice completely, but thought it should be a "last alternative."[9]

Calhoun's sense of himself as a master included displays of generosity, like a Christmas celebration in 1842 in which enslaved people were allowed to cook and dance in the Fort Hill kitchen until long after midnight.[10] In 1849, when one of the Calhouns' slaves married a slave from a neighboring plantation, they held the wedding in the main house, where the oldest Calhoun slave, "a recognized Methodist parson," performed the ceremony. At the ensuing celebration enslaved people from neighboring plantations joined in as an enslaved fiddler sawed out tunes for dancing.[11]

There were also everyday details. In the winter of 1833, Calhoun wrote James Edward that he was desperate to buy "negro shoes" since without them "the negroes lose much of the morning." Calhoun was obviously concerned about lost time and profits, but also fulfilling one of his basic obligations as a master. In 1835, he was anxious to get the molasses that James Edward purchased for him since the stock at Fort Hill was running low and molasses formed a customary part of the diet of his enslaved labor force.[12] When Aleck, the same slave whose whipping he had ordered in 1831, fell sick a few years later, Calhoun asked Anna to tend to him personally since Aleck didn't like taking medicine, which was little wonder if the "medicine" was anything like the mixture of whiskey and red pepper that another Pendleton slave got from his mistress.[13]

Yet the duties that Calhoun felt himself bound to undertake as a master could quickly give way to other demands, to duties in his capacity as a father, a debtor, or a planter. One of the prerogatives of mastery was deciding what duty, or the market, demanded. Calhoun never admitted, although he was surrounded by evidence for it, that the family metaphor that lay at the heart of paternalism quickly broke down in the face of the brutal fact that every enslaved person was valuable property subject to speculation, sale, repossession by the bank, or life events among members of the white "family." Calhoun and Floride benefited from several such divisions, in which enslaved families were broken up according to changes in family relations and fortunes. Marriages, deaths, inheritance, bankruptcies, new investments—all dictated rearrangements of people who were, suddenly, not family but property.

There is no reason to doubt that Calhoun sought to keep the families of those he enslaved together when possible, but it is also clear that this was only one of several competing priorities, and one that came in well below, for instance, the fatherly duty of ensuring an equitable inheritance for sons and daughters. As Floride's father had put it in his 1802 will, "It is recommended to keep my negroes together and work them on lands the most productive that is possible [so that] out of the profits of the crops my debts may be paid & my family supported." In the same will he divided Polydore and Monemi's children among his own children, giving their son Billy to his son William and their daughter Bina to his daughter, Floride.[14] From the 1830s until his death in 1847, Floride's brother John Ewing was repeatedly forced to sell slaves or had them sold by the local sheriff to pay his massive debts.[15] And while owners might want to keep families together, buyers, including Calhoun himself, frequently came to the market looking for single slaves to fulfill specific purposes. "Another great difficulty," Calhoun's cotton agent John Ewing Bonneau wrote him in 1828 when Calhoun was searching for three house servants, was "to procure single negroes, for in nine cases out of ten where a house servant, Cook, or chamber maid is offered for sale, you will find some family attached to them."[16] Two years later Bonneau reported that he had sold one of Calhoun's slaves, Peggy, for $338, a dollar more than Calhoun had paid for her.[17] Right alongside his professions of duty and obligation, like many other slaveholders Calhoun constantly speculated in his correspondence on the fluctuating value of "negro property."[18]

There were other contradictions, as well. The report issued by the Pendleton committee during the mail crisis, and perhaps authored by Calhoun, described slavery as "a happy patriarchal state in which in benevolence and kindness of the master, and the fidelity and affection of the slave, combine in the most bland and harmonious manner." If there was a slave rebellion, they declared, they were sure that their faithful slaves would fight alongside them.[19]

Yet running beneath all the talk of family and faithful slaves there were undercurrents of fear among the whites at Fort Hill. Floride, in particular, was often uncomfortable when Calhoun was gone, probably a result of seeing her own father poisoned by his slaves when she was a young girl. In 1827 Calhoun wrote to John Ewing asking him to check on her because the "Negroes at Clergy Hall have been in some instances disorderly. She feels quite uneasy about it." He made it clear that his brother-in-law was authorized to take any measures necessary to ensure order and safety. "I hope they have been brought into entire subjection," he wrote, "but...if not the most decided measures [should] be adopted to bring them to a sense of duty." Other incidents in the coming years would not ease Floride's mind.[20]

Old Sawney and Tilla and their children, Polydore and Monemi, "Maum Katy," Aleck, and other enslaved people at Fort Hill lived amid a network of relations on neighboring plantations that mirrored the relationships between white families in and around Pendleton, although new slaves were constantly introduced into the neighborhood by purchases. Many of the slaves at Fort Hill had friends and family at John Ewing's nearby Keowee plantation since many of them had originally been owned by Floride and John Ewing's father, and generational naming patterns at Fort Hill and Keowee in the 1850s suggest family continuities that reached back to the eighteenth century, including, of course, the family of Old Sawney, whose members would be enslaved to the family of Patrick Calhoun for three generations before freedom finally came. By the time she died, sometime between 1849 and 1854, Monemi could count dozens of her descendants who were enslaved by various members of the Calhoun family on different plantations from South Carolina to Alabama. On weekends and holidays, especially around Christmas, there was a steady flow of foot traffic between plantations in the neighborhood around Pendleton, mirroring the visiting patterns of the Calhouns. On Sundays, some of the black residents of Fort Hill accompanied their mistress to St. Paul's

Episcopal Church in Pendleton, where some of them were probably also married. Others probably went to the nearby Presbyterian church, and both churches had galleries for enslaved attendees. Today a large open space near the Presbyterian church, missing its headstones, probably marks the resting place of some of those enslaved at Fort Hill. No doubt there were also secret religious meetings and social celebrations in the woods surrounding Fort Hill where family ties, friendships, romances, rivalries, and longstanding grudges could be enjoyed or indulged beyond the gaze of the master and his family. The community of enslaved people of Fort Hill would even outlast slavery itself, and in the decades after freedom many families could still be found living in the area.[21]

In 1830 there were about twenty (out of thirty-seven total) enslaved people between the ages of ten and fifty-five living at Fort Hill, probably the core of the labor force, although younger children and older adults all had work to do. Most of them lived in the slave quarters, but a few privileged house servants, like Sawney's daughter Issey and Maum Katy, evidently lived in a small servants' quarters near the house. In 1849, a northern visitor noted small gardens in front of the slave quarters and a field of sweet potatoes, and noted that many of Calhoun's slaves grew a little cotton on their own and were allowed to keep their earnings. The gardens probably allowed some of Calhoun's slaves to supplement their weekly food rations, which probably included pork in the form of bacon, along with molasses, flour, and a little cornmeal.[22]

Old Sawney and the others at Fort Hill knew that in addition to work they could expect certain things, things like shoes, for instance, that if not provided could be held up as a reason for not going out to start work first thing in the morning. They knew that it was customary to give them time off around Christmas; to give them permission to visit other plantations in the neighborhood where they might find wives or husbands; and, within limits, they knew that their masters did not want to anger them too much since it might interfere with the white family's routines and comfort.[23] When Virgil Maxcy located a head house servant offered for sale in Baltimore, Calhoun declined the purchase because Floride believed the price was so high it would offend the other house servants, especially their cook.[24]

But Sawney, Tilla, Monemi, Polydore, Aleck, and the others also knew the weakness of the power their expectations exerted and the fragile nature of their community, which existed for the sole purpose of serving the social, economic, and material needs of a white family. The bonds of shared family history could not protect John Ewing Colhoun's slaves from his creditors, nor would they protect the Fort Hill slaves from being separated from friends, children, even spouses if Anna found a husband or Andrew found a plantation.

There was, of course, resistance. Aleck had tried running away, not to freedom but simply back to a better-known neighborhood. In 1837 Calhoun was on the lookout for one of James Edward Colhoun's slaves, a man named Scipio, who had done the same.[25] But resistance had limits if enslaved people wanted to avoid the worst. The violence of Aleck's punishment, awful as it was, was not the worst thing that the Fort Hill slaves had to fear, and there were reasons to think that being the slave of a famous and powerful man afforded some protection. During the 1820s in the wake of the Denmark Vesey plot, whites in the upcountry had brutally and publicly punished the resistance of enslaved people in a wave of hangings and burnings. One enslaved man belonging to Calhoun's cousin Alexander Colhoun was hung for trying to poison his master, echoing the 1798 poisoning attempt on Floride's father. Another enslaved woman, Tildy, was hung for allegedly murdering her master's daughter. Both hangings were done in public, one at a crossroads and the other at a militia mustering field. Other executions were even more gruesome. A Georgia runaway named William who killed a man in Greenville in 1825 was subsequently captured and sentenced to be publicly burned alive. Newspapers reported that thousands of white people from the region attended the execution, which was held a few days before the traditional July 4 festivities. James

Edward Colhoun, disgusted by the public's appetite for this "unhuman mode of punishment," hoped that it would soon become "obsolete." The South Carolina legislature banned public burning in 1833, but not before another enslaved man in Abbeville suffered the same fate after being convicted of rape. These horrific public executions were no doubt seared into the minds of the enslaved people at Fort Hill, and the lessons they drew from them marked out the limits of resistance.[26]

So, too, did their knowledge that the booming trade in slaves to the new cotton country of the Mississippi Valley made it all too easy for their master to sell them. In the resolutions passed during the mail crisis Calhoun and his neighbors had included an important qualification to their description of slavery. "In all the old States where it exists," they wrote, "it resembles…a happy patriarchal state." This was, of course, a fiction, but it showed an awareness that in newer slave states like Mississippi and Alabama the cotton revolution had grown to unprecedented industrial proportions, often employing modern accounting practices and brutal punishment to extract maximum efficiency from enslaved people. There, on sprawling plantations that sometimes resembled agricultural factories or prison camps more than farms, the enslaved people of Fort Hill knew they could expect an even harsher life far from the fragile network of friends and family that surrounded them in Pendleton. Life was an exercise in delicately balancing the resistance required to maintain their dignity and the dangers of going too far.[27]

AFTER A HARROWING TRIP back to Washington with Anna on the steamboat *South Carolina* in December 1835, Calhoun found that the Jackson administration fully shared in his constituents' anxiety about abolitionist propaganda. The administration newspaper the *Washington Globe* denounced the Tappan brothers as aristocrats who were stirring up the slavery question in an effort to divide the country and undermine the Jacksonian coalition and democracy itself.[28] In his annual message to Congress in December, Jackson called on its members to pass a law banning incendiary material from circulation in the South by empowering the Post Office to censor the mail. Jackson also proposed "severe penalties" for those who transgressed the law. On December 21 Calhoun seemed to oblige by proposing a committee to study the question and taking on the role of chair.[29]

As that committee deliberated, the South Carolina delegation staying together at Mrs. Lindenberger's boardinghouse discussed how to meet another prong of the American Anti-Slavery Society's campaign to shift public opinion, a flood of petitions to abolish slavery in the District of Columbia. The AAS had shrewdly chosen this target because article 1, section 8 of the Constitution gave Congress authority to legislate there "in all cases whatsoever." James Henry Hammond, a fiercely ambitious young nullifier who had just been elected to the House of Representatives, made the first move on December 18, proposing that the House refuse to accept the abolitionist petitions outright rather than receiving and tabling them as usual. Francis Pickens quickly supported him.[30] Hammond may have acted on his own, perhaps trying to outflank Calhoun in winning admiration back home. Indeed, throughout December and the early months of 1836 Hammond received letters from radicals like Thomas Cooper and Edward William Johnston, editor of the *Columbia Telescope*, urging him to break ranks with Calhoun, whom they thought far too moderate and considerate of his own national reputation and presidential prospects. Calhoun had co-opted and moderated their nullification movement, and they didn't want him to do it again. "I have been steadily cursing Calhoun…for precisely this thing," wrote Johnston to Hammond in a rage. "We work on…and make a doctrine popular. Of a sudden, he comes forward, seizes it…ruins the impression which might have been made on the country, by stitching the whole affair to his own political kite-tail."[31]

Either in coordination or co-option, Calhoun quickly moved onto Hammond's ground. On January 7, when Thomas Morris of Ohio presented two of the abolitionist petitions, Calhoun demanded that the Senate refuse to accept the petitions since they represented "gross, false, and malicious slander, on eleven States represented on this floor." Appealing to the Fifth Amendment and getting to the very heart of the matter, he asked directly, "Are not slaves property and if so, how can Congress any more take away property of a master in his slave in this District than it could his life and liberty? They stand on the same ground."[32]

Calhoun developed his demand throughout the session. Did his fellow southern senators really propose to humbly accept petitions that described their constituents as "pirates" and "butchers," or that equated the morality of slavery with the transatlantic slave trade? Sounding like his old foe John Randolph, he pointed across the Atlantic to Great Britain, warning, "the spirit of abolition [is] not to be trifled with. It ha[s] had its bad effect on one of the most powerful governments of Europe, and ended disastrously to its colonial possessions. It [is] commencing in the same manner here, and must be met at once with the most decided resistance." Calhoun was under no illusion that the radical abolitionists of the AAS were numerous or popular in the North—a wave of anti-abolitionist violence in the North the previous summer proved that—but he warned that there were still a great many people who "contemplated ultimate abolition," and in a battle for public opinion the "young and rising generation" were especially vulnerable to abolitionist propaganda.[33] He warned,

> The inevitable tendency of the means to which the abolitionists have resorted, to effect their object, must, if persisted in, end in completely alienating the two great sections of the Union. The incessant action of hundreds of societies, and a vast printing establishment, throwing out, daily, thousands of artful and inflammatory publications, must make, in time, a deep impression on the section of the Union, where they freely circulate, and are mainly designed to have effect. The well informed and thoughtful may hold them in contempt, but the young, the

inexperienced, the ignorant and thoughtless, will receive the poison. In process of time, when the number of proselytes is sufficiently multiplied, the artful and profligate, who are ever on the watch to seize on any means, however wicked and dangerous, will unite with the fanatics and make their movements the basis of a powerful political party.[34]

In early March 1836, Calhoun delivered his fullest contribution to the debate, a carefully prepared historical and constitutional manifesto against the principle involved in receiving the petitions. Calhoun marshaled evidence from the Senate's own journals showing that other petitions had been denied, some quite recently. Pushing the claim to its limits, he asked if the Senate would accept a petition to abolish the Constitution or the Ten Commandments. What if, he asked, "the abolition societies should be converted into a body of atheists, and should ask the passage of a law denying the existence of the Almighty Being above us, the creator of all[?]" Would his colleagues accept that petition, as well?

Calhoun knew that many of his fellow southern senators preferred a milder solution, like the one proposed by Senator James Buchanan of Pennsylvania that would accept and then automatically reject any abolitionist petitions, a procedure Calhoun ridiculed as "something like juggling."[35] The abolitionists, he warned, were waging a new kind of war, "a war of religious and political fanaticism…waged, not against our lives, but our character. The object is to humble and debase us in our own estimation, and that of the world in general; to blast our reputation, while they overthrow our domestic institutions." In this war, Calhoun announced, the petitions were only the tip of the spear. "How can it be successfully met?" he asked. "There is but one way: we must meet the enemy on the frontier, in the question of receiving; we must secure that important pass—it is our Thermopylae. The power of resistance, by universal law of nature, is on the exterior. Break through the shell, penetrate the crust, and there is no resistance within." It was the same preemptive philosophy that Calhoun had wielded against the British as a young congressman, when he had warned his colleagues that whether they liked it or not, the war had already begun.[36]

In the end Buchanan's solution finally passed the Senate 34 to 6 with the support of many southern senators, although Calhoun abstained. In the House, meanwhile, the South Carolina delegation experienced an unexpected defection when representative Henry Pinckney, a staunch nullifier, broke ranks and put forward an alternative to Hammond's hardline plan that resembled Buchanan's solution in the Senate. Pinckney's resolution passed. Other members of the South Carolina delegation put it down to Pinckney's cooperation with Van Buren or to his recent and dramatic religious conversion. "All the southerners (and indeed many of the Northerners also), are greatly enraged at Henry Pinckney's shameful conduct on the subject of abolition," Anna wrote her uncle James Edward at the end of February, perhaps more accurately capturing the mood at Mrs. Lindenberger's boardinghouse than in Congress.[37]

The so-called gag rule lasted in one form or another until 1844 in the House and 1850 in the Senate, becoming one of the most infamous ways that the power of slaveholders manifested itself in the nation's capital. Calhoun had a central role in making it happen but ironically, considering that it has become closely associated with him, he thought it yielded on a crucial principle. Even in its milder form, the gag rule backfired, generating sympathy among white northerners who disagreed with or even deplored the abolitionists but supported their right to be heard. And the gag rule did nothing to stem the tide of petitions, which only increased.[38]

ON FEBRUARY 4, IN the midst of the debate over the petitions, Calhoun reported the results of the very divided committee he had chaired on Jackson's proposal to censor the mail. The report, which Calhoun undoubtedly wrote, found that Jackson's proposal aimed for the right end—stopping abolitionist pamphlets—but proposed dangerous means to accomplish it. To give Congress the power to regulate and censor the mail, Calhoun argued, would not only violate the freedom of the press in the exact same way that the Sedition Act had in the 1790s, it would also concede a dangerous power that could just as easily be used to demand that the mail be delivered. "Fortunately Congress has no such right," he concluded. Instead, he proposed that deputy postmasters be forced to comply with state laws regarding abolitionist materials, a solution that infuriated Jackson as another form of nullification. Both Calhoun's and Jackson's solutions outraged many northerners, even those who were no friends of the abolitionists. "We cannot trample on the charter of our national freedom to assist the slaveholder in his war with fanaticism," the *New York Evening Post* announced.[39] Congress eventually passed a different bill that upheld the Post Office's responsibility to deliver the mail, but in practice Postmaster General Amos Kendall turned a blind eye to censorship at the local level, a policy that would last until after the Civil War. For Calhoun, this was another unsatisfactory outcome that aimed at a practical result while conceding an important principle.[40]

IN JUNE 1836 CALHOUN finally won a clear victory when Jackson reluctantly signed a bill to regulate federal deposits in the "pet banks" and distribute surplus revenue to the states, a bill very similar to the one Calhoun had proposed after his report on executive patronage the year before. By 1836 the treasury surplus had swelled to unprecedented levels from the proceeds of western land sales, with revenues reaching $50 million, up from $35 million the year before, and the share of government revenue from land sales outpacing revenues from the tariff for the first time in history, the result of rampant land speculation.[41] Calhoun saw in the surplus the ominous potential for executive patronage on a scale that, if artfully distributed by a figure like Van Buren to maintain party loyalty and discipline, could ensure his hold on power as effectively as a hereditary monarchy—perhaps even more so. As he had warned at the beginning of the session, "Every dollar we can prevent from coming into the treasury, or every dollar thrown back into the hands of the people, will tend to strengthen the cause of liberty, and unnerve the arm of power."[42] The Deposit Bill, as it was known, appealed to many Whigs, who still believed the Bank of the United States had performed a necessary regulatory function. And it split Jackson's supporters into groups that Calhoun called the "more honest portion of the party & the real plunder & humbug [hard money] portion." In fact, many southern and western Democrats saw the distribution of revenue to states as a desirable measure that could fund internal improvements. When the bill passed both houses of Congress with large, bipartisan majorities, Calhoun crowed that Jackson was "in a perfect rage" but dared not veto the bill for fear of splitting the party on the eve of the election. Together with nullification, which Calhoun considered a successful precedent, he believed the Deposit Bill provided the country "a new lease for our liberty." Meanwhile, and not for the last time, Duff Green had to busy himself in the *United States Telegraph* explaining why Calhoun now supported a measure that he had opposed when Jackson first proposed it. Back home in South Carolina George McDuffie, now governor, railed that the distribution of revenue to the states was simply a stopgap that did nothing to solve the root of the problem, which was the tariff.[43]

The Deposit Bill's success was a sign that despite his political independence, Calhoun could put together a coalition to push through legislation even against the wishes of so strong a figure as Andrew Jackson. For Martin Van Buren, Jackson's acknowledged successor, it was a concerning development. Earlier that year Calhoun had noted in anticipation of the fall election that with all his faults, Jackson was "bold, warlike, audacious," and that "the nominee [Van Buren]...is not...of the race of the lion or the tiger; he belong[s] to a lower order— the fox." Van Buren, Calhoun predicted as Van Buren himself sat presiding over the Senate, would not be able to play the same role on the national stage that Jackson had. Only a few weeks after the Deposit

Bill passed, Jackson proved Calhoun's point when he retaliated by issuing what became known as his Specie Circular, ordering that federal land offices only accept gold and silver in payment for public lands. The order struck a blow at the entire banking sector by effectively declaring that the government had no confidence in the paper money they issued. Jackson refused to be outflanked by Congress.[44]

Meanwhile, Calhoun had his own plans for the surplus revenue. The first railroad in the United States—the Baltimore and Ohio's twenty-three miles of track, laid in 1828—was less than a decade old, but by the end of the 1830s the United States would have twice as many miles of track as there were in all of Europe. The railroad held out the same irresistible promises of increased commerce and communication that had fired Calhoun's imagination when he dreamed of a national network of internal improvements as a younger man, and which other wonders of the modern age like the steamboat had already delivered.[45] Calhoun's views on internal improvements had changed, but in the combination of railroads and the surplus revenue distributed to the states he saw an opportunity. During the summer of 1836 Calhoun trekked through the North Carolina mountains near his upcountry home on a nine-day trip with his old War Department colleague James Gadsden, trying to find a possible route north to Cincinnati for a railroad. Throughout 1835 and 1836 he had corresponded with railroad boosters in Cincinnati about the possibility of a railroad line running from Cincinnati to Charleston, which he hoped would connect the western states commercially (and politically) to the South, instead of the North. In a letter at the end of September 1835 that was published in newspapers throughout Ohio and South Carolina, Calhoun announced his and Gadsden's discovery of a little-known gap in the mountain range that would allow the railroad to pass that way, and he touted the benefits of a southern route for the commerce of the West, including better winter weather and fewer natural obstacles than a similar route to New York. He saw the railroad as an equivalent to the Erie Canal and the Mississippi River, and as he explained to Georgia congressman Augustin Clayton in a letter seeking his support, he hoped that a bill to distribute surplus revenue could help fund it. He also corresponded with Farish Carter, one of the wealthiest planters and entrepreneurs in Georgia, with the hope that if the states of South Carolina and Georgia did not fund the railroad, Carter and a few other "strong capitalists" would.[46] Calhoun would soon become director of the Louisville, Cincinnati, and Charleston Railroad, although the financial panic of 1837 and disagreements about the route between Calhoun and Robert Hayne, the railroad's president, would eventually doom the effort. Just like his mining ventures, Calhoun's eager pursuit of one of the main harbingers of industrial modernity shows that he saw no contradiction between slavery, industrialization, and what he and many others considered the spirit of "improvement" that marked their age.[47]

THAT SUMMER FLORIDE'S MOTHER, the widow Colhoun, died on her Cold Spring plantation near Fort Hill. Calhoun owed her much. Her wealth had financed his political career, and for a good deal of his married life he had lived in houses she owned. The most direct result of her death and the division of property between Floride and her brothers, was that Calhoun received the deed for Fort Hill, and finally owned the plantation his family had been living on for a decade.[48] There was also, as always, a separation and redistribution of enslaved people who had worked on her plantations, and this is probably the reason that by 1840 the enslaved population living at Fort Hill had more than doubled, to seventy-seven.[49]

By August 1836, the prospects for Calhoun's cotton crop were dismal on account of hail, rain, and "bad management in my absence." As he wrote, "It is hard to get a good overseer anywhere, but doubly so here, where so few know anything about planting." Times were flush and cotton prices were booming in Mississippi, but in South Carolina Calhoun only went further into debt.[50] The attacks of the *Greenville Mountaineer*, a unionist paper in the upcountry that periodically addressed letters to "His Grace the Duke of Pendleton," including one that August accusing Calhoun of "seducing prominent men, and making them the instruments of revolutionizing the opinion of the South as to the value of the Union," probably did not help his mood.[51] But the abolitionist threat continued to occupy the front of his mind. At the commencement exercises of the University of Georgia in August, where his old schoolmaster Moses Waddel now served as president, Calhoun warned the graduates that many of them would be called on to resist the abolitionist threat with their "talents & perhaps with their muskets," although he hoped it would not come to that.[52]

CALHOUN HAD BEGUN OPENLY defending slavery by early 1836 during the debates over the mail crisis and abolitionist petitions, throwing aside much of his previous caution. And yet for the most part his defenses of slavery in those early speeches employed fairly traditional rhetoric. "The relation which now exists between the two races in the slaveholding states has existed for two centuries," he declared. "It has grown with our growth and strengthened with our strength." Slavery could not be destroyed without destroying southern society, and the South would resist that destruction "should it cost every drop of blood, and every cent of property."[53]

These warnings had been made before. But there were also hints in 1836 that Calhoun was thinking more broadly about a defense of slavery that could counter abolitionist propaganda more directly—a defense capable of shaping moral sentiment in favor of slavery in a way that the old "necessary evil" argument never could.

He would begin by proving that slavery was at least no worse than other forms of labor in the modern world. In the February 1836 report of his committee on Jackson's mail proposal, Calhoun addressed his northern colleagues:

> Let those who are interested remember, that labor is the only resource
> of wealth, and how small a portion of it, in all old and civilized

countries, even the best governed, is left to those by whose labor wealth is created. Let them also reflect, how little volition, or agency the operatives in any country have in the question of its distribution—as little, with a few exceptions, as the African of the slaveholding states... Nor is it the less oppressive, that in one case it is effected by the stern and powerful will of the government, and in the other, by the more feeble and flexible will of a master. If one be an evil so is the other.

Slavery was only one variation of a "universal condition," and Calhoun warned his northern colleagues that with only a "slight modification" the arguments used to condemn the exploitation of slavery could easily be turned on their factories and their banks.[54]

Calhoun's use of the term "operative" suggests that he had in mind especially the forms of labor identified with emerging industrial capitalism in places like Lowell, Massachusetts, and Manchester, England, where the cotton revolution was remaking society to fit the demands of the industrial economy. It certainly drove Calhoun's point home that in the weeks surrounding his report, New York City was experiencing a wave of labor unrest in which more than a dozen of the city's unions of journeyman laborers went on strike against the transformations wrought in recent years in many of their occupations by the market economy. These changes had transformed many small, domestic sites of artisan production in the city into, in effect, small factories, and widened the gap between owners and those who worked for them.[55]

In early 1837 he was finally prepared to go even further. Abolitionist petitions to abolish slavery in the District of Columbia were still pouring in—many northern senators and congressmen had drawerfuls of them—and the question of whether to receive them came up again in the Senate on February 6 when John Tipton of Indiana brought forward two of them, believing it was his duty to represent his constituents even though he acknowledged he thought their aims misguided and dangerous. The Senate voted to receive them, intending to follow the terms of the Buchanan compromise the year earlier.

Calhoun saw the opening he had been waiting for. Taking two petitions at random from the pile of them waiting to be presented, he read them to the Senate, repeating his argument that they should not be received. In the ensuing debate, Senator William Cabell Rives of Virginia, a conservative Democrat who had gone over to the Whigs and opposed Calhoun during the fight over the Independent Treasury, announced that he approved receiving the petitions, although as a slaveholder he objected to their "horrid pictures of misery which had no existence" in reality. Almost in passing, Rives differentiated himself from "the gentleman of South Carolina" by saying he "was not in favor of slavery in the abstract."[56]

Calhoun immediately objected, denying that he had ever defended slavery in the abstract, only as it actually existed in the South. He asked Rives directly if he considered slavery a good thing. "No," Rives replied, saying he "viewed it as a misfortune, and an evil in all circumstances, though, in some, it might be a lesser evil." That gave Calhoun his chance. Ironically, the most famous defense of slavery in American history was made not against abolitionists, at least not directly, but against a fellow slaveholder from Virginia.[57]

Calhoun began with the traditional arguments—"Be it good or bad, it has grown up with our society and institutions, and is so interwoven with them, that to destroy it would be to destroy us as a people"—but then he quickly left tradition behind:

> But let me not be understood as admitting, even by implication, that the existing relations between the two races in the slaveholding States is an evil:—far otherwise; I hold it to be a good, as it has thus far proved itself to be to both, and will continue to prove so if not disturbed by the fell spirit of abolition. I appeal to facts. Never before has the black race of Central Africa, from the dawn of history to the present day, attained a condition so civilized and so improved, not only physically, but morally and intellectually. It came among us in a low, degraded, and savage condition, and in course of a few generations it

has grown up under the fostering care of our institutions, as reviled as they have been, to its present comparative civilized condition…

In the meantime, the white or European race, has not degenerated. It has kept pace with its brethren in other sections of the Union where slavery does not exist. It is odious to make comparison; but I appeal to all sides whether the South is not equal in virtue, intelligence, patriotism, courage, disinterestedness, and all the high qualities which adorn our nature…

But I take higher ground. I hold that in the present state of civilization, where two races of different origin, and distinguished by color, and other physical differences, as well as intellectual, are brought together, the relation now existing in the slaveholding States between the two, is, instead of an evil, a good—a positive good.

Slavery was a positive good in two ways, Calhoun argued. Sharpening his earlier warning to his northern colleagues to a spear point, he continued:

There never has yet existed a wealthy and civilized society in which one portion of the community did not, in point of fact, live on the labor of the other…The devices are almost innumerable, from the brute force and gross superstition of ancient times, to the subtle and artful fiscal contrivances of modern. I might well challenge a comparison between them and the more direct, simple, and patriarchal mode by which the labor of the African race is, among us, commanded by the European.

In a brilliant rhetorical move Calhoun admitted that slavery was exploitative and turned the accusation back on its accusers, demanding that they acknowledge they were no better, and certainly less honest, than slaveholders. In no other advanced economy, Calhoun claimed, did the laborer have "so little exacted from him," and he challenged anyone to compare the condition of "old and infirm" slaves to "the tenants of the poor houses in the most civilized portions of Europe."

Calhoun then turned to the political benefits of slavery:

> And here I fearlessly assert that the existing relation between the two races in the South, against which these blind fanatics are waging war, forms the most solid and durable foundation on which to rear free and stable political institutions. It is useless to disguise the fact. There is and always has been in an advanced stage of wealth and civilization, a conflict between labor and capital. The condition of society in the South exempts us from the disorders and dangers resulting from this conflict; and which explains why it is that the political condition of the slaveholding States has been so much more stable and quiet than that of the North.

Instead of falling back on the usual examples of Athens and Rome as democratic and republican societies that depended on slavery, in a few sentences Calhoun recast the master-slave relationship for the modern world. He described it in the terms that political economists were using to describe the emerging system of industrial capitalism and its conflicts and asserted that slavery was no contradiction of political freedom but its best foundation. He closed with a call for southern unity. "Let there be concert of action, and we shall find ample means of security without resorting to secession or disunion."[58]

In its force, clarity, and content, Calhoun's argument marked a significant departure in the political debate over slavery. Although fragments of his argument could be found scattered throughout the preceding four decades—in the writings of Henry DeSaussure and Timothy Ford in the 1790s, Thomas R. Dew in 1832, in William Harper or Thomas Cooper's essays—Calhoun consciously molded these defensive elements into an aggressive political ideology designed to counter the abolitionist campaign. Racial slavery, Calhoun argued, was not a moral abomination, a hidebound anachronism, or even a necessary evil; it was an institution uniquely suited—morally, economically, politically—to the conditions of the modern world.

William Cabell Rives, for one, was shocked. Highlighting the novelty of Calhoun's argument, he replied that while he was ready to defend the South and its institutions to the death against any outside interference, he could not approve of this "new school" of slavery's defenders. Rives cited "Washington, Jefferson, Madison, Marshall," slaveholders all, who had "lamented the existence of slavery as a misfortune and an evil to their country" and looked to its eventual demise. Rives had studied law with Jefferson and knew Madison personally, lending authority to his claim. By arguing for slavery as a positive good, he scolded Calhoun, "you shock the generous sentiments of human nature, you go counter to the common sense of mankind, you outrage the spirit of the age." Rives predicted that Calhoun's revolutionary doctrines would only further inflame the sectional divide.[59] Henry Clay privately wrote that Calhoun's description of "slavery as a *blessing*" was "indefensible, unintelligible, and brings reproach upon us."[60]

Indefensible, but not unintelligible. Certainly in one sense Calhoun's critics were right. Slavery was, indeed, a putrid contradiction of the ideals of the founding generation in their purest form. But as many historians would now agree, Calhoun was accurate in his view that slavery in the United States had to a significant degree underwritten the equality, prosperity, and progress of white Americans. Instead of recoiling from this fact, lamenting it, ignoring it, or obscuring it, Calhoun followed this observation to an unsettling, iconoclastic conclusion that even some of his fellow slaveholders were unwilling to embrace.

One thing Calhoun's argument was not was old-fashioned. In one sense a profoundly conservative defense of the status quo, his argument nevertheless showed how well attuned Calhoun was to the changing intellectual currents of his world in at least three ways. Educated in the Scottish Common Sense tradition, Calhoun mixed this straightforward form of reasoning with an appeal to a utilitarian logic most closely associated with the philosopher Jeremy Bentham, who had famously described a just society as one that provides the greatest good to the greatest number of people. "I appeal to facts," Calhoun announced, describing what he considered objective evidence that both white and black races had advanced in civilization and lived in peace and prosperity under slavery. Assuming the self-evident nature of both black racial inferiority and black progress, Calhoun believed slavery had proven itself, under the present circumstances, the best system for both races. In making the utilitarian argument, Calhoun had to carefully balance the "fact" of black progress with the "fact" of continued black inferiority, ignoring the troublesome question of how much progress would be enough to justify the end of slavery.[61]

Second, at its bottom Calhoun's political and economic argument rested on the specific historical circumstances of the South, an approach that fit into a growing emphasis in southern intellectual life, and modern thought generally, on historicism—the idea that all cultural, social, and political arrangements are rooted in a specific historical context. While other proslavery thinkers like the sociologist George Fitzhugh, writing in the 1850s, would extend Calhoun's class analysis of slavery to argue that slavery might be the best option for oppressed white people throughout the industrialized world, Calhoun's defense was rooted firmly in the specific, historically determined circumstances of the South "where two races of different origin, and distinguished by color, and other physical differences, as well as intellectual, are brought together." It was not a universal prescription for the ills of industrial capitalism, or a defense of slavery in the abstract. It was an argument that the South's unique history and racial circumstances made it safe for both capitalism and democracy. It was a prescription for an alternative, uniquely southern path to modernity.[62]

Finally, Calhoun's arguments harmonized with new scientific theories of racial difference emerging across the Atlantic world, although to embrace them too fully would have undermined his argument about black progress under slavery. Racial thinking had always been part of a justification of slavery, of course, but by the 1830s this strand of the argument was thickening and acquiring a harder, more scientific edge, as some scholars rejected the older environmental theories of race and described sharper lines of distinction between the races. Since the late 1820s in South Carolina, Thomas Cooper had been publishing essays based on the "cranial capacities" theory of Samuel George Morton, a professor of anatomy at the Pennsylvania Medical College, and the writings of University of Pennsylvania's Charles Caldwell arguing that Africans were an inferior strand of the human race. Some of Cooper's essays were published in the *Southern Review*, which Calhoun had subscribed to and actively promoted from its inception.[63] By 1835 these ideas had also made it into popular discourse in the state, as can be seen from Edmund Bellinger's speech in Barnwell District, reprinted as a pamphlet, in which he declared that "the negro is from his intellectual and moral organization incapable of being civilized or enjoying freedom." A growing body of scientific literature on both sides of the Atlantic supported the conclusion, and would swell in the coming decades, so that by the 1850s some of the most famous scientific figures of the day, like Harvard's Louis Agassiz, proclaimed that black racial inferiority was a scientific fact.[64]

Where earlier generations of slaveholders usually acknowledged the theoretical possibility that black people might someday advance to a level of "civilization" that equaled whites, the new scientific racism that emerged midcentury would conveniently take this possibility off the table, prompting new conclusions about the desirability and horizons of racial oppression. Indeed, within a few years of Calhoun's death, as European imperialists implemented racialized labor regimes in colonial possessions across the globe, his argument seemed to many to have predicted with some accuracy the "spirit of the age."[65] Certainly later racial theorists professed kinship with Calhoun. When the physician Josiah Nott and Egyptologist George Gliddon published their *Types of Mankind* four years after Calhoun's death, arguing from extensive scientific evidence for Africans as a separate and inferior human species, they acknowledged that "the truth of these propositions had long been familiar to the master-mind of John C. Calhoun."[66]

CALHOUN'S AUDACIOUS ARGUMENT WAS the most prominent example of a new group of proslavery theorists who argued that slavery was the foundation of progress and civilization in the modern world. Later that same year William Harper would tell a meeting of the South Carolina Society for the Advancement of Learning that slavery had always been a building block of civilization, and that if one looked around the Western Hemisphere, slave societies like the United States, Brazil, and Cuba flourished, while Mexico and the other South American republics that had abolished slavery languished. This was a very different and more aggressive argument even from the one advanced by slavery's Christian apologists, like South Carolina Presbyterian James Henley Thornwell, who vigorously defended slavery from the Bible but stopped short of calling it good, at least in a metaphysical sense. Slavery was "not absolutely a good—a blessing," Thornwell pointedly argued. It was instead part of a fallen world—something "even the most strenuous defender of slavery ought not permit himself to deny."[67]

As Thornwell knew, John C. Calhoun was by far the most prominent American to make that argument, and its influence would only grow in the years ahead. Years later, in 1850, Calhoun's old friend and Yale tutor Benjamin Silliman would observe, "He in a great manner changed the state of opinion and the manner of speaking and writing upon this subject in the South." The effects of this change were so vast in American politics that by 1850 Silliman would lament "the mortifying and disgraceful spectacle of a great republic—the only real republic in the world—standing forth in vindication of slavery, without prospect of, or wish for, its extinction."[68]

FIFTEEN

"Dangerous and Despotic Doctrines"

I N MARCH 1837 MARTIN VAN BUREN was inaugurated president of the United States, having been nominated by a national Democratic Party convention—the second of its kind—in Baltimore. Van Buren's nomination and election confirmed Calhoun's darkest predictions about the descent of the presidency into a new type of hereditary monarchy, in which presidents hand-picked their successors. In the closing weeks of the Jackson administration Senator Thomas Hart Benton proposed that the Senate's censure of Jackson over the removal of the bank deposits be expunged from the record, prompting a passionate defense of the Senate's constitutional duty to keep accurate records from Calhoun, who called the proposal "pure, unmixed, personal idolatry." "But why do I waste my breathe? I know it is all utterly vain," Calhoun sighed.[1]

By the time Van Buren took office, Calhoun had opened an international front in his ideological war with fanaticism. Ever since the British government abolished slavery in their New World colonies and committed itself to an antislavery foreign policy in the Western Hemisphere, southern slaveholders had watched warily to see what effects the change might have. Calhoun had been paying close attention to several cases of American ships engaged in the coastal slave trade that had been shipwrecked or blown off course into British territorial waters around the Bahamas and Bermuda and seized by British authorities, who had emancipated the slaves on board and refused to compensate the slaves' owners, declaring that British policy did not recognize slavery.

Perhaps even more worrisome to slaveholders paying close attention to these developments was that northern antislavery jurists like the venerable Supreme Court justice Joseph Story and Lemuel Shaw, chief justice of the Massachusetts Supreme Court, were paying attention to such cases, too. In 1836 Shaw's landmark ruling in *Commonwealth v. Aves* refused to extend the principle of comity—recognizing the laws of another state or nation—to a Louisiana slaveholder residing in Massachusetts who had brought one of his slaves with him, arguing that the principle of comity only applied to "commodities" that were universally recognized as property. Neither the law of nations or the Constitution, Shaw argued, recognized "property in man." In the ongoing transatlantic argument over where slaves fit into Locke's scheme—were they property or persons?—Shaw took what was now the British line, adapting US law to a new Atlantic reality.[2]

Calhoun saw British actions as of a piece with the domestic threat of abolitionism, and he began moving against both of them simultaneously. In January 1837, a few weeks before his positive good speech, Calhoun requested information from the outgoing Jackson administration about the seizure of the *Encomium* and the *Enterprise* in 1834 and 1835, which he characterized as "an outrage committed on our flag and the rights of our citizens." Upon receiving the requested documentation from the administration, Calhoun discovered another, earlier case: that of the *Comet* in 1830.[3]

After reviewing the records provided by the administration, Calhoun mocked that Jackson and his administration had been "tapping gently at the door" of Lord Palmerston, the British secretary of foreign affairs, for the last five years without receiving an answer. He appealed to the law of nations and the principle of comity, arguing that the ships and their cargo were "under the protection of our flag" as much as if they had been in port in Charleston. Mere "municipal" laws could not trump the well-established principle of comity in international law. What possible reason could Britain have for not returning the slaves or compensating their owners, in clear violation of the long-established principle, Calhoun asked? There could be only one, Calhoun professed, but it was "a principle which it was scarcely credible that a Government so intelligent could assume," namely "the principle that there could not be property in persons." Once again, just as he had done in the domestic sphere, he turned the accusation implicit in Britain's policy back toward the accuser. Referring to Britain's empire, especially in India, he declared, "The principle which would abrogate the property of our citizens in their slaves would equally abrogate the dominion of Great Britain over the subject nations under her control. If one individual can have no property in another, how can one nation, which is but an aggregate of individuals, have dominion, which involves the highest right of property, over another? If man has, by nature, the right of self-government, have not nations, on the same principle, an equal right?"[4]

After Van Buren took office, Calhoun urged the new administration to press slaveholders' claims vigorously with Britain. Despite his prickly personal relationship with Calhoun, Van Buren obliged. The US minister to London, Andrew Stevenson, made much the same argument to the British foreign secretary that Calhoun had made in the Senate, but by the time they received the British response—that Britain would compensate the owners of the *Comet* and the *Encomium*, but not the *Enterprise* since it had been seized after August 1, 1834, when emancipation took effect—Calhoun had decided not to press the issue harder for the time being for fear of a full-scale war. Later in 1837 the British burned an American ship, the *Caroline*, that had been supplying arms to a minor rebellion in Canada, in a New York harbor, provoking a diplomatic crisis. Calhoun, like most southern slaveholders, had no desire for a war with a newly antislavery Great Britain, and so he let the issue lie. It was only the first salvo in an emerging contest over slavery and the balance of power between Britain and the United States in the Western Hemisphere.[5]

BY THE SUMMER OF 1837 it was clear that the financial storm that Calhoun had been predicting for the last year and a half was finally breaking. The Panic of 1837 was not well understood at the time, but it was the fruit of both domestic factors and a global economic system. A contraction of credit by the Bank of England in early 1837 put pressure on the American financial system, which did not have enough specie in its vaults to weather the storm thanks in part to Jackson's policies, which had siphoned specie out of the banking system into the federal treasury. Cotton brokers in places like New Orleans felt the pinch first as their English backers became more risk averse, but soon even American firms like Arthur Tappan and Company, which had funded much of the antislavery movement, collapsed. The economic depression seemed to lift in 1838, but came back with a vengeance in 1839 in response to a glut in the cotton market. It would ultimately last until 1843. The economic devastation wrought by the collapse provoked a realignment in American politics as the various coalitions that had made up the Whig opposition to Jackson and Van Buren coalesced in support of government intervention to ease the crisis and support economic development, while Martin Van Buren, siding with the more powerful anti-banking faction in the Democratic Party, responded by pushing to separate the government from the financial system entirely.[6]

In September Van Buren called Congress back into session to address the crisis, and Calhoun reluctantly left South Carolina, where he had been since March, for Washington. "You know how fond Papa is of home and may imagine how he disliked leaving it at this season of the year," Anna wrote to her brother Patrick, who was just beginning his education at West Point, "but you know he never complains of a duty and whatever he considers right he does cheerfully."[7]

Doing his duty may have been its own reward, but when he reached Washington, Calhoun's delight deepened when he found Van Buren ready to thoroughly reform the financial system. As Calhoun wrote to Anna, Van Buren "had no choice" if he wanted to maintain his leadership of the Democratic Party. The proposal that emerged from the administration and its supporters, known as the independent treasury or subtreasury system, was a nearly complete separation of the government from the banking system. Instead of being held in a national bank or state banks, government funds would be held in a treasury system that would have branches throughout the country.[8]

Van Buren's decision to side with the larger and more vehement anti-banking wing of his party alienated a number of conservative Democrats who thought the Independent Treasury took the traditional Democratic antipathy to banks too far, leaving the president in desperate need of allies. Since the nullification crisis Calhoun had often sided with the Whig opposition to Jackson, but, as he wrote Anna, "We disagreed on almost all points except resistance to Executive usurpation." As the special session approached, Calhoun's principles, instincts, and political interests now steered him back toward the more congenial Democratic fold.[9]

To his critics, it looked like another instance of his infinite political malleability and blatant opportunism. It was undoubtedly politically advantageous, but the shift also reflected Calhoun adjusting course to maintain his own agenda within the rapid changes in political coalitions provoked by the financial crisis. His correspondence shows clearly that Calhoun's support for the idea behind the Independent Treasury predated Van Buren's proposal that fall. In May as the financial crisis broke he had written to Samuel Ingham that it was time to make a clean break between the banks and the government. On its face it was a surprising conclusion: Calhoun had played a primary role in chartering the Second Bank of the United States in 1816, and only three years earlier he had supported a national bank, if only to "unbank the banks." But in both cases, he explained to Ingham, the bank had only been a means to an end of providing a stable currency for the country. Now it was clear that a new bank was not an option politically or financially, and the current system of deposit banks—which Calhoun had never supported—was not working. A new solution was required, and Calhoun saw it as an opportunity for wholesale reform.[10] In the Independent Treasury, he told Anna, he saw an opportunity to "throw off the last of our commercial shackles," and he delighted in the fact that his independence allowed him to follow his principles. "I stand now on my own bottom," he wrote, "with no influence acting on me but a rigid adherence to those great principles, for which I have made so many sacrifices."[11]

Calhoun's rapprochement with Van Buren was not wholesale, and never would be, but Van Buren's message to the special session of Congress that September, in which the president denounced a push for a new national bank as an example of "the constant desire among some of our citizens to enlarge the powers of the Government and extend its control to subjects with which it should not interfere," harmonized perfectly with Calhoun's sentiments.[12] His change of course may have been made even easier by the fact that during the 1836 election and the early months of his presidency, Van Buren had energetically exercised the party discipline that Calhoun so loathed to enforce a national pro-slavery position within his party, ruthlessly excising or suppressing candidates with antislavery or abolitionist feelings in the interest of sectional unity. The Whigs, meanwhile, while assuring slaveholders that they had nothing to fear, had shown themselves willing to countenance the antislavery positions of a John Quincy Adams or a William Slade of Vermont.[13]

Announcing his support for Van Buren's plan in a major speech on September 18, Calhoun told his shocked colleagues that banks had never been his preferred solution to fulfill the constitutional duty to regulate the currency. Sounding more than a little like Andrew Jackson, he declared that the connection between the government and banks was undemocratic, giving one class of citizens a disproportionate advantage over all others by their access to the use of public funds. This was not the bankers' fault, he declared. They fulfilled an essential societal function. But, he continued, through its connection with the government "we have made banking too profitable—far, very far, too profitable; and, I may add, too influential." He warned that the "legal as well as the actual connexion" between banks and the government "must be severed" and he proposed an amendment that would gradually phase out the government's acceptance of bank notes over four years.

In their place, most radically, Calhoun proposed new government notes that could circulate nationally and meet the constitutional duty to regulate the currency, allowing it to circulate at par throughout the country. Not bowing to the hard money "humbugs" (as he had once called them), Calhoun argued that "in the present condition of the world, a paper currency, in some form, if not necessary, is almost indispensable in financial and commercial operations of civilized and extensive communities." The new currency's value would rest not on gold and silver but "on supply and demand simply, which regulates the value of everything else." Although it was not adopted, the proposal showed that Calhoun was thinking well outside the alternatives of a national bank or a hard money system that preoccupied many of his colleagues.[14]

A few weeks later, in response to the accusation that he was the enemy of the banking system and the credit it offered—in other words, that he was a hard money advocate—Calhoun replied, "I am not the enemy, but the friend of credit...The question is not whether credit can be dispensed with, but what is its best possible form—the most stable, the least liable to abuse, and the most convenient and cheap?" The problem with the current system was that it allowed one subset of the people to use the government's credit, which was better than any bank's on its own, for their own use and enrichment. Since the government's credit depended in the end on taxpayers, letting banks use the government's credit for free was a kind of theft. "The credit of an individual is his property and belongs to him as much as his land and houses, to use it as he pleases, with the single restriction, which is imposed on all our rights, that they are not to be used so as to injure others," Calhoun announced.[15]

One historian has described Calhoun's political economy in the years that followed his defense of the Independent Treasury as that of an "economic liberal seeking to destroy bastions of concentrated power, special privilege, and artificial distinctions and thus free the field for the unfettered productive energies of independent citizens."[16] Preaching the gospel of the free market against the twin heresies of Henry Clay's American System on the one hand and the hard money humbugs on the other, Calhoun saw himself playing a conservative role at a crucial moment in American history. The stakes, as he made clear in the climax of his September 18 speech, were much greater than the financial system.

> We have arrived, Mr. President, at a remarkable era in our political history…The Government stands in a position disentangled from the past, and freer to choose its future course than it ever has been since its commencement. We are about to take a fresh start. I move off under the State rights banner, and go in the direction in which I have been so long moving. I seize the opportunity thoroughly to reform the Government; to bring it back to its original principles…I shall oppose strenuously all attempts to originate a new debt; to create a national bank; to reunite the political and the money power—more dangerous than that of church and state—in any form or shape; to prevent the disturbances of the compromise [of 1833], which is gradually removing the last vestiges of the tariff system; and, mainly, I shall use my best efforts to give an ascendancy to the great conservative principle of state sovereignty, over the dangerous and despotic doctrines of consolidation.[17]

The Independent Treasury passed the Senate with Calhoun's amendment to phase out government acceptance of bank notes, although it would not pass in the House for another three years. Nevertheless, Calhoun was jubilant about his return to national influence. "My situation was extraordinary," he wrote Anna near the close of the session, throwing humility aside. "I held the fate of the country, by the confession of all in my hand, and had to determine in what direction I should turn events hereafter." Only to Anna could he admit the thrill that wielding power on the national stage once more brought him.[18]

Calhoun's return to the Democratic fold momentarily divided his political base back home. Calhoun's cousin Francis Pickens and followers like the young Robert Barnwell Rhett approved of his course, but others friends and political allies from the nullification fight who had drifted into the Whig orbit on account of their opposition to Jackson were left confused and angered by Calhoun's apparent shift in loyalties and principles. Those who felt betrayed included Calhoun's fellow senator William C. Preston, Waddy Thompson, and even George McDuffie, all of whom broke with him openly by the end of the year, prompting Calhoun to publish a letter in the *Edgefield Advertiser* defending his independence, his consistency, and his adherence to principles instead of political parties. When the state legislature convened in December, Calhoun's allies brought forward resolutions supporting his positions which passed by overwhelming majorities, leaving Calhoun in a commanding position within the state. "Have you kept up with the politics of the day sufficiently to know of the glorious triumph papa has lately had in this state?" an exultant Anna wrote to Patrick, still at West Point, in late December. After rehearsing the whole course of events, including the nefarious political calculations of her father's enemies, she ended, "Indeed the effect has been exactly contrary to what they expected for papa is now stronger and more popular than he ever has been."[19] Reaffirmed in the affections of his fellow South Carolinians and ascendant in Van Buren's coalition, if not in the president's good graces, Calhoun was riding high as he returned to Washington in December. During his stop in Columbia he found himself the toast of the town. "So much for doing one's duty," he joked to Anna.[20]

IN WASHINGTON, CALHOUN WASTED no time pressing his advantage. Knowing that Van Buren would exert pressure to placate the South, and that the administration still needed his support on the Independent Treasury, which had not yet passed the House, on December 27 Calhoun introduced six resolutions that together represented his entire political creed, encompassing his views on abolition, the Union, and the need to commit the federal government to the protection of slavery. Calhoun presented his resolutions at a moment when the debate over slavery had reached a fever pitch. Abolitionist petitions continued to pour into Congress, but even more ominously, in Calhoun's view, the state legislature of Vermont had passed resolutions protesting the existence of slavery in Washington, DC, and denouncing a proposal for the admission of the one-year-old Republic of Texas as a slave state. The Vermont resolutions were not a petition from a private citizen that could simply be rejected or tabled. Instead, they came from what Calhoun had defined as the most important political unit of the Union, a sovereign state. Furthermore, only weeks before the session opened, an angry mob murdered abolitionist editor Elijah Lovejoy in Alton, Illinois, throwing his printing press into the Mississippi River in what seemed to many a perfect illustration of the spirit of the gag rule in Congress. The killing struck a nerve throughout the North, prompting a haggard, severe-looking man named John Brown to stand up at a church meeting held to protest the killing and publicly consecrate his life to the destruction of slavery. Lovejoy's murder was only the best known of dozens of acts of anti-abolitionist violence throughout the North in the preceding three years, but it was so outrageous that as Calhoun traveled back to Washington it had shifted northern opinion in favor of the bloodied radicals.[21]

Calhoun's first three resolutions laid out a state rights view of the Union: that in adopting the Constitution the states had acted by "voluntary assent" as "free, independent, and sovereign states"; that they had reserved to themselves "sole right over their domestic institutions"; and that the national government was nothing more than a "common agent" of the several states, and thus bound to act only in ways that lent "increased stability and security" to its members.

The next three resolutions focused directly on slavery and abolitionism. The fourth asserted that slavery was a central part of "Southern and Western" states of the Union and that any attacks on it would be "a violation of the most solemn obligations, moral and religious." The fifth and sixth resolutions, which would prove the most controversial, declared that "any intermeddling" of states or their citizens with slavery in the District of Columbia or "any of the Territories" would be "a direct and dangerous attack on the institutions of all the slaveholding states," and, finally, that the Union "rests on an equality of rights and advantages" and that "to refuse to extend to the southern and western states any advantage which would tend to strengthen, or render them more secure, or increase their limits or population by the annexation of new territory or States…under the pretext that the institution of slavery…is immoral or sinful…would, in effect, disfranchise the slaveholding States, withholding from them the advantages, while it subjected them to the burdens of government."[22]

Calhoun's resolutions amounted to a manifesto intended to force senators to go on the record and choose sides, something they were not eager to do. Henry Clay in particular was convinced that Calhoun was trying to ruin his chances at the presidency by forcing him on the record, and charged that the resolutions were as "abstract…as a metaphysical mind can well devise."[23] William Cabell Rives lamented "the most schoolboyish scene I have ever witnessed in a legislative body—disputing about the *abstractions* invoked in Mr. Calhoun's resolutions."[24]

Calhoun had the political leverage to force the conversation. Over the next two weeks the debate over the resolutions raged as Calhoun made small concessions to amend some of his language while doggedly fending off efforts to derail or substantially amend them. One by one the first four resolutions passed by substantial margins despite the fact that, as Daniel Webster noted during the debate, they effectively conceded the compact theory of the Constitution that Webster had waged oratorical war against during the nullification crisis (the fourth resolution as proposed and passed by the Senate specifically called the Union a "constitutional compact").[25]

The debate soon focused on the fifth and sixth resolutions, which Calhoun crafted to forestall debate over slavery in the District of Columbia and the extension of slavery into new territories. These resolutions, everyone understood, were aimed especially at easing the admission of the newly independent Republic of Texas into the Union as a slaveholding state, or perhaps several slaveholding states, which would dramatically shift the balance of power in Congress toward the South. Henry Clay and others tried to defuse the explosive issue of the territories by restricting the fifth resolution to the District of Columbia and softening the sixth. Calhoun objected and warned his southern colleagues that to yield Congress any authority over slavery in the territories would be "to give the first victory to the foe." Abolitionists, he warned, would not be satisfied with Washington, DC, or the territories. They were a new eruption of an old disease, "nothing more than that fanaticism that had carried thousands of victims to the stake...[under] the opinion that the faith of one man was criminal in the sight of another."[26] Nearly twenty years after the Missouri Compromise he had changed his mind about the authority of Congress over the territories. Back then, he acknowledged, he had thought John Randolph's extreme position "too unyielding, too uncompromising, too impracticable," but now "he had been taught his error, and took pleasure in acknowledging it." That Randolph had been dead for nearly five years probably helped.[27]

In the midst of defending his fifth resolution, Calhoun gave what would become a famous description of the antebellum South: "The Southern States are an aggregate, in fact, of communities, not of individuals. Every plantation is a little community, with the master at its head, who concentrates in himself the united interests of capital and labor, of which he is the common representative. These small communities aggregated make the State in all, whose action, labor, and capital is equally represented and perfectly harmonized."

Certainly Calhoun meant to contrast the South with the industrial societies defined by wage labor that emerged on both sides of the Atlantic. The plantation household with a beneficent master at its head was the basic unit of his political system, not the individual. But he did not mean to portray the South as somehow less modern, as his comments would often be interpreted after the Civil War through a lens that saw slavery as a relic of a previous age. He meant, instead, that the South had solved the modern conundrum of how to resolve the conflicting interests of labor and capital. This, he argued, made the South a source of political stability within the country as a whole.

> It makes that section the balance of the system; the great conservative power, which prevents the other portions, less fortunately constituted, from rushing into conflict. In this tendency to conflict in the North between capital and labor, which is constantly on the increase, the weight of the South has and will ever be found on the Conservative side; against the aggression of one or the other side, which ever may tend to disturb the equilibrium of our political system.

Slavery was not only a positive good for the South, Calhoun argued, but for the whole country.[28]

Some observers only saw one side of the coin Calhoun described, coming to believe that he advocated an alliance between northern and southern elites against the unruly masses. Decades later two northerners, Josiah Quincy of Massachusetts and Horace Binney of Pennsylvania, would recall in memoirs conversations with Calhoun from these years in which he argued, as Quincy put it, "that the interests of *the gentlemen* of the North and those of the South are *identical*." These conversations should be placed within the specific political context in which Calhoun made them—he always looked for allies and tried to show them how their interests were best served by agreeing and acting with him. They should also be treated with the caution that their authors' purposes in recording them deserve, which in Quincy's case was specifically to discredit Calhoun as antidemocratic. And yet there is no reason to doubt that they happened.[29]

The other side of the coin can be seen in a conversation a few years earlier with Richard Crallé, a newspaper editor who would later edit Calhoun's collected writings. To Crallé, Calhoun described "the tendency of Capital to destroy and absorb the property of society and produce a collision between itself and operatives." It was the capitalists' ability to bend the government to their interests that was the problem, he implied, not capitalism itself. Taking a hypothetical example of a hundred men, Calhoun described to Crallé the "tendency of the Capital to eradicate the possession of the soil, and to reduce the 90 to a state of simple operatives." Without "soil," which Calhoun probably meant literally but was also political shorthand for independence, the disadvantaged 90 percent would become a dangerous underclass, prone to either manipulation or revolution. Calhoun realized the similarity between the situation he described and slavery, in which planter capitalists wielded complete control over their "operatives," but he believed that racial difference allowed, even dictated, this scenario. Calhoun's novel conclusion was that slavery would allow the South to guard the rest of the country against *both* revolution from below *and* the exploitative tendencies of capital allied with government power that might lead to that revolution in the first place.[30]

The Senate eventually passed watered-down versions of the fifth and sixth resolutions that skirted the issue of slavery in the territories, a fact that Calhoun attributed to Henry Clay and Martin Van Buren's mutual desire to avoid sectional division in their parties ahead of the 1840 presidential election.[31]

OVERALL CALHOUN HAD ACHIEVED a significant, if symbolic, victory, winning the Senate's assent to his view of the Constitution and its condemnation of abolitionism. But it had been a vitriolic debate, and some wondered at his motives. In introducing the resolutions Calhoun declared himself a "firm, unflinching friend of the Union," arguing that his resolutions were meant to save the Union from abolitionism, the only threat that could destroy it.[32] Henry Clay, meanwhile, would write privately later that year that while he believed Calhoun's private life was "irreproachable," he was sure Calhoun would "die a traitor or a madman" and that he was purposely stoking sectional tensions to prepare the way for disunion.[33]

The idea that Calhoun worked actively for disunion was a common accusation in his day, and has had a long afterlife. Certainly by the 1830s many of his closest friends, allies, and family members had given up their attachments to the Union. His brother-in-law James Edward, who Calhoun respected and confided in more than anyone but Anna, urged him in 1835 to "give up your attachment to the Union & cease all efforts to save it: it is no longer compatible with our rights." Many others in South Carolina agreed.[34]

But Calhoun retained his faith that the Union and the Constitution, properly understood, were the best government ever devised by man, and in the late 1830s he remained optimistic about the chances of restricting power into what he viewed as its proper channels—or at least stoic about the need to do his duty until events dictated otherwise. "In my opinion you & many of our distinguished citizens yield too much to despondent feelings," Calhoun wrote to his young kinsman Francis Pickens in the summer of 1836. There were many causes for optimism, but even without them, "True wisdom, it appears to me, consists, in struggling against political disorders in a conservative sperit, without determining whether they be or be not incurable, till events themselves shall decide." Duty was its own reward.[35]

Calhoun warned his friends and family that the consequences of disunion would be dire. "You say it is better to part peaceably at once, than to live in the state of irritation we do," he wrote Anna just after his resolutions on abolition passed the Senate. "That is a natural and common conclusion, but those, who make it, do not think of difficulty involved in the word; how many bleeding pours must be taken up in passing the knife of separation through a body politik, in order to make two of one, which has been so long bound together by so many ties, political, social and commercial." The present state of things could not go on, he agreed, but before contemplating disunion, the South must "resort to every probable means of arresting the evil, and only act, when all has been done, that can be…Any other course would fail in its object, and ruin those, who may attempt it." (In the same letter Calhoun told Anna how Senator Lewis F. Linn of Missouri had nearly suffocated himself by falling asleep next to a lighted candle which then lit the curtains on fire, confirming to Calhoun his own lifelong practice "never to lie down, till all is finished, conversation and all, so that when you do, you lie down to go to sleep." Calhoun's world was full of dangers, apocalyptic and banal, which proper habits and practice could avoid.)[36]

The perception that Calhoun desired the country's demise arose from the fact that he warned about it so often beginning in the 1830s. Calhoun always conjured the specter of disunion as a dark prophecy, not as a political program to be pursued, but the line between warning and threat was a thin one. He spoke of disunion as a kind of natural process that would unfold inevitably given certain actions or inactions on the part of both the South and North. Sometimes he used this rhetoric to unify southern senators, as he did during the petitions debate and the debate over his abolition resolutions, and sometimes he used it as an accusation, conjuring the specter of hundreds of printing presses relentlessly releasing their "poison" into the bloodstream of northern public opinion as a bludgeon to beat the abolitionists with and goad northern politicians to action. The concept of disunion was one of the most potent and malleable rhetorical concepts in American political discourse, and beginning in the 1830s Calhoun became one of its master practitioners. All, in his own mind, to preserve the Union, although only on the South's terms. His contagious certainty in his own conclusions and his vivid descriptions of the disastrous future that awaited the country unless they followed his prescriptions shaped the thinking of a generation of younger southern politicians who would fulfill his prophecies in full after his death.[37]

AFTER CALHOUN'S RESOLUTIONS, THE rest of the session saw some of the most dramatic oratorical collisions of the decade between the three titans of the Senate—Calhoun, Clay, and Webster—ostensibly over the Independent Treasury bill but really rehashing the last twenty years of American politics. The Van Buren administration's Independent Treasury was under attack from both the Whigs and a few Democrats, and in early February, William Cabell Rives proposed an alternative that would have retained the use of state banks as depositories. Calhoun took the lead in defending the Independent Treasury against attacks from both sides in a February 15 speech that many observers thought one of the best of his career. "He spoke two hours & 10 minutes," Francis Pickens wrote breathlessly to his cousin Anna Maria Calhoun that night, noting that it was one of Calhoun's longest speeches. "He ought never again to utter another word in public. I never before had a full conception of his power." Recounting the full galleries completely silent as the audience listened intently to Calhoun build his argument, Pickens was swept away with the spectacle. "Traitors at home may betray him—& a cold & ungrateful world may do what they please with him, but he has impressed himself on the country forever."[38]

Clay delivered a blistering rejoinder that focused on Calhoun's sudden change in political allegiance and betrayal of his erstwhile Whig allies, leading former North Carolina senator Willie Mangum to warn Clay that he had been "a little too spicy, perhaps, towards Mr. C."[39] Calhoun responded by reminding Clay that "what the Senator charges on me unjustly *he has actually done*. He went over on a memorable occasion, and did not leave it to time to disclose his motive." Calhoun's reference to the infamous "corrupt bargain" was all the more explosive because John Quincy Adams was sitting in the Senate chamber, having come to hear the fireworks but perhaps not anticipating being hit by one. "I went into the Senate chamber," Adams fumed that night to his diary, "and found John C. Calhoun, discoursing to his own honour and glory." Adams noticed with satisfaction that when Clay called nullification "a strange, impracticable, incompressible doctrine…worthy of the puzzling theological controversies of the Middle Ages," Calhoun's colleague William C. Preston winced.[40]

Daniel Webster broke the tension when he began his own attack on Calhoun by pretending to wake up and rub his eyes, asking, "Where am I? In the Senate of the United States? Am I Daniel Webster? Is that John C. Calhoun of South Carolina, the same gentleman that figured so largely in the House of Representatives in 1816, at the time the Bill creating a National Bank passed that body?" The act drew laughs, including, according to one account, from Calhoun himself. One young observer who saw the whole drama that spring wrote to a friend from South Carolina that after seeing it all, "I was decidedly of the opinion that Calhoun beat them all out & out…Ever since I heard those speeches I have been an ultra sub Treasury man." Clay, Webster, Adams, and many of their subsequent biographers, of course, disagreed.[41]

IN BETWEEN BATTLES WITH Clay and Webster in the Senate that spring, Calhoun also corresponded with acquaintances and physicians in an effort to find a treatment that might help his daughter Cornelia, who suffered from a degenerative condition that seemed to be getting worse. Having explored experimental treatments in New York City and Philadelphia, Calhoun finally met in early 1838 with a Baltimore physician named Nathan Ryno Smith who claimed to be able to help Cornelia, and Calhoun wrote Anna asking her to accompany her sister to Washington immediately to begin the treatment. By mid-April they had arrived and Cornelia began undergoing treatment while staying with the family of Duff Green, whose political ties to Calhoun had turned personal when his daughter Margaret wed Calhoun's recently widowed son Andrew in 1836. "Sister's general health continues very good," Anna wrote to Patrick at West Point soon after their arrival in Washington, "and she seems contented and happy, but I have little hopes of a cure." Calhoun, on the other hand, with characteristic optimism, believed only a few weeks later that Cornelia had already grown two and a half inches taller and might soon be "entirely restored." Cornelia would remain in the Greens' care undergoing treatment for the next year, but it does not seem that her condition ever really improved.[42]

Anna, meanwhile, savored the joy of being back in Washington society, which she found much livelier now that her father was once again a figure of power and influence. She spent much of her time with the wife of Senator Lewis Linn (the same one that had nearly suffocated himself by falling asleep next to a lighted candle) while the senator was absent in Europe raising money for a lead mining venture back home. One of Linn's partners in that venture, a young mining engineer from Philadelphia named Thomas Green Clemson, visited Washington that summer and, perhaps after meeting her at the Linns' home, fell deeply in love with Senator John C. Calhoun's quick-witted, dark-eyed daughter. Clemson's father had been a Quaker merchant who died early but left his son an inheritance that allowed him to attend Norwich Academy and study at the Royal School of Mines in Paris. His involvement with Senator Linn's lead mine venture in Missouri reflected the fact that he already had a reputation for expertise gained in similar ventures in South America and Cuba. By July Clemson and Anna were engaged, and the lovesick Clemson, now back in Philadelphia, was writing letters calling Anna "the blessed idol of my life."[43]

Anna was not so sure, even after she agreed to the marriage. She had determined not to marry, she wrote Maria Simkins, for "I felt I was useful to my father, and was not wholly without objects in my life, while I contributed to his pleasure in the slightest degree." The prospect of leaving him was crushing, and "sometimes, even now, I set down and take a hearty cry at the idea, either that my place cannot be

altogether supplied to him, or that it should be supplied by another."
She realized that her emotions sent mixed signals about the marriage,
but wrote to Simkins, "You know my idolatry for my father, can sym-
pathize with my feelings, and imagine that such may exist, and yet be
compatible with,—what shall I call it?" She did not call it love, but
wrote that the fact that "I consent to leave my dearest father at all" was
proof of her feelings for Clemson.[44]

It seems likely that part of Anna's unusual attachment to her father
was the fact that her role as his companion and secretary allowed her
an avenue for intellectual companionship and political engagement
that she had no reason to expect as Clemson's wife. She must have
thought of this, for instance, in October as she wrote Calhoun's reply
to Henry Vethake, a professor at the University of Pennsylvania who
had sent Calhoun a copy of his new book on political economy. As
Anna wrote furiously to keep up, Calhoun, perhaps pacing back and
forth in the tiny space of his office at Fort Hill as he did on the floor of
the Senate when delivering speeches, dictated his objections to
Vethake's argument that the cost of tariffs like the one of 1828 fell
mainly on the consumer. "I lay it down as a principle," Anna wrote,
"that to determine where a tax ultimately falls, we must look not only
to the tax, but to its disbursement." Yes, she would miss this.[45]

Even as the household prepared for the wedding in November, Calhoun spent the late summer and early fall traveling around the upcountry doing the kind of stump speaking he had not done for years.
His aim was to bring down General Waddy Thompson, one of the
defectors from Calhoun's new political direction and, embarrassingly,
Calhoun's own representative. At barbecues and public meetings held
at Baptist churches and public courthouses, sometimes in bad weather,
and before audiences that reportedly reached two to three thousand
people, Calhoun debated Thompson directly, defending his support for
the Democrats and Van Buren's Independent Treasury and denouncing
any plan that would return the country to a national bank. One exchange at a church near Greenville became so heated that afterward

Thompson wrote a letter asking pointedly whether Calhoun had meant to call him a liar. Calhoun graciously replied that he had only been responding to what he thought Thompson was trying to say, and was glad to learn he had been mistaken, deftly inferring that Thompson's argument lacked precision. Despite Calhoun's efforts Thompson won the election "by a very large majority," as Calhoun reported to Duff Green, putting it down to Thompson's support from the militia (which he commanded). It was proof that Calhoun did not control South Carolina politics as completely as he hoped or as others feared.[46]

IN THE WEEKS AFTER his attempt to bring down Thompson, Calhoun turned his attention to fighting proposed changes to the South Carolina constitution. The changes would have made the office of governor popularly elected, rather than selected by the state legislature, and would have given the governorship more authority over appointments in the state government—changes that some thought would increase the state's ability to resist the federal government. Calhoun disagreed in a way that helps to illuminate his thinking about the proper sphere for democracy within a larger republic, and the safeguards required to secure its benefits and guard against its dangers. Calhoun saw in the proposed changes nothing less than the overthrow of the old Compromise of 1808 between the upcountry and the lowcountry and the seeds of a party system in the state that would undermine its main source of strength on the national stage. A popularly elected and more powerful governor with enhanced powers of patronage, Calhoun wrote to Alton Pemberton in November, would cause "two violent parties" to spring up, each one seeking the favor and patronage of the federal government in order to win control of the state government. Shift power from the legislature to a greatly empowered and popularly elected executive, and it would make South Carolina into a "wild, factious, and despotick democracy under the control of the dominant interest" instead of a "well adjusted Republick."[47]

At first glance Calhoun's fears seem to confirm the accusation that he was, at heart, antidemocratic, but this is an overly simplistic reading of a much more complicated and evolving facet of Calhoun's thinking. At the very least, his position was not completely self-interested. As he pointed out to Pemberton, it would be the upcountry with its more numerous white male voters that would benefit from the change, and under the new rules the presumptive victor of the gubernatorial contest would be Calhoun's cousin Patrick Noble.

Calhoun's experience over the past decade with what he considered majoritarian and executive tyranny had shaped his thinking about the proper sphere for the exercise of democracy, or the direct will of the people, and the limits that should be imposed on power that was too far removed from that relationship to be held accountable. As he had written Virgil Maxcy in the midst of the nullification crisis, "The rule of the majority & the right of suffrage are good things, but they alone are not sufficient to guard liberty, as experience will teach."[48] He continued to maintain that frequent and fair elections were one of the best safeguards of liberty, but in the Fort Hill Address, he had also written "that those who make and execute the laws should be accountable to those on whom the laws in reality operate."[49] To work properly, democracy must be direct, local, and, to some extent, face-to-face, the kind of democracy he knew and had experienced that summer in his debates with Waddy Thompson in the upcountry. Applied without proper safeguards at too large a scale and with control over an ever-more-powerful federal government as the prize, popular sovereignty inevitably became distorted into a form of tyranny. Distance allowed people to ignore or override the interests of others if they were allowed, or manipulated, into doing so, and excessive powers granted to branches of government, whether legislative or executive, compounded the danger.

Even a state like South Carolina, Calhoun believed, if the legislature or executive became too powerful, was too big for the exercise of a pure majoritarian will without devolving into one section oppressing the other. The Compromise of 1808 had solved this problem in the legislature, effectively requiring the two great divisions of the state to agree before passing legislation, but the proposed changes would hand the same power denied to the legislature to the executive branch and seal the devil's bargain by making the office popularly elected. "I do hope the contemplated change will not be attempted," Calhoun wrote Alton Pemberton. "It would place me in a painful situation. Come from what quarter it may, I would feel myself compelled by the highest sense of duty both to the State & Union to oppose it, with all my might."[50]

What was the proper scale, and who the proper participants in a democracy? What was the proper level at which power could, finally, be exercised, even over and against the will of others? Some clues to Calhoun's answer can be found in his description earlier that year of the South as a collection of "little communities" that together made up the state. The household was the core of what he sought to protect and the basic political unit in his conception of democracy, a concept that stretched beyond the plantation household to include nonslaveholding yeoman farmers of his state, many of whom thought of themselves, in the words of one historian, as "masters of small worlds." Beyond the household, coercive political power could be wielded only with caution, and with a legitimacy that decreased with its distance from the community on which it operated.[51]

In the twentieth century the theologian Reinhold Niebuhr would draw on the Calvinist theology of Calhoun's forebears to make observations about human nature strikingly similar to Calhoun's in his 1932 book *Moral Man and Immoral Society*, in which he noted that while individuals can be addressed through reason and as moral actors, large groups are mostly impervious to such arguments on account of their blind self-interest and "collective egoism." For Niebuhr, however, this meant that any positive social change would require "a measure of coercion," a conclusion that assumes either a shared or imposed view of the common good. Calhoun's response to the same insight was to define democracy in such a way as to seal off his society, his household, and himself from the coercion of the distant, blind masses who sought, in his view, to either exploit them or impose on him their own vision of a moral society.[52]

ANNA'S WEDDING WAS HELD at Fort Hill on November 13, attended by numerous friends and family members who traveled from throughout the area to attend. The rector of St. Paul's Episcopal Church in Pendleton, where Floride and many of the enslaved at Fort Hill attended, performed the ceremony. As she watched her daughter marry the tall, serious northerner ten years her senior, did Floride think about her own wedding to a serious young man, also ten years older, so many years before? Anna had been in Washington when she met and agreed to marry Clemson, certainly with her father's permission. Did Floride approve?

There were other feelings in the room that day, as well, no doubt. What passed through the minds of Old Sawney and his wife Tilla as they watched their master's daughter, whom they had known her whole life, marry? Perhaps they noted the similarities and differences between the slave weddings that were sometimes held in the same house and this one, and they must have thought about how the marriage of this young woman they had helped to raise might be the occasion of their own family's separation. After all, that was what happened when white people got married or died. As they hurried about serving the wedding guests, they must have thought about their own daughter Issey and young Sawney, and wondered.

Calhoun, too, was apprehensive about Anna's marriage, although for different reasons. No doubt he had agreed to it, but he would miss his daughter's company during the long winters in Washington, and her lively presence at Fort Hill. During the festivities that evening Andrew confided to one of Anna's friends how Calhoun really felt. "Observe my father," he said, "he is not as affable as usual, he is abstracted tonight, he feels that in giving up Anna, he is losing his favorite, his pride, his *confident*. The glory of the house is departing with sister Anna."[53]

Four days after the wedding Anna wrote her friend Maria Simkins, "The house really looked deserted, the day after you all left. Everything was so quiet, that it was almost impossible to realize the exciting events of the few days previous." A few days after that the house was even emptier. Calhoun, along with Floride, was on his way back to Washington for Congress. Clemson and Anna, after visiting family in Edgefield and Charleston, were on their way north to meet Clemson's relatives.

For the time being life at Fort Hill continued on, but changes were on the horizon. Before attending the wedding, Andrew had finally found a plantation to buy in Alabama, and while he was at Fort Hill he and his father and Clemson discussed how to manage the transaction. "The cain break is full of capitalists looking to invest," Andrew wrote his father from Alabama on Christmas Day, crowing that "every one wonders how I came by such a bargain."[54] But he still needed the money to fund the purchase. For some reason, perhaps to please or impress his new father-in-law, who in turn wanted desperately to set his son up as an independent planter, Thomas Green Clemson agreed to use his contacts in the North to raise the money. After considerable difficulty—banks were not eager to loan money for Alabama plantations in the wake of the recent panic—and a personal interview with Nicholas Biddle, who no doubt raised his eyebrows at the prospect of John C. Calhoun's son-in-law asking him for money, Clemson finally forwarded Andrew a certificate for $17,000 from Biddle's Philadelphia Bank of the United States, having raised part of the money by selling his stocks in northern banks and the Pennsylvania Life Insurance company. Calhoun raised an additional $3,000 himself, and together with Clemson and Andrew became joint owner of a plantation in Marengo County, Alabama, called Cane Brake. Later that year, Calhoun would incur an additional $12,000 mortgage on behalf of the group to purchase slaves from the estate of a wealthy lowcountry planter, William B. Ioor, including "a child one year old" whose mother must have been part of the purchase.

For the rest of his life Calhoun would regret his decision to support the purchase of the plantation, which would create constant tension between Andrew and Clemson, but the endeavor also had far-reaching consequences for the enslaved community at Fort Hill. After all, Andrew would need a large workforce in Alabama, and even after the purchase of slaves from the Ioor estate, part of that workforce would likely have to come from Fort Hill. If parts of the conversation between Calhoun, Clemson, and Andrew about Alabama were overheard, the news probably spread quickly through the slave quarters that night as they wondered who among them might be moving with their master's son to Alabama.[55]

SIXTEEN

"The True and Perfect Voice of the People"

I N THE SUMMER OF 1840 Calhoun wrote to his college friend Micah Sterling, "I feel but little as yet the effects of age, but I know that I have arrived at the period, when old may be well prefaced to my name." Before the end of the year, two of Calhoun's brothers, his older brother William and his younger Patrick, would die, reinforcing the fact that however he felt, Calhoun was growing older. Despite the fierce energy that he put into influencing the course of history, at fifty-eight years old Calhoun felt that its course was ultimately set, and that men had only to play their parts, do their duty, and abide the results. "I look with perfect composure on the advance of time," he wrote, "knowing that it is in the order of Providence and that it is our highest duty to acquiesce in his decrees. My confidence in his goodness and wisdom is without limits, and has sustained me through all the vicissitudes of life."[1]

And yet, at other moments, Calhoun considered the state of the modern world and its relentless pace of change with apprehension. "Modern society seems to me to be rushing to some new and untried condition," he wrote in reply to James Henry Hammond's account of his travels in Europe in 1837, which included Hammond's description of the growth of the working classes in England.[2] Indeed, there were always "revolutions" of various kinds—political, moral, financial—on the horizon in Calhoun's mind, some of them occurring before his eyes and some that he saw looming in the future. Calhoun was not afraid of change. He took it for granted as one of the essential features of his world. "I am of the progress party," he wrote to Democratic editor John L. O'Sullivan, "but events must move slowly and in their proper order, in order to move successfully."[3] Like many other Americans who considered themselves "conservative" in the mid-nineteenth century, when the term was much less controversial and more widely embraced than it is today, Calhoun saw no contradiction between conservatism and progress. Indeed, he thought they went, or should go, together. That was the only safe course. Calhoun never fully let go of the old republican fear that it was the fate of all republics eventually to degenerate and self-destruct by suicide, but he balanced this fear against the belief that if Americans could adapt the insights of their forefathers to the revolutionary changes of the modern world, including the centripetal tendency of power in all its guises, they might yet avoid that fate, perhaps for centuries.[4]

In the early and mid-1830s he had already become concerned that the republic's end was near—and that it would take the form of Andrew Jackson, Martin Van Buren, and the American Anti-Slavery Society. However, by the end of the 1830s he believed the most critical danger had passed. The Independent Treasury had passed and the Compromise of 1833 was nearing its promised conclusion as the protective tariff phased out, depriving the government of revenue that could be converted into patronage. Describing what he hoped to accomplish to Virgil Maxcy in 1839, Calhoun wrote, "It is no less, than to bring the Government back to where it was in 1789 when it started by obliterating all the intermediate acts inconsistent with the State rights principles...The work is more than half accomplished already."[5]

For the moment, at least, it seemed that abolitionism had been knocked on its heels by the gag rule, the passage of Calhoun's resolutions on slavery, and the united front of the Democratic Party. "Of all the dangers to which we have ever been exposed," Calhoun declared to the Senate in early 1839, "this has been the greatest. We may now consider it passed." He expressed confidence that his enlightened view of slavery would soon hold sway "not only in our country, but over the civilized world."[6] Paying close attention to British foreign policy, he knew that there was perhaps more danger to slavery from abroad than there was at home.

Certainly Calhoun's personal political stock, as an independent champion of his own ideals and the administration's policies, had never been higher. "As to myself," he wrote Virgil Maxcy in early 1840, "I think, I may say, that my position is strong, never more so. Time, which tests all things, acts in my favour. I in fact, put myself on time, when I took the course I did 14 years ago, and it has not deceived me." Progress as Calhoun conceived of it was inevitable, as the march of time inevitably produced revolutions—technological, social, and political—but also revealed the truth of his principles. Time would eventually vindicate the righteous. Its verdicts were not to be feared, as long as he did his duty.[7]

AFTER A SHORT AND uneventful session in Washington the winter after Anna's wedding, Calhoun, Floride, and Cornelia returned to Fort Hill in March 1839, where they would remain for most of the year. Floride was glad to leave the "monotonous life" of the "dusty and unpleasant" city, and Calhoun soon wrote Anna, who was in the North visiting Clemson's relatives, that he was "more engaged about the plantation & garden, than you have ever seen me. With the exception of meal times, I am scarcely ever in the House."[8]

Calhoun always prided himself on being a progressive farmer, advocating agricultural reforms to combat the depletion of the soil (a problem that had become increasingly common during the cotton revolution) and to render southern plantations self-sufficient by diversifying their crops. He and James Edward often exchanged letters about different techniques, including rotating crops between cotton, corn, and other grains, as well as letting land lie fallow. "But we must not neglect manure," Calhoun admonished his brother-in-law in 1832. Most of all, Calhoun lamented the effects of soil erosion, which he estimated drew off "$20,000,000 of our labour to be placed on far distant regions" like some pernicious natural version of the tariff. To fight the effects of erosion at Fort Hill, Calhoun employed a system of special ditches, especially on hillsides.[9] Virginia agricultural reformer and ardent secessionist Edmund Ruffin eagerly published Calhoun's endorsement of Ruffin's *Farmer's Register* in 1835, in which Calhoun lamented the "steady progress to sterility" of the soil across the South "from its first settlement" brought about by planters' headlong pursuit of profit. "It ought to be a principle of morals and patriotism, as well as individual economy with us," he wrote Ruffin, "that no gain is legitimate that does not leave the land as productive as it was before it was taken."[10] At Fort Hill, when he was there, Calhoun strove to put these ideals into practice, and in 1839 the progressively minded Pendleton Farmer's Society recognized his efforts by electing him its president.[11]

Calhoun's emphasis on diversified agriculture and preserving the productivity of the soil as a form of patriotism evoked the political independence that republicanism prized, but it also became an element of his argument for the South's competitiveness in the global marketplace. "A plantation is a little community of itself, which, when hard pressed, can furnish within itself almost all of its supplies," he announced in 1842 when listing the advantages that southern planters had over other labor regimes, such as India, in producing cotton. "There is not a people on earth who can so well bear the curtailing of profits, as the Southern planters, when out of debt…when prices fall and pressure comes, we gradually retire on our own means, and draw our own supplies from within." Considering the massive levels of debt that Calhoun personally carried when he made the claim, this was more of an ideal than a reality.[12]

DURING THE SUMMER OF 1839 Calhoun briefly had his whole family together back at Fort Hill, including Patrick, home from West Point. Calhoun had been pleasantly surprised by Patrick's success at the military academy over the past two years. "I wish you could have seen Papa's delighted look, as he handed the report to us," Anna had written to her brother when one of his first reports arrived at Fort Hill in 1837 showing average academic accomplishment but at least no demerits.[13] But that summer Patrick brought home evidence of a different kind of failure when it became clear he was suffering from a venereal disease that caused boils, weak eyesight, and hair loss. Calhoun was carefully measured in his reaction, and when Patrick wrote from West Point that fall that he was not fully recovered, Calhoun wrote with extensive advice on how to keep up his studies without damaging his health. "I will not for a moment suppose, that it is a new contraction of the same disease," he wrote. "I have too much confidence in your prudence & good sense, not to say morals, to suppose, that after what you have experienced you will again deviate from the paths of virtue." Warning Patrick strongly against any more "licencious intercourse," Calhoun caught himself, writing, "But I need not dwell on this. If your experience, does not keep you pure, I fear that nothing, which the deep solicitude of a father can say would."[14]

Meanwhile, in August Anna was back at Fort Hill to give birth to her first child, Calhoun's second grandchild. The little girl was born in the midst of an epidemic of fever that caused the Calhouns to temporarily abandon Fort Hill for a neighboring plantation. Calhoun wrote to James Edward two weeks after the child's birth that the baby was "quite unwell, but we hope not dangerously so." The little girl lived another week, dying at ten o'clock in the evening on September 3. Calhoun did not record what it was like to watch his daughter experience the heartbreak that he and Floride knew so well, but not long after the child's death Anna wrote to Maria Simkins of the "death of my poor little baby." "Oh! Maria I am now more reconciled to the blow but indeed it was hard to bear at first," she wrote, describing her attempts to maintain self-control "for Mr. Clemson's sake who was both very much affected & fearful of its effects on me."[15]

The experience seems to have only deepened Calhoun's concern over his daughter's health and wellbeing as she entered what was for a woman the most dangerous period of life. A few months later in Washington, after hearing from Francis Pickens that Anna was not well, he wrote to gently reproach her for not telling him. "Devoted attachment claims to know the condition of the object of its affection," he wrote, "whether it be good, or bad…and is ever pained, when either is concealed…Unless you expressly inform me hereafter, as to the state of your health by your letters, I shall infer, that it is not good." Calhoun then launched into a lament that society did not undertake to educate women on their health in the same way it did men. "I regard it," he wrote, "as one of the calamities of the age."[16]

Calhoun also tried to mend the developing rift between Thomas Green Clemson and Andrew over Cane Brake. From the very beginning, Andrew had spoken of the venture in grandiose terms—"A fortune is in our grasp," he wrote his father in December 1838 during the purchase—but in the first year he delivered little but excuses.[17] By early 1840 Clemson had become increasingly dissatisfied with the partnership and he finally complained bitterly to his father-in-law about the situation and Andrew's lax management, prompting a fatherly response from Calhoun. "I have great confidence in you both, and you ought to have in each other," Calhoun wrote, warning Clemson that "distrust & suspicion ought to be carefully avoided, particularly between those as intimately connected as you & he."[18] Clemson's frustrations were understandable; he expected regular statements of progress and a regular return on his investment, which he viewed in contractual terms. He never quite understood the tangle of land, debt, family relations, and personal honor in the southern Calhoun clan no matter how gently Calhoun tried to explain it to him.

ON THE WAY BACK to Washington in late 1839 Calhoun found himself on the same railroad car as Senator William Roane of Virginia, who offered to broker a personal reconciliation between Calhoun and Martin Van Buren. As Calhoun later described the meeting to James Edward, he was simply "making my personal, conform to my political relations."[19] It was awkward to defend the political measures of a president with whom he was not on speaking terms. "I have, in fact, changed no opinion, as to his course towards me," Calhoun wrote, but "the present is pregnant with a long train of important events," and it was vital that they be able to work together where they agreed. The meeting caused a sensation in Washington, prompting more vicious mockery from Henry Clay at Calhoun's apparently effortless political transformations. Van Buren quickly wrote to Andrew Jackson describing the meeting. "The Whigs of course hate him for it worse if that be possible than they ever did either of us," he told Old Hickory.[20] Many saw in Calhoun's actions a bid to become Van Buren's anointed successor.

In the Senate that spring Calhoun and Henry Clay sparred over the issue of public lands and the revenues from them in a debate that perfectly illustrated the differences between Calhoun's vision of a cautious, state-favoring federalism and Clay's American System. Clay proposed that the federal government distribute the revenue from public land sales back to the states to fund internal improvements and other state priorities, a proposal that Calhoun had once endorsed as a safety valve for excess revenue. But Calhoun's thinking on the matter had grown more uncompromising, and in early January 1840 he introduced a bill that would cede the public lands back to the states with a requirement that a percentage of the proceeds be paid to the federal government. Whereas Clay's proposal made the federal government the patron of the states, Calhoun's bill reversed the roles, placing the states in control of the revenue and making them the patrons of the government in Washington. Many in the western states where the land was located, including a young Illinois legislator named Abraham Lincoln, liked Calhoun's plan better. Lincoln eagerly forwarded copies of resolutions he had proposed in the Illinois legislature supporting a similar plan to Illinois congressman John T. Stuart, asking him to "show them to Mr. Calhoun." The Illinois delegation supported the bill, although the debate over the public lands would continue until after the coming election.[21]

By 1840 Calhoun was looking to renew his battle with abolitionism beyond the borders of the United States by confronting Britain's increasingly aggressive antislavery foreign policy. For Calhoun this was simply a new line in an old story—his whole life he had carried contradictory feelings of dread and admiration for the British. He had grown up in a household shaped by Irish Presbyterian and American resentment of British tyranny, entered public service during a war with Britain, built an American war machine under the assumption of another war with Britain, and helped James Monroe craft a foreign policy designed to keep Britain out of the Americas. And despite the fact the vast majority of American cotton was sold to Britain, and the fact that Calhoun was an ardent defender of free trade, it was also true that Britain's abolition of slavery in 1833 and its official antislavery stance in its foreign policy had altered the international balance of power, isolating New World slave societies like Brazil, Cuba, the United States, and, after 1836, the Republic of Texas.[22] After first raising the issue of British seizure of American ships engaged in the coastal slave trade in 1837, Calhoun had backed off as two diplomatic crises—first over the British burning of an American ship, the *Caroline* in 1837, and then a dispute over the border between Maine and Canada the following year—threatened to plunge the United States into actual war with Britain. This was a scenario that Calhoun and most other southerners wanted to avoid both because the United States was unprepared for war and for fear that the British might incite a slave revolt.[23]

By early 1840 the danger of outright war had lessened, and Calhoun again took up the same line of attack. On March 4, he submitted a series of resolutions to the Senate denouncing British harassment of American ships carrying slaves, focusing on the case of the *Enterprise*, which had been seized in 1835 after the Slavery Abolition Act took effect. A ship under the United States flag, he proclaimed, was under the protection of its laws, "as much so, as if constituting a part of its own domain," and that everyone on board, "with their property, and all the rights belonging to their personal relations, as established by the State to which they belong," were protected according to the laws of nations. The last resolution specifically denounced "the seizure and detention of negroes" as "an act in violation of the laws of nations, and highly unjust to our own citizens to whom they belong."[24]

The resolutions were Calhoun's attempt, at nearly the height of his postnullification influence, to extend his successful 1837 resolutions against domestic abolitionism into the realm of foreign policy. In his speech supporting the resolutions, Calhoun accused Britain of trying to change the long-settled law of nations when it came to slavery, an aim that would involve "no small share of effrontery for a nation which has been the greatest slave dealer on earth." Determined to demonstrate British hypocrisy, Calhoun read descriptions of slavery in Malabar in southern India and described British-occupied Afghanistan as "one magnificent plantation, peopled by more than one million slaves, belonging to a company of gentleman in England, called the East India Company." He raised the example of "subjugated Ireland," with eight million people and only ninety thousand voters. Finally, he pointed out that at the very moment they self-righteously declared the end of slavery in the Western Hemisphere, Britain was commencing a war against China—a nation that was "old and civilized before the governments of Western Europe came into existence"—in order "to force on them the use of Opium," whose sapping effects Calhoun described as worse than slavery.

Calhoun warned his colleagues not to be fooled by a false British humanitarianism, the work of British abolitionist "[William] Wilberforce, and other misguided men like him, who, although humane and benevolent, look at the surface of things, with little knowledge of the springs of human action, or the principles on which the existing social and political fabric of Europe rests; and I may add, like all other enthusiasts, without much regard as to the means employed in accomplishing a favorite object." Just look at the British colonies in the West Indies, he continued, where emancipation had simply replaced the "mild and guardian authority" of the master with "the army, the sheriff, the constable, and the tax collector" in a brutal regime of state-enforced subjugation. "Has she made her slaves free, given them the right of self-government?" Calhoun asked. "Is it not mockery to call their present subject condition freedom?" As usual, Calhoun brilliantly illuminated the inconsistencies of his opponents, but never turned the searching glare of his logic back on himself. The resolutions passed the Senate by a 33 to 0 vote, with twenty-three senators abstaining, a resounding if incomplete victory for Calhoun.[25]

In an effort to put teeth in the resolutions Calhoun soon began proclaiming the need for a stronger naval force to counteract the British dominance of the ocean. Calhoun had been an eager advocate for naval power early in his career as a result of his experience in the War of 1812, but his wariness over government expenditures had diminished his ardor in recent years. In a speech only weeks after his *Enterprise* resolutions passed, he argued that the main military threat to the country was no longer an internal one. "We must look to the ocean," he proclaimed. "That is the exposed side—the side of danger." The government should stop its spending on meaningless and wasteful internal improvements, and instead focus its resources on the navy, "our cheapest and safest defense—at once our sword and shield."[26]

Over the coming years Calhoun and a group of southerners in national government, especially the Virginian Abel Upshur, would become avid supporters of American naval power in a bid to deflect British interference with the remaining slave societies in the New World. In their minds, there was a clear constitutional difference between the federal government's powers at home, which were limited, and what Upshur in 1840 called its "ample and unquestioned" powers in foreign affairs. As Calhoun saw it, the federal government's responsibility to protect slaveholders' property meant that federal power should be restrained at home, except to restrict abolitionists or retrieve fugitive slaves, at the same time that it was actively wielded against the British threat abroad in what one historian has called a "proslavery arms race across the Western Hemisphere." There was, constitutionally speaking, no contradiction. In December 1840 Calhoun was appointed to the Senate's Committee on Foreign Relations, his first appointment to a standing committee as a senator, while in the House his kinsman and close ally Francis Pickens was appointed chair of the Committee on Foreign Affairs. These appointments, added to Calhoun's *Enterprise* resolutions and what transpired in the months after the presidential election of 1840, left little doubt as to the direction of American foreign policy.[27]

IN 1840 CALHOUN HAD one eye on British hypocrisy and the other eye on the presidential election, and both spectacles made his stomach turn. Calhoun assumed at first that Van Buren would win another term, but in 1840 the Whigs successfully adapted their approach to the age of Jackson. New-school Whigs like the newspaper editor Horace Greeley carefully crafted a message of economic and moral progress aided by government that appealed to broad swaths of the upper- and emerging middle-class electorate, and packaged it in populist rhetoric that appealed to westerners and workers. The Whigs nominated the old military hero William Henry Harrison over Henry Clay and portrayed Harrison as the candidate of ordinary people in a campaign marked by precious few policy positions, plenty of log cabin imagery (despite the fact that Harrison lived in a mansion), and copious amounts of hard cider. To Calhoun, the lack of substance at a time when the country faced so many important questions was infuriating. "I…cannot believe that the people can be humbugged by the fooleries resorted to in order to deceive them by the supporters of Harrison," he wrote Andrew in July, but "let it turn as it may, we must not despair."[28]

Part of Calhoun's disdain for the hero of Tippecanoe was his suspicion that Harrison had more principles than he let on. Nine years earlier Harrison had written a series of public letters to Calhoun in the midst of the nullification crisis supporting the tariff and denouncing nullification.[29] Calhoun was wrong about Harrison having principles, but he believed there were important questions to be decided even if the froth of the election concealed them. "If the present contest was one about men, as our opponents would have us believe," Calhoun wrote in a public letter to supporters in Greenville, "I would take neither interest nor part in it. It would be degrading to sixteen millions of freemen to be agitated on the question, whether this or that individual should be raised to highest office…The liberty and welfare of the county, and the principles and policy by which they are to be promoted and preserved, are the only considerations worthy of patriots and freemen."[30] In another public letter Calhoun sounded what had become his standard explanation of the political moment—nothing less than the culmination of the long struggle between "the school of Jefferson and the school of Hamilton."[31]

When Harrison won the election, Calhoun viewed it not as a defeat for the school of Jefferson, but as a vindication of its principles, from which the Democrats had strayed. Van Buren's defeat was "the result of a deep principle of retributive justice," he wrote Andrew in November as the result became clear. "All the old sins of Jackson's time have come back to them," he wrote. Now, he believed, the Democrats would only be able to redeem their defeat "by coming to my ground," the true ground, Jefferson's ground. Time, he believed, was doing its slow but sure work of revealing truth by punishing those who departed from the deep principles that sustained liberty.[32]

In early 1841 before the inauguration Calhoun wrote Anna from Washington that he had met with Harrison, and was not impressed. The old Indian fighter had greeted him "as if we had been old cronies" and seemed "to enjoy his elevation as a mere affair for personal vanity," Calhoun wrote in disgust. A few days later the sixty-nine-year-old president-elect wandered onto the Senate floor while it was in session and tapped a surprised Calhoun on the shoulder and immediately launched into a loud conversation before Calhoun quickly led him out to the lobby.[33]

A few weeks after that, Harrison was dead, the victim of pneumonia that set in after he delivered a two-hour inaugural address in freezing weather with no coat or hat. His unexpected death left Vice President John Tyler at the head of the federal government. Tyler was a state rights Virginian who had broken with Andrew Jackson over Jackson's nullification proclamation and joined the ranks of the emerging Whig opposition. Despite his affiliation with the Whigs and his support of Henry Clay's failed bid for the party's nomination in the last election, Tyler was known to oppose nearly everything Clay stood for, including protective tariffs, a national bank, and federal funding for internal improvements. He represented a wing of the Whig Party that consisted mainly of ex-Democrats who, not unlike Calhoun, agreed with the Whigs on narrow but important issues such as their opposition to executive power. In light of this, it was far from clear what Tyler would do in his new role. Would he go along with Clay, the clear leader of the party after Harrison's death, or would he assert his own principles? Calhoun was hopeful. "Much, very much is in his power," Calhoun wrote privately in June.[34] What soon became clear was that Tyler would be an aggressive advocate of the proslavery foreign policy positions that Calhoun had crafted in the Senate over the past few years. As 1841 progressed, it also became clear that Tyler's rogue presidency had splintered the Whigs' fragile unity and thrown their chances for reelection in 1844 into doubt. This gave Calhoun, who had emerged as one of the most prominent figures in the Democratic Party, his best chance in years to win the nation's highest office.

IN LATE SPRING OF 1841 Calhoun finally made a trip west to western Alabama to visit Andrew and see Cane Brake for himself. The rift between Thomas Clemson and Andrew had only deepened, and in an effort to bring peace to the family, Calhoun offered either to arrange new financing for Cane Brake, allowing Clemson to withdraw completely, or to change Clemson's investment into a loan, a prospect that the detail-oriented Clemson had hinted would be preferable to the vague, open-ended family partnership. "As to myself," Calhoun wrote his son-in-law, "I have no other desire in relation to the subject, but that you should be perfectly satisfied."[35]

Meanwhile, others in the Calhoun clan were becoming increasingly concerned with Calhoun's financial situation. "He is now getting old," Francis Pickens wrote James Edward Colhoun, adding that Calhoun was under "a profound delusion" about the Alabama venture, and conveying in confidence his knowledge that Andrew owed massive debts in Charleston for which Calhoun served as security. Even Anna came to agree with her husband that her father placed too much trust in Andrew, but it proved as impossible for Calhoun to admit that his son was a failure as it did for him to admit defeat in any other area of his life.[36]

His correspondence with Andrew in the months before he made the trip left Calhoun not knowing what to expect in Alabama. Perhaps trying to season his father's expectations, Andrew had written, "I am beginning to believe that the culture of cotton is incompatible with any improvement which renders a country attractive to the eye, and which generally indicates prosperity elsewhere," although he was quick to note that the "slovenly" appearance of much of the new cotton country was due to the "unequal fiscal operations of the Govt." rather than to the effects of slavery. Nevertheless, he wrote of his progress in clearing nearly 250 acres of forested land and assured his father of a "four-fold profit" on his and Clemson's investment, a promise that would never materialize.[37]

For many along Calhoun's route to Alabama it was a rare opportunity to see the famous South Carolinian in person, and local papers covered his trip extensively. In Columbus, Georgia, a curious throng filled the dining hall of the Oglethorpe Hotel to hear a short speech from Calhoun that prompted opposite responses from the local Whig and Democratic newspapers, while residents of Montgomery, Alabama, delighted for years in the story of a local man who fell into an argument with a traveling stranger about nullification, not realizing he was arguing with the head nullifier himself.[38]

Calhoun spent two weeks with Andrew, Margaret, and his grandson Duff Calhoun (named for his other grandfather) at Cane Brake, and convinced himself that the Alabama venture had promise. "The soil is rich as river bottoms," he wrote Patrick on his return, reporting that of more than 1,200 acres Andrew had cleared half, and had 400 acres planted in cotton, all the work of the eighty-six enslaved people who also lived at Cane Brake in 1840. "If the place was paid for, I should be at my ease," he wrote, "but that at present is a heavy load."[39]

By the time he left for home, news of his presence in Alabama had spread, and Calhoun found himself speaking to large audiences who packed themselves into Baptist and Presbyterian churches along his route in Marion, Selma, and Montgomery as he made his way back to South Carolina. In Marion, Calhoun's host returned home to find a crowd, with Calhoun in the middle, "more gazed at than the devil would be in the midst of a methodist revival." After dinner with prominent local citizens, Calhoun walked to the Baptist church, which was soon "crowded to suffecation" with Marion's white male population, and gave what his host thought was a "noble *conversation* (as he called an able speech) on the currency." Afterward, Calhoun walked across to the Presbyterian church, where an equally interested group of women had gathered to meet him. In the recent election Whigs had made much of an alleged affinity among American women for the Whig cause, opening a space for women to play an important, if still symbolic, role in the political drama of the presidential election. In this atmosphere the women of Marion evidently expected Calhoun's attention and he complied, walking the aisles being introduced and offering "polished and courteous" small talk to a constituency that couldn't vote but also couldn't be ignored. Thanks to Anna, the idea that women might be interested in politics was not strange to him.[40]

Knowing that he addressed a mixed political audience at these stops, and that many of the region's large planters were perfectly happy to ally with northern business interests in the Whig Party, Calhoun made his case for laissez-faire political economy against the resurgent threat of the Whig economic program in plain terms. Why would Alabamians and Mississippians, with their rich soil and abundant exports, support policies that had strangled their economic development, he asked? Just look at Cuba, he told them, which exported less than Alabama and Mississippi and paid higher taxes to their colonial center in Spain, and yet was "far more flourishing" and could support "a market city of over a hundred thousand people, while we can hardly sustain one of five thousand." Why was this the case? Because of "the fiscal action of our government," especially the tariff and its monetary policy. The South's true policy, and the nation's, Calhoun argued, was free trade and a sound currency. "We make the staple that the world must have," he told the residents of cotton country. "Let us alone, then, should be our motto."

Some in the audience certainly listened to the argument, but others only came to see the famous man. One newspaper editor who said little about the content of Calhoun's speech could not forget his "eye—restless, watchful, and penetrating, it seemed to reach into a man's very soul at a glance." Another Alabamian who saw Calhoun proclaimed that, like the biblical Simeon, he could now die in peace having seen his "God."[41]

BACK IN WASHINGTON IN the summer of 1841 for a special session of Congress, called by Harrison before his death, Calhoun could see that Henry Clay meant to make the most of the Whig's recent victory despite the minor inconvenience of Harrison's untimely demise and John Tyler's uncertain allegiance. Indeed, Clay was determined to push through not only his ambitious legislative agenda, including a national bank, a land bill, and a new tariff, but a series of measures meant to weaken the executive branch and strengthen his own position in national politics. His arrogance and fierce drive—on one occasion he tried to pass a resolution recommending his own punishing daily schedule, including directives on waking, eating, and exercising, to his Senate colleagues—would earn him the nickname "the dictator" before the year's end. To Calhoun, this was an existential threat to all his work over the last several years, and he spent much of his energy over the next year and a half desperately fighting Clay's agenda in the Senate while also tending to foreign policy and keeping a close eye on his own presidential prospects. During these running battles Calhoun articulated some of the most ambitious arguments ever made in favor of free trade and American economic imperialism in the Western Hemisphere, while also advocating for his own particular vision of a modern Jeffersonian politics based on the idea of a concurrent majority.[42]

The days in Washington that summer were long and hot. Calhoun rose early and walked, sometimes two or three miles, before preparing for Senate sessions, which sometimes stretched six hours at the hottest time of the day. It was "heavy and exhausting work," Calhoun wrote to Thomas Green Clemson, and "Clay and the whigs are exerting every nerve to carry their measures." As the summer progressed, Clay successfully moved a bill to establish a new national bank through the Senate, defeating Calhoun's last-ditch attempt to have the new bank located in New Orleans, where Calhoun argued it would at least benefit the great staple-producing region instead of some northern city or Washington.[43] When Clay tried to squelch debate on the bill with tactics that utilized the gag rule as a precedent, Calhoun objected to the general application of a rule that he viewed as only applying to abolitionist petitions, remarking that Clay was "so intoxicated with joy at the passage of his Bank bill…that he had entirely forgot all he ever knew about questions of order." Clay replied from his seat, "A good deal so," and Calhoun instantly rejoindered, "Entirely so," and expressed his hope that Clay would sober up.[44] During debate on Clay's proposal for the federal government to assume state debts and create a new national debt, Calhoun scoffed that the bill could hardly be more advantageous to the banking class "if this body, instead of being a Senate of the United States, was a deputation from Wall Street."[45]

By the end of the session, John Tyler had lived up to Calhoun's hopes, vetoing two different versions of Clay's bank and prompting the resignation of his cabinet, creating a crisis for the Whig Party.[46] Nevertheless, Clay was eventually able to push through most of his legislative agenda, including the repeal of the Independent Treasury system, whose end was celebrated by a rowdy torchlight parade of Clay supporters down Pennsylvania Avenue bearing a coffin for the deceased "Sub Treasury."[47]

Determined to cut Tyler down to size after the bank vetoes, at the next session Clay proposed a constitutional amendment eliminating the two-thirds majority required to override a presidential veto, proposing instead a simple majority on the premise that the current veto allowed the president to override the will of the American people. It was a breathtaking attempt to seize power since with Clay in firm control of Congress, the amendment would have handed him effective control of the federal government.

Having opposed Andrew Jackson's attempts to wield executive power in unprecedented ways, Calhoun now attacked Clay's attempt to usurp the proper powers of the executive, signaling to Tyler that he would support a generous application of presidential veto power against Clay's agenda. But Calhoun's speech in support of the president's veto power on February 28, 1842, was much more than that. In the midst of his running battle with Clay the previous fall, Calhoun had written to the northern editor Orestes Brownson in confidence that he was beginning work on a "scientifick development of my views of Government" that would vindicate the modern school of Jeffersonian (and Calhounian) politics.[48] The final product, two treatises titled *A Disquisition on Government* and the accompanying *Discourse on the*

Constitution and Government of the United States, would not see the light of day until after Calhoun's death, but in his speech in support of the president's veto power Calhoun gave an ingenious reading of the Constitution as the embodiment of a government of the concurrent majority.

The Constitution, Calhoun stated bluntly, did not enshrine the principle of the numerical majority, what John Randolph had once called "King Numbers," but something else entirely—the true voice of the people. The framers had devised a system by which neither the numerical majority nor a minority could easily take control of the government, but in which power was vested in "the whole—the entire people—to make it in truth and reality the Government of the people, instead of a Government of a dominant over a subject part." How had they done this? "By requiring the concurrence in the action of the government, of the greatest possible number," a bar far higher than a simple numerical majority.

Describing how the different parts of the system worked to achieve this goal, Calhoun described the House of Representatives as the expression of the will of the numerical majority, while in the Senate, which expressed the interests of states, a determined minority of the population could resist that will, requiring a greater degree of unanimity between the two bodies as a whole than either required separately. Not content to settle with this, the framers had pushed the principle of concurrence further by requiring the assent of the president before the awesome power of the federal government could be brought to bear. The president, Calhoun explained, had a different relationship to the people than any other representative, being responsible and incentivized through elections to represent the whole, or at least as many of the people as possible, instead of only those of one state, district, or section. To assure unanimity, and that the greatest possible number of interests would be consulted and represented, the framers had given to the House, Senate, and executive a veto over the other in order to prevent a numerical majority, a powerful minority, or a tyrannical executive from wielding power. The reason it required a two-thirds majority to override a presidential veto, Calhoun declared, was that only this very high bar would assure the kind of concurrence the founders sought in the absence of presidential approval. Without it, the separation of powers would be a mere "partition."

Having elaborated on all the parts, Calhoun pulled back to describe for his audience the whole glorious machine the framers had constructed in search of the elusive concurrent majority. "Such are the various processes of taking the sense of the people through the divisions and organization of the different departments of the Government," he declared, "all of which, acting through their appropriate organs, are intended to widen its basis and render it more popular, instead of less, by increasing the number necessary to put it in action." "Each," he acknowledged, "may be imperfect of itself, but if the construction be good, and all the keys skillfully touched, there will be given out in one blended and harmonious whole, the true and perfect voice of the people."

There was only one problem. The will of the numerical majority—which Calhoun conceded should have a "preponderance" of influence, but only a slight one—had been too privileged, being both embedded in the House and given the most weight in electing the executive. With the emergence of an organized party system, something the framers could not have imagined, this had left the federal government vulnerable to co-option as the numerical majority exercised more power within the system than the framers had ever intended. Fortunately, Calhoun declared, hinting at nullification, the sovereignty of the states provided a check on this tendency. With this as part of the system, Calhoun believed the Constitution expressed "the *vox populi vox Dei*; the creating voice that called the system into existence, and of which the Government itself is but a creature, clothed with delegated powers to execute its high behests."[49]

The Democratic press instantly hailed the speech as a classic, one of the "ablest, most luminous, and unanswerable ever delivered on the nature of government" in the words of Francis Blair, who had regularly lambasted Calhoun during his battles with Jackson.[50] Pleased, Calhoun wrote Anna that nearly forty-six thousand copies of the speech had been printed and circulated. "This will surprise you, when you read it," he noted, "for it comes up almost to nullification. It is in fact but the premises, from which it irresistibly follows." He was sure the nation was coming around to his point of view.[51]

BEGINNING IN THE FALL of 1840 the Clemsons took up residence at Fort Hill for about a year, to Calhoun's delight. Not only did it allow him to see his favorite daughter whenever he came home, but his dutiful and detail-minded northern son-in-law had taken over the management of the plantation, along with an overseer named Fredericks, and sent Calhoun long letters about his management and improvements.

The enslaved people at Fort Hill may have seen an opportunity in Clemson's inexperience. "The negroes have made constant complaints to me about their allowance [food], stating it not to be enough," Clemson wrote Calhoun, noting, "The quantity you mentioned has been adhered to."[52] At Christmas, Old Sawney and the others assured Clemson that they customarily received four days off, which Clemson thought, "considering the quantity of work to be done...rather much," but Fredericks the overseer assured him that Sawney and the others were correct.[53] Anna, meanwhile, wrote her father describing scenes around the house, including the invalid bookworm Cornelia reading quietly in a corner, "where she thinks she will be undiscovered."[54]

In October 1841 Clemson left for Cuba to pursue opportunities in the mining industry. Young Patrick Calhoun, who was on leave from the army, accompanied his brother-in-law. Anna soon wanted to join them, having stayed behind with little John Calhoun Clemson, who had been born in July. From Washington, Calhoun thought it was a bad idea, and worried incessantly about Anna's health, especially after she developed a painful infection in her breast soon after the birth that Anna told her friend Maria "exceeded any pain I have ever felt for intense agony" and had to be lanced. On the news of her recovery, Calhoun wrote with relief, "You do not, my dear daughter, do me and those around you justice, in imagining, that in your long indisposition our attention to you wearied us...You must expel the idea that we can ever be wearied or fatigued where you are the object of attention." He also gently chided her for not telling him about his new grandson's health, "which I regard as a great omission." But he was clear that he did not want her to go to Cuba, and he wrote to Floride discouraging the trip. Sensitive to his son-in-law's touchy temperament, Calhoun also wrote directly to Clemson, telling him that he was encouraging Anna to remain at Fort Hill. "I give you this statement, so that you may lay the responsibility on me, should she decline going," he wrote. Calhoun spent almost as much time that winter managing his family's relationships as he did fending off Henry Clay. Nevertheless, Anna, proving herself to be her father's daughter, would not be deterred, and left for Cuba in February 1842.[55]

Meanwhile, Calhoun was concerned that Patrick seemed to like Cuba too much. "Do not suppose that I distrust you," Calhoun wrote his son, urging him to return and take up his army duties and find some profitable use for his life. "It is the period of life, at which you are, that I distrust, not yourself." Always more the son of his lowcountry mother than his abstemious father, Patrick's slightly too-open embrace of life puzzled and worried his father, who continued to urge him to find the path of duty.[56] A few months later, with Patrick safely at his new post on the western frontier in Arkansas, Calhoun was still fretting, and urged Anna to use her influence on her younger brother. "I regret to see, that he forms acquaintances too hastily," Calhoun wrote, asking Anna to "put him on his guard, against being caught with young ladies who visit those distant posts from the interior. They are for the most part mere adventurers seeking husbands."[57]

AROUND THE TIME THAT Anna departed for Cuba, as cotton pick-
ing and ginning slowed at Fort Hill, a group of slaves from Fort Hill
and a white man named Davis, probably an overseer, departed for Alabama to help Andrew with his cotton crop.[58] It had been an annual
ritual since the purchase of Cane Brake, but this time "little Sawney,"
Old Sawney's son, went with them, probably to get him away from
Fort Hill. The young man had picked up a rock and threatened to
throw it at Thomas Clemson, and Floride believed he had been wearing a knife around the plantation intending to attack Fredericks, the
overseer. In any event, being sent to Alabama was either the perfect
opportunity or the last straw for young Sawney. One night only a few
days into the journey, somewhere in Georgia, he crept up to the white
man Davis's tent in the middle of the night and lit it on fire. Davis escaped, although he suffered significant burns, and young Sawney was
caught and jailed. "The Boy, that ran from Mr. Davis, is in Jaol in Georgia," Floride wrote to Margaret, Andrew's wife, in early February.
"Mr. Calhoun, writes me to have him sent out in chains to Andrew, but
I think he ought to be sold, or he will do more mischief." In one of her
rare surviving letters to her husband, Floride implored him to have
young Sawney sold "out of reach of ever coming here again." Unruly
slaves always made Floride nervous—she remembered how her father's
slaves had tried to poison him—and her solution was usually to sell
them.

Floride was also uneasy because she was sure that Sawney's father,
Old Sawney, was at the bottom of the whole thing. "I think him a *dangerous* old Negro," she wrote Margaret, "but you cannot convince his
Master of it." Having known Sawney since he was a child, Calhoun
evidently refused to believe Floride's suspicions. Sawney's long history
with Calhoun's family provided him a tenuous protection against some
of the worst fears that enslaved people faced—being sold away from
friends and family into the new cotton country and an even harsher
form of slavery—but he could not protect his family. Young Sawney
was sent to Alabama and did not return to Fort Hill.[59]

As the drama with Sawney unfolded in the early weeks of 1842, the indefatigable Duff Green wrote Calhoun from London with ominous news. Green had traveled to London to raise money for personal ventures, but his presence also reflected the unease many southerners had with a Massachusetts man, Edward Everett, representing their interests as the ambassador to England. John Tyler seems to have sent Green as a kind of unofficial ambassador for the slaveholding interest. In that role, Green was tireless. As Britain sought a treaty with France, Prussia, Austria, and Russia granting the right of search on the high seas in order to stop the slave trade—the so-called Quintuple Treaty— which would have left the United States isolated and vulnerable to British naval power, Green rushed to Paris and helped to lead a successful American campaign against French participation, a major foreign policy victory. In the process, Green believed he had uncovered Britain's true aim in their contradictory policy—to undermine slave labor in the Americas in order to eliminate the competitive advantages that it gave to cotton and sugar producers against British colonies like India and Jamaica. "Under the aspects of the case," Green wrote Calhoun at the end of January 1842, "you will find that England has much more than a work of benevolence in the suppression of the slave trade."[60]

By the time Green's letter reached Washington, there was further evidence of British malign intent in the case of the *Creole*, an American ship engaged in the coastal slave trade whose cargo, led by an enslaved man with the fantastically American name of Madison Washington, rebelled, killed one of the white crew, and steered the ship to Nassau, where the British freed most of the slaves. The case caused a furor in the slaveholding states, and Calhoun denounced Britain's perfidy in releasing the "murderers" while applauding Secretary of State Daniel Webster's prompt and aggressive response.[61]

A few weeks later Calhoun wrote back to Green in emphatic agreement on his interpretation of British antislavery as a new form of British imperialism. This view, previously held only by slightly paranoid observers such as American consul to Jamaica Robert Monroe Harrison, who had been sounding the alarm to little effect for years, would with Calhoun's imprimatur become standard among southerners in foreign policy circles. "It is surprising to me," Calhoun wrote, "that the Statesmen of the Continent do not see, that the policy of England is to get control of the commerce of the world, by controlling the labour, which produces the articles by which it is principally put in motion. Humanity is but the flimsy pretext." Britain's antislavery foreign policy, Calhoun believed, was simply a new tactic in an old struggle for control of the flow of trade across the oceans. In 1812 they had claimed the right of search to find British deserters, and now they claimed the same right to prevent the slave trade—with the same end goal in both cases.[62]

In response, under the theory that the best defense is a good offense, Calhoun and a group of highly placed southerners, especially Tyler's new secretary of the navy, Abel Upshur, a hardcore Calhounite, began to push for a strengthened American naval power focused along the Gulf Coast. Upshur frequently wrote Calhoun, who had vastly more government and foreign policy experience, asking for advice.[63] Intended to counter the new British imperialism, the policy was essentially an extension of the Monroe Doctrine that Calhoun had helped to craft decades earlier, only now it was focused on preventing British interference with New World slave societies under a kind of antebellum "domino theory," which held that in order to protect slavery in the United States it must also be protected in Cuba, Brazil, and Texas. John Quincy Adams, for one, was initially confused by the southern push for a stronger navy that began in early 1842, calling it "the most curious phenomena in our national history," but a few months later and wiser he was certain that it came "reeking hot from the furnace of slavery."[64]

When Secretary of State Webster negotiated what became known as the Webster-Ashburton Treaty later that year, settling many, but not all, of the differences between the United States and Britain, and thereby avoiding war, Calhoun breathed a sigh of relief. The treaty settled the dispute over the boundary with Maine and the Great Lakes region; the United States pledged to help Britain in its efforts to stop the slave trade along the west coast of Africa; and, most importantly, Americans interpreted the treaty to mean that Britain renounced the right of search that had served as an excuse to interfere with American trade. The British threat to slavery in the Western Hemisphere was not over, as the coming years would show, but in August 1842 Calhoun announced that while the treaty was not all he had hoped, he would vote for it. "Peace is indeed our policy," he announced. "A kind Providence has cast our lot on a portion of the globe sufficiently vast to satisfy the most grasping ambition, and abounding in resources beyond all others, which only require to be fully developed to make us the most prosperous people on earth." Fortunately, Calhoun declared, the American system of federalism—"a system of State and General Governments, so blended as to constitute one sublime whole"—would allow the United States to overstretch the continent, forgo the imperialist ambitions that drove Britain (Indians and Mexico notwithstanding), and achieve a prosperity "heretofore unequalled on the globe." Like many of his contemporaries, Calhoun believed that the United States, slavery and all, had a manifest destiny to occupy the whole North American continent.[65]

ONE AIM OF CALHOUN'S foreign policy was to convert the British to the gospel of free trade instead of antislavery interference, and during the early 1840s he was preaching the same sermons at home with increasing fervor. As 1842—the end date of the compromise of 1833—approached, and as Henry Clay made clear that he wanted a new tariff, Calhoun intensified his crusade over successive legislative sessions, arguing that in the long run free and open markets were best for everyone—cotton exporters, merchants, manufacturers, and workers.

Calhoun warned that a renewed tariff, passed under the mistaken principle of protection, would hamstring American manufacturers, limiting them to a domestic market when they could be competing for a larger hemispheric, and even global, one. "The great question for you to decide is, how to command the foreign market," Calhoun lectured his northern colleagues, dismissing Clay's pet "home market" as "too scanty for your skill, your activity, your energy, your unequaled inventive powers, your untiring industry, your vastly increased population, and accumulated capital." How could they command this foreign market? By reforming the currency, ensuring "low duties and light burdens on productions." "We have arrived at the manhood of our vigor," he declared. "Open the way—remove all constraints—take off the swaddling cloth that bound the limbs of infancy, and let the hardy, intelligent, and enterprising sons of New England March forth fearlessly to meet the world in competition." It was an expansive vision, and from the manufacturers' perspective it must have seemed suspect coming from Calhoun.[66]

Conscious of the working-class supporters of his party, Calhoun was always careful to point out that his proposal would also benefit them. "I am in favor of high wages," he announced in 1840, arguing that with a sound currency the superior productivity of American laborers would command its true value in the international market. In an 1842 speech, he drew a distinction between "real and artificial" wages, arguing that the true measure of high or low wages was not the wage itself but its purchasing power, an argument that fell like music on the ears of hard money Democrats and working-class critics of paper money.[67]

Nevertheless, in the summer of 1842, Congress passed a new tariff that many southerners believed was worse than the 1828 tariff that had prompted the nullification crisis. Calhoun fought its passage in several major speeches, in which he brought to bear a mountain of statistical data, including detailed tables back to 1820 showing annual imports, exports, manufacturing, and shipping, showing that as the tariff had gradually lowered over the past decade, the American economy responded by growing much more rapidly than it had under the protective system. Calhoun dismissed with disdain the argument that cotton growers should support the tariff because a domestic market for their cotton would protect them from global competition, including India. He noted, accurately, that the East India Company had so far failed to produce cotton on a scale that could supply the British market, and he touted the competitive advantage that slavery gave southern growers. In addition to the right climate, good soil, and cheap land, "we have a cheap and efficient body of laborers, the best fed, clothed, trained, and provided for, of any in the whole cotton growing region, for whose labor we have paid in advance." He explained, "I say paid for in advance, *for our property in our slaves is but wages purchased in advance, including the support and supplies of the laborers*…With these advantages we may bid defiance to Hindoo or Egyptian labor, at its two or three cents a day." Here Calhoun portrayed slavery as, in essence, a special category of wage labor, even though in the past he had vigorously defended the principle of property in man.[68]

As the new tariff was about to pass in August 1842, Calhoun offered a last appeal for a different path to national prosperity and American economic dominance in a swiftly developing world.

> We have, Senators, reached a remarkable point in the progress of civilization, and the mechanical and chemical arts, and which will require a great change in the policy of civilized nations. Within the last three or four generations, they have received an impulse far beyond all former example, and have now obtained a perfection before unknown. The result has been a wonderful increased facility of producing all articles of supply depending on those arts; that is, of those very articles which we call, in our financial language, protected articles…In consequence of this increased facility it now requires but a small part, comparatively, of the labor and capital of a country, to clothe its people, and supply itself with most of the products of the useful arts; and hence, all civilized people, with little exception, are producing for their own supply, and even overstocking their own market. It results, that no people, restricted to the home market, can, in the present advanced state of the

useful arts, rise to greatness and wealth by manufactures. For that purpose, they must compete successfully for the foreign market, in the
younger, less advanced, and less civilized countries. This necessity for
more enlarged and freer intercourse...at a time when the whole globe
is laid open to our knowledge...is one of the mighty means ordained
by Providence to spread population, light, civilization, and prosperity,
far and wide over its entire surface.[69]

It was an argument for an American economic empire based on free
trade, not state power. It was also evidence that Calhoun was thinking
as expansively in 1842 as he had been in 1816, if in different registers.
Calhoun lost the argument in 1842—the tariff passed—but as always
he was confident that his ideas would win out. "The gentleman from
Kentucky is behind the times," Calhoun scoffed at Clay at one point
during the tariff debate. "He might as well attempt to stop the Mississippi as to attempt to control the current of free trade." From the perspective of nearly two centuries, Calhoun's faith that free trade was the
ideology of the future seems remarkably prescient.[70]

IN MAY CALHOUN RECEIVED word that a rich vein of gold had been
discovered at his O'Bar mine in Dahlonega, Georgia. Initially reluctant
to leave Washington while Congress was in session, he was soon convinced by friends that he had to visit the mine in person to make sure
he wasn't being cheated by his overseer. The discovery and Calhoun's
whirlwind trip—eight hundred miles in four days by means of railroad,
steamboat, and horseback, according to a report in the *Pendleton
Messenger*—became a minor sensation in the newspapers. Still, on June
14 Anna, recently returned from Cuba and living back at Fort Hill,
wrote to Maria that she and Clemson had been shocked to receive a
letter from Calhoun postmarked in Augusta, announcing that he would
visit them on his way back to Washington. Calhoun had been pushing
his son-in-law to move to Dahlonega to oversee operations at the

mine—no doubt anticipating that perhaps, finally, he had gotten a financial windfall that would solve all his problems and help pay for his family's needs in his old age. But it was not to be. Rumor had it that before Calhoun's arrival at the mine it may have produced up to $24,000 of gold in thirty days, but that much of it was spirited away by two men who held a temporary lease on the property and shared profits with Calhoun. Clemson diligently took over operations of the mine, working with four slaves and three white workers, but it never produced the riches that Calhoun must have hoped it would.[71]

Only days after he arrived back in Washington, Calhoun received word that Floride had suffered what may have been a minor stroke. Anna and her children had just joined Clemson in Dahlonega, where they stayed in an unfinished cabin without windows, shutters, or a chimney, when Fredericks, the Fort Hill overseer, appeared with word of Floride's attack. Her mother requested that Anna return immediately since "she knew she would die," Clemson reported to Calhoun a few days later with a hint of annoyance. Despite a report from the doctor that the immediate danger had passed, Anna hurried home. Calhoun, having just returned to Washington, did not. As understandable as this was—by the time he heard of her attack, Floride was out of serious danger—the fact that he hurried home to attend to his gold mine but remained in Washington after Floride's health crisis seems consistent with their relationship. Anna, meanwhile, was soon worn out by her mother's constant declarations that she was dying and her midnight demands to send for the doctor. Perhaps Calhoun knew exactly what he was missing.[72]

THE ONLY REASON THAT South Carolina did not immediately nullify the new tariff passed in August 1842 was that by then Calhoun had emerged as a possible candidate for the Democratic nomination for president. Rehearsing the ways in which 1842 was different from 1828, Calhoun wrote James Henry Hammond in September, "Nullification is the extreme remedy of the Constitution, and ought never to be resorted to till all others have been fairly tried and failed." South Carolina had only nullified in 1832 after waiting for four years and until Andrew Jackson made it clear the state had no other recourse. The situation ten years later was quite different. "My impression is, if the South will act, as it ought, at the coming Presidential election," Calhoun wrote, "we shall be able certainly to repeal the act & place the duties on satisfactory grounds." What he thought the South "ought" to do was to elect him president.[73]

Looking back, we have to overcome the liabilities of hindsight to reconstruct the reasons for Calhoun's optimism, which as it turned out was as unusually well-founded as it was eventually unfulfilled. Few figures on the national scene in the early 1840s had Calhoun's stature, his name recognition, or his long and varied record of distinguished service to the Union. Harrison's death and Tyler's break with the Whigs over the bank in the summer of 1841 left the Whig Party fragmented, while the Democrats were more ideologically united but leaderless, even though Martin Van Buren still held considerable sway. By the early 1840s, despite his claim to be completely independent, Calhoun was as closely affiliated with and influential within the Democratic Party as he ever had been, and he was willing to participate in partisan politics, up to a point, for the chance to win the presidency. By November 1841 Calhoun had decided that the moment was right. "Many of my friends think the time has arrived when my name ought to be presented for the next presidency," he wrote to James Edward. "It is my own impression, that, if it is ever intended to be, now is the time."[74] Others agreed, though not without doubts. "It seems to me Calhoun must be the man," James Henry Hammond wrote in his diary after rehearsing all the possible presidential candidates, "unless he kicks over the pail, of which there is much danger."[75]

Calhoun's supporters across the country busied themselves writing letters, starting newspapers, and feeling out potential allies. During 1842 and 1843, Calhoun corresponded extensively with supporters like

New York journalist Joseph Scoville, Robert Mercer Taliaferro Hunter in Virginia, and Virgil Maxcy in Maryland. In 1842 Dixon Lewis, a legendarily obese congressman from Alabama, wrote to newspaper editor and Calhounite Richard Crallé about a "Calhoun Paper" to be established in New York City and called the *Plebian*. According to a notice announcing its publication, the paper would be "devoted to the earnest advocacy of that genuine old-fashioned Democratic Faith contended for by that revered Patriarch of Republicanism, Thomas Jefferson."[76]

Joseph Scoville engaged printmaker Nathaniel Currier to produce Calhoun campaign letterhead with an image of Calhoun titled "The People's Candidate for President" and his campaign slogan—"Free Trade; Low Duties; No Debt; Separation from Banks; Economy; Retrenchment, and Strict Adherence to the Constitution." The letterhead, as another New York supporter, J. Francis Hutton, wrote to R. M. T. Hunter, had a subliminal purpose. "Every mail will convey hundreds of these letters to all parts of the Union," he wrote, "and accustom the people to think of Mr. C whether they choose or not."[77] These efforts were all the more important since despite numerous appeals from northern and western supporters Calhoun mostly refused to campaign publicly, which may have hurt his chances but was also, to a certain kind of supporter fed up with the empty show of party politics, part of his appeal.[78]

Part of the publicity effort was an official campaign biography, *Life of John C. Calhoun*, published in 1843 along with a collection of Calhoun's most important speeches. Once considered an anonymous autobiography, the biography was a joint effort that incorporated an earlier biographical sketch of Calhoun by Virgil Maxcy with new material. The finished product was mostly the work of R. M. T. Hunter, whom Calhoun told Anna had written enough of the finished product "as fairly to be entitled to the authorship." But Calhoun had a direct hand in compiling and overseeing the project in late 1842 and early 1843, and the biography remains the only source for some of Calhoun's earliest memories about his family, especially his father. Calhoun and Anna worked together in the fall of 1842 gathering and transcribing materials before Calhoun left for Washington in November, where he gave all the materials to Hunter, who had finished a draft by the end of the year. Published by Harper & Brothers in New York in March 1843, the biography did not sell nearly as well as Calhoun or the publisher hoped, and by June Harper & Brothers complained to Virgil Maxcy that only eighteen thousand copies were in circulation, and not all of those were sold. These disappointing results, they noted pointedly, were far below the numbers achieved by William Henry Harrison's biography.[79]

Seeming to confirm James Henry Hammond's quip that Calhoun had no childhood, the biography began with a brief section on Calhoun's early life, "including the period from his infancy until he entered Congress," and then quickly got down to the business of justifying Calhoun's public life.[80] Hunter dismissed charges of inconsistency by dividing Calhoun's career into "two grand epochs," the first guided by the need to shore up a weak national government in the face of external threats, and the second in which he took up the "more difficult task" of guarding the internal workings of the American system against domestic tyranny. Different times required different measures, although Hunter delicately acknowledged that Calhoun had sometimes departed from the narrow road of state rights in his early career, even as he tried to explain away those departures. The 1816 tariff, Hunter argued, had been a revenue measure, not a protectionist scheme, justifying Calhoun's support (even though Calhoun's speech in support of the 1816 bill had not made that distinction). Knowing that Calhoun was often accused of being obsessed with abstractions at the expense of practical politics, Hunter emphasized Calhoun as a "philosophical observer of men and of their affairs" who "analyzes and reduces all things to their original elements." Also knowing that Calhoun was viewed as overly ambitious, Hunter conceded that Calhoun indeed possessed a "lofty ambition" but one that, like Greek and Roman statesmen, "prefers glory to office and power."

Most of all, Hunter portrayed Calhoun as a man whose qualities of character and mind fitted him for the task of preserving a uniquely American form of government in the swiftly changing circumstances of the modern world. Calhoun's ability to discern the deep principles of government and human action, Hunter wrote, enabled him "to decide at once not only what measures are at present necessary for a government novel in its principles, and placed in circumstances of which there is not precedent in the history of mankind, but, by discerning results through their causes, to look into futurity, and to devise means for carrying on our beloved country…to the high and glorious destiny… which awaits her." Calhoun himself often portrayed his candidacy as a campaign to reform the government, bringing it back into line with the old Jeffersonian school of politics. But he and his supporters combined this with the message that the unprecedented nature of the times required a political prodigy who could see through the confusion to discern the correct path of action. Looking back was, in fact, the best means of finding the way forward.[81]

Support for Calhoun's candidacy for the Democratic nomination was national, not sectional. One of his most interesting sources of support came from a deep vein of "left-wing Calhounism" among New York's radical Democrats, the so-called Loco Focos. Named after the brand of matches they used to keep a meeting at Tammany Hall going after the party leadership turned out the lights, and also called the Equal Rights Democrats, the Loco Focos were working-class radicals and labor activists—many had been members of the defunct Working Men's Party. They were anti-monopolist (especially when it came to manufacturers), anti-bank, anti–paper money, passionately free trade, and deeply suspicious of any connection between the government, the elite, and the financial system. As one Loco Foco pamphlet put it in 1842, who could they trust to carry the banner of "Monopolies to none. Free trade and equal rights to all"? "We have one man eminently qualified for such a position," the pamphlet continued. "JOHN C. CALHOUN." One of Calhoun's New York supporters wrote him in

September 1842 begging him to travel to New York City and give a speech in Tammany Hall, assuring him that he had strong support among the city's merchants and "hard-fisted democrats of the city," who were "inoculated very generally, with the doctrine of free trade, so you will be perfectly in your element when you meet them in the great *Wigwam*."[82] One of Calhoun's most active New York supporters, Fitzwilliam Byrdsall, started the Free Trade Association to back Calhoun's candidacy,[83] while another, Mike Walsh, leader of the so-called shirtless Democrats, attacked the "slavery of wages" in ways that echoed Calhoun's critique of industrial capitalism if not his defense of slavery. "Of all public men living," Walsh declared defiantly in his *Subterranean* newspaper, "John C. Calhoun is my favorite." Walsh and his working-class followers would continue to support Calhoun long after the election, even holding an annual "Calhoun Ball" in New York City.[84] Returning to his roots, Calhoun joined New York's Irish Emigrant Society in September 1841, writing its secretary, "I have ever taken pride in my Irish descent…As a son of an emigrant, I cheerfully join your society."[85]

The Loco Foco support for Calhoun was common knowledge, and a Whig newspaper scoffed in June 1842 that "John C. Calhoun is at present the especial favorite of Loco Focoism," sneering that "Mr. Calhoun is a man of great talents, but his ultra notions about the 'divine right' of trafficking in human flesh and blood, added to his state right nullifying doctrines, point him out as a man of the most dangerous and detestable principles."[86] Nevertheless, as one historian pointed out, the Loco Focos were bent on "upending the demagogic rule of capital by the most direct means necessary," and in 1842 that meant that many of them supported Calhoun, who had proved his devotion to severing the link between the country's financial and political systems.[87]

Calhoun appealed not only to the rank and file members of New York's labor movement, but also to some of their young, idealistic, intellectual defenders, like the brilliant young editor of the *Boston Quarterly*, Orestes Brownson. Brownson was at first glance an odd Calhoun acolyte. He burst onto the political scene during the 1840 election with an essay titled "The Laboring Classes," in which he denounced the business and manufacturing classes, advocated the Independent Treasury to insulate government from banking interests, argued that northern wage slavery was a much more efficient and brutal form of exploitation than southern slavery, and, for good measure, proposed an abolition of hereditary property. Calhoun subscribed to Brownson's publication, if not all his ideas, noting dryly in one letter, "I read with pleasure the article on distribution. My opinion on hereditary property remains unchanged."[88] The Whig victory in 1840—in Brownson's view the victory of business interests thinly packaged in popular rhetoric—convinced Brownson that a majoritarian democracy would always be manipulated by the interests of capital against those of labor, and he took up with a vengeance Calhoun's call for a firewall between government and the moneyed interests as well as Calhoun's views on the strict limits imposed on federal power by the Constitution, seeing all these as essential protections for labor against capital. Sounding very much like a philosopher's apprentice, Brownson would write Calhoun wondering if he had read the younger man's most recent article, once asking, "Have I got tolerably near right at last? I ask this question of you, for you are the only man I know, in whose answers…I should have as much confidence as even my own."[89] Overlooking slavery itself, Brownson saw slaveholders as potential allies in the battle against capital, ignoring the inconvenient implications of the fact that many large slaveholders were Whigs.[90]

In the end, two obstacles doomed Calhoun's last serious bid for the presidency. First was the fact that despite his defeat in 1840 Martin Van Buren was still firmly in control of much of the Democratic Party machinery, which seemed to guarantee his advantage when the party faithful met in Baltimore to nominate their candidate. Calhoun would have preferred not to participate in the convention at all, seeing it as nothing more than a perverse reincarnation of the old caucus system that he had opposed in 1824. But his allies convinced him he had no choice but to play the game Van Buren had invented, although Calhoun wanted to change the rules. Calhoun's supporters mounted a successful campaign to delay the convention until 1844, instead of 1843 as Van Buren wanted, but they were unsuccessful in pushing for the direct election of delegates by district, a method that Calhoun believed would show his strength among rank-and-file Democratic voters. "We go for a convention *fresh* from the people," wrote Alabama congressman Dixon Lewis, describing the strategy, "& not 2 or 3 removes from them." In the end, as had been the previous practice, party leaders in each state chose the delegates, a method that strongly favored Van Buren's vast political network.[91]

Just as significant was the eruption of a mini revolution in Rhode Island that revealed the limits of Calhoun's alliance with northern democrats. The so-called Dorr War, named after the movement's leader, Thomas Dorr, originated as a protest among Rhode Island's burgeoning industrial working classes against the state's government, which was still guided by a 1663 colonial charter that required a property qualification for the vote, and provided no bill of rights or independent judiciary. After years of conflict, in 1841 the Dorrites abandoned the normal political process and held a convention of their Rhode Island Suffrage Association at which they proclaimed a new state constitution mandating universal suffrage and other reforms. Thomas Dorr and his followers claimed the will of the people as their writ of authority, with the result that for several months in 1842 Rhode Island had two governments vying for legitimacy. In November 1842 a new, mildly reformist state constitution crafted by Dorr's Whig opponents ended the crisis, at least for Rhode Island.[92]

The Dorr War was a perfect example in miniature of the kind of revolution that Calhoun had warned would be the result of industrial capitalism's exploitation of its laboring classes. And while Calhoun sympathized with some of the reforms the Dorrites sought, he was no revolutionary. Indeed, Dorr's claim to act on behalf of a majority of the people in setting aside the state government was an extreme example of the principle of majoritarianism that Calhoun detested, even within states. So while Martin Van Buren signaled his sympathy and the aging Andrew Jackson openly proclaimed his support, Calhoun prepared resolutions against the rebellion should the question of recognizing the Dorr government come up in the Senate, lamenting in private that "a large portion of the Northern Democracy justified the move of the suffrage party [the Dorrites] on the broad principle that a majority can at pleasure set aside law & constitution."[93] Calhoun also undoubtedly connected the Dorr War to the possibility of slave revolts. The resolutions he prepared cited the Constitution's guarantee of a republican form of government to every state as well as the government's duty to help states put down domestic insurrections, both of which would have been equally applicable to a slave rebellion.[94]

When Dorr traveled to Washington to seek support for his movement, he made an ill-fated attempt to convert Calhoun in person. R. M. T. Hunter recalled that he was awakened late one night by a panicked, puffing Dixon Lewis, who had gotten wind that Dorr was on his way to see Calhoun that very night. The two men raced over to Calhoun's boardinghouse at one o'clock in the morning to warn Calhoun not to meet with Dorr, only to find that he already had. "I have given him a piece of my mind," Calhoun told them, assuring them that the truth "never hurt any man." The two men begged Calhoun not to openly oppose the rebellion, knowing it would doom his presidential chances.[95]

Word of Calhoun's opposition got out anyway, leading at least one northern newspaper that supported his candidacy to warn him publicly that if he helped suppress the Dorrites he could proclaim "a long farewell to the support of the Northern Democracy."[96] In response, while he remained opposed to the Dorrites on principle, rumors circulated that Calhoun and his lieutenants were courting senators Silas Wright of New York and Levi Woodbury of New Hampshire, both avid

Dorrites, as vice presidential running mates who would balance the ticket both ideologically and geographically. In June 1842 Joel Poinsett reported to Martin Van Buren that "the Devil" had taken Wright and Woodbury to the "summit of a lofty mountain" and tempted them to "fall down and worship John C. Calhoun." Wright and Woodbury resisted their temptation, but the attempt shows that Calhoun and those around him were conscious of the need to offset the liability imposed by his principles.[97]

In retrospect, it seems certain that Calhoun's opposition to Thomas Dorr hurt his national prospects, but Calhoun remained optimistic enough about his chances that in November 1842 he resigned his Senate seat in order to continue his campaign, although he would serve out the session, which ended in March 1843. In a foregone conclusion, the South Carolina General Assembly officially nominated him for president a few weeks later.[98]

THAT WINTER, WITH CALHOUN'S presidential campaign in full swing, Old Sawney's daughter Issey staged her own personal revolt at Fort Hill. Her enslavement itself is enough to explain what she did, but there may have been more immediate reasons. Perhaps she was angry that her family had been separated when her brother had been shipped off to Alabama the year before; or perhaps she was fed up with the constant requests that came with being a house slave. Whatever the tipping point, one evening as she prepared the beds she slipped a large, burning coal under William Lowndes's pillow, which quickly began to burn. The smell of burning feathers soon alerted the household, the fire was put out, and Issey confessed, although she claimed that she had second thoughts and was planning to remove the coal when it was discovered. A few days later Floride related the story of Issey "trying to burn us all up" to Patrick. Once more she was sure that Old Sawney was at the bottom of the whole thing, and she described how as soon as the cry of fire sounded, "He took up his hat and stick and ran off as hard as he could."

Everyone at Fort Hill understood that the consequences of Issey's act might be dire. "The Negros all appeared shocked at the act," Floride wrote, "and said she ought to have been hung," although as Floride knew, appearances could be deceiving when it came to what enslaved people said to white people.

The Calhouns were determined to keep the matter quiet. "We have kept it a profound secret," Floride wrote Patrick, adding, "If it was known she would have to be hung." Slaveholders like the Calhouns were not eager to broadcast the news of a rebellious slave, both because the death penalty meant the loss of valuable property and because it might damage their reputation as good masters. Certainly Anna, who was living at Fort Hill at the time, was politically savvy enough to know that given her father's public arguments about slavery, the news of one of his slaves being hung for arson would be explosive. Floride begged Patrick to "burn this letter as soon as read," which he failed to do.[99]

When he reached home a few days after the incident, Calhoun refused to sell Issey as Floride demanded. Not only was she the daughter of Old Sawney, but also, and perhaps more importantly for Issey's fate, she helped care for the crippled Cornelia, who made it clear that she wanted Issey to stay. After several months of arguing with both her husband and Cornelia, Floride finally succeeded in getting Issey sent away to Andrew in Alabama. But even that was not far enough for Floride. In December 1845 she wrote to Andrew's wife Margaret demanding that Issey be sold farther south. "Tell Andrew to send her to Louisianna [*sic*]," she wrote, "I prefer it, particularly, on account of their [*sic*] not being a prospect of her coming where I shall ever see her again." Floride had a "horror" of ever seeing Issey again since "she has behaved so badly to me." She also wanted the money that Issey's sale would yield to be put toward buying another slave to replace her.[100]

Andrew did not sell Issey, and a year later Floride had changed her mind and began to demand that Issey return to Fort Hill for Cornelia's sake. Andrew refused, and Floride was soon furiously writing other members of the family blaming Andrew for Cornelia's unhappiness.

Calhoun once again stepped in to play the family peacemaker. "I have expostulated with her in strong terms," he wrote to Andrew, sounding as if Floride was one of his political opponents instead of his wife. Then, in frustration, Calhoun wrote, "Nothing would do at one time, but that I must sell [Issey], which I refused to do. Then she took up the plan of taking her to Alabama to be sold, which I also opposed; & finally changed her mind not to sell her, because Cornelia objected, which by the by she did from the first." Offering a rare window into his marriage, Calhoun shared his own approach to Floride's accusations. "You must not only bear them, but forget them," he advised Andrew. "With the many good qualities of her Mother, she inherits her suspecious [sic] and fault finding temper, which has been the cause of much vexation in the family. I have borne with her with patience, because it was my duty to do so, & you must do the same, for the same reason. It has been the only cross of my life." Calhoun's rare note of self-pity ignored the fact that Floride, no doubt, had her own crosses to bear. Everyone ignored Issey, whom it appears never returned to Fort Hill.[101]

CALHOUN REMAINED IN SOUTH CAROLINA for the rest of 1843 as his presidential prospects slowly dimmed under the weight of an inferior organization and his opposition to the Dorrites, until his hopes finally sputtered out entirely by the end of the year. Some observers thought he should simply retire, that he was getting too old for politics. In 1841, with Calhoun's star still ascendant, South Carolina congressman Robert Barnwell Rhett's brother Albert wrote to him about the possibility of Calhoun failing to win the nomination. "In such a case Mr. Calhoun should quit public life," Rhett wrote. "He is getting too old to remain where he is with dignity much longer, and the best thing he can do with himself will be to withdraw into a splendid [retire] at Fort Hill and play political philosopher and sage as Jefferson did, the rest of his days."[102]

But by the time Calhoun officially withdrew from the race in January 1844 the debate over the annexation of Texas had transformed the presidential race into a referendum on the future of slavery in the United States and the Western Hemisphere. With those stakes there was little chance Calhoun would remain silent.

SEVENTEEN

"Thou Art the Man"

O N THE LAST DAY OF February 1844, Second Lieutenant Patrick Calhoun found himself sailing down the Potomac near Washington aboard the US Navy's newest weapon, the heavily armed, screw-propeller sloop *Princeton*, commanded by Robert F. Stockton. The *Princeton* was exactly the sort of vessel that Patrick's father and Abel Upshur had imagined for an updated and modernized American navy that could project American foreign policy into the Gulf of Mexico, and President Tyler had invited a large group of prominent Washingtonians, including an aged Dolley Madison, on a cruise to see this instantiation of American military might in action. As they floated down the river, Stockton fired off one of the *Princeton*'s massive twelve-inch cannons, nicknamed the Peacemaker, to the delight of all on board. Hearing that Stockton was about to fire the cannon again, Patrick was just making his way up to the main deck for a better view when he met a young woman he knew. She asked him to accompany her to the deck ("which of course I did") but refused to go near the cannon because its report was too loud for her ears. Her sensitivity, and the obliging manners that sometimes worried his father, saved Patrick's life. Touched off once more the Peacemaker exploded, transforming the deck of the *Princeton* from a pleasure cruise to a battlefield. Patrick ran forward and stooped down beside a body that, as it happened, was his father's friend Abel Upshur, lying dead on the deck. Nearby he found another of his father's closest friends, Virgil Maxcy, also dead, along with several others, including Tyler's new secretary of the navy Thomas Gilmer. Tyler himself was safely below deck when the explosion happened. "Dear Father," wrote a badly shaken Patrick that night once the *Princeton* returned to port, "I have only time to write you of the most dreadful accident that I have ever known to happen."[1]

The news of the *Princeton* explosion interrupted Calhoun in a rare moment of pessimism and self-pity brought on by the evaporation of his presidential hopes. In an address to his supporters published in the *Charleston Mercury* at the end of January he announced that he would not participate in the Democratic convention in Baltimore.[2] Although he insisted that skipping the convention was not the same thing as withdrawing from the race, the decision nevertheless plunged him into gloom. "I am the last man, that can be elected in the present condition of the country," he wrote darkly to James Edward a week later. "I am too honest & patriotic to be the choice of anything like a majority." Writing to Duff Green with a bitterness he had not shown in years, he explained that both parties had degenerated from their original principles. "The Whigs are the old federal party turn[ed] demagogue—a thing most abhorrent to their original character," he wrote. Meanwhile "the Democrats are the old Republican Party turn[ed] spoilsmen, a thing equally abhorrent…I am now disentangled from the fraudulent game of President making, and hope never to have to do anything with it again."[3] He soon began working again on the treatise on government he had begun two years earlier.[4]

Calhoun's friends in South Carolina almost immediately offered him his old Senate seat, but the *Princeton* explosion and the death of Abel Upshur opened a different, more appealing path to political redemption. Since its independence in 1836, Texans, southerners, and supporters of American continental destiny had all assumed that Texas would become part of the Union. But annexation faced fierce opposition from antislavery northerners like John Quincy Adams, who saw how annexation would shift the balance of power in Congress toward the South, giving the slaveholding states two new senators and several congressmen, or more if Texas were split into as many as five new states, as many assumed it would be. In 1837, announcing that many of his constituents, "dearly as they loved the Union, would prefer its total dissolution to the act of annexation of Texas," Adams filibustered an annexation resolution for three weeks, killing it.[5]

Another obstacle was Mexico, which refused to recognize Texas independence, making any proposal for annexation an ipso facto declaration of war. For seven years no one occupying the White House proved willing to grasp this nettle, but sensing an issue that could keep him in the White House despite having no party to support him, John Tyler threw the weight of his administration behind annexation in 1843, appointing Abel Upshur his secretary of state after Daniel Webster resigned. On February 27, 1844, the day before he died, Upshur finished negotiating an annexation treaty with representatives of the Texas government that he would present to the Senate, where it was expected to pass. Then he died on the deck of the *Princeton*, and with him, it seemed, Tyler's chances of bringing Texas into the Union in time to help himself in the election.[6]

Within hours of Upshur's death Calhoun loyalists began circulating his name as a candidate to fill the role of secretary of state.[7] The *Princeton* disaster left Tyler without two senior cabinet officials at a critical juncture in American foreign policy. Not only was Texas annexation at risk, and with it a chance to bolster the South's position in the Union, but diplomatic relations with Britain were once again in crisis over the disputed Oregon territory. Abel Upshur had begun negotiations with the British representative Richard Pakenham over Oregon the day before he died. Calhoun's vast foreign policy experience, including the fact that he had already been advising the less experienced Abel Upshur on the Texas issue, made him a natural choice. Tyler also saw the potential to win over many of Calhoun's followers in the Democratic Party now that Calhoun was no longer a candidate for president.[8]

Without consulting Calhoun, Tyler nominated him for the post on March 6. The Senate unanimously confirmed the nomination, a rare feat for Tyler appointees and proof, as George McDuffie wrote Calhoun immediately after the vote, that both Whigs and Democrats viewed him as the best candidate—Democrats and southerners because they favored Texas annexation, and Whigs because they wanted to avoid war with Britain over Oregon and trusted Calhoun's bona fides as an advocate for peace. Letters flooded in to the Pendleton Post Office from all over the country urging him to take the job. In a common sentiment, David Hale, editor of the New York City *Journal of Commerce*, wrote that the unanimous vote in Calhoun's favor showed that everyone understood the danger of the moment and the fact that "some master mind" was required to safely navigate Texas into the Union and peacefully settle the Oregon question. "You are the man," Dixon Lewis wrote from his desk in the House of Representatives of the prevailing opinion there, "& as most of them say, the only man to meet the crisis." Lewis also wrote frankly that if he accepted the post, it would place Calhoun in an "impregnable" position for the presidency in 1848. Meanwhile, some southerners saw Calhoun's nomination as providential, proof, as one correspondent wrote, that "Providence yet battles for us oppressed people of the South."[9]

For Calhoun the path of duty was clear. But first he penned a letter to his old friend Virgil Maxcy's widow. "I will not attempt to offer consolation, where I know it is impossible," he wrote. "All I can do is to mingle my grief with yours. The stroke which deprived you of the kindest & best of husbands deprived me of the most faithful of friends, whose place I can never hope to supply…I loved him, as a brother."[10]

The same day he wrote George McDuffie to say that he would accept Tyler's nomination. "I could see no motive, which could induce me to go into the State Department, except the pending negotiations," he wrote, half-heartedly raising the possibility that Tyler could place him in charge of the negotiations while appointing someone else secretary of state. Calhoun knew how much work a cabinet post could be. That Calhoun, who had just sought the Democratic nomination for president, would accept a cabinet post under an erstwhile Whig like Tyler, also showed just how fluid the political parties and coalitions of the 1840s could be. Nevertheless, the chance to serve the country in a way that furthered his image as a statesman and a patriot while also serving the South in a moment of its direst need undoubtedly appealed to Calhoun. He was soon on his way to Washington, where he took office on April 1. Eleven days later Calhoun signed a treaty of annexation with the representatives of the Republic of Texas. It would still need to be ratified by the Senate, where it needed a two-thirds majority. Abel Upshur had been confident the treaty would pass, but the events of April would transform the question of annexation, with Calhoun playing a central role.[11]

CALHOUN HAD BELIEVED TEXAS'S annexation into the Union "indispensable" for both southern interests and American destiny as soon as it achieved independence in 1836, and had even been in favor of recognizing Texas independence and bringing it into the Union all at once.[12] This placed him at the forefront of expansionist sentiment even in the South, where many planters clamored for annexation but some large slaveholders feared the acquisition of Texas would devalue the worn-out land in older cotton-producing states. By the summer of 1843 Calhoun and other influential southerners had also become convinced that Texas was the newest target of Britain's antislavery imperialism, making its annexation vital on both domestic and foreign policy grounds. During 1843 both Duff Green and Ashbel Smith, the representative for the Texas government in London, wrote Calhoun and other prominent southerners sounding the alarm that Britain was actively trying to accomplish emancipation in Texas, perhaps by guaranteeing a loan to the Texas government in return for abolishing slavery or by supporting Mexico in retaking Texas on the same condition. "I sincerely believe that the ultimate purpose is to make Texas a refuge for runaway slaves from the United States, & eventually a negro nation, a sort of Hayti on the continent," wrote Ashbel Smith to Calhoun from London, adding that Britain's ultimate purpose was the end of slavery in the whole United States.[13] Duff Green, meanwhile, reported with outrage that British foreign minister Lord Aberdeen had consented to meet with a committee that included the American abolitionist Lewis Tappan, who was in London for a meeting of the British and Foreign Anti-Slavery Society. If the United States would only vigorously resist any hint of British interference, Green believed, it might give air to the free trade, noninterference opponents of Robert Peel's Tory government and perhaps catalyze a change in British policy. Otherwise, the British might succeed in creating their "Hayti on the continent."[14]

As Calhoun worked his way through the backlog of mail addressed to his dead friend Upshur, he found what he took as ominous signs confirming what he had already suspected, that Britain was secretly at work undermining slavery in Cuba, as well as Texas. The previous August Calhoun had conveyed these suspicions to Upshur.[15] Acting in line with Calhoun's advice and on the request of the Spanish minister in Washington, the Tyler administration had gone so far as to send three warships to sit in Havana harbor that summer to discourage any British abolitionist plots. When rumors of a revolt emerged from Cuba later that year, many assumed it was the work of the former British consul in Havana, David Turnbull, who was by then stationed nearby in Jamaica. Upon taking office a few months later, Calhoun read a report from Thomas Rodney, an American representative in Cuba, who related emerging details of "a mighty plot" on the island and laid the blame on "Mr. Turnbull." In the end, the alleged revolt failed to live up to Rodney's fears, and Washington Irving, the American minister to Spain and later author of the famous story "Rip Van Winkle," reported that Spain itself suspected no British interference. But taken together with the troubling reports from London, Calhoun had little doubt that Britain was a real threat to US interests in the Americas, especially US slaveholding interests.[16]

Among Upshur's correspondence Calhoun also found an unanswered letter from Richard Pakenham, the British minister to the United States, who two days before Upshur's death had forwarded a message from his superior, Lord Aberdeen, reassuring the Tyler administration that Britain had "no occult design" on slavery in Texas, though he acknowledged that "we wish to see slavery abolished there, as elsewhere." Indeed, Aberdeen frankly acknowledged that Britain sought "the general abolition of slavery throughout the world," and would pursue this "humane and virtuous" policy openly and vigorously, although with a healthy respect for the sovereignty of slaveholding nations like the United States.[17]

Abel Upshur might have let Aberdeen's smug disavowal pass, seeing the official statement of noninterference as the most important point, but there was never any chance that Calhoun would. In the annexation treaty and their public justifications for it Tyler and Upshur had been careful to avoid the issue of slavery, which they knew would divide crucial northern support for annexation. But Calhoun apparently convinced Tyler that Pakenham's letter required an immediate reply and that the reply might be politically advantageous to Tyler, so they decided to delay sending the annexation treaty to the Senate until Calhoun could complete his response, which he did on April 18. The treaty went to the Senate four days later. The delay allowed Calhoun to reframe the issue of annexation, transforming the debate over Texas into a referendum over slavery and its place in the Union, extending his ideological offensive against abolitionism in the international sphere, and throwing Martin Van Buren's quest for the Democratic nomination into disarray in a letter that Senator Thomas Hart Benton called the "Texas bombshell."[18]

In the letter, addressed to Pakenham, Calhoun expressed "deep concern" over Aberdeen's avowal—"for the first time made to this government"—that Britain sought the abolition of slavery throughout the rest of the world, including Texas. While Britain had every right to abolish slavery within its own borders and in its colonies, it had no right to meddle in the domestic arrangements of sovereign nations. Taking Aberdeen's admission as proof that Britain was using its diplomatic and financial influence to threaten the institution of slavery in Texas, and indirectly in the United States, Calhoun explicitly cast the pending annexation treaty as a response by the Tyler administration intended to counter British policy, preserve slavery in Texas, and protect it in the existing slaveholding states. "To hazard consequences which would be so dangerous to the prosperity and safety of this Union, without resorting to the most effective measures to prevent them, would be...an abandonment of the most solemn obligation imposed by the [Constitution]." Given the chance to speak for the federal government, Calhoun made it clear exactly what he believed the Constitution demanded when it came to the protection of slaveholders' rights, which was indistinguishable from the protections it guaranteed to citizens and states.

Calhoun also directly rejected Aberdeen's claim that emancipation was a humanitarian policy, and he believed he had the numbers to prove it. Calhoun had always loved statistics, and he lived at a time when statistical data was quickly gaining cultural authority as a source of scientific knowledge that should guide public policy. He had, for example, used statistics extensively in his arguments against the tariff.[19] In his letter to Pakenham, he drew from a new source, the most recent federal census, to disprove abolitionist claims with scientific certainty. The 1840 census set a new standard for scientific measurement of populations, providing a treasure trove of data that many heralded for its usefulness to the cause of science and reform. It was the first census to be overseen by a Superintendent of the Census in the State

Department and the first to include "moral statistics" aimed at identifying patterns and challenges for public health policies. But as some hawk-eyed proslavery ideologues soon noticed, the census also seemed to clearly show the deleterious effects of freedom on black people, revealing that the numbers of "deaf and dumb, blind, idiots and insane" were a far higher percentage of the free black population in the North than they were among enslaved blacks in the South.[20] In his letter to Pakenham, Calhoun laid out the disparity at length, state by state, claiming that free blacks "invariably sunk into vice and pauperism" and pointedly noting that the percentages of infirm and insane black people were highest in states like Massachusetts, "where the change in the ancient relation of the two races was first made…[and] where the greatest zeal has been exhibited on their behalf." Thus, he concluded, if Britain actually succeeded in achieving abolition in the United States, "she would involve in the greatest calamity the whole country, and especially the race which it is the avowed object of her exertions to benefit." The numbers, he said, proved that it was the slaveholding states, and not Britain, that were humane and virtuous. Indeed the United States, half free and half slaveholding, provided the perfect experiment in testing the results of freedom on black people, and the results clearly showed exactly what Calhoun had argued since the 1830s—that slavery was a beneficial institution for both white and black alike.[21]

Even as Calhoun wielded the census against Pakenham, a controversy was brewing over its accuracy. Calhoun may have first encountered the census numbers in an 1843 article in the *Southern Literary Messenger* that made much the same argument he used against Pakenham. It is unlikely he had read an article published in the *American Journal of the Medical Sciences* in January 1844 in which Massachusetts physician Edward Jarvis systematically proved that the census numbers were wildly unreliable, in some cases recording "insane" free blacks in towns with no black residents at all and sometimes counting all the white residents of mental institutions as black. But John Quincy Adams did read Jarvis's article. Realizing its importance, and before

Calhoun's Pakenham letter appeared in public, Adams introduced a resolution in the House requesting then secretary of state Abel Upshur to provide information on how "gross errors" had made their way into the 1840 census.[22]

As fate would have it, it fell to Calhoun to comply with the request, and a few days after the Pakenham letter became public he submitted a vague and dismissive response that only acknowledged a few minor "clerical errors."[23] Determined not to let Calhoun off the hook, Adams called on Calhoun at his office, writing with bitter glee in his diary later that night that Calhoun had "writhed like a trodden rattlesnake" when Adams confronted him with the evidence. Adams did not relent, but nearly a year later Calhoun reported to the House that an internal investigation headed by the same official who had overseen the census in the first place "would seem fully to sustain the correctness of the Census on this highly important point." Unable to resist, Calhoun ended his 1845 report with the "irresistible" conclusion that for the "negro or African race" freedom was indeed "a curse instead of a blessing." By then, Calhoun's use of the census in the Pakenham letter had drawn a passionate and statistically detailed rebuttal from a group of free black New Yorkers who submitted a petition to the Senate, including statistics and tables of their own. But thanks to Calhoun's influence, both in using the census in the first place and in failing to correct it, the flawed 1840 census would continue to figure in proslavery arguments for years.[24]

The same April 27 issues of Washington newspapers that printed Calhoun's Pakenham letter, leaked by antislavery senator Benjamin Tappan of Ohio, also carried letters from both parties' leading presidential candidates, Henry Clay and Martin Van Buren, publicly opposing the annexation of Texas. Although no evidence emerged to support the accusation, the simultaneous announcement seemed to many like a ploy to defuse the issue in the presidential election, but if so both Clay and Van Buren underestimated the public appetite for annexation. Van Buren, at the head of the party of Andrew Jackson, who was inconveniently still alive and passionately in favor of annexation, had more at stake and would pay the higher price. In the meantime, the opposition of both major candidates shifted the political winds against the treaty in the Senate. So, too, did the fact that the documents accompanying the treaty showed that Tyler and Calhoun had promised Texas the protection of the American navy against Mexico while the treaty was being completed, a stretch of presidential powers Calhoun would have excoriated in other instances and that horrified even some of the most fervent expansionists.[25]

Just as decisive was the fact that Calhoun's Pakenham letter transformed the debate over annexation into a debate over slavery, alienating crucial northern supporters and, for the moment, dooming the whole project of annexation that he had ostensibly accepted office to complete. It was a confusing turn of events, and explanations were in short supply. Some observers believed that Calhoun's frustrated presidential ambitions were to blame. Van Buren's *Washington Globe*, seeing the threat posed to Van Buren by the Pakenham letter, observed, "The truth is, Mr. Calhoun, though a good and great man in many things, is a madman when the immediate aim of his ambition is thwarted. His idea of abandoning the Union to embrace Texas, and making a slave confederacy, is one of those ambitious schemes which will reduce his empire to Fort Hill, instead of making him the founder of one which he hopes to stretch from the Bay of Charleston to that of California."[26] Historians have also puzzled over Calhoun's decision to write the letter, arguing either that Calhoun never intended for the Pakenham letter to become public or that in his zeal to protect slavery he severely miscalculated what the response would be.

Neither of these explanations are plausible. From the beginning Calhoun tried to bait Pakenham into a *longer* and *more public* exchange over slavery along the lines of his literary duel with "Patrick Henry" earlier in his career.[27] And Calhoun had been in the Senate for too long not to expect that the explosive letter would become public. Instead, the Pakenham letter fits perfectly into Calhoun's belief that challenges to slavery had to be met directly and aggressively, no matter the cost, and that slavery had to be defended in positive terms, not as a necessary or temporary evil. The Pakenham letter allowed him to undermine the arguments of some of his fellow slaveholding politicians, especially Senator Robert Walker of Mississippi, who argued that Texas annexation would actually weaken slavery by diffusing it, allowing older slaveholding states like Maryland and Virginia to sell their slaves and become, eventually, free states. Furthermore, Calhoun certainly sought to preserve the Union, and saw Texas as essential to that goal, but he was not interested in preserving a Union that would not protect Fort Hill and the South from interference both at home and abroad. For him that was the whole point of annexation. "The time is come," he wrote Charleston planter John Mathewes a few days after the Pakenham letter became public, "when England must be met on the abolition question. You will have seen, that I have placed the Texan question on that issue. I am resolved to keep it there, be the consequences what it may." Just as he had in the domestic sphere with his Senate resolutions in 1837, with the Pakenham letter Calhoun strove to force a choice on the main figures in American political life: explicitly refuse to protect the South or place the positive defense of slavery at the center of American foreign policy. "Our watchwords ought to be Texas, Annexation & noninterference," he wrote. "Under them we may march to victory." Calhoun had his priorities in clear order, and unlike Henry Clay, he was not willing to compromise.[28]

The effects of the Pakenham letter were immediate and lasting. In the short term the Pakenham letter helped doom the annexation treaty, which the Senate finally and decisively rejected on June 7 in a resounding defeat for Tyler and, apparently, Calhoun. Furthermore, while nearly all northern senators voted against annexation, many southern Whigs followed Henry Clay's lead and also voted against the treaty, which to Calhoun's eyes only showed the obstacle that party loyalty represented to southern unity. Calhoun and Tyler soon began working on an alternate, and more constitutionally shaky, path to bring Texas into the Union. Instead of a treaty, they proposed a joint resolution of Congress, which would require only simple majorities in both Houses.[29]

By then Calhoun's framing of the annexation issue had helped to derail the nomination of his old enemy Martin Van Buren while committing the Democratic Party to annexation largely on Calhoun's terms. After Van Buren's public opposition to annexing Texas, Andrew Jackson withdrew his support for Van Buren's candidacy and threw his weight behind the otherwise undistinguished James K. Polk, a loyal Jackson acolyte, slaveholder, and a passionate expansionist who was nominated by the Baltimore convention just days before the Senate rejected Tyler's Texas treaty.[30] In one sense, while Calhoun failed to win the nomination himself, and refused to attend the convention, Polk's nomination was an important stride toward his goal of fusing the defense of slavery to American foreign policy. It also confirmed his judgment that the public's appetite for annexation was so vast that the American people would swallow the bitter proslavery pill he had concocted in his response to Richard Pakenham. Indeed, far from seeing the Pakenham letter as a defeat or a miscalculation, less than a year later it would look like the beginning of a victorious campaign.[31]

CALHOUN WAS DETERMINED TO use the foreign policy of the United States to counter British imperialism and protect slavery not only in Texas, or even the United States, but in the Western Hemisphere. From the State Department he had a firsthand view of what many slaveholders considered a dire warning: the disastrous effects of British emancipation in its West Indian colonies. Robert Monroe Harrison, the American consul in Jamaica, who had peppered several successive secretaries of state with his warnings of British duplicity about slavery, wrote the State Department describing the "wretched state to which this fine colony is now reduced by pseudo philanthropists." Harrison described once-grand plantations unoccupied and worthless, while a "wooly headed Mullato," a "Quadroon," and a "Bankrupt Jew" were all members of the legislature.[32] A few months earlier, Calhoun knew, the British minister in Washington had approached Abel Upshur with a private request to encourage "labourers of the free colored class" to emigrate to Jamaica to make up for the labor shortage induced by emancipation. Upshur and Calhoun considered it an audacious request to make at the same moment that Britain was denouncing American slaveholders in the most hypocritical terms imaginable.[33]

Before Upshur's death, Calhoun had floated the idea of linking arms with other slave societies in the Western Hemisphere against the British threat and enlisting the sympathies of European countries threatened by British power. Writing Upshur about Cuba and Texas, Calhoun advised, "Much can be done in France in reference to each. Would it not be well for our Govt., and that of France to enter into a Gu[ar]anty of [Cuba's] possession to Spain, against the interference of any other power?" Calhoun had been wary of the British threat to Cuba ever since his days in Monroe's cabinet, seeing the slaveholding island as a natural part of the United States, but now he was willing to ally with France just to secure Spanish rule, at least for the time being, and slavery.[34]

In office Calhoun acted on his own advice, corresponding extensively with a network of southern-born, slaveholding foreign ministers of the United States throughout the Caribbean and across the Atlantic. He instructed the American consul in Havana to investigate the means used "in exciting the blacks to rise on their masters," and particularly whether the English were involved in it.[35] In May he wrote to Henry Wise, the US minister in Brazil, instructing him to assure the Brazilian government that "between her and us there is a strict identity of interests on almost all subjects, without conflict, or even competition, on scarcely one." Describing the American policy of noninterference that he had just outlined in the Pakenham letter, Calhoun wrote, "Brazil has the deepest interest in establishing the same policy, especially in reference to the important relations between the European and African races as it exists with her and in the Southern portion of our Union…

To destroy it in either, would facilitate its destruction in the other."[36] Calhoun had once seen the emerging democratic republics of Latin America as sisters in a hemispheric movement toward liberty that deserved American sympathy and aid, even when they appeared disposed to emancipate their slaves. Three decades later he had come to see Brazil, which was still ruled by a hereditary monarchy, as the neighbor most similar to the United States in its interests, if not its form of government.[37]

Ironically, then, one of Calhoun's duties as secretary of state was suppressing the transatlantic slave trade, much of it going to Brazil. As part of the Webster-Ashburton Treaty two years earlier, the United States had agreed to help Britain patrol the west coast of Africa to stop the illegal trade. To Calhoun this was not much of a contradiction, although it did require a delicate balancing act. Many American slaveholders in the 1840s saw the transatlantic slave trade as a threat, not a support, to slavery. Calhoun had warned as early as 1842 that Brazil needed to end its slave trade for its own safety, and he probably knew that many planters in Cuba suspected the British of using the slave trade to inject slave rebels into their workforce. With Brazil, Calhoun had to strike a balance between support for a sister slaveholding society against the threat of British imperialism while also fulfilling the terms of the treaty, which required the United States to suppress a trade that Brazil believed was vital to its economy. The end goal of this seemingly contradictory American policy was a Western Hemisphere populated by stable, prosperous slave societies with naturally reproducing enslaved populations similar to the United States, which might even serve as a safer source for Brazil's labor needs in the future.[38]

The irony of the situation was compounded further by the fact that some of the ships engaged in the illegal trade came from New England. Writing from Rio de Janeiro before Calhoun took office, Henry Wise's predecessor reported that eight out of ten of the slave-trading ships arriving in that port were built in Massachusetts and flew the American flag. This meant that once Calhoun took office slave-trading ships sailing from the most abolitionist state in the Union were dodging an American navy enforcing a foreign policy directed by a South Carolina slaveholder in the waters off the west coast of Africa.[39]

The centerpiece of Calhoun's efforts to undermine European support for Britain's foreign policy was his letter to Alabamian William R. King, the new US minister to France in August 1844. Worried that France might join Britain in a declaration against the American annexation of Texas, Calhoun penned a lengthy exposé explaining what Britain was really up to, and how France's interests would be served by staying out of it. Having abolished slavery in its own colonial possessions under the sincere, but mistaken, assumption that freedom would be better for the slaves and more profitable for its empire, Calhoun asserted, Britain had now discovered its error in the plummeting productivity of its colonies and the wretched condition of its newly free workforce. Britain now sought to correct course by undermining slavery in the United States, Cuba, and Brazil to eliminate the competitive advantage that slave labor gave those countries. If they succeeded, Calhoun warned, the result would be a "war of races over all South America" and a British monopoly on products that France could now buy cheaply thanks to "competition, cheaper means of production, and nearness of market." Did the French really want to pay more for their coffee, their sugar, and their cotton clothes? Did they really want to be dependent on Britain, their old rival, as their only trading partner? In contrast, Calhoun portrayed a utopian free trade future in which "the more civilized Nations of Temperate Zone, especially Europe…exchange their products with those of the tropical regions." Free trade and a curbed British influence would give France access to both cheap "tropical" products produced by slave labor and a burgeoning New World population of consumers for its own goods.[40]

Calhoun did not lay all his cards on the table in the King letter. He kept in reserve another source of scientific support for his arguments that he had gleaned that summer from conversation and correspondence with English-born Egyptologist George Gliddon and the

Pennsylvania physician Samuel George Morton, a member of the Philadelphia Academy of Natural Sciences whose book *Crania Aegyptiaca*, published that year, argued that multiple acts of creation had produced separate and distinct human species, a theory known as polygenesis. Gliddon, whose father was the American consul in Alexandria, later claimed that Calhoun sought him out for advice that summer while Calhoun was writing the letter to William King. Gliddon referred Calhoun to Morton, who immediately sent Calhoun a copy of *Crania Aegyptiaca*, "in which, among other subjects, I have briefly inquired into the social position of the Negro race in the earliest periods of authentic history." Both Gliddon and Morton maintained that there had never been an example in history of a black civilization and that even in ancient Egypt black people had been slaves to "Caucasians," a fact that Gliddon wrote to Calhoun was "entirely confirmatory of those doctrines you have so long sustained." Calhoun chose not to include Gliddon's and Morton's arguments in his King letter, probably because he knew polygenesis was controversial even among slavery's supporters since it contradicted the biblical account of creation. But he discussed their ideas with John Tyler and asked Morton to send the president a copy of his book, sure that science was on his side. Gliddon and Morton's arguments would resurface in Calhoun's speeches in the years ahead.[41]

Calhoun had the King letter sent to American representatives throughout Europe as the definitive word on American foreign policy in regard to Texas, and he made sure it was translated into French and published in Paris. In early 1845, King wrote that Calhoun's letter had "produced quite a sensation here, as well as in England," while the American consul at the Hague reported that on his visit to Brussels, King Leopold had spoken glowingly of the letter, which had "kicked up a great row" in Europe.[42] What ultimate effect the letter had is hard to say, but France never joined Britain in condemning annexation. At home antislavery newspapers shrieked that Calhoun had proposed a "grand slaveholding League, of Brazil, Spain, and France, with the

United States at its head," while James Gadsden wrote him from South Carolina that if he succeeded in "enlightening the world on the true character of African slavery as it exists in the U.S. you will have achieved a monument of enduring fame & be richly entitled to the gratitude of the world, where trade is stimulated by the production of black & slave labor."[43]

As far-reaching as Calhoun's descriptions of the future in the letter were, he had not included his deepest fears about the results of British policy. In a "strictly confidential" follow-up to King later that year, Calhoun described a racial apocalypse in which Britain might succeed in its aims and become worldwide "the patron of the colored races of all hues" while France supported a beleaguered white race spread across the globe. Instead of a harmonious system of free trade rooted in racial slavery, the whole world would be Haiti.[44]

ONE OF THE DIPLOMATS who received Calhoun's King letter was Thomas Green Clemson, recently arrived with his family in Brussels as the new American chargé d'affaires to Belgium. When Tyler gave Calhoun the authority to choose a new minister to Belgium in May, Calhoun instantly thought of his son-in-law, whose experience living abroad and ability to speak fluent French made him unusually well suited to the post. (The incredulous British minister in Brussels later told Anna that previous American diplomats had asked him to help translate official documents into French, giving him intimate knowledge of American foreign policy.) Calhoun also suspected, rightly, that his son-in-law—half-heartedly pursuing the life of a planter on a new plantation in South Carolina—was frustrated with his current situation, often depressed, and would leap at the chance to return to Europe.[45]

It was also a chance for Calhoun to make amends with his son-in-law for involving him in the Alabama venture. The simmering crisis between Andrew and Clemson over Alabama had come to a head in early 1843. Desperately needing money to pay the debt and purchase a workforce for the new plantation he had purchased in Edgefield District, confusingly also called Cane Brake, Clemson threatened legal action against Andrew if some arrangement were not reached. Upon learning of this, Calhoun assured Clemson in a nine-page letter that "if there has been any disappointment, *the blame is mine.*" This was patently untrue, but Calhoun was eager to keep family matters out of the courts, and deftly interposed his own honor and authority as the family patriarch to keep the peace. "I would rather make a sacrafice [*sic*] myself, than you should suffer one," Calhoun wrote, and "if [Andrew] is not good for what he owes you, *I am.* You can neither doubt my solvency, or attachment to you." Two weeks later, informing Clemson of his efforts to raise the money Clemson needed, Calhoun assured his son-in-law, "If it should take every dollar I have on earth, you shall not lose a cent due you…if you have lost confidence (as I think unjustly) in him, I trust you have not in me." Realizing he had gone too far, and really having no choice once Calhoun had placed himself in the breach, Clemson quickly apologized. Later that year Calhoun and Andrew bought Clemson out of the disastrous Alabama investment by signing a statement that they owed him more than $24,000, which would be paid in three installments over the next three years. Already deeply in debt, Calhoun took on the additional financial burden to satisfy Clemson, preserve Andrew's honor, and keep the peace. "To see you & him & all my children prosperous & happy is the great object of my desire," he wrote Clemson. "I would not for all I am worth see them, including of course yourself, embroiled in feuds & conflicts to their mutual disgrace and mine." The Union was not the only thing Calhoun was trying to hold together.[46]

When Calhoun relayed the Belgium offer in May, Clemson eagerly inquired about the details while Anna wrote her father about her doubts. "Were I a few years younger or my children a few years older," Anna wrote, "I should enjoy the idea of visiting Europe much, but as it is I expect to have more of the fatigues & disagreeables of travel than the pleasures." She did not relish the "ceremonies & etiquettes" of being the wife of an American representative at a royal court, and would have preferred to remain in South Carolina. But Clemson's "constant desire" to return to Europe meant that Anna saw little chance of dissuading him, and Calhoun thought it was best even though he did not want Anna and his grandchildren separated from him by an ocean.

The Senate confirmed Clemson's nomination in June and by August the Clemsons were on their way to New York to depart for Europe after stopping briefly in Washington to see Calhoun. They finally arrived in Brussels in October along with a white nurse and a slave named Basil, whom Clemson wrote Calhoun "attracts a good deal of attention from his colour." For the next six years while she was in Belgium all of Anna's surviving letters, with only one exception, were to her father. Calhoun never traveled abroad, a deficiency for an American statesman that John Quincy Adams had once encouraged him to address, but now, through a daughter who shared his worldview more thoroughly than anyone living, he gained a window into European society and politics. "I will expect to hear from you often & fully," he wrote just after the Clemsons left Washington, "and you must give me your impressions, just as you feel them." He also sent his measurements and asked Clemson to buy him "a broad cloth coat & a pair of pantaloons, both black."[47]

AT THE SAME TIME that he was shaping American foreign policy in his own image, Calhoun had to put down a movement in South Carolina led by Robert Barnwell Rhett that threatened to undo all he hoped to accomplish on the national and global stage. Rhett was enraged by the rejection of the Texas annexation treaty and the renewal of the tariff, and he chafed at Calhoun's cautious conservatism and the older man's tight hold on South Carolina politics. At a meeting in Bluffton, South Carolina, at the end of July, Rhett openly threatened to bypass nullification and hold a secession convention to withdraw from the Union. One of the insurgents reportedly asked with scorn "if the state is to lick Calhoun's toes forever?"[48]

Friends in Charleston immediately wrote Calhoun about the new threat and he whipped off a hurried letter to his ally Armistead Burt detailing his opposition and describing how the political landscape had changed since 1832. "Then we had to contend with the Tariff alone," he wrote, "but now with that & abolition; and to decide judiciously on our course, regard must be had to both." Given that he was in the midst of writing his King letter when the Bluffton movement erupted, Calhoun no doubt had more than just domestic abolitionism on his mind. Nullification might ward off the tariff, and secession might even preserve South Carolina from the threat of homegrown abolitionism for a short time, but South Carolina could never hope to adequately counter the immense influence of Great Britain on its own. It needed to be able to simultaneously counter the power of the federal government at home and wield it abroad. In order to do that the South must be united. "The great point, toward effecting of which all our efforts ought to be directed is to unite the South," he wrote. The signs were encouraging. The annexation issue had peeled Virginia away from Martin Van Buren's New York political machine, placing it back at the head of the South where it belonged. But Thomas Ritchie's *Richmond Enquirer* made clear that Virginia disapproved of the Bluffton movement. Furthermore, only weeks earlier James Polk had won the Democratic nomination on the strength of his commitment to annexation and to lowering the tariff, as well as to other measures close to Calhoun's heart such as restoring the Independent Treasury system. "Mr. Clay must be defeated & Mr. Polk elected, which of itself is a sufficient reason why we should do nothing at present," Calhoun wrote. In the end the Bluffton movement burned out in the face of a public letter from Calhoun and the coordinated efforts of his allies in the state legislature, especially Francis Pickens, but the difficulty in restraining the radicals hinted at the shape of a future without Calhoun.[49]

In the interest of electing Polk, a few weeks later Calhoun had to address a rumor begun by Whig senator Thomas Ewing of Ohio, who announced during a meeting in St. Clairsville that summer that

Calhoun advocated slavery for poor white workers as well as blacks, essentially repeating William Cabell Rives's assertion that Calhoun defended slavery in the abstract. Recognizing an attempt to drive a wedge between the Democrats and their working-class followers, Calhoun wrote a public letter disavowing Ewing's claim as "utterly destitute of the shadow of truth." It was Whigs like Ewing and Henry Clay, advocating the same unholy marriage of capital and government that had impoverished the working classes of England, who were the enemies of the American worker, not him or the Democrats. "So far from ever having entertained such an abominable sentiment," Calhoun wrote indignantly, "my whole life has been devoted to endeavoring to uphold our free popular system of government" against "measures that must end in enslaving the laboring population of our country." Calhoun's indignation is illuminating since it sprang from his sense that he had been purposely misrepresented as being antidemocratic, something he did not believe he was despite nullification, his firm hold on South Carolina politics, and his opposition to the unvarnished principle of majority rule.[50]

Besides Texas, the most consequential foreign policy issue confronting Calhoun was the ongoing dispute between the United States and Britain over the Oregon territory, which stretched from California to Alaska and had been jointly occupied by the two countries under agreements made in 1818 and 1827. Now, with American settlers pushing into the territory and challenging the authority of the British Hudson Bay Company, the future of Oregon became a central issue in the 1844 election. Before Abel Upshur's death Calhoun had raised the idea of connecting the annexation of Texas with the Oregon question in order to enlist western support. The Democratic platform of 1844 did just that, proposing the "re-annexation" of both Texas and Oregon— which they claimed had been treacherously given away by John Quincy Adams in the 1819 Adams-Onís Treaty—as nonnegotiable policy goals of a Polk administration.[51] The term "re-annexation," in particular, got under Calhoun's skin since he had been in Monroe's cabinet when the Adams-Onís Treaty was negotiated.[52] Polk's public position was that he would settle for nothing less than the whole of Oregon, and his campaign slogan, "Fifty-Four Forty or Fight!," referred to the territory's northernmost boundary with Russian Alaska.

In reality, by the time Calhoun entered office the negotiations had narrowed to a disagreement over whether to simply extend the Webster-Ashburton line at 49° latitude to the Pacific, as the Americans wanted, or to extend the same line west to the Columbia River, and then follow the river to the Pacific, giving the British control of the "disputed triangle" that included what is today northwest Washington State. Abel Upshur had been about to enter into negotiations with Richard Pakenham on this issue when he died, and Calhoun picked up where his dead friend left off after exhaustively researching the convoluted history of various European and American claims to the region. Calhoun's exchange with Pakenham in September 1844 showed the depth of his preparation, as he laid out the history of American and British exploration in the Northwest, quoting British explorers to prove they had not entered the Columbia River (while American Robert Gray had, in 1792), and rehearsing the dizzying evolution of agreements between Spain, France, Russia, England, and the United States to show the strength of the American claim. Pakenham's response was no less impressive, but the two had not reached an agreement by the time Calhoun left Washington for a short trip to South Carolina at the end of the month.[53]

BY THEN IT SEEMED possible that James K. Polk might win the election. "Young Hickory," as Polk had long been known, was rail thin, grim-looking, and completely humorless. He had nearly limitless ambition and a work ethic that frequently pushed beyond what his frail constitution could sustain. Perhaps the only person more committed than Polk to fulfilling the country's continental destiny by annexing Texas was his wife, Sarah Childress Polk, who, unlike Floride Calhoun, was an essential advisor to her husband.[54] In September, after spending two days with the Polks, Francis Pickens gushed to Calhoun, "there are no disguises. *Everything is perfectly satisfactory.*" Polk was determined to reduce the tariff, annex Texas "at all hazards," reinstate the Independent Treasury, and reduce the spending of the government.[55] It was almost too good to be true. From Fort Hill that fall Calhoun watched with cautious optimism as Polk's narrow victory confirmed his strategy with the Pakenham letter and sealed the downfall of Martin Van Buren and Henry Clay. He regarded the defeat of his two old enemies "as a great political revolution," he wrote his friend John Mathewes in mid-October. "They give us much to hope." But as Mathewes reminded Calhoun a few weeks later, his work was not yet done. "If we are to reap we must sow," Mathewes wrote. Polk "is the soil," but "before the seed is sown, it must be prepared by a good husbandman, and as Nathan said unto David so say I unto you—'Thou art the man.'" Perhaps Mathewes did not know his Bible well enough to realize that when the prophet spoke those words, he was condemning David for stealing another man's wife.[56]

When Congress convened in December Calhoun and Tyler moved forward with their plan to annex Texas by a joint resolution of Congress instead of a treaty, a measure that had no precedent in American history. The Constitution gave Congress the authority to admit new states into the Union, but Texas was an independent republic and many doubted whether Congress had the authority to join two independent countries by a simple majority. Even Calhoun acknowledged that a treaty would have been the best method of annexing Texas, but in a striking contradiction of all his warnings about numerical majorities, in this case he was willing to wield its power to protect the South, leaving John Quincy Adams to rage in his diary that the joint resolution turned the Constitution into "a menstrous rag."[57]

The resolution sailed through the Democratic-controlled House 120 to 98 but stalled in the Senate, where it was introduced by George

McDuffie. In order to win over opponents like Thomas Hart Benton, who had opposed the annexation treaty out of loyalty to Van Buren but now saw the writing on the wall in Polk's election, an amendment was added that gave the president the authority to either admit Texas directly or to go back to the negotiating table over the terms of annexation and especially the disputed border between Texas and Mexico. The latter option was significant because it held out the narrow possibility of avoiding war between the United States and Mexico. George McDuffie assured his fellow senators that Tyler would leave the choice to the incoming president, and Polk gave the distinct impression that he would choose the so-called "Benton option." On February 27, 1845, the Senate passed the resolution 27 to 25, giving Calhoun and Tyler a victory that John Quincy Adams lamented as "a signal triumph of the Slave representation in the Constitution of the United States."[58]

With Tyler's presidency now only days from its end, and armed with the revelation that Polk would be forming an entirely new cabinet, Calhoun was determined to leave nothing to chance.[59] He was afraid that as soon as Polk took office, the English and French ministers as well as the Van Buren Democrats like Benton would exert pressure on Polk to choose renewed negotiation, which might produce a treaty that would be subject to the same two-thirds requirement that had killed his own treaty in June. In fact, he was sure that the "Benton option" was a backdoor bid to scuttle annexation by Van Buren Democrats and Texans like Sam Houston, who was rumored to favor an independent Texas. "I lost no time in preparing and giving the instructions, based on the House resolutions [i.e., immediate admittance], which I did, as the only possible means of preventing the loss of annexation," he explained months later to Andrew Jackson Donelson, a nephew of Old Hickory whom Calhoun had recently appointed minister to Texas.[60] Calhoun knew that Tyler was bitter at how Polk had co-opted the issue of Texas and eager to claim Texas annexation as his legacy, and so he determined to convince Tyler to act immediately. On Saturday, March 1, Tyler signed the joint resolutions. On Sunday he held an emergency cabinet meeting in which Calhoun made his case for immediately admitting Texas instead of leaving the decision to Polk. The other cabinet members did not need much convincing.

The next day, the day before he left office, Tyler dispatched instructions to Andrew Jackson Donelson to offer Texas immediate admission to the Union, an action that he had all but promised not to take. Texas still had to agree, of course, and Polk could still upset the apple cart by recalling the offer, but Calhoun had succeeded beyond the wildest dreams of those who saw Texas as the South's lifeline in the Union.[61] "I think it a great blessing that you are where you are," Francis Pickens had written him at the end of December. "The present generation do not see the power of your position, but after ages will pay tribute to what you are now doing." Others saw things differently. In January, even before the full scope of Calhoun's victory became apparent, John Quincy Adams observed in his diary, "John C. Calhoun and South Carolina are in the ascendant…the prospect is deathlike."[62]

CALHOUN'S MOMENT OF TRIUMPH was twinned with a grim reminder of his mortality. For the past two years the Calhoun family had listened warily as young John Caldwell, who was twenty-one years old in 1844, began exhibiting the hollow cough and irritated throat that were the first symptoms of consumption, an infection of the lungs that we know today as tuberculosis. In the early nineteenth century consumption was responsible for one out of every five deaths in America, and it ravaged whole families and communities with terrifying abandon. Indeed, one of the only things that John C. Calhoun shared with the famed abolitionist Theodore Parker besides Unitarianism was the fact that consumption killed them both, as it did thousands of their fellow Americans every year. The infection progressed slowly and unpredictably through three stages, beginning at first with a cough and irritated throat that was difficult to distinguish from other illnesses. In the next stage the cough became worse, frequently producing thick mucus and pus, accompanied by a high "hectic fever" and painful throat lesions. In the third stage, the disease earned its awful name as the victim's body appeared to waste away, consuming itself from the inside. As one physician described the final stage, "The emaciation is frightful… the cheeks are hollow…the fat of the face being most absorbed…rendering the expression harsh and painful. The eyes are commonly sunk in their sockets…and often look morbidly bright and *staring*." Death sometimes came slowly, as the victim's lungs slowly filled up and they suffocated, and sometimes all at once, with a hemorrhage of blood and mucus that poured out of the nose and mouth. In most cases, as their bodies wasted away, consumptives maintained their lucidity to the very end. While it was deadly, the disease was also cruelly unpredictable in its course. Victims could experience severe attacks punctuated by months, years, or even decades of apparent health. To have consumption in Calhoun's world was to be dealt a death sentence without knowing when it would be carried out.[63]

Mentions of young John Caldwell's cough and throat began showing up in family letters in 1842 when he left South Carolina to study at the University of Virginia, although no one openly admitted what it might be. "His throat I fear will give him much trouble. It has been very painful for some time," Floride wrote to John Caldwell's brother Patrick.[64] A year later John Caldwell left his studies to pursue a trip west with his brother Patrick in the hope that travel and the western air would cure him, a common remedy for consumption. "John looks better than when he arrived, but coughs a great deal," Calhoun wrote anxiously to Thomas Green Clemson in June 1844 from Washington, where Patrick and John were staying with him before their trip west. "I am much encouraged…of the highly beneficial effects of the excursion he is about to take."[65]

When exactly Calhoun contracted the infection is impossible to know, but in late January 1845 newspapers in Washington reported that the secretary of state had fallen seriously ill with pneumonia.[66] Floride, who had accompanied her husband to Washington for once, dismissed the report, telling their son James Edward that Calhoun had been sick but was recovering. "They say his lungs are remarkably sound," she wrote with a hint of denial, and marked his illness down to a "violent cold."[67] But three weeks later when Assistant Attorney General Francis Wharton called on Calhoun in his rooms at the US Hotel, he was frightened by Calhoun's appearance. "As he rose to meet me, on my entering the room, I was much struck with the emaciation of his frame, and the feebleness of his gait," Wharton wrote. "He was much thinner than before, his eye was glased, his cheek hectic, and his voice broken by cough." Clearly, Wharton suspected the truth.[68]

Calhoun himself must have suspected the truth, as well, but that did not stop him from pushing Tyler to annex Texas only a few days later, in his view saving it from the specter of British abolitionism, securing a balance of power for the South in the federal government, and preserving the Union. Within a year the price of prime field hands in New Orleans had risen more than 20 percent, reflecting the South's new confidence.[69]

"My health is entirely restored," Calhoun wrote Anna on March 11, just as many of the Van Buren Democrats began to realize that Calhoun and Tyler had tricked them. But a stubborn cough persisted, and his thoughts turned toward his ancestors that spring on his return to South Carolina. "I am now the last survivor of the first generation after the emigrants on my father's side," he wrote to a cousin in Alabama after the news that an aunt there had died. "Our family on the father's side emigrated in 1733. The interval is a long period to be filled up, with 2 generations." That summer he made a trip to his childhood home in Abbeville, where he visited relatives he had not seen for years and placed a "plain monument" near the graves of his father, mother, and his sister Catherine. Within days came the news that Andrew Jackson, only one generation removed from Ireland himself, had died in Nashville.[70]

EIGHTEEN

"Ours Is the Government of the White Man"

I N THE EARLY HOURS OF November 4, 1845, news reached the residents of Mobile, Alabama, that "the great Statesman of the South" would arrive in their city by noon aboard the steamer *H. Kinney*. A welcoming committee made up of "a large number of citizens" and a musical band rushed aboard their own steamboat and set off upriver to welcome him. When they met the *H. Kinney* a few miles above the city, a tall, thin figure with a shock of stubbornly erect gray hair appeared on deck and waved, prompting "loud and prolonged cheers" from the greeting party. When Calhoun reached Mobile, the docks were crowded with "thousands" of Alabamians hoping to catch a glimpse of one of the most famous Americans of the day.[1]

Calhoun was on his way to Memphis, where he had been invited to preside over a much-anticipated southern commercial convention. Everywhere he went crowds gathered to see him. In New Orleans, a military parade and procession of carriages swept him through cheering crowds to the St. Louis Hotel, and that evening he attended a dinner with more than a hundred guests, where he offered a toast to "the Valley of the Mississippi...the greatest in the world. Situated midway between the oceans, it will yet command the commerce of both."[2] At Vicksburg crowds waited in the dark as a flotilla of steamboats lit with torches and blaring music accompanied his boat toward the city. When he reached his destination, the editor of the Memphis *Weekly American Eagle* breathlessly estimated the crowd gathered to greet Calhoun at eight to ten thousand people, roughly the city's entire population.[3]

The convention's invitation to Calhoun reflected a shrewd choice on the part of its organizers. Modeled on the conventions that northern manufacturers had held since the 1820s to demand protection for their industries from the federal government, the Southern Commercial Convention was intended to demand the South's fair share of government revenue in the form of internal improvements in the Mississippi Valley, the productive core of the cotton revolution that stretched from Mobile, Alabama, to Manchester, England. Premised on Calhoun's argument that the combined effect of the tariff and unequal federal spending amounted to a redistribution of wealth from the South to the North, their demands also revealed the desire of planters in the Mississippi Valley to build up New Orleans as a direct-to-Europe commercial hub that could rival New York.[4]

The obvious problem was that many southern Democrats had spent the last fifteen years decrying federally funded internal improvements as unconstitutional, and few had been as explicit about this as Calhoun. In his address, Calhoun did not take long to ask the question on everyone's minds—"How far the aid of the General Government can be invoked to the improvement of the navigation of the Mississippi and its great navigable tributaries?" The Mississippi was no ordinary river, he pointed out. Its waters and those of its tributaries reached into eighteen states, connecting the entire South and West to the Gulf of Mexico. Furthermore, "Fulton's invention"—the steamboat—had transformed the river and its tributaries into a commercial highway amounting to an "inland sea." When it came to internal improvements, Calhoun argued, the Mississippi should be considered in the same light as the Gulf of Mexico and the Atlantic coast, where the federal government had uncontroversially established and carried out numerous aids to navigation and commerce: dredging harbors, building lighthouses, and establishing naval stations. Due to the Mississippi's vast size, such projects were "beyond the power of individuals or separate states," but would benefit a large number of states more or less equally, making the improvements an appropriate use of federal power and money. Calhoun was clear that he was "utterly opposed" to other proposals. Harbors, for instance, must remain state projects since they were essential to state sovereignty. The nullification and abolitionist mail crises had proved that.[5]

Calhoun may have drawn some of his ideas, including depth markers, lighthouses, and a canal connecting the Mississippi to the Great Lakes, from a pamphlet published before the convention by the Virginia free trader and naval booster Mathew Fontaine Maury. Calhoun knew Maury from their common efforts to bolster American naval power during the Tyler administration. A decade later, in a book that made his name as an oceanographer, Maury would famously describe the existence of "rivers in the sea," arguing that the Mississippi Valley, the Gulf of Mexico, and the Amazon all formed part of the same huge water system, resonating perfectly with Calhoun's description of the Father of Waters as an inland ocean.[6]

Nevertheless, Whig critics immediately pounced on the Memphis speech as the most perfect specimen of Calhoun's duplicity, charging that he had found an esoteric justification—the Mississippi an inland sea!—for an idea that he would have gravely opposed on principle had it come from any other quarter. The speech also horrified the so-called "Bluffton Boys" back in South Carolina, led by Robert Barnwell Rhett, as well as other strict constructionists, who thought Calhoun was playing fast and loose with the Constitution. "Your Memphis speech has given…some uneasiness," the former South Carolina congressman Franklin Elmore wrote from Columbia, reporting that many of Calhoun's allies in the state were worried "as they understood you to have changed your views on Int[ernal] Imp[rovements]."[7]

If nothing else, the Memphis speech was certainly an example of how Calhoun could still think creatively within the constraints of a limited view of federal power. He still held that the federal government could not engage in the kind of vast infrastructure projects that he had once envisioned, but at Memphis he maintained that the federal government could play a role in removing obstacles to trade and commerce too big for states to tackle alone. He still framed the project as a national, or Unionist, one, but in reality the Mississippi Valley connected the South and the West in a way that Calhoun saw as essential to counterbalancing burgeoning northern economic and political power.

Since leaving the State Department in March, Calhoun had spent the intervening months in South Carolina, but by the time he gave his Memphis address, his return to the Senate was certain. Some of his friends were clearly worried that once there he might manifest his contrarian tendencies and oppose the most Calhounite presidential platform that the country had yet seen. They were right to be worried—Polk's bellicose rhetoric about Oregon genuinely dismayed Calhoun. He believed he had been close to settling the Oregon issue peaceably, and feared that an unnecessary war with England over Oregon would also give Mexico, covertly supported by England, an opening to reclaim Texas. Without Calhoun in the Senate, James Gadsden also warned him, the Democrats would have no match for Daniel Webster. So, in November, Calhoun accepted Senator Daniel Huger's offer to step aside so that Calhoun could take his place, and the South Carolina legislature immediately elected him back to his old seat. Anna, for one, was relieved when she heard the news. "I think the life is the one you are so accustomed to," she wrote, "that your health might suffer from the change of habits." Calhoun always said that he would rather give up politics and live the life of a planter, but Anna knew him better than he knew himself.[8]

That summer Richard Pakenham—under unclear instructions from his superior, Lord Aberdeen—had rejected the Polk administration's offer to settle the Oregon boundary at the 49th parallel. Polk's offer exposed the reality that he had always been willing to compromise over Oregon, but Pakenham's unexpected rejection prompted Polk to call on Congress to revoke the joint British-American occupation of the territory, a step that would have left war as the only option to settle the dispute. Ironically, the rest of Polk's annual message to Congress that year was practically a brief for Calhoun's political agenda over the last fifteen years, and some of Calhoun's closest allies, including Francis Pickens and George McDuffie, praised the message with unrestrained enthusiasm. Meanwhile, on Wall Street, stock prices tumbled in anticipation of war with England.[9]

Calhoun arrived in Washington on December 20 and immediately called on Polk, who recorded in his diary, "The impression left on my mind is very strong that Mr. Calhoun will be very soon in opposition to my administration." Others clearly pinned their hopes for peace on Calhoun. "The balance of power between conservative and safe action and extreme ultraism probably rests with Mr. Calhoun and his friends," noted the *Baltimore American*. Across the Atlantic, the *London Times* hoped that Calhoun would be able to anchor an opposition to the administration and "defeat the party who are clamorous for war."[10]

The first decisive moment came on December 30, when Calhoun responded to resolutions from Indiana senator Edward Hannegan declaring that to settle for anything less than all of Oregon would be an "abandonment" of American honor. In response, Calhoun proclaimed that he was "for peace so long as peace can be preserved without a surrender of our national honor," and for negotiation "as long as there may be a possibility of an adjustment by negotiation." If war must come, the responsibility should lie with Great Britain.[11]

Over the next few weeks a peace party made up of Whigs like Daniel Webster and Calhounite Democrats coalesced around Calhoun, who relentlessly pressured friends and allies into line, while war hawks and those aligned with the administration fumed and guessed at his motives. Was he trying to prevent the Democratic Party from uniting around Polk to further his own presidential hopes? Had he made a secret deal with Great Britain as Tyler's secretary of state to settle for half of Oregon in return for all of Texas? Or, as one historian speculated, did Calhoun see in Oregon another opportunity to sow sectional discord?[12] Perhaps he simply wanted to avoid a war with the South's biggest trading partner at a moment when cotton prices were finally rising?[13]

The human capacity for self-deception is nearly boundless, and Calhoun's ability to rationalize his actions was virtuosic, but his own conception of himself as adhering strictly to principles no matter the consequences sometimes produced results that could seem by turns noble, stubborn, suicidal, or delusional. As R. M. T. Hunter, one of Calhoun's closest allies and the author of his 1844 campaign biography, once observed, "He in most cases thought he could defend successfully what he believed to be true. By this habit he often disturbed his friends."[14] James Henry Hammond, who had a nose for ulterior motives almost as refined as John Quincy Adams's, thought he saw this tendency in Calhoun's actions on Oregon. "Calhoun has taken a noble stand...& breasted the popular current...If he goes through with this without flinching I shall rank his qualities far higher than I have done. He is the Ajax of the peace party."[15]

There were also good reasons for Calhoun's actions besides those proposed by his political enemies. Calhoun had believed for years that the status quo—maintaining the joint occupancy arrangement with Britain in Oregon—actually worked to American advantage as American settlers streamed into the territory, making a settlement on American terms inevitable. "*Time* is acting for us," he had declared in an 1843 speech on Oregon, noting that nothing was required to accomplish American supremacy in Oregon but a "wise and masterly inactivity."[16] During the whole Oregon affair he corresponded with Louis McLane, the American minister in London, who turned to Calhoun in despair when he perceived a willingness on the British side to settle at the 49th parallel that was not being reciprocated by Polk either out of principle, politics, or pique.[17]

From McLane, Thomas Green Clemson, and Francis Lieber, a German-born political philosopher then teaching at South Carolina College, Calhoun also knew that under pressure to abate the ongoing Irish famine by opening the British market to foreign grain, British prime minister Robert Peel planned to propose a repeal of the infamous Corn Laws in England at the exact moment that Polk was pushing tariff reform in America. This held the potential to usher in the era of unrestricted free trade that Calhoun had been envisioning for nearly two decades, if only peace between the two nations could be preserved. Peel proposed this vastly consequential measure to Parliament on January 27, 1846. This aspect of Calhoun's course was understood even across the Atlantic in Ireland, where the Dublin *Freeman's Journal* explained his course to its readers by calling him "the great leader of American freetraders."[18]

After weeks of diplomatic back-and-forth, and in the face of British naval mobilization, Polk finally hinted that he would submit any British proposal to the Senate for consideration. All eyes on both sides of the Atlantic turned to the Senate, looking for a signal as to what the response to a British proposal would be.

On the morning of March 16 spectators poured into Washington as word spread that Calhoun would make a major speech. The *Richmond Enquirer* reported that "the ladies had complete possession of the circular gallery" by eight o'clock in the morning, while crowded trains and steamboats brought spectators from Baltimore, Alexandria, and as far away as New York City. Four hours before the speech the Senate galleries were packed.[19]

Calhoun had opposed the repeal of the joint occupancy agreement between the United States and Great Britain in December when it seemed tantamount to a declaration of war, but that day in the Senate he announced his support for a proposal to terminate the joint occupation agreement while also clearly stating a preference for "amicable settlement." In one of the most important speeches of his career, he gave a sweeping meditation on the relationship between principles, policy, and circumstances, the effects of war on a free society, and the engines of progress in the modern world.

Explaining his reversal, Calhoun declared, "To persist in acting in the same way under circumstances essentially different, would be folly and obstinacy, and not consistency…It is the consistency of a quack, which would be sure to kill the patient." In December, with no prospect of compromise, repeal had been unwise. Now, with public opinion in favor of compromise, the Peel and Polk governments both hinting at it, and a clear statement of the Senate's preference, repeal seemed only the necessary prelude to peace. Calhoun had been loudly criticized by Senator William Allen of Ohio for the contrast between his moderation on Oregon and his belligerence and aggressive action on Texas, while others had mocked his call for "masterly inactivity" on Oregon. Alluding to criticism, Calhoun explained that "in the case of Texas, time was against us, in that of Oregon, time was with us." With a scornful glance at Allen, Calhoun proclaimed, "He who cannot understand the difference between an inactivity like this, and mere stupid inaction…is still in the horn-book of political science."

Even if it was successful, a war with England over Oregon would have disastrous effects on American political and social institutions. By financing such a war, he warned, "we would be plunged into the paper system as deeply as we were in the days of the revolution," and the real costs would fall on "labor" while the massive profits of government contracts would go to bankers and war profiteers "who struck not a blow, nor lost a drop of blood in the contest." The demands of winning the war would "obliterate the line of distinction between…the Federal and State governments" and success itself would be no blessing since it would lend to the American mind a bent for conquest "totally inconsistent with the genius of our own system of government."

More than all this, war was the enemy of progress. During the period of peace since the War of 1812 and the defeat of Napoleon, Americans and Europeans had harnessed the energy of "the two great agents of the physical world," steam and electricity, with incredible results. Like many of his contemporaries, Calhoun was particularly struck by the recent invention of the telegraph. "Within the same period," he said, "electricity, the greatest and most diffused of all known physical agents, has been made the instrument for the transmission of thoughts. I will not say with the rapidity of lightning, but by lightning itself. Magic wires are stretching themselves in all directions over the earth, and when their mystic meshes shall have been united and perfected, our globe itself will become endowed with sensitiveness, so that whatever touches on any one point, will be instantly felt on every other." As a young man in the wake of a different war Calhoun had imagined the mail and newspapers coursing along a national transportation network, diminishing the distance and differences between citizens, and now the telegraph fired his imagination with the same possibilities.

Like many of his fellow countrymen, Calhoun imagined material, technological, and moral progress as inseparably linked, and all three in his view depended on peace. "As great as it is," he said of the progress of the past thirty years, "it is but the commencement—the dawn of a new civilization, more refined, more elevated, more intellectual, more moral, than the present and all preceding it." Did his colleagues want to be responsible for giving up this future by plunging the nation into an unnecessary war? "Although wars may at times be necessary," he warned, "yet peace is a positive good, and war is a positive evil." As Calhoun sat down, a quiet murmur of approval rippled through the galleries.[20]

To judge from his surviving correspondence, Calhoun's Oregon speech struck a chord throughout the country, but especially in the commercial centers of the North. One New Yorker "connected with the Commercial Interests of this country" gushed that Calhoun's speech, "at this crisis of our national affairs, is like the shadow of a great Rock to a weary traveler in a foreign land..."[21] Francis Lieber reported to Calhoun that he had read the speech to his senior class at South Carolina College as an example of the highest expression of statesmanship and political economy. And with a sense of relief that there was at least one sane American left, the *London Times* reported the speech as "eminently pacific and courageous."[22]

Five weeks later, on April 23, Congress approved the termination of joint occupancy with an amendment pushing for a peaceful resolution. When the British returned a proposal to settle the Oregon boundary at the 49th parallel, Polk slyly submitted the proposal to the Senate *before* signing it, something he did not have to do constitutionally but which allowed him to preserve his bona fides with the war hawks in his party by pretending to yield to the will of the coalition that Calhoun had painstakingly manufactured over the previous five months. The Senate soon approved the proposal, and Polk hurriedly sent the ratified treaty off to England.[23]

NOBODY IN WASHINGTON KNEW it—the magic wires of the telegraph had not yet stretched all the way to Texas—but the day after Congress approved ending the joint occupancy of Oregon, eleven American soldiers under the command of General Zachary Taylor were killed in a skirmish with Mexican forces on the banks of the Rio Grande in territory claimed by both the United States and Mexico.

Calhoun saw the issues of Oregon and Mexico as inseparably linked. During the whole Oregon crisis he warned that a war with England over Oregon would soon involve Mexico, which would take the opportunity to reclaim Texas, while peace with England would leave Mexico no choice but to settle its disputed boundary with the United States. "I trust," he announced in his March 16 speech, "that when we come to settle it, we will deal generously with her, and that we will prove ourselves too just and magnanimous to take advantage of her feeble condition."[24] Since Calhoun had played a central role annexing Texas, a measure Henry Clay had called "identical with war with Mexico," Calhoun's lofty hopes for peace sounded a disingenuous note. He was also significantly out of step with popular sentiment in favor of a war with Mexico, which by that spring had reached a frenzied pitch. If

Polk went to war with Mexico, nobody would be able to claim that he was going against the will of the people.[25]

When he learned earlier that year that Polk had ordered Taylor into the disputed Nueces Strip, Calhoun immediately saw that the president was trying to provoke an incident, but he was afraid that breaking with Polk openly at a crucial juncture in the Oregon debate would derail negotiations and lead to war with England, which he viewed as an even greater danger.[26] Calhoun also no doubt realized that he was on thin ice in opposing Polk since as secretary of state he had found his own justifications for sending the American military into the Republic of Texas to suppress the threat of Indians, who obligingly acted up just at the moment the United States needed to intimidate Mexico.[27]

On May 11 Polk sent a message to the Senate declaring that a state of war existed with Mexico, which he claimed had "shed American blood on American soil." His supporters ingeniously attached this declaration as a preamble to a bill appropriating support for the military, making opposition an act of political suicide. By the time the bill reached the Senate, John Quincy Adams and thirteen other antislavery Representatives had already taken a stand, voting against the bill in the House, where it nevertheless passed overwhelmingly.[28] When it reached the Senate, Calhoun asked for more time to read the documents accompanying the bill, but objected strongly to Polk's language that a war already existed. "It is *our* sacred duty to make war," he declared to his colleagues, "and it is for *us* to determine whether war shall be declared or not."[29]

The next morning, May 12, Calhoun wrote his son-in-law Thomas Green Clemson "I…have not made up my mind definitively as to the stand I shall take." A vote for the bill would affirm what he viewed as an incredibly dangerous precedent—that an American president could unilaterally declare war and belatedly ask for congressional approval. But to vote against the bill, especially as a nominal Democrat and a member of the president's party, would be to follow a principle into political terra incognita.[30]

By that afternoon he had made up his mind. Speaking several times during the extended debate Calhoun declared that he was willing to vote for supplies "on the spot," but he could no more vote for the preamble than he could "plunge a dagger into [my] own heart." Polk had usurped the war authority of Congress and now expected Congress to approve the "monstrous" act, but Calhoun declared he would not "agree to make war on Mexico by declaring war on the Constitution." The precedent was too dangerous. He would not vote for the bill. Many others who felt the same, including Thomas Hart Benton and even an ailing George McDuffie, eventually felt compelled to vote for it out of regard for public opinion and their own political existence. But as the votes were called out Calhoun sat in silent protest as the bill passed 42 to 2, making him the only Democrat to not give his assent. "The precedent is pregnant with evil," he wrote three days later in disgust to a friend in Charleston. "It sets the example, which will enable all future presidents to bring about a state of things, in which Congress shall be forced, without deliberation, or reflection, to declare war...In a word, it divests Congress virtually of the war making power, & transfers it to the president." On May 13 Polk issued a proclamation that a state of war existed between the United States and Mexico.[31]

Calhoun's stubborn stand against Polk's war threw many of his friends into despair at the thought that he had wasted all the political capital recently gained by his stand on Oregon. His old nullification ally James Hamilton Jr. wrote delicately that he was undoubtedly right on principle, "but whether it was *expedient* to be *rigorously right* is another Question." Why couldn't Calhoun have spoken out against the war but voted for the bill, as every other South Carolinian in Congress had? Another friend remarked in private that his stance was "perfectly suicidal." Calhoun agreed that his actions had made him temporarily unpopular, writing to James Edward, "It has, for the present, weakened me with the party & the unthinking portion of the community." But time would tell, as it usually did. "I have no apprehension as to the final result," he wrote.[32]

Back in South Carolina, the *Charleston Mercury* predictably applauded Calhoun's actions while the *Charleston Courier* criticized opponents of the war and issued a full-throated call for conquest of Mexico. All this Calhoun expected. More disturbing was a report that at a public meeting in Edgefield, Francis Pickens had sneeringly denounced his course on the war and proposed resolutions supporting the administration. Convened by a small group from the radical upper reaches of South Carolina politics frustrated by Calhoun's refusal to nullify the 1842 tariff, his speech in Memphis, and now his stand on the war, the meeting at Edgefield momentarily brought to the fore some of the fissures and frustrations engendered by Calhoun's attempts to keep the state unified behind him.

The moment was soon over, as even newspapers that did not usually support Calhoun rushed to denounce the meeting and prominent men in the state tripped over each other to deny their involvement. "I shall not deign to utter a word, or raise a finger against him," Calhoun wrote Anna about Pickens's "painful" betrayal, "but go on quietly discharging my duty, and leave him to his fate." When Pickens called on Calhoun in Washington that August, Calhoun received him "coldly," refusing to accept Pickens's loud protestations of innocence and loyalty. A few months later James Henry Hammond observed that when it came to South Carolina politics Pickens was "utterly dead," his example serving as a warning to others. The full repercussions of his stand on the war were yet to be seen, but Calhoun could at least be sure that South Carolina stood behind him.[33]

EVEN IN THE MIDST of the Oregon and Mexico crises, Calhoun was hard at work trying to cement an alliance between the South and the West, chairing a select committee charged with shaping a new public lands bill. He seemed determined not to let Polk out-Calhoun him altogether, although that is exactly what happened.

On June 26 he submitted the select committee's report on the Mississippi River to the Senate, taking many of the same positions he had outlined in his speech at the commercial convention in Memphis, supported by reams of research.[34] Along with the report Calhoun introduced a bill to authorize a federal survey of the Mississippi River, which was then attached to a massive internal improvement bill. In the end, though, his bill in the Senate lost out to a similar measure from the House that took a more scattershot approach, providing funding for local projects all over the West. Polk vetoed that bill, objecting that the Constitution did not give the federal government the power to directly finance "neighborhood" construction projects. Despite the fact that Polk's logic was indistinguishable from his own longstanding objections to "merely local" internal improvements, Calhoun chose to see the veto as a defeat for Polk and a potential victory for his vision of a limited but still expansive federal role in internal improvements.[35]

Polk's crowning success that summer was a reduction of tariff rates in the form of the so-called Walker tariff, which took its name from Polk's secretary of the treasury, Robert J. Walker, who wrote an eight-hundred-page report arguing that reducing tariff duties would actually increase, not decrease, government revenue. The Walker tariff also abolished the hated minimum tax on cotton textiles, the last bastion of protection for northern manufacturers. In the weeks before the tariff passed, news arrived from Britain that Prime Minister Robert Peel had successfully repealed the Corn Laws, opening a vast market to western grain farmers (who would, in turn, buy British cottons) and inaugurating an era of free trade that Calhoun had been advocating for the past two decades. When the Walker tariff seemed certain to pass that July, Richard Cobden, the leader of the Anti–Corn Law League, sent Calhoun a personal note of congratulations on achieving their common vision.[36] One American observer marveled that "the simultaneous triumph of free trade in the United States and Great Britain…is the greatest event of our age." Yet Calhoun could not help notice that Polk received most of the credit.[37]

Even more galling was the fact that Polk's tariff victory undermined Calhoun's public lands bill. After shuttling back and forth between the House and Senate for weeks, upheld by the same southern and western coalition that was also propelling tariff reform, in early August the bill was unexpectedly defeated in the House, where it had passed earlier that summer. The cause of the defeat was a group of southern Democrats, Polk loyalists, who had at first supported the bill in order to win western support for the Walker tariff, but abandoned it once the tariff was safely passed, leading to furious denouncements by westerners and fracturing the South-West coalition that Calhoun had tried so hard to forge over the previous year.[38]

By the end of the session Polk had succeeded in passing a domestic political agenda almost indistinguishable from Calhoun's, including not only tariff reform but, in the last days of the session, an Independent Treasury bill that would control the federal government's relationship to the banking system until the early twentieth century. Meanwhile, Calhoun's attempts to further his own vision of internal improvements and public lands reform and forge an enduring tie between the West and the South had failed. The contrast rankled.[39]

BY THE END OF the summer the news of American military victories on fronts in Mexico, California, and New Mexico led Calhoun and many others to hope that a speedy end to the war was at hand. After two quick victories at Palo Alto and Resaca de la Palma in early May, Zachary Taylor crossed the Rio Grande and occupied Matamoros. News of Taylor's victories sent war fever surging throughout the country. "Our people are like a young man of 18," Calhoun wrote Clemson when the news reached Washington, "full of health & vigor & disposed for adventure of any description, but without wisdom or experience to guide him."[40] By mid-August General Stephen Kearny had taken Santa Fe, in New Mexico, and in California American naval forces and an improvised force of American soldiers and settlers under the command of Captain John C. Frémont were in control of Monterey, Yerba Buena (modern San Francisco), as well as the port of Los Angeles. In September, Zachary Taylor would thrill the country with another spectacular victory at the strategically important provincial city of Monterrey in Mexico proper.

The session was about to end when Polk submitted a surprise request for $2 million for the purpose of negotiating with Mexico, the first open admission that he would seek territorial acquisitions from the war. The request was a breaking point for a group of northern Democratic representatives, including a perpetually disheveled, tobacco-chewing representative from Pennsylvania named David Wilmot, who put forward an amendment that echoed the famous Northwest Ordinance of 1787, proposing "that neither slavery nor involuntary servitude shall ever exist" in the territories gained from Mexico in the war. The House passed the amendment 83 to 64, and then narrowly approved the amended bill along starkly sectional lines, sending it to the Senate, which left the fuse burning until Congress reconvened in December.[41]

The Wilmot Proviso, as it soon became known, represented the reemergence of an impulse as old as the Northwest Ordinance and the Missouri Compromise to limit the spread of slavery on American soil. By 1846, however, this impulse had taken a new and more democratic form, adapted to the expansionist mood of the country. "I make no war upon the South nor upon slavery," Wilmot would declare at the next session of Congress. "I have no…morbid sympathy for the slave. I plead the cause of the rights of white freemen. I would preserve for free white labor a fair country, a rich inheritance, where the sons of toil of my own race and color, can live without the disgrace which association with negro slavery brings upon free labor." Advocates of "free soil," as this particular brand of antislavery came to be called, were not abolitionists, although most believed slavery was an evil and many hoped it would eventually wither away if constrained to its present geography. Their aim was stop its spread, believing that slavery devalued white labor and lent disproportionate political influence to the "slave power." It was an ideology perfectly articulated to appeal to the white working-class elements within the northern Democratic Party that had traditionally favored Calhoun, as well as the western Democrats he had hoped to weld to the South with his failed efforts at land reform and internal improvements. In an instant, David Wilmot provoked a fateful realignment in American politics.[42]

AT HOME THAT FALL Calhoun predicted that when Congress reconvened, "Wilmot's proposition will prove an apple of discord, that will do much to divide the party." He saw the proviso as a manifestation of the "taint" of abolitionism that was spreading in the North and should ideally be addressed there. "The evil is with you, & must be remedied there," he advised Henry Dearborn of Massachusetts. "The South is looking on, not without interest...but calmly & without dread for herself...She has made up her mind." If men like Dearborn did not succeed, Calhoun warned, disunion would follow.[43]

Calhoun had closely followed burgeoning antislavery sentiment in the North, including the proliferation of so-called personal liberty laws that carefully employed the antislavery jurisprudence of Supreme Court Justice Joseph Story. Story had brilliantly adapted the "freedom principle" to the American system of government in the 1842 case of *Prigg v. Pennsylvania* by simultaneously affirming the fugitive slave clause in the Constitution while also arguing that states could prohibit state officials from cooperating with its enforcement. Massachusetts passed the first law doing so in 1843, followed by Vermont and New Hampshire. By 1848 Rhode Island and Pennsylvania would follow.[44]

Calhoun also closely watched developments in national institutions like the Baptist and Methodist churches, which split into northern and southern branches over the issue of slavery in 1844 and 1845. After reading about the Methodists' fight over the nomination of a slaveholder as bishop in New York City in 1844, Calhoun invited the Reverend

William Capers of South Carolina to stop in Washington on the way home, calling the split an event of "vital importance."[45] The next year when Methodist Henry Bascom wrote a pamphlet defending slave-holding Christians and explaining that the southern Methodists had to withdraw because "the judgment of a majority became the only rule of action and standard of right," Calhoun eagerly recommended the pamphlet to Thomas Green Clemson and James Henry Hammond, urging Hammond to publicize the pamphlet in the *Southern Review*. Hammond wrote back incredulously, pointing out that Bascom had violated the most important doctrine in the proslavery catechism by calling slavery an "evil." Calhoun acknowledged Hammond's point but maintained it was the best that could be expected from Kentucky. "I concur in the opinion, that we ought to take the highest ground on the subject of African slavery," he wrote Hammond, "…but we must not break with, or throw off those who are not yet prepared to come up to our standard, especially on the exterior limits of the slaveholding states."

Calhoun reminded Hammond of how much had changed in the last ten years. "I look back with pleasure on the progress, which sound principles have made within the last 10 years in respect to the relation between the two races," he wrote. "All, with a very few exceptions, defended [slavery] a short time since on the ground of a necessary evil… S.C. was not much sounder 20 years ago, than Kentucky now is." When it came to Kentucky and the Methodists, a denomination that had publicly questioned slavery in the South when Calhoun was a young man, Calhoun would take any allies he could get.[46]

BY THE TIME CONGRESS reconvened in December, there were signs that some Americans were growing tired of the war as casualty lists lengthened and accounts of unsanitary camp conditions and atrocities against Mexican civilians began to filter back to the home front. Even the *Charleston Mercury* reprinted stories of violence and rape committed by American volunteers against unarmed Mexican men and women. Meanwhile, despite the American people's changing mood, Polk had begun raising the possibility in cabinet meetings that the United States should take all of Mexico north of the 26th parallel.[47]

A few days before Christmas 1846, Polk invited Calhoun to dinner to sound him out. Polk thought the dinner went well, writing in his diary that Calhoun was in "good humour" and willing to consider the annexation of the parts of New Mexico and California already occupied by Americans, although, according to Polk, he "cared but little" for anything south of this. On only one point had Calhoun been adamant— no treaty could include restrictions on slavery. He agreed with Polk that slavery was unlikely to spread to New Mexico and California, but warned that if the Wilmot Proviso were included, he would vote against any treaty on principle.[48]

Calhoun's warning to Polk was only one sign that by the end of 1846 the issue of the war and the sectional conflict over slavery had become intertwined in his mind. As he wrote Anna a few days after the dinner, "the scheme of the North is that the South shall do all the fighting & pay all the expense," while the North reserved all the lands gained in the war to themselves through the Wilmot Proviso. It was the mirror opposite of northern anxieties about a war to extend slavery for the benefit of slaveholders. The South must defeat the Wilmot Proviso, Calhoun wrote, "even should the Union be rent asunder." In a summation of his state of mind, he wrote, "I desire above all things to save the whole [Union]; but if that cannot be, to save the portion where Providence has cast my lot." If only Polk had not taken the "rash step of rushing into war," he lamented, the whole crisis could have been averted.[49]

Any hope that Polk may have had that Calhoun would be a loyal foot soldier soon evaporated. In February, Calhoun and a few allies opposed Polk's so-called Ten Regiments bill to raise more troops, leading Polk to fume to his diary, "I now consider him the most mischievous man in the Senate to my administration." Distracted by Polk's ire, historians have often overlooked the fact that the two men agreed on much. Their differences revolved mainly around the extent of American expansionism and the methods that Polk employed to further his goals. As he had told Polk that evening in December, Calhoun was perfectly content for the United States to take vast amounts of land from Mexico as long as the South's rights to the spoils were protected. He understood that public opinion would never settle for merely adjusting the border between Mexico and Texas, and he never joined the emerging "No Territory" coalition in the Whig Party. He had opposed the war as unwise and dangerous, and he feared its effects, but once it began Calhoun's course was to blunt the most extreme parts of Polk's ambitions on the one hand while generally supporting the military measures necessary to fight the war on the other. Certainly Calhoun was no Henry David Thoreau, who refused to pay taxes to support a war to extend slavery and wrote his famous essay on civil disobedience in the midst of it.[50]

Despite the fact that no one could mistake Calhoun for an antiwar activist, many Americans saw his independent course over the next year as nearly the only thing standing between Polk and the complete conquest of Mexico. After another dinner that December, a few weeks before their definitive break, Polk had asked Calhoun to his private office, where Calhoun listened as Polk presented his plan of a "crushing movement with a great Army upon the city of Mexico." Calhoun immediately objected, Polk wrote in his diary, and raised instead the idea of establishing a defensive line holding the territory gained so far in the war.[51] On February 9, 1847, after breaking with Polk on the Ten Regiments bill, Calhoun made the case for his defensive line to the Senate. Above all, the United States should avoid a conquest of Mexico, "a sister republic" that sought to imitate the United States. "We ought, in my opinion, to inflict the least possible amount of injury on Mexico," Calhoun declared. "I hold, indeed, that we ought to be just and liberal to her." The United States could not conquer or rule Mexico without doing irreparable moral and material damage to herself, and in any case, a failed state on her southern border would be a constant danger. "I hold that there is a mysterious connection between the fate of this country and that of Mexico," Calhoun announced, "so much so that her independence and capability of sustaining herself are almost as essential to our prosperity, and the maintenance of our institutions as they are to hers. Mexico is to us the forbidden fruit; the penalty of eating it would be to subject our institutions to political death."

Calhoun laid out the effects of eating the forbidden fruit in frightening detail. First were the massive challenges of a military campaign waged not just to take and hold territory, but to subdue a "race of people renowned above all others for their obstinacy...a people whose hereditary pride is, that they rescued their country when overrun by the Moors, after a war of seven or eight centuries." Calhoun would deploy different ethnic and racial language about Mexico to support his argument in the coming months, but here he emphasized the "pertinacity" of those Mexicans of Spanish descent shaped by the memory of the Reconquista and the certainty of a "guerrilla war" even if the United States succeeded in the formal sense.

And in the event of victory, what then? "Shall we annex the States of Mexico to our Union? Can we incorporate a people so dissimilar from us in every respect—so little qualified for free and popular government—without certain destruction to our political institutions?" He was especially doubtful that a nation of eight million Catholics, "all concentrated under a powerful and wealthy priesthood," could be assimilated into the country without provoking a religious civil war. No, if Mexico was conquered it would have to be ruled, and the executive branch would gain infinite power, influence, and opportunities for patronage from this arrangement. The effects would be disastrous. Much better to choose the certainty of the defensive line, which would "once again place us on *terra firma*, and enable us to see beyond the dark curtain which is now suspended between us and the future."[52]

Calhoun's proposal went nowhere, but the attacks on him in the Senate over the next two weeks showed that Polk's supporters feared his influence was growing at a moment when the public mood on the war was shifting. The most serious attack came from the new senator from Texas, Sam Houston. A loud dresser with a louder personality, and an expansionist of Polkian proportions, Houston had argued for years that the United States should take all of Mexico, a position he would maintain for the rest of his life. That day Houston asserted that a defensive line would require a lot more men and money than Calhoun had implied, and flourished a letter Calhoun had written as secretary of state promising military protection to Texas before its annexation. How was this any different from what Polk had done, Houston demanded? Calhoun replied dryly that the difference was simple: Polk's actions had started a war and his had not. In response to Houston's claim about the defensive line, Calhoun asked him how many men Texas had needed to prevent invasions from Mexico prior to annexation, and when Houston acknowledged that two small invasions had been easily repelled despite Texas having no standing army, Calhoun let the matter stand, having proven his point.[53]

ON THE SAME DAY he was being attacked by Houston, Calhoun took careful aim at David Wilmot's resurrected proviso, which had been successfully reattached to an appropriations bill in the House a few days before. He offered four anti-Wilmot resolutions declaring territories the common property of the states, asserting that Congress had no right to make any law depriving any state of its full and equal rights to that common territory, and maintaining that any law that deprived citizens of any state "from emigrating with their property into any of the territories of the Union" was a violation of "that perfect equality which belongs to them as members of this Union, and would tend directly to subvert the Union itself."

Introducing the resolutions, Calhoun laid out the plain facts of the changing math of representation in a deeply divided country. The slave-holding states were outnumbered in every part of the government except the Senate, where the recent additions of Texas and Florida gave them a bare equality with nonslaveholding states. Once Iowa and Wisconsin joined the Senate, the free states would hold a majority even there. In the face of these facts, did representatives of the free states really believe that slaveholding states would meekly acquiesce to an amendment that would not only deprive them of their constitutional rights but also assure their permanent minority status in the nation's government? "Can we look to their justice and regard for our interests? I ask, can we rely on that?" Calhoun asked. Would the free states be willing to abide the results if the situation were reversed?

What the South as a whole should do if the issue was pressed, he would not say:

> But I may speak as an individual member of that section of the Union. There is my family and my connexions. There I drew my first breath. There are all my hopes. I am a planter—a cotton planter. I am a southern man and a slaveholder—a kind and merciful one, I trust—and none the worse for being a slaveholder. I say, for one, I would rather meet any extremity upon earth than give up one inch of our equality— one inch of what belongs to us as members of this great republic! What! Acknowledged inferiority! The surrender of life is nothing to sinking down into acknowledged inferiority![54]

Claiming to speak only for himself, Calhoun's visceral personal reaction to the threat of shame in fact dramatized and framed the political threat of the Wilmot Proviso to the South's equal place in the Union in a way that was sure to stir deep psychological and cultural anxieties among southern white men. To submit to Wilmot's terms was to accept the truth of the personal insult it implied—that slaveholders were morally inferior to their fellow Americans—a response that every southern boy was trained from the cradle to abhor as a kind of death. Just as he had done as a young man responding to the insults of Great Britain, and just as he had done during the nullification crisis, Calhoun made clear that he would not submit, and the connection he drew between sectional and personal honor and shame meant that it would be difficult for a southern politician to argue otherwise without incurring the moral taint of submission. No other American politician of the era meditated so deeply on or framed in such stark terms the psychological effects of submission on a people, and this aspect of Calhoun's thought was rooted in his experience as a master. To submit, or to be forced to submit, to shame, was the defining characteristic of a slave.[55]

After Calhoun presented his resolutions, Thomas Hart Benton rose and objected to using up the Senate's time debating "such a string of abstractions." Calhoun immediately shot back, "The Senator says he cannot take up abstractions. The Constitution is an abstraction. Propriety is an abstraction. All the great rules of life are abstractions."[56] He did not add that honor and shame, too, were abstractions, but ones that, as every southerner understood, could have very real consequences.

The Senate never voted on Calhoun's anti-Wilmot resolutions, but they voted down the Wilmot Proviso itself and sent the appropriations bill back to the House without it, where it passed on March 3, the last day of the session. At that moment news was speeding toward Washington of Zachary Taylor's improbable victory on February 23 at Buena Vista over a vastly superior Mexican force commanded by Mexican president Antonio López de Santa Anna himself. More than seven hundred Americans were killed or wounded at Buena Vista. The dead included the young Henry Clay Jr., whose father opposed the war, as well as Illinois representative John J. Hardin, whose death left his House seat open for his young, ambitious friend, Abraham Lincoln. A few days after the session ended, on March 9, 1847, Winfield Scott landed an American army at Vera Cruz.[57]

WHEN HE ARRIVED IN Charleston on his way home from Washington, Calhoun found Floride waiting for him and large crowds gathered to welcome him home in an atmosphere electrified by the threat of Wilmot's Proviso, which everyone believed was sure to resurface at the next session of Congress. He stayed in Charleston for four days. Despite the now ever-present cough and a hoarse voice, he accepted an invitation to speak one evening to a "crammed" crowd at the Charleston Theatre building, where he ignored the war and focused exclusively on the threat to "our peculiar domestic institution." He may have demurred from charting a course for the whole South in Congress, but he did not shy away that night in Charleston.

The emerging sectional conflict had nothing to do with economic interests, he told the packed theater. "The labor of our slaves does not conflict with the profit of their capitalists, or the wages of their operatives…On the contrary, it greatly increases both" by providing raw material and a large market for the finished goods. Nor did the Wilmot Proviso originate in a fear that slave states would acquire an "undue preponderance" in the national government. (Here Calhoun ignored the fact that many antislavery northerners believed the South *already* had undue influence in the national government thanks to the three-fifths clause.) No, the problem was the two-party system. Only about 5 percent of northerners were true abolitionists, Calhoun declared, basing his estimate on votes cast for the abolitionist Liberty Party in the 1844 presidential election. Another 70 percent viewed slavery as an evil but had no desire to abolish it or to violate the Constitution. But in most northern states the two-party system was nearly equally balanced in a way that made the abolitionist bloc influential far beyond its numbers, leading calculating politicians at the state level to support policies that would appeal to both the abolitionist minority as well as the moderately antislavery majority.

The solution was simple. The South must be united in its response. "Henceforward, let all party distinction among us cease, so long as this aggression on our rights and honor shall continue," Calhoun declared.

The South could turn the cravenness of the two-party system to its advantage by copying the abolitionists in their rigid inflexibility. "As they make the destruction of our domestic institution the paramount question, so let us make, on our part, its safety the paramount question." Once the wire-pulling politicians in both parties realized that no national coalition could be built that included the abolitionists, they would put down this fanatical minority to appease the South in their insatiable lust for the presidency. "Our object," Calhoun declared, straining his weakened voice to be heard, "is to preserve the Union of these States, if it can be done consistently with our rights, safety, and perfect equality with other members of the Union. On this we have a right to insist. Less we cannot take."[58]

That evening in Charleston was another key moment in Calhoun's long and winding career. While it is easy to portray the shift as toward sectionalism, his call was not for a separate southern nation. Instead, roused by the threat of the Wilmot Proviso as he had been by the abolitionist mail crisis in 1835, the tariff in 1828, and the British in 1812, he appealed for the South to present a united front in order to change the current of northern politics and preserve the Union, which in his view was only worth saving as long as it upheld the "perfect equality" of all the states.

OVER THE SUMMER AND into the fall of 1847, as Winfield Scott marched toward Mexico City, Calhoun was focused instead on how to rally the South to meet the larger threat posed by Wilmot's amendment. The summer provided fresh examples of the danger. In June, a Maryland slaveholder named James H. Kennedy was seriously wounded, and later died, when a crowd of mostly African American men and women attacked him in the streets of Carlisle, Pennsylvania, after local officials declined to help or protect him in recovering several fugitive slaves, citing the state's recently passed personal liberty law. Slaveholders in Maryland and Virginia were outraged, not just at

Kennedy's death at the hands of black people, a slaveholder's worst nightmare, but at the potential effects on the value of their enslaved property. "The Law of Pennsylvania referred to, has rendered our slave property throughout Maryland & a large portion of Virginia, utterly insecure & will, if it continues in force a few years longer destroy any further interest that we may feel in that domestic institution," warned Virginia slaveholder Charles Faulkner to Calhoun in July. Calhoun took the Pennsylvania law and Kennedy's death as proof of the severe nature of the threat. "There is not on record a more deliberate and undisguised breach of faith and solemn obligation of Oath," he replied to Faulkner, emphasizing the Constitution as a shared commitment to comity. He then considered the combined effects of personal liberty laws like Pennsylvania's and the Wilmot Proviso in what amounted to a feverish racial nightmare, but a very different one from the race war usually conjured by white southerners. If abolition ever became a reality in such a situation, Calhoun warned, northern states would not let the freed people migrate into their states, preferring to use them as tools to oppress their former masters.

> I see clearly the whole train of calamities, which would befall us...You will be penned in with your black population, as every other slave State will be, while the non-slaveholding states will never cease their agitation until blacks are placed in all respects on an equality, political & socially with their former masters; when they would govern us and our posterity through our former slaves, and their posterity. Think not... that I am deceived. I see the future thus far, if we do not meet & repel the attack, as clearly as I do the rising of the sun tomorrow.[59]

In response to these threats Calhoun cooperated with others alarmed by the threat to start a newspaper—"an independent organ for the defense of Southern rights"—that would provide the southern point of view in Washington, instead of the Democratic or Whig Party line.[60] He also endorsed the idea of a southern convention, something he had resisted before, to show both political parties the united front of the South against abolitionism and bring them to their senses. When Benjamin F. Perry sought his help drafting resolutions for the South Carolina legislature to pass, Calhoun wrote, "I would say the more pointed and emphatick the better. I think nothing ought to be said about compromise. It is one thing to offer a compromise, with a pistol at our breast, and another to acquiesce in one offered to us, for the sake of peace." A compromise that gave anything to northern antislavery feeling would be disastrous, Calhoun warned, "and would but procrastinate the evil day & make it tenfold worse. Indeed a compromise, at best, is but a surrender on our part."[61]

As Calhoun made clear to correspondents that summer, he viewed the Wilmot Proviso as merely the representation of the real threat. "It is not sufficient to defeat the Wilmot Proviso," he wrote in September, pointing to the "late act of the legislature of Pennsylvania" and other personal liberty laws in the North, as "a more palpable, if possible, violation of the constitution." Even antislavery societies and newspapers formed in other states with "the express intention of questioning and disturbing our right in property" were "a direct breach of faith and violation of the terms of the compact." Here Calhoun went beyond a legal view of the Constitution to his sense of the Union as a kind of peace pact between sovereigns in international law, an agreement that only endured as long as both sides held up their end of the bargain, and which had no enforceable terms beyond voluntary cooperation. To defeat the Wilmot Proviso without addressing this deeper rot would be like bandaging a gangrenous wound. "It would put us off our guard, without removing or even diverting the danger."[62]

Calhoun was equally clear that the power of Congress could not be used to address the problem by coercing the states. It would have been hard for the author of nullification to openly argue anything else. "Against this flagrant breach of faith…the constitution affords no effective remedy," he wrote in a public letter to a group of planters in Alabama in October, "[and] our principles and safety will not permit us to resort, for remedy, to the principles of the Force Bill."

The trick then, as usual, was to come up with a solution that steered between the seductive appeal to federal power and the dangers of disunion. "In my opinion," he wrote to the Alabama planters, "a high and sacred regard for the Constitution, as well as the dictates of wisdom, make it our duty…not to resort to or even to look to that extreme remedy [disunion], until all others have failed."

Instead, in addition to a southern convention, Calhoun recommended closing southern ports to northern shipping and commerce while keeping open the Mississippi to avoid alienating western states. But here, too, southern unity was everything. "Without that," he wrote, "it would be ineffective."[63] Outside South Carolina, as usual, the signs were not encouraging. "This State is wide awake," he wrote in September, while lamenting to a correspondent in New Orleans that all the Deep South states seemed to be in a "state of profound torpor," insensible to the danger he saw so clearly and distracted by the war.[64] Over the summer and fall news of more American victories and a growing list of casualties steadily trickled in from Mexico. Before Calhoun departed for Washington, news arrived that Winfield Scott had taken Mexico City in September.

THE SITUATION THAT GREETED Calhoun in Washington in early December 1847 was uncertain and changing rapidly. From Fort Hill, Calhoun had watched with apprehension during the last half of the year as an "All Mexico" movement gained steam in some quarters, pushing for the Polk administration to take even more, perhaps all, land from its southern neighbor. In October, frustrated by Mexico's refusal to negotiate and emboldened by Winfield Scott's capture of Mexico City, Polk seemed to be considering whether the United States might swallow Mexico whole.

But at the same time resistance to the war was growing. Three weeks before Congress reconvened, Henry Clay had given a major speech against the war in Lexington, combining the pathos of a grieving father with an appeal to Americans' sense of justice and fair play in a performance that electrified the nation and took a principled and risky stand against the war. Clay sounded many of the same notes as Calhoun, including his doubts about the racial and religious compatibility of the Mexican and American populations, but the Kentucky slaveholder also declared that he was completely opposed to any war that would add a single slave state to the Union.[65]

Back in South Carolina, Calhoun's political allies were also divided. Some, like the alienated Francis Pickens, applauded Polk's renewed appetite for Mexican territory, while Joel Poinsett and Waddy Thompson, South Carolinians who had both served as US ministers to Mexico, both wrote Calhoun to encourage him to resist Polk's new plot at all costs. Thompson, in particular, took to South Carolina newspapers that fall to publicize his view that slavery could not spread south of the Rio Grande due to the mountainous nature of the terrain. Citing geographer and naturalist Alexander von Humboldt, Thompson argued that cotton and sugar could not be grown in most of Mexico, making the territory unfit for slavery and politically dangerous to the slaveholding states. "It is nakedly a proposition to add fifteen or twenty non slave holding States to our union," Thompson wrote to Calhoun. "Woe to the southern man who lends his aid to that." Thompson would have preferred to stop the war in its tracks and take no territory from Mexico at all, but Calhoun reminded him that large majorities of both parties had voted for the war and that the effect of subsequent American military victories on public opinion "make it impossible, in my opinion, to terminate the war in the manner you propose." In fact, advocating the "no territory" position would only strengthen the All Mexico movement by eliminating a middle ground.[66]

In Polk's annual address to Congress that December, the president denied that he wanted to take all of Mexico, but also announced the failure of negotiations and the recall of the peace commissioner, Nicholas Trist. He argued that the only way to reach an honorable peace in Mexico now was to conquer its stubborn government completely and then allow its more reasonable and peaceful citizens to form a new government under the watchful eye of the American military, after which they would presumably negotiate an acceptable (to the United States) peace. If this failed, Polk hinted strongly, the United States would simply have to occupy the country for the foreseeable future.[67]

Moving to cut off Polk's options, on December 15 Calhoun introduced a simple resolution, "that to conquer Mexico and to hold it either as a Province, or to incorporate it into our Union would be inconsistent with the avowed object for which the war has been prosecuted; a departure from the settled policy of the government; in conflict with its character and genius, and in the end subversive of our free & popular institutions." When William Allen of Ohio accused Calhoun of having joined the "No Territory" Whigs, Calhoun emphatically denied it. He agreed "we may take a part—very large parts of Mexico without touching her nationality." He only wished to avoid "the annihilation of the nationality of Mexico." The Senate scheduled the discussion of Calhoun's resolution for January 4.[68]

If Calhoun needed further evidence that more Mexican territory might result in additional free states and ultimately lead to disaster for the South, he found it in the resolutions of Daniel Dickinson of New York, offered just before his. Dickinson's resolutions proposed that any new territorial governments in Mexico should be able to decide the issue of slavery for themselves, a position that would eventually be called popular sovereignty. Ostensibly a compromise, Calhoun saw the idea as nothing less than the Wilmot Proviso in different clothes. "The Wilmot Proviso is killed," he wrote to former senator Wilson Lumpkin of Georgia, "but be assured, the North is united in the determination, that we shall not have an inch of Mexico."[69]

ON JANUARY 4, CALHOUN made his case against Polk's open-ended prosecution of the war to packed galleries in the Senate. He stood, hardly moving, hands clasped in front of him, speaking as loudly and clearly as his voice could sustain. Two years earlier a Whig newspaper in Boston noted Calhoun's lack of flowery rhetoric on such occasions— "no American eagles, 'patriotism,' and all that kind of thing"—only stripped-down, forceful constructions that drove inexorably toward the conclusion of his argument. "With him every sentence is a blow," the Whig editor observed, speculating that it would take another politician three days to deliver the kind of argument Calhoun could make in ninety minutes.[70]

The blows fell hard and fast. If the American military destroyed the only semblance of working government in Mexico, Calhoun asked, who would they make peace with? "If the war should be so prosecuted, where will be the nationality of Mexico? Where her separate existence?...Gone! We have blotted her from the list of nations. She has become a mere mass of individuals without any political existence." Ridiculing Polk's proposal that a new government could form under American auspices, he declared, "I must say I am at a loss to see how a free and independent Republic can be established in Mexico under the protection and authority of its conquerors... I had always supposed that such a Government must be the spontaneous wish of the people." Further, Calhoun doubted whether Mexico could ever form a free, stable government, even under American protection. "Where are the materials?...Where is the intelligence in Mexico for the construction and preservation of such a government?" The "intelligence and wealth" of Mexico was concentrated in its priests, not a proper population to build a new government, and he thought the planter class, "the owners of the haciendas," were "destitute of the means of forming such a government." Any government formed under such circumstances would have to be supported by American military might, and would collapse as soon as it was withdrawn.

The war had bolstered the reputation of the American military, Calhoun admitted, but it stood to lose its most important asset, the power of its moral example on the world stage. To those who wanted to make the United States into an imperial power on the model of Great Britain, Calhoun warned that instead of Great Britain, America would become Rome, gradually losing its liberties as the demands of empire slowly dragged it down into military despotism and ruin. He asked them to look at the effects of empire on Great Britain, where "the wealth derived from her conquests and provincial possessions may have contributed to swell the overgrown fortunes of the upper classes, but has done nothing to alleviate the pressure on the laboring masses below." The result of this crushing inequality, Calhoun predicted, would be a richly deserved revolution.

Calhoun's greatest fear was that Polk would conquer Mexico and try to incorporate it into the United States, and in response he fused the new racial theories of his day onto the old conservative idea of rights and forms of government as an inheritance.

> We have conquered many of the neighboring tribes of Indians, but we have never thought of holding them in subjection or incorporating them into our Union...Nor have we ever incorporated into the Union any but the Caucasian race. To incorporate Mexico would be the first departure of the kind; for more than half of its population are pure Indians, and by far the larger portion of the residue mixed blood. I protest against the incorporation of such a people. Ours is the Government of the white man.

The "great misfortune" of most of the young republics that had once composed Spanish America, Calhoun declared, was that they had made "the fatal error of placing the colored race on an equality with the white." Only Brazil—a Portuguese colony, a fellow slaveholding nation, and no republic—had escaped this error. Calhoun then took the opportunity to make a broader racial point that, along with his use of the word "Caucasian" for the first time, showed that he had been reading his racial theorists, perhaps the copy of *Crania Aegyptiaca* that Samuel George Morton had sent him four years earlier.

> It is a remarkable fact, in this connection, that in the whole history of the man, as far as my information extends, there is no instance whatever, of any civilized colored race, of any shade, being found equal to the establishment and maintenance of free Government, although by far the largest proportion of the human family is composed of them... Are we to overlook this great fact? Are we to associate with ourselves, as equals, companions, and fellow-citizens, the Indian and mixed races of Mexico? I would consider such association as degrading ourselves and fatal to our institutions.

As shocking as they are to us today, Calhoun's opinions about the capacities of the Mexican people underlay a good deal of the public opposition to a total conquest of Mexico. He was far more attuned to the mainstream of white public opinion on this than he was in his defense of slavery. In the final analysis, American government could not be exported because nonwhite people—a category created by the creation of whiteness itself as a category in the new racial science—were supposed not to have the capacity to form or sustain such a government. Calhoun believed that history and the latest scientific knowledge proved this "fact." He could support taking Oregon, California, and New Mexico on the assumption that they would one day be filled with white people, and thus could be incorporated into the United States, even if they might be free states. But the United States could not conquer and incorporate a nation of nonwhite people without destroying its form of government, and it could not safely hold them as a province or possession because to do so was antithetical to the genius and character of that government.[71]

SOME AMERICANS SAW CALHOUN standing in the breach that winter, sacrificing his presidential hopes and political popularity in order to save the American experiment. "The Caesars are forgotten but Cato lives in imperishable renown," wrote one breathless Mississippian after Calhoun submitted his anti-conquest resolution in December. "You are the true warden on the watch tower." After the January speech, William Emmons of Massachusetts echoed the image, gushing that Calhoun was "a faithful sentinal [*sic*] on the watchtower of American liberty."[72]

Frederick Douglass saw things differently. Writing in his newspaper the *North Star* a few days after Calhoun's speech in January, America's foremost black abolitionist called Calhoun a "faithful sentinel on [slavery's] bloody ramparts, ever vigilant, unwearied, and undeviating in his devotion to the American slave system." Douglass appreciated Calhoun's dissection of "the present false, foul and infernal war," which he also opposed, but what, he asked, could explain Calhoun's opposition to taking all of Mexico when he had been so keen to take Texas? The answer, Douglass believed, was that Calhoun sensed an existential threat to slavery. "Slaveholding has, for years, been the very sun of his political system. Not a measure has been proposed or adopted by him, but has been thoroughly examined in the red light of slavery." Once bold as a lion in slavery's defense, in his old age Calhoun had adopted the cunning of a fox—"He does not abandon his prey, but his mode of catching it"—and he saw that to take all of Mexico and turn it into a slaveholding empire would force a violent reaction in the North that would threaten slavery's very existence.[73]

Attempts to explain Calhoun's course during the war can fall into the trap of a false choice between assigning him the ulterior and simplistic motive of preserving slavery as an economic and social system and granting him his high-minded principles about the deleterious effects of conquest on the "character and genius" of American government. Calhoun himself never shied away from declaring that slavery was essential to the American project that he sought to preserve. As Douglass wrote in the *North Star*, slavery was to Calhoun "the very cornerstone of our republican institutions." Even the North depended on it, Calhoun believed, although indirectly. He openly argued that a "perfect equality" and a balance of power between slave and free states was essential to the preservation of the Union. New free states south of Texas would destroy that balance. Preserving slavery and a balance of power for the South was, in Calhoun's mind, preserving the Union.

Calhoun's position on the war also fit into his broader vision of a new international order, a Western Hemisphere of independent republics dominated by American, not European, influence. Open to American trade, and protective of the international rights of slaveholders, it would be an empire of free trade with America at its head. The United States could enjoy the economic benefits of empire without assuming its burdens.

At the same time it is impossible not to feel the gravity of Calhoun's insights about the unique threat that war and conquest posed to American institutions. His belief that the American system of government would be destroyed by an imperial project that would necessarily hand unprecedented power and patronage to the federal government, particularly the executive branch, is a salutary warning in our own era of endless foreign wars. Even worse, Calhoun believed the war would give American citizens a taste for subjugating neighboring nations. Overlooking what the United States had done to the Indians, he wrote to Anna the day after Christmas, "Our people have undergone a great change. Their inclination is for conquest & empire, regardless of their institutions and liberty...they think they hold their liberty by a divine tenure, which no imprudence, or folly, on their part, can defeat." Freedom, like life, as Calhoun had observed years earlier, was a forced state. It took work, effort, and wisdom to preserve. A people who took it for granted would soon lose it. Even their whiteness could not prevent that.[74]

Even as Calhoun delivered his speech against the All Mexico movement, Polk's peace commissioner Nicholas Trist was disobeying his orders and negotiating a treaty with Mexico in a desperate attempt to end the war short of total conquest. As a young man Trist had studied law with Thomas Jefferson, and he believed the war was a stain on American honor. He would pay the political price for his bravery, and he deserves most of the historical credit for frustrating Polk's boundless ambitions. Still, Calhoun's speech and his careful construction of a middle ground between no territory and total conquest meant that when Trist's treaty unexpectedly appeared in Washington in mid-February outlining a settlement much like the one Polk professed to want, Polk felt that he could not refuse it. He sent it to the Senate on February 21, where it was quickly approved. What Ulysses S. Grant would later call America's most "wicked war" was over.[75]

Two days before Polk sent the treaty to the Senate, John Quincy Adams collapsed on the House floor just after obstinately voting against a resolution commending American military officers for their service during the war. He died two days later. Despite their deep differences over the years, Calhoun served as a pallbearer at his old adversary's funeral. One can only imagine what Adams would have written in his diary about the irony of John C. Calhoun carrying his mortal remains out of the House chamber. Illinois congressman Abraham Lincoln, another opponent of the war, served on the funeral committee. Calhoun did not record his thoughts on Adams's passing, but as he accompanied Adams's casket that day, the thought of his own funeral must have, ever so briefly, run through his mind.[76]

NINETEEN

The Pillar of Fire

IN THE SPRING OF 1848, before Mexico had even ratified Nicholas Trist's treaty, news reached Washington of revolutions spreading like a contagion throughout Europe, drawing many Americans' gaze temporarily away from the brewing fight over the extension of slavery into the territories. "We all, on this side of the Atlantick, look with intense solicitude on the great events, transpiring in Europe, and no one more than myself," Calhoun wrote to Anna. In the first three months of 1848 alone, the growing unrest had already unseated Louis Philippe in France, forced absolutist rulers throughout Italy, Germany, and the Austrian Empire to grant constitutions and call national assemblies, and was in the process of destroying forever the social and political structures of feudalism in central and eastern Europe. By the end of the year the promise of these revolutions would be rolled back by the forces of reaction, but in the spring of 1848 it seemed that the whole world, at home and abroad, was trembling with change.[1]

Realizing that the political moment and his persistent cough meant that he no longer had the luxury of time, Calhoun turned his attention that spring to writing two works that would eventually be published in the year after his death as *A Disquisition on Government* and *A Discourse on the Constitution and Government of the United States*. Together, the two works gave full expression to the political theories that Calhoun had forged over his lifetime. He clearly meant them as successors to famous works of political science like Montesquieu's *Spirit of the Laws*, Locke's second treatise on government, and the *Federalist Papers*. He also meant them as a response to the 1833 and 1834 commentaries of antislavery Supreme Court justice Joseph Story, who had adapted American law to the earthshaking implications of the British Slavery Abolition Act, arguing that slavery could only be established by positive law and that states were not bound to grant slaveholders traveling through their jurisdictions comity under the Constitution.[2]

As he wrote, Calhoun viewed the progress of the European revolutions with the watchful eye of a theorist awaiting the verdict of reality. "I look…with greater solicitude for the unfolding of the great events in progress in Europe," he wrote Anna, "as they afford me an opportunity to test the truth or error, of the principles, which I have laid down in my elementary discourse on Government. It is as yet in the rough draft…I cannot doubt the correctness of the principles, I have laid down, for they are drawn from the facts of the moral world, just as certain, as any in the physical; but I am solicitous to see, how far they are subject to modification in their practical application to the present condition of the civilized world, which is so very different from any that ever preceded it in many respects." It was a dangerous time to be writing theories of government that might be proved wrong by the next steamer from Europe.[3]

CALHOUN BEGAN THE *DISQUISITION* by observing that "man is so constituted as to be a social being"—and that throughout history man had always lived in communities. There was no solitary state of nature, and any system with this idea at its root was bound to be dangerously flawed. Created as a social animal, man nevertheless had a strong sense of individual identity, and "feels more intensely what affects him directly, than what affects him indirectly through others…his direct or individual affections are greater than his sympathetic or social feelings." Calhoun was quick to insist that he was not talking about "selfish feelings," or an "excess of the individual over the social feelings…something depraved and vicious," as his Presbyterian upbringing would have taught him, but simply a "fact" or "phenomena appertaining to our nature" no different than the law of gravity in the natural world. Human beings' powers of sympathy increased or decreased depending on how directly actions affected them, or people like them. Any successful political system had to begin with this fact. Calhoun was far from the only modern theorist to recognize the importance of sympathy—Adam Smith had examined it as the basis of morality nearly a century earlier in his *Theory of Moral Sentiments*—but in the *Disquisition* Calhoun adapted the idea to constitutional theory in light of his experience as a statesman in the world's largest and most diverse republic.[4]

The tension between man's social nature and his regard for his own interests would necessarily produce conflict, Calhoun continued, making some kind of government necessary. "There is no difficulty in forming government," he wrote. "It is not even a matter of choice…Necessity will force it on all communities in some one form or another." This was because the greatest evil in human communities was not a lack of liberty, but anarchy, and governments were legitimate to the extent they prevented this unnatural state.

The most basic function of any government, on which legitimacy rested, he held, was its ability "to repel assaults from abroad, as well as to repress violence and disorders within." But for governments to perform this essential function they had to wield power, great power, which could not be diminished without compromising their purpose. (Here Calhoun rejected the solution of his old antagonist John Randolph, which was to keep government so weak that it could never threaten liberty.) The problem, as Calhoun explained, was that the power necessary to accomplish the ends of legitimate government was always liable to be usurped by those who wielded it, whether they were many or few, for their own benefit and at the expense of others.[5] In this regard, Calhoun believed, republican virtue was no match for human nature. If communities and individuals were to achieve any degree of liberty in this situation while still preserving the essential function of government, that government would need to be arranged, in Calhoun's words, "in order to resist, by its own interior structure, or to use a single term, organism, the tendency to abuse of power."[6]

This "organism" was a constitution. In contrast to forming a government, "it is one of the most difficult tasks imposed on man to form a constitution worthy of the name," Calhoun wrote, "while, to form a perfect one, one that would completely counteract the tendency of government to oppression and abuse, and hold it strictly to the great ends for which it is ordained, has thus far exceeded human wisdom, and possibly ever will."[7] The best governments were those that combined the necessary amount of power with a constitution that assured its subjects the greatest possible degree of liberty, but the balance between power and liberty depended entirely on the community being governed.

> Some communities require a far greater amount of power than others to protect them against anarchy and external dangers; and, of course, the sphere of liberty in such, must be proportionally contracted. The causes calculated to enlarge the one and contract the other, are numerous and various. Some are physical—such as open and exposed frontiers, surrounded by powerful and hostile neighbors. Others are moral—such as the different degrees of intelligence, patriotism, and virtue among the mass of the community, and their experience and proficiency in the art of self-government. Of these, the moral are, by far, the most influential.
>
> ...To allow to liberty, in any case, a sphere of action more extended than this assigns, would lead to anarchy...Liberty, then, when forced on a people unfit for it, would, instead of a blessing, be a curse...No people, indeed, can long enjoy more liberty than that to which their situation and advanced intelligence and morals fairly entitle them. If more than

this be allowed, they must soon fall into confusion and disorder—to be followed, if not by anarchy and despotism, by a change to a form of government more simple and absolute; and, therefore, better suited to their condition. And hence, although it may be true, that a people may not have as much liberty as they are fairly entitled to, and are capable of enjoying—yet the reverse is unquestionably true—that no people can long possess more than they are fairly entitled to.

Unlike those who believed that American-style democracy was aborning in Europe in the spring of 1848, Calhoun believed that governments would inevitably evolve or devolve into equilibrium with a people's ability to maintain and enjoy liberty, a fact that illuminates his understanding of the stakes of the political moment he lived in. Americans would either rise to the moment and adopt his solutions, or sink into the absolute despotism of the numerical majority. And although he did not include slavery in his taxonomy of governments, it is clear that his law of liberty and power fit seamlessly into his defense of the peculiar institution. Freedom was not man's natural state. It was, instead, a rare and ephemeral achievement in human history, resulting from the interplay between a people's innate ability to sustain it, their form of government, and especially the construction of the constitution that restrained that government. "[Liberty] is a reward to be earned, not a blessing to be gratuitously lavished on all alike," Calhoun warned. "The progress of a people rising from a lower to a higher point in the scale of liberty, is necessarily, slow; and by attempting to precipitate, we either retard, or permanently defeat it."[8]

Just as dangerous to true liberty as the assumption of natural equality, Calhoun argued, was the fever dream of "equality of *condition*." Remarkably, Calhoun almost certainly wrote this part of the *Disquisition* within a few months of Karl Marx publishing *The Communist Manifesto* amid the tumult of the 1848 revolutions, and parts of the *Disquisition* read like a brief for the capitalist argument against communism for the next century and a half. Some measure of inequality,

Calhoun argued, was essential to progress. How else would people in highly developed economies be motivated to exert their efforts and ingenuity than by the example of those around them who had succeeded in bettering themselves?

> It is, indeed, this inequality of condition between the front and rear ranks, in the march of progress, which gives so strong an impulse to the former to maintain their position, and to the latter to press forward into their files. This gives to progress its greatest impulse. To force the front rank back to the rear, or attempt to push forward the rear into line with the front, by the interposition of the government, would put an end to the impulse, and effectually arrest the march of progress.[9]

The whole *Disquisition* builds to the idea of the concurrent majority, which Calhoun believed was indispensable to free government in any of its constitutional forms, but especially in a constitutional democracy. In Calhoun's taxonomy, constitutional democracy was the most fragile and rare accomplishment in human history, and as such it required the most careful arrangement of power and restraints on that power to preserve the high degree of freedom it promised.[10]

The "indispensable and primary principle" in constitutional government was the right of suffrage, as the first safeguard against tyranny of the few. But suffrage was not sufficient on its own to ensure liberty. By itself, the best suffrage could do was to transfer the power of the government from the rulers to the ruled, and it did nothing to guard against democratic absolutism. Suffrage made the ruled into the rulers, but in so doing it also made them dangerous.[11]

A democracy governed by majority rule might work well enough in a homogenous community that had similar interests, but "the more extensive and populous the country, the more diversified the condition and pursuits of its population...the more difficult is it to equalize the action of the government—and the more easy for one portion of the community to pervert its powers to oppress, and plunder the other."

This, of course, was exactly what Calhoun believed he had seen over the course of his lifetime, and in the *Disquisition* he explained how the law of human nature had naturally produced this result. Over time different groups with compatible interests and identities would coalesce until they could achieve a majority able to impose its will on a minority different or distant enough from them that the minority's oppression did not arouse the sympathetic feelings of human nature. Indeed, the allure of using the government's power for one's own benefit was so great that even in a community with broadly similar interests, the principle of the numerical majority would by itself eventually create "two great hostile parties" vying for control, with the minority oppressed every bit as tyrannically as in any absolute monarchy.[12]

In other words, instead of a constitution designed to mitigate the influence of factions, the founders had unintentionally created a machine that amplified their influence. They had followed Montesquieu's famous prescription for preserving liberty by separating the executive from the judicial and legislative powers of government, but they could not have foreseen a party system in which crafty, power-hungry politicians would learn how to artfully combine appeals to different groups to place themselves in control of all three branches of government (the executive and legislative by elections, the judicial by appointments). True, majorities might change over time, as Madison had hoped, but instead of moderating the exercise of power, the very transient nature of a majority's power would only make the struggle more desperate and its exercise of power more ruthless.

Nor was there any hope to be had in revelation or enlightenment. "Neither religion nor education can counteract the strong tendency of the numerical majority to corrupt and debase the people," Calhoun wrote. Eventually, the whole rotten structure would collapse into itself and revert to a despotic monarchy in which the people would look to a single, strong ruler to save them from anarchy.[13]

What was the solution? To provide every element or interest in society a means of protecting itself against the blind tyranny of numbers. "Power can only be resisted by power, and tendency by tendency," Calhoun wrote. Perfect liberty could only be preserved "by taking the sense of each interest or portion of the community…separately, through its own majority, or in some other way by which its voice may be fairly expressed; and to require the consent of each interest, either to put or to keep the government in action." This unanimous consent of all the interests in a given society was what Calhoun called the concurrent majority, and constitutions that included this principle were best calculated to maintain the delicate balance between a high degree of liberty and the social order and stability provided by a legitimate government. In fact, he argued, no government was truly constitutional without it.[14]

Conservative in its effects, the concurrent majority in Calhoun's description was nothing less than utopian in its ability to create consensus, promote virtue, and safely expand the limits of democracy. Instead of a government of the few, or of the majority, a government of the concurrent majority was truly a government of the whole people, considered both as numbers and as interest groups in society. Its ability to "give a full and faithful utterance to the sense of the whole community, in reference to its common welfare, may, without impiety, be called *the voice of God*," Calhoun wrote. "To call any other so, would be impious." Calhoun argued that a government of the concurrent majority took away all the incentives to use power for self or group aggrandizement, and instead promoted considerations of a truly common good. "Its effect, then, is to cause the different interests, or portions, or orders—as the case may be—to desist from attempting to adopt any measure calculated to promote the prosperity of one, or more, by sacrificing that of others; and thus to force them to unite in such measures only as would promote the prosperity of all," he wrote. Finally, in a government of the concurrent majority, the right of suffrage could be safely extended "to every male citizen of mature age" since no part of society had anything to fear from the tyranny of numbers. Calhoun did not address the objection that under such a government the power wielded by the right of suffrage would also be diminished.[15]

Calhoun even believed that the principle could revive corrupt and dying constitutional governments. Where "cunning, fraud, treachery, and party devotion" were most prized in governments of the numerical majority, governments of the concurrent majority would by necessity prize statesmen who governed in the interest of the whole community since the alternative was that the government would cease to function and anarchy, the greatest of evils, would result. "So powerful, indeed, is the operation of the concurrent majority, in this respect," Calhoun wrote, "that, if it were possible for a corrupt and degenerate community to establish and maintain a well-organized government of the kind, it would of itself purify and regenerate them." The concurrent majority would not only reward virtue of the kind that classical republicanism had once prized, it would manufacture it by a kind of imperious, structural necessity.[16]

After two decades of defending nullification Calhoun was keenly aware of the objection that a government of the concurrent majority would produce not common action and unity, but paralysis. He acknowledged that on some, lesser issues, this might be true, implying that it was a price worth paying for the benefits of the concurrent majority, but he argued that "when something *must* be done, and when it can be done only by the united consent of all, the necessity of the case will force to a compromise." Only measures that were absolutely necessary and essential would have the ability to unite the community and put the fearful power of government into action. Secure in the knowledge that they could protect themselves, and moved by affection for a country devoted to a truly common good, "each portion would regard the sacrifice it might have to make by yielding its peculiar interests to secure the common interest and safety of all, including its own, as nothing compared to the evils that would be inflicted on all…by pertinaciously adhering to a different line of action." No doubt some of

Calhoun's critics guffawed out loud when they read this line from the father of nullification.[17]

To support his argument, Calhoun pointed to a curious hodge-podge of contemporary and historical examples. He pointed out that juries were often able to reach unanimous verdicts even in cases where "the ablest and most experienced judges and advocates differ in opinion"; he pointed to the Polish parliament, where an assembly of "one hundred and fifty to two hundred thousand" gave individual assent to elect members of the government and pass any legislation; and drawing on his time as secretary of war, he referred to the example of the Iroquois Confederacy, claiming that the strict model of consensus that governed their decision making had not prevented them from becoming "the most powerful of all the Indian tribes within the limits of our country." He spent much more time on the historical examples of the Roman Republic and Great Britain, both of which he believed had adapted the principle of the concurrent majority to fit the particular character of their people and the challenges of their times. The Roman tribunate gave plebeians a veto over any legislation that might affect them, while in Great Britain the great orders or interests of British society were all represented in parliament.[18]

The most compelling historical example of the concurrent majority in an American context, Calhoun believed, could be found in South Carolina. In *A Discourse on the Constitution and Government of the United States*, Calhoun gave an extended history of the successful Compromise of 1808, which had balanced the power of the upcountry and the lowcountry by means of a carefully calculated formula of representation that combined numbers and property value, mainly slaves. The result worked so well, he wrote proudly, that "party division and party violence...soon disappeared. Kind feelings, and mutual attachment between the two sections, took their place, and have continued uninterrupted for more than forty years." Calhoun glossed over the fact that it had been the expansion of slavery into the upcountry in the first decade of the century that had unified the state and allowed the compromise in the first place. South Carolina had not been nearly as diverse in its interests as he portrayed it.[19]

In Calhoun's view, the world now approached an unprecedented moment in history that would require constitutional democracies to adapt the principle of the concurrent majority to the new forces shaping human activity. "Numerous discoveries and inventions" that facilitated mobility and communication, including steam power, electricity, the printing press, and the telegraph, now allowed for more rapid and intense concentrations of public opinion than ever before. "Already [this phenomenon has] attained a force in the more civilized portions of the globe sufficient to be felt by all governments, even the most absolute and despotic," Calhoun wrote, no doubt with the European revolutions in mind. But without care to separate true public opinion from the "mere clamor of faction, or shouts of fanaticism," democracy was in danger of devolving into a dark age. The concurrent majority, Calhoun believed, was the fix, an old idea whose time had come again. Only a reinvention of the concurrent majority could inoculate democracy against its own excesses and preserve liberty and minority rights.[20]

Calhoun's argument for the concurrent majority was certainly an attempt to preserve the power of a slaveholding minority in the Union, but its power derived from the creative, even utopian appeal of Calhoun's ideas. It was not for nothing that so many of Calhoun's critics compared him to Milton's eloquent, fallen archangel in *Paradise Lost*, in whose mouth the poet placed arguments so rational and appealing that they called into question the reliability of reason itself. The appeal of the concurrent majority went far beyond a mere hedge against the power of numbers in a democracy. Although Calhoun claimed to work within the traditional framework of three types of government—rule by the one, the few, and the many—he in fact held out the alluring possibility of a fourth option: government by consensus. Calhoun evoked the possibility that, given the right conditions, men need not give up any part of their liberty in order to live under the blessings of government, an idea every bit as radical in its own way as the idea that all men were created equal. In its promise to virtually eliminate the possibility of tyranny in a democracy, Calhoun's concurrent majority promised that individual and communal self-determination would never be crushed simply by being outnumbered. He failed to consider how the costs of government inaction would be unequally distributed, and his theory was particularly suited to defending the interests of minority groups who already had a measure of political power. But this was just as Calhoun intended.[21]

In his *Discourse on the Constitution and Government of the United States*, which was still in draft form at his death, Calhoun moved from an abstract theory of the concurrent majority to its application in American history, outlining the changes that he believed were required to revitalize the Union's charter. The United States was "a democratic, federal republic," informed throughout its structure by "the great cardinal maxim, that the people are the source of all power," although Calhoun was clear that by "the people" he meant the people of the states. "'We, the people of the United States,'—means—We, the people of the several states of the Union," he wrote, pointing out that the people of each state ratified the Constitution in separate conventions, not as a whole. In more depth than anywhere else, he made the case for the compact theory of the Constitution: the United States was not a nation—it was a federal republic of sovereign states.[22]

Calhoun denied that the principle of "absolute democracy" was to be found anywhere in the Constitution, which he claimed had carefully implemented the principle of the concurrent majority by taking the sense of the people in multiple ways in order to capture as nearly as possible the whole voice of the community, instead of part. But having guarded against the encroachment of different parts of the federal government on one another, delicately balanced power between small states and large states, and carefully delegated certain powers to the federal government while reserving the rest to the states, the founders could not have foreseen how the forces of political parties and sectionalism would allow a numerical majority to effectively co-opt the federal government and force their will on the minority. "In a community of so great an extent as ours, contiguity becomes one of the strongest elements in forming party combinations, and distance one of the strongest elements in repelling them," Calhoun wrote, relying on the law of human nature he had laid out previously in the *Disquisition*.[23]

Nullification was, of course, one defense against this, and Calhoun defended his creation at length in the *Discourse*. Working from the principles of balance and equilibrium within the constellation of governments—federal and state—that made up the United States, Calhoun acknowledged that nullification created the possibility of disruption and even disunion—"It is a plausible objection," he wrote—but nevertheless he argued that the danger posed by nullification was no greater than that of giving the federal government a veto over the states. Besides, Calhoun argued, the forces of party loyalty, inevitable internal divisions within a state, and the possible consequences of such a desperate measure made nullification unlikely to be used in most cases. Nullification was a "high and delicate" right that should only be invoked in self-preservation.[24]

It was also, as recent history had shown, an imperfect instrument to resist federal power. Nullification had worked well to resist the tariff, but it was ineffective against the looming threat of the Wilmot Proviso, in which the northern majority could wield its power to exclude the South and assure their own dominance. History had now shown that it was not conflict between large and small states, but instead conflict between "two great sections, which are strongly distinguished by their institutions, geographical character, productions and pursuits" that posed the greatest threat to the Union. Now it was up to the American people to do "what the framers of the constitution would have done" had they foreseen the situation. "The nature of the disease is such, that nothing can reach it, short of some organic change," Calhoun wrote, "a change which shall so modify the constitution, as to give to the weaker section, in some one form or another, a negative on the action of the government." It was time to reconfigure the principle of the concurrent majority in the federal government to meet the demands of the sectional crisis.[25]

Calhoun's solution, proposed at the end of the *Discourse*, was to amend the Constitution to institute a dual executive, one from each section, with each having a veto over any Congressional legislation. It seems unimaginable that in some deep recess of his mind Calhoun did not have himself in mind for the job, although he would have denied it and perhaps even believed himself. All that was left, Calhoun wrote, was to act. Since constitutional amendments required approval from three-fourths of the states that would require the North—"the stronger section"—to put aside its territorial ambitions in order to preserve the Union by giving the South permanent veto power. In a patriotic appeal that barely veiled its threat, Calhoun wrote, "On the [North], therefore, rests the responsibility of invoking the high power, which alone can apply the remedy;—and, if they fail to do so, of all the consequences which may follow."[26]

THE FIRST REACTION OF most Americans upon hearing about the revolutions in Europe was to assume that Europe was finally following the United States' example. France drew the most attention because of its dramatic overthrow of its monarch and its special relationship with the United States. Andrew Jackson Donelson wrote Calhoun breathlessly on March 3 from Berlin. "The revolution in France has taken all the world by surprise," he wrote. "This is the fruit of our example as a free government, which is destined to do still more if it can be preserved in its original purity."[27]

Calhoun was skeptical, especially about France. As he wrote to his son James Edward Calhoun, now a student at South Carolina College, "I have no confidence that France will be able to establish a Republick. That is a task of far greater difficulty than is generally supposed."[28] He was just as cautious in public, even as many Democrats threw caution to the wind. On March 30, when William Allen of Ohio proposed a resolution on "behalf of the American people," congratulating the people of France on "their success in their recent efforts to consolidate liberty, by embodying its principles in a republican form of government," Calhoun opposed the resolution as premature. "The people of France have done much," Calhoun announced, "but the time has not yet arrived for congratulation…Whether the result shall prove to be a blessing or a curse to France and the world, depends upon what is coming, rather than upon what has already been done. A revolution in itself is not a blessing." The Senate passed the resolution over Calhoun's objection.[29]

Calhoun's skepticism was rooted in the fact that he was sure the French adhered to precisely the mistaken view of liberty he was just then denouncing in the *Disquisition*. "Indeed, her conception of liberty is false throughout," he wrote Anna in June. "Her standard of liberty is ideal; and belongs to that kind of liberty, which man has been supposed to possess in what has been falsely called a state of nature—a state supposed to have preceded the social and political, and in which, of course, if it ever existed, he must have lived apart, as an isolated individual, without society or government. In such as state…he would have, indeed, had two elements of the French political creed: liberty and equality, but no fraternity." Pronouncing the French efforts at a republic "absurd," Calhoun assured his daughter that it would end in "distraction, anarchy, and finally absolute power, in the hand of one man." Calhoun had a knack for showing how any turn of events confirmed his arguments, but he could hardly have hoped for a better apparent confirmation of his theories than the surprising election of Louis Napoleon Bonaparte in December 1848, as the French people used their new democratic powers to elect the nephew of their old hero.[30]

Unlike some European and American conservatives, Calhoun was not uniform in his views on the revolutions. In contrast to his skepticism about France, he was hopeful that the Frankfurt Assembly, building on the foundations of a preexisting confederation, would succeed in uniting Germany under a federal (not national) government. "Germany seems in a fair way to be completely revolutionized," he wrote Thomas Green Clemson in April, "and I hope permanently improved. I have much more hope for her than France. Her old institutions… furnish an excellent foundation on which to errect, if not a federal Republick like ours, a federal constitutional government…something more intimately united politically, than at present."[31] In May, when the Prussian minister to Washington, Baron Friedrich von Gerolt, asked Calhoun to review the constitution proposed as the basis for a new German union, Calhoun acknowledged his ignorance of the particulars of the German system but saw one point on which he had a definite opinion. "It seems to me, that the project errs in proposing to base the Constitution on *national unity* and to vest the union, or Empire, as it is called, with so vast an extent of power, as it does." That degree of centralization would not work "for a people divided into communities, with political institutions so very different and interests so conflicting." Instead, he advised Gerolt that Germany should work within the existing framework of the confederation as much as possible.[32]

In mid-April, Washington got a small taste of revolution itself when more than seventy slaves were spirited away down the Potomac in the middle of the night on a ship called the *Pearl* under the command of Daniel Drayton, whom it emerged had been paid by abolitionists to help the slaves escape. After the *Pearl* was quickly captured by a steamship full of angry citizens, anti-abolitionist riots burst out all over Washington. When Senator John P. Hale of New Hampshire offered a bill to compensate property owners for damages resulting from the "riotous assembly," Calhoun pointed out that Hale condemned the rioters while failing to condemn "these atrocities, these piratical attempts" by abolitionists. "If this should not rouse the South," Calhoun wrote to Wilson Lumpkin the next day, "it is to be feared that she will sleep the sleep of death."[33]

Only a few days after the *Pearl* affair, Polk, still lusting for Mexican land, sent a message to Congress directing their attention to the Yucatán Peninsula, where a conflict had recently erupted between native peoples and Spanish-descended landowners. Asking for congressional authority to "rescue the white race from extermination" on the peninsula, Polk invoked the Monroe Doctrine, which he claimed obligated the United States to intervene before a European power could do so. Opposing Polk's request as a distortion of the Monroe Doctrine, Calhoun took the opportunity to condemn the principle of false equality that he claimed had led to the conflict. "The people of Yucatan, after they threw off the Spanish yoke, acting on the idea that all men are qualified to enjoy the blessing of liberty, and ought of right to possess it, liberated the large mass of their population, consisting of aborigines in a state of ignorance and subjection, and raised them to a level with themselves, by making them citizens," he announced. "The result is such as we this day witness."[34]

In private, Calhoun had already connected the failure of the revolutions in Europe and abolitionism to what he believed were the false ideas of natural equality originating with Locke and Jefferson. "It is this false conception that is up heaving Europe," he wrote Anna. "It is at the same time threatening our institutions. Abolitionism originates in it."[35] Writing to James Edward Colhoun in April about the *Disquisition*, Calhoun speculated that the success of his ideas might depend on the failure of the revolutions, especially France, and connected the revolutions to the Dorr War in Rhode Island that had helped to doom his presidential hopes in 1844. "I do not think the publick mind is yet fully prepared for the work, nor will be, until there has been such failure and embarrassment in the French experiment…as will bring into distrust and doubt Dorrism, so as to prepare the publick mind to have its errors and consequences pointed out, and to reflect seriously on the question, What are the elements, which are indispensable to constitute a constitutional popular government?"[36]

Calhoun's fullest public condemnation of the idea of natural equality came that summer in the midst of the debate over the status of slavery in the Oregon Territory, which everyone in the country understood was the opening act in the debate over slavery in the territories gained from the Mexican war. At the end of June the House passed a bill prohibiting slavery in the Oregon Territory, citing the precedent of the Northwest Ordinance of 1787. When the Senate rejected the bill, the House passed it again. In an attempt to find a path through the impasse, on June 27 Democratic senator Jesse Bright of Indiana offered an amendment to the House bill extending the Missouri Compromise line to the Pacific Ocean.

In response, Calhoun offered one of his starkest warnings about the danger of disunion, tracing the whole conflict over slavery back to the "philanthropic but mistaken views" of Thomas Jefferson expressed in the Declaration of Independence. In the battle between the school of Jefferson and the school of Hamilton for the soul of the country, Calhoun had always placed himself on the Virginian's side of the room, at least as he understood it. He still reverenced Jefferson, but he believed that time was proving Jefferson's error on a vital point that could no longer safely be ignored. Many conservatives throughout the country still dismissed the Declaration's radical statement of human equality as a farcical distortion of reality, but it was the first time in his long career that Calhoun had criticized his political idol so harshly.

After arguing at length that slavery could not constitutionally be excluded from territories held in common by the North and the South, and that the Northwest Ordinance and the Missouri Compromise were both unconstitutional, Calhoun had the Senate secretary read Jefferson's often-quoted "firebell in the night" letter on the Missouri Compromise, in which Jefferson famously lamented that "a geographical line coinciding with a marked principle, moral and political, once conceived and held up to the angry passions of men, will never be obliterated, and every new irritation will mark it deeper and deeper."

"Mark his prophetic words!" Calhoun exclaimed. "Mark his profound reasoning!" The Sage of Monticello's prophecy had come to pass, Calhoun proclaimed, but "I hold he is not blameless in reference to this subject." Calhoun then imagined a future historian writing the history of a doomed country called the United States. The historian's first chapter would be on the Northwest Ordinance, the next on the Missouri Compromise, and the next on the present moment. "Whether there will be another beyond," Calhoun announced solemnly, "I know not."

If the future historian was of a philosophical turn of mind, Calhoun believed he would trace the origins of the conflict all the way back to Jefferson's belief, expressed in the Declaration, that all men were created equal. In the *Disquisition*, Calhoun called Jefferson's idea "unfounded and false" as well as "destitute of all sound reason."[37] Men were not born. Children were born. And they were not born alone, free, or equal, but helpless and dependent, into specific social and political contexts that would determine the amount of freedom they would enjoy in life. "For a long time it lay dormant," Calhoun said of Jefferson's famous idea, "but in the process of time it began to germinate, and produce its poisonous fruit." Jefferson had mistakenly drawn this tragically flawed conclusion, Calhoun declared, from the "hypothetical truism" of equality in a state of nature posited by "certain writers on government who had attained much celebrity in the early settlement of the States... Locke and [Algernon] Sidney." Jefferson's mistake, and that of the abolitionists and the French revolutionaries, was to compound Locke's philosophical error by trying to make it into a political and social reality, a project that could only end in disaster. In Calhoun's mind there was a direct chain of causation running from Locke's mistaken theory of man, through Jefferson's Declaration, to abolitionism, the Dorr War, the attempt to keep slavery out of Oregon, the possibility of disunion, and the ill-fated revolutions in Europe. Even as Calhoun spoke, the ruthless suppression of the June Days uprising in Paris by the new French government announced the end of the most idealistic hopes for the revolution there. Time was doing its work.

Instead of Locke's hypothetical truism or Jefferson's dangerously flawed ideal, Calhoun spoke in favor of the racial equality among white men that slavery allowed. White northerners who came South would not find free labor degraded by slavery—"There is no part of the world where agricultural, mechanical, and other descriptions of labor are more respected"—but would find instead that their status relative to other whites, even the wealthy, would improve. "With us, the two great divisions of society are not the rich and poor," Calhoun declared, "but white and black; and all the former, the poor as well as the rich, belong to the upper class, and are respected and treated as equals, if honest and industrious, and hence have a position and pride of character of which neither poverty nor misfortune can deprive them." If the North would only abide by the Constitution and leave the territories open to settlers from all the states, Calhoun assured them that slavery would likely settle in the parts of the country below an extended Missouri Compromise line, but to restrict it there would lead to disunion. "Now, I put the question to the Senators from the North," Calhoun challenged, "what are you prepared to do?"[38]

Over the next several weeks, Calhoun believed, the antislavery party of the North made clear exactly what they were prepared to do. In July, a select committee that included Calhoun produced a hard-fought compromise based on what Calhoun called "the principle of non interference." The compromise affirmed preexisting laws in regard to slavery in the Oregon Territory, assuring its exclusion, while remaining silent on slavery's future in the territories added by the war with Mexico. It was a tacit extension of the Missouri Compromise that Calhoun was willing to live with since it neither affirmed Congress's right to prohibit slavery nor instituted popular sovereignty. "I hope it will permanently settle this vexed and dangerous question," Calhoun wrote to Clemson days later. During his closing speech defending the compromise, Jesse Bright of Indiana admitted that while he had once doubted Calhoun's commitment to the Union, the South Carolinian's conduct during the negotiations of the committee had convinced him that Calhoun was at his core a devoted Union man. The compromise passed the Senate and was summarily tabled in the House by the combined strength of Free Soil Democrats and several southern Whigs, including Alexander

Stephens of Georgia, an ominous sign to Calhoun that the pull of party loyalty still had the power to frustrate his attempts at southern unity.[39]

The House sent its original bill prohibiting slavery back to the Senate in early August 1848. On August 10 Calhoun spoke against yet another amendment that would, like Jesse Bright's, extend the Missouri Compromise line to the Pacific, offering dark predictions of the future and an extended diagnosis of the changes that had led up to that moment. "There are diseases of the body politic, as well as our natural bodies, that never will stop of themselves," Calhoun announced, alluding to abolitionism but perhaps thinking of the infection raging in his own lungs. Not long ago, Calhoun pointed out, many northern states had been slaveholding states themselves, but now many considered slaveholding a sin, "notwithstanding the authority of the Bible to the contrary." This change in public opinion, coinciding with the rapid growth of federal power and the erroneous idea the United States was a single nation, had given northerners the false sense that they were somehow responsible for the continuance of slavery in the South. Abolitionists seemed to care deeply about the fate of people they had never met in states they had often never visited; in Calhoun's analysis this was a sign of their moral derangement and misapprehension of the American system of government, not true sympathy. The disease was moral and political, not economic, for when it came to slavery "the North beyond question has and is profiting by it and that to a vast extent."

The distortions of abolitionism even ran into language, Calhoun noted. Once "no people were regarded as free, who did not live under constitutional governments," while "now, every people are called free, however despotic the government," so long as they were not African slaves. It was a dangerously low bar for defining freedom, he thought, since people would be lulled into a false sense of security by the thought that at least they were not, literally, slaves.

Dwelling on the North's refusal to enforce the Constitution when it came to fugitive slaves and the "incessant agitation of the subject" in Congress, both of which he thought violated the spirit of the compact that formed the Union, Calhoun called on his southern colleagues to unite in resistance. "We must prove by our acts," he declared, "that we still have the blood of our patriotic and heroic ancestors running in our veins." If the South showed they would never join a political party that countenanced any hint of abolitionism, "a host of true and faithful allies" would materialize in the North, "unless indeed the disease has already made such progress, that the North is willing to sacrifice the union on the altar of abolition."

Knowing that "very different motives may be attributed to me," Calhoun dared his colleagues to call him an enemy of the Union. "Nearly forty years of my life have been devoted to the service of the Union," he declared. "If I shall have any place in the memory of posterity, it will be in consequence of my deep attachment to it and our federal system of Government." And then, with the next breath: "But as strong as is my attachment to the Union, my attachment to liberty and the safety of the section where Providence has cast my lot, is still stronger." He had always looked "to the good of the whole," and viewed his resistance to "aggressions," antislavery or otherwise, as a service to the whole Union, and not just his section. But his affection for the Union had a limit. "I aim not at change or revolution," he announced, evoking the events in Europe.

> My object is to preserve. I am thoroughly conservative in my politics. I wish to maintain things as I found them established. I am satisfied with them and am of the opinion that they cannot be changed for the better. I hold it to be difficult to get a good Government, and still more difficult to preserve it; and as I believe a good Government to be the greatest of earthly blessings, I would be adverse to the overthrow of ours even, if I thought it greatly inferior to what I do, in the hope of establishing better.[40]

At the moment he spoke those words, of course, Calhoun was engaged in a monumental effort to write an argument for perfecting the

American system of government that he professed to want to simply maintain. To him this was not a contradiction. Along with a deeply conservative instinct, he possessed a relentless drive toward improvement, a deep-seated belief in progress, and a sense that the world was constantly, swiftly changing. Preservation required adaptation. Conservation required re-creation. The vast numbers of Americans of every political party in the middle of the nineteenth century who called themselves conservative would have agreed. In contrast to Europe, where in 1848 many conservatives defended formal aristocracy and tradition against the tide of liberal constitutional reform, in the United States those who called themselves conservatives rarely meant that they were opposed outright to the forces associated with liberalism, progress, and improvement as they defined them, only that these forces must be carefully managed. In saying he was a conservative who abhorred revolution but favored progress, as he did on many occasions, Calhoun was appealing to the mainstream of American politics, North and South, in his day.[41]

The speech captured Calhoun's ability to narrate the history of a juncture in time in the same potent way that he developed an argument, and it was delivered with the solemn air of certainty that lent many of his prophecies their self-fulfilling power. Calhoun's lasting influence was rooted, finally, in his ability to convincingly narrate past, present, and future reality in a way that bound all three inseparably together like one of his inexorable arguments. If his listeners embraced his telling of the past, or his interpretation of the present, they would likely act on his predictions of the future. The published version of the speech, which Calhoun carefully edited and published in the *Pendleton Messenger*, was a message to the South as much as the Senate.

The day before the session ended, the Senate faced a stark choice: pass the House bill prohibiting slavery in Oregon or leave the territory without a government. To Calhoun's horror, the bill passed the Senate 29 to 25 on the votes of Thomas Hart Benton and Sam Houston, and Polk signed it. As it became clear what the Senate would do, Calhoun warned darkly, "The great strike between the North and South is ended. The North is determined to exclude the property of the slaveholder, and of course the slaveholder himself, from its territory." The victory of this principle, the principle of the Wilmot Proviso, Calhoun warned, would "convert all the southern population into slaves." And in words that caused Sam Houston to object that he had used "menacing language" on the Senate floor, Calhoun stated flatly, "This is not a question of territorial government, but a question involving the continuance of the Union."[42]

At a crowded meeting in the Charleston Theatre on his way home, Calhoun denounced Benton and Houston as traitors to the South, called the Oregon Bill a "wanton assertion of power" by the North, and warned that the Wilmot Proviso would now be applied to any new territories, "even in Cuba, should that island ever be annexed to our Union." Warning that at the next session the great question would be "California, New Mexico, and all the territory between the Nueces and the Rio Grande," Calhoun admonished South Carolinians not to be divided by the impending presidential election. "The time is coming when your united energies will be demanded for the struggle." If they lost that struggle, as he expected they would, there would be no hope left for them in the Union.[43]

DESPITE THE DARKNESS HE saw gathering on the horizon, that fall Calhoun looked forward eagerly to a visit by Anna and her family. It had been four long years since he had seen her and her children, and when Thomas Green Clemson raised the possibility that he might not have the money to bring his family home on a temporary leave of absence, Calhoun immediately borrowed the money and sent it to him. "His return without you & the children would have been a cause of great greif [sic] to us all," he wrote Anna. "Had the sum required been ten times greater, it would have been remitted to prevent it."[44]

The sacrifice was greater than Anna probably knew, since by early 1848 Calhoun's finances were in magnificent shambles and he was struggling to borrow money simply to pay the interest and payments on his other debts, including the debt he and Andrew still owed to Thomas Green Clemson.[45] When Calhoun informed him of the difficulty, Clemson wrote a frustrated and angry appeal, demanding payment of half Andrew's debt and a new arrangement with Calhoun secured by land in South Carolina. "I read with pain the part of your letter relating to our private affairs," Calhoun wrote in a rare rebuke of his son-in-law. "I certainly must have been very unfortunate in my expressions, if they be such, as to justify you in the long train of remarks in which you have indulged. I shall abstain from any comment on them. They have satisfied me, that we ought never to have any pecuniary transactions between us." Somehow, the Calhoun family's relations often seemed to mirror those of the Union.[46]

Meanwhile, cotton prices continued to sink, leading Calhoun as close as he ever came to despairing of the cotton economy. "Mobile is certainly one of the worst cotton markets in the Union," he wrote Andrew in frustration that November at the news that prices had dropped below five cents. He suggested that perhaps they should ship their cotton to New York, where they might also be able to secure a new loan to help pay their other debts.[47]

Calhoun could at least take comfort in the fact that his younger sons were finally showing signs of promise. After an earlier, abortive experiment at nearby Erskine College, and tutoring from their uncle James Edward, James and William would both be students at South Carolina College that fall under the watchful eye of Calhoun's old nullification ally William C. Preston, the president of the college. John C. Calhoun Jr., perhaps prompted by his ongoing struggle with tuberculosis, graduated from medical school in Philadelphia that summer. Only Patrick was still a source of constant worry, spending far beyond his means despite stern warnings from both Calhoun and Andrew when he regularly petitioned for more money, which his father usually gave him. "I shaped my course, with a view to control him, and to save him from certain ruin, that awaits him, unless he should reform," Calhoun wrote to Andrew in excusing his indulgence.[48]

The possibility of ruin was everywhere Calhoun looked in 1848. That summer the antislavery movement finally came of age politically with the formation of the Free Soil Party, which nominated Calhoun's old nemesis Martin Van Buren at their convention in Buffalo in August. Made up of so-called Barnburner Democrats and Conscience Whigs, and built on the foundations of the earlier abolitionist Liberty Party, the Free Soil Party represented a seismic change in American politics, the beginning of the disintegration of the Second Party System over the issue of slavery. Its platform did not call for emancipation, but forthrightly called slavery a moral evil, committed the party to stopping slavery's extension, and called for the federal government to "relieve itself of all responsibility for the existence and continuance of slavery." Convention-goers marched by torchlight through Buffalo one night carrying a banner emblazoned with the words "No Compromise."[49]

Calhoun did not underestimate the importance of these developments. He warned the crowd in Charleston that August that Van Buren always knew which way the wind was blowing, and his willingness to throw in his lot with the Free Soil Party was an ominous sign.[50] Calhoun did not comment publicly or privately on another important political development that summer, a convention to advocate women's rights held at Seneca Falls, New York, and organized by Elizabeth Cady Stanton and Lucretia Mott, but he no doubt viewed the event as rooted in the same false conception of freedom that he had denounced earlier that year. And, in a sense, he was right. Both Stanton and Mott were also abolitionists.

By September it was also clear that American hopes for the revolutions in Europe had been misplaced, just as Calhoun had warned. In all his analysis of the revolutions, Calhoun never mentioned slavery, but he clearly viewed the peculiar institution as a cornerstone of the American system of government, a felicitous ingredient in the historical happenstance that had produced American freedom. Like an experiment conducted without the catalyst, the failure of the European revolutions lent apparent confirmation to Calhoun's famous arguments about slavery. In September, a dejected Andrew Jackson Donelson wrote from Berlin, "My residence in Europe has satisfied me that this institution of ours, called slavery, has had an agency in shaping our institutions which few of us in the South sufficiently appreciate. The presence of the black race in the United States enabled the white man to treat as his equal all his own race. A basis was thus formed for liberty as broad as the population, and hence popular sovereignty was a reality, not a fiction. The absence of such a basis in Europe is the secret of the failure of all its attempts to found popular institutions." He ended, "but I could not hope to say anything new to one so familiar with the subject as you are."[51]

If the domestic skies looked dark, there was at least one point of light on the international horizon. Beginning in the late 1840s, Calhoun and other southern slaveholders began to note promising changes in international attitudes toward slavery, especially in Great Britain. After its embrace of free trade, Calhoun no longer believed Great Britain posed a serious threat to slavery. Indeed, throughout 1848 correspondents from Europe, including Andrew Jackson Donelson and the British writer Sarah Mytton Maury, informed Calhoun that public sentiment in England had soured against emancipation on account of the complete collapse of the sugar industry in the West Indies. "The question, Slavery, begins to be much better understood, and more liberally considered, than formerly," Maury wrote him in August, noting the new anti-abolitionist tone of the *London Times*. English industrialists would not risk doing to the cotton textile industry what many now acknowledged emancipation had done to the sugar business. The irony from Calhoun's perspective was that headwinds against slavery in the United States had increased at the very moment that the international winds promised smooth sailing, if only he could right the ship of state.[52]

By November it was clear that Zachary Taylor had won the presidency over the Democrat Lewis Cass and the Free Soil candidate Martin Van Buren, but unlike many southerners Calhoun took little comfort in the fact that the new president was a Louisiana slaveholder. He was a Whig, even if an ambiguous one, and his affiliation with the party of Henry Clay made him suspect. Cass, who advocated popular sovereignty in the territories as a solution to the national impasse over slavery, was no better. And Van Buren was an abomination. On his way back to Washington in December, Calhoun stopped in Edgefield at Thomas Green Clemson's Cane Brake plantation to see Anna and her children for the first time in four years. Her father's appearance must have shocked Anna, for her letters to him soon became a stream of constant pleas to take care of his health. The Clemsons would remain in America until the following May.

BY LATE 1848 TUBERCULOSIS had begun to whittle Calhoun's body and face into a strange approximation of his place in some Americans' imagination as a figure of satanic determination and brilliance—"the very incarnation of the Slaveholding idea" as the Massachusetts Anti-Slavery Society called him in its annual report that year.[53] When the young journalist Oliver Dyer traveled to Washington that winter to record the proceedings of Congress, he was by his own account "full to the brim of abolitionist bigotry and prejudice," and eagerly anticipated his first look at the famous senator from South Carolina. Calhoun's appearance did not disappoint. "He seemed to be a perfect image and embodiment of the devil," Dyer recalled of his first glimpse of Calhoun in the Senate chamber. "Had I come across his likeness in a copy of Milton's Paradise Lost, I should have at once accepted it as ... a masterpiece of some great artist who had a peculiar genius for Satanic portraiture. He was tall and gaunt, and there seemed to be an inner complexion of a dark soul shining out through the skin of the face. His eyes were large, black, piercing, scintillant. His hair was iron gray, and rising nearly straight from the scalp, fell over on all sides, and hung down in thick masses like a lion's mane. His features were strongly marked, and their expression was firm, stern, aggressive, and threatening."

The similarity to Milton's fallen angel was more than skin deep, as Dyer discovered when Calhoun rose to object to a petition from the inhabitants of New Mexico presented by Thomas Hart Benton begging that slavery not be introduced there. Taken aback by the "clearness of Calhoun's views, by the bell-like sweetness and resonance of his voice, the elegance of his diction, and the exquisite courtesy of his demeanor," Dyer found himself suddenly wishing that Calhoun was an abolitionist, "so we could have him talking on our side." Other abolitionists likewise wished their own representatives would be as honest and direct as Calhoun about slavery. At a meeting of the Massachusetts Anti-Slavery Society in January 1849, William Lloyd Garrison himself offered a resolution holding that Calhoun was "incomparably to be preferred to those Northern time-servers and dough faces, who professedly look upon Slavery with abhorrence, and yet are found ever ready to compromise." The resolution passed unanimously. At least, the society declared a year later, Calhoun defended "an actual, tangible Idea, however wicked it may be." "Even the sight of Satan himself," the report continued, "would be a welcome refreshment in the Limbo of Vanity, or Paradise of Fools" that constituted Congress.[54]

Southerners chose their allusions to Calhoun differently, although from the same biblical narrative. With a son's unique devotion but expressing a common sentiment, Andrew wrote to his father before the session began, "If your life can only be spared, the time is rapidly coming when you will occupy a position truly sublime. You who have always foreseen, foretold, and tried to avert, the terrible issue now rushing with electrick speed upon us; you will be looked to as the pillar of fire to guide us thro' the angry elements gathered up on every side, ready to envelope us."[55]

Calhoun saw his path dictated, as usual, by duty. Throughout his life, he believed, he had striven to stay on that path, though its course had been unpredictable. Others were often mystified by his kaleido-scopic interpretation of his life's imperative principle or suspicious that they detected in his interpretation of his duty the silent gravitational pull of his gigantic ambition. Yet Calhoun believed the struggle to do one's duty was its own reward. "You must not suppose," he had written Anna that spring, "that in contending against corruption & interest, that I am impelled by the hope of success...I hold, the duties of life, to be greater than life itself, and that in performing them manfully, even against hope, our labour is not lost, but will be productive of good in after times...*the reward is in the struggle, more than in victory itself.*" Time, he was confident, would prove the true worth of his efforts.[56]

BACK IN WASHINGTON ON December 22, Calhoun presided over a meeting of nearly seventy southern members of the Senate and House in a closed-door meeting in the Senate chamber. Despite the nature of the meeting, a reporter from the *Baltimore Sun* obtained an account of Calhoun urging the southern representatives to address their people regarding the stakes of the crisis in a published statement. "We are in the midst of events scarcely of less import than those of our revolution-ary era," Calhoun told his colleagues. "The question is, are we to hold our position in this confederacy upon the ground of equals, or are we to content ourselves with the condition of colonial dependence." The meeting appointed a committee of fifteen to write an address, which Calhoun evidently drafted mostly himself. Then the cracks started to show. When Calhoun presented his draft to the committee, Democrat Thomas J. Rusk of Texas, who had known Calhoun as a boy growing up on a plantation near Fort Hill in Pendleton, objected that it took too pessimistic a view of the northern people. Calhoun said he was "deeply wounded" by Rusk's objection, coming from an old acquaintance and a resident of a state he had done so much for. In the end, Rusk voted with six southern Whigs on the committee against issuing the address, though they were overruled. At a meeting of the full southern caucus two days later, now with more than eighty members present, Charles Morehead, a Whig from Kentucky, objected that the address seemed to threaten disunion, a charge Calhoun denied.[57]

A few days before Calhoun's address was finally adopted, in slightly modified form, by the southern members of Congress on January 22, Calhoun collapsed in the Senate chamber. He quickly revived, and minimized the episode in a letter to Thomas Green Clemson as the result of "the bad air & heat of the room," but reading about it in the newspapers prompted a letter from Anna imploring him not to work too hard and to take better care of himself.[58]

Even shorn of its most extreme statements by Calhoun's colleagues, the "Address of Southern Delegates in Congress, to Their Constituents" was an apocalyptic prediction of the future should the South yield an inch against northern aggression. In a foreshadowing of the secession ordinances that many southern states would pass twelve years later, Calhoun began with a frank description of "the conflict between the two great sections of the Union, growing out of a difference of feeling and opinion in reference to the relation existing between the two races, the European and the African, which inhabit the Southern Section." Restating all his arguments about slavery and the Constitution, the South's right to territories held in common by the Union, and the unconstitutional outrages of northern states in regard to fugitive slaves, Calhoun ended by pointing to the recent Oregon legislation and several measures that had been introduced in the House within the last month, including bills to exclude slavery from California and New Mexico, to abolish slavery in the District of Columbia, and, most shocking, to allow free blacks and slaves in the District of Columbia to vote. It mattered little that the bills had failed. They would soon succeed, Calhoun had little doubt, and he imagined a not-distant future in which northern majorities outlawed slavery on all federal lands and installations, even in slave states, destabilizing slave property, creating "hope" in slaves themselves, and leading eventually to emancipation, perhaps by southern states themselves as an act of desperation. But it would not stop there. Calhoun pointed to the economic ruin of the British West Indies, where at least the British government had used its power to "preserve the social and political power of the white race." The case would be different, and much worse, for the South. Seeing in the newly freed slaves a potentially powerful political constituency, northern politicians would raise them to political and social equality with southern whites in order to win their votes, "holding the white race at the South in complete subjection." "We would, in a word, change conditions with them," he warned, "a degradation greater than has ever yet fallen to the lot of a free and enlightened people."

The address was not the definitive statement of southern unity that Calhoun had hoped for, mostly because many southern members of Congress steered clear. Only two southern Whigs, members of the party about to come into power, signed the address. Among southern Democrats, the opposition of Polk, as well as Thomas Hart Benton and Sam Houston, proved formidable. In the end, slightly less than half the southern members of Congress signed it. But if it was not a complete victory, the address was proof of Calhoun's sway among southern representatives, and an ominous sign for the future. The number of signatures on the Southern Address made it clear that no final solution to the territorial or larger sectional crisis could be made without Calhoun's approval. From Calhoun's perspective, the dilemma was that only a united southern front and the prospect of disunion would force a settlement he would accept.[59]

Calhoun was uncharacteristically quiet and frequently absent from the Senate for the remainder of the session that spring, rising once to call Mississippi senator Jefferson Davis's proposal to create a new federal Department of the Interior "a monstrous bill" designed to "absorb all the remaining powers of the States."[60] Nevertheless, he watched and listened as repeated efforts to provide California a territorial government foundered on the rocks of the sectional conflict. The issue was all the more critical as thousands of Americans streamed west following the discovery of gold in the territory in early 1848, sparking one of the largest westward movements of people in the nation's history. The question of California could not be put off for long.

In late February the Clemsons arrived in Washington so that Thomas Green Clemson could ask for an extension of his leave and lobby to keep his position as chargé d'affaires in Belgium under the new administration, something Calhoun had done his best to assure by meeting with his successor in the state department, James Buchanan. In the end, Calhoun's efforts were successful—Clemson would keep his job and he and his family returned to Europe in May after a brief stay in Philadelphia. Sometime during their stay in Washington Anna accompanied Calhoun to the Washington studio of Mathew Brady, where Calhoun sat for a portrait that employed the new daguerreotype process, which he had read about and was eager to see in action. Invented just in time to capture the last living members of the second generation of American statesmen, the daguerreotype employed a chemically treated silver plate that, when carefully exposed to light, reacted to etch a delicate likeness of its subject. As Brady's workmen prepared their equipment, Calhoun described the process to Anna as she carefully rearranged his black coat and tamed stubborn strands of his shock of iron-gray hair before stepping back to let the light do its work. The day was cloudy, and it took Brady three tries to get an acceptable result. Calhoun had several daguerreotypes taken near the end of his life, but in one of them, possibly this one, the image shows an austere figure dressed all in black who could easily be mistaken for a Presbyterian minister fully capable of conjuring hell, hands clasped in front of him, his mouth tightly compressed and turned slightly down at the corners. The face is strong-boned but weathered, the cheeks gaunt, marked by lines so deep they look like scars. The deep-set, impossibly large, dark eyes, reflecting the light in the room, seem to have seared the silver plating of the daguerreotype, leaving tiny, white-hot pinpricks of light at their center. Along with similarly evocative portraits of John Brown, hand raised in an oath to extirpate slavery, or Abraham Lincoln with the bone-deep weariness of war etched on his face, it is an image that captures an era.[61]

When the Clemsons departed Washington, Anna remained deeply concerned about Calhoun's health. From Philadelphia, she wrote reminding him to continue drinking the "warm toddy" at bedtime she had prescribed for him. "Take exercise, but don't fatigue yourself," she wrote. "Study, but don't worry yourself, & don't write too much, (*except to me*)." With a fierce veneration tinged with idolatry, she reported that since their visit his grandson John Calhoun Clemson "takes great pride in being thought like you. I hope it will cause him to desire to imitate you in all things."[62]

By the time Calhoun received her letter he was back at Fort Hill, where he found the dogwoods blooming and the whole countryside turning green. On the advice of John Jr., the newly minted doctor in the family, Calhoun began a series of "wet sheet" treatments for his consumption, lying wrapped in a damp sheet and covered in blankets for an hour or more before taking a warm bath and "an effectual rubbing dry," reporting to Anna that the experience was "soothing and pleasant" and had "done much to open the pores." In his first letter to her after her departure for Europe, Calhoun came as close as he ever would to acknowledging what they both knew, but advised stoicism instead of sorrow. "We all felt, my dear daughter, as you described your feelings to be, at your departure. It is, indeed, distressing to be so far off & for so long a time from those so dear to us; but let us rather look forward, to when we shall again meet, than indulge in unavailing sorrows." He advised her that his grandchildren should not spend much more than two more years in Europe. "Their habits & mode of thinking will, by that time, begin to be formed; and it is important, that they should be such, as to conform to the condition of the country, which is to be their home." He did not say whether he meant the United States, the South, or South Carolina, but he told Anna that he often imagined her children "enjoying themselves in our green & shady yard." South Carolina was their true home, and certainly he hoped that they would be shaped by her "habits & mode of thinking," including slavery, rather than by their father's northern birthplace. Slaveholding and mastery were so deeply a part of South Carolina's culture and Calhoun's identity that he could not imagine what a Calhoun would be without them. That spring he began addressing his letters to Anna *Calhoun* Clemson, rather than Anna Maria Clemson. "I hope you will adopt the change," he wrote. Anna soon did.[63]

AS THE SUMMER PROGRESSED, southern hopes stirred by having a slaveholder in the nation's highest office evaporated. Hoping to short-circuit the debate over slavery in the territories, Zachary Taylor encouraged California to write a constitution and proposed to skip the territorial stage altogether and admit California directly to the Union as a new state. By the fall of 1849 California had ratified a constitution that excluded slavery and elected a state legislature that immediately petitioned for statehood, setting the stage for a cataclysmic congressional session that December. From the little office behind Fort Hill that summer, in between wet sheet treatments and his customary morning rides, Calhoun finally finished his *Disquisition* and began serious work on the *Discourse*. "I finished yesterday, the preliminary work," he wrote Anna in June, "which treats of the elementary principles of the Science of Government...I am pretty well satisfied with its execution."[64]

He had to delay his work for a couple of weeks to write a public reply to Thomas Hart Benton, who gave a scorching denunciation of Calhoun early that summer back home in Missouri, portraying Calhoun as a virulent disunionist who was secretly aiding the Free Soilers and abolitionists and had deceived the South for his own aggrandizement. In the kind of rhetorical excess that Benton specialized in and Calhoun despised, the Missouri senator charged that the Wilmot Proviso should actually be called the Calhoun Proviso. In reply to Benton's accusation that Calhoun had been attacking him for twenty years, Calhoun retorted bitingly, "I never thought of such a thing. We move in different spheres."[65]

Benton's speech came as he nervously contemplated the consequences of having opposed Calhoun's Southern Address, which might not have united southern members of Congress but was proving a rallying point for southern state legislatures, especially as Taylor's betrayal of his fellow slaveholders became clear and southern Whigs found it difficult to defend their man. Watching the movement from Fort Hill, Calhoun urged correspondents in Mississippi to call for a southern convention that would provide a show of unity and, perhaps, force both political parties to tame their abolitionist and Free Soil factions and come to a permanent compromise. Or the convention could be the beginning of a separate southern nation. As Calhoun wrote Mississippi senator Henry Foote that summer, "Fortunately for us, the road which leads to both yet lies in the same direction. We have not reached the fork yet, if we are ever to do it." The convention ought to be informal, Calhoun thought, "such as those often called by both parties at the North, in taking some new political position." A formal convention of the states in their official capacity, which in Calhoun's view would have the authority to withdraw from the Union and declare a new one, ought not to be called "short of the last extremity." But, if forced to choose between resistance and submission, as he thought they might be, the choice was clear. "We should take resistance, at all hazards." In October a convention of slaveholders in Mississippi issued a call for a southern convention to be held in Nashville the following June. Some, like James Henry Hammond, hoped that it would be an opportunity to coordinate a simultaneous southern secession, and in an even more ominous sign, state legislatures in Mississippi and South Carolina began appropriating money for military defense. As usual, Calhoun trod the razor's edge between preserving the Union on his own terms and destroying it, but as he left Fort Hill for Washington in late November, there was at least one good sign. Cotton prices had begun to rise.[66]

In Washington Calhoun took rooms at an old brick building at First and A Streets that had once served as a temporary capital after the British burned the city in 1814. It was the same building where as a young man he had urged his countrymen to conquer the limitless space of their continent, a project that now threatened to tear the country apart.

Just as there had been when Calhoun was the new congressman from South Carolina, the first session of the Thirty-First Congress involved a changing of the guard. From Calhoun's generation, both Henry Clay and Daniel Webster had returned to the Senate. Meanwhile, William Seward had taken the seat of John Adams Dix of New York, and Salmon Chase had replaced William Allen of Ohio. Seward's antislavery opinions were energetic and well known, while Chase had defended fugitive slaves and played a central role in the formation of the Free Soil Party. Along with returning senator John P. Hale of New Hampshire, Chase and Seward represented a new group of northern senators whose defining political issue was the fight against the slave power. Then there was Senator Stephen Douglas of Illinois, still in his first term.

The crisis that Zachary Taylor had hoped to avoid did not take long to erupt. A bitter battle over appointing the speaker of the house—which the South won—showed the depths of sectional distrust as southern members of Congress made it clear they were ready to act on the threat of secession if Taylor's plan for admitting California succeeded. Congressman Robert Toombs of Georgia announced openly that if California were admitted, "*I am for disunion,*" and his Whig colleague Alexander Stephens immediately concurred. In the Senate, Jefferson Davis portrayed the admission of California as the last stage of the North's bid for dominance over the South. As one historian puts it, "A vanguard among the defenders of slavery and states' rights was moving inimitably toward the embrace of disunion as a *program,*" rather than a threat or a process.[67] During the fight over the House speakership, an actual fight erupted when William Duer of New York called Richard Meade of Virginia a disunionist, and then a liar when Meade denied it. When Meade lunged at Duer, chaos ensued, leading the House sergeant at arms to grab his mace and make for Duer's side to protect him from his southern colleagues.[68]

Calls for disunion came from the North, as well. Hoping to illustrate southern bellicosity and hypocrisy, a few weeks into the session Senator John Hale introduced a petition from residents of Pennsylvania and Delaware asking Congress to implement the "peaceful dissolution of the Union," prompting impassioned responses from southern senators on the limits of congressional authority to do so. The petition Hale presented was not the only northern appeal for disunion that winter, although many northerners dismissed these calls as dangerous.[69]

Determined to save the Union, as well as the Whig Party that he led, on January 29, 1850, Henry Clay proposed a series of eight resolutions that combined several measures proposed on either side along with some of his own in an attempt to forestall disaster. Clay had played a key role in resolving the Missouri crisis as a younger man, and now thirty years later he laid the foundations for another great compromise. The first six resolutions were in counterbalanced pairs—California would be admitted as a free state, but the rest of the territories gained from Mexico would be organized without any restrictions on slavery; a border dispute between Texas and New Mexico would be resolved in New Mexico's favor, yielding less territory that might become a future slave state, but the federal government would assume debts incurred by the Republic of Texas before annexation; the slave trade would be outlawed in the District of Columbia, but slavery itself affirmed. The last two resolutions were aimed squarely at the South. The first maintained that Congress had no authority over the interstate slave trade, and the second proposed a greatly strengthened fugitive slave law that empowered the federal government to intercede on slaveholders' behalf when states refused. In explaining his resolutions, the seventy-three-year-old Clay, seriously ill with end-stage tuberculosis himself, contended that neither side would yield any important principle or set any precedent by agreeing to the resolutions. They would only be exercising "mutual forbearance" in a spirit of "conciliation and concession" in order to preserve the Union. Clay knew, of course, that this was exactly how

Calhoun now portrayed the Missouri Compromise. Now, he asked his fellow southerners, especially his old rival, to do it again.[70]

In mid-January, newspapers throughout the country carried news that an attack of "pneumonia" had left Calhoun greatly weakened and confined to his rooms. When the young Virginian and future congressman John Randolph Tucker visited him at the Old Capitol in February Tucker found Calhoun seated in a large arm chair, frequently resting the back of his head against it to catch his breath, with his long, gray hair "falling upon his shoulders in massive folds" around a face which was "emaciated and pale." But from the wasted face there still shone "those fiery, restless, brilliant eyes."[71] In Brussels, Anna read news of his attack in American newspapers and wrote her father in desperation. "You must quit Washington, my dear father, & resign," she wrote in what she must have known was a futile plea. "You have spent a long life in the service of your country, & now it is time to take care of yourself for our sakes."[72]

Others only hoped Calhoun would die before he had the satisfaction of seeing the country fall apart. "May he never live to see the disruption of the Union, which he has so often threatened," wrote the editor of the *Boston Recorder*, while the *Washington National Era* decried "men who are ready to pull down the pillars of the Union, because they are thwarted in their attempt to enslave a continent."[73]

The spectacle of Calhoun approaching death in the midst of what many believed were the final days of the Union may have even fired the imagination of Herman Melville, who was hard at work on a book about an ill-fated whaling voyage as the American ship of state seemed about to splinter into pieces that spring. The previous year Melville had based a character named Nulli in his novel *Mardi* fairly explicitly on Calhoun, describing the character, whose name was an unsubtle reference to nullification, as a "cadaverous, ghost-like man; with a low ridge of forehead; hair, steel-gray; and wondrous eyes." Now, in what would eventually become the quintessential American novel of its century, Melville described the doomed voyage of the ship *Pequod*, a vessel of "democratic dignity" manned by thirty "isolatoes…federated along one keel." Ahab, the ship's monomaniacal captain, Melville wrote, "looked like a man cut away from the stake, when the fire has overrunningly wasted all the limbs without consuming them." When Melville's narrator Ishmael first sees this haunted figure, he discerns "an infinity of firmest fortitude, a determinate, unsurrenderable willfulness, in the fixed and fearless, forward dedication of that glance."[74]

Beginning on February 5, Henry Clay gave a sweeping, two-day appeal for the Union and his compromise measures. Calhoun was too sick to attend the Senate to hear it, but after reading Clay's speech he was determined to use his last shred of strength to force a final settlement of the slavery question, one way or another. With the help of Joseph Scoville, a New York journalist who had visited Fort Hill the previous summer and written a glowing profile of Calhoun for the *New York Herald*, Calhoun drafted a speech and took the unusual step of having ten thousand copies printed the day before he gave it.[75] Young North Carolina congressman Abraham Venable, who was with Calhoun often in those final days, later recorded the deep impression left on him by witnessing Calhoun's mind struggling against his body's decay. "The menstruum retained all its powers of solution while the frail crucible that contained it was crumbling to atoms," Venable recalled, comparing the experience to watching a steamboat engine churn on as the wooden frame of the vessel splintered around it.[76]

When Calhoun arrived in the Senate on March 4, it was clear to everyone that he was dying. From the gallery, as a crowd of well-wishers and colleagues gathered around Calhoun, a young military officer named William Tecumseh Sherman could see that the South Carolinian was "evidently approaching his end, for he was pale and feeble in the extreme."[77] After briefly apologizing that he was too ill to give his speech, Calhoun moved to his seat, wrapped his wasted figure in a black cloak, and listened as Senator James M. Mason of Virginia read out his ultimatum.

The Senate faced a monumental question—"How can the Union be preserved?" Calhoun admitted that the threat to the Union arose from the southern states, but why, he asked his northern colleagues, had the Union fallen from the South's affections? Calhoun was ready with answers. Comparing the census of 1790 with that of 1840, he showed that while there had once been an equilibrium between the southern and northern states, with the upcoming census of 1850 and the pending admission of Oregon, Minnesota, and perhaps California, the North was poised to hold a substantial majority in both the ways that mattered to control of the federal government: the number of states and population. He predicted that over the next decade, "this great increase of Senators, added to the great increase of members of the House of Representatives and electoral college…will effectually and irretrievably destroy the equilibrium which existed when the Government commenced."

Taken alone, this loss of equilibrium would not have given the South cause to fear, but combined with legislation that made a mockery of the federal government as the "common agent of all," it had soured the affections of the South. Calhoun listed the acts—the Northwest Ordinance of 1787, the Missouri Compromise, and the recent Oregon bill—"by which the South has been excluded from the common territory belonging to all of the States." He described the way that a purportedly equal tax, the tariff, combined with unequal distribution of federal revenue, had quietly siphoned off "hundreds of millions of dollars" of wealth from the South and transferred it to the North. Even those used to Calhoun's recent predilection for dark prophecies must have been shocked by his depiction of the situation that now confronted them. "What was once a constitutional federal republic, is now converted in reality, into one as absolute as that of the Autocrat of Russia, and as despotic in its tendency, as any absolute government that ever existed."

At this critical juncture in history the South now faced the existential threat of the slavery question. There was in fact a deep divide over the morality of slavery, Calhoun acknowledged, and he made little distinction between the immediate abolitionist and Free Soil positions. Both, he was confident, aimed at the eventual extinction of slavery and the expansion of federal power had made them feel obligated to end slavery in any way they could, something that was now within their reach.

But Calhoun did not call for secession. Not yet. Instead, he painstakingly described exactly where the Union stood in the process of disunion so that his colleagues would understand what he believed they had to do: "It is a great mistake to suppose that disunion can be effected by a single blow. The cords which bound these States together in one common Union are far too numerous and powerful for that. Disunion must be the work of time. It is only through a long process and successively, that the cords can be snapped, until the whole fabric falls asunder."

Already some of those cords had snapped. Calhoun described the fracture of the Methodist and Baptist churches over slavery, and pointed to the way that the two great national political parties were disintegrating under the strain of sectional conflict. Like an astronomer describing great, unseen celestial forces, he continued: "If the agitation goes on, the same force, acting with increased intensity, as has been shown, will finally snap every cord, when nothing will be left to hold the States together except force. But, surely, that can, with no propriety of language, be called a Union when the only means by which the weaker is held connected with the stronger portion is force."

How then could the Union be saved? Not by "eulogies on the Union, however splendid." Nor by appeals to "the illustrious Southerner whose mortal remains repose on the western bank of the Potomac." Washington had been a slaveholder—"one of us"—and although devoted to the union with Britain, when that union became an instrument of oppression "he did not hesitate to draw his sword." Nor could Clay's compromise save the Union, Calhoun was certain, since it did not go to the root of the problem.

The only thing that could save the Union was "a full and final settlement, on the principle of justice, of all the questions at issue between the two sections." The more powerful section, the North, must act to save the Union by granting the South equal rights to acquired territory, faithfully enforcing the fugitive slave clause of the Constitution, and providing an amendment to the Constitution "which will restore to the South in substance the power she possessed of protecting herself, before the equilibrium between the sections was destroyed by the action of this Government." Certainly Calhoun had in mind his proposal for a dual executive, recently outlined but as yet unpublished in the *Discourse*. Calhoun's demand for a constitutional amendment was a complete surprise to everyone, even his southern colleagues.[78]

And if the North would not act? Then "say so and let the States we both represent agree to separate and part in peace. If you are unwilling we should part in peace, tell us so, and we shall know what to do, when you reduce the question to submission or resistance. If you remain silent, you will compel us to infer by your acts what you intend." California was the "test question," and if she were admitted as a free state, "We would be blind not to perceive in that case, that your real objects are power and aggrandizement, and infatuated not to act accordingly."[79]

THE SPEECH WAS CALHOUN'S final act of defiance, and even some of his southern colleagues thought he had gone too far. The next day Henry Foote of Mississippi rose and practically apologized to his northern colleagues for Calhoun's portrayal of them as tyrants, assuring them that Calhoun had not consulted with his southern colleagues. As Foote spoke Calhoun entered the Senate chamber in time to hear the end of his speech, and asked, "Did he accuse me of disunion? Did he mean to insinuate that?" Foote quickly apologized.[80]

Four days later Calhoun sat listening in the Senate to a more formidable foe when Daniel Webster gave his own speech contesting Calhoun's account of history and southern oppression. The entire founding generation, North and South, had believed slavery an evil, Webster asserted, and looked to its eventual demise. What had changed this? Cotton. "The age of cotton became a golden age for our southern brethren," Webster announced. And with slaveholders in charge of the American government for most of its early and recent history, they had been able to fully gratify their desire for wealth and land. Webster pointed to the Louisiana Purchase in 1803, the cession of Florida in 1819, and, especially, Texas in 1845. If the North had entire control of the government, as Calhoun charged, and had been using that control to diminish and oppress the South, they had done a remarkably poor job of it. No, Webster contended, despite the tariff the South had little to complain about when it came to the actions of the federal government. But, and here the speech turned, signaling Webster's willingness to compromise, the South did have cause to complain when it came to the fugitive slave clause. In that case, Webster announced, "the South, in my judgment, is right, and the North is wrong." Hailed by conservative northerners, and many southerners, Webster's speech showed a path toward compromise and earned him the undying scorn of many in the antislavery camp.[81] Calhoun saw in Webster's speech "a yielding on the part of the North" that might produce a short-lived compromise, but he was sure no mere legislative compromise could solve the heart of the problem. "Indeed," he wrote Thomas Green Clemson a few days later, "it is difficult to see how two people so different & hostile can exist together in one common Union."[82]

There was a pregnant moment in the midst of the speech when Calhoun interrupted Webster to contest his assertion that the Union could not be dissolved. "Am I to understand," Calhoun said weakly from his chair, "that no degree of oppression, no outrage, no broken faith, can produce the destruction of this Union?" If that were true, Calhoun held, the Union itself would become a tool of oppression. "No, sir! The Union can be broken. Great moral causes will break it... it can only be preserved by justice, good faith, and a rigid adherence to the Constitution." Webster replied that what Calhoun was describing was revolution, not peaceable disunion.[83] The argument would outlive both of them. Henry Clay's efforts at compromise would eventually fail in the Senate that summer, but they lasted just long enough to defuse the threat of secession. By the time the southern convention Calhoun had worked for met in Nashville that June, the appetite for radical action had dissipated in anticipation of a compromise. After the failure of Clay's so-called "omnibus bill" and the unexpected death of Zachary Taylor in July, Senator Stephen Douglas of Illinois, with the support of now-president Millard Fillmore, shepherded each of Clay's resolutions through the Senate separately, cobbling together the appearance of a compromise that, for the moment, staved off disunion.[84]

JOHN C. CALHOUN JR. arrived in Washington a few days after Calhoun's exchange with Webster, alerted to his father's deteriorating condition by Joseph Scoville, who also wrote Thomas Green Clemson, warning him to expect the worst.[85] Whether because she did not really think he was dying (after all there had been other serious attacks of the unpredictable disease), or for her own reasons, Floride stayed in South Carolina. For the next two weeks visitors came and went from Calhoun's rooms at the Old Capitol, old friends and old enemies alike, and he refused few of them. On Saturday evening, March 30, he began coughing up large amounts of mucus with intense effort and had difficulty breathing, signs that the end was near. His mind remained clear. "If I could have but one hour to speak in the Senate," John recalled him saying that day, "I could do more good than on any previous occasion of my life." John and Scoville sat by the fire into the evening as Calhoun lay in his bed nearby. A little after midnight Calhoun asked John if he was concerned, and when John said he was, Calhoun answered, "I feel I am sinking." He pointed to his dresser where the manuscripts of the *Disquisition* and *Discourse* sat, and asked his son to put them in his trunk for safekeeping. When John asked if he was in pain, Calhoun replied, "I am perfectly comfortable." Hours passed in silence. About six in the morning, Calhoun gestured for John to come to his bedside and, grasping his son's hand firmly, looked into his eyes for a long time, lips moving silently. Perhaps doubting his own abilities, John sent for North Carolina congressman Abraham Venable, who had been trained as a physician, and Venable soon appeared with two other members of the South Carolina delegation, James Orr and Daniel Wallace. As dawn broke on Washington, Calhoun raised his hand and ran it through the thick mass of gray hair that covered his pillow, then placed his hand on his chest. He strained to take one last deep breath and then quietly breathed his last "without a pang or struggle." As Abraham Venable reached to close Calhoun's eyes, Joseph Scoville noticed that they had, finally, dimmed.[86]

The magical wires that Calhoun had so admired soon flashed the news across the nation. Within hours the bells at St. Michael's Church in Charleston began ringing, continuing throughout the day, and the ships in Charleston harbor lowered their flags to half-mast, a pattern of mourning repeated in port cities and towns throughout the South.[87] During the two days before the funeral in Washington a steady stream of visitors waited in line to enter the room at the Old Capitol where Calhoun's body lay encased in a newly invented metal coffin featuring a glass window in the top through which curious onlookers could see the dead senator, dressed in the same black suit he had worn in the Senate, his face still "quite natural." Visitors marveled at the spartan simplicity of the famous senator's living quarters.[88]

The *Richmond Enquirer* noted that Calhoun had died a philosopher's death, calmly meeting his end without the comfort of religion or the presence of a minister, although Floride privately assured Anna that Calhoun had begun closing his letters with "God, bless you all" near the end of his life, "which was never done before." Scanning newspaper accounts of his famous pupil's death, Calhoun's old Yale tutor Benjamin Silliman noted, "No remark is quoted regarding his soul and his prospects for another life."[89]

In the Senate, Henry Clay and Daniel Webster eulogized their departed colleague of nearly forty years. "I was his senior, Mr. President, in years—in nothing else," Clay lamented graciously. Webster compared Calhoun to a "Senator of Rome" and marveled, "I have not, in public nor in private life, known a more assiduous person in the discharge of his appropriate duties. I have known no man who wasted less of life in what is called recreation." But in what became a running theme in the eulogies that day, Webster noted that the only exception to Calhoun's relentless work ethic was "the pleasure of conversation with his friends."[90]

The barely concealed sense of relief running just beneath the surface of both Clay's and Webster's eulogies echoed many who believed Calhoun's death had saved the Union. Even in South Carolina there were more than a few sighs of relief. His old Senate colleague William C. Preston considered Calhoun's death "the interposition of God to save the country," while South Carolina College professor Francis Lieber thought Calhoun's death would be "healing" for the nation.[91] Others, meanwhile, foresaw Calhoun exercising an influence from beyond the grave. "He is not dead, sir,—he is not dead," Thomas Hart Benton predicted with a prescience Calhoun would have thought uncharacteristic. "There may be no vitality in his body, but there is in his doctrines."[92]

Still others discerned a different manifestation of divine providence in Calhoun's death. "It is possible," mused the Reverend James Henley Thornwell to the students at South Carolina College, "that our confidence in the great statesman...may have been such as to provoke the jealousy of that God, who will not give His glory to another." Thornwell hinted that while the great man was a worthy political hero, the rising generation should avoid Calhoun's unorthodox religious beliefs.[93]

Six US senators, including Jefferson Davis, accompanied Calhoun's body on the steamship *Nina*, which arrived in Charleston harbor on April 25. Governor Whitemarsh Seabrook had convinced Calhoun's sons to let their father be buried in Charleston, instead of at Fort Hill, as Floride and Anna had assumed he would be, and as Calhoun probably would have preferred. A procession more than a mile long followed a hearse pulled by eight black horses along crowded, silent streets to City Hall, where Calhoun lay in state before his funeral at St. Philip's Episcopal Church the next day. Long into the day, and early the next until the funeral, a line of visitors formed, snaking its way through City Hall. White and black Charlestonians came that day, but not for the same reasons. Even as flowers brought by the women of Charleston piled up on the coffin, one white attendee overheard some black observers declare, "Calhoun was indeed a wicked man, for he wished that we might remain slaves."[94]

At the funeral ceremony the next day the Reverend James Warley Miles quoted Lord Byron, ushering Calhoun into the company of "those dead, but sceptered sovereigns who still rule our spirits from their urns." Then an honor guard bore the metal coffin to a new section of the church's cemetery and lowered Calhoun's remains into the stone tomb prepared to receive them, covering it with a massive marble slab engraved with a single word—"Calhoun." Then they left, the crowds dispersed, and the only movement in the silent cemetery was a flag, the flag of the Union, which hung down from a flagpole beside the grave, fluttering in the passing breeze.[95]

"Nations...Are but the Monuments of Deathless Men"

A T THE END OF THE Civil War the poet Walt Whitman over-heard two wounded Union soldiers talking in a Washington hospital. The younger man said that he had been to Charleston and seen "Calhoun's monument," by which he meant Calhoun's tomb. The other soldier, an "old veteran," interrupted. "I have seen Calhoun's monument," he told his young friend. "That you saw is not the real monument. But I have seen it. It is the desolated, ruined south; nearly the whole generation of young men between seventeen and thirty destroyed or maim'd; all the old families used up—the rich impoverish'd, the plantations cover'd with weeds, the slaves unloos'd and become the masters, and the name of southerner blacken'd with every shame—all that is Calhoun's real monument."[1]

If, as the old veteran intimated, Calhoun's real monument was the devastated South, it was because the decade after his death saw a degree of southern unity that Calhoun had been unable to conjure during his lifetime. During the 1850s almost the only disagreement among white South Carolinians was whether South Carolina should secede alone or wait for other slaveholding states to join them, and both sides claimed Calhoun. In 1852 leading separatists established the Calhoun Monument Association to raise a tribute to their hero, but they were soon elbowed aside by the Ladies' Calhoun Monument Association, formed in 1854, which became one of the first examples of the important role women would play in memorialization after the Civil War. The women even managed to squeeze a donation out of an aging James Petigru, who had vigorously opposed Calhoun during the nullification crisis. When the association laid the cornerstone of the new monument in 1858 they placed a cannonball from the Revolutionary War and a lock of Calhoun's hair at its base and invited the fire-eating secessionist Laurence M. Keitt to give the oration. But the monument remained unfinished when the war came.[2]

The Calhoun monument was part of a larger process that white southerners embarked on in the 1850s of imagining a separate, southern nation. The 1850s saw the rise of romantic nationalism on both sides of the Atlantic as separatist movements in Hungary, Poland, Ireland, and the American South came to see a shared culture, language, and history as a justification for separate nationhood. Located in different parts of the globe, the common thread connecting these movements was a sense of grievance, of being oppressed by means of an unnatural union with a people who were not countrymen.[3] Nobody had articulated the South's complaint as influentially as Calhoun, and in 1851 the South Carolina legislature recognized this fact by placing a copy of his final speech, alone, beneath the cornerstone of their new statehouse. When the writer, poet, and southern nationalist William Gilmore Simms wrote an 1855 ode to Calhoun that began, "Nations themselves are but the monuments / Of deathless men," it was clear he was not referring to the Union.[4]

The southern nation that Calhoun came to symbolize in the 1850s was a prosperous, modern, slaveholding nation, if only it could be protected from the new Republican Party and the abolitionists. White southerners looking at the world around them in the 1850s believed that they were seeing the confirmation of Calhoun's belief that slavery was compatible with progress. The 1850s saw not only booming global demand for cotton, but the apparent triumph of the free trade doctrines that Calhoun had championed and a growing acceptance among Europeans bent on industrial growth and colonial domination that some form of unfree labor—Chinese, Indian, African—was acceptable and even necessary for economic progress. The failure of the 1848 revolutions in Europe seemed to confirm Calhoun's contention that slavery was the best basis for free white government, and a growing consensus of racist scientific research, including by towering northern authorities like Harvard's Louis Agassiz, seemed to confirm that slavery was indeed the best condition for black people.[5]

That explains why a statue of Calhoun commissioned in the 1840s before his death and sculpted by Hiram Powers seemed so wrong to those who first saw it in 1850. Powers's statue, which was not connected to the efforts to build a monument, presented Calhoun as a figure of classical virtue clad in a toga. White South Carolinians hated it. Their hero was no antiquated figure from the distant past. He was the venerated prophet of an alternative, southern slaveholding modernity. When the Powers statue was destroyed in Columbia during the Civil War, few white South Carolinians missed it.[6]

When the state secession convention met in Charleston at the end of 1860, Calhoun looked on from a banner behind the president's chair, invoked as the spiritual father of secession and the founder of a new nation.[7] Whether that moment finally came because of Calhoun or because of his absence is an interesting but ultimately unanswerable question. Calhoun's entire aim to the end of his life had been to maintain slavery and southern power within the constitutional framework of the Union, but he always feared that secession might be inevitable in the course of events. How he would have weighed the major political victories that slaveholders won in the 1850s—the repeal of the Missouri Compromise, the Dred Scott decision, federal enforcement of the new Fugitive Slave Act—against the election of Abraham Lincoln is impossible to know. But surely he bore a large degree of the blame for secession. Without Calhoun, a generation of southern politicians like Robert Barnwell Rhett picked up the weapons he had forged for the preservation of the Union on southern terms and used them instead to destroy it.

Significantly, Calhoun's closest confidante in life looked on secession with deep foreboding. Anna wrote to her own daughter Floride in November 1860 that the South had been "pushed to extremity" and "could not perhaps draw back from their solemnly expressed determination without dishonor, but the alternative is a dreadful one, & and I look upon it as the beginning of the end."[8]

Nevertheless, the Confederacy adopted Calhoun as one of its founding fathers. Many of the secession ordinances passed by southern state legislatures rehearsed the arguments in Calhoun's final speech nearly blow by blow. Already by 1860 half the states that would secede had counties named after Calhoun. During the war the Confederate government put his image on currency and war bonds and named ships after him, while on the battlefield units with names like the Calhoun Avengers fought for the separate, slaveholding nation they believed, not without reason, that Calhoun would have wanted.[9]

In March 1861, the new Confederacy's vice president, Alexander Stephens of Georgia, explained the new nation's essence to a crowd in Savannah. Denouncing the outdated "error" that slavery was an evil and all men were equal, Stephens declared, "Our new government is founded upon exactly the opposite idea; its foundations are laid, its corner-stone rests, upon the great truth that the negro is not equal to the white man." The Confederate nation would be the "first, in the history of the world, based upon this great physical, philosophical, and moral truth," Stephens announced with pride, while acknowledging "this truth has been slow in the process of its development, like all other truths in the various departments of science. It has been so even amongst us. Many who hear me, perhaps, can recollect well, that this truth was not generally admitted, even within their day." Everyone in

Savannah that day knew exactly who had been responsible for opening the South's eyes.[10]

While Confederates celebrated Calhoun's intellectual remains as the basis of their new nation, his physical remains were treated like national relics. When Union warships threatened Charleston in 1863, two merchant brothers, Henry and Robert Gourdin, fearing that Union soldiers might desecrate the great man's grave, opened Calhoun's tomb in the middle of the night and carried the metal coffin back across the street to St. Philip's church, hiding it under an old scrap of carpeting before later reburying it in a different section of the church graveyard. There Calhoun lay for the remainder of the war.[11]

BY THE TIME THE Gourdins disinterred her father's remains, Anna had become accustomed to death for reasons that had nothing to do with the war. During the 1850s three of her brothers—John Jr., Patrick, and William—died, apparently of the same disease that killed their father. Her sister Cornelia died unexpectedly in 1857. In the early 1850s James went to California, continuing a long Calhoun family tradition of following opportunity to the edge of empire. He died there in 1861.[12]

After Andrew purchased Fort Hill from Floride in 1854, the widow Calhoun moved to a neighboring property, Mi Casa, where she lived until her death in 1866. Having learned the independence that widowhood could offer from her mother, Floride reported to Andrew months after Calhoun's death that she was "getting along far better than I had calculated. So far from feeling the least loneliness, or fear, at being alone, I am surprised, at my bravery...You would be surprised to find how much of a business person, I have become." Always sure she was about to die, Floride outlived all her children but Anna.[13]

In March 1865, with Grant encircling Richmond and Columbia in ruins, Andrew Pickens Calhoun died of a heart attack at Fort Hill. The inventory of his estate, made two weeks after Lee's surrender at

Appomattox courthouse, listed "one hundred and twenty-seven ne-groes" valued at $54,000, many of them from the Cane Brake planta-tion in Alabama that Andrew had finally sold two years earlier. First on the list, along with his wife Tilla, was seventy-one-year-old Sawney, still listed as property although he was now legally a free man, as his father Adam may have been before being sold into slavery to a man named Calhoun in the British colony of South Carolina. The inventory also revealed the ties that bound the Fort Hill freedpeople together, listing a four-year-old girl named after Sawney and Tilla's departed daughter Issey, and an eight-year-old girl named after Tilla, perhaps grandchildren. Issey and Young Sawney were not listed, and whether their parents ever discovered their fate is unknown.

Whatever ties bound them to each other, many of the Fort Hill freedpeople soon made it clear that they did not feel bound to the Cal-houn family. "All negroes have asserted their freedom now," wrote Floride Clemson, Anna's daughter, in her diary a few months later. "At Ft. Hill all have left but some fifteen hands."[14]

When the abolitionist William Lloyd Garrison visited Charleston in 1865 to see the American flag raised once more above Fort Sumter, he made a point to visit Calhoun's grave, where he placed his hand on the marble slab and solemnly announced to a small crowd that had gathered, "Down into a deeper grave than this slavery has gone, and for it there is no resurrection."[15] The irony was that in 1865, because the Gourdin brothers had moved Calhoun's body for safekeep-ing during the war, the tomb that Garrison laid his hand on was empty. Calhoun and his doctrines were not as dead as Garrison might have hoped. In fact, the years after the war would see a kind of resurrection of Calhoun's ideas.[16]

Soon after the war ended, Andrew Johnson's administration de-cided to put Jefferson Davis on trial for treason in an effort to publicly and decisively discredit the doctrine of state sovereignty and the constitutionality of secession. Yet they soon had to abandon the trial in order to forestall the disastrous possibility that Davis might be acquitted by a sympathetic jury.[17] Meanwhile, ex-Confederates like Alexander Stephens wasted little time vindicating the South's course in the late war by appealing to Calhoun's theories, writing in 1868 that Calhoun's *Disquisition* was "one of the few books of this age, that will outlive the language in which it was written."[18]

At times it seemed that Calhoun was winning legal victories from the grave. In 1873 the Supreme Court drastically restricted the new Fourteenth Amendment, which guaranteed equal protection under the law. In the famous *Slaughterhouse* case, the court declared that the amendment only applied to federal rights specifically enumerated in the Constitution since the main source of citizenship and rights remained in the states. In his dissent from the majority, Justice Stephen Field complained that the court had adopted "the opinion of Mr. Calhoun and the class represented by him."[19]

Still, the demise of the Confederacy and slavery posed a problem for the ongoing effort to memorialize Calhoun in Charleston. White southerners could no longer hold up Calhoun as the avatar of a modern, slaveholding nation, and his death in 1850 precluded the kind of veneration that white southerners heaped on battlefield heroes like Stonewall Jackson and Robert E. Lee. But as Walt Whitman famously said of himself, Calhoun contained multitudes. When the women's association in Charleston dedicated their finished Calhoun monument in 1887, they emphasized Calhoun's stature as a national, not sectional, leader, a figure whose fight to preserve the Union could serve the imperative of sectional reconciliation. They sent invitations to President Grover Cleveland, his cabinet, the governors of every state in the Union, and the famous nurse of the Union, Clara Barton. On the day of the dedication they draped the statue in a gigantic American flag. The crowd gathered on Citadel Square heard L.Q. C. Lamar praise Calhoun as a figure whose spirit could mend the severed bonds of affection between the North and South.

Just as the choice of the fire-eating secessionist Laurence Keitt had thirty years earlier, the choice of Lamar sent a message. He was a Confederate veteran, but also Grover Cleveland's secretary of the interior, the first white southerner to serve in a presidential cabinet since the end of the war, although perhaps nobody grasped the irony that Calhoun had opposed the creation of Lamar's office with almost his dying breath. Most strikingly for someone charged with paying tribute to Calhoun, Lamar was a Republican, the party of Abraham Lincoln, and most Americans knew him for his stirring eulogy of the abolitionist senator Charles Sumner. Unsurprisingly, Lamar was a controversial figure in the white South, and the women's invitation to him represented a conscious decision to portray Calhoun in shades of reconciliation and compromise. That day Lamar assured the audience that had Calhoun lived, "his great talents would have been, as they had ever been before, directed to save this people from the horrors of disunion and war."[20]

Charleston's black residents saw the Calhoun monument in starkly different terms. From its unveiling, many saw the statue as part of a larger effort to reimpose a racial order on Charleston after the white South's successful resistance to Reconstruction, which in South Carolina had ended in 1876 with the election of ex-Confederate Wade Hampton as governor. Sculptor Albert E. Harnisch's statue of Calhoun rising from his seat to defend South Carolina in the Senate nowhere mentioned slavery, but putting up a statue to Calhoun at the moment that white southerners were carefully constructing the intricate legal and social framework of Jim Crow sent a clear message. "Blacks took that statue personally," an elderly Mamie Garvin Fields recalled of her childhood as an African American in Charleston in the 1890s. "As you passed by, here was Calhoun looking at you in the face and telling you, 'Nigger, you may not be a slave, but I am back to see you stay in your place'...I believe white people were talking to us about Jim Crow through that statue." In response, Fields recalled, "We used to carry something with us, if we knew we would be passing that way, in order to deface that statue—scratch up the coat, break the watch chain, try to knock off the nose…" Originally, Harnisch had planned to ring the base of the Calhoun monument with four allegorical figures representing Truth, Justice, the Constitution, and History, but he only ever delivered the figure of Justice. White observers soon noted with discomfort that black Charlestonians had taken to calling the statue of Calhoun towering over a lone, diminutive female figure, "Calhoun and 'he wife."[21]

Black hostility and sarcasm aimed at the monument, along with aesthetic objections—one critic called it "a statue of an arm-chair, with a tall gentleman standing beside it"—may have played a role in the decision to replace the Harnisch statue in 1896 with a new statue cast by New York sculptor John Massey Rhind.[22] Rhind's creation featured a fluted column rising more than a hundred feet in the air, with a caped Calhoun standing, looking grimly down over the square. At its base a plaque commemorated Calhoun's commitment to "Truth, Justice, and the Constitution," still with no mention of slavery. Mamie Garvin Fields recalled with some satisfaction how black Charlestonians interpreted the change. "Children and adults beat up John C. Calhoun so badly that the whites had to come back and put him way high up," she recalled, "so we couldn't get to him."[23]

THE CAMPAIGN THAT MAMIE GARVIN Fields and others waged against the Calhoun statue in Charleston was part of a long-running seam in American memory, running back at least to Frederick Douglass, in which black Americans forthrightly identified Calhoun's real monument as his defense of slavery and white supremacy. In 1884, former slave and Calhoun's fellow South Carolinian Archibald Grimké announced to an audience in a Washington, DC, lecture that Calhoun's had been "the master hand that directed the horrible chorus of slavery."[24] In his novel *The Marrow of Tradition*, a fictionalized version of the 1898 Wilmington, North Carolina, race riot that was published in

1901, the black writer Charles Chesnutt imagined a group of white characters who gathered to drink "Calhoun Cocktails" mixed from a recipe handed down by Calhoun himself to one of their fathers. As they drink this "nectar of the gods," they lay plans to maintain the South's racial hierarchy and drink toasts to "White Supremacy!... White Supremacy Everywhere...Now and Forever!"[25] Several decades later, in a speech given at the closing of the Southern Negro Youth Congress held in Columbia, South Carolina, in 1946, the black scholar and intellectual W. E. B. Du Bois pointed to Calhoun as the beginning of a "long series of men whose eternal damnation is the fact that they looked *truth* in the face and did not see it...men whose names must ever be besmirched by the fact that they fought against freedom and democracy in a land which was founded upon democracy and freedom."[26]

Between Grimké's lecture in 1884 and Du Bois's indictment in 1946, however, black claims on Calhoun's legacy lost out to rival claims by white Americans who believed that the interests of national unity and sectional reconciliation overrode the imperative of racial justice and an accurate telling of history. When the last aging, tottering Union and Confederate veterans gathered to celebrate the fiftieth anniversary of Gettysburg in 1913, they celebrated a version of the war in which both sides had been in some sense right, both sides fought valiantly for principles deeply held, and in which slavery played, at most, a secondary role. In perhaps the best sign that the national mood was open to a positive view of Calhoun, D. W. Griffith's blockbuster 1915 film *Birth of a Nation* told a story of Reconstruction that mirrored exactly Calhoun's fervid prophecies in the 1840s of the South's fate should abolitionists succeed.

Indeed, there were clear signs that Calhoun had been ushered back into the nation's good graces as one of its premier, if controversial, constitutional thinkers, whose memory could be honored in part because history had proved him wrong. When the state of South Carolina donated a statue of Calhoun to be placed in the National Statuary Hall in the US Capitol building in 1910, Massachusetts senator Henry Cabot Lodge praised Calhoun's intellectual prowess, his courage as a statesman, and absolved him of the old charge of inconsistency. Then, completely contradicting Calhoun's own descriptions of himself and his society, Lodge portrayed Calhoun as a lonely figure fighting against the flow of history. Calhoun "must have known," Lodge surmised, that "the world of civilized man was demanding a larger freedom, and slavery, economically unsound, was a survival and an anachronism," and that "the principle of separatism, of particularism, was at war with the spirit of the time," which Lodge identified as a deepening sense of nationalism.[27]

One of the main signs of Calhoun's resurgent national stature came from his alma mater, Yale University, which named a new residential college for Calhoun in 1933. The committee recommending Calhoun's name called him "Yale's most eminent graduate in the field of Civil State," passing over more recent graduates like president and chief justice of the Supreme Court William Howard Taft as too controversial. The decision to go with Calhoun was in effect a diversity initiative: Yale leaders hoped that Calhoun's name would attract southern students, and perhaps with this in mind the university included a series of stained glass windows in the completed college depicting contented slaves in fields white with cotton, and, in one, a shackled black man kneeling at Calhoun's feet. Indeed, although one donor's family objected to his name being associated with a "secessionist," nobody objected to Calhoun's defense of slavery until the 1933 dedication ceremony for the new college, when the writer Leonard Bacon, whose great-grandfather had been an antislavery minister and a professor at Yale, observed in verse written for the occasion:

> *I suppose that I ought*
> *To have bayed at the moon*
> *Singing the praises*
> *of John C. Calhoun.*

But I cannot, although
He was virtuous and brave,
And besides my great-grandfather
Would turn in his grave,
If he dreamed of a monument
Raised to renown
Calhoun in this rank
Abolitionist town.[28]

IN THE MIDDLE DECADES of the twentieth century several different strands of American conservatism, but not all, looked to Calhoun as an example of their ideals, usually minimizing his defense of slavery as secondary to his constitutional or conservative principles. About the same time that Yale named a residential college for Calhoun, a group of southern writers known as the Nashville Agrarians published a manifesto titled *I'll Take My Stand* in which they warned against the effects of industrialization on a traditional, agricultural southern society. Some of the agrarians, like the writer Andrew Lytle, saw in Calhoun's battle with the tariff and the abolitionists a prototype of their own struggle to preserve a way of life from the ravages of modern industrial capitalism and an all-powerful federal government. More mainstream than the agrarians, in 1953 the conservative writer Russell Kirk included Calhoun alongside John Randolph as exemplars of a uniquely southern conservatism in his widely influential book *The Conservative Mind*. Kirk approvingly portrayed Calhoun as a chastened Jeffersonian, "unalterably opposed to 'progress,' centralization, and abstract humanitarianism," who had resisted "a consolidated and industrialized new order." Kirk viewed the "partisan controversy over slavery" as separable from Calhoun's conservative ideas, and *The Conservative Mind* helped launch an intellectual resurgence that shaped the modern conservative movement.[29]

In 1957 freshman senator John F. Kennedy of Massachusetts, no conservative, chaired a committee tasked with selecting five distinguished senators from American history whose portraits would be placed in the Senate reception room. The committee settled on "leadership in national thought and constitutional interpretation as well as legislation" as their criteria and agreed that the decisions had to be unanimous. They polled 160 scholars who returned 65 names, eventually agreeing on Henry Clay, Daniel Webster, and John C. Calhoun, along with Robert Taft and Robert La Follette Sr.[30]

One of the scholars whose opinion Kennedy sought out was Yale historian C. Vann Woodward. A native southerner but no southern apologist, in 1955 Woodward had published *The Strange Career of Jim Crow*, detailing the historical construction of racial segregation in the American South in the hope that it could be dismantled. Martin Luther King Jr. called the book "the historical Bible of the Civil Rights movement." When Kennedy wrote to Woodward asking his opinion on the five greatest senators in American history, Woodward included Calhoun "for his contributions in constitutional theory," although he did put Calhoun last on his list.[31]

Along with scholarly opinion, the committee's decision may have been influenced by one of its members, Senator Richard Russell, a Democrat from Georgia who played a central role in resisting the civil rights movement. The year before serving on Kennedy's committee, Russell had cooperated with another freshman senator, Strom Thurmond of South Carolina, in crafting a resolution denouncing the Supreme Court's landmark 1954 decision in *Brown v. Board of Education*, which struck down the "separate but equal" doctrine that lay at the heart of Jim Crow. Although it stopped well short of Calhoun's apocalyptic rhetoric in the Southern Address, this resolution, which came to be known as the Southern Manifesto, nevertheless raised the specter of state interposition and characterized the *Brown* decision as "a clear abuse of judicial power." After the reading of the manifesto in the

Senate chamber on March 12, 1956, Senator Wayne Morse of Oregon declared in disbelief, "On the basis of the arguments...of southern Senators, you would think today Calhoun was walking and speaking on the floor of the Senate." Some of the southern senators took Morse's comment as a compliment.[32]

For some white Americans, Calhoun's association with resistance to the civil rights movement spelled the end of an era in which he could be celebrated as primarily a brilliant constitutional thinker. In a 1968 foreword to his massive three-volume biography of Calhoun, first published in the 1940s, Dartmouth College professor Charles M. Wiltse noted the change. He had originally written about Calhoun in a different era, when "numerical majorities" had recently handed power to figures like Mussolini and Hitler, and American voters had given unprecedented power to Franklin D. Roosevelt, whose New Deal, Wiltse observed, "did not appear to differ in essentials from the dictatorships of Europe." Twenty years later, in 1968, the main problem confronting the United States was the "paradoxical survival in portions of our country of the social mores of the old south." In this new historical moment, Wiltse realized, it was Calhoun's defense of slavery that mattered, and readers should understand that his interpretations of Calhoun "represent a history of the first half of the nineteenth century as seen from the fifth decade of the twentieth." The times were changing, and as they did, different parts of Calhoun's legacy rose to the surface, although they were the very parts that black Americans had been pointing to all along.[33]

IN THE LAST HALF of the twentieth century Calhoun's real monument continued to shift, although in ways that both confirmed and confounded other layers of his memory. In 1979 the Yale-educated Dutch political scientist Arend Lijphart published a book titled *Democracy in Plural Societies* in which he explicitly drew on Calhoun's theory of the concurrent majority to found the field of "consociational democracy," which examines methods of political power-sharing to sustain democracy within societies deeply divided along religious, ethnic, or ideological lines. One of the ideas Lijphart examined was the minority veto, which he wrote "is synonymous with John C. Calhoun's concurrent majority."[34]

Lijphart's work was widely influential, and one of his early readers was the white South African politician Frederik van Zyl Slabbert, leader of the anti-apartheid Progressive Federal Party in South Africa, who came to believe that the minority veto was the only means of winning white support for the end of apartheid. In his 1979 book, *South Africa's Options: Strategies for Sharing Power*, Slabbert proposed a new South African constitution in which universal suffrage would be coupled with minority veto power for any group garnering 10 to 15 percent of the electorate. Meanwhile, the ruling National Party in South Africa saw in the minority veto a means to maintain white power, and floated several less sincere versions of the idea, including rotating the presidency between white and non-white presidents. Unsurprisingly, the idea of a minority veto was consistently rejected by Nelson Mandela and the African National Congress, which saw the veto as a blatant attempt for a white minority to maintain power. South Africa eventually would follow a majoritarian model.[35]

Through Lijphart, Calhoun's theories also exerted an influence on his family's ancestral home of Northern Ireland, where the 1998 Good Friday Agreement instituted a consensus model of government and a so-called "diarchy," a dual executive along the lines proposed by Calhoun, between nationalist and unionist camps in the conflict. One recent scholar of Calhoun's political theories has written that if the agreement continues to succeed, it will be "better evidence indeed [for the viability of Calhoun's theory] than anything that occurred in Calhoun's original antebellum U.S. context."[36]

Perhaps the most fascinating twist in the recent history of Calhoun's legacy came in 1993 when Bill Clinton nominated a University of Pennsylvania Law School professor named Lani Guinier to head the Justice Department's civil rights division. After an outcry from Republicans and even a few Democrats about the content of Guinier's scholarship, Clinton withdrew the nomination, acknowledging that he had found some of her writings "anti-democratic" and "very difficult to defend."[37]

Guinier went on to become the first woman of color tenured at Harvard Law School, and the year after Clinton withdrew her nomination she published a book titled *Tyranny of the Majority: Fundamental Fairness in Representative Democracy*, in which she outlined how a democratic process based on supposedly color-blind majoritarian principles could reinforce racial inequality. "Sometimes, even when rules are perfectly fair in form they serve in practice to exclude particular groups from meaningful participation," Guinier wrote, describing how even substantial minorities could be completely shut out of representation on county boards, city councils, or multimember state legislative districts when voting consistently followed racial lines. "When majorities are fixed," she wrote, "the minority lacks any mechanism for holding the majority to account or even to listen…The permanent majority simply has its way." Many of Guinier's solutions—including cumulative voting, her proposal to give minority representatives' votes more weight on issues directly affecting them, or requiring supermajorities, "or its equivalent, a minority veto on critical minority issues"—echoed Calhoun's argument that for democracy to work, a minority must have a meaningful voice in determining its fate. Like Calhoun, Guinier also believed that these changes could restore the element of genuine deliberation to democracy where it had been lost or intentionally suppressed by blind majoritarianism.[38] One of the book's reviewers pointed out the "fundamentally conservative" nature of Guinier's proposals, including "her quite genuine concern, which pervades the book, that unless public policy begins to address the needs of the African American community, that community will become increasingly disaffected from national politics, with disorder to follow."[39]

As Guinier discovered, this was not a version of conservatism that many American conservatives in the 1990s recognized. In an attack on Guinier in the *Wall Street Journal* during the nomination fight, columnist Paul Gigot compared Guinier to Calhoun and portrayed both as fundamentally antidemocratic. "The root American principle, over which Lincoln fought a war, is that rights inhere in individuals, not groups," Gigot wrote. "In the Guinier view, some voters are more equal than others." In effect, Gigot accused Guinier of wanting the same special rights for the descendants of slaves that Calhoun had once wanted for slaveholders. It seems unlikely that Guinier's ideas will ever form the foundations of a real monument to Calhoun, one exactly the opposite of what he wanted, but if they ever do, it will be as undeniably his as the one Whitman's old veteran identified.[40]

THE MOST RECENT CHAPTER in the long history of Calhoun's memory and America's long national failure to reckon with its history began on the evening of June 17, 2015, when a thin, boyish-looking white man named Dylann Roof turned off Calhoun Street in Charleston, South Carolina, entered Emanuel African Methodist Episcopal Church, one block from where the Calhoun monument sat on Marion Square, and joined a Bible study in progress. "Mother Emanuel," as the church is known, was a historic site of black resistance—the revolutionary Denmark Vesey, leader of the failed 1822 slave rebellion, had once been a member. After sitting for nearly an hour, Roof opened fire when the group stood to pray, killing nine of the church's congregants, including pastor Clementa Pinckney. In a picture discovered after the shooting, Roof held a Confederate battle flag, and according to witnesses in the church that day, before he began shooting he said, "I have to do this, because you're raping our women and y'all taking over the world."[41]

In the weeks after the shooting a reevaluation of Confederate symbols and monuments swept the country, and much of the attention soon settled on Calhoun, especially his connection to the Confederacy and his defense of slavery. In Charleston, activists continuing a long pattern of local resistance spray painted the words "racist" on the Calhoun monument in Marion Square and added the word "slavery" alongside "Truth, Justice, and the Constitution."[42] In Minnesota a lengthy list of signatures petitioned for the renaming of Lake Calhoun outside Minneapolis, named by one of the expeditions Calhoun sponsored as secretary of war. Meanwhile at Yale University, a petition calling Calhoun "one of the most prolific defenders of slavery and white supremacy in American history" demanded that Calhoun College be renamed. It quickly swelled with signatures.[43]

Yale president Peter Salovey initially resisted the proposed change. In his address to the freshman class at Yale that fall Salovey warned against attempts "to efface or distance ourselves from our own history," and announced a series of conversations and campus events to consider Calhoun's legacy and connection to Yale. Salovey asked his audience, "Are we perhaps better off retaining before us the name and the evocative, sometimes brooding presence of Yale graduate John C. Calhoun?"[44]

Over the next year many members of the Yale community made it very clear they would rather not be haunted by John C. Calhoun, including a black dishwasher in Calhoun College named Corey Menafee, who used a broom to break out one of the college's stained glass windows depicting slaves carrying cotton. "It's 2016," Menafee told an interviewer, "I shouldn't have to come to work and see things like that."[45] A few months later a black Yale student named Tobias Holden from Anderson, South Carolina—not far from Fort Hill—wrote an opinion piece in the *New York Times* revealing that he had recently learned of a family oral tradition that he was descended from Calhoun and an enslaved Cherokee woman named Liza Lee. Holden made it clear that he, too, wanted his ancestor's name removed from the college.[46]

In August 2016 Salovey convened a distinguished committee to establish principles to guide renaming for the whole campus, with Calhoun College as the test case. The committee produced a detailed and carefully reasoned report in which they argued for the criteria of a "principle legacy" as the test for renaming. They described Calhoun's distinguished record of public service, and pointed out that while Calhoun's constitutional theories were controversial, they nevertheless "attracted widespread attention and respect as the work of a man with unusual analytic talents." They even recognized that "devices designed by Calhoun to protect the interests of white slaveholders are now deployed as institutional defenses of minority interests against majoritarian tyranny." Yet the committee argued that Calhoun's principle legacy, his real monument, was his defense of slavery.[47] In 2017 Yale renamed Calhoun College for Rear Admiral Grace Hopper, a pioneering naval officer and computer scientist. In 2020, after a fresh wave of protests, the mayor and city council of Charleston announced that they would take down the monument to Calhoun erected by the Ladies' Calhoun Monument Association in Marion Square.

IN THE FIRST QUARTER of the twenty-first century, John C. Calhoun has become once again what he was to some even in his own lifetime, a heretic. Indeed, to many Calhoun seems to represent the antithesis of the American idea of equality, inclusion, and popular democracy. It is a testament to our current era that a broader swath of Americans are finally coming around to a conclusion that black Americans reached long ago. But as the Yale committee fully realized, there are dangers inherent in the ritual of proclaiming heretics, who often go to the stake to expiate the anxieties of those who watch them burn. Heretics, in history and historical memory, usually function to reveal and reinforce the official orthodoxy of their societies, which are usually not as orthodox as they claim to be. We cannot forget that changing the name of

Calhoun College does not change Yale's history, any more than removing the Calhoun monument in Charleston changes the history of that city, the South, or the United States of America. We must be careful to avoid what the Yale committee called "the problem of erasure," of not acknowledging how the past is always present.[48]

That problem can take many forms, obscuring Calhoun's continued relevance in our world. Reinforced by a healthy dose of American exceptionalism, there are those who believe that Calhoun's constitutional arguments are ineluctably linked to and constrained by the purposes for which he made them. Certainly, we should never forget that Calhoun wrought his theories in defense of slaveholders, and that in an American context they have mostly been used to defend racial inequality. On that point our history is clear. We should also realize that Calhoun's particular formulations were designed to protect an already powerful minority. And yet the powerful refashioning of arguments quite similar to Calhoun's by modern advocates for minority rights proves this is not an ironclad rule, as does the fact that his solutions, or solutions like them, continue to attract attention in deeply divided democratic societies around the world. As one political scientist writes, "Political systems granting veto rights to one or more interests have existed, continue to exist today, and will be created or at least proposed in the future." In this light, Calhoun's theories, though indelibly shaped by his time and place, were a response to a perennial problem in democratic societies, and even if these systems do not explicitly draw from Calhoun, he is part of their history in our world.[49]

Moreover, the years since the 2016 presidential election have proved with abundant clarity that it is not only putative conservatives who need to worry about the excesses of popular democracy or the defense of state and local rights in the face of executive or federal power.[50] We have hardly outlived the debate, in the United States and elsewhere, over how to restrain the excesses of democracy while maintaining its vitality. Nor have we definitively solved the riddle of the relationship between states and the federal government. We do not have to eat the apple Calhoun offered in his theory of the concurrent majority, the prospect of democracy with no dangers, in order to learn from his critiques.[51] Honoring and understanding are two very different things. The English philosopher John Stuart Mill, who in 1861 rated Calhoun the best "speculative political thinker" America had produced since the founding generation, once argued that the act of silencing religious or political heretics deprives us of an opportunity to strengthen the basis of our beliefs. In Mill's terms, if we dismiss, forget, or mischaracterize Calhoun, we deny ourselves a useful critic of many of our most basic, and therefore unexamined, assumptions.[52]

There is also the stubborn fact that secession remains a prominent tendency in our world. Americans tend to associate secession so strongly with the failed state of the Confederacy that we assume the forces of separatism and secession died at Appomattox. In fact, far from breaking the spell of secession, the Civil War instead marked the beginning of an era in which "political divorce"—as philosophers, legal scholars, and political scientists now prefer to call it—would become one of the root causes of large-scale slaughter all over the world, making the morality and legality of secession, including the construction of peaceful constitutional processes to accomplish it, a source of major debate. Surveying this global phenomenon, one historian concludes that for the last two centuries "state breaking has been the primary method of state making around the world."[53] There is no reason to expect that this will not continue. Indeed, even as Yale inched toward removing the name of Calhoun College, the Catalan parliament declared independence in defiance of the Spanish central government, sparking a protracted constitutional crisis. Even today within the United States there are numerous secession movements advocating state, county, or local secession, and it would be naïve in the extreme to think that the Civil War has inoculated the United States forever from what it revealed—in one historian's words, "the possibility for national disintegration and the astonishing compulsion of modern nations to resist fragmentation." In this context, Calhoun appears as one of the first figures in the age of the modern nation-state to contemplate the causes and the processes by which nations are unmade.[54]

Finally, it is not difficult to draw a straight line that runs from Calhoun through the Confederacy and Massive Resistance in the civil rights era to Dylann Roof's evil act and the most extreme elements of our society today. But by the time that line reaches us, it is suspiciously faint, as if the forces in our history that Calhoun represents have attenuated to the point that they only exercise their force on radical extremists, instead of continuing to operate powerfully and silently in the structures of our society, our governments, and ourselves. In excising Calhoun's name from buildings, toppling monuments to his memory, and associating him with fringe elements of our society, we should be careful not to forget his central role in our past and, unavoidably, our present. If we excommunicate Calhoun by casting him as the defender of a rejected path in American history, the antidemocratic defender of an antiquated brutality, and the father of the failed Confederacy, we will be unable to see the lines running from Calhoun's America to our own. And if we reduce him to his defense of slavery, which set him apart even in his own day, we may miss the fact that when Calhoun proclaimed the United States, not the Confederacy, "the government of the white man," it was possibly one of the least controversial things that he ever said.

We do not have to honor John C. Calhoun, nor should we. But he has not left us the luxury of forgetting him. Perhaps that, as much as anything else, is his real monument.

ACKNOWLEDGMENTS

THE FIRST DEBT THAT ANY biographer of John C. Calhoun owes is to the editors of Calhoun's published papers, who painstakingly collected, edited, and published those documents over the course of more than half a century, finishing in 2003. Without the diligent and careful work of Robert L. Meriwether, W. Edwin Hemphill, Shirley A. Cook, and Clyde N. Wilson, I could not have written this book. Their contribution to preserving the American past is a testament to the quiet, patient, meticulous work that sometimes goes unnoticed and is certainly underappreciated in our distracted digital age.

This book would also have been impossible without the work of a whole host of other historians who have transformed our understanding of Calhoun's world, and our own, over the past twenty years. Thanks to them I often had the feeling that I was plowing in furrows that had already been prepared for me. Their names are in the endnotes.

Many other generous colleagues and friends have helped along the way. Don Doyle, Beth Schweiger, Vernon Burton, and Jim Roark all generously encouraged the project and gave of their time to write recommendations for various grant proposals. At the South Caroliniana Library, Henry Fulmer, Graham Duncan, and the rest of the Caroliniana staff pointed me in the right direction, patiently explained the ins and outs of their invaluable archive, and provided me with one of the best environments a scholar could ask for to simply sit and think. On one of my several trips to Columbia, Alex Moore took the time to enlighten me about the inner workings of the *Papers of John C. Calhoun*. At Clemson University, Will Hiott proved a fount of information on the Calhoun family and Fort Hill that would have taken me ages to discover otherwise. Kate Armstrong patiently answered my questions about her brilliant dissertation on grieving, loss, and antebellum motherhood. Michael Kimmage sent me Alan Heimert's wonderful article on political symbolism in Herman Melville's *Moby-Dick*. When Daniel Domingues arranged for me to present material from the last chapter at the Kinder Institute on Constitutional Democracy at the University of Missouri, Jeff Pasley and Jay Sexton were warm and insightful hosts.

I started the research for this book during a semester's leave as a university research professor at Valparaiso University, where I left behind a wonderful community and a group of exemplary friends and colleagues. Heath Carter, in particular, was a constant source of camaraderie and questions. At Baylor, Barry Hankins and the history department gave me the time to complete the book, including crucial course releases during my first year. My colleagues, especially fellow "basement dwellers" Dan Barish, Dan Watkins, and Elesha Coffman, dealt graciously with my often-closed door. Tommy Kidd proved a wise guide to trade publishing, as well as all things Baylor. Mike Parrish, who must read in his sleep, sent me several articles that significantly shaped parts of the book. Jim SoRelle passed on the anecdote, which appears in the epilogue, from Charles Chesnutt's novel *Marrow of Tradition*. Caleb Cruseturner compiled articles about Calhoun in British newspapers, several of which are cited in the book, for an honors project.

Whether he remembers it or not, Joe Crespino first suggested to me in an offhand comment that a biography was a good second book project. I'm still not sure he was right, but he has been a steady source of encouragement over the past few years, and his insightful comments on the epilogue improved it tremendously. Other colleagues, including Rod Andrew, Mark Cheathem, Matt Karp, and Rachel Shelden, read significant parts of the book manuscript, pointing out embarrassing mistakes, imprecise wording, and lazy or misguided arguments. I am sure they did not always agree with my conclusions, but their intellectual rigor and generosity made the book much better than it would have been otherwise.

I've been lucky to work with two wonderful editors at Basic Books. Dan Gerstle had the idea for this book about the same time I did, and once we found each other, he proved a savvy and reliable guide in the book's early stages before departing for a new job. Connor Guy faithfully and patiently pushed me to keep writing, and never once complained or lost his imperturbable cool. His advocacy for the reader during the editing process was nothing short of heroic. Bill Warhop's formidable eye greatly improved the manuscript during copyediting. Basic's publisher, Lara Heimert, terrifies me, and she knows it, but she never took advantage of that fact. Basic is lucky to have her at the helm.

Nobody should have to share a household with a writer, let alone one who spends his days with John C. Calhoun. Catherine Elder did much more than that. She read draft chapters, pointed out when I was being too wordy, made me go running when I was grumpy, and put life back into perspective on the many occasions when I lost my frame of reference. Philip, Dalton, Henry, and Caroline, with varying degrees of actual interest, dutifully asked me what chapter I was writing, and what the book was about, over and over and over again for five years. Their questions were an invaluable reminder that for them the book was not the most important thing about me. For that, I dedicate it to them.

Unless noted otherwise, correspondence and speeches are from Robert L. Meriwether et al., eds., *The Papers of John C. Calhoun*, 28 vols. (Columbia: University of South Carolina Press, 1959–2003). For recent authoritative overviews of the era and further reading, readers can follow notes below to Daniel Walker Howe's *What Hath God Wrought: The Transformation of America, 1815–1848* (Oxford University Press, 2007) and Sean Wilentz's *The Rise of American Democracy: Jefferson to Lincoln* (W.W. Norton & Company, 2006).

Abbreviations

AC United States Congress, *Annals of Congress*, Web Edition (Washington, DC: Library of Congress, 1999), http://memory.loc.gov /ammem/amlaw/lwac.html
SCL South Caroliniana Library at the University of South Carolina
SCDAH South Carolina Department of Archives and History

Preface
  1. Joseph Scoville to Thomas Green Clemson, April 1, 1850; George Park Fisher, *Life of Benjamin Silliman*, vol. 2 (Philadelphia: Porter & Coates, 1866), 99.
  2. "'Take It Down': Calhoun Monument Will Be Moved from Marion Square, Charleston Mayor Says," *Charleston Post and Courier*, June 17, 2020, https://www.postandcourier.com/news/take-it-down-calhoun-monument-will

-be-relocated-charleston-mayor-says/article_e091943a-afdc-11ea-9ff0-a7abea
2a3199.html.

3. Sam Tanenhaus, "Original Sin," *New Republic*, February 9, 2013; Nancy MacLean, *Democracy in Chains: The Deep History of the Radical Right's Stealth Plan for America* (New York: Penguin Books, 2018); Lincoln Caplan, "The White-Supremacist Lineage of a Yale College," *Atlantic*, October 5, 2015; "Lake Calhoun Name Change Gets Another Look in Minneapolis," *Minneapolis Star-Tribune*, June 23, 2015.

4. Richard Hofstadter, *The American Political Tradition: And the Men Who Made It* (New York: Vintage, 1948), 89–90.

5. J. William Harris, "Last of the Classical Republicans: An Interpretation of John C. Calhoun," *Civil War History* 30 (September 1984): 267.

6. Irving H. Bartlett, *John C. Calhoun: A Biography* (New York: W.W. Norton, 1993), 382. The exception to this trend is the historian Lacy Ford, whose brilliant essays on Calhoun have shaped my own interpretation in what follows.

Chapter One: The People with No Name

1. Rod Andrew, *The Life and Times of General Andrew Pickens: Revolutionary War Hero, American Founder* (Chapel Hill: University of North Carolina Press, 2017), 156–161. The title of this chapter is taken from Patrick Griffin, *The People with No Name: Ireland's Ulster Scots, America's Scots Irish, and the Creation of a British Atlantic World, 1689–1764* (Princeton, NJ: Princeton University Press, 2001).

2. John C. Calhoun and R. M. T. Hunter, *Life of John C. Calhoun* (New York: Harper & Brothers, 1843), 3. A wealth of family tradition and genealogical research can be found in Orval O. Calhoun, *800 Years of Colquhoun, Colhoun, Calhoun, and Cahoon Family History in Ireland, Scotland, England, United States of America, Australia, and Canada* (Baltimore: Gateway Press, 1976), including the number of Calhouns (or Colhouns) who lived in and around Strabane and Newtownstuart in County Tyrone.

3. Griffin, *People with No Name*, 19.

4. John Abernethy, "Scarce and Valuable Tracts and Sermons" (Dublin, 1751) 28; John Abernethy, "The Nature and Consequences of the Sacramental Test Considered" (Dublin, 1731), 50; Griffin, *People with No Name*, 3, 9–36, 62–64.

5. Henry F. May, *The Enlightenment in America* (New York: Oxford University Press, 1978), 346–350.

6. Ronald Hamowy, "Jefferson and the Scottish Enlightenment: A Critique of Garry Wills's *Inventing America: Jefferson's Declaration of Independence*," *William and Mary Quarterly* 36, no. 4 (1979): 506–510. For the influence and circulation of Hutcheson's argument, see Caroline Robbins, "'When It Is That Colonies

May Turn Independent': An Analysis of the Environment and Politics of Francis Hutcheson (1694–1746)," *William and Mary Quarterly* 11, no. 2 (1954): 243–244.

7. Griffin, *People with No Name*, 78–79. See also David Hackett Fischer, *Albion's Seed: Four British Folkways in America* (New York: Oxford University Press, 1989), 610–612, although Fischer is treating a larger "borderlands" migratory pattern that includes the Ulster migrants as well as Scottish and English migration.

8. Robert V. Remini, *Andrew Jackson and the Course of American Empire, 1767–1821* (New York: Harper & Row, 1977), 1, 2–3.

9. E. R. R. Green, "The 'Strange Humors' That Drove the Scotch-Irish to America, 1729," *William and Mary Quarterly* 12, no. 1 (1955): 118; Griffin, *People with No Name*, 96–97.

10. Griffin, *People with No Name*, 104–106. The cemetery records of the Chestnut Level Presbyterian Church list a number of Calhouns, including a "James Patrick Calhoun" who died in 1741. http://chestnutlevel.org/cemetery, accessed July 19, 2017.

11. *Pennsylvania Gazette*, November 17, 1729; Hector St. John de Crèvecœur, *Letters from an American Farmer* (London: 1782), 78–79; Griffin, *People with No Name*, 3, 102–103.

12. Exact data and estimates for the Atlantic slave trade are available from the Transatlantic Slave Trade Database at www.slavevoyages.org. For overall estimates on the slave trade in the eighteenth century, see www.slavevoyages .org/estimates/jP0CCLv5, accessed July 18, 2017. For data on the slave trade to North America in the eighteenth century, see www.slavevoyages.org/voyages /amTyIPXg, accessed July 18, 2017. For the 1730s, see www.slavevoyages.org /voyages/eJdAl3zu, accessed July 18, 2017. See also David Eltis, *The Rise of African Slavery in the Americas* (New York: Cambridge University Press, 1999).

13. Olaudah Equiano, *The Interesting Narrative of the Life of Olaudah Equiano* (London, 1789), 78–79, 87–88, http://docsouth.unc.edu/neh/equiano1/equia no1.html, accessed July 18, 2017.

14. Ira Berlin, *Many Thousands Gone: The First Two Centuries of Slavery in North America* (Cambridge: Harvard University Press, 1998), 54–55, 178–179; Darold D. Wax, "Negro Imports into Pennsylvania, 1720–1766," *Pennsylvania History* 32, no. 3 (June 30, 1965): 267.

15. Griffin, *People with No Name*, 134, 155.

16. David Brion Davis, *Inhuman Bondage: The Rise and Fall of Slavery in the New World* (New York: Oxford University Press, 2008), 64–70.

17. Davis, *Inhuman Bondage*, 48–76, Hume quoted on 75; George Fredrickson, *Racism: A Short History* (Princeton, NJ: Princeton University Press, 2002),

56–64, quote on 56. See also Winthrop B. Jordan, *White over Black: American Attitudes toward the Negro, 1550–1812*, 2nd ed. (Chapel Hill: University of North Carolina Press, 2012).

18. Quoted in Manisha Sinha, *The Slave's Cause: A History of Abolition* (New Haven: Yale University Press, 2016), 12.

19. John Woolman, *A Journal of the Life, Gospel Labours and Christian Experiences, of That Faithful Minister of Jesus Christ, John Woolman* (Philadelphia, 1845), 215, 219, 221, 239, 249, 254. Opposition to the Seven Years War, 1756–1763, eventually pushed many Quakers in Pennsylvania and abroad further toward opposition to slavery, or at least the slave trade, and in 1758 Woolman played a central role when the Philadelphia Yearly Meeting condemned both slave trading and slaveholding. Sinha, *The Slave's Cause*, 19–20.

20. Estate Inventory of Patrick Calhoun, 1743, Lancaster County Historical Society; A. S. Salley, "The Grandfather of John C. Calhoun," *South Carolina Historical and Genealogical Magazine* 39, no. 1 (1938): 50.

21. The first mention of the Calhoun family in Augusta County is on September 19, 1746, when James, Ezekiel, William, and Patrick were accused in the county court by a man named James Patton of being "divulgers of false information to the great detriment of the inhabitants of the colony." Perhaps as punishment, they were put to work building a road from their settlement on Reed Creek to another nearby settlement, but as the eldest brother James was assigned the overseer, their offense must have been slight or negligible. Augusta County Court Records, Order Book 1, 113, 129. See also A. S. Salley, "The Calhoun Family of South Carolina," *South Carolina Historical and Genealogical Magazine* 7, no. 2 (1906): 81.

22. Augusta County Court Records, Surveyors Book 1, 34.

23. Acreage estimate calculated from Salley, "Calhoun Family of South Carolina," 81–83. In his account of an 1846 visit to Wytheville, John C. Calhoun referenced "3,000 acres" of land that his family owned in Augusta County, but he may have been including extended family beyond the four brothers. JCC to James Edward Colhoun, September 15, 1846.

24. "A List of Tithables Sent to the Lords of Trade, 1756," in Robert Dinwiddie, *The Official Records of Robert Dinwiddie, Lieutenant-Governor of the Colony of Virginia, 1751–1758* (Richmond, 1883), 2:352. Turk McClesky provides an in-depth account of slavery in Augusta County in *The Road to Black Ned's Forge: A Story of Race, Sex, and Trade on the Colonial American Frontier* (Charlottesville: University of Virginia Press, 2014), 123–143. For religious affiliation in Augusta County during this period, see Nathaniel Turk McCleskey, *Across the First Divide: Frontiers of Settlement and Culture in Augusta County, Virginia, 1738–1770* (PhD thesis, College of William and Mary, 1990), 174.

25. Slave Voyages Database, http://www.slavevoyages.org/estimates/N8pgwWNs, accessed February 27, 2018.

26. Edmund S. Morgan, *American Slavery, American Freedom: The Ordeal of Colonial Virginia* (New York: W.W. Norton, 2003), 381–385.

27. Charles Wiltse painstakingly reconstructed the Calhouns' probable route from a journal kept by William Calhoun, Patrick's brother, on a business trip back to Virginia a few years later. Charles M. Wiltse, *John C. Calhoun: Nationalist* (Indianapolis: Bobbs-Merrill, 1944), 14.

28. JCC to Charles H. Allen of the *Abbeville Banner*, November 21, 1847.

29. David Ramsay, *The History of South-Carolina: From Its First Settlement in 1670, to the Year 1808* (Charleston, 1809), 2:598.

30. Walter B. Edgar, *South Carolina: A History* (Columbia: University of South Carolina Press, 1998), 68.

31. Edgar, *South Carolina*, 35–46, quote on 46.

32. Edgar, *South Carolina*, 69.

33. Slave Trade Voyages Database, http://www.slavevoyages.org/estimates/s7V4JPQn, accessed March 8, 2018.

34. Edgar, *South Carolina*, 74–75.

35. *South Carolina Gazette*, December 8, 1759.

36. The first land plat in Patrick's name is for his neighbor, William Morris, who received 350 acres on June 23, 1758. This is followed quickly by plats for Patrick's brothers William, Ezekiel, and James, and a plat for Patrick himself for 200 acres. South Carolina Colonial Plat Books, vol. 6, 350, 382, 390, 404. Accessed on SCDAH online March 2, 2018, http://www.archivesindex.sc.gov/online archives/Thumbnails.aspx?recordId=97175. Rachel Klein identified surveying as a source of wealth for several backcountry settlers from this period, see Rachel Klein, *Unification of a Slave State: The Rise of the Planter Class in the South Carolina Backcountry, 1760–1808* (Chapel Hill: University of North Carolina Press, 1992), 28–36.

37. See Charleston Wills, Book QQ, 181–182, SCDAH.

38. J. Franklin Jameson, *Correspondence of John C. Calhoun*, Annual Report of the American Historical Association for the Year 1899 (Washington, DC: Government Printing Office, 1899), 71–72. This is from the W. Pinckney Starke sketch, an early biography of John C. Calhoun composed after the Civil War. Starke grew up and lived in the Calhoun settlement, and many of his stories seem to have circulated among the web of Calhoun, Noble, and Pickens families there.

39. *South Carolina Gazette*, February 9 and February 23, 1760; JCC to Charles Allen, November 21, 1847; Salley, "Calhoun Family of South Carolina," 86.

40. Richard J. Hooker, ed., *The Carolina Backcountry on the Eve of the Revolution: The Journal and Other Writings of Charles Woodmason, Anglican Itinerant* (Chapel Hill: University of North Carolina Press, 1953), 214.

41. Hooker, *The Carolina Backcountry*, 27. Also see Klein, *Unification of a Slave State*, 62–63.

42. Hooker, *The Carolina Backcountry*, 215.

43. Edgar, *South Carolina*, 212–216. The classic work on the Regulator movement is Richard Maxwell Brown, *The South Carolina Regulators* (Cambridge, MA: Belknap Press of Harvard University Press, 1963), see 47–52, quote from Woodmason on 52. See also Rachel N. Klein, "Ordering the Backcountry: The South Carolina Regulation," *William and Mary Quarterly* 38, no. 4 (1981): 661–680.

44. Brown, *Regulators*, 97.

45. Gilbert Tennent journal, September 2, 1775, SCL; Edgar, *South Carolina*, 223.

46. See 1784 tax receipt in Patrick Calhoun Papers, SCL.

47. Edgar, *South Carolina*, 230.

48. Calhoun and Hunter, *Life of John C. Calhoun*, 4.

49. David Waldstreicher, *Slavery's Constitution: From Revolution to Ratification* (New York: Hill and Wang, 2010), 39–41, 60–61. See also Joseph T. Murphy, "The British Example: West Indian Emancipation, the Freedom Principle, and the Rise of Antislavery Politics in the United States, 1833–1843," *Journal of the Civil War Era* 8, no. 4 (2018): 621–646.

50. Quoted in Edgar, *South Carolina*, 249–250.

51. Quoted in Waldstreicher, *Slavery's Constitution*, 115.

52. Quoted in Waldstreicher, *Slavery's Constitution*, 85.

53. See Sean Wilentz, *No Property in Man* (Cambridge: Harvard University Press, 2018), Madison quoted on 3. See also Murphy, "The British Example."

54. *Debates Which Arose in the House of Representatives of South-Carolina, on the Constitution Framed for the United States* (Charleston, 1831), 52, 59, 83. Patrick's vote to hold the convention does not necessarily mean he favored the Constitution. Another anti-Federalist, Acdanus Burke, also voted to hold the convention but opposed ratification. Edgar, *South Carolina*, 250–252.

55. On this see Jonathan Gienapp, *The Second Creation: Fixing the American Constitution in the Founding Era* (Cambridge, MA: Harvard University Press, 2018), introduction. Madison to Thomas Jefferson, June 30, 1789, https://founders.archives.gov/documents/Jefferson/01-15-02-0221, accessed January 16, 2020.

56. 1790 US Census, Abbeville, South Carolina, series M637, roll 11, page 452, image 270, Family History Library Film 0568151. Patrick Calhoun Estate Inventory, January 25, 1797, Calhoun Family Papers, SCL.

57. George Howe, *History of the Presbyterian Church in South Carolina* (Columbia, 1870), 1:654.

58. Patrick Calhoun to John Ewing Colhoun, September 30, 1795, Patrick Calhoun Papers, SCL.

59. Calhoun and Hunter, *Life of John C. Calhoun*, 4–5.

Chapter Two: Educations

1. John C. Calhoun and R. M. T. Hunter, *Life of John C. Calhoun* (New York: Harper & Brothers, 1843), 5.

2. Calhoun and Hunter, *Life of John C. Calhoun*, 5; Elizabeth Fox-Genovese and Eugene D. Genovese, *The Mind of the Master Class: History and Faith in the Southern Slaveholders' Worldview* (Cambridge: Cambridge University Press, 2005), 263, 764. Calhoun may also have read Rollin at Yale, where Rollin was part of the curriculum at the turn of the century. Calhoun's future teacher at Yale, Timothy Dwight, reportedly read Rollin at age ten. William Gribbin, "Rollin's Histories and American Republicanism," *William and Mary Quarterly* 29, no. 4 (1972): 613.

3. For the description of Voltaire I am indebted to Ryan Bennett's fine senior seminar paper, completed under my direction, on popular depictions of Charles XII. Ryan J. Bennett, "How Changing Portrayals and Uses in Popular Media Reflect Overall Interest and Knowledge of Charles XII, King of Sweden," Senior Seminar Paper, Valparaiso University, 2018 (in author's possession). On the prominence of Robertson's histories and his role in spreading knowledge about South America, particularly Mexico and Peru, see Caroline Winterer, *American Enlightenments: Pursuing Happiness in the Age of Reason* (New Haven, CT: Yale University Press, 2016), 84–86.

4. Calhoun and Hunter, *Life of John C. Calhoun*, 5; Henry F. May, *The Enlightenment in America* (New York: Oxford University Press, 1978), 7–10, 19.

5. On Martha Calhoun, see Pinkney Starke's sketch in J. Franklin Jameson, *Correspondence of John C. Calhoun*, Annual Report of the American Historical Association for the Year 1899 (Washington, DC: Government Printing Office, 1899), 69; Patrick Calhoun Will, February 7, 1797, Estate Record Book 1, 153, Estate Packet Box 19, Pkg. 393, SCDAH, accessed online June 11, 2018.

6. Thomas Jefferson, *Notes on the State of Virginia* (Boston, 1801), 240–241.

7. Jefferson, *Notes on the State of Virginia*, 204–207.

8. Walter B. Edgar, *South Carolina: A History* (Columbia: University of South Carolina Press, 1998), 64–66; Inventory of the Estate of Patrick Calhoun, February 7, 1797, South Carolina Wills and Probate Records, 1670–1980, Ancestry.com, accessed January 29, 2020. On origins of slaves sold in Charleston between 1760 and 1790, see Slave Voyages Database: http://www.slavevoyages

.org/voyages/WLHjEI1j, accessed June 18, 2018; Patrick Calhoun to John Ewing Colhoun, September 30, 1795, Patrick Calhoun Papers, SCL; Calhoun and Hunter, *Life of John C. Calhoun*, 5.

9. Sven Beckert, *Empire of Cotton: A Global History* (New York: Knopf, 2014), 29–48, esp. 47–48 and 56–57, 66.

10. Beckert, *Empire of Cotton*, xv, 88–97.

11. Beckert, *Empire of Cotton*, 102–103. On the history of cotton production in South Carolina and the way tobacco paved the way for cotton, see Joyce E. Chaplin, "Creating a Cotton South in Georgia and South Carolina, 1760–1815," *Journal of Southern History* 57, no. 2 (1991): Hampton on 194.

12. Washington's Farewell Address (1796), Avalon Project, Yale University, https://avalon.law.yale.edu/18th_century/washing.asp, accessed June 21, 2018.

13. Gordon S. Wood, *Empire of Liberty: A History of the Early Republic, 1789–1815* (New York: Oxford University Press, 2011), 268–271; Jefferson's Draft of Kentucky Resolutions of 1798, before October 4, 1798, in Barbara Oberg et al., eds., *The Papers of Thomas Jefferson* (Princeton, NJ: Princeton University Press, 2003), 30:531–532, 536–541; Jefferson to Madison, August 23, 1799, in Oberg et al., eds., *The Papers of Thomas Jefferson*, 31:172–174.

14. See Forrest McDonald, *States' Rights and the Union: Imperium in Imperio, 1776–1876* (Lawrence: University Press of Kansas, 2000), 27–46.

15. Calhoun and Hunter, *Life of John C. Calhoun*, 6.

16. Nearly a century later, Pinckney Starke found the newspaper, the May 10, 1798, edition, among Calhoun's papers. See Jameson, *Correspondence of John C. Calhoun*, 76.

17. JCC to Andrew Pickens Jr., September 6, 1801. See note.

18. JCC to William B. Sprague, May 19, 1849. Calhoun initially attended Waddel's first school, which dissolved with the death of Waddel's wife, Calhoun's sister. Calhoun later returned to another of Waddel's schools to prepare for his entrance to Yale. Augustus Baldwin Longstreet, *Master William Mitten: Or, a Youth of Brilliant Talent, Who Was Ruined by Bad Luck* (Macon, GA, 1864), 71–72.

19. JCC to Anna Maria Calhoun, April 3, 1834.

20. James Lewis MacLeod, *The Great Doctor Waddel* (Easley, SC: Southern Historical Press, 1985), 56, 60. Polybius was one of the rare sources that Calhoun cited. See Speech on the Dangers of Factious Opposition, January 15, 1814.

21. David Ramsay, *The History of South-Carolina: From Its First Settlement in 1670, to the Year 1808* (Charleston, 1809), 2:370–371; Augustus B. Longstreet, *Georgia Scenes, Characters, Incidents, &c., in the First Half Century of the Republic by a Native Georgian* (Augusta, GA, 1835), 144–157.

22. JCC to William B. Sprague, May 19, 1849; Augustus Baldwin Long-street, *Eulogy on the Life and Services of the Late Rev. Moses Waddel, D.D.* (Augusta, GA, 1841); Longstreet, *Master William Mitten*, 72.

23. JCC to A. D. Wallace, December 17, 1840.

24. Chandos Michael Brown, *Benjamin Silliman: A Life in the Young Republic* (Princeton, NJ: Princeton University Press, 2014), 56–58.

25. Lyman Beecher and Charles Beecher, *Autobiography, Correspondence, Etc., of Lyman Beecher, D. D.* (New York, 1864), 43.

26. Henry F. May, *The Enlightenment in America* (New York: Oxford University Press, 1978), 189–190; Robert J. Imholt, "Timothy Dwight, Federalist Pope of Connecticut," *New England Quarterly* 73, no. 3 (2000): 386–411. Imholt is mostly an account of Dwight's critics, and he concludes, as does May, that most of the criticism was unjustified.

27. Brown, *Benjamin Silliman*, 89–92; Charles E. Cunningham, *Timothy Dwight, 1752–1817: A Biography* (New York: Macmillan, 1942), 328–330.

28. Cunningham, *Timothy Dwight*, 298–303; May, *Enlightenment in America*, 346.

29. Cunningham, *Timothy Dwight*, 199, 193–195, 298; quote is from Imholt, "Federalist Pope," 400.

30. Kevin M. Gannon, "Escaping 'Mr. Jefferson's Plan of Destruction': New England Federalists and the Idea of a Northern Confederacy, 1803–1804," *Journal of the Early Republic* 21, no. 3 (2001): quote on 442. During the conspiracy, Calhoun's future teacher Tapping Reeve wrote to Uriah Tracy, "I have seen many of our friends; and all that I have seen, and most that I have heard from, believe that we must separate, and that this is the most favorable moment," 437.

31. James Henry Hammond, *Selections from the Letters and Speeches of the Hon. James H. Hammond of South Carolina* (New York, 1866), 244.

32. JCC to Andrew Pickens Jr., May 23, 1803.

33. JCC to Joseph Swift, October 26, 1823; John D. Gardiner to JCC, June 17, 1844.

34. Remarks upon the Query: Would it be politic to encourage the immigration of foreigners into the U. States, November 2, 1803, and note. Calhoun's classmates John D. Gardiner and Micah Sterling both named boys "Calhoun." See John D. Gardiner to JCC, June 17, 1844; Micah Sterling to JCC, June 9, 1843. On the format of the debates, see Cunningham, *Timothy Dwight*, 239.

35. Cunningham, *Timothy Dwight*, 242–244.

36. Hugh Blair, *Lectures on Rhetoric and Belles Lettres* (Boston, 1802), 1:2, 131–132.

37. William Paley, *The Principles of Moral and Political Philosophy* (Boston, 1801), 23–55, quotes on 23, 51; May, *Enlightenment in America*, 342–347.

38. Paley, *Principles of Moral and Political Philosophy*, 34, 161–164.

39. Brown, *Benjamin Silliman*, 30–35, 55.

40. Larry E. Tise, *Proslavery: A History of the Defense of Slavery in America, 1701–1840* (Athens: University of Georgia Press, 2004), 210–211, 217.

41. Cunningham, *Timothy Dwight*, 311; Brown, *Benjamin Silliman*, 44. On Samuel Stanhope Smith and Jefferson, see Nell Irvin Painter, *The History of White People* (New York: W.W. Norton, 2011), 110–117.

42. Cunningham, *Timothy Dwight*, 245; Calhoun and Hunter, *Life of John C. Calhoun*, 6.

43. JCC to Alexander Noble, October 15, 1804. Giving one of the commencement addresses was considered a very high honor. See Cunningham, *Timothy Dwight*, 290.

Chapter Three: The Science of Law

1. JCC to Alexander Noble, October 15, 1804.

2. The Colhouns retained or recovered the Scottish spelling of the name, but Calhoun paid little attention to this in his letters to Floride.

3. See "Cash Payments and Remittances Made to Mrs. Floride Colhoun" from 1803 to 1811 in John Ewing Colhoun Papers, SCL. The document records yearly sums paid by the estate to Mrs. Colhoun, including $3,625 in 1804.

4. See "Cash Payments and Remittances Made to Mrs. Floride Colhoun" from 1803 to 1811 in John Ewing Colhoun Papers, SCL. See also a note from Theodore Dehon, rector of Trinity Church in Newport, thanking Floride for her "skill and kindness in performing upon the organ of the Church, while the church is unavoidably destitute of an organist." Theodore Dehon to Floride Colhoun, March 17, 1810, Editorial Records of the John C. Calhoun Papers, SCL.

5. JCC to Floride Colhoun, June 12, 1810.

6. Floride Colhoun to JCC, September 14, 1805; Floride Colhoun to A. M. Alston, April 23, 1810, Editorial Records of the John C. Calhoun Papers, SCL; Floride Colhoun to James E. Calhoun, April 21, 1819, John Ewing Colhoun Papers, SCL.

7. JCC to Floride Colhoun, January 19, March 3, 1806.

8. Anna Calhoun Clemson to Charles Edward Leverett, April 22, 1867, in Catherine Taylor Matthews, J. Tracy Power, and Frances Wallace Taylor, eds., *The Leverett Letters: Correspondence of a South Carolina Family, 1851–1868* (Columbia: University of South Carolina Press, 2000), 426–427. Also quoted in Meriwether et al., *Papers of John C. Calhoun*, 27:254–255.

9. See JCC to Alexander Noble, October 15, 1804. Also see copy of a page from the cashbooks of DeSaussure and Ford law firm in Charleston entry on

December 24, 1804, that reads "John C. Calhoun…entered our office as a student for 100 guineas." Editorial Records of the John C. Calhoun Papers, SCL.

10. Joseph W. Cox, *Champion of Southern Federalism; Robert Goodloe Harper of South Carolina* (Port Washington, NY: Kennikat Press, 1972), 33–35.

11. Quoted in Walter B. Edgar, *South Carolina: A History* (Columbia: University of South Carolina Press, 1998), 257.

12. Henry W. DeSaussure, *Letters on the Questions of the Justice and Expediency of Going into Alterations of the Representation in the Legislature of South-Carolina, as Fixed by the Constitution* (Charleston, SC, 1795), 18.

13. Timothy Ford, *The Constitutionalist: Or, an Enquiry How Far It Is Expedient and Proper to Alter the Constitution of South-Carolina* (Charleston, SC, 1794), 39. See also Jack P. Greene, "'Slavery or Independence': Some Reflections on the Relationship Among Liberty, Black Bondage, and Equality in Revolutionary South Carolina," *South Carolina Historical Magazine* 101, no. 1 (2000): 27.

14. DeSaussure, *Letters*, 15–16, 19.

15. Henry William DeSaussure, ed., *Reports of Cases Argued and Determined in the Court of Chancery of the State of South Carolina*, vol. 4 (Columbia, SC: Printed by Cline & Hines, 1817). William Lowndes Yancey, among others, noted Calhoun's devotion to the phrase in his eulogy for Calhoun. Yancey, *Life and Character of John C. Calhoun* (Montgomery, AL, 1850), 5. For the quote, see Francis Bacon, *The Works of Francis Bacon, Baron of Verulam, Viscount St. Alban, and Lord High Chancellor of England* (London: Printed for J. Johnson, 1803), 6:149.

16. JCC to Floride Colhoun, April 13 and June 2, 1806.

17. Henry DeSaussure to Robert Goodloe Harper, May 13, 1805, Editorial Records of the John C. Calhoun Papers, SCL.

18. JCC to Andrew Pickens Jr., June 25, 1805.

19. For descriptions of Jefferson, see Henry Adams, *History of the United States of America During the First Administration of Thomas Jefferson*, vol. 1 (New York: Scribner, 1921), 185–186.

20. For James Edward Colhoun's memory of the meeting, which he thought occurred at Monticello, see Charles M. Wiltse, *John C. Calhoun: Nationalist, 1782–1828* (Indianapolis: Bobbs-Merrill, 1944), 36. Wiltse, who did not have the letter from Calhoun to Andrew Pickens, did not think the meeting with Jefferson happened.

21. JCC to Floride Colhoun, July 22, 1805. The description of Reeve is from Andrew M. Siegel, "To Learn and Make Respectable Hereafter: The Litchfield Law School in Cultural Context Note," *New York University Law Review* 73 (1998): 2002–2004.

22. Siegel, "To Learn and Make Respectable Hereafter," 1979–1980, 2021.

23. Siegel, "To Learn and Make Respectable Hereafter," 1981, 1990–1991.

24. The only hint we have of Calhoun's attire in Litchfield is a receipt for "2 yds Super Black Sedan B cloth." Meriwether et al., *Papers of John C. Calhoun*, 1:31n20.

25. JCC to Floride Colhoun, July 22, 1805.

26. Reeve himself relied on the notes of his lectures compiled by his son, Aaron Burr Reeve, as a guide to his lectures. Siegel, "To Learn and Make Respectable Hereafter," 2012n161.

27. JCC to Floride Colhoun, August 12, 1805.

28. Siegel, "To Learn and Make Respectable Hereafter," 2005–2008. Also see Marian C. McKenna, *Tapping Reeve and the Litchfield Law School* (New York: Oceana, 1986), ch. 4, and on Gould, ch. 5. For a list of books in the Litchfield library, 112.

29. Maxcy, Biographical Memoir, in Meriwether et al., *Papers of John C. Calhoun*, 1:51n2.

30. Siegel, "To Learn and Make Respectable Hereafter," 2006.

31. McKenna, *Tapping Reeve*, 63–67.

32. McKenna, *Tapping Reeve*, 64.

33. Siegel, "To Learn and Make Respectable Hereafter," 2016–2017.

34. Siegel, "To Learn and Make Respectable Hereafter," 2016n190.

35. William Blackstone, *Commentaries on the Laws of England* (Buffalo, NY: W.S. Hein, 1992), 1:123; David Brion Davis, *Inhuman Bondage: The Rise and Fall of Slavery in the New World* (New York: Oxford University Press, 2008), 234.

36. Blackstone, *Commentaries*, 1:411.

37. Blackstone, *Commentaries*, 2:402.

38. Blackstone, *Commentaries*, 2:2.

39. JCC to Floride Colhoun, December 23, 1805, and editor's note. Osborn later supported Calhoun for president.

40. Quoted in Siegel, "To Learn and Make Respectable Hereafter," 2008.

41. Quoted in Siegel, "To Learn and Make Respectable Hereafter," 1998.

42. Siegel, "To Learn and Make Respectable Hereafter," 2017–2018.

43. JCC to Floride Colhoun, January 19, 1806. See also Mark Boonshoft, "The Litchfield Network: Education, Social Capital, and the Rise and Fall of a Political Dynasty, 1784–1833," *Journal of the Early Republic* 34, no. 4 (2014): 561–595.

44. JCC to Floride Colhoun, April 13, 1806.

45. JCC to Floride Colhoun, July 3, September 11, 1806.

46. JCC to Floride Colhoun, December 22, 1806.

Chapter Four: "I Am Your True Lover, John C. Calhoun"

1. JCC to Floride Colhoun, December 22, 1806.

2. Resolutions on the Chesapeake-Leopard Affair, August 3, 1807. On

honor as a motivating impulse in foreign affairs, including the War of 1812, see Bertram Wyatt-Brown, *A Warring Nation: Honor, Race, and Humiliation in America and Abroad* (Charlottesville: University of Virginia Press, 2014).

3. Resolutions on the Chesapeake-Leopard Affair, August 3, 1807, note 23. John C. Calhoun and R. M. T. Hunter, *Life of John C. Calhoun* (New York: Harper & Brothers, 1843), 7. Bowie's recollection can be found in "Brief Sketch of Mr. Calhoun," *Camden Weekly Journal*, October 24, 1854.

4. See Application for Admission to Practice in the Chancery Courts, March 7, 1808, note 25 accompanying lays out the likelihood that Calhoun had been examined and admitted to the bar the preceding December.

5. JCC to Floride Colhoun, October 1, 1807.

6. Lacy K. Ford, *Origins of Southern Radicalism: The South Carolina Upcountry, 1800–1860* (New York: Oxford University Press, 1988), 24n66.

7. See Donald G. Mathews, "The Second Great Awakening as an Organizing Process, 1780–1830: An Hypothesis," *American Quarterly* 21, no. 1 (Spring 1969): 23–43. On population shifts, see Rachel Klein, *Unification of a Slave State: The Rise of the Planter Class in the South Carolina Backcountry, 1760–1808* (Chapel Hill: University of North Carolina Press, 1992), 251.

8. Klein, *Unification of a Slave State*, 238–246.

9. Sven Beckert, *Empire of Cotton: A Global History* (New York: Knopf, 2014), 74; Ford, *Origins of Southern Radicalism*, 7–11.

10. David Ramsay, *The History of South-Carolina: From Its First Settlement in 1670, to the Year 1808* (Charleston, 1809), 2:448–449; Ford, *Origins of Southern Radicalism*, 12. Rachel Klein gives a more detailed account of the rising levels of slaveholding in several counties, noting that in some levels did not change dramatically between 1790 and 1810. See Klein, *Unification of a Slave State*, 250–254.

11. Margaret DesChamps, "Antislavery Presbyterians in the Carolina Piedmont," *Proceedings of the South Carolina Historical Society*, 1954, 9.

12. Henry DeSaussure to Floride Colhoun, June 18, 1807, Editorial Records of the John C. Calhoun Papers, SCL.

13. Actual (not estimated) numbers for 1807 from Slave Voyages Database, www.slavevoyages.org, accessed November 16, 2018.

14. Henry William DeSaussure, ed., *Reports of Cases Argued and Determined in the Court of Chancery of the State of South Carolina* (Columbia, SC: Printed by Cline & Hines, 1817), 4:26–33. See also record of a case in October 1810 in Editorial Records of John C. Calhoun Papers, SCL.

15. JCC to Floride Colhoun, April 6, 1809.

16. Ford, *Origins of Southern Radicalism*, 108–113.

17. Ford, *Origins of Southern Radicalism*, 112; Edward Hooker, *Diary, 1805–1808* (Washington, DC: American Historical Association Annual Report, 1897), 894, 896, 900–902.

18. Ford, *Origins of Southern Radicalism*, 106–107; Walter B. Edgar, *South Carolina: A History* (Columbia, SC: University of South Carolina Press, 1998), 261–263.

19. JCC to Alton Pemberton, November 19, 1838.

20. *A Discourse on the Constitution and Government of the United States*, in Meriwether et al., *Papers of John C. Calhoun*, 28:236–239.

21. Edgar, *South Carolina*, 262; Ford, *Origins of Southern Radicalism*, 106–108.

22. DeSaussure quoted in Ford, *Origins of Southern Radicalism*, 105.

23. Edgar, *South Carolina*, 262.

24. Maryland would eliminate property and tax qualifications in 1810, as well, and Kentucky had joined the Union in 1792 without them. See Alexander Keyssar, *The Right to Vote: The Contested History of Democracy in the United States* (New York: Basic Books, 2000), Appendix Table A.2; Ford, *Origins of Southern Radicalism*, 108.

25. Ira Berlin, *Generations of Captivity: A History of African-American Slaves* (Cambridge, MA: Belknap Press, 2004), Table 1.

26. On the role of slavery in convention debates over suffrage, see Keyssar, *Right to Vote*, 38, 46.

27. Carl Lawrence Paulus, *The Slaveholding Crisis: Fear of Insurrection and the Coming of the Civil War* (Baton Rouge: Louisiana State University Press, 2017), ch. 1.

28. See Edmund S. Morgan, *American Slavery, American Freedom: The Ordeal of Colonial Virginia* (New York: W.W. Norton, 2003). On parallels with Greece and Rome, see Elizabeth Fox-Genovese and Eugene D. Genovese, *The Mind of the Master Class: History and Faith in the Southern Slaveholders' Worldview* (Cambridge: Cambridge University Press, 2005), 249–304, although the Genoveses would not completely agree with the characterization of South Carolina as a distinctly modern type of democracy.

29. Reports from Committee on Claims of the SC Genl. Assembly, December 8, 11, 1809, Editorial Records of the John C. Calhoun Papers, SCL. See John Earle's Petition, December 2, 1809, SCDAH, Archives ID: Series: S165015 Year: 1809 Item: 00089, http://www.archivesindex.sc.gov/, accessed November 28, 2018.

30. Barton, Timothy, Petition, December 4, 1809, SCDAH, Archives ID: Series: S165015 Year: 1809 Item: 00085; William Smith Petition, December 8, 1809, Archives ID: Series: S165015 Year: 1809 Item: 00098; Elizabeth and James

Kennedy Petition, November 2, 1809, Archives ID: Series: S165015 Year: 1809 Item: 00087, http://www.archivesindex.sc.gov/, accessed November 28, 2018.

31. Trial Transcript, August 29, 1798, John Ewing Colhoun Papers (1763–1951), SCL.

32. JCC to Floride Colhoun, June 25, 1809.

33. JCC to Floride Colhoun, July 18, 1809; October 1, 1809; January 20, 1810.

34. JCC to Floride Colhoun, June 25, 1809, and note.

35. JCC to Floride Colhoun, June 30 and September 7, 1810.

36. JCC to Floride Colhoun, July 27, 1810.

37. JCC to Floride Colhoun, July 27 and August 24, 1810.

38. JCC to Floride Colhoun, June 12, 1810.

39. JCC to Floride Colhoun, September 13, 1810.

40. For Bowie, see *Camden Weekly Journal*, October 24, 1854; JCC to Floride Colhoun, July 18 and July 27, 1810, and note.

41. JCC to Floride Colhoun, September 28, 1810.

42. JCC to Floride Colhoun, September 7, 1810. Calhoun evidently got his way. See Meriwether et al., *Papers of John C. Calhoun*, 1:61n43. Calhoun's objection to a marriage settlement illustrates the argument of historian Peter Bardaglio that as the nineteenth-century North moved toward a more "contractual" model of marriage and household, the South held to a more "organic" view of the institution. See Peter Winthrop Bardaglio, *Reconstructing the Household: Families, Sex, and the Law in the Nineteenth-Century South* (Chapel Hill: University of North Carolina Press, 1995), xii. Meanwhile, Stephanie Jones-Rogers has given the most thorough recent description of marriage contracts in slaveholding families. See Stephanie E. Jones-Rogers, *They Were Her Property* (New Haven, CT: Yale University Press, 2020), 31–37.

43. JCC to Floride Colhoun, September 28, 1810.

44. *Charleston City Gazette*, October 20 and 22, 1810.

45. *Charleston City Gazette*, December 25, 1810; Marriage License from the Charleston District Court of Ordinary, December 27, 1810, Editorial Records of the John C. Calhoun Papers, SCL.

46. JCC to Floride Colhoun, September 7, 1810.

Chapter Five: "The Road That All Great Nations Have Trod"

1. JCC to Floride Colhoun, May 8, 1811.

2. JCC to Floride Colhoun, May 23, 1811.

3. Alan Taylor, *The Civil War of 1812: American Citizens, British Subjects, Irish Rebels, & Indian Allies* (New York: Knopf Doubleday, 2011), 115–119.

4. See, for instance, *Carolina Gazette*, May 3, June 15, June 22, August 17, and August 24, 1811.

5. *Carolina Gazette*, February 22, 1811; Caitlin Fitz, *Our Sister Republics: The United States in an Age of American Revolutions* (New York: Liveright, 2016), 3–4, 28–36, and Appendix.

6. William Lowndes, Calhoun's fellow congressman from South Carolina, took the Philadelphia packet from Charleston. See Harriot Horry (Rutledge) Ravenel, *Life and Times of William Lowndes of South Carolina, 1782–1822* (Boston, 1901), 82.

7. *AC*, 12th Congress, 1st Session, 11–16 (Madison's message), 331 (Calhoun seated). On Tippecanoe, see Taylor, *Civil War of 1812*, 127.

8. Ravenel, *William Lowndes*, 84–87; JCC to Floride Colhoun, December 21, 1811.

9. Ravenel, *William Lowndes*, 84–87; Robert V. Remini, *Henry Clay: Statesman for the Union* (New York: W.W. Norton, 1993), on physical appearance, 12–13; on voice, 21; on expansion, 66.

10. Gordon S. Wood, *Empire of Liberty: A History of the Early Republic, 1789–1815* (New York: Oxford University Press, 2011), 660–661.

11. Henry Adams, *History of the United States of America During the First Administration of James Madison,* vol. 2 (New York: Scribner, 1890), 122–123.

12. This is Alan Taylor's interpretation. See Taylor, *Civil War of 1812*, 5–6, quote on 120.

13. *AC* 12–2, 782.

14. David Johnson, *John Randolph of Roanoke* (Baton Rouge: Louisiana State University Press, 2012), 68–74.

15. Johnson, *John Randolph*, 2–4; Ruggles quoted in William K. Bolt, *Tariff Wars and the Politics of Jacksonian America* (Nashville: Vanderbilt University Press, 2017), 12.

16. Johnson, *John Randolph*, quote on 141; Remini, *Henry Clay*, 78–79.

17. Other committees were charged with the more specific preparations for war. *AC* 12–1, 342–343.

18. Calhoun's subsequent speeches, even on different topics, used language similar to the report. See, for instance, Speech on the Apportionment Bill, December 5, 1811.

19. Report on Relations with Great Britain, November 29, 1811. On the portrayal of impressed sailors as white slaves, see Taylor, *Civil War of 1812*, 135–136.

20. Ravenel, *William Lowndes*, 88.

21. Speech on the Apportionment Bill, December 5, 1811.

22. *AC* 12-1, 409. On the Constitution, see, for instance, Speech on the Revenue Bill, January 31, 1816, 318–319.

23. *Carolina Gazette*, December 21, 1811.

24. *AC* 12-1, 441–455. For the events Randolph referenced, see Alan Taylor, *The Internal Enemy: Slavery and War in Virginia, 1772–1832* (New York: W.W. Norton, 2013), 113–142.

25. This was Henry Adams's opinion. See Adams, *History of the US During the First Administration of James Madison,* vol. 2, 137–143.

26. See *Alexandria Gazette* (VA), December 12, 1811, which reported that Calhoun asked for another day because he did not feel well enough to speak. For "rapid in his delivery," see the *Columbian* (NY), December 14, 1811.

27. Speech on the Report of the Foreign Affairs Committee, December 12, 1811. On Louisiana, see Adam Rothman, *Slave Country: American Expansion and the Origins of the Deep South* (Cambridge, MA: Harvard University Press, 2007), 109–117, 123–124. For Virginia, see Taylor, *Internal Enemy,* 113–142.

28. Speech on the Report of the Foreign Affairs Committee, December 12, 1811.

29. Adams, *History of the US During the First Administration of James Madison,* vol. 2, 143.

30. *Columbian Gazette* (Utica, NY), December 24, 1811.

31. *Richmond Enquirer,* December 24, 1811.

32. For "unfledged political pedagogue," see *AC* 12-1, 542; Johnson, *John Randolph,* 146–147.

33. Ravenel, *William Lowndes,* 90–92. Lowndes attended the French ball, although he also mostly stayed in. JCC to Floride Colhoun Sr., December 21, 1811.

34. On January 10, when Randolph presented a resolution that would have allowed the president to use the troops raised by Congress to build roads and canals, probably as a discouragement to enlistment, Calhoun objected that this was beneath the dignity of the "yeomanry of our country." See Comment on Randolph's Resolution, January 10, 1812.

35. Comment on the Bill for an Additional Military Force, January 2, 1812.

36. Adams, *History of the US During the First Administration of James Madison,* vol. 2, 156–158.

37. JCC to Patrick Calhoun, January 24, 1812.

38. JCC to James Macbride, February 16, 1812; Fitz, *Our Sister Republics,* 4; Comment on the Resolution for Relief of Caracas, April 29, 1812, and note.

39. JCC to Floride Calhoun, March 1, 1812.

40. Adams, *History of the US During the First Administration of James Madison,* vol. 2, 227. Also, see Remarks on the Question of Restriction of Debate, May 29, and note. The exchange between Calhoun and Randolph, for instance, was reported by the *Boston Weekly Messenger* on June 26, 1812.

41. Taylor, *Civil War of 1812*, 132–137; Report on the Causes and Reasons for War, June 3, 1812; Bill to Declare War on Great Britain, June 3, 1812; JCC to Patrick Noble, June 17, 1812.

Chapter Six: "The Great Gun of the Party"

1. Speech on the Army Bill, January 14, 1813, 154.

2. Speech on Embargo Repeal, May 6, 1812, 104–105.

3. Hull surrendered on August 16. See Gordon S. Wood, *Empire of Liberty: A History of the Early Republic, 1789–1815* (New York: Oxford University Press, 2011), 679; *Charleston City Gazette*, September 7, 1812.

4. Wood, *Empire of Liberty*, 677–681.

5. *Charleston Investigator*, October 21, 1812.

6. Speech on Non-Importation, June 24, 1812.

7. Speech on Merchants' Bonds, December 8, 1812.

8. Henry Adams, *History of the United States of America During the First Administration of James Madison*, vol. 2 (New York: Scribner, 1890), 233.

9. See, for example, Comment on the Bill to Enforce Non-Importation, February 23, 1813.

10. JCC to James Macbride, December 25, 1812, and February 2, 1813; also, JCC to Patrick Calhoun, January 13, 1813.

11. Archibald S. Foord, *His Majesty's Opposition, 1714–1830* (Oxford: Clarendon Press, 1964), 1–12.

12. Speech on the Bill for an Additional Military Force, January 13, 1813.

13. The observer was George Ticknor, quoted in Robert V. Remini, *Daniel Webster: The Man and His Time* (New York: W.W. Norton, 1997), 184, Emerson on 29.

14. Memorial to James Madison, president of the United States, as published in the *Trenton Federalist*, October 19, 1812; Remini, *Daniel Webster*, 98–100.

15. Remini, *Daniel Webster*, 108; Speech on Webster's Resolutions, June 16, 1813. Calhoun did object to Webster's assertion that the Orders in Council were the main point of contention, restating that impressment, not the rescinded orders, were the issue.

16. *AC* 13-1, 333–347; Comment on the Massachusetts Memorial, June 29, 1813.

17. JCC to James Macbride, June 23, 1813.

18. John Forsyth of Georgia and Robert Wright of Maryland would threaten force in early 1814 during the debate over the Loan Bill. See *AC* 13-2, 1609, 1670.

19. Episode and Clay's response can be found in Charles M. Wiltse, *John C. Calhoun: Nationalist, 1782–1828* (Indianapolis: Bobbs-Merrill, 1944), 83–84.

20. Mary Elizabeth Moragne Davis, *The Neglected Thread: A Journal from the Calhoun Community, 1836–1842* (Columbia: University of South Carolina Press, 1951), 3; Survey of an 840 acre tract of land "Situated in Abbeville District on branch of Savannah River," May 30, 1817, Editorial Records of the John C. Calhoun Papers, SCL.

21. See JCC to Eliza Pickens, October 26, 1813.

22. Wood, *Empire of Liberty*, 684–686; *Pendleton Messenger*, October 9, 1813.

23. See Henry Adams, *History of the United States During the Second Administration of James Madison*, vol. 1 (New York: Scribner, 1891), 367; John C. Calhoun and R. M. T. Hunter, *Life of John C. Calhoun* (New York: Harper & Brothers, 1843), 13–14.

24. This was Alexander Contee Hanson, quoted in Bartlett, *John C. Calhoun*, 79.

25. Reprinted in the *Northern Whig*, January 4, 1814; for original, see *New York Evening Post*, December 24, 1813.

26. *Boston Repertory*, January 4, 1814; *Daily National Intelligencer*, December 28, 1813. Also see Henry Clay to William Thornton, December 24, 1813, in James F. Hopkins, ed., *The Papers of Henry Clay: The Rising Statesman, 1797–1814* (Lexington: University Press of Kentucky, 1959). Clay acknowledges the duel and laments that it will happen, but despairs that anything can be done to stop it.

27. Adams, *History of the US During the Second Administration of James Madison*, vol. 1, 370–371.

28. Speech on the Dangers of a Factious Opposition, January 15, 1814; and for "wise and virtuous people," see Speech on the Loan Bill, February 25, 1814, 211.

29. For Stockton comment, see *AC* 13-2, 1013.

30. JCC to Floride Calhoun, February 7, 1814.

31. *AC* 13-2, beginning on 1269.

32. James H. Kettner, *The Development of American Citizenship, 1608–1870* (Chapel Hill: University of North Carolina Press, 1978), 10.

33. Linda K. Kerber, "The Meanings of Citizenship," *Journal of American History* 84, no. 3 (1997): 841.

34. Taylor, *Civil War of 1812*, 4, 10. Denver Brunsman examines impressment during the war as a kind of "forced migration." See Denver Brunsman, "Subjects vs. Citizens: Impressment and Identity in the Anglo-American Atlantic," *Journal of the Early Republic* 30, no. 4 (2010): 557–586.

35. *AC* 13-2, 1389.

36. Remarks on the Maryland Memorial, February 2, 1814. For Grosvenor, see *AC* 13-2, 1223. For other statements of support for the "perpetual allegiance"

position, see *AC* 13-2, 1015, 1389, 1508. For the history of "volitional allegiance" in the early United States, see Kettner, *Development of American Citizenship*, 173–210. In 1816, Calhoun opposed a resolution to restrict directors of branch banks of the national bank to native-born citizens, calling the resolution "odious" and unconstitutional. See Speech on the Bank Bill, March 6, 1816, 342. On July 7, 1813, Calhoun's Foreign Relations Committee reported a Senate bill that modified the naturalization acts to make clear that individuals residing in the United States at the start of the war were still eligible for naturalized citizenship. The bill was ratified on July 30, 1813. See *AC* 13-1, 396, 465, 2738. In January 1814 the House debated whether a right of expatriation was implied by the Constitution, with some arguing that it was simply the mirror image of naturalization. Calhoun was one of those who asked for more time to study the question, which was tabled. See *AC* 13-2, 1097–1098.

37. The correspondent's letter, dated February 18, was published in the *Boston Daily Advertiser*, February 28, 1814.

38. Robert V. Remini, *Henry Clay: Statesman for the Union* (New York: Norton, 1993), 105.

39. Speech in Defense of the Republican Foreign Policy, April 6, 1814.

40. *New York Spectator*, March 5, 1814; *Poulson's American Daily Advertiser* (Philadelphia), March 2, 1814; *AC* 13-2, 1798.

41. Speech on Encouragement for Manufactures, April 7, 1814.

42. *Daily National Intelligencer*, April 18, 1814.

43. Adam Rothman, *Slave Country: American Expansion and the Origins of the Deep South* (Cambridge, MA: Harvard University Press, 2007), 138–139.

44. Sven Beckert, *Empire of Cotton: A Global History* (New York: Knopf, 2014), xv. Beckert argues that war capitalism was central to the emergence of industrial capitalism.

45. Taylor, *Civil War of 1812*, 387–389, 405, 413.

46. Calhoun and Hunter, *Life of John C. Calhoun*, 16; Speech on the Military Situation, October 25, 1814.

47. Taylor, *Civil War of 1812*, 415.

48. JCC to Andrew Pickens, November 1, 1814; Taylor, *Civil War of 1812*, 415–416.

49. Taylor, *Civil War of 1812*, 417–419, "We lose no territory" on 419. For Calhoun, see Speech on Results of the War, February 27, 1815, esp. 281.

50. JCC to Patrick Noble, February 11, 1815; JCC to John E. Colhoun, February 26, 1815.

51. Taylor, *Civil War of 1812*, "fixed determination" on 414, 420–421, 437.

52. JCC to Floride Calhoun, April 9, 1815. On grief and gender differences between southern men and women, see Katherine McVane Armstrong, "Thy

Will Lord, Not Mine: Parents, Grief, and Child Death in the Antebellum South" (PhD dissertation, Emory University, 2011), 87–88, 149–183. Armstrong also points out that for all the rhetoric about "my family, black and white," enslaved members of a household were rarely part of the circle of grief.

Chapter Seven: "Let Us Conquer Space"

1. JCC to Floride Calhoun, November 29, 1815.

2. Walter Johnson, *River of Dark Dreams: Slavery and Empire in the Cotton Kingdom* (Cambridge, MA: Belknap Press, 2017), 73–96; Adam Rothman, *Slave Country: American Expansion and the Origins of the Deep South* (Cambridge, MA: Harvard University Press, 2007), 180.

3. Sven Beckert, *Empire of Cotton: A Global History* (New York: Knopf, 2014), 94–97, 98–122.

4. Speech on the Revenue Bill, January 31, 1816, 330.

5. Speech on the Military Peace Establishment, February 27, 1815, 277; Speech on Revenue Bill, January 31, 1816, 321.

6. For instance, when the Ways and Means Committee determined that the creation of a national bank would violate the Constitution by creating a corporation within states without their consent, Calhoun proposed a resolution instructing the committee to look into establishing the bank in Washington since the Constitution gave Congress complete authority there. The resolution passed, even though this early effort to establish a bank did not pass during that session. See Resolution on the Question of a National Bank, February 4, 1814; for "The single fact," see Speech on the Military Situation, October 25, 1814, 255.

7. Speech on the Bank Bill, November 16, 1814, and note.

8. Samuel Taggert to John Taylor, November 22, 1814, Editorial Records of the John C. Calhoun Papers, SCL.

9. John C. Calhoun and R. M. T. Hunter, *Life of John C. Calhoun* (New York: Harper & Brothers, 1843), 16.

10. John Jacob Astor to JCC, November 23, 1814, Editorial Records of the John C. Calhoun Papers, SCL.

11. *AC* 14-1, 1064.

12. Eric Lomazoff, *Reconstructing the National Bank Controversy: Politics and Law in the Early American Republic* (Chicago: University of Chicago Press, 2018), 94–120; *Charleston City Gazette*, April 24, 1816.

13. Randolph "rats" in David Johnson, *John Randolph of Roanoke* (Baton Rouge: Louisiana State University Press, 2012), 173.

14. JCC to Alexander Dallas, December 21, 1815, Editorial Records of the John C. Calhoun Project, SCL; Ralph C. H. Catterall, *The Second Bank of the United States* (Chicago: University of Chicago Press, 1903), 15–16, 21.

15. First and Second Speeches on the Military Academies Bill, January 2 and 3, 1816.

16. Speech on the Revenue Bill, January 31, 1816; for Randolph comment, see *AC* 14-1, 841.

17. Speech on the Revenue Bill, January 31, 1816, 327.

18. Randolph quoted in William K. Bolt, *Tariff Wars and the Politics of Jacksonian America* (Nashville: Vanderbilt University Press, 2017), 14.

19. Daniel Walker Howe, *What Hath God Wrought: The Transformation of America, 1815–1848* (New York: Oxford University Press, 2007), 84.

20. Beckert, *Empire of Cotton*, 158–159. On South Carolina, see Joyce E. Chaplin, "Creating a Cotton South in Georgia and South Carolina, 1760–1815," *Journal of Southern History* 57, no. 2 (1991): 171–200.

21. Bolt, *Tariff Wars*, 7–14.

22. Randolph, *AC* 14-1, 842.

23. Speech on the Tariff, April 4, 1816. For Calhoun's later statement about the circumstances of the speech, see Speech on the Force Bill, February 15 and 16, 1833, 53–54; and Calhoun and Hunter, *Life of John C. Calhoun*, 19. For reference to it in 1823, see JCC to Virgil Maxcy, November 2, 1823.

24. Bolt, *Tariff Wars*, 14–16.

25. Calhoun openly admitted in 1833 that the 1816 bill was protectionist in some respects, but claimed that he had "overlooked" this at the time. Speech on the Force Bill, February 15, 1833, 52, 55.

26. Beckert, *Empire of Cotton*, 38, 47–48, 158.

27. JCC to Alexander Dallas, June 15, 1816; Speech on Compensation of Members, March 8, 1816, and note.

28. Calhoun and Hunter, *Life of John C. Calhoun*, 23; Charles M. Wiltse, *John C. Calhoun: Nationalist, 1782–1828* (Indianapolis: Bobbs-Merrill, 1944), 124–126; John Noble to JCC, August 21, 1816.

29. Speech on the Compensation Law, January 17, 1817. For Burke's famous speech after the Bristol election, see James Prior, *Memoir of the Life and Character of Edmund Burke* (London: H. and E. Sheffield, 1839), 164–166. For Grosvenor, *AC* 14-2, 621–622; *Camden Gazette*, February 6, 1817.

30. Speech on the Neutrality Bill, January 25, 1817; Caitlin Fitz, *Our Sister Republics: The United States in an Age of American Revolutions* (New York: Liveright, 2016), 80–91, with "only one class of men" on 87.

31. Lacy K. Ford, *Deliver Us from Evil: The Slavery Question in the Old South* (New York: Oxford University Press, 2011), 174–179.

32. For "diffusion" in Virginia, see Alan Taylor, *The Internal Enemy: Slavery and War in Virginia, 1772–1832* (New York: W.W. Norton, 2013), 404–409.

33. Speech on the Commercial Treaty, January 9, 1816, 312.

34. Ford, *Deliver Us from Evil*, 188–194, "remorseless, merciless traffic," 189; "It would be a blessing," 193.

35. Calhoun's original letter to Briggs does not survive, but see JCC to James Barrel, September 22, 1816, in which he calls McCalla a "good judge of cotton"; Isaac Briggs to JCC, December 19, 1816.

36. JCC to William Poindexter, January 30, 1817, and receipt included with the letter, in Editorial Records of the John C. Calhoun Papers, SCL; Walter Johnson, *Soul by Soul: Life Inside the Antebellum Slave Market* (Cambridge, MA: Harvard University Press, 1999), 117–134.

37. See Jeff Forret, *Williams' Gang: A Notorious Slave Trader and His Cargo of Black Convicts* (New York: Cambridge University Press, 2020), ch. 1, for further examples.

38. JCC to William Poindexter, January 30, 1817, Editorial Records of the John C. Calhoun Papers, SCL; William Wirt to JCC, August 22, 1816.

39. John C. Calhoun v. Jacob Fowler and William Hix, Goochland Co. Superior Court of Law Order Book, April 19, 1820, 365, Library of Virginia.

40. JCC to Alexander J. Dallas, June 15, 1816.

41. Motion to Form a Committee to Plan a Fund for Internal Improvements, December 16, 1816; Internal Improvements Bill, December 23, 1816.

42. Speech on the Tariff, April 4, 1816.

43. Speech on Internal Improvements, February 4, 1817.

44. *AC* 14-2, 880.

45. Calhoun and Hunter, *Life of John C. Calhoun*, 21. On Madison's residence, see Jeff Broadwater, *James Madison: A Son of Virginia & a Founder of the Nation* (Chapel Hill: University of North Carolina Press, 2012), 172. Calhoun would claim in his 1843 campaign biography that he "never committed himself, in any speech or report, as to the extent of the Constitutional powers of Congress over internal improvements," but confessed that he had wrongly believed these powers were included in the "money-power of the government." Calhoun and Hunter, *Life of John C. Calhoun*, 21.

46. For one published version of Madison's statement, see the *Columbian* (New York), March 12, 1817; Martin Van Buren, *The Autobiography of Martin Van Buren*, ed. John Clement Fitzpatrick, Annual Report of the American Historical Association for the Year 1918 (Washington, DC: Government Printing Office, 1920), 513.

47. For Clay's vote and its significance, see Robert V. Remini, *Henry Clay: Statesman for the Union* (New York: W.W. Norton, 1993), 143.

48. For Madison's veto as a mistake from a nationalist perspective, see John Lauritz Larson, *Internal Improvement: National Public Works and the Promise of Popular Government in the Early United States* (Chapel Hill:

University of North Carolina Press, 2001), 63–69; Howe, *What Hath God Wrought*, 89.

49. See *AC* 14-2, 761–762; John Trumbull to JCC, February 10, 1817.

50. "First Inaugural Address of James Monroe," March 4, 1817, the Avalon Project at Yale Law School, https://avalon.law.yale.edu/19th_century/monroe1 .asp, accessed August 30, 2020; Howe, *What Hath God Wrought*, 93.

51. JCC to James Monroe, November 1, 1817; Calhoun and Hunter, *Life of John C. Calhoun*, 24–25.

52. JCC to Floride Colhoun, November 15, 1817.

Chapter Eight: Secretary of Improvement and Empire

1. See JCC to James Monroe, August 29, 1818, forwarding two possible designs for the new flag. For the law, see Richard Peters, ed., *The Public Statutes at Large of the United States of America, from the Organization of the Government in 1789, to March 3, 1845* (Boston: Little and Brown, 1845), 3:415.

2. Daniel Walker Howe, *What Hath God Wrought: The Transformation of America, 1815–1848* (New York: Oxford University Press, 2007), 125–127; Adam Rothman, *Slave Country: American Expansion and the Origins of the Deep South* (Cambridge, MA: Harvard University Press, 2007), 165–216, price of cotton and land sales in Huntsville on 171; Daniel S. Dupre, *Transforming the Cotton Frontier Madison County, Alabama, 1800–1840* (Baton Rouge: Louisiana State University Press, 1997), 80–87; Ira Berlin, *Generations of Captivity: A History of African-American Slaves* (Cambridge, MA: Belknap Press, 2004), 168. For an extended account of the boom in Mississippi, see Joshua D. Rothman, *Flush Times and Fever Dreams: A Story of Capitalism and Slavery in the Age of Jackson* (Athens: University of Georgia Press, 2014). William Bibb to JCC, January 23, 1818.

3. *City of Washington Gazette*, November 21, 1817.

4. James Edward Colhoun to JCC, November 10, 1817. See Watt Stewart, "The South American Commission, 1817–1818," *Hispanic American Historical Review* 9, no. 1 (1929): 43.

5. *City of Washington Gazette*, December 4, 1817.

6. John Quincy Adams, *Diaries*, ed. David Waldstreicher, vol. 1 (New York: the Library of America, 2017), February 6, 1818, 433.

7. Robert V. Remini, *Andrew Jackson and the Course of American Empire, 1767–1821* (New York: Harper & Row, 1977), 342.

8. Waldstreicher, *Diaries*, 1:427; General Orders concerning the Issuance of Orders, December 29, 1817; JCC to Andrew Jackson, December 29, 1817; *City of Washington Gazette* and *Daily National Intelligencer*, December 31, 1817.

9. JCC to Edmund P. Gaines, December 16, 1817; Andrew Jackson to George Graham, December 16, 1817 (Jackson was apparently unaware that Calhoun was the new secretary of war and addressed his letter to the interim secretary); JCC to Andrew Jackson, December 26, 1817. On the cabinet meeting, see Waldstreicher, *Diaries*, December 26, 1817, 1:429.

10. JCC to Andrew Jackson, December 26, 1817; Jackson to Monroe, January 6, 1818, in Andrew Jackson, *The Papers of Andrew Jackson*, Harold Moser et al., eds., vol. 4 (Knoxville: University of Tennessee Press, 1994); Howe, *What Hath God Wrought*, 98–107; Monroe to JCC, January 30, 1818. Calhoun would later recall coming into Monroe's room while the president was seriously ill and feverish and Monroe handing him the letter, which he looked over and told Monroe would require a response. Jackson would later claim he got that response, while Monroe would always deny it. Historians have generally taken Monroe's side. However, on January 30 Monroe did write Calhoun a brief note instructing him to tell Jackson "not to attack any post occupied by Spanish troops." Calhoun evidently believed Jackson was already so instructed and did not repeat the order, but at least one historian has questioned whether Monroe's January 30 letter, which almost seems like an afterthought, was added to the written record later to cover the administration's tracks; see Howe, *What Hath God Wrought*, 104. Robert Remini plausibly suggested that Monroe fully understood what Jackson intended but maintained official distance through his careful silence. Remini, *Andrew Jackson and the Course of American Empire*, 346–350.

11. Jürgen Osterhammel, *The Transformation of the World: A Global History of the Nineteenth Century*, trans. Patrick Camiller (Princeton, NJ: Princeton University Press, 2014), 573.

12. JCC to John Gaillard (President of the Senate) and Henry Clay (Speaker of the House), January 24, 1818.

13. Thomas L. McKenney to JCC, March 2, 1818.

14. Lurton Dunham Ingersoll, *A History of the War Department of the United States* (Washington, DC, 1879), 78–79.

15. Peters, *Public Statutes at Large*, 3:407–408, 412, 463–464. See also Meriwether et al., *Papers of John C. Calhoun*, 2:xlix–li.

16. JCC to William Crawford, November 3, 1818. For instance, Calhoun estimated that in 1820 the government's spending would be about $16.5 million. See JCC to Samuel Ingham, November 6, 1820.

17. John C. Calhoun and R. M. T. Hunter, *Life of John C. Calhoun* (New York: Harper & Brothers, 1843), 25. For "literal chaos," see Thomas L. McKenney, *Memoirs, Official and Personal* (New York, 1846), 53.

18. JCC to Charles Ingersoll, December 14, 1817.

19. Calhoun and Hunter, *Life of John C. Calhoun,* 26. Calhoun's 1843 estimate is confirmed by a report given to Congress by Peter Hagner, an auditor in the War Department, in 1823. See *Daily National Intelligencer,* April 10, 1823.

20. For Crawford see *American State Papers: Documents, Legislative and Executive, of the Congress of the United States* (Washington, DC: Gales and Seaton, 1832), 1:636; Calhoun and Hunter, *Life of John C. Calhoun,* 30.

21. JCC to Jacob Brown, December 17, 1817.

22. JCC to Charles Tait, July 20, 1818.

23. See JCC to John Williams, February 5 and February 18, 1818; John Williams to JCC, February 11, 1818, inviting him to write the bill. "Very much my own conception," see JCC to Virgil Maxcy, March 27, 1827. For the bill, see Peters, *Public Statutes at Large,* 3:426–427. On rations, see Joseph Lovell to JCC, August 22, 1818; JCC to James Monroe, August 22, 1818. For the organization of the War Department after the reorganization, see Ian C. Hope, *A Scientific Way of War: Antebellum Military Science, West Point, and the Origins of American Military Thought* (Lincoln: University of Nebraska Press, 2015), 63. "Much more congenial," see JCC to Henry Clay, December 11, 1818, 384.

24. "Entombed in some abyss," Thomas Waide to JCC, September 24, 181. See, for instance, regulations governing allowances to officers, issued August 10, 1818, and regulations for substantiating claims to pensions, issued December 23, 1818. Calhoun obviously asked subordinates to provide input on proposed regulations: see Trueman Cross to JCC, July 30, 1819, in which Cross objects that proposed regulations would complicate instead of simplify the department's work. "Moved of itself," Calhoun and Hunter, *Life of John C. Calhoun,* 30.

25. Ingersoll, *History of the War Department,* 85–86. Hope, *Scientific Way of War,* 51–52. For the Post Office reorganization along Calhoun's lines, see McKenney, *Memoirs,* 53.

26. Hope, *Scientific Way of War,* 59–75; JCC to John Taylor, December 12, 1820, 489–490.

27. First and Second Speeches on the Military Academies Bill, January 2 and 3, 1816; JCC to James Monroe, September 3, 1818; James Monroe to JCC, September 9, 1818; William H. Fitzhugh to JCC, February 7, 1824; Hope, *Scientific Way of War,* 64; John Wood et al. to JCC, April 1, 1824.

28. Peters, *Public Statutes at Large,* 7:176–200.

29. Jonathan Jennings to JCC, October 28, 1818. See also JCC to James Monroe, November 27, 1818.

30. JCC to Jasper Parrish, May 14, 1818; JCC to Joseph McMinn, July 29, 1818.

31. Frederick E. Hoxie, *This Indian Country: American Indian Political Activists and the Place They Made*, Penguin History of American Life (New York: Penguin Press, 2012), 66–69.

32. JCC to Speaker Henry Clay, December 5, 1818.

33. See Thomas McKenney to JCC, August 19, 1818.

34. JCC to Speaker Henry Clay, December 5, 1818.

35. Caroline Winterer, *American Enlightenments: Pursuing Happiness in the Age of Reason* (New Haven, CT: Yale University Press, 2016), 110–141.

36. JCC to Return Meigs, July 19, 1820.

37. JCC to Jasper Parrish, May 14, 1818.

38. JCC to Joseph McMinn, July 29, 1818. Calhoun was so concerned to convince the Cherokee to move that he wrote McMinn two letters on the same day. "Extreme liberty," see Return Meigs to JCC, October 10, 1818.

39. See McKenney's report to Calhoun on the schools in January [n.d.], 1822.

40. Ronald N. Satz, *American Indian Policy in the Jacksonian Era* (Lincoln: University of Nebraska Press, 1974), 247–249; See Louis William Dubourg, Bishop of New Orleans, to JCC, March 17, 1823, and Calhoun's reply on the twenty-first.

41. Jedidiah Morse, *A Report to the Secretary of War of the United States, on Indian Affairs: Comprising a Narrative of a Tour Performed in the Summer of 1820* (New Haven, CT: S. Converse, 1822), 11.

42. JCC to James Monroe, February 8, 1822; Monroe's eighth annual message to Congress, December 7, 1824, in James D. Richardson, ed., *A Compilation of the Messages and Papers of the Presidents, 1789–1897* (District of Columbia: Published by Authority of Congress, 1899), 2:257.

43. Other young Choctaw at the academy were reportedly named for Henry Clay and Andrew Jackson. *Cherokee Phoenix*, reprinting an article from the *National Intelligencer*, August 13, 1828.

44. JCC to James Monroe, February 8, 1822.

45. See James McDonald to JCC, October 13, 1823; McKenney, *Memoirs*, 115.

46. Hoxie, *This Indian Country*, 71–75; McKenney, *Memoirs*, 116.

47. Hoxie, *This Indian Country*, 94. Also see John Demos, *The Heathen School: A Story of Hope and Betrayal in the Age of the Early Republic* (New York: Vintage, 2014).

48. Herman J. Viola, *Thomas L. McKenney: Architect of America's Early Indian Policy, 1816–1830* (Chicago: Sage Books, 1974), 198–200.

49. JCC to Charles Ingersoll, August 4, 1818; JCC to Charles Ingersoll, October 1, 1818.

50. Waldstreicher, *Diaries*, vol. 1, May 4, June 9, June 25, 1818, 440-441, 442, 443-444; Andrew Jackson to JCC, May 5, 1818; *Camden Gazette*, June 27, 1818; *Charleston City Gazette*, June 22, 1818; Howe, *What Hath God Wrought*, 100–103.

51. Waldstreicher, *Diaries*, vol. 1, July 15, July 20, 1818; JCC to Charles Tait, July 20, 1818.

52. Howe, *What Hath God Wrought*, 103–111; James Monroe to Andrew Jackson, August 19, 1818 (included in Calhoun's papers); James Monroe to JCC, September 9, 1818, and Calhoun's reply, September 12.

53. James Monroe to Andrew Jackson, October 20, 1818 (included in Calhoun's papers); JCC to Monroe, September 12, 1818; Waldstreicher, *Diaries*, vol. 1 February 9, 1819, 474; Floride Calhoun to Mrs. Patrick Noble, February 4, 1819, in Alice Noble Waring, "Letters of John C. Calhoun to Patrick Noble, 1812–1837," *Journal of Southern History* 16, no. 1 (1950): 67–68.

Chapter Nine: "To the Western Confines of the Continent"

1. JCC to Patrick Noble, November 17, 1818; Andrew H. Browning, *The Panic of 1819: The First Great Depression*, Studies in Constitutional Democracy (Columbia: University of Missouri Press, 2019), 3–7.

2. The House voted down the proposed censures of Jackson on February 8, and Tallmadge offered his amendment on February 13. Robert V. Remini, *Andrew Jackson and the Course of American Empire, 1767–1821* (New York: Harper & Row, 1977), 374; Daniel Walker Howe, *What Hath God Wrought: The Transformation of America, 1815–1848* (New York: Oxford University Press, 2007), 147.

3. Cobb quoted in Howe, *What Hath God Wrought*, 148.

4. John Craig Hammond, "President, Planter, Politician: James Monroe, the Missouri Crisis, and the Politics of Slavery," *Journal of American History* 105, no. 4 (March 2019): 849; Howe, *What Hath God Wrought*, 147–160.

5. John Quincy Adams, *Diaries*, ed. David Waldstreicher, vol. 1 (New York: Library of America, 2017), December 13, 1819, 514.

6. Waldstreicher, *Diaries*, February 24, 1820, 1:534–535.

7. Waldstreicher, *Diaries*, vol. 1, March 3, 1820, 537-545.

8. Pauline Maier, *American Scripture: Making the Declaration of Independence* (New York: Vintage Books, 1998), 175–189, 197–206.

9. Waldstreicher, *Diaries*, vol. 1, March 3, 1820, 537-545.

10. Waldstreicher, *Diaries*, vol. 1, January 10, March 3, 1820, 523-524, 537-545. For "genius of the age," see JCC to Charles Tait, April 23, 1821.

11. William K. Bolt, *Tariff Wars and the Politics of Jacksonian America* (Nashville: Vanderbilt University Press, 2017), 27–38, "create and support a new interest," 29; "on one side," 36. For Calhoun's opposition to the tariff, see JCC to Virgil Maxcy, November 2, 1823.

12. JCC to Henry DeSaussure, April 28, 1820, in supplement to Meriwether et al., *Papers of John C. Calhoun*, found in vol. 27.

13. JCC to Andrew Jackson, June 1, 1820.

14. JCC to James Edward Colhoun, May 7, 1820.

15. Margaret (Bayard) Smith, *The First Forty Years of Washington Society* (New York, 1906), 149–151. Calhoun mentioned the miscarriage to Floride's brother John Ewing Colhoun in a November 8, 1818, letter. In the same letter he mentioned they had bought a house.

16. The John Quincy Adams Digital Diary Project, Massachusetts Historical Society, April 22, 1824, https://www.masshist.org/publications/jqadiaries /index.php/document/jqadiaries-v35-1824-04-22-p142, accessed June 13, 2019.

17. Smith, *First Forty Years*, 147, 148; JCC to Joseph Swift, March 19, 1821.

18. Smith, *First Forty Years*, 147, 148.

19. Anna Maria Calhoun Journal, October 1, 1838, Thomas Green Clemson Papers, Clemson University Special Collections, https://tigerprints.clemson .edu/cgi/viewcontent.cgi?article=1375&context=tgc, accessed June 14, 2020.

20. Lewis quoted in Irving H. Bartlett, *John C. Calhoun: A Biography* (New York: W.W. Norton, 1993), 250.

21. Varina Howell Davis, *Jefferson Davis, Ex-President of the Confederate States of America, A Memoir by His Wife* (New York: Belford Company, 1890), 1:213–214.

22. JCC to John Ewing Colhoun, November 18, 1818.

23. Smith, *First Forty Years*, 158–160.

24. Copy of Subscription List, September [n.d.] 1820, Editorial Records of the John C. Calhoun Papers, SCL.

25. Channing in Dan McKanan, ed., *A Documentary History of Unitarian Universalism* (Boston: Skinner House Books, 2017), 1:181.

26. Josephine Seaton, *William Winston Seaton of the "National Intelligencer"* (Boston: James R. Osgood and Co., 1871), 156–158.

27. Ballston Spa in *Boston Patriot and Daily Chronicle*, September 7, 1820.

28. Boston and Hull in *New York Evening Post*, September 18, 1820.

29. *Commercial Advertiser* (NY), September 25, 1820.

30. *National Advocate for the Country* (NY), September 26, 1820.

31. JCC to Virgil Maxcy, August 12, 1820.

32. JCC to Charles Tait, October 26, 1820, October 1, 1821.

33. William W. Freehling, *Prelude to Civil War: The Nullification Controversy in South Carolina, 1816-1836* (New York: Oxford University Press, 1992), 98; JCC to Charles Tait, October 1, 1821.

34. JCC to Henry Wheaton, September 2, 1821; George McDuffie, *Defence of a Liberal Construction of the Powers of Congress* (Philadelphia, 1832); Freehling, *Prelude to Civil War*, 89–106.

35. See JCC to Edward Everett, November 30, 1822, in which Calhoun thanks Everett for sending a copy of his brother Alexander Hill Everett's recent book on European politics, and references Theodore Lyman's 1820 book on Italian politics.

36. JCC to Charles Tait, April 23, 1821.

37. For Vesey conspiracy, see Lacy K. Ford, *Deliver Us from Evil: The Slavery Question in the Old South* (New York: Oxford University Press, 2009), 207–214; Thomas Bennett to JCC, July 15, 1822; JCC to Major James Bankhead, July 22, 1822. For American attitudes and the initial failure to connect Latin American antislavery to domestic antislavery, see Caitlin Fitz, *Our Sister Republics: The United States in an Age of American Revolutions* (New York: Liveright, 2016), 80–155, "free womb" law on 93.

38. JCC to Andrew Jackson, March 30, 1823; also July 31, 1823, on the same topic; John Quincy Adams Digital Diary Project, September 27, 1822, https://www.masshist.org/publications/jqadiaries/index.php/document/jqadiaries-v32-1822-09-27-p364, accessed June 14, 2020.

39. Jefferson quoted in Jay Sexton, *The Monroe Doctrine: Empire and Nation in Nineteenth-Century America* (New York: Hill and Wang, 2011), 51; John Quincy Adams Digital Diary Project, especially November 15 and 26, 1823, https://www.masshist.org/publications/jqadiaries/index.php/document/jqadiaries-v34-1823-11-15-p149, accessed September 2, 2020.

40. See Andrew Jackson to JCC, ca. August 20, 1823.

41. Sexton, *The Monroe Doctrine*, 47–65.

42. See Sexton, *The Monroe Doctrine*, 47–65, "conducive to its political system," 60.

43. John C. Calhoun and R. M. T. Hunter, *Life of John C. Calhoun* (New York: Harper & Brothers, 1843), 27–28.

44. JCC to Thomas Smith, March 16, 1818.

Chapter Ten: "I Am with the People, and Shall Remain So"

1. John Quincy Adams Digital Diary Project, Massachusetts Historical Society, June 2, 1823, https://www.masshist.org/publications/jqadiaries/index.php/document/jqadiaries-v34-1823-06-02-p075#sn=4, accessed September 2, 2020; Calhoun portrait reproduced in front of vol. 2 of Meriwether et al., *Papers of John C. Calhoun*; Sarah Mytton Maury, *The Statesmen of America in 1846* (Philadelphia, 1847), 181.

2. Josephine Seaton, *William Winston Seaton of the "National Intelligencer"* (Boston: James R. Osgood and Co., 1871), 162.

3. Mark R. Cheathem, *The Coming of Democracy: Presidential Campaigning in the Age of Jackson* (Baltimore: Johns Hopkins University Press, 2018), 35.

4. JCC to John Ewing Colhoun, April 14, 1823.

5. Michael F. Holt, *The Rise and Fall of the American Whig Party: Jacksonian Politics and the Onset of the Civil War* (New York: Oxford University Press, 2003), 4–6; Daniel Walker Howe, *What Hath God Wrought: The Transformation of America, 1815–1848* (New York: Oxford University Press, 2007), 203–211.

6. Howe, *What Hath God Wrought*, 203–211.

7. Harriot Horry Ravenel, *Life and Times of William Lowndes of South Carolina, 1782–1822* (Boston, 1901), 223–229; JCC to Virgil Maxcy, December 31, 1821.

8. See JCC to Andrew Jackson, March 7, 1821.

9. John Quincy Adams Digital Diary Project, April 22, 1822, https://www.masshist.org/publications/jqadiaries/index.php/document/jqadiaries-v32-1822-04-22-p261, accessed September 2, 2020.

10. JCC to Virgil Maxcy, May 6, 1822.

11. John Quincy Adams Digital Diary Project, October 5, 1822, https://www.masshist.org/publications/jqadiaries/index.php/document/jqadiaries-v32-1822-10-05-p385, accessed September 2, 2020.

12. JCC to Micah Sterling, June 17 and June 18, 1822; JCC to Virgil Maxcy, December 9, 1822. See Joseph B. Cumming, "The Cumming-McDuffie Duels," *Georgia Historical Quarterly* 44, no. 1 (1960): 18–40.

13. JCC to Virgil Maxcy, March 13, 1823.

14. JCC to Jacob Brown, August 8, 1823.

15. A Citizen of New York, *Measures, Not Men: Illustrated by Some Remarks upon the Public Conduct and Character of John C. Calhoun* (New York, 1823).

16. Cheathem, *Coming of Democracy*, 33.

17. See degree on September 9, 1822, and Calhoun's reply, December 2, 1822.

18. JCC to Lewis Cass, December 9, 1821.

19. JCC to John Ewing Colhoun, March 19, 1822.

20. JCC to Virgil Maxcy, December 31, 1821.

21. See JCC to Virgil Maxcy, June 9, 1822, in which Calhoun sends a prospectus for the paper.

22. *New York Statesman*, reprinted in *Ithaca Journal*, October 29, 1823.

23. *Richmond Enquirer*, December 11, 1823.

24. Neither Irving Bartlett or John Niven mention the visit, although Wiltse does so in passing. Charles M. Wiltse, *John C. Calhoun: Nationalist, 1782–1828* (Indianapolis: Bobbs-Merrill, 1944), 275.

25. Daniel Raymond, *The Elements of Political Economy*, 2nd ed. (Baltimore, 1823), 1:85.

26. John Taylor, *Tyranny Unmasked* (Washington City: Davis and Force, 1822), esp. preface, 260, 267, 299.

27. See, for instance, the *National Intelligencer*, March 20, 23, and 28, 1822; and the *Washington Gazette*, March 21, 22, and 26, 1822.

28. JCC to Virgil Maxcy, November 2, 1823.

29. Taylor, *Tyranny Unmasked*, 332.

30. JCC to Virgil Maxcy, April 24, 1823.

31. JCC to John McLean, August 4, 1828; Speech in Reply to Daniel Webster's Rejoinder, March 22, 1838, 240.

32. JCC to Joseph Swift, August 24, 1823.

33. On Montesquieu, see David Lynn Scribner, "A Study of the Antecedents, Argument, and Significance of John C. Calhoun's 'South Carolina Exposition'" (PhD, University of Houston, 1997), 239n23; JCC to Robert Garnett, July 3, 1824. For Garnett's prominent role in opposing the tariff, which passed Congress in May, see William K. Bolt, *Tariff Wars and the Politics of Jacksonian America* (Nashville: Vanderbilt University Press, 2017), 41–42.

34. JCC to John Jackson, December 23, 1823.

35. JCC to Virgil Maxcy, September 9, 1825.

36. JCC to Micah Sterling, January 30, 1824; Howe, *What Hath God Wrought*, 206.

37. JCC to Thomas Rogers, March 12, 1823; JCC to Virgil Maxcy, March 13, 1823.

38. JCC to Virgil Maxcy, February 27, 1824.

39. *Daily National Intelligencer*, April 12 and 13, 1824; Meriwether et al., *Papers of John C. Calhoun*, 9:lii.

40. JCC to Lewis Cass, April 24, 1824.

41. Margaret (Bayard) Smith, *The First Forty Years of Washington Society* (New York, 1906), 164.

42. JCC to John Ewing Colhoun, October 8, 1822.

43. JCC to James Edward Colhoun, August 7, 1823. See Walter Muir Whitehill, *Dumbarton Oaks: The History of a Georgetown House and Garden* (Cambridge, MA: Belknap Press, 1967).

44. JCC to John Ewing Colhoun, May 27, 1823.

45. George Ticknor, *Life, Letters, and Journals of George Ticknor* (London: S. Low, 1876), 1:349–350.

46. Irving H. Bartlett, *John C. Calhoun: A Biography* (New York: W.W. Norton, 1993), 123. As Bartlett cites an unpublished letter from Wilkes, which he evidently discovered, I have chosen to cite him instead of the letter.

47. JCC to James Edward Colhoun, February 20, 1825.

48. Catherine Taylor Matthews, J. Tracy Power, and Frances Wallace Taylor, eds., *The Leverett Letters: Correspondence of a South Carolina Family, 1851–1868* (Columbia: University of South Carolina Press, 2000), 424–425.

49. JCC to John Ewing Colhoun, January 16, 1823.

50. JCC to John Ewing Colhoun, May 27, 1823.

51. John Quincy Adams Digital Diary Project, July 31, 1824, https://www
.masshist.org/publications/jqadiaries/index.php/document/jqadiaries-v35
-1824-07-31-p213, accessed September 2, 2020; August 4, 1824, https://www
.masshist.org/publications/jqadiaries/index.php/document/jqadiaries-v35
-1824-08-04-p226, accessed September 2, 2020.

52. James L. Haley, *Sam Houston* (Norman: University of Oklahoma Press,
2015), 24.

53. See Richard Peters, *The Public Statutes at Large of the United States of
America, from the Organization of the Government in 1789, to March 3, 1845* (Boston: Little and Brown, 1845), 4:22–23.

54. See *Daily National Intelligencer*, August 19, September 3, September 11,
and September 14, 1824.

55. JCC to Virgil Maxcy, January 23, 1825.

56. JCC to James Monroe, October 20 and October 28, 1824.

57. *Daily National Intelligencer*, February 10, 1825, 3, col. 2.

58. JCC to Lewis Cass, April 24, 1824.

59. JCC to Joseph Swift, November 20, 1824.

60. JCC to Unknown, November 20, 1824.

61. JCC to Andrew Jackson, March 30, 1823.

62. Howe, *What Hath God Wrought*, 208–209.

63. JCC to Virgil Maxcy, February 18, 1825.

64. Harry L. Watson, *Liberty and Power: The Politics of Jacksonian America*
(New York: Hill and Wang, 2006), 81–82.

65. John Quincy Adams Digital Diary Project, February 11, 1825, https://
www.masshist.org/publications/jqadiaries/index.php/document/jqadiaries-v33
-1825-02-11-p066; February 13, 1825, https://www.masshist.org/publications
/jqadiaries/index.php/document/jqadiaries-v33-1825-02-03-p066, both accessed
September 2, 2020.

66. JCC to Samuel Ingham, October 25, 1838.

67. Robert V. Remini, *Andrew Jackson and the Course of American Freedom,
1822–1832* (New York: Harper & Row, 1981), 102.

68. JCC to Joseph Swift, March 10, 1825.

Chapter Eleven: "The Impression, That I Acted Under the Force of Destiny"

1. JCC to Christopher Vandeventer, April 14, 1825.

2. Speech at Abbeville, South Carolina, May 27, 1825.

3. William K. Bolt, *Tariff Wars and the Politics of Jacksonian America* (Nashville: Vanderbilt University Press, 2017), McDuffie on 41, Jefferson on 42.

4. Walter B. Edgar, *South Carolina: A History* (Columbia: University of South Carolina Press, 1998), 326–329.

5. William W. Freehling, *Prelude to Civil War: The Nullification Controversy in South Carolina, 1816–1836* (New York: Oxford University Press, 1992), 114–115.

6. *Richmond Enquirer*, "The Slave Question," March 25, 1825.

7. Freehling, *Prelude*, 111–118.

8. JCC to Christopher Vandeventer, September 22, 1825.

9. JCC to Joseph Johnson, June 24, 1825; JCC to Floride Bonneau Colhoun, October 5, 1825.

10. Thomas Cooper, *Consolidation: An Account of Parties in the United States, from the Convention of 1787, to the Present Period.*, 2nd ed. (Columbia, SC: Printed at the "Times and Gazette" Office, 1830), 19.

11. Freehling, *Prelude*, 117–118.

12. Robert V. Remini, *Andrew Jackson and the Course of American Freedom, 1822–1832* (New York: Harper & Row, 1981), 55–56.

13. Josiah Quincy, *Figures of the Past from the Leaves of Old Journals* (Boston: Roberts Brothers, 1884), 263.

14. George H. Haynes, *The Senate of the United States, Its History and Practice*, vol. 1 (Boston: Houghton Mifflin Company, 1938), 273–274. For Calhoun's response to the rule change, see Speech on the Rules of the Senate, April 15, 1826.

15. JCC to Joseph Swift, June 27, 1825.

16. John C. Calhoun and R. M. T. Hunter, *Life of John C. Calhoun* (New York: Harper & Brothers, 1843), 31.

17. *Journal of the Senate of the United States*, 19th Congress, 1st Session, December 6, 1825, 27.

18. JCC to Joseph Swift, December 11, 1825.

19. *Senate Journal*, 19th Congress, 1st Session, December 6, 1825, 17, 26.

20. JCC to Samuel Southard, August 16, 1825.

21. *Senate Journal*, 19th Congress, 1st Session, 113, 118, 131–132.

22. *Senate Journal*, 19th Congress, 1st Session, 405–406; "A Western Senator," *Daily National Intelligencer*, April 24, 1826; Mahlon Dickerson to Gales and Seaton, April 24, 1826 (in Calhoun's published papers), and published in *Daily National Intelligencer* the next day.

23. Although Patrick Henry's identity has never been confirmed, and may well have been one of Adams's surrogates, three scholars who have collected the essays produced by the ensuing debate point out that Calhoun would not have responded unless he really believed that his opponent was Adams. H. Lee Cheek, Sean R. Busick, and Carey M. Roberts, *Patrick Henry–Onslow Debate:*

Liberty and Republicanism in American Political Thought (Lanham, MD: The Rowman & Littlefield Publishing Group, Lexington Books, 2013), xiii.

24. See JCC to Floride Bonneau Colhoun, April 23, 1826.

25. Cheek, Busick, and Roberts, *Patrick Henry–Onslow Debate*, quotes on 9, 27, 95.

26. JCC to Floride Colhoun, April 23, May 28, 1826.

27. JCC to John Ewing Colhoun, June 14, 1826.

28. JCC to James Edward Colhoun, December 24, 1826.

29. John Thackston, *Primary and Secondary Education in South Carolina* (PhD thesis, New York University, 1908), 20.

30. Anya Jabour, *Scarlett's Sisters: Young Women in the Old South* (Chapel Hill: University of North Carolina Press, 2007), 46–82, quote on 45, 54.

31. JCC to James Edward Colhoun, January 23, 1828.

32. JCC to James Edward Colhoun, December 24, 1826. See Clemson University's history of the Fort Hill property, https://www.clemson.edu/about /history/properties/fort-hill/, accessed September 27, 2019.

33. See *New York Herald*, July 26, 1849; Sawney is listed as fifty-nine years old in the 1854 inventory produced by the sale of Fort Hill to A. P. Calhoun. Tilla's age is listed as fifty. See inventory at https://www.clemson.edu/about/his tory/properties/documents/slaves-at-FH.pdf, accessed September 2, 2020, and Clemson Special Collections.

34. JCC to Micah Sterling, December 16, 1826.

35. Report of the Minority of the Select Committee, February 13, 1827; JCC to James Edward Colhoun, February 14, 1827.

36. Bolt, *Tariff Wars*, 61–63.

37. Quoted in Bolt, *Tariff Wars*, 67.

38. Freehling, *Prelude*, 126–128; Robert J. Turnbull, *The Crisis: Or, Essays on the Usurpations of the Federal Government* (Charleston, SC: Printed by A. E. Miller, 1827), 127, 131, 137.

39. *Niles Weekly Register*, September 8, 1827, 28.

40. JCC to Samuel D. Ingham, October 28, 1827.

41. JCC to Virgil Maxcy, July 1, 1827.

42. JCC to Littleton Tazewell, July 1, 1827; Toast at Pendleton, July 3, 1827.

43. JCC to Littleton Tazewell, August 25, 1827.

44. See Lacy K. Ford, "Inventing the Concurrent Majority: Madison, Calhoun, and the Problem of Majoritarianism in American Political Thought," *Journal of Southern History* 60, no. 1 (1994): 19–58; Daniel Walker Howe, *What Hath God Wrought: The Transformation of America, 1815–1848* (New York: Oxford University Press, 2007), ch. 6.

45. JCC to Littleton Tazewell, August 25, 1827. See also Maurice Culp, "A Survey of the Proposals to Limit or Deny the Power of Judicial Review by the Supreme Court of the United States," *4 Indiana Law Journal 386 (1929)* 4, no. 6 (March 1, 1929).

46. Remini, *Andrew Jackson and the Course of American Freedom*, 113–115. See Martin Van Buren to Thomas Ritchie, January 13, 1827, Papers of Martin Van Buren (digital edition), ed. Mark R. Cheathem et al., http://vanburenpapers .org/document-mvb00528, accessed August 7, 2020.

47. James Monroe to JCC, February 26, 1827, and March 16, 1828; JCC to James Monroe, February 30 [*sic*], 1827, March 7, 1828, and May 1, 1828; Andrew Jackson to JCC, May 25, 1828; JCC to Andrew Jackson, July 10, 1828.

48. John Quincy Adams Digital Diary Project, February 23, 1828, https:// www.masshist.org/publications/jqadiaries/index.php/document/jqadiaries-v37 -1828-02-23-p419, accessed December 20, 2019.

49. Speech on Internal Improvements, April 10, 1828.

50. Bolt, *Tariff Wars*, 76–90, McDuffie quoted on 77.

51. JCC to James Edward Colhoun, May 4, 1828.

52. Bolt, *Tariff Wars*, 76–90, Tazewell quoted on 89. Bolt makes a convincing case that there must have been an agreement between Van Buren, Wright, and Calhoun.

53. Speech on the Bill to Reduce the Duties on Certain Imports, February 23, 1837, 457.

54. *Charleston Mercury*, November 10, 1828.

55. JCC to Micah Sterling, May 15, 1828.

56. John Ewing Bonneau to JCC, May 28, 1828.

57. Freehling, *Prelude*, 148–149.

58. *Charleston Mercury*, June 25, 1828.

59. Toast at Independence Day Dinner, July 4, 1828.

60. Samuel Smith to JCC, July 5, 1828.

61. Duff Green to JCC, August 4, 1828.

62. Duff Green to JCC, September 23, 1828.

63. James Monroe to JCC, August 4, 1828.

64. JCC to Samuel Ingham, July 23, 1828.

65. JCC to Samuel Smith, July 28, 1828.

66. JCC to John McLean, August 4, 1828.

67. JCC to John McLean, August 4, 1828.

68. JCC to John McLean, August 4, 1828.

69. See, for instance, JCC to John McLean, October 4, 1828. On the construction of the office, the current interpretation of the Fort Hill site is that the office was probably constructed sometime in 1827 or 1828, certainly by 1830.

Email to author from William Hiott, executive director of Historic Properties, Clemson University, September 12, 2019, in author's possession.

70. JCC to William C. Preston, November 6, 1828.

71. Bolt, *Tariff Wars*, 2.

72. Rough Draft of What Is Called the *South Carolina Exposition*, November 25, 1828, 456, 460.

73. John A. James, "The Optimal Tariff in the Antebellum United States," *American Economic Review* 71, no. 4 (1981): 726–734; Bennett D. Baack and Edward J. Ray, "Tariff Policy and Income Distribution: The Case of the U. S., 1830–1860," *Explorations in Economic History; New York* 11, no. 2 (winter 1973): 103–121; Mark Bils, "Tariff Protection and Production in the Early U.S. Cotton Textile Industry," *Journal of Economic History* 44, no. 4 (1984): 1033–1045. For the conclusion that US manufacturers could have survived without the tariff after 1830, see Douglas A. Irwin and Peter Temin, "The Antebellum Tariff on Cotton Textiles Revisited," *Journal of Economic History* 61, no. 3 (2001): 777–798.

74. James Monroe to JCC, August 4, 1828.

75. Rough Draft of What Is Called the *South Carolina Exposition*, November 25, 1828, 504.

76. JCC to John McLean, October 4, 1828.

77. Rough Draft of What Is Called the *South Carolina Exposition*, November 25, 1828, 520–522; see Freehling, *Prelude*, 167–169.

78. John Taylor, *Tyranny Unmasked* (Washington City: Davis and Force, 1822), 256.

79. Rough Draft of What Is Called the *South Carolina Exposition*, November 25, 1828, 522.

80. Protest, December 19, 1828.

81. Madison quoted in James H. Read, *Majority Rule versus Consensus: The Political Thought of John C. Calhoun* (Lawrence: University Press of Kansas, 2009), 46.

82. JCC to William C. Preston, November 6, 1828.

83. Rough Draft of What Is Called the *South Carolina Exposition*, November 25, 1828, 530.

Chapter Twelve: "There Shall Be at Least One Free State"

1. John F. Marszalek, *The Petticoat Affair: Manners, Mutiny, and Sex in Andrew Jackson's White House* (New York: Free Press, 1997), 45–54, "married his mistress" on 48, 73; Reply to John Eaton's Address, October 19, 1831, also published in the *Pendleton Messenger*.

2. Marszalek, *Petticoat Affair*, 65.

3. Marszalek, *Petticoat Affair*, 101–103.

4. Virgil Maxcy to JCC, April 6, 1829.

5. Quoted in Robert V. Remini, *Andrew Jackson and the Course of American Freedom, 1822–1832* (New York: Harper & Row, 1981), 240.

6. Quoted in Marszalek, *Petticoat Affair*, 111.

7. JCC to Christopher Vandeventer, March 14, 1829.

8. JCC to Christopher Vandeventer, March 14, 1829; JCC to Virgil Maxcy, June 21, 1829.

9. JCC to Samuel Ingham, July 26, 1829.

10. JCC to Littleton Waller Tazewell, April 14, 1829.

11. JCC to William Cabell Rives, June 21, 1829.

12. Charles Wiltse made this point long ago. See Charles M. Wiltse, *John C. Calhoun: Nullifier, 1829–1839* (Indianapolis: Bobbs-Merrill, 1949), 24.

13. JCC to Jeremiah Day, James L. Kingsley, or Benjamin Silliman, October 12, 1829.

14. *Register of Debates*, 21st Congress, 1st Session, Appendix, 8–9, 15–16, 18.

15. Hayne's Speech on January 19, 1830, in Herman J. Belz, ed., *The Webster Hayne Debate on the Nature of the Union: Selected Documents* (Indianapolis: Liberty Fund, 2007), 3–14. For context on the debate, see Christopher Childers, *The Webster-Hayne Debate: Defining Nationhood in the Early American Republic* (Baltimore: Johns Hopkins University Press, 2018).

16. Webster's Speech, January 20, 1830, in Belz, *Webster Hayne Debate*, 15–34.

17. Hayne's Speech, January 25, 1830, in Belz, *Webster Hayne Debate*, 35–80.

18. Webster's Speech, January 26 and 27, 1830; Belz, *Webster Hayne Debate*, 81–154.

19. Robert V. Remini, *Daniel Webster: The Man and His Time* (New York: W.W. Norton, 1997), 317–331.

20. Remini, *Andrew Jackson and the Course of American Freedom*, 233–234.

21. Remini, *Andrew Jackson and the Course of American Freedom*, 235; Martin Van Buren, *The Autobiography of Martin Van Buren*, ed. John Clement Fitzpatrick (Washington, DC: Government Printing Office, 1920), 415.

22. Van Buren, *Autobiography*, 416; Remini, *Andrew Jackson and the Course of American Freedom*, 235–236.

23. *Daily National Intelligencer*, April 19, 1830; Wiltse, *Calhoun: Nullifier*, 71–72, fn17. Lillian Adele Kibler, *Benjamin F. Perry, South Carolina Unionist* (Durham, NC: Duke University Press, 1946), 96.

24. Remini, *Andrew Jackson and the Course of American Freedom*, 244–247.

25. John Forsyth to William Crawford, April 16, 1830 (included in Calhoun's published papers). For Crawford's reply, see Andrew Jackson to JCC, May 13, 1830.

26. Andrew Jackson to JCC, May 13, 1830.

27. JCC to Andrew Jackson, May 13, 1830.

28. JCC to James Monroe, May 17 and 26, 1830; James Monroe to JCC, May 21 and May 27, 1830; William Wirt to JCC, May 28, 1830; JCC to William Barry, May 28, 1830.

29. JCC to Andrew Jackson, May 29, 1830.

30. Remini, *Andrew Jackson and the Course of American Freedom*, 246.

31. Remini, *Andrew Jackson and the Course of American Freedom*, 246; Andrew Jackson to JCC, May 30, 1830.

32. Andrew Jackson to William Lewis, August 25, 1830, in Daniel Feller, ed., *The Papers of Andrew Jackson*, vol. 8 (Knoxville: University of Tennessee Press, 2010).

33. JCC to Virgil Maxcy, August 6, 1833.

34. Toast at Pendleton Independence Day Celebration, July 4, 1830; for first use of Fort Hill, see JCC to John Branch, August 6, 1830.

35. Duff Green to JCC, August 15, 1830.

36. JCC to Virgil Maxcy, September 11, 1830.

37. JCC to Virgil Maxcy, September 11, 1830; William W. Freehling, *Prelude to Civil War: The Nullification Controversy in South Carolina, 1816–1836* (New York: Oxford University Press, 1992), 196–197.

38. JCC to James Edward Colhoun, January 13, 1831; JCC to John Quincy Adams, February 11, 1831; Duff Green to John Eaton, February 16, 1831; *United States Telegraph*, February 17, 1831; *Correspondence Between Gen. Andrew Jackson and John C. Calhoun: President and Vice-President of the U. States, on the Subject of the Course of the Latter, in the Deliberations of the Cabinet of Mr. Monroe, on the Occurrences in the Seminole War* (Washington, DC: Printed by Duff Green, 1831).

39. On reactions, including Clay, see Wiltse, *Calhoun: Nullifier*, 96.

40. Memorandum by Virgil Maxcy, February 28, 1831.

41. Memorandum by James H. Hammond, March 18, 1831, in Robert Y. Hayne, "Letters on the Nullification Movement in South Carolina, 1830–1834," *American Historical Review* 6, no. 4 (1901): 736–765.

42. "Mr. Mcduffie's Speech, Delivered at a Public Dinner Given to Him at Charleston, on May 19, 1831," *Banner of the Constitution*, June 8, 1831, 217. Accessed via Proquest American Periodicals Series, 1829–1832.

43. Duff Green to JCC, May 31, 1831.

44. Constans Freeman Daniels, June 11, 1831, published in *Camden Journal*.

45. Freehling, *Prelude*, 224.

46. JCC to Virgil Maxcy, June 16, 1831.

47. Fort Hill Address, July 26, 1831.

48. See note to Fort Hill Address, July 26, 1831, for a list of locations and publications.

49. JCC to Virgil Maxcy, August 6, 1831.

50. JCC to Samuel Ingham, May 27, 1832.

51. Freehling, *Prelude*, 224; State Rights and Free Trade Association, *Catechism on the Tariff for the Use of Plain People of Common Sense* (Charleston, 1831), Newberry Library (Chicago) General Collections.

52. JCC to Francis W. Pickens, August 1, 1831.

53. JCC to James Edward Colhoun, August 27, 1831.

54. Howe, *What Hath God Wrought,* 323–327; *Richmond Enquirer,* August 26, 1831.

55. JCC to Samuel Ingham, July 31, 1831; JCC to James Edward Colhoun, August 27, 1831; JCC to James Edward Colhoun, September 10, 1831.

56. Bill from Hiram Keller, August 27, 1831.

57. JCC to Armistead Burt, September 1, 1831. Aleck's running away and his punishment conform to patterns in the upcountry. See W. J. Megginson, *African American Life in South Carolina's Upper Piedmont, 1780–1900* (Columbia: University of South Carolina Press, 2006), 81–85.

58. Fort Hill Address, July 26, 1831, 428.

59. Thomas Hart Benton, *Thirty Years' View; or, a History of the Working of the American Government for Thirty Years, from 1820 to 1850* (New York: D. Appleton and Co., 1886), 1:219; Michael F. Holt, *The Rise and Fall of the American Whig Party: Jacksonian Politics and the Onset of the Civil War* (New York: Oxford University Press, 2003), 11.

60. Bolt, *Tariff Wars,* 112–116; JCC to Waddy Thompson Jr., July 8, 1832.

61. JCC to James Hamilton Jr., August 28, 1832; see also Freehling, *Prelude,* 164, where Freehling points out some of the problems and contradictions inherent in Calhoun's argument.

62. Freehling, *Prelude,* 252–253.

63. For the nullification revivals, see Stephanie McCurry, *Masters of Small Worlds: Yeoman Households, Gender Relations, and the Political Culture of the Antebellum South Carolina Low Country* (New York: Oxford University Press, 1995), ch. 4, Petigru quoted on 154.

64. Anonymous, *Memoirs of a Nullifier* (Columbia, 1832), 104–110, Newberry Library (Chicago), General Collections. The author was probably either Algernon Sydney Johnston or, possibly, Thomas Cooper.

65. JCC to Virgil Maxcy, October 8, 1832.

66. Bolt, *Tariff Wars,* 119–120; Robert Hayne to JCC, December 22, 1832; JCC to H. Edward Livingston, December 28, 1832.

67. Robert V. Remini, *Andrew Jackson and the Course of American Democracy, 1833–1845* (New York: Harper & Row, 1984), 20–21.

68. Bolt, *Tariff Wars,* 125, 127; Remini, *Andrew Jackson and the Course of American Democracy,* 29.

69. Margaret Bayard Smith, *The First Forty Years of Washington Society* (New York, 1906), 341–342.

70. Quoted in David Johnson, *John Randolph of Roanoke* (Baton Rouge: Louisiana State University Press, 2012), 224–225.

71. JCC to Armistead Burt, January 16, 1833.

72. Charles Cotesworth Pinckney, "The Great Debate of 1833" (n.p., 1899), 108, originally published in *Lippincott's Magazine*, vol. 63 (1899), held in SCL.

73. Remarks on the President's Message on South Carolina, January 16, 1833.

74. JCC to James Hamilton Jr., January 16, 1833; Bolt, *Tariff Wars*, 131, 133. See also JCC to William C. Preston, February 3, 1833.

75. David S. Heidler and Jeanne T. Heidler, *Henry Clay: The Essential American* (New York: Random House, 2011), 253–254; Pinckney, "Great Debate," 112–113.

76. Bolt, *Tariff Wars*, 128–137; Remarks on the Compromise Tariff Bill, February 12, 1833; Heidler and Heidler, *Henry Clay*, 253–254.

77. Remini, *Daniel Webster*, 377.

78. Speech on the Force Bill, February 15 and 16, 1833.

79. Remini, *Daniel Webster*, 378–380.

80. Pinckney, "Great Debate," 110–111.

81. Speech in Reply to Daniel Webster on the Force Bill, February 26, 1833.

82. Quoted in Johnson, *John Randolph*, 226.

83. Pinckney, "Great Debate," 111; Alexander H. Stephens, *A Constitutional View of the Late War Between the States* (Philadelphia, 1868), 1:387.

84. Remini, *Daniel Webster*, 381n37.

85. JCC to Virgil Maxcy, October 8, 1832.

86. John C. Calhoun and R. M. T. Hunter, *Life of John C. Calhoun* (New York: Harper & Brothers, 1843), 48–49; Howe, *What Hath God Wrought*, 408; Wiltse, *Calhoun: Nullifier*, 195.

87. JCC to Christopher Vandeventer, March 25, 1833.

88. See Richard E. Ellis, *The Union at Risk: Jacksonian Democracy, States' Rights, and Nullification Crisis* (New York: Oxford University Press, 1989).

89. See Sven Beckert, *Empire of Cotton: A Global History* (New York: Knopf, 2014), 224–226; JCC to Samuel Ingham, September 26, 1829.

90. See, for instance, Nancy MacLean, *Democracy in Chains: The Deep History of the Radical Right's Stealth Plan for America* (New York: Penguin Books, 2018), prologue; Manisha Sinha, *The Counterrevolution of Slavery: Politics and Ideology in Antebellum South Carolina* (Chapel Hill: University of North Carolina Press, 2000), ch. 1 and 2. These are only two examples of a view that is fairly common (see preface above).

91. JCC to James Hamilton Jr., August 28, 1832. As the historian Lacy Ford once wrote, the nullification crisis, secession, and the Civil War were, in part, "a

struggle between two competing conceptions of a shared American ideal, popular sovereignty." Lacy K. Ford, "Inventing the Concurrent Majority: Madison, Calhoun, and the Problem of Majoritarianism in American Political Thought," *Journal of Southern History* 60, no. 1 (1994): 21.

Chapter Thirteen: "I Think, I See My Way Clearly on the Slave Question"

1. JCC to Anna Maria Calhoun, December 30, 1831.

2. Anna Maria Calhoun to Maria Simkins, May 2, 1833, in Julia Wright Sublette, "The Letters of Anna Calhoun Clemson, 1833–1873" (PhD dissertation, Florida State University, 1993); AMC to James Edward Colhoun, July 4, 1833; JCC to AMC, March 10, 1832; JCC to AMC, February 18, April 3, 1834.

3. JCC to James Kingsley, August 30, 1830; JCC to Stephen Twining, February, 12, 1831; Andrew Calhoun to James Edward Colhoun, February 19, 1834; Ernest M. Lander, *The Calhoun Family and Thomas Green Clemson: The Decline of a Southern Patriarchy* (Columbia: University of South Carolina Press, 1983), 7–8.

4. Oliver Dyer, *Great Senators of the United States Forty Years Ago* (New York, 1889), 168–170; AMC to Patrick Calhoun, August 27, 1837, in Sublette, "Letters of Anna Calhoun Clemson"; JCC to AMC, February 7, February 24, and June 7, 1838.

5. John Ewing Colhoun to James Edward Colhoun, June 17, 1832, in John Ewing Colhoun (1792–1847) Papers, SCL. Ten years later James Edward refused to act as security for his brother. See letter on February 10, 1843, between the two in the same collection.

6. Sherry L. Boatright, *The John C. Calhoun Gold Mine: An Introductory Report on Its Historical Significance* (Atlanta: Historic Preservation Section, Dept. of Natural Resources, State of Georgia, 1974), 10, 18–19, Appendix A14, SCL; AP Calhoun to James Edward Colhoun, July 6, 1833; Nicholas Biddle to JCC, September 11, 1833; Samuel Morse to JCC, December 20, 1833. Andrew also cooperated with David C. Gibson, Calhoun's overseer at Bath, where Andrew had spent the first year of his ill-fated marriage. Gibson sued Calhoun over the ownership of the mine, charging he had been cut out. See Boatwright, *Calhoun Gold Mine*, Appendix 20–30.

7. Speech at Charleston, November 22, 1833, note.

8. See Michael O'Brien, *A Character of Hugh Legaré* (Knoxville: University of Tennessee Press, 1985), 169.

9. JCC to AMC, April 3, 1834.

10. JCC to James Edward Colhoun, December 25, 1831.

11. See JCC to James Edward Colhoun, February 16, 1834, for a typical example.

12. JCC to Francis W. Pickens, December 12, 1833.

13. Daniel Walker Howe, *What Hath God Wrought: The Transformation of America, 1815–1848* (New York: Oxford University Press, 2007), 373–388.

14. Charles Wiltse, ed., *Papers of Daniel Webster: Correspondence*, vol. 3 (Hanover, NH: University Press of New England, 1974), 306.

15. Speech on the Removal of the Deposits, January 13, 1834.

16. See *Register of Debates*, 23rd Congress, 1st Session, 876, 1526, for examples of memorials before and after Calhoun's speech. *Washington Globe* reprinted in *New York Evening Post*, March 24, 1834.

17. Michel Chevalier, *Society, Manners and Politics in the United States* (Boston, 1839), 70.

18. Speech on the Bill to Continue the Charter of the Bank of the United States, March 21, 1834. *Washington Globe* reprinted in *New York Evening Post*, March 24, 1834.

19. Speech in Support of Repeal of the Force Act, April 9, 1834.

20. Speech on the President's Protest, May 6, 1834.

21. JCC to AMC, May 14, 1834.

22. JCC to AMC, April 3, 1834.

23. JCC to AMC, June 23, 1834.

24. AMC to Maria Simkins, April 5, 1834, in Sublette, "Letters of Anna Calhoun Clemson."

25. AMC to Maria Simkins, December 18, 1835, in Sublette, "Letters of Anna Calhoun Clemson."

26. AMC to Maria Simkins, December 18, 1835, in Sublette, "Letters of Anna Calhoun Clemson."

27. AMC to Maria Simkins, January 6, March 5, 1836, in Sublette, "Letters of Anna Calhoun Clemson."

28. Melvin Rosser Mason, "'The Lion of the West' Satire on Davy Crockett and Frances Trollope," *South Central Bulletin* 29, no. 4 (1969): 143–145. AMC to Patrick Calhoun, April 30, 1838, in Sublette, "Letters of Anna Calhoun Clemson." Other biographers, including Irving Bartlett, have confusingly called the play *The Kentuckian*, a novel published about the same time, but Anna's reference to the Wildfire character proves it was *The Lion of the West*.

29. Harriet Martineau, *Retrospect of Western Travel* (London: Saunders and Otley, 1838), 1:243–245.

30. AMC to Maria Simkins, January 23, March 5, 1836, in Sublette, "Letters of Anna Calhoun Clemson." See Amy S. Greenberg, *Lady First: The World of First Lady Sarah Polk* (New York: Knopf, 2019).

31. AMC to Maria Simkins, July [?], August 24, 1836, in Sublette, "Letters of Anna Calhoun Clemson."

32. Josiah Quincy, *Figures of the Past from the Leaves of Old Journals* (Boston: Roberts Brothers, 1884), 264.

33. Motion on Executive Patronage, January 5, 1835; Remarks on Motion on Executive Patronage, January 6, 1835. For national debt, see Robert V. Remini, *Andrew Jackson and the Course of American Democracy, 1833–1845* (New York: Harper & Row, 1984), 222–224.

34. See, for instance, JCC to John Forsyth, January 22, 1835, requesting information on the Judiciary Department that Forsyth had not included in his original report.

35. Martineau, *Retrospect of Western Travels*, 1:245.

36. Remarks on the Death of Warren R. Davis, January 29, 1835.

37. Remini, *Andrew Jackson and the Course of American Democracy*, 227–229.

38. Remarks on an Article in the *Globe*, February, 2, 1835.

39. Report of the Select Committee on Executive Patronage, February 9, 1835.

40. Bill to Amend the Tenure in Office Act, Bill to Regulate the Deposits of the Public Money, Resolution Proposing a Constitutional Amendment to Provide for a Distribution of Surplus Revenue, February 9, 1835.

41. Remarks on the Executive Patronage Report in Exchange with Thomas H. Benton, February 13, 1835; Martineau, *Retrospect of Western Travel*, 1:245–246.

42. Lacy K. Ford, *Deliver Us from Evil: The Slavery Question in the Old South* (New York: Oxford University Press, 2009), 359–389, 447–480, quote on 359.

43. Ford, *Deliver Us from Evil*, 359–389, quotes on 379, 381.

44. Manisha Sinha, *The Slave's Cause: A History of Abolition* (New Haven, CT: Yale University Press, 2016), 34–96, 195–227.

45. JCC to Francis Pickens, January 4, 1834.

46. Speech on the Removal of the Deposits, January 13, 1834, 205.

47. David Brion Davis, *Inhuman Bondage: The Rise and Fall of Slavery in the New World* (New York: Oxford University Press, 2008), 218–220, 231–249.

48. Joseph T. Murphy, "The British Example: West Indian Emancipation, the Freedom Principle, and the Rise of Antislavery Politics in the United States, 1833–1843," *Journal of the Civil War Era* 8, no. 4 (2018): 621–646.

49. Ford, *Deliver Us from Evil*, 481–495; for Mississippi, see Joshua D. Rothman, *Flush Times and Fever Dreams: A Story of Capitalism and Slavery in the Age of Jackson* (Athens: University of Georgia Press, 2014), 91–153.

50. Report and Resolutions of a Public Meeting at Pendleton, September 9, 1835. The language of the report doesn't read as if Calhoun alone authored it, but for some similar language, at least on slavery, see JCC to James T. Austin, December 28, 1837.

51. JCC to Francis Pickens, May 19, 1835.

52. JCC to James Edward Colhoun, September 23, 1835.

53. On honor, shame, and moral change, see Kwame Anthony Appiah, *The Honor Code: How Moral Revolutions Happen* (New York: W.W. Norton, 2010); Corey Robin, *The Reactionary Mind: Conservatism from Edmund Burke to Donald Trump*, 2nd ed. (New York: Oxford University Press, 2017), 4.

Chapter Fourteen: "It Is Our Thermopylae"

1. Sven Beckert, *Empire of Cotton: A Global History* (New York: Knopf, 2014), 118–123.

2. Beckert, *Empire of Cotton*, 217–224, quote on 220; Joshua Rothman, "Contours of Cotton Capitalism," in Sven Beckert and Seth Rockman, eds., *Slavery's Capitalism: A New History of American Economic Development* (Philadelphia: University of Pennsylvania Press, 2016), esp. 126, 127, 131.

3. JCC to Andrew Pickens Calhoun, December 13, 1834; on John Ewing's financial trouble, see John Ewing Bonneau to JCC, September 24, 1834.

4. John J. Chappell to Andrew Pickens Calhoun, December 21, 1835, and note.

5. JCC to Virgil Maxcy, March 18, 1822.

6. J. Franklin Jameson, *Correspondence of John C. Calhoun*, Annual Report of the American Historical Association for the Year 1899 (Washington, DC: Government Printing Office, 1899), 73–74.

7. See conjectural drawing of the Fort Hill plantation, https://www .clemson.edu/about/history/properties/fort hill/african-americans.html, accessed December 12, 2019; 1830 and 1840 US Census, Pickens District, Pickens, South Carolina, Ancestry.com, accessed December 12, 2019; 1854 Fort Hill estate inventory available at https://www.clemson.edu/about/history/proper ties/documents/slaves-at-FH.pdf, accessed December 12, 2019; "A Visit to Fort Hill," *New York Herald*, July 26, 1849.

8. JCC to William C. Brown, November 14, 1844.

9. JCC to Thomas Green Clemson, October 27, 1845.

10. Thomas Green Clemson to JCC, December 30, 1842.

11. "A Visit to Fort Hill," *New York Herald*, July 26, 1849.

12. JCC to James Edward Colhoun, November 17, 1833; JCC to James Edward Colhoun, April 26, 1835.

13. AMC to Patrick Calhoun, August 18, 1838, in Julia Wright Sublette, "The Letters of Anna Calhoun Clemson, 1833–1873" (PhD dissertation, Florida State University, 1993); W. J. Megginson, *African American Life in South Carolina's Upper Piedmont, 1780–1900* (Columbia: University of South Carolina Press, 2006), 165.

14. Will of John Ewing Colhoun of Saint John's Parish, November 18, 1802, SCDAH.

15. See, for instance, John Ewing Colhoun to James Edward Colhoun, February 10, 1843, John Ewing Colhoun (1791–1847) Papers, SCL; Megginson, *African American Life*, 150–151.

16. John Ewing Bonneau to JCC, March 13, 1828.

17. John Ewing Bonneau to JCC, September 25 and October 23, 1830.

18. JCC to Andrew Pickens Calhoun, December 13, 1834.

19. Report and Resolutions, September 9, 1835.

20. JCC to John Ewing Colhoun, January 15, 1827.

21. Megginson, *African American Life*, 140–156.

22. W. J. Megginson notes that other slaves in the upper Piedmont grew and sold their own cotton. Megginson, *African American Life*, 46.

23. On Christmas, see Thomas G. Clemson to JCC, December 27, 1840. Clemson writes the absent Calhoun that they are on "Christmas vacation," which Calhoun's overseer assured him the slaves expected and was usually given. See also Clemson to JCC, December 20, 1840, where he writes that "the negroes have made constant complaints to me" about their rations not being enough. Clemson didn't intend to increase it.

24. JCC to Virgil Maxcy, November 10, 1822.

25. JCC to James Edward Colhoun, May 12, 1837.

26. Megginson, *African American Life*, 80–81.

27. See Walter Johnson, *Soul by Soul: Life Inside the Antebellum Slave Market* (Cambridge, MA: Harvard University Press, 1999); Walter Johnson, *River of Dark Dreams: Slavery and Empire in the Cotton Kingdom* (Cambridge, MA: Belknap Press, 2017); Anthony E. Kaye, "The Second Slavery: Modernity in the Nineteenth-Century South and the Atlantic World," *Journal of Southern History* 75, no. 3 (2009): 627–650; Caitlin Rosenthal, *Accounting for Slavery: Masters and Management* (Cambridge, MA: Harvard University Press, 2019); Joshua D. Rothman, *Flush Times and Fever Dreams: A Story of Capitalism and Slavery in the Age of Jackson* (Athens: University of Georgia Press, 2014).

28. Robert V. Remini, *Andrew Jackson and the Course of American Democracy, 1833–1845* (New York: Harper & Row, 1984), 271.

29. Motion and Remarks on That Portion of the President's Message Concerning the Incendiary Publications of the Abolitionists, December 21, 1835.

30. Lacy K. Ford, *Deliver Us from Evil: The Slavery Question in the Old South* (New York: Oxford University Press, 2009), 500–501; *Register of Debates*, 24th Congress, 1st Session, 1969.

31. Drew Gilpin Faust, *James Henry Hammond and the Old South: A Design for Mastery* (Baton Rouge: Louisiana State University Press, 1982), 168–175, Johnston quoted on 174.

32. First Remark on Receiving Abolition Petitions, January 7, 1836.

33. Remarks on the Reception of the Ohio Abolition Petition, January 19, 1836; Remarks in Debate on the Reception of Abolition Petitions, February 12, 1836.

34. Report from the Select Committee on Incendiary Publications, February 4, 1836.

35. For "juggling," see Remarks on the Reception of the Ohio Abolition Petition, January 19, 1836, 43.

36. Speech on Abolitionist Petitions, March 9, 1836.

37. Ford, *Deliver Us from Evil*, 500–501; AMC to James Edward Colhoun, February 26, 1836, in Sublette, "Letters of Anna Calhoun Clemson."

38. Elizabeth R. Varon, *Disunion! The Coming of the American Civil War, 1789–1859* (Chapel Hill: University of North Carolina Press, 2010), 113–114.

39. Quoted in Sean Wilentz, *The Rise of American Democracy: Jefferson to Lincoln* (New York: W.W. Norton, 2006), 412.

40. Report from the Select Committee on Incendiary Publications, February 4, 1836; Wilentz, *Rise of American Democracy*, 410–412.

41. William K. Bolt, *Tariff Wars and the Politics of Jacksonian America* (Nashville: Vanderbilt University Press, 2017), 2, Table 1.

42. Remarks on Motion to Reduce or Repeal Certain Tariff Duties, December 29, 1835.

43. JCC to Samuel Ingham, June 21, 1836; Charles M. Wiltse, *John C. Calhoun: Nullifier, 1829–1839* (Indianapolis: Bobbs-Merrill, 1949), 267.

44. Daniel Walker Howe, *What Hath God Wrought: The Transformation of America, 1815–1848* (New York: Oxford University Press, 2007), 499–503.

45. Howe, *What Hath God Wrought*, 562–563.

46. JCC to John S. Williams of Cincinnati, September 30, 1835; JCC to Farish Carter, November 26, 1835; JCC to Augustin S. Clayton, November 24, 1835; JCC to James Edward Colhoun, September, 19, 1836.

47. JCC to Frederick W. Symmes, editor of the *Pendleton Messenger*, September 22, 1836; JCC to Samuel Ingham, December 18, 1836. For Calhoun's resignation, see JCC to Robert Hayne, October 28, 1838; on railroads as agents of modernity, see William G. Thomas, "'Swerve Me?': The South, Railroads, and the Rush to Modernity," in L. Diane Barnes, Brian Schoen, and Frank Towers, eds., *The Old South's Modern Worlds: Slavery, Region, and Nation in the Age of Progress* (New York: Oxford University Press, 2011).

48. See deed, executed October 22, 1836.

49. 1840 US Census, Pickens, Pickens District, South Carolina, Ancestry .com, accessed September 4, 2020.

50. JCC to Francis Pickens, August 17, 1836.

51. "Foederatus to His Grace the Duke of Pendleton," August 13, 1836, *Greenville Mountaineer* and in Calhoun's published papers.

52. Remarks at the University of Georgia, August 3, 1836.

53. Speech on Abolitionist Petitions, March 9, 1836.

54. Report from the Select Committee on Incendiary Publications, February 4, 1836.

55. Sean Wilentz, *Chants Democratic: New York City and the Rise of the American Working Class, 1788–1850*, 20th anniversary ed. (Oxford: Oxford University Press, 2004), 286–294.

56. Remarks on Receiving Abolition Petitions (First Report), February 6, 1837.

57. *Register of Debates*, 24th Congress, 2nd Session, 721–722.

58. Remarks on Receiving Abolition Petitions (Revised), February 6, 1837. There are two versions of Calhoun's response, one printed the next day in the *National Intelligencer*, probably taken down by a reporter, and later reprinted in the Senate's official *Register of Debates*, and a longer, more polished version that Calhoun himself prepared and that was published two months later in the short-lived paper *Washington Reformer*—Calhoun's new newspaper arm under the editorship of Richard Crallé—and also as a pamphlet. Like many of his colleagues, after giving an important speech Calhoun would often spend days preparing a polished text of the speech for publication. I have drawn from the revised and subsequently published version, both because it represents Calhoun's thinking more fully than the first shortened version taken down hurriedly in the Senate chamber, and because it would become the most widely circulated.

59. *Register of Debates*, 24th Congress, 2nd Session, 721–722. Rives could easily have quoted and may have had in mind the influential French philosopher Montesquieu's pronunciation in *The Spirit of the Laws* that "the state of slavery is bad of its own nature: it is neither useful to the master nor to the slave." See Caroline Winterer, *American Enlightenments: Pursuing Happiness in the Age of Reason* (New Haven, CT: Yale University Press, 2016), 153–154.

60. Quoted in Robert V. Remini, *Henry Clay: Statesman for the Union* (New York: Norton, 1993), 507.

61. Whether Calhoun read Bentham directly we cannot know, but by 1835 Thomas Cooper was explicitly using Bentham's theories and appealing to self-evident "facts" to justify slavery despite the fact that Bentham had explicitly condemned slavery. Daniel Kilbride, "Slavery and Utilitarianism: Thomas Cooper and the Mind of the Old South," *Journal of Southern History* 59, no. 3 (1993): 478n15.

62. On historicism, and a growing emphasis on history in southern life in general during the first half of the nineteenth century, see Michael O'Brien,

Conjectures of Order: Intellectual Life and the American South, 1810–1860 (Chapel Hill: University of North Carolina Press, 2004), 2:591–653, 1178–1183.

63. See JCC to James Iredell, March 28, 1828. Kilbride, "Slavery and Utilitarianism," 482n21; Paul Erickson, "The Anthropology of Charles Caldwell, M.D," *Isis* 72, no. 2 (1981): 252–256.

64. Ford, *Deliver Us from Evil*, 509–511. For the ways that science and racial theories supported an "enlightened" view of slavery, see Winterer, *American Enlightenments*, 142–170. On scientific racism, see George M. Fredrickson, *The Black Image in the White Mind: The Debate on Afro-American Character and Destiny, 1817–1914* (New York: Harper & Row, 1971), ch. 3; David Brion Davis, *Inhuman Bondage: The Rise and Fall of Slavery in the New World* (New York: Oxford University Press, 2008), 75–76.

65. Matthew Karp, *This Vast Southern Empire: Slaveholders at the Helm of American Foreign Policy* (Cambridge, MA: Harvard University Press, 2016), 150–172.

66. Josiah Clark Nott and George R. Gliddon, *Types of Mankind* (Philadelphia: Lippincott, Grambo, 1854), 50.

67. William Harper, *Memoir on Slavery* (Charleston, 1838), 3–6, 42–44; Karp, *This Vast Southern Empire*, 57–58; Ford, *Deliver Us from Evil*, 523.

68. George Park Fisher, *Life of Benjamin Silliman* (Philadelphia: Porter & Coates, 1866), 2:98.

Chapter Fifteen: "Dangerous and Despotic Doctrines"

1. Remarks on the Motion to Expunge the Senate's Censure of Andrew Jackson, January 13, 1837.

2. Joseph T. Murphy, "The British Example: West Indian Emancipation, the Freedom Principle, and the Rise of Antislavery Politics in the United States, 1833–1843," *Journal of the Civil War Era* 8, no. 4 (2018): 629–630, quotes on 630; Andrew Delbanco, *The War Before the War: Fugitive Slaves and the Struggle for America's Soul from the Revolution to the Civil War* (New York: Penguin Press, 2018), 170–173.

3. Motion in Regard to *Encomium* and *Enterprise*, January 28, 1837.

4. Remarks on the Correspondence with Great Britain, March 2, 1837.

5. Matthew Karp, *This Vast Southern Empire: Slaveholders at the Helm of American Foreign Policy* (Cambridge, MA: Harvard University Press, 2016), 17–19, 51–57.

6. Daniel Walker Howe, *What Hath God Wrought: The Transformation of America, 1815–1848* (New York: Oxford University Press, 2007), 502–505; Michael F. Holt, *The Rise and Fall of the American Whig Party: Jacksonian Politics and the Onset of the Civil War* (New York: Oxford University Press, 2003), 64–70.

7. AMC to Patrick Calhoun, August 27, 1837, in Julia Wright Sublette, "The Letters of Anna Calhoun Clemson, 1833–1873" (PhD dissertation, Florida State University, 1993).

8. JCC to AMC, September 8, 1837.

9. JCC to AMC, September 8, 1837; Holt, *Rise and Fall of the American Whig Party*, 65–67.

10. JCC to Samuel Ingham, May 25, 1837.

11. JCC to AMC, September 8, 1837.

12. Special Session Message, September 4, 1837, Miller Center, University of Virginia, https://millercenter.org/the-presidency/presidential-speeches/september-4-1837-special-session-message, accessed August 11, 2020.

13. Howe, *What Hath God Wrought*, 508–512. That Calhoun well understood this about the difference between the two parties, see Remarks on the Right of Petition, February 13, 1840, 101.

14. Speech on the Bill Authorizing an Issue of Treasury Notes, September 18, 1837.

15. Speech on Amendment to Separate the Government and the Banks, October 3, 1837.

16. Lacy K. Ford, "Republican Ideology in a Slave Society: The Political Economy of John C. Calhoun," *Journal of Southern History* 54, no. 3 (August 1, 1988): 418.

17. Speech on the Bill Authorizing an Issue of Treasury Notes, September 18, 1837.

18. JCC to AMC, September 30, 1837.

19. JCC to John Bauskett et al., Edgefield district, SC, November 3, 1837; AMC to Patrick Calhoun, December 24, 1837, in Sublette, "Letters of Anna Calhoun Clemson."

20. JCC to AMC, December 10, 1837.

21. Manisha Sinha, *The Slave's Cause: A History of Abolition* (New Haven, CT: Yale University Press, 2016), 228–237. On John Brown, see Tony Horwitz, *Midnight Rising: John Brown and the Raid That Sparked the Civil War* (New York: Picador, 2012), 25.

22. Resolutions on Abolition and the Union, December 27, 1837.

23. Quoted in Robert V. Remini, *Henry Clay: Statesman for the Union* (New York: Norton, 1993), 509.

24. Rives quoted in Irving H. Bartlett, *John C. Calhoun: A Biography* (New York: W.W. Norton, 1993), 241.

25. *Congressional Globe*, 25th Congress, 2nd Session, 59–98, Webster on 74.

26. *Congressional Globe*, 25th Congress, 2nd Session, 74.

27. Remarks on His Fifth Resolution, January 10 and 11, 1838.

28. Remarks on His Fifth Resolution, January 10 and 11, 1838.

29. Charles Chauncey Binney, *The Life of Horace Binney, with Selections from His Letters* (Philadelphia, London: J.B. Lippincott Co., 1903), 313–314; Josiah Quincy, *Figures of the Past from the Leaves of Old Journals* (Boston: Roberts Brothers, 1884), 263–264.

30. Richard Crallé memorandum, December 4, 1831, in Calhoun's published papers.

31. JCC to Armistead Burt, January 24, 1838.

32. *Congressional Globe*, 25th Congress, 2nd Session, 73.

33. Clay in Remini, *Henry Clay*, 518–519; *National Intelligencer* republished in New York *Evening Star*, January 5, 1838.

34. James Edward Colhoun to JCC, February 1, 1835.

35. JCC to Francis Pickens, August 17, 1836.

36. JCC to AMC, January 25, 1838.

37. Elizabeth R. Varon, *Disunion! The Coming of the American Civil War, 1789–1859* (Chapel Hill: University of North Carolina Press, 2010), 11, 116–121, 133–134.

38. Francis Pickens to AMC, February 15, 1838.

39. Mangum quoted in Remini, *Henry Clay*, 513.

40. Calhoun Response to Henry Clay, March 10, 1838; Remini, *Henry Clay*, 515–516; John Quincy Adams, *Diaries*, ed. David Waldstreicher (New York: Library of America, 2017), March 10, 1838, 2:429–430.

41. Remini, *Henry Clay*, 517; Charles M. Wiltse, *John C. Calhoun: Nullifier, 1829–1839* (Indianapolis: Bobbs-Merrill, 1949), 384.

42. JCC to AMC, February 24, 1838; AMC to Patrick Calhoun, April 14, 1838, in Sublette, "Letters of Anna Calhoun Clemson"; Ernest M. Lander, *The Calhoun Family and Thomas Green Clemson: The Decline of a Southern Patriarchy* (Columbia: University of South Carolina Press, 1983), 8; JCC to Armistead Burt, May 27, 1838.

43. Lander, *Calhoun Family*, 1–4.

44. AMC to Maria Simkins, August 2, 1838, in Sublette, "Letters of Anna Calhoun Clemson."

45. JCC to Henry Vethake, October 11, 1838. The editors note that the manuscript is in Anna's hand.

46. Remarks at a Barbecue in Greenville District, SC, August 28, 1838, "like every other business" on 407; Waddy Thompson Jr. to JCC, August 30, 1838; JCC to Waddy Thompson Jr., September 2, 1838; Remarks at a Public Dinner at Pickens Court House, September 12, 1838; Remarks at Anderson, SC, September 27, 1838; JCC to Duff Green, October 11, 1838.

47. JCC to Alton Pemberton, November 19, 1838.

48. JCC to Virgil Maxcy, August 6, 1831.

49. Fort Hill Address, July 26, 1831.

50. JCC to Alton Pemberton, November 19, 1838.

51. On households, see Stephanie McCurry, *Masters of Small Worlds: Yeoman Households, Gender Relations, and the Political Culture of the Antebellum South Carolina Low Country* (New York: Oxford University Press, 1995).

52. Reinhold Niebuhr, *Moral Man and Immoral Society: A Study in Ethics and Politics* (New York: Scribner, 1941), introduction and ch. 1, xii, xx, 3.

53. Lander, *Calhoun Family*, 1.

54. APC to JCC, December 25, 1838.

55. Lander, *Calhoun Family*, 6–9; for Biddle interview, see Thomas Green Clemson to JCC, January 22, 1839; TGC to Andrew Calhoun, February 2, 1839; Bond and Mortgage executed by Calhoun, Clemson, and Andrew, October 19, 1839, SCDAH.

Chapter Sixteen: "The True and Perfect Voice of the People"

1. JCC to Micah Sterling, July 1, 1840.

2. JCC to James Henry Hammond, February 18, 1837.

3. JCC to John L. O'Sullivan, October 14, 1838. O'Sullivan had written Calhoun about the idea of abolishing the legal enforcement of contracts, leaving credit to rest solely on its "natural basis of confidence" in the contracting parties, an idea that took free market ideals to an extreme of which Calhoun was skeptical.

4. On conservatism in nineteenth-century America, see Adam I. P. Smith, *The Stormy Present: Conservatism and the Problem of Slavery in Northern Politics, 1846–1865* (Chapel Hill: University of North Carolina Press, 2017), 6–8.

5. JCC to Virgil Maxcy, February 28, 1839.

6. Remarks on Abolition, February 7, 1839.

7. JCC to Virgil Maxcy, March 28, 1840.

8. Floride quoted in Ernest M. Lander, *The Calhoun Family and Thomas Green Clemson: The Decline of a Southern Patriarchy* (Columbia: University of South Carolina Press, 1983), 10; JCC to ACC, April 6, 1839.

9. JCC to James Edward Colhoun, February 26, 1832.

10. JCC to Edmund Ruffin, August 17 and October 8, 1835, both published in *Farmer's Register* 3, no. 8, in December 1835.

11. Proceedings of the Pendleton Farmer's Society, October 3, 1839.

12. Speech on Henry Clay's Resolutions, March 16, 1842.

13. ACC to Patrick Calhoun, November 6, 1837, in Julia Wright Sublette, "The Letters of Anna Calhoun Clemson, 1833–1873" (PhD dissertation, Florida State University, 1993).

14. JCC to Patrick Calhoun, December 4, 1839.

15. JCC to James Edward Colhoun, August 27, 1839; ACC to Maria Simkins Calhoun, September 19, 1839, in Sublette, "Letters of Anna Calhoun Clemson."

16. JCC to ACC May 30, 1840.

17. APC to JCC, December 25, 1838.

18. JCC to TGC, February 22, 1840; Lander, *Calhoun Family*, 23.

19. JCC to James Edward Colhoun, February 1, 1840.

20. Martin Van Buren to Andrew Jackson, February 2, 1840, Papers of Martin Van Buren [digital edition], ed. Mark R. Cheathem et al., http://vanburenpapers.org/document-mvb02913, accessed September 6, 2020.

21. Bill to Cede the Public Lands, January 3, 1840; Abraham Lincoln to John T. Stuart, January 1, 1840, Papers of Abraham Lincoln Digital Library, https://papersofabrahamlincoln.org/documents/D200197, accessed January 22, 2020.

22. Matthew Karp, *This Vast Southern Empire: Slaveholders at the Helm of American Foreign Policy* (Cambridge, MA: Harvard University Press, 2016), ch. 1.

23. See JCC to Joel Poinsett, April 28, 1839, in which Calhoun says he would have introduced the issue earlier if not for the "Maine question."

24. Motion in Regard to the Brig *Enterprise*, March 4, 1840.

25. Speech on the Case of the Brig *Enterprise*, March 13, 1840; Joseph T. Murphy, "The British Example: West Indian Emancipation, the Freedom Principle, and the Rise of Antislavery Politics in the United States, 1833–1843," *Journal of the Civil War Era* 8, no. 4 (2018): 632.

26. Remarks on the Cumberland Road Bill, April 1, 1840, 171.

27. Karp, *This Vast Southern Empire*, 48–49; John B. Edmunds, *Francis W. Pickens and the Politics of Destruction* (Chapel Hill: University of North Carolina Press, 1986), 60–61.

28. JCC to APC, July 5, 1840. On the election, see Mark R. Cheathem, *The Coming of Democracy: Presidential Campaigning in the Age of Jackson* (Baltimore: Johns Hopkins University Press, 2018), 136–153.

29. See William Henry Harrison to JCC, November 29, 1831.

30. JCC to Tandy Walker et al., August 24, 1840.

31. JCC to James Scott et al., August 11, 1840, 331.

32. JCC to APC, November 22, 1840.

33. JCC to ACC, February 17, 1841.

34. JCC to Orestes Brownson, June 6, 1841.

35. JCC to TGC, January 26, 1841.

36. Francis Pickens to James Edward Colhoun, May 6, 1842; ACC to Patrick Calhoun, March 8, 1843, in Sublette, "Letters of Anna Calhoun Clemson."

37. APC to JCC, August 2, 1840.

38. *Columbus Times*, April 22, 1841, 2; John Witherspoon Du Bose, *The Life and Times of William Lowndes Yancey* (Birmingham, AL: Roberts & Son, 1892), 98–99.

39. JCC to Patrick Calhoun, June 9, 1841; 1840 US Census, Marengo Co., Alabama, Ancestry.com, accessed September 6, 2020.

40. Samuel Townes to George Franklin Townes, July 25, 1841, Townes Family Papers, SCL; Meriwether et al., *Papers of John C. Calhoun*, 15:xix–xx. For women's role in the 1840 election, see Elizabeth Varon, "Tippecanoe and the Ladies, Too: White Women and Party Politics in Antebellum Virginia," *Journal of American History* 82, no. 2 (1995): 494–521.

41. Remarks at Montgomery, May 8, 1841. For "God," see Samuel Townes to George Franklin Townes, July 25, 1841, Townes Family Papers, SCL.

42. Robert V. Remini, *Henry Clay: Statesman for the Union* (New York: Norton, 1993), 585; Sean Wilentz, *The Rise of American Democracy: Jefferson to Lincoln* (New York: W.W. Norton, 2006), 523–529.

43. Further Remarks on the Fiscal Bank of the United States, July 7, 1841.

44. Further Remarks in Debate on Points of Order, August 7, 1841.

45. Speech on the Loan Bill, July 19, 1841.

46. Wilentz, *Rise of American Democracy*, 524–525.

47. Remini, *Henry Clay*, 586.

48. JCC to Orestes Brownson, October 31, 1841.

49. Speech in Support of the Veto Power, February 28, 1842.

50. Blair quoted in Wilentz, *Rise of American Democracy*, 528.

51. JCC to AMC, March 20, 1842.

52. TGC to JCC, December 20, 1840.

53. TGC to JCC, December 27, 1840.

54. ACC to JCC, December 21, 1840.

55. ACC to Maria Calhoun, September 16, 1841, February 23, 1842, in Sublette, "Letters of Anna Calhoun Clemson"; JCC to ACC, January 3, 1842; JCC to TGC, December 31, 1841.

56. JCC to Patrick Calhoun, March 20, 1842.

57. JCC to ACC, May 30, 1842.

58. "If the negroes have not yet started, they had better wait for the first good spell of weather." JCC to ACC, December 23, 1841.

59. Floride Calhoun to Margaret Calhoun, February 8, 1842; Floride Calhoun to JCC, February 15, 1842. Sawney is not listed on an inventory of Andrew's estate in 1865 that included both Fort Hill and Cane Brake slaves.

60. Duff Green to JCC, January 24, 1842. For more on Green, see Edward Bartlett Rugemer, *The Problem of Emancipation: The Caribbean Roots of the American Civil War, Antislavery, Abolition, and the Atlantic World* (Baton Rouge: Louisiana State University Press, 2008), 205–208; Karp, *This Vast Southern Empire*, 25–27.

61. Remarks on the *Creole* Affair, February 3, 1842.

62. JCC to Duff Green, April 2, 1842; Rugemer, *Problem of Emancipation*, 180–221; Karp, *This Vast Southern Empire*, 26–27.

63. See, for instance, JCC to Abel Upshur, August 27, 1843.

64. Karp, *This Vast Southern Empire*, 32–49, Adams quoted on 34.

65. Speech on the Treaty of Washington, August 19, 1842.

66. Speech on Felix Grundy's Report, February 5, 1840. For a comprehensive account of Calhoun's economic views in the late 1830s and early 1840s, see Lacy K. Ford, "Republican Ideology in a Slave Society: The Political Economy of John C. Calhoun," *Journal of Southern History* 54, no. 3 (August 1, 1988): 405–424.

67. Speech on Felix Grundy's Report, February 5, 1840; Speech Before the Passage of the Tariff Bill, August 5, 1842, 371.

68. Speech on Henry Clay's Resolutions, March 16, 1842.

69. Speech Before the Passage of the Tariff Bill, August 5, 1842.

70. Remarks on the Tariff, February 3, 1842, 106.

71. JCC to John Mathewes, May 22, 1842; ACC to Maria Calhoun, June 14, 1842; TGC to JCC July 9, 1842; *Pendleton Messenger*, July 1, 1842; Sherry L. Boatright, *The John C. Calhoun Gold Mine: An Introductory Report on Its Historical Significance* (Atlanta: Historic Preservation Section, Dept. of Natural Resources, State of Georgia, 1974).

72. TGC to JCC, July 15, 1842; JCC to ACC, July 16, 1842; Lander, *Calhoun Family*, 48–49.

73. JCC to James Henry Hammond, September 24, 1841.

74. JCC to James Edward Colhoun, November 1, 1841.

75. Carol K. Bleser, *Secret and Sacred: The Diaries of James Henry Hammond, a Southern Slaveholder* (New York: Oxford University Press, 1988), 109.

76. Dixon Lewis to Richard Crallé, June 20, 1842.

77. Joseph Scoville to R. M. T. Hunter, February 16, 1843, and note; J. Francis Hutton to R. M. T. Hunter, February 18, 1843.

78. See, for instance, Robert Barnwell Rhett to JCC, August 25, 1843, in which Rhett writes hopefully that Calhoun's refusal to campaign is popular with many voters.

79. James L. Anderson and W. Edwin Hemphill, "The 1843 Biography of John C. Calhoun: Was R. M. T. Hunter Its Author," *Journal of Southern History* 38, no. 3 (1972): 469–474; JCC to ACC, February 6, 1843; Harper Brothers to Virgil Maxcy, June 13, 1843.

80. James H. Hammond, *Selected Letters and Speeches* (New York, 1866), 244.

81. John C. Calhoun and R. M. T. Hunter, *Life of John C. Calhoun* (New York: Harper & Brothers, 1843), 3, 18–19, 70–74.

82. Pamphlet reprinted in *Auburn Journal and Advertiser*, June 29, 1842; James Auchincloss to JCC, September 22, 1842.

83. Wilentz, *American Democracy*, 534–535.

84. The *Subterranean*, December 26, 1846.

85. JCC to Gilbert Rice, September 13, 1841.

86. *Jamestown Journal* (NY), June 30, 1842.

87. Wilentz, *American Democracy*, 533–537.

88. Orestes Brownson, *The Laboring Classes* (Boston, 1840). For Calhoun's subscription, see JCC to Orestes Brownson, March 10 and June 6, 1841.

89. Orestes Brownson to JCC, October 13, 1841.

90. Wilentz, *American Democracy*, 499–500, 535–539.

91. See An Appeal to the Democratic Party, January 1843, written by Robert Barnwell Rhett, in Meriwether et al., *Papers of John C. Calhoun*; Dixon Lewis to Richard Crallé, December 28, 1842.

92. Wilentz, *American Democracy*, 539–545.

93. JCC to John Mathewes, May 22, 1842.

94. Resolutions on Rhode Island, ca. May 1842.

95. R. M. T. Hunter, manuscript memoir of John C. Calhoun, 269–271, R. M. T. Hunter Papers, Library of Virginia.

96. *New York Democratic Republican New Era*, May 26, 1842; also, in Meriwether et al., *Papers of John C. Calhoun*, 16:xvii.

97. Joel Poinsett to Martin Van Buren, June 5, 1842, Papers of Martin Van Buren [digital edition], ed. Mark R. Cheathem et al., http://vanburenpapers .org/document-mvb03370, accessed August 17, 2020; Donald B. Cole, *Jacksonian Democracy in New Hampshire, 1800–1851* (Cambridge, MA: Harvard University Press, 1970), 234–235.

98. To the South Carolina House of Representatives, November 26, 1842; Resolution of the South Carolina General Assembly, December 19, 1842. Sean Wilentz attributes Calhoun's loss of northern support to his opposition to the Dorr War. Wilentz, *American Democracy*, 545.

99. Floride Calhoun to Patrick Calhoun, April 3, 1843.

100. Floride Calhoun to Margaret Calhoun, December 3, 1845.

101. JCC to APC, June 3, 1846, April 12, 1847. Issey does not appear in the list of Fort Hill slaves from Andrew's purchase of Fort Hill from his mother in 1850 after Calhoun's death. See https://www.clemson.edu/about/history/properties /documents/slaves-at-FH.pdf, accessed February 19, 2020.

102. Albert Moore Rhett to Robert Barnwell Rhett, October 19, 1841, SCL.

Chapter Seventeen: *"Thou Art the Man"*

1. Patrick Calhoun to JCC, February 28, 1844.

2. Address of Mr. Calhoun to His Political Friends and Supporters, January 29, 1844.

3. JCC to James Edward Colhoun, February 7, 1844; JCC to Duff Green, February 10, 1844.

4. JCC to Virgil Maxcy, February 12, 1844.

5. Adams quoted in Sean Wilentz, *The Rise of American Democracy: Jefferson to Lincoln* (New York: W.W. Norton, 2006), 561.

6. Amy S. Greenberg, *A Wicked War: Polk, Clay, Lincoln, and the 1846 U.S. Invasion of Mexico* (New York: Vintage, 2013), 8–17.

7. George McDuffie to JCC, March 1, 1844.

8. See Abel Upshur to JCC, August 14, 1843; JCC to Abel Upshur, August 27, 1843.

9. George McDuffie to JCC, March 6, 1844; John Tyler to JCC, March 6, 1844; David Hale to JCC, March 7, 1844; John Mathewes to JCC, March 17, 1844; Dixon Lewis to JCC, March 6, 1844.

10. JCC to Mary Galloway Maxcy, March 9, 1844.

11. JCC to George McDuffie, March 9, 1844; Treaty of Annexation Between the United States of America and the Republic of Texas, April 12, 1844.

12. JCC to Samuel Ingham, June 21, 1836.

13. Ashbel Smith to JCC, June 19, 1843.

14. Matthew Karp, *This Vast Southern Empire: Slaveholders at the Helm of American Foreign Policy* (Cambridge, MA: Harvard University Press, 2016), 86–87; W. Stephen Belko, *The Invincible Duff Green: Whig of the West* (Columbia: University of Missouri, 2006), 362–365. See also Memorandum Communicated by Texan Ministers to Mr. Calhoun, April 4, 1844.

15. JCC to Abel Upshur, August 27, 1843.

16. Karp, *This Vast Southern Empire*, 61–65; Thomas Rodney to the Secretary of State, March 28, 1844; Washington Irving to Secretary of State, April 2, 1844.

17. Richard Pakenham to Abel Upshur, February 26, 1844.

18. Wilentz, *Rise of American Democracy*, 567. On the delay, see John Tyler to Andrew Jackson, April 18, 1844, Library of Congress, http://hdl.loc.gov/loc .mss/maj.01111_0262_0265, accessed September 6, 2020.

19. On the rise of statistics as a source of authority, see Patricia Cline Cohen, *A Calculating People* (New York: Routledge, 1999). See, for example, Speech on Henry Clay's Resolutions, March 16, 1842.

20. On the 1840 census see Paul Schor, *Counting Americans: How the U.S. Census Classified the Nation* (New York: Oxford University Press, 2017), 30–39.

21. JCC to Richard Pakenham, April 18, 1844.

22. Albert Deutsch, "The First U.S. Census of the Insane (1840) and Its Use as Proslavery Propaganda," *Bulletin of the History of Medicine* 15, no. 5 (1944): 469–482. For Adams's resolutions, see *House Journal*, 28th Congress, 1st Session, 471; 2nd Session, 291.

23. JCC to John W. Jones, Speaker of the House of Representatives, May 1, 1844.

24. John Quincy Adams diary 44, page 329 [electronic edition], May 18, 1844, *The Diaries of John Quincy Adams: A Digital Collection* (Boston: Massachusetts Historical Society, 2004), http://www.masshist.org/jqadiaries, accessed September 6, 2020; JCC to John W. Jones, Speaker of the House of Representatives, February 8, 1845; Schor, *Counting Americans*, 30–39.

25. Greenberg, *Wicked War*, 17–20.

26. *Washington Globe*, May 2, 1844, 1.

27. See JCC to Richard Pakenham, April 27, 1844.

28. JCC to John Mathewes, May 9, 1844.

29. Wilentz, *Rise of American Democracy*, 575–578.

30. On Polk's nomination, see Greenberg, *Wicked War*, 38–43.

31. Wilentz, *Rise of American Democracy*, 566–570.

32. Robert Monroe Harrison to Abel Upshur, March 8, 1844; Harrison to JCC, May 4, 1844; Edward Bartlett Rugemer, *The Problem of Emancipation: The Caribbean Roots of the American Civil War, Antislavery, Abolition, and the Atlantic World* (Baton Rouge: Louisiana State University Press, 2008), 204–221.

33. Karp, *This Vast Southern Empire*, 87.

34. JCC to Abel Upshur, August 27, 1843.

35. JCC to Robert Campbell, June 26, 1844.

36. JCC to Henry Wise, May 25, 1844.

37. Karp, *This Vast Southern Empire*, 70–72.

38. Karp, *This Vast Southern Empire*, 72–81; for another argument, see Gerald Horne, *The Deepest South: The United States, Brazil, and the African Slave Trade* (New York: New York University Press, 2007).

39. George Proffit to Abel Upshur, February 27, 1844.

40. JCC to William King, August 12, 1844.

41. George Gliddon to JCC, May 9, August 2, 1844; Samuel George Morton to JCC, May 9, 1844; JCC to Samuel George Morton, circa September 1844,

689. Josiah Clark Nott and George R. Gliddon, *Types of Mankind* (Philadelphia: Lippincott, Grambo, 1854), 50–52. Ibram Kendi notes important dissent from Morton's findings. See Ibram X. Kendi, *Stamped from the Beginning: The Definitive History of Racist Ideas in America* (New York: Nation Books, 2016), 179–180.

42. William King to JCC, January 29, 1845; Christopher Hughes to JCC, January 31, 1845.

43. "Grand slaveholding league," Karp, *This Vast Southern Empire*, 96, 101; James Gadsden to JCC, December 14, 1844.

44. JCC to William King, December 13, 1844.

45. JCC to ACC, May 10, 1844; ACC to JCC, December 5, 1844.

46. TGC to JCC, December 30, 1842; JCC to TGC, January 8 and 21, 1843; Ernest M. Lander, *The Calhoun Family and Thomas Green Clemson: The Decline of a Southern Patriarchy* (Columbia: University of South Carolina Press, 1983), 60–63, 71.

47. ACC to JCC, June 1, 1844; Julia Wright Sublette, "The Letters of Anna Calhoun Clemson, 1833–1873," (PhD dissertation, Florida State University, 1993), 385; TGC to JCC, October 20, 1844; JCC to ACC, August 29, 1844; Lander, *Calhoun Family*, 78–81; JCC to TGC, September 14, 1844.

48. Francis Pickens to James Edward Colhoun, December 7, 1844.

49. Elizabeth R. Varon, *Disunion! The Coming of the American Civil War, 1789–1859* (Chapel Hill: University of North Carolina Press, 2010), 170–171; JCC to Armistead Burt, August 7, 1844; JCC to William Porter, president of the Young Men's Democratic Association of Charleston, August 19, 1844; James Hamilton Jr. to JCC, August 20, 1844; Francis Pickens to JCC, November 27, 1844.

50. JCC to Robert I. Alexander et al., September 12, 1844.

51. JCC to Abel Upshur, August 27, 1843.

52. See Memoranda by Robert J. Walker, December, 1844, 432–433.

53. JCC to Richard Pakenham, September 3, 1844; Richard Pakenham to JCC, September 12, 1844; Daniel Walker Howe, *What Hath God Wrought: The Transformation of America, 1815–1848* (New York: Oxford University Press, 2007), 711–718.

54. Greenberg, *Wicked War*, 27–33.

55. Francis Pickens to JCC, September 9, 1844.

56. JCC to John Mathewes, October 14, 1844; John Mathewes to JCC, December 1, 1844.

57. John Quincy Adams, *Diaries*, ed. David Waldstreicher (New York: Library of America, 2017), 2:607.

58. Howe, *What Hath God Wrought*, 699; Waldstreicher, *Diaries*, 2:607.

59. Polk informed Calhoun of the cabinet decision on February 27, the same day the Senate resolution passed. JCC to James K. Polk, February 28, 1845.

60. JCC to Andrew Jackson Donelson, May 23, 1845.

61. JCC to Andrew Jackson Donelson, May 23, 1845; Charles Sellers, *James K. Polk: Continentalist, 1843–1846* (Norwalk, CT: Easton Press, 1987), 215–220. In a different context, and for political points, Thomas Hart Benton would place the responsibility for the war with Mexico entirely on Calhoun as the one responsible for annexing Texas. See *Congressional Globe*, 29th Congress, 2nd Session, 498–501. See also Speech in Reply to Thomas H. Benton on the Mexican War, February 24, 1847.

62. Francis Pickens to JCC, December 28, 1844; Waldstreicher, *Diaries*, January 20, 1845, 2:604; Wilentz, *Rise of American Democracy*, 566–570.

63. Sheila M. Rothman, *Living in the Shadow of Death: Tuberculosis and the Social Experience of Illness in American History* (Baltimore: Johns Hopkins University Press, 1995), 13–17.

64. Floride Calhoun to Patrick Calhoun, April 3, 1843. See also JCC to ACC, February 6, 1843, and January 3, 1842.

65. JCC to Thomas Green Clemson, June 4, 1844.

66. *Washington Constitution*, January 31, 1845; see Meriwether et al., *Papers of John C. Calhoun*, 21:132.

67. Floride Calhoun to James Edward Calhoun, February 1, 1845.

68. Memorandum by Francis Wharton, February 18 and 20, 1845.

69. Howe, *What Hath God Wrought*, 700.

70. JCC to ACC, March 11, 1845; JCC to John Alfred Calhoun, April 2, 1845; JCC to James Edward Colhoun, June 9, 1845.

Chapter Eighteen: "Ours Is the Government of the White Man"

1. *Mobile Daily Advertiser*, November 5, 1845; Account of Calhoun's Visit to Mobile, November 4, 1845.

2. *Mobile Register and Journal*, November 11, 1845; Account of Calhoun's Voyage from Mobile to New Orleans, November 7, 1845; Toast, November 8, 1845.

3. *Jackson Southern Reformer*, November 15, 1845; *Vicksburg Daily Sentinel*, November 11, 1845. For Memphis, *Weekly American Eagle*, November 14, 1845. Account of Calhoun's Arrival at Memphis, November 12, 1845. In 1850 Memphis had a population of 8,841 according to the US Census, https://www2.census.gov/library/publications/decennial/1850/1850a/1850a-38.pdf, accessed September 8, 2020.

4. Walter Johnson, *River of Dark Dreams: Slavery and Empire in the Cotton Kingdom* (Cambridge, MA: Belknap Press, 2017), 280–302, esp. 297.

5. Address on Taking the Chair of the Southwestern Convention, November 13, 1845.

6. Matthew Karp, *This Vast Southern Empire: Slaveholders at the Helm of American Foreign Policy* (Cambridge, MA: Harvard University Press, 2016), 35–39; Johnson, *River of Dark Dreams*, 296–302.

7. Franklin Elmore to JCC, December 16, 1845.

8. JCC to James Henry Hammond, August 30, 1845; James Gadsden to JCC, September 19, 1845; Francis Pickens to JCC, September 29, 1845; R. M. T. Hunter to JCC, October 17, 1845; ACC to JCC, November 10, 1845.

9. Charles Sellers, *James K. Polk: Continentalist, 1843–1846* (Norwalk, CT: Easton Press, 1987), 339–348, 357, Pickens quoted on 347.

10. Polk quoted in Sellers, *Polk: Continentalist*, 363–364; *Baltimore American*, December 23, 1845; Meriwether et al., *Papers of John C. Calhoun*, 23:312; *London Times*, December 2, 1845.

11. Remarks and Resolutions on Oregon, December 30, 1845.

12. Sellers, *Polk: Continentalist*, 363–372.

13. Daniel Walker Howe, *What Hath God Wrought: The Transformation of America, 1815–1848* (New York: Oxford University Press, 2007), 719.

14. R. M. T. Hunter memoir of John C. Calhoun, 269, R. M. T. Hunter Papers, Library of Virginia.

15. Carol K. Bleser, ed., *Secret and Sacred: The Diaries of James Henry Hammond, a Southern Slaveholder* (New York: Oxford University Press, 1988), February 14, 1846, 153.

16. Speech on the Bill for the Occupation and Settlement of the Territory of Oregon, January 31, 1843, 643. For one validation of Calhoun's view, see David L. Dykstra, *The Shifting Balance of Power: American-British Diplomacy in North America, 1842–1848* (Lanham, MD: University Press of America, 1999).

17. See, for instance, Louis McLane to JCC, January 3, 1846. McLane also sent Calhoun several London newspapers.

18. TGC to JCC, January 31, 1846; Francis Lieber to JCC, March 16, 1846; Dublin *Freeman's Journal*, April 23, 1846.

19. *Richmond Enquirer*, March 20, 1846; *Baltimore American and Commercial Advertiser*, March 17, 1846; Meriwether et al., *Papers of John C. Calhoun*, 22:xiv.

20. Speech on the Abrogation of the Joint Occupancy of Oregon (Revised), March 16, 1846, and note; "a positive good," Speech on the Abrogation of the Joint Occupancy of Oregon (First Version), March 16, 1846, 697.

21. Tilly Allen to JCC, March 19, 1846.

22. Francis Lieber to JCC, March 27, 1846; *London Times*, April 11, 1846; Meriwether et al., *Papers of John C. Calhoun*, 22:xv.

23. Sellers, *Polk: Continentalist*, 397–415.

24. Speech on the Abrogation of the Joint Occupancy of Oregon (Revised), March 16, 1846, 711.

25. Amy S. Greenberg, *A Wicked War: Polk, Clay, Lincoln, and the 1846 U.S. Invasion of Mexico* (New York: Vintage, 2013), 96–98.

26. JCC to APC, May 14, 1846. See also JCC to TGC, May 29, 1846.

27. See JCC to Andrew Jackson Donelson, September 17, 1844; Karp, *This Vast Southern Empire*, 97. Arkansas senator Ambrose Sevier raised this very issue when Calhoun opposed Polk's actions. See Remarks on the President's War Message, May 11, 1846.

28. In the House, Isaac Holmes and Robert Barnwell Rhett previewed arguments that Calhoun would make in the Senate, showing that the South Carolinians were talking. Ernest McPherson Lander Jr., *Reluctant Imperialists: Calhoun, the South Carolinians, and the Mexican War* (Baton Rouge: Louisiana State University Press, 1980), 6–8.

29. Remarks on the President's War Message, May 11, 1846.

30. JCC to TGC, May 12, 1846.

31. Remarks on the Declaration of a State of War with Mexico, May 12, 1846; JCC to Henry Conner, May 15, 1846; Greenberg, *Wicked War*, 109–110.

32. James Hamilton Jr. to JCC, May 25 and June 21, 1846. See also James Gadsden to JCC, May 18, 1846; JCC to James Edward Colhoun, May 29, 1846; "perfectly suicidal," Wilentz, *American Democracy*, 583.

33. JCC to ACC, June 11, 1846; JCC to TGC, August 8, 1846; Lander, *Reluctant Imperialists*, 15–21, "utterly dead" on 21.

34. Report on the Memphis Memorial, June 26, 1846; Bill to Authorize a Mississippi River Survey, June 26, 1846.

35. JCC to James Edward Colhoun, August 8, 1846.

36. Clement Biddle to JCC, July 6, 1846. The ACLL publication *The Anti Bread Tax Circular* published glowing reports of Calhoun's positions on free trade during his 1844 presidential run, and applauded his attempts to keep the peace during the Oregon crisis. In 1845, when ACLL vice president George Wilson sent Calhoun a collection of ACCS publications, Calhoun replied in words that rang like a liturgy in every free trader's ears. "I regard free trade, as involving considerations far higher than mere commercial advantages, as great as they are," he wrote. "It is, in my opinion, emphatically the cause of civilization & peace." Simon Morgan, "The Anti–Corn Law League and British Anti-Slavery in Transatlantic Perspective, 1838–1846," *Historical Journal* 52, no. 1 (2009): 87–107; JCC to George Wilson, March 24, 1845.

37. On the Walker tariff, see William K. Bolt, *Tariff Wars and the Politics of Jacksonian America* (Nashville: Vanderbilt University Press, 2017), 174–186, "simultaneous triumph" on 185.

38. See Amendment to the Public Lands Bill, June 30, 1846; Remarks on His Amendment to the Public Lands Bill, July 8, 1846.

39. Sellers, *Polk: Continentalist*, 468–476.

40. JCC to TGC, May 29, 1846.

41. Wilentz, *Rise of American Democracy*, 596–597; Sellers, *Polk: Continentalist*, 479–484.

42. Sellers, *Polk: Continentalist*, 480–481; Wilentz, *Rise of American Democracy*, 586–601.

43. JCC to Lewis Coryell, November 7, 1846; JCC to Henry Dearborn, November 8, 1846.

44. Wilentz, *Rise of American Democracy*, 590. On the freedom principle in Atlantic context, see Joseph T. Murphy, "The British Example: West Indian Emancipation, the Freedom Principle, and the Rise of Antislavery Politics in the United States, 1833–1843," *Journal of the Civil War Era* 8, no. 4 (2018): 621–646.

45. JCC to Rev. William Capers, June 4, 1844.

46. JCC to TGC, June 23, 1845; JCC to James Henry Hammond, July 7, August 2, August 30, and September 28, 1845; James Henry Hammond to JCC, August 18, 1845.

47. Greenberg, *Wicked War*, 127–135.

48. Milo Quaife, ed., *The Diary of James K. Polk* (Chicago, 1910), 2:281–284.

49. JCC to ACC, December 27, 1846.

50. Quaife, *Diary of James K. Polk*, 2:371; on agreement between Polk and Calhoun see Karp, *This Vast Southern Empire*, 118–122. For Calhoun's own interpretation: "But after the war was declared…I acquiesced in what I could not prevent, and which it was impossible for me to arrest; and I then felt it to be my duty to limit my efforts to giving such direction to the war as would, as far as possible, prevent the evils and danger with which it threatened the country and its insertions." Speech on the War with Mexico (Revised), January 4, 1848.

51. Quaife, *Diary of James K. Polk*, 2:293.

52. Speech on the War with Mexico, February 9, 1847.

53. Speech in Reply to Hopkins Turney, February 12, 1847; Further Remarks on the Mexican War, February 19, 1847.

54. Speech and Resolutions on the Restriction of Slavery from the Territories, February 19, 1847.

55. See Orlando Patterson, *Slavery and Social Death: A Comparative Study* (Cambridge, MA: Harvard University Press, 1982), and Bertram Wyatt-Brown, *Southern Honor: Ethics and Behavior in the Old South* (New York: Oxford University Press, 1982).

56. Remarks in Reply to Thomas Hart Benton, February 19, 1847.

57. Greenberg, *Wicked War*, 156–161.

58. Speech at a Meeting of Citizens of Charleston, March 9, 1847; JCC to TGC, March 19, 1847.

59. Charles James Faulkner to JCC, July 15, 1847; JCC to Charles James Faulkner, August 1, 1847.

60. JCC to Eustis Prescott, September 5, 1847; Isaac Hayne to JCC, September 15, 1847.

61. JCC to Benjamin F. Perry, September 21, 1847.

62. JCC to Henry Peronneau, September 28, 1847.

63. JCC to Percy Walker, October 23, 1847. See also JCC to Charles James Faulkner, August 1, 1847.

64. JCC to Eustis Prescott, September 5, 1847; JCC to Pierre Soule, July 8, 1847.

65. Greenberg, *Wicked War*, 231–236.

66. JCC to Waddy Thompson, October 29, 1847.

67. "December 7, 1847: Third Annual Message," Miller Center, University of Virginia, https://millercenter.org/the-presidency/presidential-speeches/december-7-1847-third-annual-message, accessed September 8, 2020.

68. Resolutions on the Mexican War, December 15, 1847; Remarks on Resolutions, December 20, 1847.

69. JCC to Wilson Lumpkin, January 8, 1847.

70. Meriwether et al., *Papers of John C. Calhoun*, 23:ix–x.

71. Speech on the War with Mexico (Revised Version), January 4, 1848. See Joshua A. Lynn, *Preserving the White Man's Republic: Jacksonian Democracy, Race, and the Transformation of American Conservatism* (Charlottesville: University of Virginia Press, 2019).

72. Franklin Smith to JCC, December 22, 1847; William Emmons to JCC, January 9, 1848.

73. "John C. Calhoun," *North Star*, January 14, 1848, Library of Congress, https://www.loc.gov/item/mfd.21013/, accessed September 8, 2020.

74. JCC to ACC, December 26, 1847.

75. Greenberg, *Wicked War*, 256–271.

76. Fred Kaplan, *John Quincy Adams: American Visionary* (New York: Harper Perennial, 2015), 570; "Order of the Procession for the Funeral of the Hon. John Quincy Adams, a Representative in the Congress of the United States from the State of Massachusetts, and Ex-President of the United States…February 24, 1848," Library of Congress, Washington, DC, https://www.loc.gov/resource/rbpe.23204500/, accessed April 8, 2020.

Chapter Nineteen: The Pillar of Fire

1. JCC to ACC, April 28, 1848. On the 1848 revolutions, see Jonathan Sperber, *The European Revolutions, 1848–1851* (New York: Cambridge University Press, 2005).

2. Joseph T. Murphy, "The British Example: West Indian Emancipation, the Freedom Principle, and the Rise of Antislavery Politics in the United States, 1833–1843," *Journal of the Civil War Era* 8, no. 4 (2018), 628.

3. JCC to ACC, April 28, 1848.

4. *Disquisition*, in Meriwether et al., *Papers of John C. Calhoun*, 28:7–8.

5. *Disquisition*, 11.

6. *Disquisition*, 13.

7. *Disquisition*, 11.

8. *Disquisition*, 36–38.

9. *Disquisition*, 38–39.

10. *Disquisition*, 11, 27.

11. *Disquisition*, 13–14.

12. *Disquisition*, 14–18.

13. *Disquisition*, 35.

14. *Disquisition*, 13, 20–21.

15. *Disquisition*, 28, 32.

16. *Disquisition*, 34–35.

17. *Disquisition*, 43–45.

18. *Disquisition*, 43–66.

19. *Discourse on the Constitution and Government of the United States*, in Meriwether et al., *Papers of John C. Calhoun*, 28:236–239; Rachel Klein, *Unification of a Slave State: The Rise of the Planter Class in the South Carolina Backcountry, 1760–1808* (Chapel Hill: University of North Carolina Press, 1992).

20. *Disquisition*, 56–58.

21. See James H. Read, *Majority Rule Versus Consensus: The Political Thought of John C. Calhoun* (Lawrence: University Press of Kansas, 2009), 1–2.

22. *Discourse*, 71–74, 81.

23. *Discourse*, 104, 140.

24. *Discourse*, 160–161, 167–168.

25. *Discourse*, 231.

26. *Discourse*, 233–234.

27. Andrew Jackson Donelson to JCC, March 3, 1848.

28. JCC to James Edward Calhoun, March 23, 1848.

29. Speech on the Revolution in France, March 30, 1848.

30. JCC to ACC, June 23, 1848.

31. JCC to Thomas Green Clemson, April 13, 1848.

32. JCC to Baron Friedrich von Gerolt, May 28, 1848.

33. Remarks on the Disturbances in the District of Columbia, April 20, 1848; JCC to Wilson Lumpkin, April 21, 1848.

34. Remarks on the Occupation of Yucatán, April 29, 1848.

35. JCC to ACC, June 23, 1848.

36. JCC to James Edward Colhoun, April 15, 1848.

37. *Disquisition*, 39.

38. Speech on the Oregon Bill, June 27, 1848.

39. JCC to TGC, July 23, 1848; *Charleston Mercury*, July 31, 1848; For Bright's comment, see Charles M. Wiltse, *John C. Calhoun: Sectionalist, 1840–1850* (Indianapolis: Bobbs-Merrill, 1951), 352.

40. Speech on the Proposal to Extend the Missouri Compromise Line to the Pacific, August 10, 1848.

41. Adam I. P. Smith, *The Stormy Present: Conservatism and the Problem of Slavery in Northern Politics, 1846–1865* (Chapel Hill: University of North Carolina Press, 2017), esp. introduction.

42. Further Remarks on the Oregon Bill, August 12, 1848.

43. Remarks at a Public Meeting in Charleston, August 19, 1848.

44. JCC to ACC, July 30, 1848.

45. See Ker Boyce to JCC, March 20, 1848; JCC to APC, April 16 and 26, 1848. Ernest M. Lander, *The Calhoun Family and Thomas Green Clemson: The Decline of a Southern Patriarchy* (Columbia: University of South Carolina Press, 1983), 107–111.

46. TGC to JCC, April 26, 1848; JCC to TGC, July 23, 1848.

47. JCC to APC, November 25, 1848.

48. JCC to APC, November 25, 1848; Lander, *Calhoun Family*, 109.

49. Sean Wilentz, *The Rise of American Democracy: Jefferson to Lincoln* (New York: W.W. Norton, 2006), 617–628.

50. Remarks at a Public Meeting in Charleston, August 19, 1848.

51. Andrew Jackson Donelson to JCC, September 27, 1848.

52. Andrew Jackson Donelson to JCC, March 3, 1848; Sarah Maury to JCC, August 15, 1848; Matthew Karp, *This Vast Southern Empire: Slaveholders at the Helm of American Foreign Policy* (Cambridge, MA: Harvard University Press, 2016), 134–141; Seymour Drescher, *The Mighty Experiment: Free Labor Versus Slavery in British Emancipation* (New York: Oxford University Press, 2002), 158–201.

53. Quoted in Andrew Delbanco, *The War Before the War: Fugitive Slaves and the Struggle for America's Soul from the Revolution to the Civil War* (New York: Penguin Press, 2018), 242.

54. Oliver Dyer, *Great Senators of the United States Forty Years Ago* (New York, 1889), 148–149. Abolitionist meeting quotes in Delbanco, *War Before the War*, 242.

55. APC to JCC, September 2, 1848.

56. JCC to ACC, March 7, 1848.

57. Remarks at a Meeting of Southern Members of Congress, December 22, 1848; Remarks at a Meeting of the Committee of Fifteen, January 13, 1849; Remarks at a Meeting of the Southern Caucus, January 15, 1849.

58. JCC to TGC, January 22, 1848; ACC to JCC, January 27, 1848.

59. Address of Southern Delegates in Congress, to Their Constituents, January 22, 1849, and note.

60. Remarks on a Bill to Create an Interior Department, March 3, 1849.

61. Thomas Bangs Thorpe, "Webster, Clay, Calhoun, and Jackson: How They Sat for Their Daguerreotypes," *Harper's New Monthly Magazine* (New York: Harper & Bros., 1869). For the image described here, see daguerreotype of John C. Calhoun, ca. 1849, by Mathew Brady, at Yale Beinecke Rare Book and Manuscript Library, https://brbl-dl.library.yale.edu/vufind/Record/3438518, accessed September 8, 2020.

62. ACC to JCC, April 15, 1849.

63. JCC to ACC, April 10 and June 15, 1849.

64. JCC to ACC, June 15, 1849.

65. To the People of the Southern States, July 5, 1849.

66. JCC to Henry Foote, August 3, 1849; William W. Freehling, *The Road to Disunion* (New York: Oxford University Press, 1990), 480–482; on cotton prices, see JCC to James Edward Calhoun, November 11, 1849.

67. Elizabeth R. Varon, *Disunion! The Coming of the American Civil War, 1789–1859* (Chapel Hill: University of North Carolina Press, 2010), 209–210; Wilentz, *Rise of American Democracy*, 636–638.

68. Joanne B. Freeman, *The Field of Blood: Violence in Congress and the Road to Civil War* (New York: Picador, 2019), 144–145.

69. Varon, *Disunion*, 213–215.

70. Robert V. Remini, *Henry Clay: Statesman for the Union* (New York: Norton, 1993), 731–733.

71. Memorandum by John Randolph Tucker, February 1850.

72. ACC to JCC, February 18, 1850.

73. See *Schenectady Reflector*, January 25, 1850; *Boston Recorder*, February 7, 1850; *Washington National Era*, December 13, 1849. Most reports agreed that Calhoun's attack came on Wednesday, January 16.

74. Alan Heimert, "Moby-Dick and American Political Symbolism," *American Quarterly* 15, no. 4 (1963): 498–534. My thanks to Michael Kimmage, who alerted me to this wonderful essay.

75. JCC to John Towers, March 3, 1850.

76. *Congressional Globe*, 31st Congress, 1st Session, 622.

77. William Tecumseh Sherman, *Memoirs of General W. T. Sherman* (New York: Library of America, 1990), 107; Delbanco, *War Before the War*, 238.

78. *Congressional Globe*, 31st Congress, 1st Session, 462.

79. Speech on the Slavery Question, March 4, 1850.

80. *Congressional Globe*, 31st Congress, 1st Session, 463.

81. *Congressional Globe*, 31st Congress, 1st Session, 476–484.

82. JCC to TGC, March 10, 1850.

83. Remarks During Daniel Webster's Speech, March 7, 1850.

84. Varon, *Disunion*, 222–231.

85. Joseph Scoville to TGC, March 13, 1850.

86. "The Last Moments of Mr. Calhoun's Life," by Joseph Scoville, March 31, 1850; John C. Calhoun Jr. to Richard Crallé, May 19, 1850.

87. See *Daily National Intelligencer*, April 11, 1850.

88. *Boston Recorder*, April 11, 1850.

89. *Richmond Enquirer*, April 12, 1850; Floride Calhoun to ACC, April 4, 1850; George Park Fisher, *Life of Benjamin Silliman* (Philadelphia: Porter & Coates, 1866), 2:97.

90. *The Death and Funeral Ceremonies of John Caldwell Calhoun* (Columbia, SC: Printed by A. S. Johnston, 1850), 18–24.

91. Quoted in Lillian Adele Kibler, *Benjamin F. Perry, South Carolina Unionist* (Durham, NC: Duke University Press, 1946), 244.

92. John Wentworth, *Congressional Reminiscences* (Chicago, 1882), 23–24.

93. James Henley Thornwell, *Thoughts Suited to the Present Crisis: A Sermon, on Occasion of the Death of Hon. John C. Calhoun* (Columbia, SC, 1850), 33.

94. Fredrika Bremer, *The Homes of the New World; Impressions of America* (New York, 1853), 1:312; Ethan J. Kytle and Blain Roberts, *Denmark Vesey's Garden: Slavery and Memory in the Cradle of the Confederacy* (New York: New Press, 2018), 97.

95. James Warley Miles, *The Discourse on the Occasion of the Funeral of the Hon. John C. Calhoun* (Charleston, 1850), 24; Thomas J. Brown, *Civil War Canon: Sites of Confederate Memory in South Carolina* (Chapel Hill: University of North Carolina Press, 2015), 40; *Death and Funeral Ceremonies of John Caldwell Calhoun*, 107.

Epilogue

1. "Calhoun's Real Monument," Walt Whitman, *Specimen Days in America* (London, 1887), 118.

2. Thomas J. Brown, *Civil War Canon: Sites of Confederate Memory in South Carolina* (Chapel Hill: University of North Carolina Press, 2015), 51–63.

3. Paul Quigley, *Shifting Grounds: Nationalism and the American South, 1848–1865* (New York: Oxford University Press, 2014), ch. 2.

4. Brown, *Civil War Canon*, 43, 55.

5. Matthew Karp, *This Vast Southern Empire: Slaveholders at the Helm of American Foreign Policy* (Cambridge, MA: Harvard University Press, 2016), ch. 6; on Agassiz, see William Stanton, *The Leopard's Spots: Scientific Attitudes Toward Race in America, 1815–59* (Chicago: University of Chicago, 1982), 104–112.

6. Brown, *Civil War Canon*, 41–44.

7. Brown, *Civil War Canon*, 62.

8. ACC to Floride Clemson, November 11, 1860, in Julia Wright Sublette, "The Letters of Anna Calhoun Clemson, 1833–1873" (PhD dissertation, Florida State University, 1993).

9. Brown, *Civil War Canon*, 63.

10. Stanley Harrold, ed., *The Civil War and Reconstruction: A Documentary Reader* (Malden, MA: Blackwell Publishing, 2008), 61.

11. Brown, *Civil War Canon*, 65–66.

12. Ernest M. Lander, *The Calhoun Family and Thomas Green Clemson: The Decline of a Southern Patriarchy* (Columbia: University of South Carolina Press, 1983), 150–185.

13. Floride Calhoun to Andrew Calhoun, November 13, 1850, Floride Calhoun Papers, SCL.

14. Lander, *Calhoun Family*, 223–224; Ernest M. Lander and Charles M. McGee, eds., *A Rebel Came Home: The Diary of Floride Clemson* (Columbia: University of South Carolina Press, 1961), 93; Andrew Pickens Calhoun Estate Inventory, April 26, 1865, Fort Hill Historical Site, Clemson University, https://www.clemson.edu/about/history/properties/documents/Enslaved%20Persons%20at%20Fort%20Hill%201854%20and%201865.pdf, accessed May 16, 2020.

15. Quoted in Brown, *Civil War Canon*, 66.

16. Calhoun's remains were returned to their original resting place in 1871. Ethan J. Kytle and Blain Roberts, *Denmark Vesey's Garden: Slavery and Memory in the Cradle of the Confederacy* (New York: New Press, 2018), 99.

17. Cynthia Nicoletti, *Secession on Trial: The Treason Prosecution of Jefferson Davis* (Cambridge: Cambridge University Press, 2017), 1–19.

18. Alexander H. Stephens, *A Constitutional View of the Late War Between the States* (Philadelphia, 1868), 1:341.

19. "Slaughterhouse Cases," Legal Information Institute, https://www.law.cornell.edu/supremecourt/text/83/36, accessed May 19, 2020.

20. Brown, *Civil War Canon*, 77–79; Ladies' Calhoun Monument Association, *A History of the Calhoun Monument at Charleston, S.C.* (Charleston, SC: Lucas, Richardson, Printers, 1888), 72, SCL.

21. Mamie Garvin Fields and Karen Fields, *Lemon Swamp and Other Places: A Carolina Memoir* (New York: Free Press, 1983), 57; Kytle and Roberts, *Denmark Vesey's Garden*, 107.

22. Brown, *Civil War Canon*, 80–84, quote on 83.

23. Fields, *Lemon Swamp*, 107; Kytle and Roberts, *Denmark Vesey's Garden*, 107–113.

24. Quoted in Kytle and Roberts, *Denmark Vesey's Garden*, 103.

25. Charles W. Chesnutt, *The Marrow of Tradition* (Boston, 1901), 38–39.

26. W. E. B. Du Bois, *W.E.B. Du Bois Speaks: Speeches and Addresses*, ed. Philip S. Foner (New York: Pathfinder Press, 1970), 2:197.

27. On Civil War memory, see David W. Blight, *Race and Reunion: The Civil War in American Memory* (Cambridge, MA: Belknap Press, 2002); Henry Cabot Lodge, *The Democracy of the Constitution: And Other Addresses and Essays* (New York: C. Scribner, 1915), 179.

28. Report of the Committee to Establish Principles of Renaming, 12–14, Yale University, https://president.yale.edu/sites/default/files/files/CEPR_FINAL _12-2-16.pdf, accessed May 20, 2020.

29. See Andrew Nelson Lytle, "John C. Calhoun," *Southern Review* 3, no. 3 (1938): 510–530; Russell Kirk, *The Conservative Mind: From Burke to Eliot*, 7th revised ed. (Washington, DC: Regnery Publishing, 1986), 152. Meanwhile, other conservative intellectuals rejected Calhoun. See, for instance, Harry V. Jaffa, *A New Birth of Freedom: Abraham Lincoln and the Coming of the Civil War*, reprint edition (Lanham, MD: Rowman & Littlefield Publishers, 2018), 403–472.

30. "The Famous Five," United States Senate, https://www.senate.gov/artand history/history/minute/The_Famous_Five.htm, accessed September 8, 2020.

31. C. Vann Woodward to John F. Kennedy, February 25, 1957, in C. Vann Woodward, *The Letters of C. Vann Woodward*, ed. Michael O'Brien (New Haven, CT: Yale University Press, 2013), 161. For MLK quote, see John Herbert Roper, *C. Vann Woodward, Southerner* (Athens: University of Georgia Press, 1987), 198.

32. Joseph Crespino, *Strom Thurmond's America* (New York: Hill and Wang, 2013), 105–107.

33. Charles M. Wiltse, *John C. Calhoun: Nationalist, 1782–1828* (New York: Russell & Russell, 1968), foreword.

34. Arend Lijphart, *Democracy in Plural Societies: A Comparative Exploration* (New Haven, CT: Yale University Press, 1977), 37; James H. Read, *Majority Rule Versus Consensus: The Political Thought of John C. Calhoun* (Lawrence: University Press of Kansas, 2009), 197.

35. Read, *Majority Rule Versus Consensus*, 196–197, 216–221.

36. Read, *Majority Rule Versus Consensus*, 204–208, quote on 208.

37. "Clinton Dumps Nominee," *Chicago Tribune*, June 4, 1993, https://www .chicagotribune.com/news/ct-xpm-1993-06-04-9306040115-story.html, accessed September 8, 2020.

38. Lani Guinier, *The Tyranny of the Majority: Fundamental Fairness in Representative Democracy* (New York: Free Press, 1994), 1, 9; Read, *Majority Rule Versus Consensus*, 222–224.

39. Mark Tushnet, "The Tyranny of the Majority, by Lani Guinier (Review)," *Boston Review*, 1994, https://bostonreview.net/archives/BR19.3/tushnet.html, accessed September 8, 2020.

40. Paul A. Gigot, "Hillary's Choice on Civil Rights: Back to the Future," *Wall Street Journal*, May 7, 1993.

41. Kytle and Roberts, *Denmark Vesey's Garden*, 337–339; Jelani Cobb, "Inside the Trial of Dylann Roof," *New Yorker*, February 6, 2017, https://www .newyorker.com/magazine/2017/02/06/inside-the-trial-of-dylann-roof, accessed September 8, 2020.

42. "John C. Calhoun Statue Vandalized in Downtown Charleston," https://www.live5news.com/story/29386563/john-c-calhoun-statue-vandalized -in-downtown-charleston/, accessed June 23, 2020.

43. "Lake Calhoun Name Change Gets Another Look in Minneapolis," *Minneapolis Star-Tribune*, June 23, 2015; Calhoun Petition, in author's possession, and https://docs.google.com/document/d/1XIsgJjSddobqQZSdW_72q5 m4A63pWYe-6H16StE-2D8/edit, accessed May 27, 2020.

44. "Launching a Difficult Conversation," August 29, 2015, https://presi dent.yale.edu/speeches-writings/speeches/launching-difficult-conversation, accessed September 8, 2020.

45. "Worker Smashes 'Racist' Panel, Loses Job," *New Haven Independent*, July 11, 2016.

46. Tobias Holden, "Get My Racist Ancestor's Name Off of Yale's Campus," *New York Times*, February 11, 2017. Although I have discovered no documentary evidence to support Holden's claim, it should not be dismissed out of hand. Oral tradition has proved reliable in other cases, most famously that of Thomas Jefferson.

47. Report of the Committee to Establish Principles of Renaming, 10–14, https://president.yale.edu/sites/default/files/files/CEPR_FINAL_12-2-16.pdf, accessed May 20, 2020.

48. Report of the Committee to Establish Principles of Renaming, 22, https://president.yale.edu/sites/default/files/files/CEPR_FINAL_12-2-16.pdf, accessed May 20, 2020.

49. Read, *Majority Rule Versus Consensus*, 161.

50. See, for example, Jeffrey Rosen, "States' Rights for the Left," *New York Times*, December 4, 2016.

51. For an example, see Read, *Majority Rule Versus Consensus*, conclusion.

52. John Stuart Mill, *On Liberty*, 2nd ed. (London, 1859), esp. ch. 2; John Stuart Mill, *Considerations on Representative Government* (London, 1861), 306–307.

53. David Armitage in Don Doyle, ed., *Secession as an International Phenomenon: From America's Civil War to Contemporary Separatist Movements* (Athens: University of Georgia Press, 2010), 37.

54. Doyle, ed., *Secession as an International Phenomenon*, 6. On other types of secession, see Glenn Harlan Reynolds, "Splitsylvania: State Secession and What to Do About It," *Notre Dame Law Review Online* 94, no. 2 (January 1, 2019): 90.

ROBERT ELDER is an assistant professor of history at Baylor University, where his research focuses on the American South. He holds a PhD from Emory University and lives in Waco, Texas.